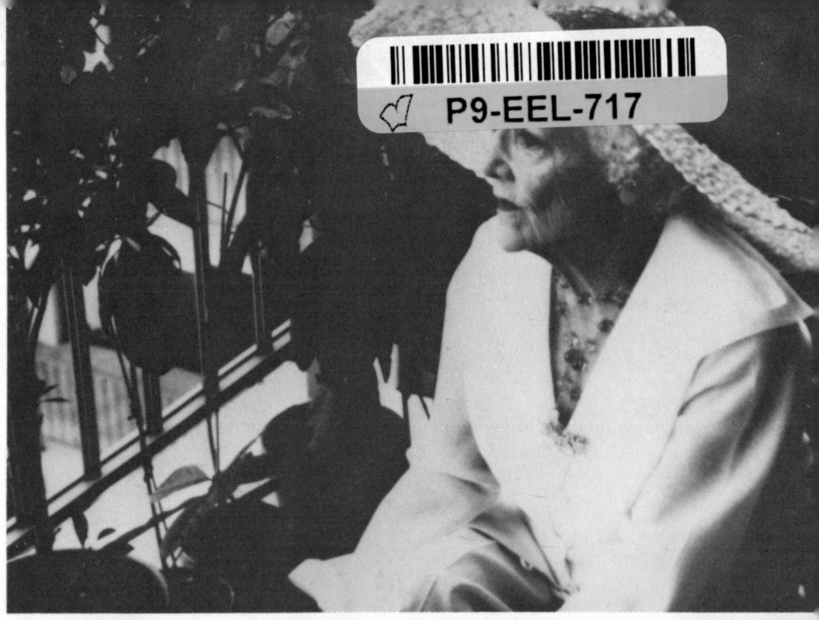

P9-EEL-717

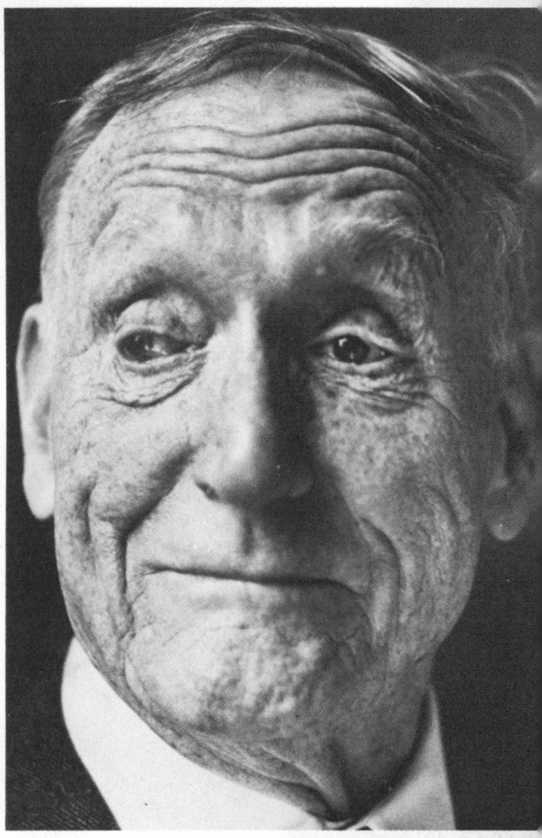

9221

For Reference

Not to be taken from this room

LIBRARY
St. Michael's College Prep H.S.
19292 El Toro Rd., Silverado, CA 92676

DICTIONARY OF LITERARY BIOGRAPHY YEARBOOK: 1980

Dictionary of Literary Biography

1: *The American Renaissance in New England,*
ed. Joel Myerson (1978)

2: *American Novelists Since World War II,*
ed. Jeffrey Helterman and Richard Layman (1978)

3: *Antebellum Writers in New York and the South,*
ed. Joel Myerson (1979)

4: *American Writers in Paris, 1920-1939,*
ed. Karen Lane Rood (1980)

5: *American Poets Since World War II,* 2 volumes,
ed. Donald J. Greiner (1980)

6: *American Novelists Since World War II,* Second Series,
ed. James E. Kibler, Jr. (1980)

7: *Twentieth-Century American Dramatists,* 2 volumes,
ed. John MacNicholas (1981)

8: *Twentieth-Century American Science-Fiction Writers,* 2 volumes,
ed. David Cowart and Thomas L. Wymer (1981)

9: *American Novelists, 1910-1945,* 3 volumes,
ed. James J. Martine (1981)

Dictionary Of Literary Biography
Yearbook: 1980

Edited by
Karen L. Rood
Jean W. Ross
and
Richard Ziegfeld

A Bruccoli Clark Book
Gale Research Company • Book Tower • Detroit, Michigan 48226
1981

Planning Board for
DICTIONARY OF LITERARY BIOGRAPHY

John Baker
William Emerson
A. Walton Litz
Orville Prescott
William Targ
Alden Whitman

Matthew J. Bruccoli, *Editorial Director*
C. E. Frazer Clark, Jr., *Managing Editor*
Richard Layman, *Project Editor*

Manufactured by Braun-Brumfield, Inc.
Ann Arbor, Michigan
Printed in the United States of America

Copyright © 1981
GALE RESEARCH COMPANY

ISBN 0-8103-1600-5

Contents

New Entries

Introduction

The purpose of the *Dictionary of Literary Biography*, as stated in the first volume in the series, is to provide a "comprehensive scholarly treatment of the lives and work" of literary figures. In the three years since the first volume of *DLB* was published, some 7,000 new works of fiction, well over 100 literary biographies, 3,000 volumes of literary criticism, and many thousands of critical articles have appeared, contributing to a vast, in many instances overwhelming, fund of knowledge about authors and their works. Literary scholars have never been more active, and contemporary literature thrives, a circumstance that increases the challenge of keeping informed about this vitally important aspect of our culture. Because the *Dictionary of Literary Biography* is an attempt to record the history of a living, expanding literature and to synthesize the best that is written about it, there is a constant need for augmenting, updating, and reviewing entries already published and for supplementing the series with entries on newly prominent writers, or writers who were omitted from *DLB* volumes. That is the purpose of the *Dictionary of Literary Biography Yearbook*.

DLB Yearbook is divided into two sections: Updated Entries and New Entries. Updated Entries are designed to complement the *DLB* series with current information about the literary activities of living authors and reports about the most recent scholarship on deceased ones. Each Updated Entry takes as its point of departure an already published *DLB* entry, adding primary and secondary bibliographical information, providing descriptions and assessments of new works, and, when necessary, reevaluating an author's works. Subjects of the entries are offered the opportunity to comment on their recent writings (see the Louis Auchincloss, Mark Harris, Walker Percy, and William Styron entries in this volume) or to respond to previously published entries in *DLB* (as inthe case of Thomas Berger here). The death of a major writer prompts a summation of his achievement. One of the functions of Updated Entries is to provide fresh, authoritative appraisals of the careers of recently deceased authors and to solicit comments from the authors' contemporaries. (See the entries for Marc Connelly, Henry Miller, and Katherine Anne Porter.) Newly published material that contributes significantly to the understanding of a deceased author's life or work—such as letters, journals, notebooks, or a biography—will also be discussed. The form of entry in Updated Entries is similar to that in the standard *DLB* series. Each Updated Entry is preceded by a reference to the *DLB* volume in which the basic entry on the subject appears. Readers seeking information about an author's entire career must consult the basic entry along with the Updated Entry for complete biographical and bibliographical information.

The second section is devoted to New Entries, on figures not previously included in *DLB*. Emphasis is placed on biography and syntheses of the critical reception of the authors' works. Bibliographies of the authors' writings and the critical writings about them are selective. The lists of books at the beginnings of entries are intended to give an overview of the subjects' book-length work in all genres; major books are included, but ephemeral works such as chapbooks or pamphlets are normally omitted. Primary bibliographies at the ends of entries are selected to include works other than original book-length writings, such as screenplays, translations, and contributions to books and periodicals. The most useful books and articles about the authors are selected for the secondary bibliographies. If there are significant public collections of an author's papers, the information is listed at the end of the entry.

Samuel Johnson's observation that "the chief glory of every people arises from its authours" was endorsed by the *DLB* advisory board, editors, and publishers in the first volume of the *DLB* series. *DLB Yearbook* is a further affirmation of that belief. *Yearbook* is designed to augment the *Dictionary of Literary Biography* so that the series may more fully realize its obligation to make the achievements of literature better understood and more accessible to students, while at the same time serving the needs of scholars and teachers.

Permissions

The following people and institutions generously permitted the reproduction of photographs or manuscripts: Nancy Sirkis, p. 4; Thomas Victor, pp. 9, 13, 22, 26, 33, 61, 93, 97, 253; James Zampathas, p. 18; Culver Pictures, Inc., p. 29; Debra Bailin, p. 37; Martin Dwyer, p. 41; Jim Santana, p. 45; Jerry Bauer, pp. 54, 267; Janna Malamud, p. 64; Tom Corcoran, p. 68; Diana H. Walker, pp. 72, 215; The Humanities Research Center, University of Texas at Austin, p. 76; Maclean Dameron, courtesy of Alfred Appel, Jr., p. 80; Joe McTyre, p. 88; Paul Porter, p. 95; Mark Morrow, pp. 100, 315; Duke University Library, p. 103; Michael Chikiris, p. 108; Robert A. Ballard, Jr., p. 121; David Baumbach, p. 129; Michael E. Bry, p. 136; Terry Hardy, p. 145; Alan Fortney, p. 158; David Cherryh, p. 166; Jade Albert, p. 170; Christopher Cox, p. 175; Jerome Liebling, p. 179; Bob Crawford, p. 184; Richard Robinson, p. 191; Madame Robert Champigny, p. 207; Robert Reed, p. 209; Martha Kaplan, p. 222; James Leonard, p. 227; Karen Huie, p. 236; Roger Ressmeyer, p. 243; Alen MacWeeney, p. 270; Atlanta Historical Society, p. 277; Jef Wright, p. 298; Chester Simpson, courtesy of Bantam Books, p. 302; Nancy Rica Schiff, p. 305; Victoria Sorrentino, p. 311.

Acknowledgments

This book was produced by BC Research. The production staff included Linda E. Beattie, Janet E. Black, Mary Bruccoli, Anita Dunn, Joyce Fowler, Stacy Gibbons, Robert H. Griffin, Chad W. Helms, Patricia S. Hicks, Sharon K. Kirkland, Cynthia D. Lybrand, Mary V. McLeod, Shirley A. Ross, Walter W. Ross, Robin A. Sumner, Cheryl A. Swartzentruber, Julia Tilley, Margaret A. Van Antwerp, Carol J. Wilson, and Lynne C. Zeigler.

Anne Dixon and Jacquelyn Price did the library research with the valuable assistance of the following librarians at Thomas Cooper Library: Michael Freeman, Dwight Gardner, Michael Havener, David Lincove, Donna Nance, Harriet Oglesbee, Jean Rhyne, Paula Swope, Jane Thesing, Ellen Tillett, Gary Treadway, and Beth Woodard. Photographic copy work for this volume was done by Pat Crawford of Imagery, Columbia, South Carolina.

Finally, grateful acknowledgment is due the subjects of entries in this book who were kind enough to read their entries for accuracy. Without the assistance of all these people, this book would not have been possible.

Updated Entries

Dictionary of Literary Biography

Louis Auchincloss
(27 September 1917-   )

The *DLB* entry on Louis Auchincloss appears in *Dictionary of Literary Biography*, volume 2, *American Novelists Since World War II* (1978), pp. 7-14.

NEW BOOKS: *The Country Cousin* (Boston: Houghton Mifflin, 1978; London: Weidenfeld & Nicolson, 1978);

Persons of Consequence: Queen Victoria and Her Circle (New York: Random House, 1979; London: Weidenfeld & Nicolson, 1979);

Life, Law and Letters: Essays and Sketches (Boston: Houghton Mifflin, 1979);

The House of the Prophet (Boston: Houghton Mifflin, 1980; London: Weidenfeld & Nicolson, 1980).

Louis Auchincloss continues both to inhabit the world of New York professionals through his association with a law firm and to write novels, literary criticism, and social history. The fact of his two careers, as partner in the Wall Street firm Hawkins, Delafield & Wood and as a widely published writer, is, Auchincloss told C. D. B. Bryan, who interviewed him for a *New York Times Magazine* feature, "the only thing about me that does not interest me at all." While not the only fact about him that interests others, as Auchincloss said he suspects, it is invariably cited, as was poet Wallace Stevens's work with an insurance company, perhaps because success in two arenas is rare for American writers. For his fiction Auchincloss sometimes draws on his specialized knowledge of the practice of law in New York, but his fiction's distinctiveness results less from that aspect than from the authority of his wry analyses of the moral dilemmas of the affluent. In his nonfiction he not only makes use of the skill in observation that informs his fiction but also of significant themes from his fiction, such as the importance of money, power, and work in human experience.

From 1947 to the end of 1980 Auchincloss has had twenty-three works of fiction and twelve books of nonfiction published. Of these works, in 1980 fourteen were available in new editions and fourteen were still in print in their original editions. Few serious American writers of literary stature have written so much. Perhaps the sheer amount of writing has led some critics to question the quality of Auchincloss's latest works, but he continues to be taken seriously and to be admired for his particular talents by major reviewers such as Abigail McCarthy and Benjamin DeMott.

Auchincloss continues to draw upon his good eye for material detail; his inside knowledge about a specialized world of work; his strong narrative talents; his merciless ability to recognize the bogus, pretentious, and righteous; and his rueful sympathy for idealists who must compromise. All these qualities are on display in his newest works. The novel *The Country Cousin* (1978) takes readers into the world of New York law firms and a conflict between passion and ethics. *Persons of Consequence: Queen Victoria and Her Circle* (1979) displays a world of extraordinary egotism, dogmatism, and power. *Life, Law and Letters: Essays and Sketches* (1979) makes parallels and distinctions among authors of literary and legal works. A recent short story, "The Sea Gull," which appeared in the *Atlantic Monthly* for May 1979, details the self-induced troubles of a clergyman. *The House of the Prophet* (1980) focuses on a fictional journalist who grows increasingly unable to separate his ego from what he calls respect for truth.

The Country Cousin centers on the ethical conflict of Jamey Coates, the respected senior partner of a New York law firm, who for love of his wife, Amy Hunt, has concealed the fact that she destroyed the codicil to a will, a painful violation of what he calls his delicate lawyer's conscience. Like many characters in Auchincloss's novels, Jamey is sincere in seeing himself as a lawyer of the highest principles whose position and knowledge entitle him to make fine distinctions. Some months before his own test comes, Jamey assures himself that he can be proud of his high ethical standards, even though he understands that in the case of the fixed traffic ticket, gentlemen are expected not to be "Galahads of trivia." His view, as Abigail McCarthy noted in her review in the *New York Times Book Review*, relates to current interest in "bribery and chicanery among those in whom society places its trust." Jamey tells Amy that she is more important to him "than all of morals and law and life." When he is threatened with exposure for that act, he almost welcomes it, acknowledging to himself that he should be disbarred. He feels cheated of self-sacrifice by his decision to remain silent. It is a mark of Auchincloss's skillful tone that this punishment seems appropriate for one so smug.

Smugness untroubled by doubt emerges as the central characteristic of the Victoria and Albert whom Auchincloss examines in *Persons of Consequence: Queen Victoria and Her Circle*. In a history filled with personages difficult to like, Albert, with his stubborn will, self-satisfaction, and dogmatic moralism, would be the strongest candidate, were this a novel, for the role of villain. Auchincloss notes that the same Albert who gained control over Victoria through the power of sex brought the prudery that bears Victoria's name to England, and Albert's irrational response to his son's first affair "was considered just as odd in the British male world of 1861 as it would be today." For Albert, unlike Jamey Coates, no doubt shades his righteous domination, petty dogmatism, pious exploitation of the lives of others, and contempt for the divergent opinion.

Auchincloss's recognition of the significance of the ideas of others is apparent in *Life, Law and Letters: Essays and Sketches*. In the eighteen essays, two-thirds of which appeared previously in various publications, he shares the pleasure he has found in a wide variety of writing, ranging from social history to judicial style to different aspects of British, American, and French literature. Some material is familiar. He tells again, with new examples, the story he related in *A Writer's Capital* (1974), of his delighted discovery of the legal language of Justice Benjamin Cardozo and the novelistic characteristics of cases he decided. Auchincloss extends the remark of a character in *The Country Cousin* about the validity of Emily Dickinson's lack of interest in the publication of her poetry because it was intended for one reader only.

An even more familiar theme to Auchincloss's readers is the significance of money. Auchincloss noted in *A Writer's Capital* that while he was a student at Yale he became interested in money and how it is "made, inherited, lost and spent." In *Life, Law and Letters*, he sympathetically describes Jane Austen's characters' need for the affluence that provides space, and he correctly notes that poverty causes the wretchedness of Theodore Dreiser's characters.

When Auchincloss describes himself in an essay on the composition of *The Rector of Justin* (this account was first published in 1969, and the process was also discussed in *A Writer's Capital*), it is mostly as a writer interested in language and the problems of his craft. He describes his tone as that neither of "a satirist nor a cheerleader" but strictly that of an observer of the values of his characters.

No one would call Auchincloss a cheerleader for the central character of his short story "The Seagull." Denis Sanders's tale is cast in the form of a letter of explanation to his bishop in which he

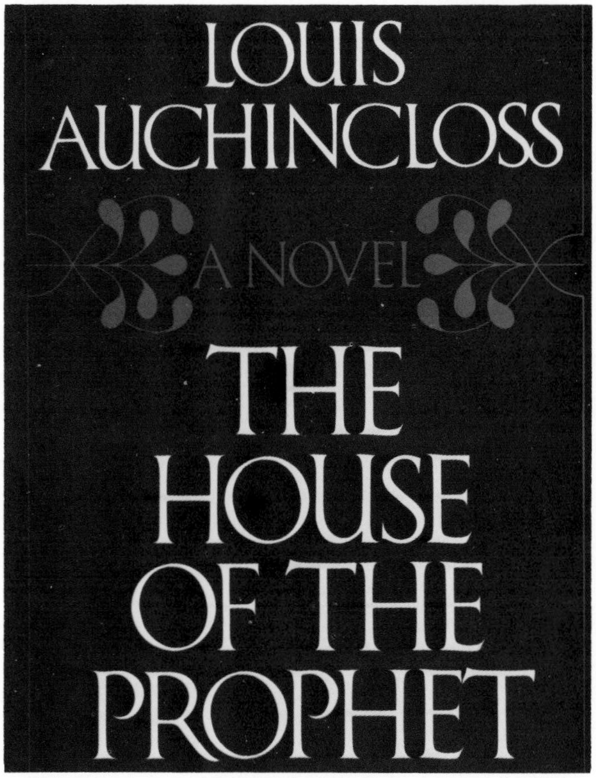

Dust jacket

recounts the events that led to the breakup of his marriage, his dismissal as rector of a suburban church, and his decision to give up the ministry. Sanders recalls without the least irony how he felt "the Episcopal Church was living again in Christ" when the bishop invited a ballet company to dance in the cathedral, led a peace march, and ordained a lesbian priest. Sanders sees himself throughout as a good man victimized and learns nothing from his experience, but Auchincloss's marvelously funny tale veers toward the satire he denies as his method.

Auchincloss's tone is far more objective toward another self-satisfied protagonist, Felix Leitner of *The House of the Prophet*. Felix, a self-styled devotee of truth, is presented through a point of view similar to that used by Auchincloss in his earlier successful portrait of single-minded dedication, *The Rector of Justin*. Roger Cutter, a loyal follower whose life has been absorbed by Felix, provides his own memories and collects accounts from Felix and his circle. Felix's life is traced from his comfortable childhood in New York through his successes as a student, lawyer, presidential adviser, and columnist, to his death in old age. Although all accounts of him stress his intellect, they also show a person who uses friends to advance his position, has no feeling for or interest in his children, leaves his intelligent first wife whose social position he had once needed, then marries the frivolous wife of an old friend, writes a book on the Constitution that embarrasses his law partners, and pettily attacks an old friend for the sake of a good column. Some praise his loyalty to truth, and Felix tells the admiring Roger that he would sacrifice everything, "health, love, vigor, family, friends," if he had to choose between them and the uses of his intellect. Before his life ends, he has made that choice and tells Roger: "Nobody has ever really been able to accept the fact that I can have no friend but truth."

The House of the Prophet was attacked in a review in the *Christian Science Monitor* for involving characters who "carry ideas, rather than blood in their veins," and conversely by Robert Kiely in the *New York Times Book Review* for providing a character described as a genius with mundane ideas of neither "striking originality nor unusual elegance." Felix is indeed one for whom ideas matter more than blood, and if his ideas are mundane, as Kiely asserts, he has sacrificed much for an illusion of greatness.

In his certainty about his choices, Felix resembles Auchincloss's portrait of Prince Albert more than that of Jamey Coates. It is Roger, not Felix, who needs to justify Felix's behavior. A telling, perhaps symbolic, instance of Felix's imperviousness to alternative views occurs when he dismisses as "too neat" his aunt's interpretation of an El Greco portrait of an Inquisitor as revealing the face of one "trapped into one dimension of reality by the horrible things he thinks God wants him to do." The externals of Felix's life suggest a comparison to Walter Lippman, but his character, his stepdaughter observes, is like that of Henry David Thoreau, who pretended to need little but the chance to use his mind while he depended on others to supply material wants. Felix, like the Inquisitor and others certain of their truths, remains trapped in one dimension of reality by what he believes truth requires of him.

Auchincloss is neither cheerleader nor satirist in his account of Felix. The fictional chronicler of Felix, Roger Cutter, decides not to attempt an assessment of Felix's life but to deposit his material with Felix's papers at Harvard. He turns with relief to Felix's columns, where for him the words "redeemed all, saved all," and where he could be "alone with Felix at last." Roger treats Felix's story as Auchincloss says Dickinson did her poetry: "as the product of two persons," the writer and the reader. Neither needs a wider audience.

Auchincloss's reputation as a writer has been influenced by factors somewhat external to it. Both the novel of manners and the fictional characters called WASPs are not fashionable. Perhaps in reply to misinformed objections, Auchincloss has a character in *The House of the Prophet* comment about a movie company that, while filming in his brokerage house, rejected the actual customer's men as extras because they did not look the part. "Chronicles of fashion," he complains, are either "a generation behind the times, or else they try to give the public what the public likes to think is truth." Disciple of Henry James that Auchincloss is, he might well wish that critics followed James's dictate that they should grant a writer his subject and direct comments to the execution of it. Auchincloss came close to making such a request himself when he observed in *A Writer's Capital* that he chooses the background of his characters simply because it is familiar and available, but their problems are "personal or psychological, and would have existed in a multitude of other geographical areas and other social strata."

Benjamin DeMott, writing of Auchincloss's nonfiction in an essay review for the *New York Times Book Review*, addresses the oversimplification that results when Auchincloss is seen merely as a chronicler of the New York rich and "proper." DeMott praised Auchincloss for his cool and straightforward style in both essays and fiction, for his suggestive writing about pride, for his skill in creating intelligent women characters, and especially for his portraits of "self-regard under pressure."

In employing the theme of "self-regard under pressure," Auchincloss works with a universal topic, especially appropriate for an American writer. Ralph Waldo Emerson was as much describing Americans as announcing a principle of nonconformity when he observed that nothing is at last sacred but the integrity of one's own mind. When doubts assail that integrity, or when they should, whatever the occupation or social class of the person under pressure, the result is the self-conflict that makes great art. Observing that conflict, neither as a cheerleader nor a satirist, in his well-crafted fiction Auchincloss proves himself an important American writer.

—Patricia Kane

Periodical Publications:

FICTION:

"The Seagull," *Atlantic*, 243 (May 1979): 52-57.

NONFICTION:

"The Long Life and Broad Mind of Mr. Justice Holmes," *American Heritage* (June 1978): 69-75;

References:

C. D. B. Bryan, "Under the Auchincloss Shell," *New York Times Magazine*, 11 February 1979, pp. 35-37, 61-64;

Benjamin DeMott, "In Praise of Louis Auchincloss," *New York Times Book Review*, 23 September 1979, pp. 7, 32.

AN INTERVIEW
with LOUIS AUCHINCLOSS

DLB: In *A Writer's Capital* you describe your early development of what you've called "the sense that the world was packed with drama and the warning sense at the same time that this drama was not a thing that could be used." Has it often been a problem in writing your fiction to decide what elements of real experience could be used?

AUCHINCLOSS: No, for two reasons. One is that as you develop the craft of fiction, you learn to digest the drama into your material in such a way that there's no dangerous or distressing similarity to events in real life. In the second place, as you live to be older, so many of the dramas that you have witnessed have retreated so far into the past that they don't have to be disguised to save anyone's feelings today.

DLB: You've written more than thirty books now. Are you always writing, or are there pauses between books?

AUCHINCLOSS: There used to be pauses between books, but I must say they have diminished. I think it's true with many writers that their volume increases as they get older. Of course John O'Hara is a conspicuous, perhaps rather appalling example of that. I'm a great admirer of his early works, but I think almost all critics would agree that his ability did not increase with his volume. With Henry James, the volume remained about the same, but I think the quality increased.

DLB: Do you enjoy writing fiction and writing nonfiction equally?

AUCHINCLOSS: I find them very, very different. I think I probably enjoy writing fiction more.

DLB: Like Trollope, another man who worked steadily at two jobs, you write the sort of prose that seems effortless to the reader. Does the actual writing come without major struggles, writer's block, and extensive revision?

AUCHINCLOSS: It does not come without revisions. I revise quite extensively. The novel that I've just completed, for example, went to the publisher and then I took it back and added at least twenty percent to its length. I did some very drastic and fundamental rewriting to it, and that was after it had already been through two or three drafts. I write quickly and I revise quickly, but that doesn't mean I don't revise constantly—three or four drafts. Because I'm a person with a nervous personality, I operate in all things with a certain amount of speed. But I come back to them.

DLB: I know that you're bored with the interest people express in your having two careers. May I just ask if they have enhanced each other in ways that might not be obvious to readers?

AUCHINCLOSS: I think my practice in law has enhanced my writing in providing all kinds of thoughts, ideas, and inspirations; and of course I've written a good deal about the law. I would not think my writing has in any way enhanced or helped my practice of law.

DLB: In the company of other fine writers you've been accused by some critics of dealing in your fiction with a world of limited scope. How do you feel about this criticism?

AUCHINCLOSS: Critics only criticize you for that if they happen to have a scunner against the particular field that you're concentrating on. If I limited myself to a small county in Mississippi, like Faulkner, no one would say anything against it at all. Or if I limited myself to the housemaids and their employers in a large house in Kent, like Ivy Compton-Burnett, nobody would mind. It's only if you limit yourself to a world that people think is a world that has power that *shouldn't* have power. There's an awful lot of social consciousness in the criticisms of my books; I have no doubt about that.

DLB: Do you see much of other writers now?

AUCHINCLOSS: I used to when I was young, but I don't now for the simple reason that the writers who are my contemporaries are pretty well scattered around; they don't form a unit the way we used to in the White Horse Tavern, for example. I knew all sorts of writers who have since become very famous like Mailer and Styron and Gore Vidal. Now Norman Mailer doesn't live in New York, Styron is up in Roxbury, Connecticut, and Gore Vidal lives in Italy. Secondly, the law practice takes a lot of time. Thirdly, I'm very much involved in the New York cultural scene, being president of the Museum of the City of New York, so a large part of my social life is with people who work in and out of museums and other cultural institutions. It doesn't leave much time for literary parties. Then there's another factor—as I get older, I don't like the late hours that many writers keep who don't have to get up in the morning.

DLB: Are there any plans or books in progress that you'd like to talk about?

AUCHINCLOSS: I have two books finished now. One is due out in March, and it's called *The Cat and the King*. It's a departure; I've never done anything like it. It's an historical novel taking place during the reign of Louis XIV and cast in the form of an addendum to the memoirs of the Duc de Saint-Simon. It's a very tight, accurate little book with two large genealogical charts of actual people, the royal family of France, that really have to be studied with it, and it takes place completely from the point of view of the seventeenth century. There are no modern lessons or analogies to be drawn. It's an effort at a complete capsule for a particular moment in history. I'm quite excited about it.

There's another book I expect to have out for Christmas 1981. It takes place in 1859 and goes on into the Civil War. It's a book I've long planned, and I regard it as rather a success. I think that I'm reaching a new dimension and depth in my writing. Just as a certain number of critics think I'm written out, I think I'm just beginning. But there we are—there is always room for wide differences of opinion on that.

—*Jean W. Ross*

Donald Barthelme

(7 April 1931-   )

The *DLB* entry on Donald Barthelme appears in *Dictionary of Literary Biography*, volume 2, *American Novelists Since World War II* (1978), pp. 34-39.

NEW BOOK: *Great Days* (New York: Farrar, Straus & Giroux, 1979; London: Routledge, 1979).

"There's very little difference between Donald Barthelme the person and Donald Barthelme the writer," former *New Yorker* fiction editor Roger Angell has said of one of the most highly acclaimed innovators working in a type of fiction that has been labeled variously avant-garde, postmodern, and experimental—the latter an epithet Barthelme eschews, identifying it with "that which is not successful." There is, to be certain, a strong sense of authorial presence in Barthelme's fiction, as there must be when the absence of traditional linear plot and well-developed character thwarts the illusion of an independent, lifelike world. The individual human responses to certain circumstances are there in his fiction, as is the subsequent exposure of personal human values, but these values are more apt to be identified with the author rather than with any fictional character. Barthelme's reader observes the author's mind at work and at play, exposing in a richly comic, often satiric manner the bewilderment and insecurity of man as he copes with the perplexities of contemporary life—all within a framework of technical and linguistic innovation peculiarly Barthelmeic.

The concerns of Donald Barthelme the person often mirror those of Donald Barthelme the writer. The quiet, unextraordinary life-style the red-bearded and bespectacled author is reported to enjoy with his third wife, Danish-born Birgit, and daughter, Anne, in their Greenwich Village apartment belies the activist in Barthelme. In February 1979 the author, long a political satirist in his fiction, protested in the columns of the *New York Times* the government's treatment of writer Grace Paley and the other "White House Lawn 11." Paley, Barthelme's friend, neighbor, and fellow vice-president of the P.E.N. (Poets, Playwrights, Essayists, Editors and Novelists) American Center, faced sentence on a misdemeanor conviction involving a Labor Day 1978 protest against nuclear power and weaponry. She and ten associates left a White House tour to unfurl a banner reading, "No nuclear weapons, no nuclear power USA or USSR." Barthelme, representing the P.E.N. American Center, charged the government with "proceeding in a somewhat ham-handed fashion here. The demonstrators offered no threat whatsoever to the President, to the White House, to America as an idea, or even to the grass," adding that "the authorities might also bear in mind that getting a message to the authorities is a difficult business, and sometimes *requires* walking on the grass." Barthelme's political satire often focuses on government's ineffectualness and unresponsiveness. Speaking to John F. Baker of *Publishers Weekly*, the author said that the political pieces in his nonfiction collection, *Guilty Pleasures* (1974), were "inspired by extreme exacerbation. I feel a sense of outrage at the prevailing spirit of helplessness, the feeling that there's nothing we can do. Well, one thing we can do is to write a nasty piece about it."

From September through October 1979, Barthelme wrote a brief but intense series of movie reviews for the *New Yorker* magazine, where most of his short stories first appear. In the short story "The New Music," collected in *Great Days* (1979), a character labels film "the great medium of this century" because of its value as an avenue of surrogate experience. Barthelme's affection for the medium is longstanding, evident from his early career as a journalist, when during the first half of the 1950s he wrote reviews for the University of Houston student newspaper, the *Cougar*, and for the *Houston Post*. And it is film to which Barthelme partially attributes the new directions in which he and similar contemporary authors have taken prose fiction. Movies, Barthelme noted during an authors' panel discussion at Washington and Lee in October 1975, have "forced us to think about what we've been doing very much harder than we might ordinarily have done." Analogizing the impact of the still photograph on painting and the impact of film on writing, the author explained that "the painters had to go out and reinvent painting because of the invention of photography and I think films have done something of the sort for us."

Barthelme's own "reinvention" of fiction

Donald Barthelme

propels prose toward poetry. In the absence of the intrigue inherent in traditional plot and character development, Barthelme relies largely upon the tools of the poet to engage and maintain his reader's attention, which accounts for the compression of his work. The reader is engaged through the reciprocative device of allusion, through oftentimes startling figures of speech, and through Barthelme's fond preoccupation with the language. Barthelme's logophilia is evidenced in his invention of words and word combinations, his frequent use of obsolete, archaic, and poetic diction, and his parody of jargon and argot. The author has said that "one of the funny things about experimentalism in regard to language is that most of it has not been done yet." Speaking of the possibilities of the more or less random coupling of words and phrases, that which he attempts in the generally misunderstood and unappreciated story "Bone Bubbles" (*City Life,* 1970), Barthelme explains, "There's a lot of basic research which hasn't been done because of the enormous resources of the language and the enormous number of resonances from the past which have precluded this way of investigating language." Barthelme's verbal pluck appears to be aimed at jolting his reader out of psittacism. "He knows that there are only the same old words in the world," Denis Donaghue writes about Barthelme in the *Saturday Review,* "but that an accomplished word-man can upset their complacency, set them free from their attachment to objects, convert them to a new music. . . . He uses English as a second language, hoping to release us from the preoccupations of the first."

Of the sixteen entries in *Great Days,* Barthelme's sixth collection of short stories, thirteen appeared originally in the *New Yorker,* all but one of these between 1977-1978. There is much in the collection familiar to the Barthelme reader. There are the linguistic lagniappes ("—Think you're the mule's eyebrows don't you? —No. I feel like Insufficient Funds") and the incongruities of style ("He who hath not love is a sad cookie"). There are the surrealistic situations, with zombies who converge on a village to buy wives and a sculptor who lives in a steel Butler building and welds four-thousand pound steel artichokes. In "The Death of Edward Lear" and "Cortés and Montezuma," there are Barthelme's perverse revisions of history. And there is experiment with form. An author's note reveals that "The Question Party," in which a coquettish parlor game climaxes in the shooting death of a bachelor participant, is an *objet trouvê* that appeared in *Godey's Lady's Book* in 1850 under the pseudonym Hickory Broom. Barthelme shortens the piece and adds several new lines. In "Concerning the Bodyguard," Barthelme explores the professional and private life of the titular character via seven pages of questions. The question format, much like the left-hand portion of a letter printed in "Eugénie Grandet" (*Guilty Pleasures*), engages the reader by requiring him to participate in the actual composition of the story. Diane Johnson observes that one might label this "a stone-soup method of writing, recalling the folk tale in which a wily stranger puts a stone in some water, announces that he is making soup, and invites the villagers to improve the flavor by putting in carrots and onions of their own. Of course Barthelme, unlike the stranger, is far from destitute—is rather a miracle of variousness and vigilance in the matter of our times, and he puts strange objects in instead of stones."

Seven of the stories in *Great Days* suggest something of a new formalistic direction for Barthelme. These stories progress by means of alternating voices, with only a dash replacing the customary speech tag and quotation marks. Some are clearly dialogues; others can be as legitimately read as the operations of a single psyche. As Marc Granetz notes in a review of *Great Days,* "Interviews and catechisms have appeared before in Barthelme's work, but these new pieces are different, mysterious," and several critics point to the influence of Joyce, Beckett, and Pinter.

Angst pervades most of the seven stories, and the self-questioning introspection and paralyzing indecision of many of the voices are reminiscent of earlier Barthelme characters, including those in *Snow White* (1967). Representative is the speaker in "The Crisis," who notes that "we feel only 25 percent of what we ought to feel" and asks, "Is something wrong with me?" In these seven colloquies, Barthelme concerns himself with what Diane Johnson calls "Great Subjects (fear, faith, hope, sexual contention)." Several explore the fragility and transiency of human relationships. "The affair ran the usual course. Fever, boredom, trapped," says one of the speakers in "On the Steps of the Conservatory," and her companion commiserates, "Hot, rinse, spin dry." Others address the problem of religious faith. The speakers in "The Leap," Barthelme's version of Wallace Stevens's "Sunday Morning," attempt to meditate in preparation for the embracement of faith: "We are but poor lapsarian futiles whose preen glands are all out of whack and who but for the grace of God's goodness would—." But "the leap to faith" falls short as one announces, "Can't make it. I am a double-minded man," and attention is redirected to the heavenly joys of corporeal life. The somberness evoked by the contemplation of such "Great Subjects" is tempered by Barthelme's playfulness and the inability, shared by his protagonists, to take himself too seriously. "The typical Barthelme protagonist," says Joe David Bellamy, "whistles along good-naturedly in the teeth of the boredom, despair, absurdity, moral decay, and deplorable behavior surrounding him." Looming in the background of all of Barthelme's work is the dictum from *Snow White* that "ANATHEMATIZATION OF THE WORLD IS NOT AN ADEQUATE RESPONSE TO THE WORLD."

Critical reaction to *Great Days* has been mixed. Many complain that the further Barthelme penetrates the frontiers of form and language, the more cryptic he becomes and the more difficult to read. Marc Granetz accuses him of moving "away from the pains and elations of the heart toward fiction that is increasingly thin, enigmatic and obscure" and claims that *Great Days* "celebrates life less and less." Diane Johnson finds the collection "bare Barthelme at his best, quite inimitable, with a new kind of calm confidence, a new depth of subject. . . ." The disparity among critical opinions may be partially attributable to Barthelme's luxury of two readerships.

Dust jacket

As Richard Schickel explains, one can "enjoy the intellectual effort required to catch his meanings," but, "on the other hand, it is sometimes amusing merely to let his stuff 'wash over you.' " And Johnson notes, "It's nice that Barthelme's stories are equally fun for the light reader browsing through the New Yorker looking for fables, laughs, punch lines, and also for someone who wishes to brood, reread and make connections. Good writing, like religion, no doubt, develops complexity and interest in proportion to the attention you give it."

—*David M. Taylor*

Periodical Publications:

"As Grace Paley Faces Jail with 3 Other Writers," *New York Times*, 2 February 1979, section 1, p. 25;

"The Current Cinema: The Earth as an Overturned Bowl," *New Yorker*, 55 (10 September 1979): 120-122;

"The Current Cinema: Parachutes in the Trees," *New Yorker*, 55 (17 September 1979): 132, 134-135;

"The Current Cinema: Special Devotions," *New Yorker*, 55 (24 September 1979): 132-133;

"The Current Cinema: Dead Men Comin' Through," *New Yorker*, 55 (1 October 1979): 103-104;

"The Current Cinema: Three Festivals," *New Yorker*, 55 (8 October 1979): 164, 167-168;

"The Current Cinema: Peculiar Influences," *New Yorker*, 55 (15 October 1979): 182-184.

References:

John F. Baker, "Donald Barthelme," *Publishers Weekly*, 206 (11 November 1974): 6-7;

Donald Barthelme, William Gass, Grace Paley, and Walker Percy, "A Symposium on Fiction," *Shenandoah*, 27 (Winter 1976): 3-31;

Joe David Bellamy, "Barthelme and Delights of Mind-Travel," *Washington Post*, 11 February 1979, section 6, pp. 1, 4;

Denis Donaghue, "For Brevity's Sake," *Saturday Review*, 6 (3 March 1979): 50-52;

Marc Granetz, "Great Days," *New Republic*, 180 (17 February 1979): 37-38;

Alexandra Johnson, "Barthelme's Language to Name the Unknown," *Christian Science Monitor*, 7 March 1979, p. 18;

Diane Johnson, "Possibly Parables," *New York Times Book Review*, 4 February 1979, pp. 1, 36-37;

Christopher Lehmann-Haupt, "Books of the Times," *New York Times*, 31 January 1979, section 3, p. 21;

Richard Schickel, "Freaked Out on Barthelme," *New York Times Magazine*, 16 August 1970, pp. 14-15, 42, 44, 47-48.

Thomas Berger

(20 July 1924-   )

The *DLB* entry on Thomas Berger appears in *Dictionary of Literary Biography*, volume 2, *American Novelists Since World War II* (1978), pp. 50-56.

NEW BOOKS: *Arthur Rex* (New York: Delacorte/ Seymour Lawrence, 1978; London: Magnum, 1979);

Neighbors (New York: Delacorte/Seymour Lawrence, 1980; London: Magnum, 1981).

For the past twenty years, reviewers have expressed surprise and dismay that Thomas Berger's novels have not found the large audience they deserve. Following publication in 1977 of *Who Is Teddy Villanova?*, the *Nation* ran two articles that attempted to account for his neglect by isolating some of the challenges of Berger's unique style and radical vision. Frederick Turner, speaking of *Little Big Man* (1964) in terms that apply to all of Berger's writing, observed that its daring lay in taking a "position beyond sentimentality, beyond classic American liberalism." The companion essay noted that Berger, to the befuddlement of reviewers and readers alike, has "persisted in the writing of novels that are aggressively intelligent, and consistently resistant to the twin sentimentalities of idealism and despair." In 1978 *Arthur Rex* was published, and the praise of Berger's skills continued. But it was the 1980 publication of Berger's tenth novel, *Neighbors*, that seems to have permanently raised the ante for appraising his career. Frederick Busch, writing in the *Chicago Tribune*, simply stated that "this is a novel by Thomas Berger, and everything he writes should be read and considered." Thomas R. Edwards showed even less restraint in the *New York Times Book Review*, concluding of Berger's work that "our failure to read and discuss him is a national disgrace."

To a great extent, Berger's distinctive talents explain his lack of greater popular acclaim. His fiction swells with paradoxes, seeming to embrace what it exposes as delusion, to celebrate what it seems to parody, absolutely refusing to subscribe to any codified philosophy, whether romantic, existential, or absurd. His style challenges the reader with precise, but often elaborate or serpentine sentences, and those sentences are as full of surprises as Berger's characters and plots. If we can be sure of only one thing in his writing, it is that expectations are meant to be disproved. To this end, Berger tries to make of each novel an "independent existence," an alternative reality he hopes the reader will approach "without the luggage of received ideas, *a priori* assumptions, sociopolitical axes to grind, or feeble moralities in search of support."

Despite his efforts, two such "received ideas" have dogged Berger's career—that his novels are parodies or that they are social criticism. To the first of these claims Berger responds: "My conscious intention is always to write as conventional an example (of whichever genre) as I can manage to do. Thus I never begin with the intention to deride a genre; my purpose is always to celebrate it, to identify and applaud its glories." In a recent interview with Richard Schickel, Berger chided those who mistake him "for a merry-andrew with an inflated pig's bladder," because such readers "can never understand that I adore whichever tradition I am striving to follow, and that what results is the best I can manage by way of joyful worship—not the worst in sneering derision." To the second notion—that his novels should be taken as satires on society, Berger responds less patiently: "The naive invariably believe that I strive, and fail, to write social criticism for the delectation of the illiterates who take the daily newspapers seriously and for the semiliterates who make up their staffs. They assume there is a consensus of men of good will and believe that I am trying to associate myself with it." Berger never displays the blithe conviction of the true satirist. Douglas Hughes has pointed out that while Berger "delights in exposing affectation, hypocrisy, and other foibles, he refrains from unrelieved ridicule based on an implicit absolute, that idealism on which the satirist draws his strength." He admits that he has never known quite what it is that he does in his fiction, but Berger insists his aim is simply to amuse himself, citing Nabokov's comment that what he sought in his work was simply "aesthetic bliss." Berger explains: "I have never believed that I work in the service of secular rationalism . . . (the man of good will, the sensible fellow, the social meliorist who believes the novel holds the mirror up to society, etc.). I am essentially a voyeur of copulating words."

Indeed, for Berger the novel is first and foremost

a progression of words, a series of sentences that characteristically combine exuberance with precision. He believes that "the sentence is the cell beyond which the life of the book cannot be traced, a novel being a structure of such cells: most must be vital or the body is dead." A glimpse of what "vitality" may mean to Berger can be gained from his description in *Arthur Rex* of a would-be assassin who follows Arthur down a winding stairway: " 'Dost descend?' King Arthur asked hollowly from below.

" 'I do,' said the lady, holding the dagger sinistrally against a fold of skirt as with her dexter hand she followed the curve of the wall and felt with her dainty feet the stone treads, of which she used the broadest portion, at the maximum of their centrifugation, and the masons had laid them with such marvelous exactitude that each conformed to the rule of all, so that having found the pace, one could misstep only willfully, unless the constant revolution ever downwards agitated the humors causing vertigo." Berger has said that he looks for himself through the English language and that for him language is "a morality and a politics and a religion." He explains that he cannot maintain interest in a narrative "unless it is a continuum, not of plot or character or philosophy . . . but of language." Cheerfully, he adds that he will apply himself "with the same ardor in composing a note to the milkman as in writing a novel."

Berger's concerns in his novels are no more nor less than whatever he finds himself writing about, with the manner and matter of that writing always one. His ten novels seem as unalike as ten novels written by the same hand could possibly be. However, two intertwined, equally ambiguous terms, *language* and *freedom*, may suggest the threads that make of his works one cloth. The intersection of these two concepts forms as much of a pattern as can be safely maintained of Berger's fiction: the lives of his characters are affected more by words than by actions, and insofar as true freedom might be defined by Berger as "the ability to be consistent with oneself," his characters are enslaved by language. They are victimized by definitions that exclude or threaten them, by rhetoric that makes them lose sight of physical facts, and by language designed more to preclude than to encourage clear thinking. For this reason, the plot of a Berger novel typically chronicles the efforts of the protagonist to free himself from someone else's verbal version of reality. In this sense, Berger's novels have all explored the processes of *victimization*, with Berger approaching his subject much as a jeweler might examine all of the facets of some bright and terrible diamond.

From Carlo Reinhart to Jack Crabb to Russell Wren to Arthur and now to Earl Keese in *Neighbors*, Berger's characters live blurring lives in which they oscillate between being victims and victimizers, between manipulating and being manipulated by the kinds of rhetoric or language codes that organize human life. Each Berger protagonist struggles, whether consciously or unconsciously, to free himself from the inexorable tendency to think of himself as a victim of outrages and impositions, both humorously small and tragically large. Almost never in control of the situation around them, these characters consistently find themselves outmaneuvered, outsmarted, insulted, and imposed upon. Their victimization is usually funny, but always serious, often seemingly trivial, but always with an underlying pattern that falls little short of an old-fashioned naturalistic determinism.

To note this pattern in Berger's writing, however, is neither to describe his ten novels nor to account for their differences, for what the reader surely notices first of Berger's novels is their almost manic dissimilarity. His two most recent works,

Arthur Rex and *Neighbors,* indicate the wide range of Berger's subjects and the flexibility of his style. On their surfaces, these two books could hardly be less alike. *Arthur Rex,* as the book jacket informs us, is "Thomas Berger's salute to the Age of Chivalry from his own enmired situation in the Time of the Cad." *Neighbors* is a contemporary domestic tale of harassment, in which, its jacket announces (in prose which can only be Berger's), "the truth is often exposed as brutally as the shame of an exhibitionist who lifts his raincoat in a park, and there are scenes in which the droll, the horrid, and the merely humiliating are inextricably intermingled." *Arthur Rex* is Berger's homage to Sir Thomas Mallory; *Neighbors* tips its hat to Franz Kafka, with a nod to the older masters, Pierre Choderlos de Laclos and the Marquis de Sade.

In *Arthur Rex,* Berger inevitably brings modern scrutiny and his sense of humor to the legend of King Arthur, but he does so in keeping with his "genuine hunger for gallantry and a passion for panache." Accordingly, Berger's retelling of the legend has a double focus. He indicates the complicated nature of this focus with the observation that "we now know that greatness, wisdom, and courage are necessarily conjoined with selfishness, childishness, and petulance—had not Winston Churchill been an egomaniac, Britain would have fallen to Hitler, to give a political example." Or, as Berger puts this dichotomy another way, "The Arthurian legend is essentially infantile: and you must understand that I believe children are naturally vicious." One of Berger's most compelling characters, Gawaine, most human and ultimately the wisest of Arthur's knights, suggests some of the effects of Berger's belief when, late in his life, he is asked by a brother if he does not long for the old days of action: " 'Nay,' said Sir Gawaine. 'I am happy to have had them in my proper time, but of a life of adventure it can be said that there is no abiding satisfaction, for when one adventure is done, a knight liveth in expectation of another, and if the next come not soon enough he falleth in love, in the sort of love that is an adventure, for what he seeketh be the adventure and not the lovingness. And methinks this sequence is finally infantile, and beyond a certain age one can no longer be interested in games.' "

Berger's retelling of the Arthur legend in no way diminishes the glory of Arthur's attempt or the measure of his achievement, but it does devote greater attention to the cause of the legend's final tragedy. In one sense, that tragedy centers not on the dissolution of the Round Table nor on the estranging of Arthur, Guinevere, and Launcelot, but on the erosion of the innocent belief that life can be governed by the simple principle of opposing good to evil. Complexity finally overwhelms Arthur and even the wicked who oppose him. Having had little success in her schemes against Arthur, the crafty Morgan la Fey enters a nunnery, "for after a long career in the service of evil she had come to believe that corruption were sooner brought amongst humankind by the forces of virtue, and from this moment on she was notable for her piety."

Arthur knows when he formulates his code of chivalry that his efforts, being human, will ultimately fail, but he insists that they can fail gloriously, since glory "doth come only from a quest for that which is impossible of attainment." What he does not know is that strict adherence to a rigid code of conduct may create more problems than it solves, threaten order more than ensure it. One problem is that Arthur and his men define themselves precisely by the evil they oppose, and in ridding the land of evil they call their own existence into question more than they affirm it. When the young Percival's mother challenges his wish to become a knight, she observes that "for all the brave men in the world who fight for the good, there is no less of evil anywhere." He can only answer, "if there were no evil, then what would become of bravery?" And, when Sir Percival, the most naive of knights, searches for the Holy Grail, he encounters a kind of relativity that Arthur's rule cannot assimilate: "And some of the men he met were fairly good, and some were very evil, but most were a mixture of virtues and vices whether they wore silk or rags, or lived in a palace or a hut or a cave, and taking them all in all, all were corrupt to a great degree, but none was without some small virtue, and all were equal in that they lived in Time."

What dawns too slowly on Arthur and some of his knights is the realization that the Code of Chivalry, like any system of abstract principles, comes into conflict with itself if pursued too blindly. After Gawaine's honor demands that he avenge his father's death, even though that death, at the hands of another knight, was itself justified by honor, Arthur sadly notes that the code's guidance begins to blur because "distinctions are sometimes hard to draw, for our obligations do oft war each on each." To Launcelot, Arthur admits that "evil doing hath got more subtle, perhaps even to the point at which it can not properly be encountered with the sword." The warring of obligations to equally compelling rationales for action leads the two greatest knights of all, Launcelot and Gawaine, to fight each other. During that sad fight, Launcelot suddenly understands that "if Gawaine's morality were complex, it was because chivalry in general was more complicated than it seemed, for it is not easy always to know what is the noble thing, or what is brave and generous or even simply decent." In Berger's hands, Arthur's most anguishing discovery is not that he has been betrayed by his queen and his most trusted knight, but that his philosophy has been shallow, because "to the profound vision there is no virtue and no vice, and what is justice to one, is injustice to another."

Arthur recognizes the flaw in his great dream, but Berger makes it clear that Arthur's legend is not to be judged by the success or failure of that dream. The Lady of the Lake assures the dying Arthur that he could not have done better in his life than he did, and the ghost of Sir Gawaine offers to his king the Round Table's poignant epitaph: "we sought no easy victories, nor won any. And perhaps for that we will be remembered."

From Camelot to suburbia is quite a jump, but Berger's *Neighbors* shares several of the concerns of *Arthur Rex*. Berger has jokingly remarked that "the most difficult thing in life is to maintain one's belief in one's hoax." While lightly made, his comment has a serious edge to it: substitute *myth* or *legend* for *hoax* and Arthur's greatest burden becomes clear; substitute *self-image* or *style* for *hoax* and this most difficult of tasks falls to Earl Keese, Berger's protagonist in *Neighbors*. Keese, a quiet, reasonable forty-nine-year-old suburbanite, tells people that his home sits "at the end of the road," because that construction sounds less "dispiriting" than would his saying he lives at a "dead end." But, when Harry and Ramona—new neighbors—move next door, within twenty-four hours Keese is faced with a sequence of situations so outrageous that he can find no rhetorical constructions to mask their threat or to maintain the hoax of his previously complacent life.

Mysterious and maddening, Harry and Ramona are, by turns, forward, friendly, rude, flattering, insulting, and provoking. Their words and actions are always unexpected and usually contradictory; they are *not* good neighbors. Their visits more and more seem like assaults. Their comings and goings produce a series of off-balance events, each more preposterous than the last, gradually stripping Keese of his easy assumptions and habitual responses. Harry and Ramona seem committed to tweaking Keese's sensibility, to pushing him to see how far he will go to avoid humiliation, to pestering, haunting, and ultimately rearranging his life. Their behavior stuns him, placing him at such disadvantage in all his dealings with them that he is driven to respond in thoughts and actions even more outlandish than theirs. He desperately sighs, "I am trying to adjust to

Dust jacket

a life in which chance encounters can be brutal."

In this absurd context, Harry's firing a shotgun at Keese and offering him a dirty coffee cup seem equally offensive, and Harry and Ramona sting Keese as much by accusing him of sarcasm as they do by falsely accusing him of attempted rape. Yet as Keese's experiences increasingly blur the line between comedy and nightmare, his relations with all those around him begin to undergo subtle changes—a metamorphosis. He realizes that his life had grown so stale that Harry's and Ramona's crazy-seeming aggravations may actually offer him a salvation of sorts—the chance to take control of his life, to team up with them and "roam the boulevards with a supercilious smile for all, and glide through smart shops exchanging glib remarks."

In his glowing review of *Neighbors,* Thomas R. Edwards has pointed out how Keese rises to Harry and Ramona's insidious challenge: "What begins as a practical defense of what he takes to be his life—social decency, worldly goods, family and home—shifts, under their ruthless pressure, toward something more essential, a new sense of self that can survive the loss of the people and things and styles his old self had seemed to require." And this change is not beyond Keese's notice, as he finally admits to Harry, "Every time I see you as a criminal, by another light you look like a kind of benefactor."

Madcap physical changes punctuate Berger's plot—entrances, exits, fights, a damaged car, a destroyed house—but for all its action, *Neighbors* might best be described as a series of functions of language: puns, platitudes, theories, definitions, excuses, accusations, rationalizations, promises, questions, threats—all acts performed with words. Keese, Berger notes "is a prisoner of what he believes to be his responsibilities, in language as in all else." Because he suffers from "outlandish illusions," Keese knows enough never to trust completely what he sees. However, he does believe his ears, consistently confusing rhetoric with reality. Language explicitly fascinates Keese and implicitly dupes him, so much so that when a wrecker driver suddenly starts cursing him, Keese protests, "You can't be getting nasty. You were just so nice."

Neighbors may offer the most verbal world Berger has created; like his *Little Big Man* it is a book in which language becomes the only operating reality. Perhaps for this reason, it is also Berger's favorite of his novels: "It is for me the absolutely pure fiction that I have lately aspired to, with no taint of journalism, sociology, and the other corruptions." He describes *Neighbors* as his translation of *The Trial,* explaining "it was Kafka who taught me that at any moment banality might turn sinister, for existence was not meant to be unfailingly genial." Calling *Neighbors* "a story of harassment—another of the sadomasochistic situations in which, I think, my peculiar strength lies," Berger concludes: "The suspense comes in trying to identify who's the kicker and who the kickee, *sub specie aeternitatis* or even only in terms of the local supermarket."

Thomas Berger continues to be one of America's most perplexing and most productive writers. Since, as he puts it, he does nothing but write novels, no more than a couple of years usually passes between the appearance of one of his novels and the next. Of his steady regimen, he explains: "I never take a vacation, because what would it be *from*? I became a novelist many years ago so that I might live in a continuum of make-believe in which there are no weekends and, more importantly, no Monday mornings." The only interruptions to his writing are his occasional moves, the most recent of which was from an island in Maine back to the New York area. His most recently completed project is a fourth novel following the misadventures of Carlo Reinhart, the protagonist of *Crazy in Berlin, Reinhart in Love,* and *Vital Parts.* Berger promises that in this outing, to be titled "Reinhart's Women," Reinhart finally becomes a winner. He says of his Reinhart books: "They are as near as I can come to the standard novel-as-slice-of-life. I do one now and again to keep in touch with reality, for my connections to society get ever feebler."

—Brooks Landon

Interviews:

Douglas Hughes, "Thomas Berger's Elan: An Interview," *Confrontation,* 12 (Spring-Summer 1976): 23-39;

Richard Schickel, "Interviewing Thomas Berger," *New York Times Book Review,* 6 April 1980, pp. 1, 21-22.

References:

Thomas Edwards, "Domestic Guerrillas," *New York Times Book Review,* 6 April 1980, pp. 1, 23;

Brooks Landon, "The Radical Americanist," *Nation* (20 August 1977): 151-153;

Michael Malone, "American Literature's Little Big Man," *Nation* (3 May 1980): 535-537;

Leonard Michaels, "If Hammett and Chandler Were Written by Perelman," *New York Times Book Review,* 20 March 1977, pp. 1, 25-26;

John Romano, "Camelot and All That," *New York*

Times Book Review, 12 November 1978, pp. 3, 62;

Richard Schickel, "Bitter Comedy," *Commentary*, 50 (July 1970): 76-80;

Stanley Trachtenberg, "Berger and Barth: The Comedy of Decomposition," in *Comic Relief*, ed. Sarah B. Cohen (Urbana: University of Illinois Press, 1978), pp. 45-69;

Frederick Turner, "Melville and Thomas Berger: the Novelist as Cultural Anthropologist," *Centennial Review*, 13 (Winter 1969): 101-121;

Turner, "The Second Decade of *Little Big Man*," *Nation* (20 August 1977): 149-151.

Papers:

The Boston University library has a collection of manuscripts and related correspondence.

A STATEMENT

by THOMAS BERGER

In the *Dictionary of Literary Biography*, volume 2, *American Novelists Since World War II* (1978), the author of the entry on Thomas Berger is of course welcome to his tastes in fiction and did not need a license from me to assess my first eight novels. But it almost goes without saying—not quite, else I should not be saying it—that I should find inadequate his no doubt earnest or at any rate solemn attempt to approach my work as of 1977. How anyone, however pedestrian, could plod through my career without noticing that each of my books is written in another style cannot easily be explained—until one understands that what this man looks for exclusively is the sociological and not the literary and boldly demonstrates his immunity to infection by language by ignoring all linguistic considerations throughout these many pages except for the line or two of naive commentary on the styles of *Little Big Man* (lavishly praised by others) and *Who Is Teddy Villanova?*, of which Leonard Michaels, in the *New York Times Book Review*, said, "[the] style . . . is one of the great pleasures of the book . . . educated, complicated, graceful, silly, destructive in spirit. . . . Essentially then, Berger's style is like itself insofar as it is like other styles. And [the] whole novel—in its wide ranging reference to cultural forms both high and pop—is like a huge verbal mirror."

It should be said that Mr. Michaels's enthusiastic notice was on the front page of the *Book Review* and that John Leonard praised the book in the daily *New York Times*, and that prominent favorable reviews appeared in *Time* and *Newsweek* and in newspapers all across the land—a piece of fact that would seem to expose as fanciful the bald statement of our local authority to the effect that *Who Is Teddy Villanova?* received a "poor critical reception."

But then our critic tends consistently to record only that which would support his biases, an all-too-human and perhaps even fetching trait which can be found in us all, but I cannot allow him smugly to pretend that—aside from Richard Schickel, in *Commentary*, which identification, incidentally, is missing, though an adverse reviewer is painstakingly named, along with his periodical—in his judgment of *Killing Time* he is joined by the world, when the book was called by Arthur Koestler, in the *Observer*, the best novel of its year of publication, and by Leo Braudy, in the *New York Times Book Review*, "Berger's most brilliant effort to engage in the most truly poetic task of renovating the language we speak," and praised by Guy Davenport in the *National Review*, Brooks Landon in the *Nation*, and, again, on and on.

To deal with the eccentricities of this study, which would so often render the work under examination as unrecognizable to him who wrote it, is beyond my patience (e.g., I am not a "satirist" who offers "bits of promise amidst decay"; *Killing Time* is no more "ambitious" than anything else I have ever written; and *Sneaky People* is not a "comic novel"), but let me penultimately state some facts that cannot be controverted by the fancy of poor scholarship: *Little Big Man*, the sales of which on its first publication scarcely exceeded 10,000 copies, was hardly a "popular" success and except for specialists in Western history received little serious critical attention. Indeed, not until the release of the multimillion-dollar motion picture of the same name, six years after the publication of the book, did the paperback edition, which had gone out of print but was reissued, begin to sell in appreciable quantities. And not until the same time did I begin to hear, from the persons who prefer images on film to words on paper, that the novel was to be commended: for in our lamentable culture many literary intellectuals are quite as vulgar as lesser breeds. Nor was *Sneaky People* any more of a "popular and critical success" than *Who Is Teddy Villanova?*—!

And it should be noted that the confident assertion with which this study of an imaginary author concludes, viz., "Most critics believe that Berger has yet to produce a work which adequately expresses his . . . gifts," is as pure an invention as anything else in the essay. Readers are advised to understand that the judgment enunciated applies only to the lone name signed thereunder.

Richard Brautigan

(30 January 1935-   )

The *DLB* entries on Richard Brautigan appear in *Dictionary of Literary Biography*, volume 2, *American Novelists Since World War II* (1978), pp. 65-70 and *Dictionary of Literary Biography*, volume 5, *American Poets Since World War II, Part I: A-K* (1980), pp. 96-99.

NEW BOOKS: *June 30th, June 30th* (New York: Delacorte/Seymour Lawrence, 1978);
The Tokyo-Montana Express (New York: Delacorte/Seymour Lawrence, 1980).

Richard Brautigan

Noted for his taciturnity about biographical information, Richard Brautigan perhaps views his personal life as a work-in-progress, an appropriate view in light of the highly autobiographical character of his most recent works, *June 30th, June 30th* (1978) and *The Tokyo-Montana Express* (1980). Brautigan is currently headquartered at his small ranch outside of Livingston, Montana, seat of Park County, which is bordered on the south by Yellowstone National Park. The sparsely populated, mountainous region with its protean horizons and bountiful fishing is congenial to an author who is frequently compared to Hemingway in his affection for nature. "I get a lot of my work done at the ranch. There's isolation here, a beautiful relationship to the fierce, stark hugeness of the land," Brautigan tells *New York Times Book Review* columnist Herbert Mitgang. Brautigan leaves the pastoral Montana setting for occasional readings and for frequent trips to San Francisco and Tokyo. "One day I'm here, the next day I'm there," he tells Mitgang. "And I find a kinship between Montana and Japan; the people are dynamic in both places."

June 30th, June 30th, a collection of poetry in diary form, records Brautigan's first visit to Japan in the spring of 1976. The title is based on the date of departure for the United States after his seven-week sojourn, the date repeated because the day is recaptured as the airplane crosses the international date line. Brautigan's introduction to the collection explains the evolution of his "deep affection" for the Japanese. The six-year-old Richard Brautigan, growing up in Tacoma, Washington, at the advent of World War II, adopted the adult world's attitude toward the Japanese. His imaginary slaughter of the enemy is the kernel for "The Ghost Children of Tacoma" in *Revenge of the Lawn* (1971). His hatred was brought into sharp focus by the death of his Uncle Edward, "indirectly" attributed to the Japanese. Brautigan writes of the death in the poem "1942," collected in *The Pill Versus the Springhill Mine Disaster* (1968) and repeated in the introduction of *June 30th, June 30th.* As he matured into his midteens, Brautigan says, the hatred gave way to a self-righteous and patronizing forgiveness, and as he approached his twenties, a growing awareness of Japanese culture—through Japanese literature, paintings, scrolls, religion, food, movies, and friends—brought an admiration and affection that led inevitably to the visit.

The tone of the seventy-three poems and four fragments in *June 30th, June 30th* shifts at fairly identifiable junctures in correspondence with the author's changes in mood. Most of the poems written during the first five days of the visit are marked by a childlike naivete and awe occasioned by the speaker's confrontations with ordinary Japanese life. Brautigan commemorates his first Japanese bird and fly, celebrates his first solo order from a Japanese menu, and, upon winning a game of pachinko (vertical pinball), exuberates, "I feel wonderful, exhilarated, child-like, / perfect." As the novelty of the cultural encounter wanes, the tone becomes increasingly one of loneliness. The language barrier heightens the sense of isolation, but the speaker notes, "I've been there before / in Japan, America, everywhere when you / don't understand what somebody is / talking about." The speaker's depression diminishes as the diary progresses and human contacts are made, relationships formed. Dispersed throughout *June 30th, June 30th* are panegyrics upon Oriental pulchritude ("If there are any unattractive / Japanese women / they must drown them at birth."), reminiscent of the romanticized descriptions of Yukiko, the estranged mistress of the American humorist protagonist of *Sombrero Fallout* (1976). Also included are denunciations of smug Caucasians in Japan and Brautigan's familiar musings on time—recognition of the past's fateful gestation of present and speculation on the enigma of future.

Critics have noted the disparate quality of the poems in *June 30th, June 30th*. Some equal or surpass the best of Brautigan's earlier poetry; a few are solipsistic indulgences that serve primarily to mark times and places in the diary. A reviewer for *Choice* suggests that the volume, "an often good book," will be "served well by the winnowing process that will eventually take place." In his introduction, Brautigan himself acknowledges that "the quality . . . is uneven," but adds, "I have printed them all anyway because they are a diary expressing my feelings and emotions in Japan and the quality of life is often uneven."

The Tokyo-Montana Express, which Brautigan says took three years to compose, shows promise of providing literary taxonomists with hours of activity—as did *Trout Fishing in America* (1967). Called by Brautigan in his interview with Mitgang a "novel" but more prudently labeled a "book" on the dust jacket, *The Tokyo-Montana Express* is a pastiche of 131 entries, several previously published, set primarily in Tokyo, Montana, and San Francisco. The entries, unrelated by plot, are held together tenuously by the metaphor of the train. Brautigan explains to Mitgang, "The novel is arranged like a train trip. There are stops along the way, and the 'I' in the story is the voice of the stations along the tracks of the Tokyo-Montana Express. Each chapter is separated by a photo of a medallion of the last coal-burning train that I saw in the transportation museum in Tokyo." Providing greater cohesiveness, though, are the strong identity of the narrator and the elaboration of his concerns. The work appears largely autobiographical, more so perhaps than any of Brautigan's earlier novel-length

Richard Brautigan and Shiina Takako lolling in a small boat off the coast of Japan. It was a hot afternoon and they were tired of fishing.
Photograph © 1980 Nakai Keisuke
ISBN: 0-440-08770-8
RICHARD BRAUTIGAN
The TOKYO-MONTANA EXPRESS
DELACORTE PRESS
LAWRENCE
The TOKYO-MONTANA EXPRESS
D51
A BOOK BY
RICHARD BRAUTIGAN
Dust jacket

prose, but, as Robert Novak cautions in *Dictionary of Literary Biography*, volume 2, although Brautigan's "stories often seem to have . . . many autobiographical details, he obviously invents freely."

There is a fair sprinkling of the celebrated Brautigan humor in *The Tokyo-Montana Express*, but the tone is more often one of melancholy nostalgia, and common motifs are unfulfilled dreams, aging, and death. It is a book fraught with endings: failed business ventures—pale epitaphs to the illusionary American Dream, discarded Christmas trees, dead and abandoned animals, a death-row menu, drowning, and suicide. Past decades are recalled, the 1960s with a vignette of a middle-aged Indian woman searching in the snow in New Mexico for a lost tire chain as her brother casually waits with his foot propped on the running board of his "blue Age-of-Aquarius pickup truck," and the 1970s with a poignant metaphor of a caged wolf, the "pet" of an insensitive owner, aimlessly but persistently pacing his life away. The narrator, often preoccupied with gloomy thoughts about aging, eschews the complexities of the modern world, trades his Sunday *New York Times* for the *National Enquirer*, and announces that "sometimes all I want to do is have a little mindless fun with the years that are left in my life." The desire for simplicity is evident in the subject matter of the work, drawn largely from the quotidian. With varying degrees of artistry, Brautigan unleashes his fertile imagination on discarded chocolate wrappers and rubber bands, on umbrellas and an empty popcorn jar—a validation of the narrator's comment that "I spend a lot of my life interested in little things, tiny portions of reality like a pinch of spice in a very complicated recipe that takes days to cook, sometimes even longer. Any more spice than the single pinch and you're walking on dangerous ground." The penchant for the uncomplicated is also apparent in Brautigan's figurative language. The vehicles are Frostian in their simplicity; it is the elaboration that marks a figure as Brautigan's: "My mind is racing forward at such a speed that compared to it, a bolt of lightning would seem like an ice cube in an old woman's forlorn glass of weak lemonade on some front porch lost in Louisiana. She stares straight ahead at nothing, holding the glass of lemonade in her hand."

After a lengthy excursion into more traditional plot handling in his novels published in the 1970s—several of them parodies of popular forms—Brautigan may be flirting in *The Tokyo-Montana Express* with a return to the method of his first-written and most highly acclaimed novel, *Trout Fishing in America*, the work which critics have been wont to use as a yardstick in pointing out shortcomings of subsequent works. In *City of Words* (1971), Tony Tanner describes *Trout Fishing in America* as "self-dissolving or self-cancelling writing," and his comments on the work befit *The Tokyo-Montana Express*: "Each chapter is a separate fragment, unpredictable because unrelated in any of the usual ways. Each one engages us for a moment with its humour, or strangeness, or unusual evocation, and then fades away. . . . It is one of Brautigan's distinctive achievements that his magically delicate verbal ephemera seem to accomplish their own vanishings."

Brautigan still courts—and attracts—a limited audience, largely the high-school and college reader who is near the age of Brautigan's daughter, Ianthe, born in 1960. In 1978 his works became the center of a book-banning controversy in a northern California high school. The American Civil Liberties Union and Brautigan's hardcover publisher, Seymour Lawrence, Inc., joined several students and teachers in a suit against the Shasta County school board after several of Brautigan's works were removed from the classroom. The publisher reports that the case was decided in Brautigan's favor.

In his fourth novel, *The Abortion: An Historical Romance 1966* (1971), Brautigan introduces himself as a character in the form of a contributor to the unique library of the novel. "The author was tall and blond and had a long yellow mustache that gave him an anachronistic appearance," Brautigan writes about himself. "He looked as if he would be at home in another era. This was the third or fourth book he had brought to the library. Every time he brought in a new book he looked a little older, a little more tired." In *The Tokyo-Montana Express* the narrator describes himself in one entry as looking "like a fading middle-aged hippie" and in another comments that "what makes you older is when your bones, muscles and blood wear out, when the heart sinks into oblivion and all the houses you ever lived in are gone and people are not really certain that your civilization ever existed." Popularly identified as a chronicler of the youth movement of the 1960s, Brautigan displays in his recent work a sense of displacement in time and a longing for halcyon days. "Now, at 45," he reports to Mitgang, "I feel that I'm maturing and weathering. The weather is very nice in Montana."

—*David M. Taylor*

Periodical Publication:

"Great Golden Telescope," *Redbook*, 153 (August 1979): 57.

References:

Patricia Holt, "Judge Advances Fight Against Brautigan Book Ban," *Publishers Weekly* (9 April 1979): 19-20;

Holt, "Seymour Lawrence and ACLU Fight Ban on Brautigan Books," *Publishers Weekly* (16 October 1978): 32;

Herbert Mitgang, "Home on the Range," *New York Times Book Review*, 26 October 1980, p. 59.

Truman Capote

(30 September 1924-)

The *DLB* entry on Truman Capote appears in *Dictionary of Literary Biography*, volume 2, *American Novelists Since World War II* (1978), pp. 81-88.

NEW BOOK: *Music for Chameleons* (New York: Random House, 1980).

From the vantage point of 1980, any assessment of Truman Capote must be tentative. There has been a fifteen-year hiatus between the publication of *In Cold Blood* (1965) and the just released *Music for Chameleons*, a collection of short pieces all written since 1975. Still uncertain is the status of the long awaited nonfiction novel, "Answered Prayers." By all accounts, the decade of the 1970s has been a difficult one for Truman Capote, both personally and professionally. Capote's candor in essays and interviews over the last few years has made it clear that somewhere in the neighborhood of his fiftieth year, he underwent a profound crisis.

Capote's initial difficulties surfaced as a kind of writer's block. He had been working on, and had received a handsome advance for, "Answered Prayers" ("more tears are shed over answered prayers than unanswered ones."—Saint Theresa), but by 1973, the novel was five years overdue, and he had become bogged down by what he calls an "obsessive perfectionism" that caused him to redo thirty pages in order to change twenty words. Months would go by without any writing at all. In an effort to break through the block, he decided to publish several sections of the novel in *Esquire*, hoping to rekindle his own enthusiasm, but it only seemed to make things worse. One published section, "Le Côte Basque: 1965," was filled with the names of and unpleasant stories about the rich and famous, and those who had been his close friends soon ceased to be so. Although his treatment of them seemed both indiscreet and unkind, Capote nevertheless professed to be genuinely shocked by their reactions: "[It] was unbelievable. I might just as well have killed the Lindbergh baby." There were other losses as well: the death of his Palm Springs housekeeper and longtime confidante, Myrtle Bennett; the death of his paternal grandmother, a pivotal figure in his childhood; and the end of a four-year love affair with a married man. In addition, there were legal troubles: Gore Vidal filed a one-million-dollar lawsuit for an unflattering anecdote Capote told in *Playgirl* about Vidal's insulting Jacqueline Kennedy at a White House dinner and subsequently being asked to leave.

In May 1976, Capote was involved in what he described as a "near fatal" automobile accident and pled guilty to a charge of drunk driving. By June 1976 he was experiencing severe emotional pain, which led him to seek help from a series of five psychiatrists. He committed himself to the Silver Hill Hospital in Connecticut for a month to rid himself of his dependency on drugs and alcohol, but his recovery was only temporary. He sought treatment again, this time at the "fortress-like" Smithers Alcoholic Rehabilitation Center in New York City. That fall, he appeared at Towson State University in Maryland on one stop of a projected college lecture tour. Obviously unsteady on his arrival, he left the stage almost immediately,

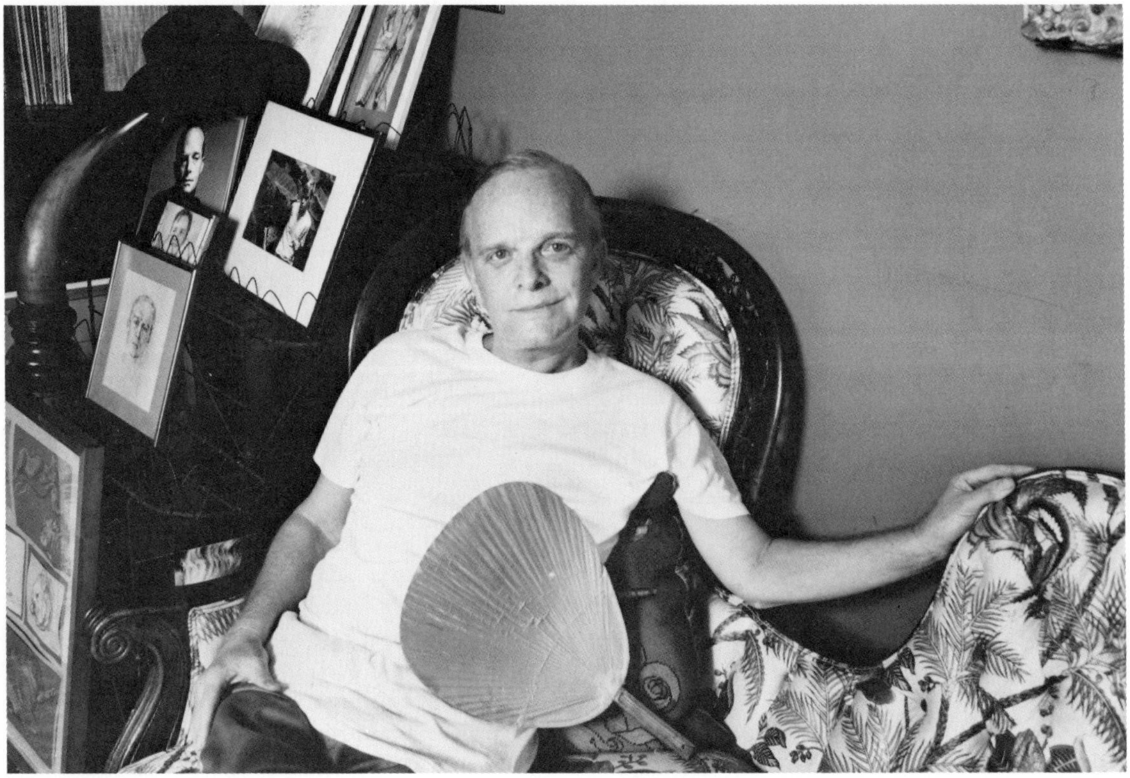

Truman Capote

announcing that he was an alcoholic and would not appear again in public until he was well.

In general, Capote has kept that promise. His own most recent comments indicate that he has spent the last few years taking stock of himself and his work, although he minimizes the relationship between his personal and professional troubles. In September 1977, he stopped work on "Answered Prayers"—by his estimate two-thirds to three-quarters complete—not so much, he claims, because of his personal problems, or the reaction to "Le Cote Basque: 1965," but because of a growing uneasiness about the writing itself; "My writing was becoming too dense," he notes. "Slowly, but with accelerating alarm, I read every word I'd ever published, and decided that never, not once in my writing life, had I completely exploded all the energy and esthetic excitements that material contained." As Capote continued to analyze his work, it began to present a major aesthetic issue, "an apparently unsolvable problem, and if I couldn't solve it, I might as well quit writing. The problem was: how can a writer successfully combine within a single form—say the short story—all he knows about every other form of writing? . . . A writer ought to have all his colors, all his abilities available on the same palette for mingling (and, in suitable instances, simultaneous application). But how?"

As Capote describes it, he was envisioning a technique that would incorporate all his previous development in his craft but would also represent a departure from his most recent triumph, *In Cold Blood*. He saw himself at the beginning of a crucial fourth and final phase in his career. In his eyes, the first phase, concluding with the publication of *Other Voices, Other Rooms* (1948), had been spent mastering a polished fictional technique. The second phase was one of experimentation, developing a variety of techniques, which culminated in *The Muses Are Heard* (1956), a collection of articles in which for the first time Capote utilized the novel form to write about factual material. The third phase, "a gamble," which extended the application of fictional technique to fact, resulted in *In Cold Blood*. The fourth began with Capote's attempts to write "Answered Prayers." His description of these attempts and the aesthetic problems that arose sheds light on the interplay between his personal and professional crises.

His first task in undertaking "Answered Prayers" involved "rewriting and indexing my own letters, other people's letters, my diaries and journals (which contain very complete accounts of hundreds of scenes and conversations) for the years 1943 through 1965." It was, then, to be not only nonfictional, but autobiographical as well, and thus

Capote found himself trying to write an autobiographical novel, trying to incorporate his own viewpoint, at precisely the time when his sense of self was in real jeopardy. So it was that in 1977 he set aside "Answered Prayers" and embarked on experiments with a new style of writing, incorporating this element of self: "I set myself center stage, and reconstructed, in a severe, minimal manner, commonplace conversations with everyday people: the superintendent of my building, a masseur at the gym. . . ." Out of these exercises, Capote developed a form which he calls "Conversational Portraits," "a framework into which I could assimilate everything I knew about writing. . . . using a modified version of this technique, I wrote a nonfiction short novel (*Handcarved Coffins*) and a number of short stories."

These comments on the fourth phase of his career first appeared in *Vogue* (December 1979) and now serve as the preface to his collection of "new writing," *Music for Chameleons*, encompassing with one exception virtually all he has published since stopping work on "Answered Prayers." (The exception is "Mojave," an apparently discarded section of "Answered Prayers," which is still described as forthcoming.) A discussion of three pieces—"Music for Chameleons," "Dazzle," and "Mojave"—should be sufficient for gauging the impact of Capote's experimentation on his work.

The title piece, "Music for Chameleons," is a particularly striking and haunting piece set in Martinique: on the surface an idle, amiable conversation between Capote and a nameless but elegant woman, a Martinique aristocrat; lurking under the surface a *basso ostinato* of present and past violence, notably the murder of Capote's friend Marc Blitzstein in a Martinique bar fifteen years before. Clearly the piece is nonfictional and autobiographical, for it first appeared in the *New Yorker* column "Our Far Flung Correspondents." Just as clearly it is masterful in its fictional technique. It marks the woman's chilling elegance that she performs a Mozart piece for an audience of chameleons in order to show Capote that they are music lovers: "They skittered across the terrace and scampered into the salon, a sensitive, absorbed audience for the music played. And then not played, for suddenly my hostess stood and stamped her foot, and the chameleons scattered like sparks from an exploding star."

As the dialogue continues, Capote stares at his hostess's "black mirror" in which "there is nothing there to be read or seen—except the mystery of one's own image projected by the black mirror's surface before it recedes into its endless depths. . . ." The black mirror, used by artists like Van Gogh and

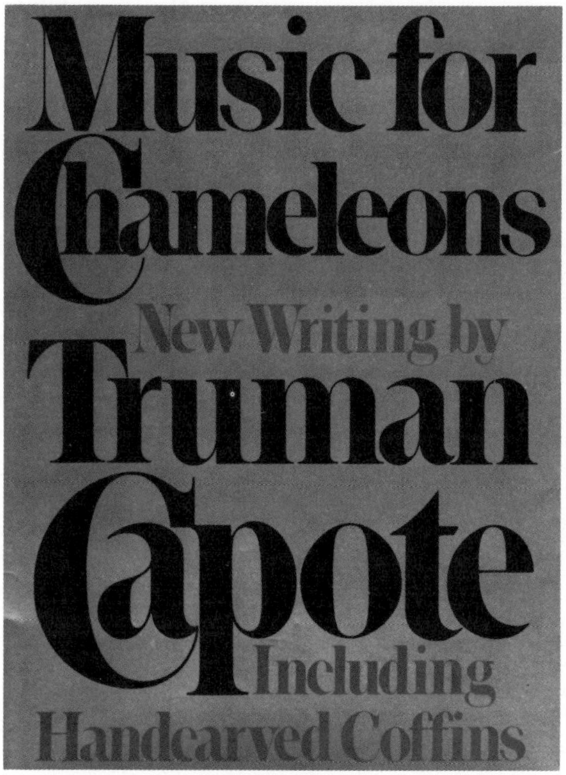

Dust jacket

Gauguin "to refresh their vision," now serves as an objective correlative for Capote's reluctant reentry into this nightmare of his past: "all the while the black mirror has been lying in my lap, and once more my eyes seek its depths. Strange where our passions carry us, floggingly pursue us, forcing upon us unwanted dreams, unwelcome destinies." The dialogue ends as Capote's hostess returns to her piano and her Mozart, and the chameleons assemble as her audience.

As Capote suggests, the strength of the piece has much to do with our awareness of an actual history underlying the dialogue, and an autobiographical presence. The piece lives because of the irreconcilable tension of point-counterpoint: the aristocrat's tolerance for and icy pleasure in her culture versus Capote's horror and melancholy. "Music for Chameleons" is first-rate Capote.

"Dazzle," on the other hand, written in the same experimental manner, is less successful. On the occasion of its appearance in *Esquire*, Capote observed, "I couldn't have written 'Dazzle' before this [new technique], because I wasn't prepared to fit something as psychologically complicated into such a short space. I think I've now arrived at what I call a swift simplicity. I've been working on speeding up my effects." Yet except for Capote's insistence on its autobiographical validity, it seems a throwback to far earlier Capote. The story is an episode from Capote's boyhood in New Orleans. Eight years old, he is haunted by a wish to become a girl and is convinced that Mrs. Ferguson, a New Orleans laundress with a reputation for magical powers, can grant it. Mrs. Ferguson becomes interested in him as well when she discovers that his grandmother possesses a gaudy gemstone which Mrs. Ferguson mistakenly assumes to be valuable. Not knowing his wish specifically, she nevertheless sends her son Skeeter to negotiate: his wish for the pendant. The atmosphere surrounding Mrs. Ferguson is explicitly sexual. When Skeeter ushers Capote, with the pendant, into Mrs. Ferguson's house, he tells him, "Walk right in. And if you catch her in the middle of a hump, keep your eyes open: that's how I got be a champion humper." Capote gives her the stone, but delays in telling her his wish. When he finally blurts it out, "her voice was soft and hissing and serpentine. 'You don't know what you want, boy. I'll show you what you want. Look at me, boy.' " All the while she spins the stone—"Spindazzlespinspindazzledazzledazzle"—and whether from the stone's movement or the emotions of the moment, Capote blacks out, coming to only when he is back at his house.

Capote describes his story: "at the climactic moment in 'Dazzle,' when Mrs. Ferguson lifts the gem, I do a quick cut. Bang! I'm back in my house in the next paragraph, and the story ends in three more. A lot happens in those final paragraphs, in fact the whole point of the story is there, but it all moves *very fast.*" The whole point is that forty-four years later, when his grandmother dies, Capote suddenly realizes that since this episode, he has had no access to his feelings for his grandmother, because thoughts of her have been inextricably connected with the sinister Mrs. Ferguson and his own act of theft. It is this realization that makes his grief surface. Yet the "swift simplicity" is too swift, too simple. The grief is not felt or conveyed, nor is there a coming to terms with the sexual atmosphere, which disturbs the child Capote far more than concerns over rightful possession. Last paragraphs aside, "Dazzle" does not seem so much a piece of "new writing" as another episode in the life of Joel Knox of *Other Voices, Other Rooms,* written in first person, rather than third.

"Mojave," however, written before Capote's experiments, has all the explosiveness one could ask. The story is complex, haunting, and masterful in its denouement, a series of stories within stories turning on a series of sexual triangles. The plot is simple: Sarah Whitelaw's day, which is made up of encounters with three men: Jaime, her hairdresser; Dr. Bentsen, her analyst turned gigolo: and her husband, George. Each man shares with her the end of an affair. In George's case, it prompts him to tell her about George Schmidt, an old blind masseur he met in the Mojave Desert thirty years before. The old man had just been marooned there by his wife and her nineteen-year-old lover, and he told Whitelaw the sordid details of love, duplicity, betrayal, and abandonment. As Whitelaw retells the story, he so successfully mimics the masseur that he becomes him, "a man fixed in another man's mind," a man who observes, "Snakes and Women. One thing they have in common is: the last thing that dies is their tails." Only after he ends the story does Whitelaw inform Sarah (as well as the reader) that once again the mistress she has provided for him, out of guilt for her own frigidity, has left him. "We all, sometimes, leave each other out there under the skies and we never understand why," he concludes. Dutifully, Sara responds, "*Please,* darling. We'll think of somebody."

"Mojave" is a portrait of people in sterile relationships, operating at cross purposes, and revealing their aloneness in dialogues which are really two-voice monologues, different only in surface content. With its parallel plots like "an echo, caverns resounding," "Mojave" has the strengths of both his new and old writing: the ability to convey in tightly focused and precise language, the gratuitousness of life, the universal chill which isolates each of us, regardless of what alliances and bonds we construct in our defense. And if there is little evidence to support Capote's claim to the mastery of a "new writing," there is comfort to be drawn from the fact that he has lost none of his previous power.

Perhaps Capote owes his recovery from his crisis simply to his ability to create a new credo for his writing. "He writes now for many hours at a stretch," Catherine Medwick reports, "in a room he has acquired just for the purpose. The room is all white, with just some photos taped to the walls. A view of the river. . . . " "For the last year or so," Capote tells her, "I really have been doing nothing but work work work work work. I work at writing ten, eleven hours a day. I mean, I've never done that in my life. And I know it's going to go on that way." Given Capote's present Spartan regimen, the long-awaited arrival of "Answered Prayers" may be close at hand, a worthy culmination, one hopes, to his "fourth and final" phase. *—J. Douglas Perry, Jr.*

References:

J. DeBelles, "Visions and Revisions: Truman Capote's *In Cold Blood,*" *Journal of Modern Literature,* 7 (September 1979): 519-536;

Ann T. Fleming, "The Private World of Truman Capote," *New York Times,* 9 July 1978, p. 22ff; 16 July 1978, p. 12ff;

John Hallowell, *Between Fact and Fiction: New Journalism and the Non-Fiction Novel* (Chapel Hill, N.C.: University of North Carolina Press, 1977);

Catherine Medwick, "Truman Capote," *Vogue,* 170 (December 1979): 263ff.;

L. Zacharias, "Living the American Dream: Children on their Birthdays," *Studies in Short Fiction,* 12 (Fall 1975): 343-350.

John Cheever

(27 May 1912-)

The *DLB* entry on John Cheever appears in *Dictionary of Literary Biography,* volume 2, *American Novelists Since World War II* (1978), pp. 88-100.

NEW BOOKS: *The Stories of John Cheever* (New York: Knopf, 1978);

The Day the Pig Fell into the Well (Northridge, Cal.: Lord John Press, 1978);

The Wapshot Chronicle and the Wapshot Scandal (New York: Harper & Row, 1979); previously published separately as *The Wapshot Chronicle* (1957) and *The Wapshot Scandal* (1964).

RECENT AWARDS: Pulitzer Prize, National Book Award, National Book Critics Circle Award, and the Edward McDowell Medal, 1979, for *The Stories of John Cheever.*

"When I was younger I didn't care about the audience," John Cheever said to Arthur Unger for the *Christian Science Monitor.* "The idea of an audience simply didn't cross my mind. An opinion of my age now is that writing is a mutual thing. I can't write without a reader. It's precisely like a kiss—you can't do it alone." Cheever's most recent novel, *Falconer* (1977), and *The Stories of John Cheever* (1978), which won major critical awards, brought him a celebrity he had never courted.

Certainly Cheever's late public recognition can be attributed partly to his own reclusiveness. In the past, he habitually avoided attention, even to the extent of leaving the country when his books were published. This kind of behavior stemmed from an attitude his parents helped instill in him. When he was twelve, he was given their permission to become a writer only after he promised, "I have no idea of becoming famous or wealthy." But the attitude seemed to undergo some revision with the success of *Falconer,* which celebrated his victory over depression and alcoholism. After its publication, a *Newsweek* interview by his oldest child, Susan Cheever, marked the beginning of a new accessibility. Cheever's openness in the interview and others that followed provided additional information about his life and insights into his work.

The Cheevers have lived for the past twenty years in an eighteenth-century house in Ossining, New York. Cheever has never had a real study—not even a desk, he says—but has worked in the rooms gradually vacated as his three children have left home. He bicycles in the mornings before writing and relaxes after the day's work by walking in his garden and the woods nearby. Cheever is Episcopalian and attends church regularly—"to make my thanksgivings. Period." Most of the Cheever family are writers. Susan Cheever's first novel, *Looking for Work,* was published in 1979 by Simon & Schuster. Benjamin is an editor for *Reader's Digest.* The youngest child, Fred, graduated last year from Stanford. Cheever's wife, the former Mary Winternitz, is a teacher and published poet. Cheever has said of their marriage, "That two people of our violent temperament have been able to live together for nearly 40 years as we have seems to me a splendid example of the richness and diversity of human nature . . . and in the 40 years there's scarcely a week in which we haven't planned to get a divorce." Susan Cheever observes, "Both are very strong, smart, independent. . . . They are together because they don't need each other."

In the lean early days of his writing, Cheever

went to Yaddo, the writers' colony in Saratoga Springs, New York, where he could work while getting free room and board. He has paid that debt by serving as a director for Yaddo for more than thirty years now. His generosity to new writers extends to reading as many as a hundred new books a year. In 1979 he went as a guest of the government to Bulgaria, the only Communist country that has published *Falconer* in translation. Although the novel is banned in all the other Communist countries, many of the short stories are available in Russian.

Shortly after the publication of *The Stories of John Cheever,* Cheever wrote for *Newsweek* a defense of the form in which he has been most prolific: "A collection of short stories appears like a lemon in the current fiction list. . . . but so long as we are possessed by experience that is distinguished by its intensity and its episodic nature, we will have the short story in our literature. . . ." Despite that modest apology, the book became one of the few short-story collections to make the best-seller lists. *The Stories of John Cheever* brings together in chronological order all of the stories from five earlier collections (*The Enormous Radio and Other Stories,* 1953; *The Housebreaker of Shady Hill,* 1958; *Some People, Places and Things That Will Not Appear in My Next Novel,* 1961; *The Brigadier and the Golf Widow,* 1964; and *The World of Apples,* 1973). There are in addition four stories that had not previously appeared in a book: "The Common Day," "The Day the Pig Fell into the Well," "The Bus to St. James," and "Another Story," all of which appeared originally in the *New Yorker.*

In his preface to the collection, Cheever writes: "It would please me if the order in which these stories are published had been reversed and if I appeared first as an elderly man and not as a young one who was truly shocked to discover that genuinely decorous men and women admitted into their affairs erotic bitterness and even greed. . . . A writer can be seen clumsily learning to walk, to tie his necktie, to make love, and to eat his peas off a fork. He appears much alone and determined to instruct himself. Naive, provincial in my case, sometimes drunk, sometimes obtuse, almost always clumsy, even a selected display of one's early work will be a naked history of one's struggle to receive an education in economics and love." He also pays tribute to editors Harold Ross, Gus Lobrano, and William Maxwell of the *New Yorker,* where many of these stories were first published. These men, he writes, "gave me the inestimable gifts of a large, discerning, and responsive group of readers and enough money to feed the family and buy a new suit every other year."

John Irving calls Cheever "the best storyteller living" and says in summarizing the collection: "Sixteen of *The Stories of John Cheever* moved me as if they had been incredibly lovely and compressed novels. At least 50 stories are stories you'll want to read again, and all 61 have something good enough in them to make you laugh or cry." Richard Locke, writing in the *New York Times Book Review,* called the stories "a gift at once sweet and sad, nourishing, voluptuous and nostalgic." Among the titles most frequently praised are "Goodbye, My Brother" (which opens the collection), "A Country Husband," "The Enormous Radio," "The Death of Justina," "The Brigadier and the Golf Widow," "Marito in Citta," and "The Swimmer," the basis for a 1969 movie and the story Robert Morace calls in *Dictionary of Literary Biography,* volume 2, Cheever's finest structural achievement.

Inevitably the publication of these stories as a group has revived the earlier criticism of Cheever's fictional milieu as narrow, dealing, in Locke's words, with "the classic subjects of the New Yorker magazine, . . . the manners and morals of upper

John Cheever

Dust jacket

middle-class and upper-class New Yorkers and suburbanites." This puts Cheever in the excellent company of such writers as Jane Austen and Henry James, as Paul Gray points out in a review for *Time*. Gray defends the scope of Cheever's subjects: "Well outside the mainstream, the Cheever people nonetheless reflect it admirably. What they do with themselves is what millions upon millions would do, given enough money and time. And their creator is less interested in his characters as rounded individuals than in the awful, comic and occasionally joyous ways they bungle their opportunities. The best Cheever stories act like fulcrums; they translate considerable social weight into emotional power."

Cheever's fiction reflects his own personal blend of bleakness and hope. In the stories, a difficult optimism creeps through despite the frailties of his characters. "What makes the affirmation of humanity in Cheever's work so successful is that he never chooses easy subjects for love," Irving writes. Cheever's characters are "difficult to forgive, but he usually forgives them." Jesse Kornbluth, in a *New York Times Magazine* article, states that the greatest strength of Cheever's fiction lies in "the remarkable discipline of its creator, for Cheever's stories and early novels are not about people scrapping for social position and money, but about people rising toward grace."

On 24 October 1979 and the two succeeding Wednesday nights, dramatizations of three Cheever stories appeared on PBS television, opening the "Great Performances" series. Cheever had no hand in the project. The selection was made by Peter Weinberg of WNET in New York from stories of suburban Shady Hill characters. When Cheever turned down the opportunity to write the adaptations, each story was assigned to a different playwright in an effort to achieve a variety of textures. "The Sorrows of Gin," which opened the series, was adapted by Wendy Wasserman. A. R. Gurney, Jr., whose Off-Broadway play *Children* was suggested by a Cheever story, adapted "O Youth and Beauty!" The last of the series, "The Five Forty-Eight," was done by Terrence McNally. John J. O'Connor, who reviewed the series in the *New York Times*, found the first of the three adaptations "curiously lifeless" on television, but concluded that the series was "on the whole . . . a worthy accomplishment for public television, demonstrating that American literature can serve as an important source of dramatic material."

Cheever himself has written a one-hour television play, set, like the televised adaptations, in the fictional suburb Shady Hill. It is planned to be broadcast as a part of the WNET-TV "New Drama Project" series. Cheever explained to the *Christian Science Monitor* that he had done the drama only as an experiment in writing four- or five-minute scenes that could be visually arresting. Asked if he saw himself as "a forerunner in the movement of creative writers into television," he responded, "No, not a forerunner. Just a workman in the field."

Cheever has a new novel in progress, but he is reluctant to discuss it. He will ask his children to pass judgment on it, he says. In closing the *Newsweek* interview by Susan Cheever, he read from prepared notes: "Since I have no clear and responsible sense of the seasons of life, and since I would not want to be one of those old men who claim to be burgeoning and burdened when there's not a leaf in sight, I count on you and your brothers to keep me posted."

—*Jean W. Ross*

Periodical Publications:

FICTION:

"The Night Mummy Got the Wrong Coat," *New Yorker* (21 April 1980): 35.

NONFICTION:

"Why I Write Short Stories," *Newsweek* (30 October 1978): 24-25.

Interviews:

Christopher Lehmann-Haupt, "Talk with John Cheever," *New York Times Book Review*, 26 March 1978, pp. 3, 31-32;

Arthur Unger, "John Cheever's Long View," *Christian Science Monitor*, 24 October 1979, pp. 17-18.

Television Adaptations:

"The Sorrows of Gin," adapted by Wendy Wasserman, WNET, New York, 24 October 1979;

"O Youth and Beauty," adapted by A. R. Gurney, WNET, New York, 31 October 1979;

"The Five Forty-Eight," adapted by Terrence McNally, WNET, New York, 7 November 1979.

References:

Paul Gray, "Inescapable Conclusions," *Time* (16 October 1978): 122, 125;

John Irving, "Facts of Living," *Saturday Review* (30 September 1978): 44-46;

Jesse Kornbluth, "The Cheever Chronicle," *New York Times Magazine*, 21 October 1979, pp. 26-29, 102-105;

Richard Locke, "Visions of Order and Decency," *New York Times Book Review*, 3 December 1978, pp. 3, 78;

Charles Nicol, "The Truth, the Impartial Truth," *Harper's*, 258 (June 1979): 93-95;

John J. O'Connor, "TV," *New York Times*, 24 October 1979, section 3, p. 28; 31 October 1979, section 3, p. 31; 7 November 1979, section 3, p. 32;

Christina Robb, "Cheever's Story," *Boston Globe Magazine*, 6 July 1980, pp. 11-13, 27-31, 35;

Martha Smilgis, "Bio," *People* (23 April 1979): 78-83;

Ralph Tyler, "How a Trio of Cheever Stories Made It to TV," *New York Times*, 14 October 1979, pp. 1, 33.

Marc Connelly

(13 December 1890-21 December 1980)

The *DLB* entry on Marc Connelly appears in *Dictionary of Literary Biography*, volume 7; *Twentieth-Century American Dramatists, Part 1: A-J* (1981), pp. 124-130. This eulogy was delivered at the funeral on 23 December 1980.

A TRIBUTE

from GARSON KANIN

I have been asked to speak for the Dramatists Guild, which on Sunday last, lost its oldest, most distinguished and beloved member—indeed, the last of the founders of our revered fraternity.

The death of friends has never caused me to mourn or to grieve. In these lugubrious times, I feel not sadness, but anger, rage, fury.

This is especially so in the case of the death of Marc Connelly, because, in dying, he has not only deprived me of a rare friendship, but he has made me the senior member of the Dramatists Guild Council—and I doubt that I shall ever be able to fill those stylish, elegant shoes.

Marcus Cook Connelly. What a man. What a playwright. His innate sense of construction did not desert him, even at the very end. It has been said that the theater experience is akin to the sexual one. A play must woo the audience, then excite it, delight it, and finally provide a climax. Observe, then, how Marc constructed the drama of his life, providing it not only with a gratifying and satisfying third act, but a spectacular final curtain.

Consider the parties and pieces and praises, the celebrations and appreciations which have been going on for the past several months. Marc took them all in benign stride. It was no more than he deserved and he knew it.

Not long ago, a few hundred of us waited in the Blue Room at City Hall, where Marc was to receive the city's highest medal from Mayor Koch and Governor Carey. As he entered the room, we all rose and gave him an ovation. When it subsided, he looked around and asked, "What's that for, *survival?*"

At that same City Hall occasion, Helen Hayes told me that Marc had just a few days earlier read her his new play with the hope of convincing her to play the lead. Think of it! Sixty years ago, this very same playwright was reading to this very same actress a play called *To The Ladies*, which he had written with George S. Kaufman and which she eventually played with great success. I asked Helen if he still read his plays aloud in the same way. Like this . . .

(Marc reads)
TOM
Good morning, Anna.
(Marc looks up, proud and pleased, then continues to read)
ANNA
Good morning, Tom.
(Marc looks up for approval, reads again)
TOM
You're looking a little peaked today, Anna. Why?
(Marc looks up, reads on)
ANNA
You know why.
(Marc looks up, mysteriously)

And so on . . .

There were those who teased and twitted Marc about this method, but they were people who understood neither plays nor playwrights. Marc simply *loved* playwriting and plays—particularly his own. Everything he wrote astonished and surprised him. He was delighted at what ran down his sleeve every day and he wanted to share that joy.

He once invited me to hear him read a new play to a group of friends at the Garden of Allah in Hollywood. I accepted, of course, and said, "I can hardly wait! What's it about?"

Marc laughed and said, "I don't *know* what it's about, but I read it to Dottie Parker and she told someone that it was 'A fantasy about an aviator who takes off in his plane and crashes right into the middle of the dullest part of American history.' " Then he added, "And Dottie ought to know. She *is* the dullest part of American history."

They were tough babies, that Algonquin bunch. They sharpened their wits on one another.

Once when I was working with Dorothy Parker, someone asked her what I was like and she said, "Oh, he's a sort of Jewish Jed Harris."

My head has been a jumbled album of snapshots all morning.

Marc's beloved Bob Benchley was once an hour late getting to the celebrated poker game, and said, "Sorry to be late, fellas, but I've been cuing June Walker."

"Now, now," said Marc, "no baby talk!"

I remember one late night in the Cub Room of the Stork Club, Marc coming in tie-less, distraught, going from table to table asking everyone, friends and strangers alike, "What's your blood type?" "What's your blood type?" And those who replied,

Marc Connelly

"A Positive" were whisked off to provide blood transfusions for Bob Benchley.

A few weeks ago, an interviewer asked him, "Do you think conversation is as fascinating now as it was in the twenties?"

"*Mine* is," said Marc.

At Charlie Brackett's apartment in Hollywood, I once spent a long, rainy Sunday afternoon watching Marc teach Charlie how to cheat at backgammon. When we left and went over to the Troc to have a drink, I asked, "What was the point of all that? Why teach him to cheat instead of to play well?"

"Because, my child," said Marc, "backgammon is a game principally played by extremely wealthy lay-abouts who've got nothing else to do and who *deserve* to be cheated!"

He was stubborn, as are most dedicated artists. In New Haven during a tryout of *Beggar On Horseback,* the second act curtain line failed completely. George Kaufman said they had better think of a new one.

"No, no," said Marc, "it's hilarious and I'll tell you why." Whereupon, he explained it to Kaufman. The next night, it bombed again! Marc again explained why it had to stay; why, if given a chance, eventually it would gò over. The next night, nothing!

They took a walk around New Haven the following morning, talking it over. Suddenly, George darted into Malley's Department Store and asked a clerk if they had any good second act curtains.

Finally, Marc became desperate, and asked George, "What do you think we ought to do?" And George said, "Simple. Let's call the audience in for a ten o'clock rehearsal."

Felix Frankfurter once promised his mother that he would never "commit wealth." And he never did. Neither did Marc. He was more interested in excellence than he was in excess profits, and his generosity is proverbial.

Some of you were at The Players the other night when at the end of the evening, our remarkable old friend brought down the house with his spirited rendition—alas, his *final* rendition of *Spartacus At The Gates.*

He loved the Dramatists Guild and the Dramatists Guild loved him. At our meeting last week, he sat at the head of the table, drinking beer and munching peanuts and raising hell. The last sentence I ever heard him utter came during a discussion of theater ticket marketing, the Duffy Square booth, cut-rates, two-fers, and the like. Marc got mad and shouted, "Damn it all, they're turning Broadway into one big Gray's Drug Store." Some of the younger members of the Council had no idea what he was talking about. Some of us did. He was bridging the gap of time.

At ninety, at eighty-nine, at eighty-eight, he always attended our sessions and through them he constantly kept looking at his watch. He seldom stayed to the end. He always had something else to do.

Playwright, journalist, humorist, memoirist, director, actor, screenwriter, wit, gentleman, and all-around jolly good fellow, he will never be replaced because he is irreplaceable.

He was a constantly prolific and creative man. Of all his productions and creations, surely the greatest was the one he called Marc Connelly. Unique, valuable, adorable. And, characteristically, he went out, not with a whimper, but with a beautiful bang.

We have been told that in his last hours, Marc was exceptionally and visibly cheerful.

His nurse asked, "What makes you so happy, Mr. Connelly?"

Marc beamed, clapped his hands together, and said, "We've got the money! We go into rehearsal tomorrow morning!"

Was it true? Does it matter? Marc thought it was true and that is true enough.

Two errors to correct and I have done.

Some of the public prints yesterday reported: "Mr. Connelly leaves no immediate family." Wrong. Mr. Connelly leaves one of the largest immediate families of any man who ever lived. He leaves the whole of the theater community.

The second error was in the coroner's report which states that Marc Connelly died of congestive heart failure due to pneumonia. Don't you believe it. Our incomparable friend died of living. There's a lesson there for all of us. Thank you, Marc. Darling Marc.

E. L. Doctorow

(6 January 1931-)

NEW BOOKS: *Drinks Before Dinner* (New York: Random House, 1979);

Loon Lake (New York: Random House, 1980; London: Macmillan, 1980).

RECENT AWARDS: National Book Critics Circle Award, 1976, for *Ragtime*.

The publication of *Ragtime* (1975) plummeted the generally unrecognized but accomplished novelist E. L. Doctorow into the literary limelight. A best-seller, Book-of-the-Month Club selection, and winner of a National Book Critics Circle Award, Doctorow's fourth novel brought him great commercial success. The paperback rights went for $1.9 million, and the film, with the heralded return of James Cagney to the movies, is anticipated at the end of 1981. Doctorow was delighted with *Ragtime*'s success and with the idea of reaching many readers but shied away from the resulting literary lionizing. In response to the hoopla, he went back to work. While he was working on *Ragtime*, he taught creative writing at Sarah Lawrence College in Bronxville, New York, but upon completing the novel, he began work as a playwright. Commissioned by the Yale Repertory Theatre under a fellowship from the Columbia Broadcasting System, Doctorow became a creative writing fellow for the Yale School of Drama for one year and then went on to teach at the University of Utah. For the 1980-1981 school year he taught at Princeton University.

After *Ragtime*, while Doctorow worked with drama, he brought to it some of the same fascination and concern with language that distinguish his novels. In an essay entitled "The Language of Theater" (originally published in the *Nation* for 2 June 1979, and later as the introduction to the play), Doctorow explains that *Drinks Before Dinner* "originated not in an idea or a character or a story, but in a sense of heightened language, a way of talking. . . . The language preceded the intention. . . . Writers live in language, and their seriousness of purpose is not compromised nor their convictions threatened if they acknowledge that the subject of any given work may be a contingency of the song."

Doctorow attributes the inspiration of the play's "style of language" to the writings of Gertrude Stein and Mao Tse-tung. Their "rhythm of repetition" and "flexible language with possibilities of irony and paradox" appealed to his modernist ear. Thus he began with sound first, "the words second, and the names third." According to his conception of dramaturgy, characters are "formal expressions of the basic passion of the play"; they remain abstractions. No biographies are given. They gain identity only from "their positions in the dialogue." Doctorow explains that "the idea of character as we normally celebrate it on the American stage is what this play seems to question." Indeed his acknowledged intention is to abandon the theater of psychology and biography and to align himself with the theater of language and ideas.

The formal design of *Drinks Before Dinner* ideally suits Doctorow's intention. The characters in the play are all guests at a chic dinner party and are engaged in cocktail-hour conversation. The three couples, gathered in an expensive Manhattan penthouse, await the arrival of a celebrity—a secretary of something (probably state), who has won the Nobel Peace Prize. Edgar, a member of this elite group, is clearly unhappy about everything and announces, "Let's not have the evening we expect to have." Suffering from great dissatisfaction, Edgar denounces all their life-styles in a barrage of iconoclastic wit. Then he casually pulls a gun from his jacket pocket. This action dramatizes Edgar's despair as he shifts from his intellectual speculations about the end of the world to an irrational effort to bring the apocalypse right into their living room. He insists he holds the gun "for all of us."

The second act opens with the long-awaited guest of honor, Alan, tied to a straight-back chair. As Edgar nonchalantly wields his gun, the two engage in intellectual byplay about the world's destruction. Alan proves to be a good match. He too is convinced the end is near, but he admits to Edgar that the government has contingency plans to save the world from its own annihilation. Edgar would rather have destruction. Realizing that the survivors of the apocalypse "will have the vision of the world's end imprinted on their [children's] brains," he suggests that "those memories will erupt at night in terrible dreams. And one day again in the universe these dreams will come true. The dreams will again come true because the children of the survivors will be made in their image and will build a new earth with the genius of the conspiracy of survival. Everything that has happened will happen again. The ark will be built to resemble a lavish apartment overlooking a ruined city. The ark will look like this room. We are on the ark now. The world has already ended." With this statement he squeezes the trigger, and the unloaded gun emits a hollow click. This anticlimatic moment of black comedy dramatizes Edgar's inconsolable agony over the world's disregard for its own blind destruction. The play's ending underscores the irony when the guests do sit down to dinner.

Joseph Papp presented the original production of *Drinks Before Dinner* at the New York Shakespeare Festival in the Public Newman Theatre on 22 November 1978. Mike Nichols directed, and Christopher Plummer played Edgar. Drama critics praised the production of the play. However, Doctorow and the play itself received rather negative notices. The main charge levied against the play was its over reliance on rhetorical fun and games and an inability to dramatize the ideas. As the critic for *Time* magazine complained, Edgar only talked his hostages to death. More typical of critical opinion was Michael Feingold's salute in the *Village Voice* to Doctorow's ambitions "to put the whole case against civilization in a nutshell," but Feingold wished "he had found a way to say it fully, genuinely, and dramatically." In the *New York Times* Richard Eder responded more positively: "Mr. Doctorow's turns of thought can be odd, witty and occasionally quite remarkable. His theme . . . is hardly original, but certainly worth saying. And he finds thoughtful and striking ways of saying it, even though eventually the play becomes an endless epigram. . . . Still, a play of ideas is rare enough nowadays, and Mr. Doctorow's are sharp enough to supplement intellectual suspense when the dramatic suspense bogs down."

Much of the criticism directed at *Drinks Before Dinner* resembles the critical reservations concerning *Ragtime*. Whereas most critics considered the play and the novel genuinely experimental, some criticized Doctorow's work for being mere stylish surface. For example, Anthony Burgess assessed his rereading of *Ragtime* and found it lacking: "I find that most of the initial impact has been blunted: Literary shocks are subject to the law of diminishing returns. I find, too, a certain vacuity of literary display. What once seemed verbally startling is now revealed as mostly tinsel." Indeed after the original excitement generated over *Ragtime*, a critical backlash developed. In an article in the *New Republic*, John Seelye suggested that the novel's popular success endowed it with "an aura of trashiness." Thus some literary critics developed a certain skepticism about Doctorow and a "show-me" attitude in regard to his next work of fiction.

As a result of the critical controversy surrounding *Ragtime*, the publication of *Loon Lake* in the fall of 1980 marked an important point in Doctorow's career. In this fifth novel the author pushes his experiments with technique further. As he explained to John F. Baker in a *Publishers Weekly* interview, in *Ragtime* he deliberately concentrated on "the narrative element" and "wanted a really relentless narrative, full of ongoing energy. . . . the sense of motion." And indeed this novel's vigorous prose style with its rhythmic "ragtime" effect accounted for much of its success—proving it to be both accessible and entertaining. However, in *Loon Lake* Doctorow is more formally ambitious, again focusing on narration. In a *New York Times Book Review* interview with Victor S. Navasky, Doctorow notes that in *Loon Lake* "the narrator throws his voice, and the reader has to figure out who and what he is. The convention of the consistent, identifiable narrative is one of the last conventions that can be assaulted, and I think it has now been torpedoed. For the first time, I've made something work without the basic compact between narrator and reader, and technically I'm pleased at being able to maintain a conventional story despite giving up that security."

In *Loon Lake* Doctorow intentionally provides no conventional narrative exposition. Time sequences are not only juggled, but shifts in narrative viewpoint occur so frequently that the reader does not always know who is talking. At times the point of view switches suddenly from first to third person or vice versa. In his interview with Navasky, Doctorow explains his purpose: "Here you don't know who's talking so that's one more convention out the window. That gives me pleasure, and I think it might give pleasure to readers, too. Don't underestimate them. People are smart, and they are not strangers to discontinuity. There's an immense amount of energy attached to breaking up your narrative and leaping into different voices, times, skins, and making the book happen and then letting the reader take care of himself. It's a kind of narrative akin to television—discontinuous and mind-blowing."

As in *Ragtime*, Doctorow evokes a period in American history, in this case the 1930s. Although the novel glances back to the 1920s and looks to the 1970s, the present action takes place in 1936, during the Great Depression. The action is narrated mainly by Joe Korzeniowski of Paterson, New Jersey, who has left his impoverished home and is on the road.

E. L. Doctorow

Having toured hobo camps and worked as a carnival roustabout, he finds himself lost in the woods one night near a single-track railroad in the Adirondack Mountains. A private train goes by, and through the window, he catches a glimpse of a naked girl reflected in a mirror. As if propelled by a vision, he follows the tracks until he comes to Loon Lake, a hidden wilderness estate of 30,000 acres owned by one of the country's richest men, F. W. Bennett. An industrial tycoon of the robber baron variety, Bennett plays host at his grand retreat to gatherings of celebrated people. Rather eccentric, Bennett takes a liking to Joe, who stays on as one of the estate's workers.

Also present at Loon Lake are Bennett's wife Lucinda, a world-famous aviatrix who occasionally flies in on her hydroplane, and Warren Penfield, a great-hearted poet and drunkard in residence, who narrates some of the action in a poetic form that resembles blank verse. The girl whose image on the train captivated Joe turns out to be a guest also. A tough blond beauty, Clara Lukács is the moll of the gangster Tommy Crapo, who works for Bennett as a strikebreaker. While visiting Loon Lake on business, Crapo gives Clara to Bennett, who in turn leaves her to Warren Penfield's care.

Eventually Joe helps Clara escape from Loon Lake with Penfield's aid and a Mercedes stolen from

Dust jacket

Bennett. Their destination is California, and on their cross-country tour they witness the nightmare of the Depression. Afraid that Bennett is pursuing them, they hide out most of the time until Joe decides he must take a job to earn some cash. He decides that one of the last places Bennett would look for him is on the assembly line at one of his own auto plants. For a while he and Clara live a domesticated life in an Indiana factory town. However, violent union disputes soon erupt. A neighbor and friend, Red James, who is an active union member, turns out to be a fink, a company operative under the employ of Tommy Crapo. When his role as a double agent is discovered, Red is killed—not by union members but by Crapo's thugs. Joe, who is implicated by his friendship with Red, is badly beaten by these thugs at the same time, but is later accused of Red's murder. Tommy Crapo arrives at the police station and spirits Clara away while Joe pleads innocence and professes to be Bennett's true son.

The hoax works and Joe eventually struggles back to Loon Lake, stripped of everything and feeling "dispossessed." Although desiring revenge, Joe declares that "no simple motive could fill the totality of my return." At Loon Lake he discovers Bennett wasting away, grieving over the plane-crash death of his wife and Penfield. Rather than satisfying his urge for revenge, Joe marks his return by a baptismal plunge into Loon Lake and emerges with a new identity. The novel concludes with a biographical sketch outlining the remainder of Joe's career—as soldier (an officer in strategic services), deputy assistant director of the Central Intelligence Agency, ambassador, and chairman of the board of the steel corporation and the Bennett Foundation. These accomplishments are catalogued in the best Horatio Alger tradition. Joe Korzeniowski of Paterson becomes Joseph Paterson Bennett, not only the adoptive son of F. W. Bennett but now the "Master of Loon Lake."

Loon Lake presents Doctorow's ironic comment on the traditional American dream, for Joe pays his dues to the system and becomes a material success as well as a moral failure. Clearly what Joe earlier ran away from—the corruptibility of wealth's impersonal force—he epitomizes at the end. As George Stade analyzes the novel's ending, Joe "triumphs over his adoptive father by becoming him, only worse—" for his is "revenge through usurpation." Stade concludes: "In America, . . . the sons win; they destroy the past only to preserve the worst of it in themselves, and thereby destroy the future. Such is Doctorow's variation on the conventional American success story."

Doctorow underscores the violent contrast between the American dream and the reality of the American experience through his stylistic manipulation of structure, narration, and symbol. The title of the novel itself holds the novel's prevailing symbols. The lake with its shimmering reflections suggests the use of corresponding images in the novel as well as what Robert Towers refers to as the "concentrically expanding ripples of implication." In his review in the *New York Times Book Review*, Towers calls *Loon Lake* "a world of mirrors, a fascinating, tantalizing novel in which nearly every image or episode has its counterpart somewhere else in the book." Likewise functioning as a symbol, the loon is a bird which hunts fish by diving into the lake, shattering its surface, and then rising with its catch. Doctorow certainly suggests the process of diving and rising with the novel's fragmented structure, the radical alternations in time sequence and narrative viewpoint, and especially with the two extremes of Joe's life.

In the *New Statesman* Nicholas Shrimpton argues that Doctorow's stylistic methods of "vertiginous alternations" serve to intensify the novel rather than complicate it. On the other hand, Robert Towers "felt trapped in a Barthian funhouse of mirrors" and suggests that the "loon-lake symbol" is not enough to give the novel shape. However, he concludes on a positive note: "Yet the novel is so rich in its disorder that I can regret only to a point the lack of a final coherence. The experience of reading *Loon Lake* . . . was exhilarating."

Although many reviewers noted the structural flaws in *Loon Lake*, most praised Doctorow's formal ambitions. As Paul Gray says in *Time* magazine, "Doctorow may try to do too much in *Loon Lake*. . . . But the author's skill at historical reconstruction, so evident in *Ragtime*, remains impressive here; the novel's fragments and edgy, nervous rhythms call up an age of clashing anxiety. *Loon Lake* tantalizes long after it is ended." In the *New York Review of Books*, Diane Johnson likewise gives a positive assessment: "Doctorow's faith in his version of American history, and his willingness to run the large artistic risks involved in asserting it, make him one of the bravest and most interesting of modern American novelists. . . ."

Although *Loon Lake* has not generated the same enthusiastic acclaim as initially greeted *Ragtime*, it has nevertheless been a critical and commercial success. Like *Ragtime*, it too had a large first printing, is a best-seller, and a Book-of-the-Month Club selection. Thus Doctorow seems to have maintained his popular support while continuing to pursue his formal experiments, perhaps proving his faith in his reader's willingness to explore with him. Anthony Burgess may best explain Doctorow's accomplishment in *Loon Lake* when he says that "the serious novelist's problem is to be uncompromising and yet to find an audience. Doctorow has found an audience and nothing could be less of a fictional compromise than *Loon Lake*." In this respect, *Loon Lake* is something of a milestone for Doctorow. Because this fifth novel confirms Doctorow as a serious contemporary novelist and a commercial success, it stands as an important addition to his literary accomplishments.

—*Carol MacCurdy*

Play:

Drinks Before Dinner, 22 November 1978, Public/Newman Theatre, New York.

Periodical Publications:

"The Language of Theater," *Nation*, 228 (2 June 1979): 637-638;

"Loon Lake," *Kenyon Review*, new series, 1 (Winter 1979): 5-13;

Review of *The Scapegoat* by Mary Lee Settle, *New York Times Book Review*, 26 October 1980, pp. 1, 40-42.

Interviews:

John F. Baker, "E. L. Doctorow," *Publishers Weekly*, 207 (30 June 1975): 6-7;

Victor S. Navasky, "E. L. Doctorow: 'I Saw a Sign,' " *New York Times Book Review*, 28 September 1980, pp. 44-45;

Hilary Mills, "E. L. Doctorow," *Saturday Review*, 7 (October 1980): 44-48.

References:

Anthony Burgess, "Doctorow's 'Hit' is a Miss," review of *Loon Lake, Saturday Review*, 7 (September 1980): 66-67;

Richard Eder, "Doctorow's 'Drinks Before Dinner,' " *New York Times*, 24 November 1978: C4;

David Emblidge, "Marching Backward into the Future: Progress as Illusion in Doctorow's Novels," *Southwest Review*, 62 (Autumn 1977): 397-409;

Michael Feingold, "Not with a Bang," review of *Drinks Before Dinner, Village Voice*, 23 (4 December 1978): 121;

Paul Gray, "The Nightmare and the Dream," review of *Loon Lake, Time*, 116 (22 September 1980): 81;

Diane Johnson, "Waiting for Righty," review of *Loon Lake, New York Review of Books*, 27 (6 November 1980): 18-20;

T. E. Kalem, "Party Pooper," review of *Drinks Before Dinner, Time*, 112 (4 December 1978): 108;

Joseph Moses, "To Impose a Phrasing on History," *Nation*, 221 (4 October 1975): 310-312;

John Seelye, "Doctorow's Dissertation," *New Republic*, 174 (10 April 1976): 31;

Nicholas Shrimpton, "New Jersey Joe," review of *Loon Lake, New Statesman*, 100 (31 October 1980): 27;

George Stade, "Types Defamiliarized," review of *Loon Lake, Nation*, 231 (27 September 1980): 285-286;

Robert Towers, "A Brilliant World of Mirrors," review of *Loon Lake, New York Times Book Review*, 28 September 1980, pp. 1, 45-47.

Stanley Elkin

(11 May 1930-)

The *DLB* entry on Stanley Elkin appears in *Dictionary of Literary Biography*, volume 2, *American Novelists Since World War II* (1978), pp. 131-136.

NEW BOOKS: *The Living End* (New York: Dutton, 1979; London: Cape, 1980);

Stanley Elkin's Greatest Hits (New York: Dutton, 1980).

"I don't think of myself in categories," Stanley Elkin will frequently tell inquisitive interviewers, refusing to be assigned some pigeonhole for the convenience of literary critics. Is he a Jewish writer, a black humorist, a metafictionist, all or none of the above? Understandably disturbed by Elkin's categorical evasiveness, scholars have only recently granted his work close critical scrutiny. Such recognition has lagged behind Elkin's public acclaim in journalistic reviews. Elkin's resistance to anything that would compromise the integrity of his work is reflected in his handling of Hollywood commissions for screenplays: when his dialogue for the movie *Demon Seed* was rejected on the basis of its being "too intellectual" for the computer that was supposed to speak it, Elkin refused to lower his standards.

Since Elkin's major literary breakthrough with *The Franchiser* (1976), however, a measure of fame has finally come to an author who does not seem easy to pin down. While the writer's integrity may have stood in the way of his fame, his personal accessibility has done much to counteract his otherwise disadvantageous publicity strategy. Elkin is not shy about advertisements for himself. With self-irony, he will sell himself, an art he learned from his much admired salesman father and shares with his storekeeping and franchising protagonists. Elkin is a compellingly dramatic reader of his own work. Like the salesman buttonholing his customer until he buys the product, Elkin holds his audience by dramatically, dazzlingly, exhaustingly adopting his protagonists' different voices and concerns. Remarkably, Elkin can read spellbindingly despite the fact that he—like his franchiser, Ben Flesh—is stricken with what he calls a "poetic disease" (multiple sclerosis).

Elkin's fellow writers have done much to pave the way for an appreciation of his fiction, its style in particular. At Washington University in Saint

Louis, Elkin is stimulated by a coterie of writers that includes William Gass, Howard Nemerov, and Mona Van Duyn. The sensibility of a fellow stylist has enabled Elkin's colleague/friend/neighbor William Gass to recognize the verbal versatility, "such rich wild oratory," that expresses Elkin's unorthodox vision. For Gass, Elkin's writing is "the naming of names." He sees Elkin as a writer whose foremost concern is language, the *logos* that may conquer all that is distasteful, evil, painful in our lives. Although they seem to be worlds apart in their choices of plots, characters, and diction, the relationship between Gass and Elkin has been fruitful.

Apart from the steady admiration of his colleagues and fellow writers, the support of his family is an encouragement to creativity. Elkin's wife Joan is herself an accomplished artist whose paintings capture the awkwardness, the comedy, and the sweetness of people posing for the photographer. Her intentionally "primitive" style accentuates the difference between ordinary portrait painting and painting inspired by a different artistic medium, namely photography. Whether consciously influenced by his wife's work or not, Elkin too has been fascinated by the interplay of artistic media. His involvement in screenplay writing has already been mentioned; among his unproduced scripts is "The Art of War," based on the relationship between novelist Ernest Hemingway and photographer Robert Capa. More striking still, the whole middle section of his radio-inspired novel, *The Dick Gibson Show* (1971), might easily be turned into a radio play, reversing the original act of transformation through which the novel was created.

Although Elkin has accepted writer-in-residence positions all over the United States and has attended numerous summer writers' workshops, Saint Louis has remained his home base. To him the Midwest signifies the "neutral decent feel of the law of averages." It is precisely the Midwest's lack of narrowly regional atmosphere that attracts a novelist whose supraregional professional protagonists symbolize and even celebrate the homogenization of America.

Like the three novellas in *Searches and Seizures* (1973), Elkin's newest fiction, *The Living End* (1979), is a triptych of related stories bound together by a common theme rather than by common characters. In *The Living End* Elkin ventures beyond the supraregional to the surrealistic. Characters go back and forth from Minneapolis-Saint Paul to Heaven and Hell. A strong dichotomy is suggested in the title—*The Living End*. The

Dust jacket

Throughout the Underworld the nine thousand, six hundred and forty three Ladlehauses who had died since the beginning of time, not excepting the accomplice to Ellerbee's murder, looked up, acknowledged their presence in thirty tongues. These are my family, Ladlehaus thought, and
three four
glanced in the direction of the ~~one~~ or ~~two~~ he could actually see. Their blackened forms, lathered with smoke and fire damage, were as meaningless to him, as devoid of kinship, as the dry flinders of ancient bone in museum ~~xxxxx~~ display cases. Meanwhile God was still out there. "Not you," he said petulantly to the others, "the old timer."
in His summer linens
He means me, Ladlehaus thought, this shaved and showered squire God/means me. He means me,
and
this commissioned officer Lord with his myrrh and frankincense colognes and aromatics~~, Whose~~ His Body ~~tingles with~~ tingling with ~~agency,~~ morning dip and agency, all the prevailing moods of
fettle he had
~~health~~ and immortality. He means me, and even though ~~Ladlehaus~~ knew there~~'d~~ been a mistake, that he'd not been the one who'd sounded off, Ladlehaus held his tongue. He means me, he makes mistakes.
you're the fellow who spouts grafitti to God, are you?" kneeling be-
"So ~~you want to know if there's life before death?"~~ God said~~,~~ and Ladlehaus was ~~standing next~~ neath Him, *hocus pocus'd through Hell,* "Be off."
~~to Him,~~ terrified and clonic below God's rhetorical attention. "Go," God said. ~~XXXXXXXXXX~~
And Ladlehaus's ~~and~~ quiet "yes" was as [illegible] the [illegible] in God's [illegible] ~~[illegible]~~ [illegible] mistake.
And Ladlehaus thought Well, why not? He didn't know me any better when He sent me here. He didn't know my heart. I was an accomplice, what's that? No hit man, no munitions or electron-
sent from far, and certainly no mastermind. a lookout,
ic~~s~~ expert~~,~~ no big deal Indy wheel man ~~sent from far,~~ Only an accomplice,/a man by the door, ~~say,~~
say,
like a sentry or a commisionaire~~,~~ little more than an eye witness really~~, or the first man on~~
Almost a mascot.
~~the scene after the break in~~ /And paid accordingly, his always the lowest share, sometimes no-
taken place
thing more than a good dinner and a night on the town. The crimes would have ~~occurred~~ without
redcap, a of
him. An accomplice, a ~~red or~~ skycap, a shuffler of suitcases, ~~handle bags of~~ doggybags of ~~boodl~~ boodle, someone with a ~~bi~~ station wagon, ~~with~~ seats that folded down to accommodate ~~the~~ cartons
the business of his
of TV sets, stereos. What was the outrage? Even ~~his boasting about~~ having been an accomplice
though ~~it was~~ true,
to Ellerbee's murder was ~~more~~ ~~tak~~ talk ~~than~~ anything else, something to give him cachet in his
buddy's *as much* *as* a *a pal's* ~~The killer had~~
~~pal's~~ eyes, ~~a way of~~ an assertion that he'd left ~~his~~ mark on ~~his buddy's~~ life. ~~XXXXXXXXXXX~~
~~been high~~
~~really happened was~~ And God said "Be ~~@~~ off," and he was off.

#

A blow of blackness---speleological.
The first thing he was aware of ~~was~~ the darkness. He was some~~place~~ secret, somewhere doused.
quenched *where* ~~A blow of blackness,~~
Not void but void's/wilderness. All null subfusc gloom's bleak eclipse. ~~Feeling blackness like~~
~~a speleological~~
~~a blow~~ Hell was downtown by comparison---unless this was Hell too, some lead-lined,
(And Ladlehaus afraid of the dark.) still
heavy curtained outpost of it. ~~Was it even the universe?~~ Was it ~~even~~ the universe?
4

The Living End, *revised typescript*

contrast between the ordinary and the supernatural is further complicated by the bifurcation of the latter into the irreconcilable poles of Heaven and Hell. If we rearrange the sequence in our minds, we can imagine humdrum America as the centerpiece and Heaven and Hell as the triptych's two diametrically opposed side panels, gaudy pictures of fulfilled cliches and crushed hopes. Surrealistic as these dichotomies are, they force a reconsideration of the "real" world of ordinary pains and pleasures.

The first section, entitled "The Conventional Wisdom," begins with Ellerbee's hopeless struggle to protect his liquor store from robbers and murderers. His extremely good-natured attempts to care for former employees victimized in holdups and his equally heroic efforts to reassure his wife May, who nags him about their "financial reversals," come to an end when Ellerbee himself is killed in yet another holdup. He is sent from a theme-park Heaven full of green pastures and angelic choirs straight to a Hell populated by pitchfork-wielding devils. Why? Because even Ellerbee had his flaws and God's supreme justice is both relentless and petty. (Is staying open on Sunday really punishable by eternal damnation?) The first section ends with despair about the injustice of man's fate and with a bitter recompense: Ellerbee can "look for himself in Ladlehaus's glowing blisters."

Ladlehaus is the accomplice of Ellerbee's killer. Having died of natural causes, a case of poetic injustice, Ladlehaus becomes the central character of the second section, "The Bottom Line." Quiz, the earthly groundskeeper, is angry at the buried Ladlehaus's voice from underground. Children pretend to fight a war between the Twin Cities on Ladlehaus's grave. God's role as arbitrary arbiter is continued with a sense of growing frustration.

"The State of the Art," the final section, begins with Quiz's encounter with Heaven and Hell. Now that he too is dead, he seeks a posthumous justification of his suffering, and he is sorely disappointed. The divine motivation for the world's creation and for the Fall from Eden is perplexing; asked why, God replies, *"Because it makes a better story is why."* At Judgment Day, God complains that he "never found [His] audience," and annihilates everything.

With an unorthodox story like this, one could easily mistake Elkin's compassion for man's suffering as "blasphemy," as one reviewer has. However, *The Living End* is a rejection of the myth, the cliche, the dichotomy of Heaven and Hell. It is rather an affirmation of the intertwining of pleasure and pain. It is possible to extract elixir from gall, pleasure from pain, in this world too, by taking "God's" advice and turning suffering into fiction, the "better story."

The Living End was greeted with the greatest critical acclaim accorded any Elkin book to date. For the first time, reviewers praised Elkin's successful blend of form—his language a "literary jazz band"—and content: "three discrete narratives whose characters and themes bleed into one another." *The Living End,* with its condensation of style and character portrayal—referred to by one enthusiastic reviewer as "Elkin's economy"—is his most popular fiction so far, and it may well attract an eager audience for his forthcoming novel, "George Mills."

—Doris Bargen

Other:

The Best American Short Stories 1980, edited by Elkin and Shannon Ravenel, with an introduction by Elkin (Boston: Houghton Mifflin, 1980).

Periodical Publication:

"Why I Live Where I Live," *Esquire,* 94 (November 1980):108-111.

References:

Doris G. Bargen, *The Fiction of Stanley Elkin* (Bern & Frankfurt: Lang, 1980);

Robert Edward Colbert, "The American Salesman as Pitchman and Poet in the Fiction of Stanley Elkin," *Critique,* 21, no. 2 (1979): 52-58;

William Gass, "Stanley Elkin's *The Franchiser,*" *New Republic* (28 June 1980): 29-32;

Paul Gray, "Two Serious Comic Writers," review of *Stanley Elkin's Greatest Hits, Time* (10 November 1980): 102, 104;

Francine O. Hardaway, "The Power of the Guest: Stanley Elkin's Fiction," *Rocky Mountain Review of Language and Literature,* 32 (1978): 234-245;

John Irving, "An Exposé of Heaven and Hell," review of *The Living End, New York Times Book Review,* 10 June 1979, pp. 7, 30;

Frank Kermode, " 'Love and Do as You Please,' " review of *The Living End, New York Review of Books* (16 August 1979): 44-45;

Christopher Lehmann-Haupt, Review of *The Living End, New York Times*, 25 May 1979, C27;

Larry McCaffery, "Stanley Elkin's Recovery of the Ordinary," *Critique*, 21, no. 2 (1979): 39-51;

Peter S. Prescott, Review of *The Living End, Newsweek* (18 June 1979): 83, 86;

R. Z. Sheppard, "Life after Afterlife," review of *The Living End, Time* (4 June 1979): 74, 76;

Geoffrey Wolff, "Hell and Superhell: Elkin's Vision of the Afterlife," review of *The Living End, Esquire* (19 June 1979): 13-14.

Irvin Faust

(11 June 1924-)

The *DLB* entry on Irvin Faust appears in *Dictionary of Literary Biography*, volume 2, *American Novelists Since World War II* (1978), pp. 142-148.

NEW BOOK: *Newsreel* (New York & London: Harcourt Brace Jovanovich/Bruccoli Clark, 1980).

Now rounding out twenty years as a guidance counselor in a high school in Garden City, Long Island, Irvin Faust continues also to live and write in the Morningside Heights neighborhood of Manhattan near Columbia University. He lives there, he says, surrounded socially and ideologically by liberals, who challenge him for not committing his counseling energies to the uplift of struggling minorities in areas like Bedford-Stuyvesant. His response to such challenges may declare something about the major thrust of his stories and novels as well as their fate with readers and reviewers.

Like his father before him, Faust is a steadfast Roosevelt liberal . . . a political position not so narrow as some zealots feign. "Middleclass kids need help, too," he says of his responsibilities in Garden City. And though he inhabits what may be the only district in America that went five to one for McGovern in the 1972 presidential election, his sympathies presently go with the New York mayor who is himself at odds with the minorities and their liberal spokespersons for his inclinations to middle-class values. "If the middle class doesn't make it here, New York is not going to make it," Faust says, leaving it to his fiction to articulate more decisively both what he means by middle-class values and what it means to "make it" amid the crepitations of culture shock, historic disorder, and what is called in *Newsreel* (1980), the "Finestone luck"—an eponym for a disjunction in the nature of things, which forever isolates desire from the conditions of its fulfillment.

Newsreel is the personal history of Manny (Speed) Finestone, who was transformed by his participation in World War II from a timorous boy into a true-blue, self-confident soldier in the crusade led by Dwight D. Eisenhower. The security of this latter identification is severely shaken by postwar circumstances, and—because a major part of the author's interest lies in retrieving the successive popular formulas and catch cries of the postwar decades—Manny is implicated in most of the flagrant political, sociological, and cultural sensations of these times. His allegiance to the soldierly virtues he has learned from and projected on the fictive persona of the Supreme Commander keeps him tethered away from the gratifications of full commitment to the liberal passions of the men and women with whom he associates and at the same time sustains him—in half-mad suspension above reality—when their ploys and causes go sour. The necessarily picaresque range of his experiences as actor, writer, husband, and political activist is given coherence chiefly by the continuity of his predicament, a division in his loyalties that reappears in all new circumstances, and by the constant deterioration of his options. His last chance at redemption as he gets older and the options have been used up appears in his love for a girl who figures in the design of the novel as avatar and embodiment of the American dream. The thematic proposition is, in the end, clearly posed: *if* he can marry Maureen O'Brien then he will embrace and possess in the flesh those fugitive and miraculous riches for which he has always spurned the mundane offerings of his time. This proposition is stated in the language and terms of comedy, and the comedy of the whole is heavily laced with outright farce, as befits the tale of a pilgrim whose eschatological vocabulary has been gleaned from sports pages, movies, political rhetoric, military slang, and sentimental romances. Thus his ultimate leap for salvation is presented in terms of a polling booth choice between voting for Nixon or Humphrey. The Faustian dilemma is resolved by a choice to vote for Humphrey—a choice permitting readers and reviewers who confuse the surface of farce with the substance of bitter comedy to breathe easier and assure each other that Manny is back in the fold prepared by all those who have throughout his life betrayed him.

The reviews which greeted the appearance of *Newsreel* acknowledged the merits, charms, and novelistic skill which have by now been fairly well adumbrated in the reception of Faust's previous novels and stories. Writing in the *Saint Louis Globe-Democrat* Robert K. Morris says: "Faust has absorbed . . . the history of the last thirty years. Names, dates, places, songs, movies, events click, click, click through the pages with the recall and vigor of Dos Passos's camera eye. Through allusions that teem, America's past is recaptured." Ivan Gold in the *New York Times Book Review* notes: "this is probably Irvin Faust's most ambitious book, attempting, as it does, to come to terms with four decades of American history, as well as describe the passage of its protagonist through those often horrific years. Nostalgia, the theater, war, movies, politics, sports, Jews, sex, families, fathers, writing, the city, madness, history—these have always been the author's ingredients and themes. . . ."

Then, having gone so far with admiration and comprehension of what Faust handles and how he works, the bulk of the reviews hang up in that curious bafflement about what he is driving at, which must be kin to the distress of his liberal neighbors in Morningside Heights who can't believe such a nice, serious, committed, and perceptive fellow has not seen the unworthiness of middle-class values so readily apparent to them.

Thus, in Dick Roraback's review of *Newsreel* in the *Los Angeles Times* we finally come on this appraisal of the girl Manny Finestone lost almost in the moment of possession. The girl, says Roraback, is "a thoroughly apolitical young checkout clerk with an old-fashioned round body, whose single-minded ambition is to work in a shopping center. . . ." From this he goes on to remark: "Faust's descriptions of the girl are a fair measure of his talent. Anyone who can so delightfully consider a creature of such surpassing lack of originality is

himself possessed of rare imagination."

The enormity of such praise appears when we note that it is only made possible by a diametric inversion of the meaning of the novel, by a willful misreading of a character so carefully drawn by the author to focus the anguish of Finestone's plight. It is precisely this "apolitical young checkout clerk," Maureen O'Brien, who permits, in the resolving passages of the story, Manny Finestone to preserve his platonic identity as "Speed" at a time when he knows the others he has counted on throughout his life thus far have "betrayed poor little Manny and all his dreams." It is Maureen's voice (*O, hypocrite lecteur*) which pleads for him to "be a *mensch*" in the face of this betrayal. It is by responding to "that quiet, serious voice" that Speed remains undefeated amid the betrayals.

It is hard to believe that a reviewer acquainted with the proximate tradition of "the undefeated" in the work of Hemingway or Faulkner (or the longer tradition going back to Cervantes's absurd old Don) could so perfectly misunderstand what has happened in the polling booth when Speed rejects the temptation to vindictiveness, vengefulness, and

Dust jacket

despair equated in his mind with voting for Nixon on that particular occasion. What is easy to understand is that the reviewer felt that since Maureen in her simplicity is an incarnation of middle-class American values, Faust *shouldn't* be saying what he says about her and her role in Speed's refusal to be defeated. To carry this a little farther and spell it out in language any cat and dog and even Ivan Gold can read, reviewers must have felt that since Faust's "ingredients and themes" are those on which the liberal establishment enforces agreement, it would be doing the author a good turn with his potential readers to pass the word that he had not deviated from the faith that a vote for Hubert Horatio Humphrey was, in itself, a sign of grace.

It is easy to believe something like this because it has happened before in the reception and critical sanitizing of Faust's best work. Once the hard-edged liberal calipers had been applied to Willy Kleinhans of *Willy Remembers* (1971), and it was sufficiently determined Willy was a bigot, then the good turn done the author was the pretense that he had (almost successfully) duplicated the Archie Bunker formula—i.e. had set up a straw bigot as the target for derision of the bigot-hunting witches of the intellectual establishment. What followed from this was that any ambiguities which might suggest real virtue and heroism in Willy were either flaws of execution or forgivable excesses of farce.

Thus, in general, we handle our deviationist writers on this side of the Iron Curtain—whistling past their hard-won findings and tolerantly misreading their lapses from cliches taken to be self-evident.

But at least John Leonard, reviewing *Newsreel* in the *New York Times* (8 April 1980) was reckless enough to state more exactly what the engagement of this novel is: " 'Newsreel' brilliantly portrays the Jewish romance with American popular culture. It ends in schizophrenia. That the fathers of the Hollywood studios that gave us our images of the American family and the American way were mostly Jewish is not peculiar; it is sad. They took it upon themselves to invent everything to which they wanted to belong. As Maureen tells Manny: 'You had a terrific shock. It was as if you lost the war instead of winning it.' "

After this lightning flash of precision Leonard's review goes on tentatively and impressionistically to tick off some of the "echoes and emendations" linking *Newsreel* with the work of other contemporary Jewish writers in America. The emendations—in which Faust's particular merit and perhaps his

TWENTY-SEVEN

I took a deep breath, flexed my head, ~~and~~ set myself up on 108th Street, went for long walks alongside the Hudson, from the piers in the 40's up to Inwood in the 200's, and I opened up all my creative pores and invited my new career to step in. The only problem was that '61 was a tough year for America, which meant a tough year for Speed Finestone. Eisenhower was brooding down on the farm after blasting his bread and butter in the military-industrial complex so you knew the condition ~~it~~ was serious. Kennedy was still trying to pull out of his ~~Cuba~~ Bay of Pigs tailspin, the Nobel in Literature and the first space orbit went to the ~~Commies,~~ Reds, the Davis Cup went to Australia, Carry Back, my favorite horse since Equipoise, lost the Belmont and blew the triple crown, and ~~before the year was out~~ Hemingway and Gary Cooper ~~had~~ both made it to the barn. I began to get extremely itchy, to long mightily for a winner; Speed could only go so long out of first place. So on July 4 I went up to the Stadium; there, at least, you could count on some victorious stability.

Newsreel, *revised typescript*

greatest claim on the attention of the serious reader consist—are not spelled out. To spell them out would probably, in these times and circumstances, be to make trouble with Faust's fans and neighbors in Morningside Heights. So he remains, as this new decade begins, the real Dangling Man among Jewish novelists, admired at the price of misrepresentation, passing by the tolerance of his misreaders.

Frozen in this "sad" ambiguity (as Leonard so brilliantly and tantalizingly tagged it) the author presently shares the plight of his latest protagonist. I ventured to suggest earlier that this is a Faustian plight in more senses than one—a plight to be resolved perhaps not by the belated will or choice of the individual but by the contention of the good angels and the demons who clamor to possess him for their respective domains.

The tangible historic record of the century begun in *Willy Remembers* is brought at least to the brink of the 1970s by *Newsreel* and it is a record of the tangible disappointment of those middle-class codes and ambitions which guided Willy Kleinhans and Manny Finestone in their generations. The prophecy of what follows is ambiguously given in the last sentence of *Newsreel.* There we are told that Manny, "grinning Speed's crooked grin," sits down to write *The Girl in the Mall.* Either this means that the vindication of Maureen O'Brien and her class is still to be written by our common history and Faust's interpretation of it—or that it has been written here for those with eyes to see. This ghostly and doubly fictive novel hovers at the periphery of our comprehension, either a promise or a clue. The happy choice might be to take *The Girl in the Mall* as the secret, cabalistic title of what was published as *Newsreel*; as the cipher permitting us to decode the whole work cheerfully, perceiving the lineaments of the great American girl therein like the "bride immortal in the maize" as Hart Crane put it when he scanned the meaning of the American experience.

—R. V. Cassill

Ernest J. Gaines

(15 January 1933-)

The *DLB* entry on Ernest J. Gaines appears in *Dictionary of Literary Biography*, volume 2, *American Novelists Since World War II* (1978), pp. 170-175.

NEW BOOK: *In My Father's House* (New York: Knopf, 1978).

When *The Autobiography of Miss Jane Pittman* proved such an extraordinary success on television, its author, Ernest J. Gaines, became something of a celebrity. No longer was his name familiar only in literary circles. Nevertheless, the growing reputation of Gaines and his work has not changed the man or his life-style. He still lives in the same neighborhood in San Francisco he moved into seventeen years ago when he was a struggling writer, a neighborhood some (not Gaines) would call a ghetto. Although he has lived in California twice as long as his sixteen years in Louisiana, he still turns to that southern land of his birth for his fiction. Gaines has said, "When I try to write about California it just doesn't ring true." When he turns to Louisiana, however, he returns to a culture he calls "rich with tradition, stories, myth, superstition." Not surprisingly, his most recent novel, *In My Father's House* (1978) is set in fictional St. Adrienne, a small community across the Mississippi River from Baton Rouge.

The novel explores a familiar subject of Gaines's, the alienation between father and son. The father in this instance is sixty-year-old Rev. Phillip Martin, sometimes called "King" Martin (the echo of Martin Luther King's name here no doubt intended), a prominent and deservedly admired civil-rights leader. Thirty years earlier when Phillip Martin spent his days drinking, fighting, and womanizing, he met and had an extended affair with Johanna Rey, a union which produced three children. Eventually Johanna and the children leave St. Adrienne and Phillips's life. Later God changes Phillip, and he becomes a minister, a married man with a second family of three children, and a nationally known civil rights leader of the 1960s.

But in 1970 a ragged and half-crazed twenty-eight-year-old calling himself Robert X—really Phillip's elder son Etienne whom he has not seen in twenty years—appears in town to confront and kill the father who abandoned him so long ago. In his disturbed heart, Robert/Etienne sees his father as guilty of both the abandonment of children and the rape of their mother, since Phillip neglected to marry her. Etienne's grievance is aggravated by a personal sense of failure and inadequacy because, some ten years previously, he let his adolescent younger brother fill his role as family avenger by killing the rapist of their sister. When the father and son finally confront each other, Etienne is unable to carry out his plan to kill Phillip, but he does force Phillip to undergo a long and painful odyssey through his own past and the labyrinthine streets of Baton Rouge to learn what really happened to his first family. The full revelation is made in the climactic final chapters of the novel, when Phillip understands how his earlier immaturity has led to the imprisonment of one son, the rape of a daughter, and the isolated poverty of their mother, Johanna.

Readers familiar with Gaines's earlier work will recognize his considerable skills. As always, he displays his mastery of dialogue, and among contemporary writers there are few as attuned as Gaines to the speech of the people in his imaginative world. His humor, a feature of his writing too often neglected by critics and reviewers, invariably springs from his control of the speaking voice. While Gaines himself seldom makes jokes, his characters can be uproariously funny. In this latest novel, the portrayal of character is competent, sometimes brilliant, as in the case of Chippo Simon, a minor character who appears only in the last two chapters. Like Faulkner, to whom he is frequently compared, Gaines is adept at withholding revelations of plot and character until the proper dramatic moment. And in this novel he shows himself once again master of the intense emotional scene which never becomes melodrama. The final two chapters stand as a fine and moving example.

In My Father's House presents the problem of manhood for black males, a recurring theme in *Of Love and Dust* (1967), *Bloodline* (1968), and *The Autobiography of Miss Jane Pittman* (1971). Phillip Martin's failure to keep his first family whole, to honor his and Johanna's love by marriage, and the dissipation of the first half of his adult life—these unfortunate events are clearly a consequence of Martin's fear of accepting the responsibilities of black manhood. Etienne suffers from the same malady. He views himself as a eunuch, and through the murder of his father he hopes to regain the manhood he symbolically lost when his sister was raped.

Addressing the problem of manhood, Gaines has said: "You must understand that the blacks who were brought here as slaves were prevented from becoming the men that they could be. . . . A *man* can speak up, he can do things to protect himself, his home, and his family . . . eventually the blacks started [saying], 'Damn what you think I'm supposed to be—I will be what I ought to be. And if I must die to do it, I'll die' and for a long time they did get killed. Once they stepped over that line there was always that possibility, and quite a few of my characters step over that line."

As Gaines's statement indicates, the difficulty black males have in maintaining their manhood is largely due to the destructiveness of racism. Commenting on Gaines's first two novels, William Grant in *Dictionary of Literary Biography*, volume 2, notes that "social determinism shapes the lives of all the characters, making them pawns in a mechanistic world order rather than free agents." This bleak appraisal has been alleviated to some degree in Gaines's later work, but his characters' ability to act freely is practiced at a terrible cost. In this most recent novel Etienne has been crushed by mechanistic forces; his father struggles to overcome them.

Another destructive consequence of the black male's difficulty in claiming his manhood is the failure of male and female relationships. In *In My Father's House* as well as in his earlier works, romantic love does not survive the dehumanizing ethics governing Louisiana political and social life.

Ernest J. Gaines

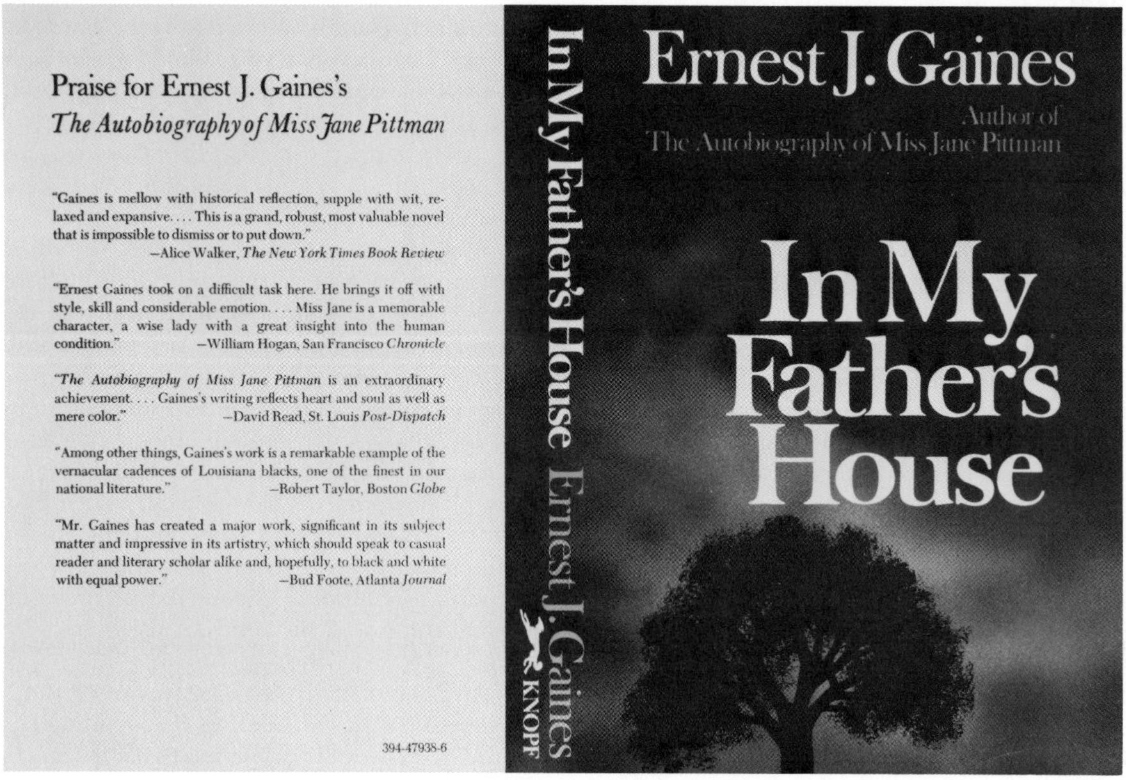

Dust jacket

Not only does Phillip abandon Johanna, he doesn't really talk to Alma, his second wife. Minor characters, Beverly and Shepherd, are unmarried lovers, youthful versions of Phillip and Johanna. Other male-female exchanges are marked by friction and anger. In Gaines's work, black women generally receive respect and tribute from men when, like Angelina in this novel, they are no longer sexually available.

In My Father's House has received generally favorable reviews. Novelist Larry McMurtry in the *New York Times Book Review* calls it a "mature and muscular novel"; it is "a book that attempts a large theme, and is fully adequate to it." A minority report is filed by V. M. Burke in the *Library Journal* who says the novel has "a weak plot, stick figures, and flat redundant writing." Although the plot line slackens in places, especially in the early chapters, McMurtry's appraisal seems a far more sensitive and accurate judgment than Burke's.

Whatever the final assessment of this novel, Gaines admits that it presented technical difficulties. In his work generally he favors the first-person narrator: "Usually, once I develop a character and 'hear' his voice I can let him tell the story. My writing is strongest when I do that." In this novel, however, he tackled what is for him a more technically difficult problem, the use of a third-person narrator. It is Gaines's belief that form, accomplished technique, becomes as or more important than content. The challenge is "putting that story down so that a million people can read, and feel, and hear it." In this novel he succeeds admirably.

Although *In My Father's House* has not received either the attention or acclaim of *The Autobiography of Miss Jane Pittman,* it marks an interesting new development. Like Dostoevski in *The Brothers Karamazov,* Gaines parallels the relationship of Phillip and his children with God and the human family. The "father" in the title refers to both Phillip and the creator of the universe. Although Gaines has always paid attention to the religious persuasions of his characters, he has not until this last novel developed fully and consistently the metaphysical implications of such religious belief. This concern should prove fruitful in the future.

And Gaines is writing again. After finishing a book, he says, "you always feel that you've failed" so "you're forever going to that next book . . . so you never really finish. Not if you are a writer. And it never gets any easier."

—William Burke

References:

John Callahan, "Image Making: Tradition and the Two Versions of *The Autobiography of Miss Jane Pittman*," *Chicago Review*, 29 (1977): 45-62;

P. Desruisseaux, "Ernest Gaines: A Conversation," *New York Times Book Review*, 11 June 1978, pp. 13, 44-45;

Jack Hicks, "To Make These Bones Live: History and Community in Ernest Gaines's Fiction," *Black American Literature Forum*, 11 (1977): 9-19.

Mark Harris

(19 November 1922-)

The *DLB* entry on Mark Harris appears in *Dictionary of Literary Biography*, volume 2, *American Novelists Since World War II* (1978), pp. 215-222.

NEW BOOKS: *Henry Wiggen's Books* (New York: Avon, 1977); previously published separately as *The Southpaw* (1953), *Bang the Drum Slowly* (1956), and *A Ticket for a Seamstitch* (1957);

Short Work of it: Selected Writings of Mark Harris (Pittsburgh: University of Pittsburgh Press, 1979);

It Looked Like For Ever (New York: McGraw-Hill, 1979);

Saul Bellow: Drumlin Woodchuck (Athens: University of Georgia Press, 1980).

A boxer-writer character in Mark Harris's novel *Wake Up, Stupid*, felt that a writer had to write a little every day, as a boxer had to punch a bag a little every day, just to keep his hand in. Harris, who has recently taken a new position as director of creative writing at Arizona State University at Tempe, has certainly heeded this injunction himself, and is continuing an active writing career that has seen a new book published, on the average, every two years for the past thirty-five years. The books have all been good, but four or five—*The Southpaw* (1953), *Something About a Soldier* (1957), *Wake Up, Stupid* (1959), *Killing Everybody* (1973), and perhaps *Bang the Drum Slowly* (1956)—have been distinguished. This raises a question: why has Harris not received the major critical attention accorded many lesser one- and two-book writers who have caught the popular fancy for a day, then faded away? No American writer of comparable stature has had so little written about him, beyond newspaper and magazine reviews.

The answer is cloudy and complex. First, Harris was strongly affected by his experiences in the army during World War II. His best friend (to whom his first novel was dedicated) was killed in that war. Harris himself went AWOL after basic training, was arrested, and finally discharged as "psychoneurotic." The story is told with some accuracy, if considerable poetic coloring, in *Something About a Soldier*. Perhaps this was the beginning of Harris's lifelong pacifism, a stance which has not been popular until recently. Henry Wiggen, the protagonist of *The Southpaw*, voiced criticism of the Korean War, which was not done in 1953 when the book was published. Wiggen's sentiments were praised in a review in the Communist *Daily Worker*, but other reviewers suggest that Harris was as immature as Wiggen. In 1956, when he wrote *Something About a Soldier*, which made heroes out of the young men in basic training who shot their fingers off in order to avoid going overseas, and which had as its sympathetic protagonist the deserting young soldier Epp, the sensible survivor, for the first time in his career Harris had a manuscript rejected by his publisher, a sobering shock for a writer who must have known he had just written one of his best books. He wrote and had another novel published before *Something About a Soldier* finally appeared.

If his political views possibly made critics stay away from him (Granville Hicks was one of his few champions), so perhaps did Harris's writing style. His novels seem so simple and readable on the surface that the exegetical critics of our time may have felt there was little for them to spend their ingenuity on. Such an impression, however, is deceptive, for if the novels do not require intricate decoding, they do require intelligence and attention to keep one from misreading them or missing what is good in them.

Finally, some of the books have baseball players as major characters, and Harris frequently has run into the attitude that naturally no book about baseball players can be serious literature. In "Easy Does It Not," published in Granville Hicks's *The Living Novel* (1957), Harris says, "If the reader is himself without ears (which is to say, untrained to read) he will think Henry . . . is nothing but a baseball player."

Harris's books, over the years, have fallen into three easily identifiable categories: four of his novels are narrated by baseball player Henry Wiggen and have baseball settings; six of his novels have writers or intellectuals as heroes; five of his books are mainly nonfictional autobiography. What is striking about them, however, is how much all these books have in common. Henry Wiggen, for instance, is the ostensible writer of the four baseball books ("Author" Wiggen, his teammates call him), and what he is writing is his autobiography. Some of the protagonists of the other novels, as well as being writers or intellectuals, are also powerful athletes, and many of them are self-consciously concerned with their autobiographies. And in all the books, fiction or nonfiction, we are at some level being presented with the ongoing autobiography of Harris himself, as the "disguised person in my books."

As we knock away the surface differences of the books we begin to see also the common themes underlying them. First is the absolute value of the individual as opposed to society or any other collective body. From this major theme come all the others: the antiwar theme, for example, for what is war but a vast machinery in which the individual is exhorted to sacrifice himself to the greater good of the society? Also linked to this emphasis on the individual is the tendency toward biography or autobiography, for what is more important to record than the life of the individual—particularly the radical, maverick individual? And if a biography or autobiography is to show the uniqueness of the individual, what individuals are more exemplary than writers, who, working in their solitary studies, find themselves more often than not in postures where they single-handedly stand against the great society outside them. Because the writer is a loner with nothing to write about but what he first filters through his consciousness, he is more likely than those from any other occupation to be self-conscious, to be fully aware of himself as an individual. Now, if the individual is all-important, then he has an existential obligation to be the best, most fully conscious and aware individual possible. Harris chooses professional athletes or writer/intellectuals as protagonists because for him these are perhaps the individuals who work the hardest, lifelong, to perfect their given abilities, and in this process, they define themselves as human beings. Over and over again in Harris's books—baseball novels, other novels, biographical or autobiographical works—the protagonists work to test and measure and perfect themselves. Harris's characters are flawed—like all humans—but because they are also people of great gifts, which is to say, exceptional powers and high expectations, their gifts and flaws together can thrust them into temptations, hasty judgments, and great disillusions. Typically in a Harris book the protagonist strives, not at first very successfully, to find his best self, while his friends wait on the sidelines with diminishing patience, sometimes offering advice, though they know that it will be unheeded and that the protagonist is involved in a personal struggle he must work out for himself.

Harris's most recent books continue in this pattern. *It Looked Like For Ever* (1979) is a fourth Henry Wiggen novel. The first novel in the series, *The Southpaw*, shows young Henry during his first season in the major leagues. He has not done much thinking about himself before, and he finds he has a great deal of growing up to do very quickly. Will he, for the sake of easy rewards, become merely a cog in the machinery of the baseball organization, winning at all costs, even at the sacrifice of his integrity, or will he realize in time that everything he does in life is done for its own sake, with himself and his closest friends as the judges he must live with? The next novel, *Bang the Drum Slowly* (one of Harris's most popular novels, and one from which a first-rate movie was made), shows Wiggen several seasons later as a seasoned professional who is suddenly faced with the fact of death (one of his teammates is dying of cancer). As the men one by one learn of the coming death, they drop their bickering and petty squabbles and pull together as an unbeatable team, the baseball team in this case a metaphor for the union of common humanity we must muster against the great leveler, death. The third, *A Ticket for a Seamstitch* (1957), again deals with maturing: with learning how to reconcile unrealistically high expectations with the reality that follows.

The new book, which is cast in a pattern very similar to *Bang the Drum Slowly*, suggests that growing, maturing, is not just something for young men, but is lifelong. Henry Wiggen is now forty (thirty-nine and a half, he quickly corrects us). His manager, Dutch Schnell, drops dead while out playing golf, and Henry, who has lost his fast ball, and is not completing very many games anymore, takes it for granted he will be selected to replace Dutch as manager of the team. But he is not; in fact,

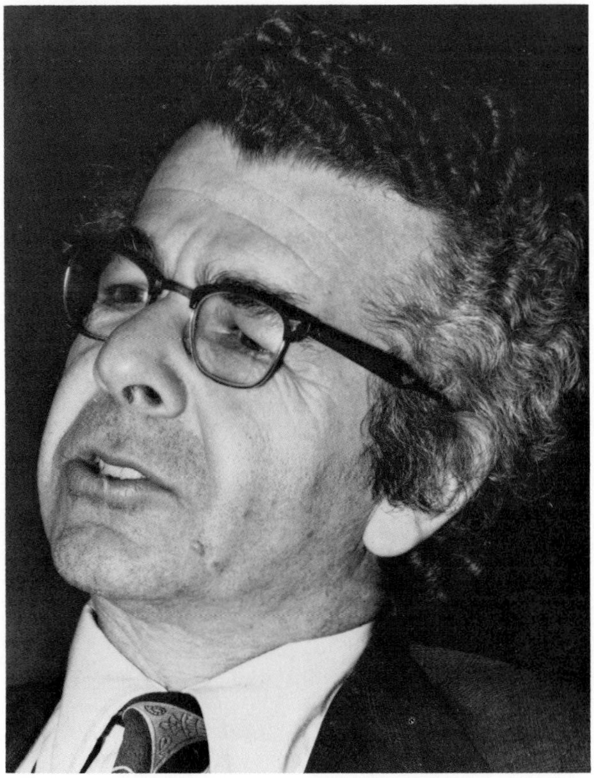

he is simply cut from the team and thrust into what he considers premature retirement. The reason he has not been chosen manager, he finds, is that he is not considered inhuman enough for the job. The world is divided into "electric chair men" and "permission men," and he is one of the latter. The good manager should get the best out of his players, then discard them without a second thought when they pass their peaks—as has happened to Henry himself.

Henry has been taking his youngest daughter to a child psychiatrist because she stands in public places and screams at the top of her voice claiming she will not stop until she sees him play in a game. She is expressing outwardly his own inward scream. With the mid-life crisis fully upon him, Henry toys with the idea of having affairs with several women to prove his prowess (trying to ignore the fact that his prostate—"prostrate" as he spells it—is suddenly almost crippling him) and tries desperately to be taken on by another team as a relief pitcher. Finally he gets his chance, and, though his fast ball has gone, his twenty-one years of experience stand him in good stead, as he is put in during the final innings to save a number of games by carefully outthinking each batter. In the first game, however, a ball has been hit hard back to the box. He has fielded it and made the out at first, but has been bothered because it all happened so quickly, he hardly saw the ball coming. He puts the incident out of his mind, but, several games later, a terrific hit comes back at him, and this time he wakes up in the hospital with severe bruises. It is a typical Harris climax, a moment of definition: "This was no accident," Henry says, "This is Nature speaking." He now sees what he could not admit to himself before: he has gotten too old for a young man's game. His young daughter, meanwhile, gives up her screaming and her interest in baseball: she has moved on to the next stage in her development and is now wild about horses. No man, Henry sees, can stop time, but he can learn how to accept it.

Just as in many other Harris books, there is a particular richness of secondary characters, most of them providing negative examples of what Henry might become if he cannot face reality. We see the managers and owners of the various teams Henry tries to join, and catch glimpses of their home lives that are as bizarre as any in a novel by Dickens. Those who stay in this kid's game of professional athletics beyond the time of their youth can only stay through the sheerest distortion of values: their home lives are crippled, and their professional lives depend upon their becoming "electric chair men." Other characters live in complete dream worlds in which fantasies are more real than facts. The wife of Wiggen's manager, for instance, fantasizes that she has had torrid affairs with all of the big-name baseball players. Other characters will go to any lengths to deny to themselves that they are aging. A woman athlete Wiggen knows, for instance, dresses more youthfully and behaves more foolishly than her own daughter, in an attempt to exchange roles with her. Pointedly, Henry's daughter's psychiatrist is so effective because she gets down on the level of the daughter and behaves just as childishly, and the daughter, seeing how foolish that is, quickly matures.

If *It Looked Like For Ever* is a characteristic Harris novel, *Saul Bellow: Drumlin Woodchuck* (1980) is just as obviously a characteristic Harris nonfiction book, which is to say, it is a book about the writing of the book. When a writer reaches a certain stage in his development, Harris once said, "the work itself is experience," by which he means the actual act of writing is a major portion of his life.

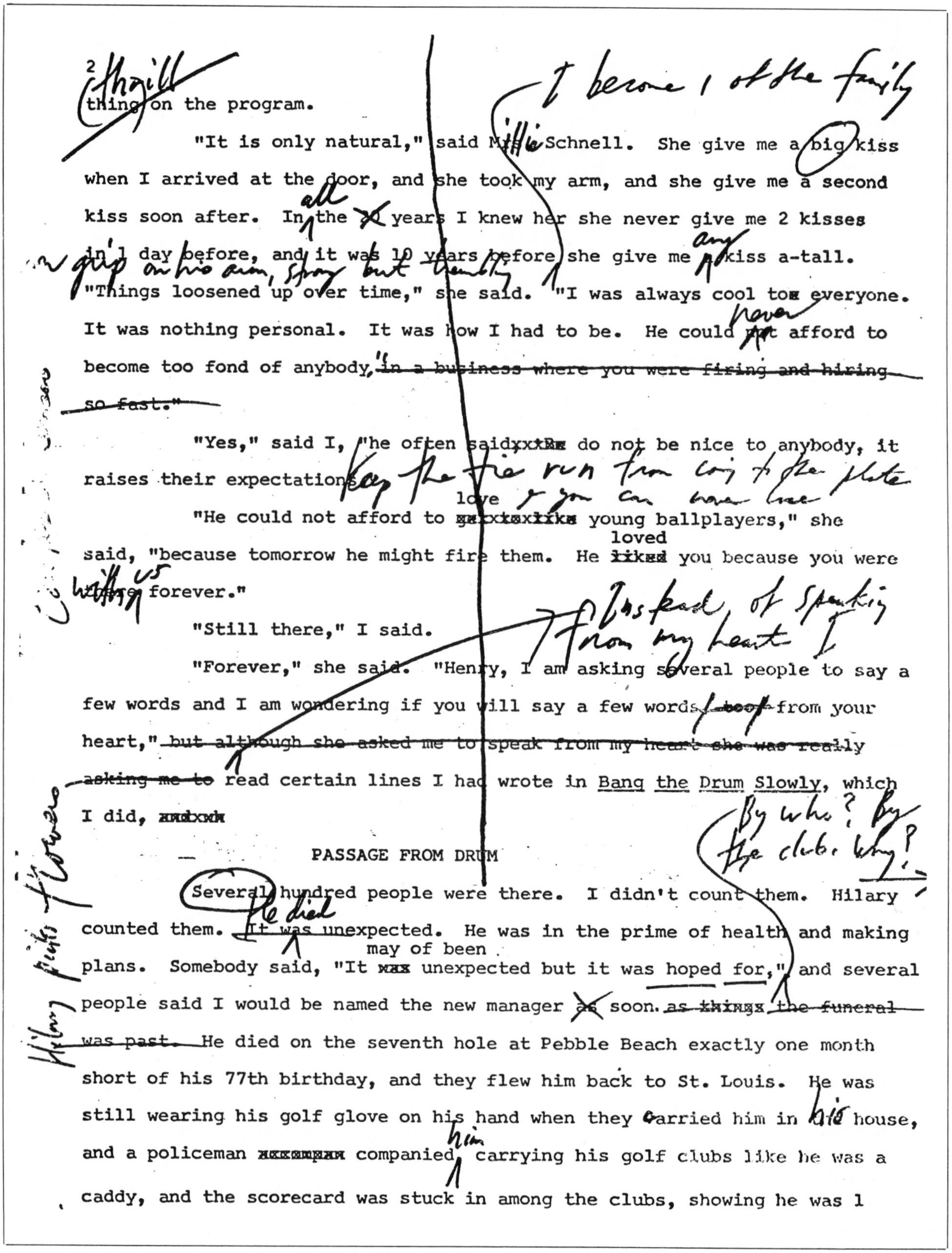

2

thing on the program.

"It is only natural," said Mrs. Schnell. She give me a big kiss when I arrived at the door, and she took my arm, and she give me a second kiss soon after. In the 30 years I knew her she never give me 2 kisses in 1 day before, and it was 10 years before she give me a kiss a-tall. "Things loosened up over time," she said. "I was always cool to everyone. It was nothing personal. It was how I had to be. He could not afford to become too fond of anybody in a business where you were firing and hiring so fast."

"Yes," said I, "he often said do not be nice to anybody, it raises their expectations."

"He could not afford to like young ballplayers," she said, "because tomorrow he might fire them. He liked you because you were there forever."

"Still there," I said.

"Forever," she said. "Henry, I am asking several people to say a few words and I am wondering if you will say a few words from your heart," but although she asked me to speak from my heart she was really asking me to read certain lines I had wrote in Bang the Drum Slowly, which I did,

PASSAGE FROM DRUM

Several hundred people were there. I didn't count them. Hilary counted them. It was unexpected. He was in the prime of health and making plans. Somebody said, "It may of been unexpected but it was hoped for," and several people said I would be named the new manager as soon as things the funeral was past. He died on the seventh hole at Pebble Beach exactly one month short of his 77th birthday, and they flew him back to St. Louis. He was still wearing his golf glove on his hand when they carried him in the house, and a policeman companied him, carrying his golf clubs like he was a caddy, and the scorecard was stuck in among the clubs, showing he was 1

It Looked Like For Ever, *revised typescript*

Harris's play, *Friedman & Son* (1963) is somewhat autobiographical, and when he had it published, he included with it a purely autobiographical preface as long as the play, in which he discusses the circumstances surrounding the writing of the play. Later, *Life* commissioned Harris to follow the Nixon-Brown gubernatorial race in California. After he wrote a brief article on the campaign for *Life,* he wrote a full-sized book, *Mark the Glove Boy* (1964), discussing the events leading up to his writing the article. Similarly, *Twentyone Twice* (1966), ostensibly Harris's account of an investigative mission he went on for the Peace Corps in Africa, has for half the volume an autobiographical account of how he was chosen for the assignment. It is a method of operation that suits Harris well, writing his life by indirection, putting his own life against the wider canvas of the times he has been living through. Ironically, his direct autobiography, *Best Father Ever Invented* (1976), is curiously flat by comparison. One is tempted to say that Harris as a man is less interesting than Harris as a highly self-conscious and engaged observer of his times.

Saul Bellow: Drumlin Woodchuck is actually an autobiographical account of Harris in the process of trying to write a biography of Bellow. It is certainly Harris's finest nonfiction book. Like half a dozen or so of his earlier books, this one too will probably be perennially republished. Harris begins by saying that Bellow's writings and life had always filled him with admiration, had always taught him new things about his own writing and his own life. "That I was thinking so much about Bellow," he realized early in 1966, "suggests that by this time I had firm thoughts about writing his biography." He had corresponded with Bellow on various occasions over the years, finally met him a few times, and it seemed they would be friends. But after he went to Bellow with his proposal to write a biography of him, their friendship became strained. Harris felt himself behaving artificially in front of Bellow, trying to impress him, and he was constantly worried that Bellow was trying to avoid him. Bellow was evasive on the idea of the biography, saying a biography should be written only when the man is finished: "I'm not finished, not done, not *fini.* I'm still groping." Years went by and Harris felt he was learning nothing. The single hard fact he thought he had was Bellow's birthdate, then he found he had even missed that by a month. But each time he was at the point of quitting, his friends, and sometimes Bellow himself, suddenly encouraged him to continue.

Although the book seems to be mainly about Harris himself and his problems writing the book, almost unexpectedly there are indeed insights into Bellow's personality. Neither Harris nor Bellow seems entirely attractive. Harris, the single-minded biographer, often seems slow on the uptake, often seems singularly lacking in personal pride. Of course, he is consciously depicting himself in this way, and the feeling—it is one of the strengths of the book—of Boswell is often close at hand. How can one be anything but a bit silly running about writing down the words of the great man? And Bellow the private man comes across as irritable, evasive (though why shouldn't he be: everyone seems to be after him. The drumlin woodchuck of the title—a character in a Robert Frost poem—is an animal with several exits, several escape routes from his burrow). The theme emerges that Bellow the public man needs his evasiveness, his escape routes, in order to preserve for Bellow the private man a quiet corner for him to do his writing in.

The extremely fine long section near the end of the book, the story of Bellow's coming to Purdue (where Harris is teaching at the time) to give a talk, shows another side of Bellow's demand for privacy. In the midst of the rising protest against the Vietnam War, Bellow has been having obscenities hurled at him at every school he speaks at, because he has refused to speak out against the war. Bellow the solitary thinker can only say what he thinks and refuses to give easy answers for the sake of popular praise. At Purdue he voiced his distrust of the young demonstrators, finding their violence as bad as any other violence: "You don't found universities in order to destroy culture. For that you want a Nazi party." Harris, at that time leading demonstrations himself, found Bellow's position inexplicable, but over time began to feel more drawn to it. And so he should, for Bellow is like the quintessential hero of one of Harris's novels: the querulous private man with a chaotic family life is publicly a man with considerable dignity in his refusal to be merely what others want him to be.

This is a rich book, told in the way only Harris could have told it. Harris, approaching his sixtieth year, continues his non-stop writing life, at last word preparing a Boswell reader abridged from the six-volume Yale edition of Boswell's private papers. Long before it is completed, he will be casting around for a new book to write.

—*Norman Lavers*

Television Play:

The Man That Corrupted Hadleyburg, adapted from Mark Twain's short story, PBS, 1980.

Other:

"How to Write," in *Afterwords,* ed. Thomas McCormack (New York: Harper & Row, 1969), pp. 65-79.

Periodical Publications:

"Old Enough to Know, Young Enough to Care" [interviews with Robert Frost and Carl Sandburg], *Life* (1 December 1961): 101ff;

"The Last Article," *New York Times Magazine,* 6 October 1974, pp. 20ff.

Reference:

Norman Lavers, *Mark Harris* (Boston: Twayne, 1968).

AN INTERVIEW
with MARK HARRIS

DLB: In real life and in fiction you've dealt with the difficulties of a dual career—teaching and writing. Has the balancing act become any easier with time?

HARRIS: Yes, I feel very comfortable with doing both now. I don't feel a contradiction.

DLB: Do they tend to feed on each other in constructive ways?

HARRIS: Oh yes, I think that's what is easy about it. When I'm talking to students or colleagues about writing, that's what I'm thinking about privately too. I think the act of composition and the act of teaching are very close to each other, at least the way I teach and the way I compose. I find them still compatible, as, in effect, I realize they always were, even though I felt friction from time to time.

DLB: Recently you've moved to Tempe, Arizona, to serve as director of creative writing at Arizona State University. Have the moves in your teaching career been a major stimulus to your writing?

HARRIS: I suppose. It's hard to tell whether they're the result of it or whether they stimulated it. I think a sense of discontent in one place, moving around—that is part of a writing energy, you might say. For me it's become habit or a way of life. I think it has contributed. It's a bother but it seems to go with my territory.

DLB: Is there any one academic situation that stands out as having been most conducive to creative endeavors?

HARRIS: The years in San Francisco were very formative. I was more impressionable; I was younger. But every place really did give me different images. It might have all been the same if I had stayed in one place all my life, but it seems to me that I drew from each place. It was what I had instead of travel. I think settling in different places did bring out different aspects of what I was feeling.

DLB: In an essay collected in *Short Work of It: Selected Writing by Mark Harris,* you wrote of readers, "There are people whose ears have never grown, or have fallen off, or have merely lost the power to listen. And there are people with ears." Are you finding more people with ears now than earlier in your writing career?

HARRIS: I'm not sure that I would state it in terms of ears anymore. I think now I would assess it in terms of self-awareness. I don't know. I can't tell if things are different or the same. To be able to apprehend writing, a reader has to be able really to believe that the characters there are different from himself or herself. You have to be able to shed your own skin for a moment and be in somebody else's skin—even if you don't fully understand what is being said, at least to know that something is being said which may be different from what you came to the book with. So I can't generalize about people. You meet people who seem to be brilliant readers at a very young age, other people at an advanced age who are still down with their assumptions and can't get out of them.

DLB: Much of your writing is about writing itself, and *Saul Bellow: Drumlin Woodchuck* is no exception. You set out to write a traditional biography of Bellow—with some implicit encouragement from Bellow—but found him an elusive subject. Are you happy with what the book became?

HARRIS: Yes, I feel that I observed a dictum that somebody once offered about building: you work with available materials. If he wasn't going to help make any more available, that was going to be the limit of it. So I did work with what I had. I feel that was sensible, and I think it's a humorous and meaningful book as it is, and somebody else will have to do the definitive biography.

DLB: In the preceding essay, Norman Lavers describes as the basic common theme underlying all your books "the absolute value of the individual as opposed to society or any collective body." Has this been your major concern as a writer?

HARRIS: That's a nice way to put it. Most people would say it's egotistic to think that the individual should be basic, but I really do think so. For a moment there I stopped at the word *absolute* because I think I do tend to have certain absolute values rather than a kind of thought like "this person could be sacrificed for the good of society." I think that no one should be sacrificed. I agree with the idea that the highest criterion of moral determination is the preservation of life, and no abstract ideas, in my opinion, can override that. I feel that the phrase Lavers uses is close to it.

DLB: How do you respond to errors or misconceptions in print about your work?

HARRIS: I find the best thing to do when I think about those errors is to put them out of my mind because I don't like to keep ruminating over them. There are a lot of things that I've seen that I've been distressed with at the time, but they seem to pass. There's nothing along that line I would want to address myself to now.

DLB: What are you working on now?

HARRIS: Right now I'm at the end of a different work. I just sent off today a screenplay that's based on a journal of Boswell's, his defense of a poor man for stealing sheep. It hopefully will be produced as a film this year by the BBC. In the same shipment I sent back to McGraw-Hill some galleys of a one-volume book I have done that's a distillation of the first six volumes of Boswell's journal.

I wish I could tell you something definite, but now I go into a kind of miserable time when I don't really have any work in front of me yet. That gets to be very gloomy and frustrating, and then I do start to brood on all the things that I want to correct. That's where writing begins for me, in anger. So when I'm not working I get angry about things again until I can get writing. I really do feel unhappy and depressed when I'm not writing. I didn't used to say that because I felt I was dramatizing myself, but it's just a fact.

—Jean W. Ross

John Hawkes

(17 August 1925-   )

The *DLB* entries on John Hawkes appear in *Dictionary of Literary Biography,* volume 2, *American Novelists Since World War II* (1978), pp. 222-231, and *Dictionary of Literary Biography,* volume 7, *Twentieth-Century American Dramatists, Part 1: A-J* (1980), pp. 263-268.

NEW BOOK: *The Passion Artist* (New York: Harper & Row, 1979).

RECENT AWARD: elected to the American Academy and Institute of Arts and Letters, 1980.

John Barth, a friend and fellow novelist, says of Hawkes's books, "They wear me out. . . . they hurt my head. They provoke, though, the kind of love that one feels only for amazing things that could not come out of one's own imagination at all. One loves them the more for that fact." Readers of John Hawkes agree. They like their fiction nightmarish but comic; disturbing yet poetic; erotic but lyrical; unconventional yet highly structured. Hawkes has been having such fiction published since 1949. Along with a few other contemporary novelists such as John Barth and Thomas Pynchon, Hawkes offers an originality of vision that extends the boundaries of fiction. In the *New York Times Book Review* a few years ago Tony Tanner called Hawkes "one of the very best living American writers," and Thomas McGuane argued that Hawkes is "feasibly our best writer."

Hawkes's canon, including eight novels and three novellas, has come under increasing critical attention, especially since the publication of *Second*

John Hawkes

Skin (1964), the runner-up for the National Book Award. Yet his critical reputation has not carried over to the general reading public. Although he has been publishing fiction for over thirty years, he has not gained the popular acclaim earned by Saul Bellow, Norman Mailer, Joseph Heller, and William Styron. Sensitive to the charge that his books are "inaccessible," Hawkes has eased some of the demands that the early, surreal fiction made on the reader. In fact, his triad, which includes *The Blood Oranges* (1971), *Death, Sleep & the Traveler* (1974), and *Travesty* (1976), takes on some of the trappings of the conventional novel with recognizable characters, setting, and plot. In 1976 when *Travesty* came out, Hawkes had high expectations for its success and was bitterly disappointed with its lack of recognition. The result was a crisis in his artistic career. Feeling the pressure of middle age and the number of years dedicated to his writing, Hawkes acknowledged his desire to reach more readers. He frankly admitted, "I am tired of being called America's best unknown writer."

Part of Hawkes's effort to gain a larger audience led to a change of publishers. All of his fiction from "Charivari" (1949) to *Travesty* (1976) had been published by New Directions, a small yet highly respected New York literary house headed by his old friend James Laughlin. Because of New Direction's limited national distribution and promotion, Laughlin encouraged Hawkes to seek a bigger audience, telling him that he deserved to be more than a cult writer. In 1979 the novelist changed to Harper & Row, a major trade publisher with access to book outlets and an interest in advertising promotion. When *The Passion Artist* came out in 1979, Hawkes unquestionably received more attention. A full page ad appeared in the *New York Times Book Review*, and *Time* reviewed the novel—the first of Hawkes's novels to be mentioned by *Time* since 1950.

A new start for Hawkes, *The Passion Artist* is his most accessible novel to date. It exchanges the use of an unreliable first-person narrator, evident in the triad, for a relatively straightforward, third-person account of the central character Konrad Vost. Hawkes explained to Thomas LeClair that one of his goals in *The Passion Artist* was "to create a man who is more unsympathetic than any other character I've created and to make the reader share in artistic sympathy for him by the end of the novel." Like many of Hawkes's other middle-aged protagonists, Vost is enslaved by the repressions, fears, desires, and nightmares from his childhood and his past, which are locked up in his unconscious. Excessively rigid and obsessed with control, this timid man lives in an anonymous European city whose bleakness and deathly uniformity reflect the protagonist's desolate existence.

La Violaine, the local women's prison, dominates the city, the landscape of the novel, and its protagonist. A symbol of repression and sterility, the prison suggests the sexual deprivation of a modern authoritarian society where eroticism is the enemy of order. Unlike the lush landscapes of sexual vitality described in *Second Skin* and *Blood Oranges*, the fictive world of *The Passion Artist* is reminiscent of Hawkes's earlier works, like *The Cannibal* (1949), *The Beetle Leg* (1951), and *The Owl* (1954), where the oppressive modern world imprisons the individual spirit and imagination.

Neither passionate nor an artist, Konrad Vost belies the novel's title with his sexual celibacy and precise action. Ignorant of women, yet obsessed by them, he cares for his schoolgirl daughter Mirabelle, in actuality a teenage prostitute; frequents the grave of the adulterous Claire, his deceased wife; and thinks often of his mother Eva, a prisoner in La Violaine for the murder of his father. Characterized as a "man who does not know the woman," Vost remains "faithful to the landscape of his mother's punishment."

After suggesting the resemblance between Vost and his sterile environment, Hawkes disrupts this ordered existence. Within twenty-four hours Vost accidentally learns that his daughter is a prostitute, submits to one of her prostitute friends, and after turning his daughter in to the police, answers the public call for help in suppressing the women's prison riot. Along with other male volunteers armed with sticks, he tries to beat the women inmates into submission, all the while wishing "that the rioting all around him would never cease." About the eruption in the prison (suggestive of Vost's own repressed unconscious), Hawkes writes, "the prison had exploded, so to speak; interior and exterior life were assuming a single shape." Similar to other gothic enclosures that contain nightmares of sex and death, the prison embodies Vost's worst fears as well as his only hope of releasing his demons. The ultimate prisoner of his restrictive environment and, more significantly, his own unconscious desires, Vost must break out of his private cell if he is to experience life's mysteries.

During the riot when Vost is wounded and loses consciousness, he dreams of traveling into a "dead marsh," the sole passenger on a night train carrying a coffin. At this point *The Passion Artist* suggests Hawkes's post-1964 fiction, in which landscape often mirrors the narrator's psyche. Although not filtered through a first-person narrator, this novel turns inward and follows Vost into his world of dream. His night train ride toward death corresponds with his actual trip to the outlying marsh in search of female escapees from prison. Not able to determine which direction he is taking in the "fog-covered marsh," he finds an empty stone barn of "slimy roughness." In this damp enclosure Vost lies in the dung beneath a frightening horse and later two more frightening women who simultaneously arouse and repulse him. Placed at the novel's center, the trip into the marsh and the night in the abandoned barn continue Vost's "disordering" and suggest his beginning release. The description of this classic interior journey reminds Albert Guerard of the "old Hawkesian entropies" and "imaginative attraction to decay." According to Guerard, these fears energize Hawkes's return "to the tension and stylistic power of the best earlier fiction."

Made prisoner by the two women, Vost is taken back to La Violaine. He acknowledges the inevitability of his return and the irony that his freedom will come only through imprisonment. Confined to the darkness of his private cell, Vost relives the sexual traumas of his youth and exchanges this nightmare for erotic liberation. In the

Dust jacket

presence of "women he had spent his life avoiding," this man of precision and rigid self-control feels "at last the transports of that singular experience which makes every man an artist: the experience, that is, of the willed erotic union." For Vost passion releases his imaginative vitality and allows him to achieve the ultimate artistic experience—the union of the self and the other. *The Passion Artist* thus continues Hawkes's preoccupation with the relationship between sex and the imagination—a theme which pervades his work.

Although Hawkes allows Vost to be initiated into the art of passion, he does not unite the extremes represented by the sterile order of a repressive society and the irrational power of sexuality. Exploding in violence, *The Passion Artist* ends with Vost being shot as he emerges from the prison gates. Even though Hawkes closes the novel on a severe note, he nevertheless suggests the importance of plumbing the interior depths where the irrational, imaginative, and erotic lie.

Most reviews of *The Passion Artist* praise Hawkes's artistic skills but find the novel ultimately unsatisfying. The review in the *New York Times Book Review*, entitled "A Detour to Nihilism," grants that Hawkes "remains among the most innovative and original American writers" yet argues that in *The Passion Artist* "his virtuosity leads to superficiality." Likewise, Paul Gray in *Time* writes that the book "does not so much explore sex as mime its mysteries." On the other hand, fellow novelists John Barth and John Irving applaud the book, with Barth calling it Hawkes's best since *Second Skin*. Also in praise, Hawkes's former teacher, Albert Guerard writes, "The later sections of *The Passion Artist* are among the most poignant and most powerful in Hawkes's now extensive and truly classical *oeuvre*." Further recognition followed in 1980 when he was elected to the American Academy and Institute of Arts and Letters.

The T. B. Stowell University Professor at Brown University, Hawkes lives in Providence, Rhode Island, with Sophie, his wife of thirty-three years, to whom he gives great credit for the quality of his work. His academic post at Brown allows him to teach two years with a third off for writing. Whether teaching or writing, he totally concentrates on that specific activity, unable to integrate the two. He and Sophie Hawkes usually spend the third year overseas, where he writes three hours a day, usually from eight to eleven in the morning. Explaining his work regimen to Carol McCabe, Hawkes says, "It's a matter of energy and the sense of the page being as white as the day . . . I don't try to prepare myself emotionally for writing, but while shaving I may be thinking. What a writer has to do is to achieve a sense of detachment, an emotional separation from what's going into the writing. . . . Writing is a very disciplined matter."

Pleased with his new publisher and given a solid advance for his next novel, Hawkes left in June 1980 for his year in France. Staying at the home of a friend of James Laughlin's, he is working on his next novel, tentatively titled "Don Quixote's Daughter." Planned as a parody of erotic literature, the new novel is set in a futuristic, decayed Paris and has a fourteen-year-old girl as its first-person narrator. Hawkes believes he has time to write three more novels before he retires from teaching. In his conversation with John Barth, he admits to looking forward to retirement: "I love the university, but I want to go to a Greek island or the south of France and eat grapes and olives and swim, or at least float in the ocean, and get clean again if I can. I want to get sex or the eroticized landscape out of my system once and for all." "Don Quixote's Daughter" may achieve this ambition, but certainly Hawkes's fiction will always shatter habitual responses and offer a beauty of language Dionysian in its energy.

From the very beginning of his writing career Hawkes has pursued innovation. In 1964 he described "the function of the true innovator" as keeping "prose alive," testing "in the sharpest way possible the range of our human sympathies," and constantly destroying "mere surface morality." *The Passion Artist* furthers Hawkes's reputation as an innovator and marks his new start.

—Carol MacCurdy

Interviews:

"Hawkes and Barth Talk About Fiction," *New York Times Book Review*, 1 April 1979, pp. 7, 31-33;

Thomas LeClair, "The Novelists: John Hawkes," *New Republic* (10 November 1979): 26-29.

References:

Paul Gray, "Harrowing Sex," review of *The Passion Artist, Time* (24 September 1979): 82, 84;

Donald J. Greiner, *Comic Terror: The Novels of John Hawkes*, enlarged edition (Memphis: Memphis State University Press, 1978);

Albert J. Guerard, Review of *The Passion Artist*, *New Republic* (10 November 1979): 29-30;
Josephine Hendin, "A Detour to Nihilism," review of *The Passion Artist*, *New York Times Book Review*, 16 September 1979, pp. 7, 36;
Carol A. Hryciw, *John Hawkes: An Annotated Bibliography*, with "Four Introductions" by John Hawkes (Metuchen, N.J.: Scarecrow Press, 1977);
Thomas LeClair, "A Pair of Jacks," *Horizon*, 22 (November 1979): 64-71;
Carol McCabe, "Portrait of the Artist as a Middle-Aged Man," *Providence Sunday Journal*, 18 November 1979, pp. 6, 8, 12, 14.

Joseph Heller

(1 May 1923-)

The *DLB* entry on Joseph Heller appears in *Dictionary of Literary Biography*, volume 2, *American Novelists Since World War II* (1978), pp. 231-236.

NEW BOOK: *Good As Gold* (New York: Simon & Schuster, 1979; London: Cape, 1979).

Joseph Heller, like Bruce Gold, the protagonist of his newest work, gets ideas for his writing while jogging. Like Gold, Heller worries neurotically about heart attacks, cancer, and death; also like Gold, he loves to eat and to engage in the rapid repartee his friend Mel Brooks has called "verbal Ping-Pong." The slashing, slanting, aggressive strokes of that game make it an apt metaphor for his (Heller-Gold's) prose style as well.

Good As Gold is written in the manner familiar from *Catch-22* (1961) and *Something Happened* (1974), Heller's previous novels. The paradox, the contradiction, the double bind are the central devices on which these tragicomedies are constructed. Bruce Gold plans to write a book about the "Jewish Experience in America" that will be both sensational and serious; Joseph Heller has written a book about one kind of American experience, and it too is at once sensational and serious—sensational in its vulgar language, its sexual escapades, its glaring confessions, and its excoriation of our political leaders; serious in its social concerns, its psychological depths, and its literary self-consciousness.

Good As Gold focuses on a middle-aged professor of English, a respected writer of books, essays, and reviews. The product of a Jewish immigrant neighborhood in Coney Island, now grown up to Manhattan's West Side, Gold travels on the lecture circuit. He has children at private schools and a dull marriage from which he escapes into adulterous adventures. The Gold clan is headed by an eighty-two-year-old cantankerous tyrant of a father and includes a veritable menagerie of brothers, sisters, and in-laws. Leonard Michaels, in the *New York Times Book Review*, has called this family "exquisitely realistic—that is, grotesque, witty, lugubriously banal." This Jewish family that is lovingly but abrasively protective of its members while gleefully stabbing them in the back has become practically a stereotype in American humor. The reviewer Gene Lyons has suggested in the *Nation* that "Heller should give Woody Allen a cut of the take, who should pass most of it on to Philip Roth." Bruce Gold is the spoiled child prodigy of his Jewish family; throughout the novel one or another of his relatives is taking him aside to tell him that everyone is immensely proud of him. But for Gold the family dinners are sessions of malicious abuse from his father, maniacally hostile pronouncements from his stepmother, painfully idiotic debates with his brother, Sid, and trivial, noisy contributions by the others, to all of which he responds with helpless rage and frustration.

To escape from the black comedy of Jewish Brooklyn, Gold rushes to the tantalizing possibility of real respect in an important position in Washington, D.C. His WASP college friend Ralph Newsome, now an adviser at the White House, offers him a series of jobs like "spokesman," "unnamed source," "senior official," director of NATO and the CIA, and cabinet positions ranging from secretary of agriculture to secretary of the treasury to secretary of state. To improve his chances of success Ralph suggests Gold get rid of his dumpy, aging wife Belle and marry Andrea Conover, a tall, blond heiress with "connections."

The world of political glory to which Gold now seeks entry is characterized by an Orwellian (or today, Hellerian) doublespeak which, through narrative voice and dialogue, reveals one of the novel's main themes. Disbelief, outrage, and horror grow as the reader looks into a world where institutions are facades standing in front of nothing, where political figures have no qualifications other than self-interest, where language conveys no meaning and only hinders communication, and where chaos parades as order. John W. Aldridge, writing in *Harper's*, has called the Washington sections of the novel a "masterful burlesque" producing an "effect of derangement from conditions of order, sanity and meaningful causality." The result, he has written, is one of "psychotic arbitrariness. In the absence of clear and unavoidable imperatives that fix the nature of reality and control one's perception of it, reality can become anything one wishes it to be or decides it is."

When Gold is first offered a job, he asks, "What would I have to do?" Ralph Newsome tells him, "Anything you want, as long as it's everything we tell you to say and do in support of our policies, whether you agree with them or not. You'll have complete freedom." And he continues, "This President doesn't want yes-men. What we want are independent men of integrity who will agree with all our decisions after we make them. You'll be entirely on your own."

Gold decides he just might fit in, for he considers himself a "radical moderate" who advocates "fiery caution and crusading inertia." Unfortunately, the stumbling block to an actual appointment comes in the form of a "catch": Gold tells Newsome that Andrea Conover will not marry him until he is "somebody important in government," but Newsome responds that for Gold to get an appointment quickly, he must be married to Andrea because "The Conover connection is crucial." So

Dust jacket

Gold returns to New York for a few more frustrating family dinners, only to flee again to Washington for meetings with Andrea and visits to her father, Pugh Biddle Conover, an obnoxious, rich anti-Semite with whom Gold hopes to curry favor. Conover receives Gold on his Maryland estate and, while Andrea goes off to pursue that gentile pastime of horseback riding, Gold is subjected to the venomous harangues and the contempt of her father. So strong is the language of these passages that they reveal a passionate hatred almost unreal, an overt vilification of Jews so blatant that Conover becomes unbelievable, and Gold comes to be seen more than ever as a spineless opportunist for allowing it to continue.

The climax to all the hectic activity comes after Gold meets his daughter's schoolteacher and falls madly in love with her. Having already planned to sneak away for a trip to Acapulco with Andrea, he now decides to take the teacher along as well. A wildly surrealistic chapter ensues in which, as he jogs around the track at the gym in New York, Gold imagines himself racing from one woman's hotel room to the other's, eating and fornicating for all he's worth. Finally, he collapses on the track and is taken to the hospital with what his doctor calls either an attack of anxiety or a mild heart attack. He does recover, but his brother, Sid, dies at the book's end, an event that brings Gold back to the Jewish fold, for the time being at least. The ambiguity of his identity problem is hardly resolved, but Heller does seem to offer at least a temporary point of rest.

Before Gold's collapse, as the shifts of scene between Brooklyn and Washington are accelerating in pace, Gold studies his clippings on Henry Kissinger in preparation for the book he is planning to write on "The Little Prussian." In the excerpts he quotes and in his running commentary, a vitriolic attack is built up against the writer, intellectual, and Jew Kissinger who has achieved the political and social power that is denied Gold. Kissinger becomes an alter ego onto whom Gold projects his self-hatred, in Leonard Michaels's words, in a fashion "so rich in moral revulsion as to seem like a voodoo incantation . . . Bruce Gold yearns to escape what he is so that he can become what he isn't, which is precisely what he hates." Alienation from self, alienation from one's background and people is in Michaels's view the novel's "deepest subject," and he calls it an up-to-date and American version of Kafka's agonies of personal identity.

As Michaels goes on to point out, Heller himself is implicated. The indictment of the intellectual Jew who goes to Washington and sells himself to corrupt politics is the same as the indictment of the Jew "who wants to escape his identity while exploiting it, particularly by making a lot of money on a big book about Jews." And Heller, of course, is quite aware of, indeed self-conscious about, the dilemma. He has said of his own success, "I don't think I deserve all this money. It puts me into a class for which I have very little sympathy." In "On America's Inhuman Callousness," an article he wrote for *U.S. News & World Report*, Heller levels a similar charge against our entire society: "I'm not sure anything can work without major modifications in our economic system, and nobody doing well wants to make those modifications."

It appears that essentially one issue—the depth and validity of Heller's social critique—has determined (and divided) the response to *Good As Gold*. Reviewers like John Aldridge and Leonard Michaels have praised the book and treated it to serious discussions of its themes and its literary significance. The work's particular merit, according to Aldridge, is that Heller's black humor and his scathing comedy are always grounded in the "actualities of the observable world," and that Heller (unlike Pynchon and Barthelme) provides, as a kind of fulcrum of sanity, a reliable narrator whose rationality the reader can identify with. Aldridge's main reservation is that "Heller tends . . . to ring too many changes on what is essentially one good joke," a criticism also raised by others who have found the book repetitive and derivative. But basically Aldridge believes that Heller's vision of American culture is correct and that *Good As Gold* is a powerful statement about our society.

Benjamin DeMott, reviewing the novel for *Atlantic Monthly*, thought it "unsatisfying" and "rather listless and dispirited." He takes the author to task for not probing sufficiently beneath the surface he satirizes and for not making the hero's and the world's troubles very consequential to the reader. DeMott charges Heller with "judgmental ambiguity" and an attitude of "stylized unresponsiveness" toward that which he portrays. In a similar vein, Gene Lyons finds that *Good As Gold* lacks the "emotional resonance" of Heller's previous novels, and that its stereotypical pictures of Jews and gentiles are "peasant superstition and ought to be dismissed as such." In other words, both DeMott and Lyons seem to believe that *Good As Gold* relies on superficial means to make its point and that it fails in any case to make the reader care.

This response was not at all shared by critics in Germany, where the novel appeared in a translation by Gunter Danehl. Lengthy reviews in major German newspapers and magazines treated the novel as a particularly biting and successful political and social satire. Helmut Heissenbüttel, one of Germany's major contemporary poets, wrote in *Die Zeit* that the work may be taken generally as a "Swiftean satire of political activity in the second half of the twentieth century" and might more concretely be seen as a roman a clef of the late 1970s. German reviewers have essentially shared John Aldridge's view that the novel "is indeed comic, often hilariously so, but it is also comedy of the bleakest and blackest kind. It is all about a society that is fast going insane, that is learning to accept chaos as order, and unreality as normal. The horror is that the time may soon come when the conditions Heller depicts will no longer seem to us either funny or the least bit odd."

—Katherine Elias

Periodical Publications:

"On America's Inhuman Callousness," *U.S. News & World Report,* 86 (9 April 1979): 73.

References:

John W. Aldridge, "The Deceits of Black Humor," *Harper's,* 258 (March 1979): 115-118;

Benjamin DeMott, "Heller's Gold and a Silver Sax," *Atlantic Monthly,* 243 (March 1979): 129-132;

Barbara Gelb, "Catching Joseph Heller," *New York Times Magazine* (4 March 1979): 14-16, 42-49;

Helmut Heissenbüttel, "Dunkle Machenschaften im Weissen Haus," *Die Zeit* (30 May 1980): Overseas Edition, p. 19;

Hellmuth Karasek, "Billard gegen Henry Kissinger," *Der Spiegel,* 34 (10 March 1980): 216-219;

Gene Lyons, "Contradictory Judaism," *Nation,* 228 (16 June 1979): 727-728;

Leonard Michaels, "Bruce Gold's American Experience," *New York Times Book Review,* 11 March 1979, pp. 1, 24-25.

Norman Mailer

(31 January 1923-)

The *DLB* entry on Norman Mailer appears in *Dictionary of Literary Biography,* volume 2, *American Novelists Since World War II* (1978), pp. 278-290.

NEW BOOKS: *The Executioner's Song* (Boston: Little, Brown, 1979; London: Hutchinson, 1979);

Of Women and Their Elegance (New York: Simon & Schuster, 1980).

RECENT AWARD: Pulitzer Prize for *The Executioner's Song,* 1980.

The apex of Norman Mailer's recent literary career is undoubtedly *The Executioner's Song,* which he chose to call "a true life novel." Published in 1979, the 1056-page book was widely reviewed, receiving an eight-to-one majority of favorable notices. Many of the book's negative critics questioned the morality of devoting so much dispassionate attention to a murderer with no apparent redeeming social merits. Positive critics, on the other hand, argued that Mailer's nonjudgmental treatment of a probable psychopath gained force from its reportorial accuracy. All the reviews agreed that *The Executioner's Song* was a substantial book produced by a literary master. The more laudatory notices accented what they called Mailer's artistry.

Virtually every review, including that in the *Times Literary Supplement,* noted that Mailer had been hired to write the book by Lawrence Schiller, a freelance journalist who had purchased the rights to the stories of the book's principals for a large sum, and disclosed that Schiller paid him $250,000. In interviews and in the book, Mailer acknowledged Schiller's paramount role in the genesis of the book.

The unusual arrangement between Schiller and Mailer raised questions in the literary community. Schiller's purchase of exclusive rights to the principals' stories was generally criticized as "checkbook journalism," and his hiring of Mailer was scored as further evidence of his eagerness to exploit the principals' "sordid" stories for private gain. Mailer's willingness to write for Schiller also stirred some controversy, but this died down when he explained that he had complete freedom to handle Schiller's material in any fashion he chose.

"This book does its best to be a factual account of the activities of Gary Gilmore and the men and women associated with him from April 9, 1976, when he was released from the United States Penitentiary at Marion, Illinois, until his execution a little more than nine months later in the Utah State Prison," Mailer writes in the book's afterword. After stating that his book is based on interviews, documents, court records, and other original material, Mailer adds: "Out of such revelations was this book built and the story is as accurate as one can make it. This does not mean it has come a great deal closer to the truth than the recollections of the witnesses. While important events were corroborated by other accounts wherever possible, that could not, given the nature of the story, always be done, and, of course, two accounts of the same episode would sometimes diverge. In such conflict of evidence, the author chose the version that seemed most likely. It would be vanity to assume he was always right."

Recited by a masterly reporter and an

enthralling storyteller whose own point of view is notably absent, *The Executioner's Song* is a stark and socially realistic chronicle of the last nine months in the life of Gary Gilmore, one of the outcasts of American society who spent eighteen of his thirty-five years in various prisons for a variety of crimes. Many involved ill-conceived thefts. Asocial and strongly given to fantasy, he was released on parole to his Mormon cousins in Provo, Utah, in April 1976. Motivated by good-heartedness, the cousins accepted Gilmore into their home and introduced him to their circle of friends. They found him work and they probed gently for ways to fit him into the routines of their lives.

But Gilmore's basic violence often broke through. To the dismay of his relatives and their friends, he engaged in fights and contests of physical strength with violent overtones. He also stole six-packs of beer and once proposed stealing a two-ton truck and repainting it for sale. In Mailer's telling, Gilmore seems pathetic as he alternated between conforming to community values and flouting them; at times he expressed repentance for his behavior and pledged not to repeat it. He won a certain sympathy for himself as "a guy [who] has been locked up a long time [and] takes a while to get used to being out."

At the same time, he caused uneasiness by cadging loans, overindulging in beer, and buying a secondhand car with only flimsy means. The car, a Mustang, made him feel like somebody as he raced it around the countryside.

His attitude toward the law also disturbed his acquaintances. Irked by the complications of getting a driver's license, he nonetheless declined to sign up for a required training course. "I'm a grown man and it's beneath me," he said. A friend attempted to reason with him. "The law is for everybody. They're not singling you out," the friend argued. "Do you think you're better than I am?" "Excuse me," Gary said at last. . . . As he walked off, he said, "real good advice." Quick to get away, adds Mailer.

The contradictions of Gilmore's life amount to a social statement in the Theodore Dreiser or Frank Norris mode. A sense of inevitable tragedy hovers over Gilmore; events portray him as a loser, one who has been buffeted and whose perhaps creative nature has been stunted from childhood. Although it is possible to perceive Gilmore as a hardened criminal, psychotic, misshapen by his parents and thus meriting little compassion, it can also be argued that he is largely the product of uncaring prison regimes—that his antisocial tendencies and easy acceptance of violence were reinforced in jail. There

Norman Mailer

Dust jacket

16933$$$26

92—Of Women and Their Elegance—Mailer/Greene—14/17 Caslon 540 x34

We weren't on the movie two days before I was unhappy. I usually don't know ~~when~~ things are going ~~in a good direction~~ for me, personally, so I need someone like ~~Natasha Lytess, or Milton, or Amy, or~~ Paula Strasberg to point me in the right direction or ~~at least say,~~ You're on ~~the way already~~. On the other hand, I can always ~~feel if someone else~~ is headed for disaster. So I began to worry ~~that~~ what the world's greatest actor was doing ~~with~~ this picture as a director ~~might be a big error~~. I was playing an American music-hall girl on tour in Europe, and he was playing a Balkan prince who was visiting London for the marriage of Prince George and Princess Mary. "Pure turn of the century," said Sir Laurence to the crew, as if ~~like a good~~ British ~~team~~ they need know more. Sir Laurence Olivier was so good ~~that way~~ that he could ~~change~~ his posture j~~ust a little bi~~t and immediately switch the year. Right now, he was playing a perfect prince, stiff as steel, ~~and he had a wonderful accent~~. He sounded like he learned German with a Bulgarian accent, and then ~~learned~~ his English with a German-Bulgarian accent. ~~Except it was Carpathia.~~ It was like Sir Laurence Olivier ~~could~~ start with a mark of 99 and then ~~work to get~~ 100. I never acted before with somebody who was so perfect in their role. He didn't seem to know about others actors having trouble with contact. Why, as the director, he would talk to the cameraman ~~about a problem~~, then light a cigarette. Presto, he was the Prince. I couldn't believe it. I had to concentrate for hours just to get near ~~to the American showgirl~~, Elsie, ~~that~~ I was playing, and Elsie was a lot like me in the first place.

In that sense, if that's what acting was, Sir Laurence Olivier was the world's greatest actor. He was a true Prince. There was only one thing wrong. This Prince didn't like me. He kept looking at me like I was a place where a dog had just done his duty.

Of course, in the script he wasn't supposed to like me in the beginning, and was bothered a lot by my lack of royal manners. But ~~what~~ I thought was missing ~~in~~ his performance ~~was~~ the feeling that this Prince ~~wasn't perfect but~~ had a little crack in him, and ~~through that opening~~ I might be able to reach in and touch him. No, he played it as if he was made of metal and they polished it every morning. That gave me a dull feeling. Nobody would ever believe I could make him fall in love. So I would look silly. I could give a good performance and yet it would still look like a bad performance. I always know. I can feel trouble before it has a name.

Then he'd want to rush through a scene. I'd want to slow him up, make him more human. He acted like we were all garage mechanics. The English always want everybody to be a machine anyway. That way, if you're expensive, ~~you can marry~~ another expensive machine. He was used to playing the part with Vivien Leigh. She could pretend to be an American showgirl and he would probably think it was ~~all~~ delicious. Like a husband and wife playing ~~secret~~ games in bed. He could enjoy a scene with Vivien Leigh, but not with me, the real article. ~~I felt that~~ all he wanted was for me to know the lines, and not be late. Get into character quickly. T~~hat was practically his motto~~. I felt as if he was directing me with a stopwatch. ~~Whereas~~ I liked to get to know each word, ~~kind of come up on it. "Hello, who are you,~~ what do you have to say for yourself?" ~~As~~

Of Women and Their Elegance, *corrected galley proof*

is no evidence that Gilmore benefited from rehabilitation, if indeed he was significantly exposed to it.

The first section of the book, "Western Voices," carries Gilmore from his parole and introduction to Provo through a crude sexual liaison with Nicole to two cold-blooded killings. The first was of a gas-station attendant and the second, the following night, was of a motel clerk. Both were exhibitions of Gilmore's rage.

Almost immediately captured, he was back in prison after three and a half months of freedom. What stands out in this period is Gilmore's striving for quick and easy gratification of animalistic desires: food, drink, and sex. His tempestuous affair with Nicole was made possible in large measure because both partners were sexually voracious. Both also liked the excitement of violent actions.

"Western Voices" is written with great tautness and suspense. Paragraphs are seldom more than one sentence long, as if Mailer were a busy newspaper rewrite man working against a deadline and turning out copy one "take" at a time. The literary artistry in sustaining this style without making the narrative seem jerky is of a very high level. The power and the realism of the prose are remarkable.

By deft description and telling use of quotation, Mailer evokes both the goodwill and the banality inherent in lower-middle-class life in Provo. The American scene is painted without enhancement; its dependence on television for stimulation and diversion are starkly reported, as is the vacuity of its conversations, which are limited to concepts gleaned from television or the movies. Equally though, Mailer is at pains to represent Provo's (and America's) human kindness. Although members of Gilmore's circle repeatedly suffer from him, they are reluctant to send him back to jail; they are baffled and hurt by his erratic conduct. Even Nicole, slapped and knocked about, "could feel a lot of ugliness beginning to collect in her" only after repeated instances of abuse.

The second portion of *The Executioner's Song*, called "Eastern Voices," deals with the events from November 1976, after Gilmore's conviction, to his execution by a firing squad on 17 January 1977. There is a marked shift in tone as Mailer takes the reader into the criminal justice bureaucracy and into the world of the news media. Once Gilmore enters the Utah criminal justice system and once he declares his determination to die for his killings, he becomes the focus of a "story" for the electronic and the pencil press, both of which symbolize the East. The East is also the headquarters of those groups and organizations that oppose capital punishment and intervene in vain to save Gilmore.

By quoting extensively from police and court documents, Mailer demonstrates the impersonality of the criminal-justice system; the drama of the otherwise bleak legal proceedings is transformed by the media. "The Gilmore case" is brought into being, particularly as Gilmore's final days tick off. In depicting members of the press as hawks and vultures, seekers after sensation, Mailer includes Schiller among them. Once initiated, "the Gilmore case" creates its own momentum; it accumulates a bureaucracy, assessments from the psychiatric profession, a legal corps, and recorders of the phenomenon from the national and world press. Indeed, as the firing squad's guns bark, reporters are within a couple of feet of the action.

Mailer's detachment, his role as a panoptic observer after the case was closed, was confirmed in an interview for this article. Noting that the book relied heavily on research materials supplied by others, he said the novel was "probably the least personal of my books.

"There is an irony in this," he continued, "and it is that *The Executioner's Song* is my most intense work since *The Naked and the Dead.*

"And there is a further irony: All my personal books—and they were terribly personal—repelled as many critics as they attracted. With this book, however, the criticism has been that it is impersonal. I think this demonstrates that critics cut their cloth to fit their biases.

"When I sat down to write this book, I decided to skip experimentation and to follow well-charted paths. In this sense the book displays my skills, but not necessarily my talents as a writer. Since the Gary Gilmore story was not my own experience, I could not feel as near to it as if it had been something that had arisen out of my life."

There is an argument to be made that the book's impressive strength derives from the absence of a clear authorial voice. By letting the Gilmore story speak for itself, the unappealing and seedy side of American life is presented without palliatives. Mailer leaves it up to the reader to decide whether Gilmore is representational of criminal conduct, or whether his conduct reflects the failure of our prison system, or whether the criminal justice system functions with compassion, or whether the press distorts and sensationalizes such cases as his. Descriptive, but not prescriptive, *The Executioner's Song* raises a host of social questions.

In doing so, it adds luster to Mailer's standing as one of our foremost writers. —*Alden Whitman*

Bernard Malamud

(26 April 1914-   )

The *DLB* entry on Bernard Malamud appears in *Dictionary of Literary Biography,* volume 2, *American Novelists Since World War II* (1978), pp. 291-304.

NEW BOOK: *Dubin's Lives* (New York: Farrar, Straus & Giroux, 1979; London: Chatto & Windus, 1979).

Always a patient craftsman, Bernard Malamud took five and a half years, two years longer than usual,to finish his latest novel, *Dubin's Lives* (1979). Never satisfied, he drove his publisher crazy revising even the final proofs, as he searched for the texture and substance of a man's life and surroundings. Malamud said of the writing process: "Working with words is working with water, trying to make something solid, to make something that never was before."

William Dubin, the hero of the novel, has a good deal of Malamud in him. Like his creator, Dubin is approaching his sixties, lives in relative isolation in rural Vermont, and earns his living as a free-lance writer, though of biography rather than fiction. Malamud saw his novel as a chance to sum up what he has learned about the experience of living. Although Dubin lives in the present, almost all his actions are filtered through what he knows of his own past and the pasts of others.

Dubin is another of Malamud's protagonists who lives on the margins of either art or life. Many Malamud heroes live one step away from the real thing; they are art critics, high-school biology teachers, literary critics, floorwalkers in book departments, and their stories depend on whether or not they can make a full commitment and take the final step. William Dubin is a biographer who has gradually cut himself off from life, as he studies the lives of others. He had hoped that his work would give him new perspective on his own life, but as he approaches the end of middle age, his life seems without sufficient reward.

When the novel opens, Dubin has completed four books of biography: one each of Lincoln, Twain, and Thoreau, and *Short Lives,* a collection of lives of geniuses who died young. His current project is a biography of D. H. Lawrence. The Lincoln and Twain works do not weigh heavily in the novel, but the others tell us a good deal about

Dubin. Malamud said of his subject matter, "I could use the stuff and material of biography for its many sources of harmony and counterpoint." What happens to Dubin is that he strives for harmony with the lives he writes and ends up at counterpoint, which often extends itself to pointed irony. The biographer of "Honest Abe" spends half of the novel lying to his wife about his sex life, and the Thoreau scholar never can quite make peace with nature. Dubin lives in a Thoreauvian setting in rural New England, and though he wants to love nature the way Thoreau did, he is never completely comfortable outside his study. After years in the country, he is still learning the names of much of the commoner flora and fauna. As he goes out into wintry weather to cure a state of depression, Dubin scoffs at Thoreau: "Thoreau was wrong in saying nature doesn't sympathize with sorrow." The winter assails him with a blizzard that almost kills him, until he is rescued by a mechanized version of a St. Bernard—

his wife driving the family car: "something . . . a truck, or car, its wheels churning in the slush, brights on, wipers flapping as it loomed up like a locomotive out of the raining snow." Dubin begins the novel by taking long walks through the countryside; he ends by taking his "walks" in the car. If Dubin cannot reach a feeling of oneness with nature, the same cannot be said of Malamud. His descriptions of rural New England in all seasons are wonderfully precise and evocative. He says of writing these passages: "If it is winter in the book, spring surprises me when I look up." For a novelist who has been thought of as an urban poet, Malamud knows the country well—which is not really surprising since he has spent the last third of his life in rural Oregon and Vermont.

Dubin offers a copy of his first work, *Short Lives,* in which no one lives to the age of forty, as a love gift to the woman who will become his mistress. From these lives of truncated genius, he had originally gleaned a philosophy which saw the brilliance of their work as just compensation for the brevity of their lives. As he matures, however, the lesson he learns is reversed: "If you don't live life to the hilt, or haven't for whatever reason, you will regret it—especially as you grow older—every day that follows."

None of these earlier biographies influences Dubin as much as his work-in-progress, the life of D. H. Lawrence. Dubin begins to measure his life by Lawrence's theories of passion and finds it lacking. He has never known the kind of passion Lawrence writes about in his novels, and at this stage in his life he feels he has only one more chance at it, a chance which is offered to him by Fanny Bick, a girl young enough to be his daughter. Although the illicit courting of Fanny is filled with much of the comic misadventure found in both *A New Life* (1961) and *Pictures of Fidelman* (1969) and though Dubin does not consummate the affair until almost two-thirds through the novel, Dubin's problem is not so much how to get Fanny as, having gotten her, whether to keep her in a perpetual Lawrentian fantasy or return to his long-suffering wife, Kitty. His decision in this matter depends in large measure on what he makes of Lawrence. Though it would seem that a biographer of Lawrence would choose the life of the body, the decision is complicated by the facts of Lawrence's own life. Lawrence, the advocate of absolute passion, was impotent by the time he was forty, so he could, in fact, not live the life of passion projected in his novels. Early in the book, Dubin warns himself "one writes lives he cannot live." This stricture seems at first to apply solely to his own occupation, making it a vicarious parasitism on the lives of others, but it also applies to his subjects' lives. Lawrence was not the passionate man he creates in his novels. Thoreau, likewise hungered for absolute communion with nature, but as Dubin notes, "the man went home often to see his mama." What happens then if the biographer tries to live the lives he writes? Which life does he live? The projected, pulse-pounding, lambent-loined fictive Lawrence, or the real, wife-dominated impotent Lawrence.

For William Dubin, the choice of two such lives comes down to the choice between the two women in his life. His wife Kitty (a namesake perhaps of Levin's wife, Kitty, in *Anna Karenina,* an intelligently domestic counterweight to the passionate heroine of that novel) has carefully nurtured Dubin's talent, providing him with the domestic surrounding that allows him to write. Theirs is a marriage built on a modicum of love, but little passion. The marriage came relatively late in life for both partners (Kitty was a widow with a child) so that it is a merging of two already defined lives. Kitty's nurturing is enough for writing the lives of Lincoln, Twain, and Thoreau, but when Dubin comes up against Lawrence, he feels he cannot get to the core of his subject unless he understands passion.

It is from Fanny (who tells us she is named for a

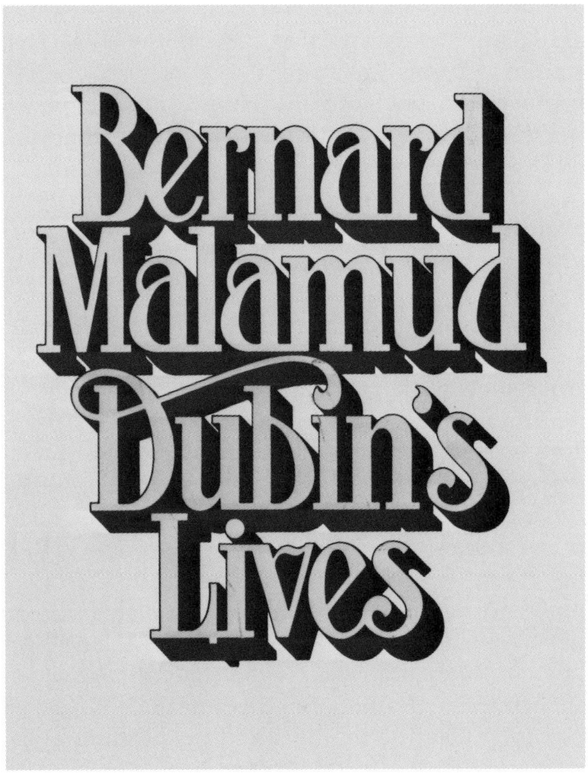

Dust jacket

Jane Austen character, Fanny Price, but seems a more likely namesake of another eighteenth-century heroine, Fanny Hill) that Dubin learns about passion. Dubin is too controlled to respond to Fanny's first, unpremeditated, sexual offer, and thus dooms himself to a series of missed assignations that culminate in a comically humiliating week in Venice. The episode has the tone of a tale out of Boccaccio in which the jealous old husband is deceived by his randy, young wife. Dubin is the *jaloux* who is cuckolded by Fanny and a gondolier. Instead of ending Dubin's search for passion, however, the episode teaches him desire and forces him beyond the confines of his work, perhaps for the first time in his life. Eventually, Dubin does get Fanny and believes he has reached the Lawrentian ideal in which passion equals life. Fanny is passionate, but despite a large amount of sexual experience, she is relatively unformed. She is filled with potential, but has not finished school, has not embarked on a career, has not had a child. Though she is vitally alive, Fanny Bick has not yet lived.

Dubin, a careful observer of others' lives, is not insensitive about his own. He understands that much of his attraction to Fanny is part of the pursuit of fading youth, a pursuit that also takes the form of his regimen of exercise and diet. Like Thoreau, Dubin strives to keep off the spectre of Death, in his case by clinging to things that are young—Fanny and what is left of his own still healthy body. His concern with his lost youth is not merely for what has once been, but is also the yearning for what never was. "Middle age . . . is when you pay for what you didn't have or couldn't do when you were young."

What Dubin has to learn is perhaps Lawrence's greatest lesson: true passion does not fear the onslaught of death, but embraces it. Only through death can there be resurrection and in a thematic pattern omnipresent in Malamud's earlier novels Dubin undergoes symbolic death and rebirth that corresponds to the change of seasons.

Dubin's first winter after the botched Venetian affair is a spiritual dying with his creative juices drying up even as the sap freezes in the trees. He thinks of his writing as an act of procreation which he cannot perform: "Sentences breed sentences. But the notes tensed him." Eventually this creative impotence leads to sexual impotence with his wife so that ironically she shares the worst part of Lawrence's sexuality—*his* impotence with *his* wife. The winter's culmination is a death for Dubin as he loses his identity in the blinding blizzard. The biographer has tried to shape lives against the ravages of time, but finds that he has lost the battle. "I'm like a broken clock—works, time, mangled." Dubin, like Keats's woebegone knight (Keats is one of the subjects of *Short Lives*), has become the thrall of La Belle Dame sans Merci, so that he exists "alone and palely loitering."

With the spring, Fanny returns, now as a different aspect of the beautiful woman without pity. She becomes to Dubin what Fanny Brawne was to Keats, a 'warm, white lucent, million-pleasured breast." As they make love for the first time among the springtime flowers, Dubin comes alive again, feeling "this evens it . . . for the cruel winter." His writing revives as well as he understands at last Lawrence's belief in the blood and the flesh.

Dubin discovers, however, that he is not the Lawrentian hero, partly out of his knowledge that Lawrence was not either. As he gets involved with Fanny, he brings Lawrence's impotence to his own marriage. The cause of his sexual failure with his wife is the growing number of lies he is forced to tell her. The duplicity necessary to maintain the affair cuts not only against all of Lawrence's dicta about honesty to the blood, but also against Dubin's own honesty that has served him well as a biographer. Dubin is enough of a man of principle to have refused Lyndon Johnson's request that he write the Texan's biography because he knew he couldn't please Johnson and tell the truth at the same time. When he deceives his wife, Dubin dreams that Richard Nixon comes to him and asks him to write a flattering biography, one liar to another, so to speak. The negative aspects of the affair are partly responsible for Dubin's turn away from the pure life of the flesh that he shares with Fanny. The other force is his nature and profession.

Dubin is a biographer who lives upon lives. He devours the lives of others. Fanny has no life yet, none of the complications and nuances that make biography interesting. Kitty, on the other hand, has both her own life and the life she has shared with Dubin. Two troubled children—one theirs, one hers—have become an integral part of his life. His dealings with these grown children, both Fanny's age, help convince him that his wife is a woman of his complexity with a life comparable to his own.

Fanny belongs in a Lawrence novel, not in Dubin's life. Only by being honest with himself and his wife can Dubin avoid the impotence that plagued Lawrence's last years. At the end of the novel, he makes a distinction which escapes Fanny as he explains why he will return to his wife:

"But do you love her?"

"I love her life."

Dubin loves Fanny, but it is not enough for the biographer. She doesn't yet have a life for him to share. Though the novel ends with Dubin about to return to his wife, a "bibliography" of Dubin's works tells us the move was the right one. Dubin completes the biography of Lawrence and goes on to write several other works.

Malamud's novel has an autumnal sense of completeness about it. He asks the same questions about Dubin that Dubin asks about all of his subjects: What does a man's life add up to? In *Dubin's Lives,* Malamud makes clear that even the most ordinary of lives is worth a biography.

—Jeffrey Helterman

Interview:

Ralph Tyler, "A Talk with the Novelist," *New York Times Book Review,* 18 February 1979, p. 1.

References:

Leslie Fiedler, "Malamud's Travesty Western," *Novel,* 10 (1977): 212-219;

Leslie Field, "Malamud-Dubin's Discontent," *Studies in American Jewish Literature,* 4, no. 1 (1978): 77-78;

Edward Friedman, "The Paradox of the Art Metaphor in Bernard Malamud's 'The Pimp's Revenge,' " *Notes on Contemporary Literature,* 9, no. 2 (1979): 7-8;

Marcia Gealy, "A Reinterpretation of Malamud's *The Natural,*" *Studies in American Jewish Literature,* 4, no. 1 (1978): 24-32;

Arnold Goldsmith, "Nature in Bernard Malamud's *The Assistant,*" *Renascence,* 29 (1977): 211-223;

Steven Kellman, "*The Tenants* in the House of Fiction," *Studies in the Novel,* 8 (1976): 458-467;

Irving Malin, "*The Fixer*: an Overview," *Studies in American Jewish Literature,* 4, no. 1 (1978): 40-50;

Herbert Mann, "The Malamudian World: Method and Meaning," *Studies in American Jewish Literature,* 4, no. 1 (1978): 2-12.

Thomas McGuane

(11 December 1939-)

The *DLB* entry on Thomas McGuane appears in *Dictionary of Literary Biography,* volume 2, *American Novelists Since World War II* (1978), pp. 325-328.

NEW BOOK: *Panama* (New York: Farrar, Straus & Giroux, 1978).

In 1973, immediately after Thomas McGuane's third novel, *Ninety-Two in the Shade,* was published, L. E. Sissman wrote in the *New Yorker* that McGuane was "one of the best young novelists in America" and added that "it's cheering to watch him approach his apogee." Just three years later, after the disastrous appearance of two movies that he was closely associated with (a film version of *Ninety-Two in the Shade,* which he wrote and directed, and *The Missouri Breaks* for which he wrote the script), Tom McGuane's personal life and artistic reputation were in shambles. In 1981, some eight years after McGuane was seemingly approaching his "apogee," he has had published only a single additional novel—*Panama,* which was released in 1978 to mixed reviews—and written one more film script (for *Tom Horn,* a movie that will probably be remembered mainly as Steve McQueen's last picture). But there are public and artistic indications that all has not been lost for McGuane. Indeed, there is some striking evidence that McGuane has begun to mature as both an individual and an artist—and that now that he has made peace with himself, he can reclaim some of the respect that his earlier novels had won him.

McGuane worked extremely hard on his first three novels, *The Sporting Club* (1969), *The Bushwhacked Piano* (1971), and *Ninety-Two in the Shade* (1973). Thomas Carney quotes McGuane in a 1978 *Esquire* article: "I had been so determined to be a successful writer, so sure it took insane dedication, that from twenty to thirty I did nothing else but read and write." But after finishing *Ninety-Two in the Shade* over the Christmas holidays in 1972, McGuane had an experience which altered his whole outlook on life and art. Heading south from Montana to Key West in his 911 Porsche with Scott Palmer, a sixteen-year-old boy living with the McGuanes, McGuane lost control of his car at 140 miles per hour, just outside Dalhart, Texas. Turning to Palmer as the car began to richochet off a truck, McGuane said quietly, "We're dead." Miraculously, the Porsche ended up in a cornfield almost undamaged, but several hours later Palmer got out of the car, called McGuane's wife Becky, and told her that she'd better meet them in Key West. The reason for the urgency: McGuane had been unable to speak since the accident. "I kept thinking I had died," McGuane told Carney, "I kept thinking about all the things I hadn't done."

Thomas McGuane

This accident became a clear turning point for McGuane and his artistic career—a turning point which *did not,* however, lead to artistic success and personal fulfillment. As McGuane puts it, "In Key West after the accident, I finally realized I could stop pedaling so intensely, get off the bike and walk around the neighborhood. The changes that came were irresistible but it was getting unthinkable to spend another year sequestered like that, writing, and I just dropped out. I quit fighting my way through marriage and through the Sunday N.Y. *Times.*" The most obvious effect of McGuane's decision to "get off the bike and walk around the neighborhood" was involvement in movies and his temporary abandonment of fiction. Despite the widespread critical success of his first three novels, McGuane had discovered that his books had little mass-market appeal. (*The Bushwhacked Piano* won the Rosenthal Award, given each year to the best novel that has not been a commercial success.) So when Elliot Kastner, the movie producer, contacted McGuane after his accident, saying how much he admired his writing and asking if he might be interested in a movie project, McGuane was quick to say yes.

A summary of the next several years in McGuane's life reads like an especially lurid column out of the *National Enquirer.* After being taken to London by Kastner to meet Candice Bergen, Nickolas Roeg, and other notables, McGuane was soon hobnobbing with Hollywood superstars. Robert Altman was the original choice to direct a film version of *Ninety-Two in the Shade,* but after Kastner and Altman argued, Martin Ritt and then Sam Peckinpah became compromise candidates. Meanwhile McGuane, with some financial assistance from Kastner, began another screenplay about a bored, rich kid in the modern Wild West and his adventures with a young Indian. When the movie, *Rancho DeLuxe* (directed by Frank Perry), was released in 1975, Paul Zimmerman noted in his *Newsweek* review that "the film's ironies, original vision and wacky dialogue belong to screenwriter Thomas McGuane, who arrives as a major film talent." The movie was shot in and around McGuane's home town, Livingston, Montana, and as Thomas Carney describes what happened, "Everybody loved everybody. Jeff Bridges fell in love with a local girl and married her. Elizabeth Ashley fell in love with McGuane. It was Hollywood come to the Yellowstone Valley and national magazines were sending reporters out to find out what was going on (drugs, wife swapping). But the atmosphere for *Rancho Deluxe* wore out a lot of the participants and the toll began to show up on film."

Perry has since commented that, "The trouble with McGuane is he's a star. He could write, direct, you name it. He's a star. But I think the film business was pernicious for him." Soon, like his main character in *Panama,* McGuane could refer to "a pile of scandal sheets to see what had hit friends and loved ones." McGuane, working on the filmscript of *The Missouri Breaks,* managed to convince Kastner that the best possible director for *Ninety-Two in the Shade* would be Tom McGuane. Soon he found himself involved in an affair with leading lady Margot Kidder, and with Elizabeth Ashley also starring in the movie, certain fight scenes among the main participants in the movie take on an authentic intensity. To continue the scenario, McGuane's wife Becky began an affair with Scott Palmer. As if this were not enough, McGuane was heavily into drugs, and when Margot Kidder returned to Los Angeles after the filming, she discovered she was pregnant.

McGuane was granted a divorce from Becky in 1975. Some nine months after their child Maggie was born, McGuane and Margot Kidder began an ill-fated marriage that was terminated in May 1977. During this same two-year period, McGuane's sister Marion and his father suddenly died. *The Missouri Breaks* (directed by Arthur Penn and starring Jack Nicholson and Marlon Brando) opened to disastrous reviews. Things were falling apart, both professionally and personally, for Tom McGuane.

Gradually, however, things began to right themselves. The summer after Margot Kidder left, Laurie Buffett, the sister of popular singer Jimmy Buffett, came to McGuane's ranch in Livingstone, and in September 1977 they were married. McGuane began busying himself with a new novel, *Panama,* a book which it is almost irresistible to read as an autobiographical commentary on what had been happening to McGuane during the past several years. Indeed, in many ways *Panama* appears to be a kind of heightened, surreal portrayal of McGuane's own suffering, self-delusion, and eventual self-understanding—a book which moves beyond his earlier novels' satiric and ironic stances to produce a work filled with what the narrator describes as "the sense of humor that is the mirror of pain, the perfect mirror, not the trick mirror of satirists."

Perhaps closest in tone to the hot-wired style and dark humor of *The Bushwhacked Piano, Panama* tells the story of Chester Hunnicut Pomeroy, an exhausted overnight sensation who proclaims himself as "the most sleazed-out man in America." Pomeroy, like McGuane, is a thirtyish celebrity who has made a career of acting out the fantasies of a freaked-out, bewildered America. As Gary Fisketjon summarized in his sympathetic review in the *Village Voice,* Chet "has lost the greater portion of his teeth, not to mention Catherine, his estranged wife and possible redeemer. Worse yet, he's no longer in complete possession of his memory and all 52 cards; on occasion he speaks with his dead brother, communes with and is obsessed by the spectre of Jesse James, and suffers crying jags. . . . The meteoric career of this overnight sensation has passed its peak, fallen, and bottomed out. . . . Victim of fame and corruption, Chet is now somewhat below the stars thick with aspirations of success, in a land of bad sinuses and worse dreams."

Narrated in Pomeroy's highly personalized first-person style, *Panama* retains several of McGuane's earlier thematic concerns: the nature of masculine rivalries, the despair at seeing our Republic corrupted by materialism, and the need for sensitive outsiders to discover some refuge, some excuse for not committing suicide. And McGuane's biting humor, sharp eye for detail, and wonderfully rich prose are still very much in evidence here: "When they build a shopping center over an old salt marsh, the seabirds sometimes circle the same place for a year or more, coming back to check daily, to see if

Dust jacket

there isn't some little chance those department stores and pharmacies and cinemas won't go as quickly as they'd come. Similarly, I come back and keep looking into myself, and it's always steel, concrete, fan magazines, machinery, bubble gum; nothing as sweet as the original marsh." Still, there is a difference in tone here, a scathing honesty and painfully introspective quality that were missing from his earlier novels. In Carney's *Esquire* article, Perry is quoted as complaining of McGuane that "his overriding quality is coldness. *Rancho Deluxe* was a beautifully structured film, but it was totally cold and cerebral. I think McGuane is that way, too, despite all the charm." As if to answer such charges, McGuane infuses *Panama* with a desperate, nightmarish intensity of emotion. Pomerory's attempts to win back the affections of his wife, Catherine, are at once pathetic and outrageous (his opening ploy is to nail himself to her door, for example). Vowing that "If Catherine and I find a way to be happy together, we'll step aside when desolation roars past," Chet adamantly stalks her throughout the novel, gamely attempting to ignore the effects of his own evident despair, drug usage, and insanity. Like so many other heroes of recent fiction, Chet is unable to confront directly the ugliness, smallness of spirit, and moral indifference of his age. One measure of his need to escape from these realities is his reliance on drugs—"Given the objective conditions of our lives, how can we avoid taking the drugs?" he comments at one point. More significantly, he also adopts the same escape mechanism employed by Vonnegut's Billy Pilgrim, by Coover's J. Henry Waugh, by Nabokov's Humbert Humbert and Kinbote: he retreats into the private realm of his imagination where he can deny the existence of his father (a snack-food magnate) and can conjure up the mythic presence of Jesse James presiding over a landscape where men can still be men.

As the novel draws to a conclusion, Catherine makes the inevitable decision that there can be no future with Chet, whose humpty-dumpty life is scattered in so many pieces that even love offers no hope for reassemblage. But, remarkably, the unfolding of this love affair—pointless and doomed as it is since they lack such tools as hope and memory which we usually rely on to deal with the big issues in our lives—retains the power to move us. As Fisketjon comments, "It is Chet's comic and appalling struggle against her almost inevitable departure that makes this novel more than a tour de force through broken lives and heartaches by the million. . . . And it is Chet's exploding realization of what he has really lost that makes his case more than just another fall through their funhouse."

Perhaps due to all the adverse publicity that McGuane had received during the previous five years, *Panama* received little public notice when it was released in 1978, and most reviewers who did examine the book were negative in their appraisals. The unsigned review in *Time* was typical of these unsympathetic reactions in claiming that, "*Panama* is fairly minor McGuane. . . . *Panama* may be intended as a dithyramb of exhaustion—Pomeroy's and, grandiosely, the American culture's. But Despair loses something when it is unearned and vaguely cute. The novel savors of cocaine, narcissism, and a certain impenetrable smugness." Such comments to the contrary, McGuane's despair hardly can be judged to be "unearned." Although *Panama* indeed retains the same kind of "smugness" that characterizes McGuane's earlier books—condescension toward rich New Yorkers vacationing in Key West and toward mediocre, unappreciative sailors and fishermen; disdain toward those who build taco stands and Moped rental drops "where Hart Crane and Stephen Crane had momentarily coexisted on a mildewed shelf"—it also powerfully presents a vision of America difficult to shrug off. Pomeroy announces in the novel's opening words that, "This is the first time I've worked without a net. I want to tell the truth." It seems obvious that in *Panama* McGuane is aiming for much the same results.

—*Larry McCaffery*

Screenplay:

Tom Horn, United Artists, 1980.

Periodical Publications:

"Ressurection Waltz," *Esquire*, 90 (7 November 1978): 79-84;

"Big Sky, Big Swaps," *Esquire*, 93 (15 March 1980): 82-83.

Bibliography:

Larry McCaffery, "Thomas McGuane: A Bibliography, 1969-1978," *Bulletin of Bibliography*, 35 (October-December 1978): 169-172.

References:

Thomas Carney, "McGuane's Game," *Esquire*, 89 (6 June 1978): 4-46;

D. R. Cohen, "After *Panama*, McGuane Steps Out of the Shade," *Feature* (February 1979): 20;

Gary L. Fisketjon, "Holes in the Head," review of *Panama*, *Village Voice*, 11 December 1978, pp. 115-116.

Larry McMurtry

(3 June 1936-)

The *DLB* entry on Larry McMurtry appears in *Dictionary of Literary Biography*, volume 2, *American Novelists Since World War II* (1978), pp. 328-331.

NEW BOOK: *Somebody's Darling* (New York: Simon & Schuster, 1978).

In a biting 1975 essay in the *Atlantic*, "The Texas Moon, And Elsewhere," Larry McMurtry bade a not-so-fond farewell to the region his novels had so richly mined. "I was halfway through my sixth Texas novel," he explained, "when I suddenly began to notice that where place was concerned, I was sucking air. The book is set in Houston, but none of the characters are Texans." Pinning his fatigue on "the kind of mental and emotive inarticulateness" he found in Texas, McMurtry concluded: "The move off the land is now virtually completed, and that was the great subject that Texas offered writers of my generation. The one basic subject it offers us now is loneliness, and one can only ring the changes on that so many times." In 1978 McMurtry put away his "Minor Regional Novelist" T-shirt (actually, he reports he lost it in a laundromat) and published his seventh novel, *Somebody's Darling*—leaping from the frying pan of Texas literature into the well-stoked fire of novels about Hollywood.

Somebody's Darling, a comedy of manners and of vulgarity, is about movie people and movie-making and has all the earmarks of the Hollywood novel: hopeless dreamers, bitchy stars, cynical writers, artless directors, colorful has-beens, and sad hangers-on. McMurtry's Hollywood is all about "frippery, pretense, indulgence, overconspicuous overconsumption." It is a place where gofers hold elevators for their bosses and a dalmatian can, unnoticed, eat $800 worth of caviar at a director's party. It is a place where *whatever* is the word to end all conversations and equivocation is the order of the day.

It should come as no surprise to his readers that McMurtry would set a novel in Hollywood. As early as 1968 he was indicating in his essays that California and Texas had much in common, going so far as to predict that "the new Texas is probably going to be a sort of kid brother to California, with a kid brother's tendency to imitation." And McMurtry was quick to acknowledge the challenge this "big brother" posed: "California, whether as a subject or a place to live, is almost too taxing. There the confusion is greater, the rivalries of manners more intense: the question is whether anyone can live in California and comprehend it clearly now. Nathanael West would have a harder time with the state today than he had in 1939."

Certainly, McMurtry's knowledge of Hollywood is extensive. Charles Peavy, author of the most systematic study of McMurtry's work, notes that "few contemporary American novelists have been as intimately associated with motion pictures" as has McMurtry. Three of his novels have been made into movies (*Horseman, Pass By* as *Hud*, 1963; *The Last Picture Show*, 1971; and *Leaving Cheyenne* as *Lovin' Molly*, 1973); two others sent Texas characters to Hollywood, and McMurtry—an avowed aficionado of "bad movies"—has been a contributing editor of *American Film* magazine. One critic has claimed that his involvement with Hollywood makes him "a pivotal figure who demonstrates how an exchange between film and fiction can each enrich the other."

Against such a background, the surprising thing about *Somebody's Darling* is that it never really tries to be much of a Hollywood novel: Hollywood provides its context, but not its subject. While Jonathan Yardley contended in the *New York Times Book Review* that the novel's "principal concern is the ambiguous relationship between craft and art as it manifests itself in Hollywood," *Somebody's Darling* seems much more concerned with familiar McMurtry themes, ringing one more change on the subject of loneliness. Indeed, everything about the book is familiar: its three-narrator structure is very similar to that of *Leaving Cheyenne* (1963); two of the three narrators—Joe Percy and Jill Peel—and a couple of minor characters reappear from *Moving On* (1970) and from *All My Friends Are Going To Be Strangers* (1972); and the third narrator—Owen Oarson—is a Texan, a slightly more urbane and complicated version of Paul Newman's Hud. Two of the most memorable characters in *Somebody's Darling*, Elmo Buckle and Winfield Gohagen, are good ol' boy screenwriters from Austin, Texas, and that native Texas delicacy, chicken-fried steak, even makes a guest appearance. In one humorously self-conscious moment, one of McMurtry's narrators laments: "There's no getting away from cowboys, no place

I've ever been." In another such moment, one of the two puckish Texan screenwriters counsels that "Texas is the ultimate last resort. . . . It's always a good idea to go to Texas, if you can't think of anything else to do."

Somebody's Darling, a frequently hilarious, finally sad, always engaging book, does indeed "go to Texas" twice, but not because McMurtry runs out of ideas. (Some of the novel's most effective scenes are set in New York and much of its important action occurs in Rome.) McMurtry has acknowledged the danger of self-imitation ("that monster that lurks eternally outside the writer's window") and in this wide-ranging story he studies the love that is friendship in a way not seen before in his novels.

Somebody's Darling tells the story of thirty-seven-year-old Jill Peel, Hollywood's first female director, a woman somewhat randomly catapulted by her directorial debut into success and out of her longstanding and deep friendship with Joe Percy, a sixty-three-year-old contract screenwriter. Joe, the first of the novel's three narrators and easily its most endearing character, has been reduced to writing plots for a television series based on the song "Witchita Lineman." He is a dapper widower, a self-styled "pseudo-sage," who manages to be both avuncular and sybaritic. One of Hollywood's last gentlemen, Joe is a man whose consideration and simple kindness prove irresistible to a string of young Hollywood wives. Joe feels himself to be the last of an old breed, but unlike so many of McMurtry's earlier patriarchal dinosaurs, he can accept change: he misses the old days of Hollywood, but does not delude himself that they were idyllic. Joe lives his life knowing that at any moment, in any relationship, "the bottom could always drop out." And, when Jill begins an affair with Owen Oarson, an opportunistic ex-football star now determined to become a Hollywood producer by bedding the right women, the bottom does drop out of their long friendship. "Friendship, too, is ruinable," Joe sadly notes, "and can be destroyed as quickly and as absolutely as love."

Owen detests Jill's respect for old-timers such as Joe and, in fact, detests most of her characteristics. She is as principled as he is not, as sentimental as he is callous. However, Jill has an intellectual toughness that Owen grudgingly admires, a kind of integrity he cannot understand since "a woman like her destroys all the simple appetites." For all his

Larry McMurtry

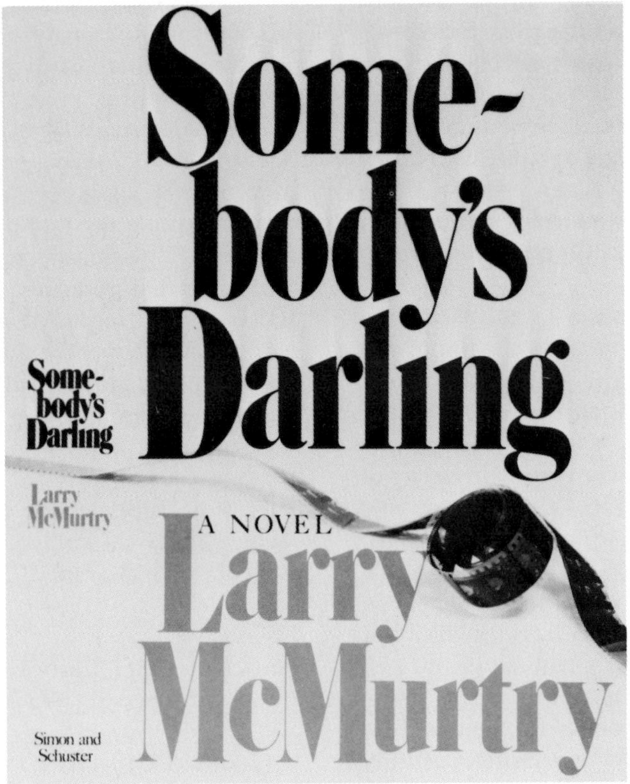

Dust jacket

unpleasantness and cruelty, Owen remains the book's most pathetic figure: his hustling never slows, but his own recalcitrant complexity keeps betraying him. "I've always aspired to pure opportunism," he complains, "but I never make it."

Jill Peel is the momentary darling of the movie industry, the recipient of "more general love than anybody." But specific love has always been her special problem, a chronic victim of her complicated principles and pride. She recognizes all of Owen's flaws, but his crude attraction to her counters her debilitating need for overintellectualizing relationships. Jill is one of McMurtry's most complex characters, paradoxically strong and weak at the same time. Recently, McMurtry told interviewer Patrick Bennett that his women characters give him the problem of "finding men worth having in the same book with my women." McMurtry elaborates: "Women are always the most admirable characters in my novels. . . . I feel I write about them well, but that's not necessarily to say that I understand them. My writing frequently convinces women that I understand them, but I don't know whether that means I really do, or whether it means they are easily persuaded, or that my writing is especially persuasive when it comes to descriptions of women."

Although she is torn by her conflicting feelings for Owen, Jill's greatest concern is for her old friend Joe Percy. Even more than she had disapproved of Joe's affairs with young wives, Joe had disapproved of her involvement with Owen, and Joe and Jill had quietly grown apart. Jill worries: "We're such old friends we've forgotten how to be friends. Maybe we really aren't friends any more and just don't want to admit it." The nearly symbiotic Texan screenwriters, Elmo Buckle and Winfield Gohagen, remind Jill that friends should complement each other. ("When one was down, the other could be counted on to be up. They were sometimes both up, but never both down.") However, the problem facing Jill and Joe is that *both* of them are down: a stroke has robbed him of his potency and spirit; her relationship with Owen and various studio intrigues have robbed her of precision and purpose.

The most compelling scenes in *Somebody's Darling* deal with Jill's and Joe's fumbling attempts to make sense once more of "the little roads that lead people up to and then away from one another." The great poignancy of their final scene together probably stems, at least in part, from the pivotal role his endings play in McMurtry's writing. He explained to Patrick Bennett: "I consider it a process of discovery, writing a novel. But I always start with an ending. My novels begin with a scene that forms itself in my consciousness, which I recognize as a culminating scene. . . . It's been to the point where I see the people, and I hear the conversation, and I know what the last words are going to be, and I know that something's ended. I don't know exactly what's ended, and the writing of the novel is a process in which I discover how these people got themselves to this scene."

While reviewers variously grumbled that *Somebody's Darling* failed to answer "important questions," or that it set its sights too low, the novel's critical reception was by and large genial, as critics acknowledged the appeal of both McMurtry's characters and his prose. McMurtry uses the device of multiple narrations to refract his characteristic concerns with kinds of initiation, with loneliness, and with the passing of old orders through the prism of Jill's relationships with Joe and Owen. In Joe Percy and Jill Peel, McMurtry has created two of his most mature and most fully realized characters. In Elmo and Winfield ("neither of them quite trusted a woman until she'd slept with them both"), McMurtry has created two screamingly funny characters—crazy but endearing Texans.

Yet, McMurtry was not satisfied with *Somebody's Darling*, seeing it as "an enjoyable read," but as no more than an interesting failure. Calling it the only unpleasant writing experience that he had ever had, McMurtry specified in the Bennett interview: "I've often wished that I had done only the first section and used it as a short novel or something. The first section has life. I struggled with several technical problems in that novel that I don't think I overcame. Perhaps my approach was a bit conservative. That first section should have been the last section somehow, and it should have been the only section in the first person. . . . I always felt there was something misfitting about the conception of that book. Oh, well, water under the bridge. I'm not one to brood."

Currently, McMurtry divides his time among his writing, his prolific reviewing and incidental journalism, and his Washington, D.C., rare-book shop, Booked Up. His exploits as a book scout have been detailed in a 1976 *New Yorker* article by Calvin Trillin. Indeed, talking about his book collecting, McMurtry wryly notes, "the strange thing is that in the book trade my reputation as a dealer is a good deal better than my reputation as a novelist." McMurtry has indicated his interest in writing a serious novel about Washington and has recently worked on a screenplay about coal development in Montana, but he says only that his current projects are "vague."

—Brooks Landon

Periodical Publications:

"The Texas Moon, And Elsewhere," *Atlantic Monthly* (March 1975): 29-36.

Interviews:

Patrick Bennett, "Larry McMurtry: Thalia, Houston, & Hollywood," *Talking With Texas Writers: Twelve Interviews* (College Station: Texas A & M University Press, 1980),pp. 15-36;

David W. McCullough, "Larry McMurtry," *People Books & Book People* (New York: Harmony Books, 1981),pp. 117-118.

References:

E. Pauline Degenfelder, "McMurtry and the Movies: *Hud* and *The Last Picture Show*," *Western Humanities Review*, 29 (Winter 1975): 81-91;

Charles D. Peavy, *Larry McMurtry* (Boston: Twayne, 1977);

Dorey Schmidt, ed. *Larry McMurtry: Unredeemed Dreams* (Living Author Series, 1), (Edinburg, Texas: School of Humanities, Pan American University, 1978);

Calvin Trillin, "US Journal: Washington, D.C.—Scouting Sleepers," *New Yorker* (14 June 1978): 86-92.

Henry Miller

(26 December 1891-7 June 1980)

The *DLB* entry on Henry Miller appears in *Dictionary of Literary Biography,* volume 4, *American Writers in Paris, 1920-1939* (1980), pp. 282-294.

NEW BOOKS: *Henry Miller's Book of Friends* (Santa Barbara: Capra, 1976; London: Allen, 1978);

Gliding Into the Everglades and Other Essays (Lake Oswego, Oreg.: Lost Pleiade Press, 1977);

Mother, China, and the World Beyond (Santa Barbara: Capra, 1977);

The World of Lawrence: A Passionate Appreciation (Santa Barbara: Capra, 1980).

RECENT AWARD: Legion of Honor, 1975.

Although Henry Miller did not write anything of enduring literary value during the last forty years of his life, he is a genuinely great American writer. Because his fall from literary grace was so extended and obvious, we can easily lose sight of the enormous contribution he made to twentieth-century literature in the decade of his first book, his masterpiece, *Tropic of Cancer* (1934). He long outlived the artist he had been, but coming generations, at least, may forgive him the sin of longevity. Certainly Miller forgave himself. He was not bothered by—or interested in—reviewers who complained of his failure to live up to the bright promise he had shown in Paris. The Paris work had fulfilled the man, and the artist became secondary. "I wrote in order to live," Miller told his biographer Jay Martin a few years ago, echoing a declaration made almost thirty years before: "The highest art is the art of living . . . writing is but a prelude or form of initiation for this purpose." Miller satisfied his demon in Paris; gradually he renounced his dedication to the rigors of his craft—but only after leaving an indelible mark on the history of modern letters.

His death was the ordinary one we might have anticipated for "just a Brooklyn boy." He died in his sleep in that fiercely respectable house in Pacific Palisades which always affronted our image of the down-and-out rogue, the Henry Miller type. According to one account, he left not with a bang or whimper, but at most with a peaceful snore.

The last three decades of his life delighted literary gossips. In the 1950s, he was cast as the guru of Big Sur, bathing naked in the hot springs near his coastal mountain cottage. In the 1960s, as the vindicated hero of the last great censorship trials of this century, he appeared in the media as a scandalous septuagenarian. In the 1970s, he sold his watercolors by the hundreds, invited numerous young women callers inside for Ping-Pong matches, and turned his life into a coffee table book published by Playboy Press. He seemed to indulge himself in the follies of life to the fullest, without apology, as death inched nearer.

Even in his dotage and decline, however, Miller continually emerged as an important literary figure. Over the past thirty years, he (or his publishers) constantly cashed in portions of a vast literary capital accumulated earlier. *The Rosy Crucifixion,* a trilogy (*Sexus, Plexus,* and *Nexus*), appeared in Paris between 1947 and 1960. This recounting of Miller's life before Paris in Brooklyn of the 1920s had been outlined by the author much earlier and described in less detail in *Tropic of Capricorn* (1939). While this work was rather too easily dismissed by reviewers as self-indulgent dribble, it does contain some of Miller's most humorous sexual episodes and finest surrealistic fantasies. This would be Miller's last extended autobiographical narrative. *Quiet Days in Clichy* (1956) was a better effort, a companion piece to *Tropic of Cancer*; but it did not represent Miller's later writing since it had been composed and misplaced in 1940. The legal publication of Miller's Paris work in England and America during the 1960s resurrected the artist and made him a popular success nearly thirty years after the fact. Also in Miller's vault were thousands of letters which, when skillfully edited, made marvelous reading. His correspondence with Anaïs Nin (*Henry Miller: Letters to Anaïs Nin,* 1965) and Lawrence Durrell (*Lawrence Durrell/Henry Miller: A Private Correspondence,* 1963) detail the inner workings of a modern artist.

The original work of these later years was minor. Slight pieces were regularly published by small, independent presses. Almost without exception, Miller had always published first with houses outside the mainstream; he continued to do so until his death, most notably with Capra Press through its editor, Noel Young. It is perhaps doubly fitting, then, that the author's final work would be published by Capra Press and that it was a selection

Henry Miller

from unpublished manuscripts Miller composed in the early 1930s. *The World of Lawrence* (1980) was intended to commemorate the fiftieth anniversary of D. H. Lawrence's death; it now also commemorates the death of the author he influenced so strongly, Henry Miller.

The marriages and divorces, triumphs and follies, the repatriation and death of the man will be of less concern ultimately than the essential achievements of the artist. Miller's claim to a major role in modern art is established by his earliest published writings. *Tropic of Cancer* is the volcanic event; *Black Spring* (1936) and *Tropic of Capricorn* are powerful aftershocks; *The Colossus of Maroussi* (1941), although often praised, is a feeble tremor from the initial eruption which grows increasingly dormant through a hundred or more minor efforts. The early work is what endures and continues to influence the literature of our century.

Among notices of Miller's death on the front pages of leading American newspapers was an appreciation by Anatole Broyard in the *New York Times*, which suggested that Miller's importance could not be measured by his later work or even by his celebrated, pioneering use of frank language. Instead, Broyard praised Miller as "one of the earliest American writers to perfect a vernacular, conversational style and to use it to write an impressionistic, anecdotal novel about a comic, antiheroic character." No writer has drawn more directly or profoundly from the American vernacular tradition, and from its chief figure, Mark Twain. Miller's version of the colloquial voice and vision was a brilliant twentieth-century extension of Twain's deeply serious, disarmingly comic satirical genius. In Miller's version, Huck Finn's innocence was inverted, raft and river became whorehouse and sewer, and the whole North American continent became the shoreline of corruption and enslavement from which the hero hightailed it. Miller also adapted and darkened Twain's apocalyptic strains, but he added a Rabelaisian twist, a sidesplitting belly laugh of acceptance, which transformed the crude and the cataclysmic into life-affirming experiences.

With this voice and vision before him, Miller was able at the same time, quite naturally and effortlessly, to introduce Surrealism and Dadaism into the modern American narrative. These techniques made possible Miller's sometimes brilliant burlesques and wild pastiches, his dissolutions of logic and convention which reflected a whole culture on the brink of annihilation. Miller's Surrealism had a decidedly native flavor; it was more instinctive, active, immediate, humorous, and personal than the ascendant European version. Increasingly since the 1940s, many American novelists, poets, and dramatists have employed surrealistic techniques; in such experimentation, Miller stands out as the father and master.

The vernacular, the surreal, and the anarchical received a coherent shape in Miller's masterpieces only when the author drew upon two venerable American traditions—the one literary, the other intellectual. Miller was a great autobiographical artist; he was also an energetic transcendentalist thinker. The autobiographical form and the transcendentalist idea combined in *Tropic of Cancer* to unify the vulgar voice, the crude experience, the nihilistic gesture. While Miller revitalized the transcendentalist tradition for his time, he also headed the literary drive of autobiography toward fictional narrative forms—toward antiheroic, nihilistic, avant-garde modes. Finding himself in an age of discontinuity and cultural disintegration, Miller was compelled to modulate the shattered elements of life through his personal voice. He accepted anarchy in art as in life. "In an age marked by dissolution, liquidation seems to me a virtue, nay a moral imperative," Miller explained in *The Wisdom of the Heart* (1940). "I have always looked upon decay as being just as wonderful and rich an expression of life as growth."

The formal model for *Tropic of Cancer* was Whitman's *Song of Myself*. The American Transcendentalists were Miller's greatest influence; the personal narrative was their form; it was always Miller's form. His intent was thoroughly autobiographical, as he explained to Anaïs Nin in 1932: "I must be the one person in the world to risk everything, tell everything . . . and not to leave out anything because of principles, art, or whatever it may be that has constrained man heretofore." Wanting to reveal himself "as openly, nakedly and unashamedly as possible," Miller was at one with Whitman; his urge to describe and expose himself in frank detail was his way of "rendering back life, enhanced and exalted, to those who read me." Miller's *Tropic of Cancer* did not simply repeat *Song of Myself*, however; it recast an American classic for a darker time with renewed power.

Miller was born a few months before Whitman died. They grew up in the same city. Their achievements were less than a century apart, yet the difference in America was astonishing, especially during the Depression. Even so, the Miller hero begins in perfect health at middle age, holding

"Creeds and schools in abeyance," content to "loafe," determined to make himself perfect in the present moment, to live "without check with original energy." Miller's heroic self is sensual, fleshly, and "divine inside and out"—a Whitmanesque monster with even franker sexual appetites. But the shape of the world has changed. Whitman could declare that "all goes onward and outward, nothing collapses," and he could embrace every element of his world. Miller found the world itself in collapse; but the transcendental impulse obliged him to embrace it, and his art was the savage expression of that embrace. The art was quite unlike anything of its time, although at bottom it was almost completely conventional and its roots were those of the extreme individualism and native idealism the modern world had outgrown—or at least rejected.

The story in Miller's autobiography was the story we still find in Whitman's personal poem. In the course of seemingly aimless episodes, the hero is reborn in superhuman, procreative form. Then the autonomous hero begins a steady reintegration with the material world and surrenders to the natural cycle of life. Whitman comes to this conclusion: "I effuse my flesh in eddies, and drift in lacy jags/ I bequeath myself to the dirt to grow from the grass I love." Miller comes to a similar conclusion: "I love everything that flows, everything that has time in it and becoming, that brings us back to the beginning where there is never end." As Whitman translated the positive reality of his America, so Miller translated the negative reality of his time into the substantial and significant outlines of his self-creative art.

Beneath the irascible, ribald, word-drunk, slightly off-key voice of Henry Miller, one could almost hear Walt Whitman as he might have sung in a nightmare world. In *The Books in My Life* (1952) Miller noted the resemblance, for he too sought a "revaluation of all human values" and a "revolutionizing of art," and he wished beyond that to make himself and his art inseparable so that he might emerge "with *all* his sluices open—like some monstrous creature of the deep . . . adrift in the stream of life."

Although in life the man outlived the artist, in death the artist will outlive the man. Always at odds with his culture, his nation, and his literary tradition, Henry Miller was—as he said of Whitman—"more *America* than America itself." Or as he declared on another occasion: "I'm even more American than you, only against the grain. Which, if you will think a moment, serves to put me in the tradition." Yes—in the tradition and at its forefront as autobiographer, innovator, and desperado.

—*J. D. Brown*

A TRIBUTE

from JAMES LAUGHLIN

People who only read the Tropics books, may well have thought of Henry Miller as some sort of a sex fiend or monster. Nothing could be further from the truth. He was, as a person, mild, charming and enormously generous to others. Most of his royalties he gave away to help writers who were in difficult straits. The great quality of his writing was that it was truly American. He worked out an idiom for his expression which was in complete accord with colloquial American speech, and therein lay a great part of its power. One should not overlook the wide ecumenism of his interests. He was truly an international writer in the very best sense.

Vladimir Nabokov

(23 April 1899-2 July 1977)

The *DLB* entry on Vladimir Nabokov appears in *Dictionary of Literary Biography*, volume 2, *American Novelists Since World War II* (1978), pp. 350-364.

NEW BOOKS: *Details of a Sunset and Other Stories* (New York: McGraw-Hill, 1976; London, Weidenfeld & Nicolson, 1976);

Stikhi [Poems] (Ann Arbor: Ardis, 1979);

The Nabokov-Wilson Letters, ed. Simon Karlinsky (New York: Harper & Row, 1979; revised edition, New York: Harper Colophon, 1980);

Vladimir Nabokov: Lectures on Literature, ed. Fredson Bowers (New York & London: Harcourt Brace Jovanovich / Bruccoli Clark, 1980; London: Weidenfeld & Nicolson, 1980);

Lectures on Ulysses*: A Facsimile of the Manuscript* (Bloomfield Hills, Mich. & Columbia, S.C.: Bruccoli Clark, 1980).

Of the forty-eight short stories which Vladimir Nabokov wrote in Russian (1924-1939), forty-one were rendered into English under their author's supervision. They appeared in four volumes—*Nabokov's Dozen* (1958), *A Russian Beauty* (1973), *Tyrants Destroyed* (1975), and *Details of a Sunset* (1976)—the last of these appearing the year before his death. Nabokov thus succeeded in completing the self-appointed task of bringing the full array of his Russian prose fiction to his English-reading audience. The seven stories dating to the earliest part of his career which he chose not to translate were referred to as "two or three broken crackers and some mouseturdies at the bottom of the barrel."

Nabokov's short fiction is an important, and to date little studied, segment of his complete works. Asked to proffer a definition of the short-story genre, Nabokov provided the following specific and elegant response: "Many widespread species of Lepidoptera produce small, but not necessarily stunted, races above timberline. In relation to the typical novel the short story represents a small Alpine, or Polar, form. It looks different, but it is conspecific with the novel and is linked to it by intermediate clines." Indeed, his best stories, such as "Cloud, Castle, Lake," "Spring in Fialta," and "The Vane Sisters," demonstrate the same level of wit, sensibility, acute perception, and masterful style which one finds in his best novels. As with them, the themes are those of exile and loss, love and death, the artist and the nature of art, and "the burden and pressure of human consciousness."

At the time of his death in 1977, Nabokov was working on a number of projects. "Original of Laura," which his son, Dmitri, claims "would have been Father's most brilliant novel," was substantially but not totally completed, and Nabokov "expressly forbade" its publication in incomplete form. Also left incomplete was a voluminous illustrated history of the butterfly in art, a project on which Nabokov had worked for many years. Research for this project surely brought him the special bliss of scholarship so well described in *Pnin* (1957) and earlier provided by his work on Pushkin's *Eugene Onegin*. Moreover, as he explained, it gave a reason to abandon Montreux to the summertime tourist hordes while pursuing butterfly incarnations in distant museums.

For the special delight of those who read Russian, Nabokov did complete the selection of poems to be included in a large volume of collected verse. An introduction and notes were subsequently provided by his wife, Vèra, and the volume, *Stikhi*, appeared posthumously in 1979. Though he had ceased writing prose in Russian upon arriving in the United States in 1940, he did continue to write an occasional poem in Russian. The two-hundred-odd poems in this collection (of the more than three hundred which he wrote and published) date from 1917 to 1974. Thirty-nine of them were translated by Nabokov into English and can be found in *Poems and Problems* (1970).

This largest single collection of Nabokov's poems testifies to the various stages of his versificatory art as he himself describes them: 1) "an initial one of passionate and commonplace love verse"; 2) "a period reflecting utter distrust of the so-called October Revolution"; 3) "a period (reaching well into the 1920s) of a kind of private curatorship, aimed at preserving nostalgic retrospections and developing Byzantine imagery"; 4) "a period during which I set myself to illustrate the principle of making a short poem contain a plot and tell a story"; 5) "a sudden liberation from self-imposed shackles, resulting both in a sparser output and in a belatedly discovered robust style." This final period which dates from the late 1930s until his death is represented by some twenty-five poems in the collection. Nabokov's fame rightfully derives from his work as a

Vladimir Nabokov

novelist, and his stature as a poet has not yet been measured, though the four cantos which provide the core of *Pale Fire* have been qualified by some as among the highest achievements in English verse of the twentieth century.

A major literary event of 1979 was the publication of *The Nabokov-Wilson Letters.* Interest was stirred by recollections of the heated dispute of 1965 when Edmund Wilson attacked Nabokov's literal translation of, and notes to, *Eugene Onegin* in the pages of the *New York Review of Books,* imprudently challenging, among other things, Nabokov's command of the Russian language. Nabokov countered Wilson's attack point by point in the pages of *Encounter.* "If told I am a bad poet," he wrote, "I smile; but if told I am a poor scholar, I reach for my heaviest dictionary." In the succeeding months, Slavists and others picked sides and added their words, providing the literary-academic world with considerable entertainment. What was not generally known then was that Nabokov and Wilson had been friends since 1940, when Nabokov, shortly after arriving in America and at the suggestion of his cousin Nicholas, wrote to Wilson a letter of introduction, seeking a meeting. During the following decades the Nabokov and Wilson families met regularly, though apparently less frequently than either wished. Distance, familial obligations, illnesses, and separate careers made meetings infrequent and the gaps, as it were, were filled in by an epistolary interchange of news and views.

The correspondence covers the period from August 1940 through spring 1958, with seven letters dating 1959-1971. The sparsity in the latter period was due to an estrangement between the two men stemming from Wilson's dislike of *Lolita* ("I like it less than anything else of yours I have read") while championing Pasternak's *Doctor Zhivago* (disliked by Nabokov), Wilson's criticism of Nabokov's *Onegin* ("an uneven and sometimes banal translation"), his disparaging remarks on the Nabokovs in *Upstate: Records and Recollections of Northern New York* (1971), and his less than complimentary summary view of Nabokov's stature as a writer in *A Window on Russia* (1972). Thanks are due to the wives of these two men, Vera Nabokov and Elena Wilson, for setting aside past differences and making the letters public. The bonds between Nabokov and Wilson were strong enough that Nabokov could write in his last letter in this volume (2 March 1971): "A few days ago I had the occasion to reread the whole batch of our correspondences. It was such a pleasure to feel again the warmth of your many kindnesses, the various thrills of our friendship, that constant excitement of art and intellectual discovery."

Wilson provided Nabokov with introductions to various editors and publishers and advice on how to deal with them, while Nabokov served Wilson as a valuable source of knowledge on Russian language, literature, and culture. As Simon Karlinsky points out in his excellent introduction, "it was during his period of closeness with Nabokov that Wilson's thoroughgoing involvement with Russian literature and culture hit its full stride. The beginnings of Nabokov's second literary career (as an American writing in English) can hardly be imagined without Wilson's help, advice, and literary contacts." Nabokov had great difficulty finding publishers and obtaining equitable remuneration. The theme of small fees and insufficient livelihood, which had been equally bothersome throughout his European period (1919-1940), runs throughout the correspondence until the phenomenal success of *Lolita* (1955) brings financial security and the freedom to work at writing full time.

The letters are rich in details of chronology and background for Nabokov's "American period," with specifics relative to editors and publishers, family life, employment, and travel. The topic which preoccupies the two men is, naturally, literature. Their range of literary sampling was wide, and while they could agree on the merits of some writers, their divergences in taste were frequent. "You and I," Wilson writes in exasperation, "differ completely, not only about Malraux, but also about Dostoevsky, Greek drama, Lenin, Freud, and a lot of other things . . . so that we'd better, I suppose, stick to the more profitable discussion of Pushkin, Flaubert, Proust, Joyce, etc." During these years, aside from novels and stories, Nabokov was teaching literature, writing a book on Gogol (1944), and translating various Russian poets, Lermontov's *A Hero of Our Time* (1958), *The Song of Igor's Campaign* (1960), and *Eugene Onegin* (1964). ("Russia," he writes, "will never be able to repay all her debts to me.") Wilson was also translating from the Russian ("Why don't we write together a scholarly prose translation of *Evgenii Onegin* with copious notes?" Wilson inquires in 1948) and writing essays on Pushkin, Gogol, Chekhov, Turgenev, and Tolstoy. Their shared enthusiasm for Russian literature pervades the correspondence, though they never agreed on the distinctions between English and Russian prosodic systems, nor was Nabokov successful in changing Wilson's conceptions regarding the Russian revolution, the person of Lenin, and the realities of the Soviet state.

Though in his first letter Wilson admonished

Dust jacket

Nabokov for his propensity for punning, a singular delight in reading the correspondence is the profusion of word games, multi-lingual punning, stylistic one-upmanship, and the strong strain of humor practiced by both men. For example, Wilson wrote to Nabokov: "I hope that *Lolita,* as a study of amorous paternity and delinquent girlhood, will touch the American public to the point of making your fortune. If you can get her married to Pnin in Alaska and bring them home to life tenure and the American way of life in some comfortable Middle Western university, you may be able to compete in popularity with *Marjorie Morningstar* and be lecturing on young people's problems from Bangor to San Diego."

"Next year I am teaching a course called 'European Fiction,' " Nabokov wrote Wilson on 17 April 1950. "What English writers (novels or short stories) would you suggest? I must have at least two. Am going to lean heavily on the Russians, at least five broad-shouldered Russians, and shall probably choose Kafka, Flaubert and Proust to illustrate West-European fiction." "In my opinion," Wilson replied, "the two incomparably greatest (leaving Joyce out of account as an Irishman) are Dickens and Jane Austen." Though the suggestion was at first resisted, Wilson's advice prevailed and those two writers led off Nabokov's fabled course, "Masters of European Fiction." Nabokov taught at Wellesley College and Cornell Univerity, with guest stints elsewhere, from 1941 though 1958. His reputation as a teacher grew over the years, and though he on occasion promised to polish his lectures into a collection of essays he never started the project. Unexpectedly and happily the Nabokov estate decided to do so and provided Nabokov's mostly handwritten class lectures, notes, and marginally annotated classroom texts for editing and publication.

The lectures are appearing in two volumes, the first devoted to British, French, and German writers; the second, to Russian writers. The first volume (published in 1980) contains Nabokov's lectures on Austen's *Mansfield Park,* Dickens's *Bleak House,* Flaubert's *Madame Bovary,* Stevenson's "The Strange Case of Dr. Jekyll and Mr. Hyde," Proust's *The Walk by Swann's Place,* Kafka's "The Metamorphosis," Joyce's *Ulysses,* and three lectures given on special occasions—"Good Readers and Good Writers," "The Art of Literature and Commonsense," and "L'Envoi." As noted by John Updike in his fine introduction, a "striking, enveloping quality of pedagogic warmth" suffuses the pages. And though the written word cannot convey the timbre and modulation of Nabokov's theatrical delivery, as recalled by this ex-student, one will agree with Updike's observation that "the intonation, the twinkle, the sneer, the excited pounce are present in the prose, a liquid speaking prose effortlessly bright and prone to purl into metaphor and pun: a dazzling demonstration. . . ."

In his last semester of teaching, in the autumn of 1958, when this writer was a student in Nabokov's two courses at Cornell University, the European fiction course drew an overflow crowd into Goldwin Smith B Lecture Hall, while his survey course on Russian literature attracted only some thirty-five students to a smaller classroom down the corridor. In both courses Nabokov was an inspiring teacher despite his intimidating stature, despite the arduous demands he made of his students, and despite his plaints as found in the Nabokov-Wilson correspondence ("I am tired of teaching, I am tired of teaching, I am tired of teaching"). His pedagogic point of departure is suggested by an anecdote he related to his students: asked by a woman what *Finnegans Wake* was about, Joyce is said to have replied: "It took me seventeen years to write, Madame. Now why don't you read it for seventeen years." Nabokov's vantage point was that of the writer, the creator of fictions, and not that of the literary critic or historian. His concern was with the literariness of literature, its matter and substance. He demanded the close intimacy with texts that could come only from careful rereading.

The published lectures lead the reader, guided by the unique sensibilities of Nabokov, through the artfullness of selected masterpieces: the geography of Mansfield Park, the Jarndyce-jaundice and mystery themes of *Bleak House,* the counterpoint and layer-cake techniques of Flaubert, the special fantasy of Kafka, the metaphorical imagery of Proust. The focus is on language, style, theme, and structure—and always the detail. Though not always appreciated by his students, Nabokov's aim was high. "I have tried to teach you to read books for the sake of their forms, their visions, their art. I have tried to teach you to feel a shiver of artistic satisfaction, to share not the emotions of the people in the book but the emotions of its author—the joys and difficulties of creation. We did not talk around books, about books; we went to the center of this or that masterpiece, to the live heart of the matter."

Detail, so carefully woven into Nabokov's own fictions, is of paramount importance in his aesthetic. The attention to detail by fictional character, author, and reader, exemplified in these lectures, though considered by some to be sterile work and an irrational standard for judgment, receives its

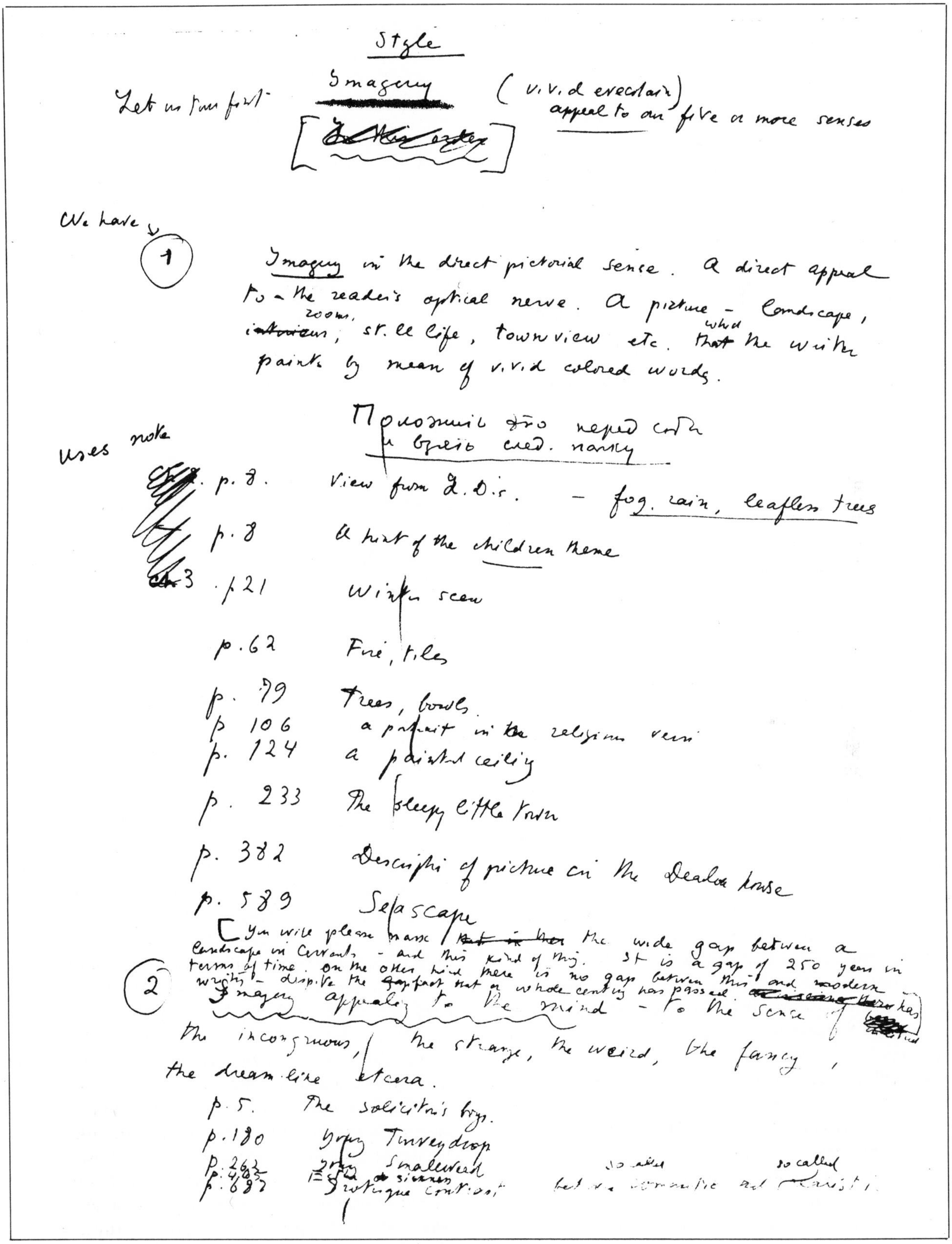
Style

Let us turn first — Imagery (vivid evocation) appeal to our five or more senses

We have ↓

1 Imagery in the direct pictorial sense. A direct appeal to the reader's optical nerve. A picture – landscape, rooms, still life, townview etc. which the writer paints by means of vivid colored words.

Положить это перед собой и брать след. пачку

uses note

p. 8. View from L.D.'s. – fog, rain, leafless trees
p. 8 A hint of the children theme
3 p. 21 Winter scene
p. 62 Fire, tiles
p. 79 Trees, boughs
p 106 a portrait in the religious vein
p. 124 a painted ceiling
p. 233 The sleepy little town
p. 382 Description of picture in the Dedlock house
p. 589 Seascape

[You will please mark the wide gap between a landscape in Cervantes – and this kind of thing. It is a gap of 250 years in terms of time. On the other hand there is no gap between this and modern writing – despite the fact that a whole century has passed.

2 Imagery appealing to the mind – to the sense of the incongruous, the strange, the weird, the fancy, the dream-like etcetera.

p. 5. The solicitor's boys.
p. 180 Young Turveydrop
p. 263 Young Smallweed
p. 483 sisters
p. 683 Grotesque contrast between so called romantic and so called realistic.

Notes for Bleak House *lecture*

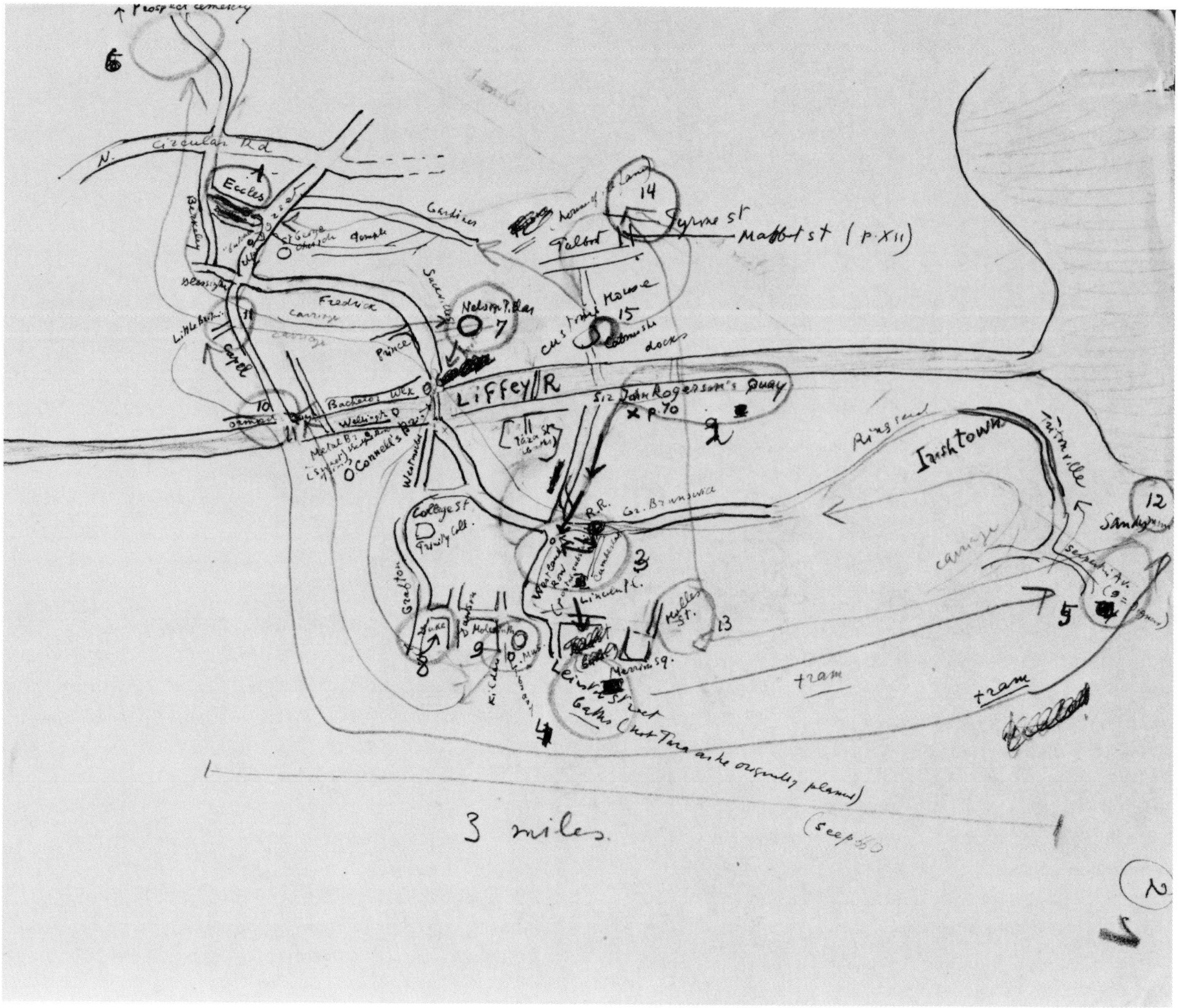

Map of Dublin for Ulysses *lecture*

eloquent justification in Nabokov's occasional lecture, "The Art of Literature and Commonsense" when Nabokov refers to "the supremacy of the detail over the general, of the part that is more alive than the whole, of the little thing which a man observes and greets with a friendly nod of the spirit while the crowd around him is being driven by some common impulse to some common goal . . . . This capacity to wonder at trifles," he continues, "no matter the imminent peril—these asides of the spirit, these footnotes in the volume of life are the highest forms of consciousness, and it is in this childishly speculative state of mind, so different from commonsense and its logic, that we know the world to be good."

Also appearing in 1980 were Nabokov's actual lecture notes for *Ulysses. Lectures on* Ulysses*: A Facsimile of the Manuscript* was published in a limited edition of 500 copies. Carefully prepared, revised, and rearranged over the years, these notes include fully written-out passages, brief comments to be expanded upon in class, notations about passages to be read aloud, a diagram of Bloom's house at 7 Eccles Street, and several hand-drawn maps of Dublin on which Nabokov traces the characters' movements.

Having read Nabokov's lectures, we might agree with John Updike's happy speculation: "It is pleasant to suspect that the rereading compelled by the preparation of these lectures at the outset of the decade, and the admonitions and intoxications rehearsed with each year's delivery, contributed to the splendid redefining of Nabokov's creative powers; and to detect, in his fiction of these years, something of Austen's nicety, Dickens's *brio*, Stevenson's 'delightful winey taste' added to and spicing up the Continental stock of Nabokov's own inimitable brew."

—*Stephen Jan Parker*

References:

Modern Fiction Studies, special Nabokov issue, ed. Charles S. Ross, 25 (Autumn 1979);

A. D. Nakhimovsky and V. A. Paperno, *An English-Russian Dictionary of Nabokov's Lolita* (Ann Arbor: Ardis, 1979);

Marina Naumann, *Blue Evenings in Berlin: Nabokov's Short Stories of the 1920s* (New York: New York University Press, 1978);

Stephen J. Parker, ed., *The Vladimir Nabokov Research Newsletter* (Fall 1978-);

Ellen Pifer, *Nabokov and the Novel* (Cambridge & London: Harvard University Press, 1980);

Peter Quenell, ed., *Vladimir Nabokov: A Tribute to His Life, His Work, His World* (London: Weidenfeld & Nicholson, 1979);

William M. Rowe, *Nabokov and Others: Patterns in Russian Literature* (Ann Arbor: Ardis, 1979);

Samuel Schuman, *Vladimir Nabokov: A Reference Guide* (Boston: G. K. Hall, 1979);

Dabney Stuart, *Nabokov: The Dimensions of Parody* (Baton Rouge: Louisiana State University Press, 1978).

AN INTERVIEW
with FREDSON BOWERS

DLB: How did the lectures come to be published?

BOWERS: The lectures came to be published because students of Nabokov recalled the thrill when they had heard the lectures at Cornell. A search was conducted to find out if the copy for the lectures was still in existence and in shape to be published. The search led to Montreux and to Nabokov's widow Vèra and her son Dmitri. Negotiations were successful for the rights, and the original manuscripts were brought back. I was then asked if I would undertake the editing and preparation of these lectures for publication.

DLB: How were you able to reconstruct classroom lectures delivered twenty-five years ago?

BOWERS: Each set of lectures presented its own problems. So far as I could tell, the manuscripts were complete but a number were in various stages of preparation. The most polished had been typed in major sections by Mrs. Nabokov, who had smoothed out various roughnesses in the process and made something of an orderly arrangement. These sections Nabokov himself would normally have read over and revised from time to time with some additions but chiefly by tinkering with the style to improve it by the test of his fastidious ear. Most sections, however, were in his own handwriting. Some of these sections showed not a great deal of reworking during the writing out, and these may have been his own fair copies of earlier drafts. Other pages were heavily corrected, obviously while he was first writing, as well as later when he came to read over the lectures at different times. The general order of the sections was usually in no doubt, although the page numbering in the lectures is not continuous and was often much revised as additions or subtractions were made. Reconstruction involved trying to straighten out the very mixed nature of the manuscripts, getting the discourse in its right order, distinguishing revisions from early versions, adding comments from his marked teaching copies, as well as quotations, and then, in extreme cases, really making an editorial lecture version out of disordered and incomplete working notes never fully written out in lecture delivery style.

DLB: Nabokov taught in the United States from 1942 to 1958. Did he always teach the same courses and did he always give these same lectures?

BOWERS: Although he hyperbolically boasts of having a hundred lectures, some two thousand pages, prepared before coming to America, this amount seems excessive and so far as I know the lectures represented in the two volumes of this series are all that are preserved. A few students' notes from his courses have been located and compared to the preserved lectures. They follow the general outlines, and sometimes show the exact phrases of his manuscripts but do vary slightly in their internal order and content. We have no means of knowing what parts of lectures he destroyed when he revised one in a new form. My impression is that in general he taught the same lectures and novels from year to year, as represented in the now published series. For special occasions he must have provided others that are now, apparently, lost. There are references in some of these lectures to lectures that he gave at Harvard on Cervantes, for instance. This is to ignore, of course, his public lectures on a number of subjects, several of which are preserved and reprinted here, and to confine speculation strictly to the set lectures on authors that would have formed part of a college course.

DLB: The distinction is often made between a teacher and a scholar. Which was Nabokov, or did he combine the traits of each?

BOWERS: Nabokov's acquaintance with published criticism of the authors he treated was limited to relatively few books, and the world of learned journals was closed to him. He does not seem to have been especially interested in literary theory. He relied almost exclusively on his own peculiar knowledge of the literary art as a writer himself: his own convictions gained by experience were to him the ultimate criteria. Professional scholarship, indeed, generally received a somewhat contemptuous reaction, and he was capable of curious forms of quirkiness of a nonscholarly variety such as his insistence that Joyce did not shape *Ulysses* on the events of the *Odyssey*. It is unlikely that Nabokov ever performed an act of literary research that in any way resembled scholarship. Instead, he was his own authority and his reactions were the touchstones for his theories.

DLB: A criticism often leveled against Nabokov's later work is that although he was a brilliant writer and a stunning artist, he wrote for himself, in a style so rich and complex that only he could fully comprehend his works. Was this man able to communicate with an undergraduate audience, to speak on their level?

BOWERS: When Nabokov addressed an audience, whether or not of students, he was acutely conscious that he must make himself clear and explicit. His public lectures like "The Art of Literature and Commonsense" are highly polished but by no means involuted or obscure. In his manuscript lectures to students, what might be described as sotto voce comments to the students (omitted in the editing) show that he had no exaggerated idea of their background of information when he felt impelled, for instance, to add that Paris was in France and Trieste in Italy, and that they must look up in a dictionary every word they did not understand.

DLB: From your knowledge of Nabokov's classroom style, how would you rate him as a teacher?

BOWERS: All student accounts of his lectures are rhapsodic in their admiration. This is understandable because his chief purpose seems to have been to foster in his students the relation in a novel between art and life, the magic of the fairy tale as he expressed it. Since he felt this magic so keenly himself, he was able to communicate it by frequent references and by his gift for bringing to life by quotation the specific point he wanted to make about the art behind the events of the novel. His combination of narrative and of quotation was masterly in presenting these novels and could not fail to enthrall an undergraduate audience by the narrative spell that he wove.

DLB: Aside from proximity with a celebrity, at least after publication of *Lolita* in 1956, were there special benefits to be gained from Nabokov's classes? Was he able to explain the worth of literary masterpieces any better than other less celebrated teachers?

BOWERS: As a writer Nabokov could speak with authority on some matters that a nonwriter critic could not touch. Being himself a creator, he understood the creative process and was often singularly successful in formulating the understanding in terms that could be comprehended by the general reader. His analysis of Flaubert as a writer is masterly and extraordinary for its insights into the methods by which an artist shapes his material. Nabokov was the foe of all critics and readers who identify with the fictional characters and their plot. He hammered home constantly the theme that everything that happens in a book takes place in the author's mind. However, in his insistence that social conditions do not shape the characters, but only the author as manipulator, he may sometimes have lost sight of the fact that social conditions may have shaped the writer himself, as he partly suggests with Jane Austen. Nabokov's intuitive understanding of literature, since he was one of the producers of literature himself, enabled him to deal with authors on an equal basis, whereas a critic may always feel himself an outsider. His strength lay chiefly when he admired the author and could penetrate deeply into his mind and art. No one can read these lectures without being enlightened in an almost unique manner in the best of them, as in the Flaubert and often the Proust and Joyce, as to qualities in the novels and their authors that represent special insights. Even the less congenial authors will receive some appreciation and understanding that contribute to one's pleasure in them. Nabokov knew what a literary masterpiece was, and what was a fake or inflated work of reputation, and his reactions, expressed in vivid and often memorable terms, cannot fail to illuminate the worth of the masterpieces to which these lectures are devoted.

—*Richard Layman*

Flannery O'Connor

(25 March 1925-3 August 1964)

The *DLB* entry on Flannery O'Connor appears in *Dictionary of Literary Biography*, volume 2, *American Novelists Since World War II* (1978), pp. 382-387.

NEW BOOK: *The Habit of Being: Letters*, ed. Sally Fitzgerald (New York: Farrar, Straus & Giroux, 1979).

RECENT AWARDS: Special National Book Critics Circle Award, Christopher Award, and Bowdoin College Award for *The Habit of Being*, 1980.

With the publication of the collection of Flannery O'Connor's letters in 1979, we are reminded that the dynamism of faith and region was every bit as much the substance of her life as we had come to know it was in her fiction. The passage from her 15 September 1955 letter to Andrew Lytle is sure to become a classic reference: "To my way of thinking, the only thing that keeps me from being a regional writer is being a Catholic and the only thing that keeps me from being a Catholic writer (in the narrow sense) is being a Southerner."

It is hard to believe that if Flannery O'Connor had been alive in 1979, she would have been only fifty-four, a little older than John Updike and Jerzy Kosinski, but younger by almost a decade than Walker Percy and John Cheever, roughly the same age as William Styron, James Baldwin, and Truman Capote. Although scarcely more than a quarter of a century had passed since the publication of her first novel, *Wise Blood* (1952), Flannery O'Connor has gained the lasting attention, if not the acceptance, of lovers of fiction the world over. What has made her position indisputably clear is the reception her collected letters received when they were released by Farrar, Straus & Giroux on 16 March 1979. Robert Towers wrote in the *New York Review of Books*: "Despite the small body of her work and the narrowness of its range, [she] seems as permanently seated among the American immortals as Emily Dickinson or Hawthorne."

Sally Fitzgerald, who selected, edited, and wrote the introduction to *The Habit of Being*, is the former wife of Robert Fitzgerald, O'Connor's literary executor, and was a close personal friend of O'Connor. The chasteness and precision of her portrait of O'Connor are typical of the integrity she brings to her whole project: "calm, slow, funny, courteous, both modest and very sure of herself, intense, sharply penetrating, devout but never pietistic, downright, occasionally fierce, and honest in a way that restores honor to the word." Fitzgerald has been acclaimed for the sensitivity and good judgment that she demonstrated in preparing the collection.

Two months before the collection was released, *Publishers Weekly* heralded it as "a trove of pleasure and information." Quentin Vest in *Library Journal* called *The Habit of Being* "a magnificent addition to one of the most unique achievements in 20th-century American literature," adding, "there is nothing else like it anywhere." Vest considers the letters the tongues of a personal pentecost: "They speak to us with a clarity, a directness, an energy, an intensity of intelligent purpose that one knows better than to try to describe. . . . Above all else they speak her faith as it has rarely been spoken in our time." In relating the letters to their genre, reviewers were lavish in their praise. Richard Gilman, writing for the *New York Times Book Review*, was sensitive though to O'Connor's renowned scorn of "interleckchul talk": "To compare her with the great letter writers in our language may seem presumptuous and would have elicited from her one of her famous steely glances, but Byron, Keats, Lawrence, Wilde and Joyce come irresistibly to mind: correspondence that gleams with consciousness." Robert Towers, more cautious in this respect than in his linking O'Connor with Dickinson and Hawthorne, concluded: "While it would be excessive to place Flannery O'Connor's letters with those of Keats, D. H. Lawrence, or Virginia Woolf in their literary significance, they are certainly among the most valuable produced by any twentieth-century American writer—only a handful by F. Scott Fitzgerald come to mind as their equal."

This extraordinary collection of letters spans Flannery O'Connor's productive years as a writer, from 1948 until her premature death at the age of thirty-nine in 1964. For fourteen of these sixteen years, the lupus that she inherited from her father forced her to live at her home, Andalusia, in the Georgia countryside that she made immortal in her stories; increasingly confined and immobile, she candidly admitted: "Mail is very eventful to me." For what it tells us of her, *The Habit of Being* is far superior to an autobiography: it lacks a self-conscious design. Together with Robert Fitzgerald's brief biographical introduction to *Everything that Rises Must Converge* (1965), it could satisfy too our need for a biography inasmuch as it leaves the excitement of interpretation to the reader. Sally Fitzgerald, however, is at work on a commissioned biography.

Whereas O'Connor is characteristically reticent in the letters about her illness, the critics have been quick to cite the irony of its relationship to her prolific correspondence. "Probably the O'Connor letters would not have been as numerous, varied, or profound had she not been circumscribed by disease," the poet Robert B. Shaw noted in the *Nation*. When O'Connor addresses the subject of her illness directly in a letter to "A" (the anonymous friend to whom some of the most brilliant letters are written), she uses an image that occurs again and again in *Mystery and Manners* (1969), the collection of her occasional prose pieces edited by Sally and Robert Fitzgerald, to specify the genuine source of artistic creativity—knowledge of place, awareness of being somewhere: "I have never been anywhere but sick. In a sense sickness is a place, more instructive than a long trip to Europe, and it's always a place where there's no company, where nobody can follow. Sickness before death is a very appropriate thing and I think those who don't have it miss one of God's mercies." If O'Connor's spiritual place was

Flannery O'Connor

sickness, the South was of course the geographical place of her artistic inspiration. Over and over again, as in the letter to Andrew Lytle, cited earlier, she attributed the unique flavor of her fiction to the interaction of her Southern countryside and the true country of her faith.

The Habit of Being has put to rest the confused estimates of O'Connor as an anti-intellectual. Everyone familiar with her work is aware of the fun that she regularly poked at critics and teachers who destroyed fiction by picking it to pieces (she referred to it as the why-is-the-Misfit's-hat-black? problem), but this was nothing more than the reasonable sensitivity of a young artist who wrote for the whole person and not just the mind. *Mystery and Manners* made it clear that O'Connor could handle abstractions, if not as comfortably and artfully as the concrete, certainly with no less clarity and force. What emerges in the letters is the undeniable impression of a keen mind that was formed carefully by ideas—just as her artistic vision was instructed by the reality she perceived—and that shaped ideas with precision, especially those ideas related to the faith that grounded her "habit of being." (Fitzgerald's title appeals to Jacques Maritain's *Art and Scholasticism* (1962), which treats *art* as a habit or quality of mind.) There is clear evidence here that the articulation of faith came more easily to her than the formulation of her theory of fiction, but that is no doubt as it should be inasmuch as her habit of art flowed from her habit of being.

O'Connor's letters to "A" and to Alfred Corn, a student at Emory who heard her talk two years before her death, are among the best examples of her sensitive and intelligent dedication to that faith which is so evident in her fiction. The first correspondence covered nine years, the second was spent in four letters, showing respectively the endurance and the intensity of her faith and love. She urges "A" not to come into the church until she feels "it would be an enlargement of [her] freedom" and Corn "to find out about faith" by reading "the most intelligent ones" who have it, recommending in one letter Cardinal Newman, Etienne Gilson, and Teilhard de Chardin. With characteristic humor, she calls herself "a hillbilly Thomist" and "a Thomist three times removed," explaining the latter to John Hawkes as one "who doesn't read Latin or St. Thomas but gets it by osmosis."

The letters provide indispensable clues to the everyday source of her artistic material—events at Andalusia that found their way into fiction—and an essential confirmation of the soundness of her judgment about her own work. She voices repeated

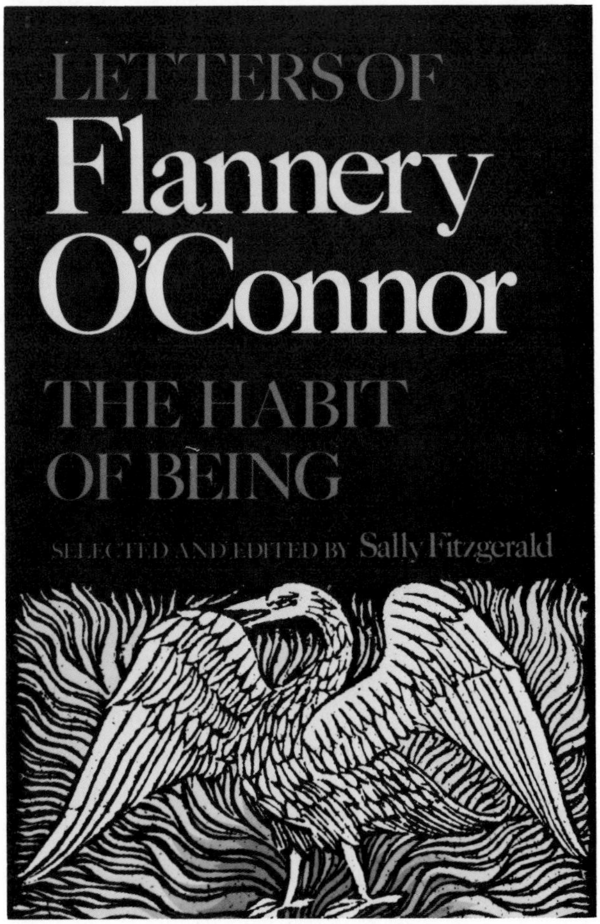

Dust jacket

satisfaction, for example, with "The Artificial Nigger" and "Good Country People" and consistent regrets about "A Stroke of Good Fortune" and "The Partridge Festival." There is clarification of her intentions about the design of most of her stories, and an illuminating exchange with Hawkes over his misunderstanding of the demonic in her fiction.

Infinitely more rewarding, however, is the disclosure of her personal and artistic asceticism. She was "a full-time believer in writing habits," she confesses to Cecil Dawkins, admitting that she forced herself to sit at her desk, without conscious distraction of any sort, at the same time every day for two hours, even if no inspiration came. "Sometimes I work for months and have to throw everything away, but I don't think any of that was time wasted. Something goes on that makes it easier when it does come well." Describing Simone Weil's life to "A" as both "comical" and "truly tragic," she acknowledges a desire to write a comic novel about a woman. "What is more comic and terrible," she asks, "than the angular intellectual proud woman approaching God inch by inch with ground teeth?" Humor aside, and with apparent knowledge of the limits to energy and life her illness would impose, she wrote as early as 1953 to Robert Lowell: "What you have to measure out, you come to observe closer."

The release of major screen and television adaptations of two of O'Connor's works—"The Displaced Person" (1979) and *Wise Blood* (1980)—accompanied the appearance of *The Habit of Being.* "The Displaced Person," adapted for Public Television's "American Short Story" series, has three memorable performances. Shirley Stoler, who became widely known as a character actress for her role as the commandant of the Nazi concentration camp in Lina Wertmuller's *Seven Beauties,* offers a portrayal of Mrs. Shortly that will be hard to forget or surpass; equally fine are Irene Worth as Mrs. McIntyre and John Houseman as Father Flynn.

Wise Blood, the thirty-third feature film of John Huston, its director, is a classic cinematic adaptation of a novel because it is faithful both to the spirit of the work as well as to the substance of the narrative and is an exuberantly fine film in its own right. Coproduced by Michael and Benedict Fitzgerald (sons of Sally and Robert Fitzgerald) from a screenplay by Benedict Fitzgerald, *Wise Blood* is clearly a work of love. The excellence and success of both these adaptations herald a new era of O'Connor's popularity as more of her fiction is brought to the screen.

—John R. May

Film Adaptation:

Wise Blood, adapted by Benedict Fitzgerald, New Line Cinema, 1980.

Television Adaptation:

"The Displaced Person," adapted by Horton Foote, "American Short Story Series," PBS, 1979.

References:

Shannon Burns, "The Literary Theory of Flannery O'Connor and Nathaniel Hawthorne," *Flannery O'Connor Bulletin,* 7 (Autumn 1978): 101-113;

Michael Cleary, "Environmental Influences in Flannery O'Connor's Fiction," *Flannery O'Connor Bulletin,* 8 (Autumn 1979): 20-34;

Robert Coles, *Flannery O'Connor's South* (Baton Rouge: Louisiana State University Press, 1980);

Mary Gordon, "The Habit of Genius," *Saturday Review* (14 April 1979): 42-45;
John R. May, ed., "Blue-Bleak Embers: The Letters of Flannery O'Connor and Youree Watson," *New Orleans Review* 6 (1979): 336-356;
James H. McCown, "Remembering Flannery O'Connor," *America* (8 September 1979): 86-88;
Barbara McKenzie, "Flannery O'Connor Country on Film: A Photo Essay," *Georgia Review*, 31 (Summer 1977): 404-426;
Marion Montgomery, "Flannery O'Connor and the Jansenist Problem in Fiction," *Southern Review*, 14 (July 1978): 438-448;
Robert Phillips, "On Being Flannery O'Connor," *Commonweal* (13 April 1979): 216-220;
Robert B. Shaw, "Jane Austen in Milledgeville," *Nation* (28 April 1979): 472-474;
Carol Shloss, *Flannery O'Connor's Dark Comedies: The Limits of Inference* (Baton Rouge: Louisiana State University Press, 1980);
Robert Towers, "Flannery O'Connor's Gifts," *New York Review of Books*, 3 May 1979, pp. 3-6;
Ralph Wood, "From Fashionable Tolerance to Unfashionable Redemption: A Reading of Flannery O'Connor's First and Last Stories," *Flannery O'Connor Bulletin*, 7 (Autumn 1978): 10-25;
Judith F. Wynne, "The Sacramental Irony of Flannery O'Connor," *Southern Literary Journal*, 7 (Spring 1975): 33-49.

Walker Percy
(28 May 1916-)

The *DLB* entry on Walker Percy appears in *Dictionary of Literary Biography*, volume 2, *American Novelists Since World War II* (1978), pp. 390-397.

NEW BOOK: *The Second Coming* (New York: Farrar, Straus & Giroux, 1980; London: Secker & Warburg, 1981).

Since the appearance of *Lancelot* in 1977, Walker Percy has had a single book published: a novel entitled *The Second Coming* (1980), which he considers his "first unalienated novel." While *Lancelot* was accorded a mixed critical reception, *The Second Coming* has been almost unanimously hailed with such words as "masterly" and "superior." In the *New York Times Book Review*, John Romano lauded the work as "Walker Percy's best since *The Moviegoer*," and there has been general critical acclaim for the novelist's increasing deftness.

Such effusive praise must be a source of bemusement as well as satisfaction to the sixty-five-year-old writer whose undergraduate and graduate training was in science and medicine rather than in the arts, whose first publications were scholarly philosophical essays rather than fiction, and whose first published novel appeared a mere twenty years ago when he was already forty-five. Walker Percy is not the stereotypical writer. Percy and his wife live comfortably and unassumingly near their two married daughters and grandchildren in the pleasant Southern backwater of Covington, Louisiana. "Nothing," says Percy with immense satisfaction, "has ever happened here." Percy is not—and never has been—a driven man: having never practiced the medical profession for which he was trained, he spent a number of quiet years reading and thinking and living on his inheritance before happening onto a career as a writer. Along with many other successful contemporary novelists, Percy has done a little university teaching and continues to read fledgling authors' manuscripts, but unlike many others, he refuses to disrupt his life-style for such activities as publishers' promotional tours for his books. "A morning of work is enough," Percy says. "I'm happy to leave [it], be with my family."

Finally, for Percy even more than for many other so-called novelists of ideas, his concern with the craft of fiction has often seemed less, or at least no more, intense than his fascination with the eternal problems of theology, philosophy, and language, for which his novels occasionally appear to be vehicles of expression. As a young man, during several years of convalescence from pulmonary tuberculosis, Percy steeped himself in Sören Kierkegaard, Gabriel Marcel, Martin Heidegger, Jean-Paul Sartre, and Albert Camus; many of his diagnoses of the problems of contemporary life—everydayness, inauthenticity, abstraction—resulted from this study. So did many of the key questions that Percy has raised in various forms in all of his writing to date: Is there a God, and, if there is, how can we know him? Is it possible for us to truly know ourselves, or others? What impulses, both scientific and humanistic, shape us? Is ours an age of madness, newly awakening belief, apocalyptic signs? What do the words with which we attempt to communicate mean? And, over and over again: Why are we here?

A comparison of Percy's five novels to date shows plainly the existence of a typical Percy protagonist. He is a roughly middle-aged man, at least reasonably comfortable in material circumstances, but plagued by depression and/or other psychological and/or physical problems. This cerebral main character shares many of his author's insights and obsessions: he is keenly aware of the paradoxes of being alive, the critical significance of language, and the corruption of contemporary American life. His story is the story of his coming to terms with the donnee of his existence.

Such a generalized description easily fits Walker Percy's latest protagonist, Will Barrett resurrected (hence, the title *The Second Coming*) from *The Last Gentleman* (1966), and about twenty-five years older. In the earlier book, Will is portrayed as a searcher of answers to the unanswerable questions. He encounters the Vaught family, falls in love with Kitty, and travels around the country finding answers to some of his questions about life through his companionship with her two brothers. In the second novel, the adult Will confides to Kitty's older brother Sutter his plans for a scientific experiment in search of God, only to discover not God but at least indirect proof of his existence in the guise of Kitty's schizophrenic daughter Allison Huger (Kitty's "second coming"), whom he plans to marry as the narrative ends.

To all outward appearances, Will Barrett is the quintessence of the successful man: "Not only did he marry a Peabody, he also made it on his own, from editor of the *Law Review*, straight into the top Wall Street firm, one of the Ten Most Promising Young Attorneys, early retirement, man-of-the-year. . . ." Yet, in private he wonders whether or not life is worth living. Will's father committed suicide when Will was twelve; Will agonizes over whether death might not be a preferable alternative to the death-in-life that he feels is his existence. His easy socializing with friends, camaraderie on the golf course, overseeing his late wife's good works projects have become meaningless to him, and he begins to suffer brief petit mal trances, brief hallucinatory flashbacks to moments in his past. In his state of depression, he begins to wonder if there is any way to determine definitively if God exists, ruling out the "maybe." And he is inspired by an idea.

Will decides to enter a limestone cave near the golf course and wait for God to give a sign of his existence. If God does so, Will reasons, he will gladly reenter the world, infused with new desire and purpose for living. If God chooses to make no sign or does not exist, there is no reason for living, and he will cheerfully opt for suicide, remaining in his self-imposed entombment until he dies.

Before acting on his plan, Will writes two letters, the first a note to a local friend designed to eliminate the impression of suicide and the second a letter to Sutter Vaught that outlines the whole experiment. He tells Sutter where to find his body should the experiment fail and gives him instructions to collect his life insurance benefits and to use them to continue the quest for evidence of God's existence. Outfitted with a flashlight and spare batteries, fortified with plenty of sleeping pills to help him endure a potentially long wait, Will enters the cave and settles down to watch for a sign. However, ironically the supposedly foil-proof plan is foiled by the pain of an abscessed tooth that sends Will wildly backtracking toward the cave entrance. Losing his way, he finds another opening and ludicrously knocks himself unconscious by falling through it into a greenhouse sheltered on one side by the mountain. It is secretly occupied by Allison, recently escaped from a mental institution.

Some time earlier, Will has come across Allison and her secret hideaway while searching for golf balls that he has hit into the woods. Allison has, in her terms, "flunked ordinary living"; she cannot find the language to explain to her parents and psychiatrist that before she can be like the "giant red star Betelgeuse . . . trying to expand and fan out and take in and please the whole universe," she must collapse "down to the white dwarf Sirius . . . diamond bright and diamond hard, indestructible by comets, meteors, people." She believes she must find the essence of herself before she can hope to "come back up" to normal living, despite the risks to her mental well-being that such a journey entails. During a lucid interval between electroshock treatments, Allison has learned of land she has inherited from an aunt's friend. Through torturous concentration and reliance on notes to herself written during her clearer mental periods, she has successfully effected her flight from the hospital, located part of the acreage that is now hers, and set up basic housekeeping in the greenhouse, feeling and acting like a wide-eyed alien from another planet. Estranged from most of humanity, Allison has come to recognize and partially trust Will before he falls through her roof; in nursing him back to

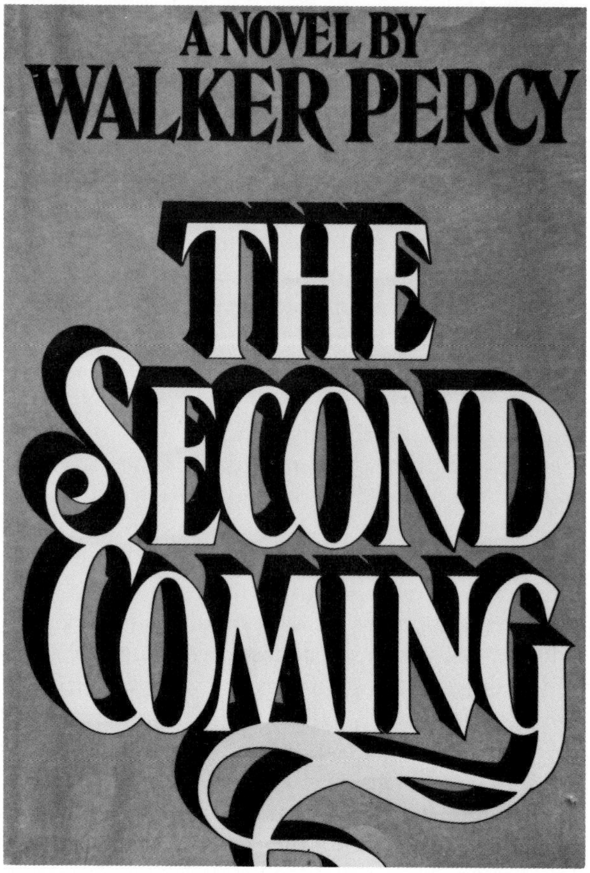

Dust jacket

health, she falls in love with him and he with her.

The explicitness, yet sensitivity, with which Percy describes Will and Allison's first tentative sexual encounter and their increasing delight in discovering each other's bodies is new in Percy's writing. New, too, is the idyllic happy ending of the novel: stiff parental opposition to the pair's marital union dissipates without explanation; Allison discovers with joy that lovemaking solves the problem of how to pass the time of the interminable "four o'clock longens" (her term for the inactive part of late afternoon when she begins to feel sad). Together, Will and Allison plan a life of simple natural living, developing her property by employing the talents of several skilled but partially disabled men from the local old folks' home. Love for Will gives Allison an all-consuming interest outside herself for the first time, helping to lessen her hypersensitivity; his love for her increases her self-confidence and sense of self-worth. Love for Allison gives Will a reason for living: he sees her to some extent as the sign that God had not given him while he was in the cave. *The Second Coming* concludes with hope: love and life triumph over death.

Though the essentially happy ending of *The Second Coming* is something of a departure for Percy, avowed fans of the novelist will find that both the themes of the novel and its style vary but little from his earlier works. As is usual with Percy, there is satire of contemporary American life: of Californians, of nursing homes (as in *Love in the Ruins* and *Lancelot*), of religious beliefs and clergymen and religious retreats (as in Jack Curl's description of "an ecumenical retreat" that includes "a wonderful bunch of guys"). There is, once again, a sense of impending apocalypse, reminiscent of *Love in the Ruins*: references to signs of the Last Days, a jeremiad in Will's letter to Sutter, Will's vision of "the great black beast of the apocalypse" as he falls from the cave. Also, Percy's characters continue to include comic types among the lesser players: the clergyman reluctant to discuss God, Allison's money-conscious parents, the comically ingratiating Pakistani doctor who counsels Allison in the hospital.

Much of *The Second Coming* is Percy at his best: the crisp detail of his descriptions of autumn on the golf course; the short, sharp, uncluttered dialogue; the beautifully interwoven flashbacks relating Allison's background and the critical hunting incident that ended in Will's father's suicide. Percy's most recent novel has a complexity and a surety that were not consistently there before; he has always had the provocative ideas, but *The Second Coming* unites thought and vehicle in the most felicitous way to date.

For much of his writing career, Percy has moved from writing nonfiction to fiction and back again; it is not surprising, therefore, that his present project is a sequel to *The Message in the Bottle* (1975), an essay collection with the working title "Lost in the Cosmos, or the Last Self-Help Book." Linda Whitney Hobson reports in an August 1980 issue of *Horizon* that the work deals "with semiotics, with consciousness, with the problems scientists have, and with the impact of television sit-coms—with their easy solutions to complex problems—on the minds of an entire culture." Percy's work is a determined undertaking for a writer quoted in the same article as saying, "Writing is the loneliest goddamn life in the world." "I'm bloody sick of making up stories," he told James Atlas for a piece in the 29 June 1980 *New York Times Book Review*. "When you get through with a novel, you think, 'This is not a respectable occupation for a grown man.' "

For all such outbursts, Walker Percy steadily keeps on with his writing. He told Hobson, "I think the only thing that keeps the novelist going, and I'm not sure that any other novelist would admit this, is the thought that you are going to do the really big one." Most critics would say that *The Second Coming* is the closest Walker Percy has yet come to "the really big one." If he should never achieve that aim, however, Walker Percy has suggested in his modest way that he would be content with another goal: "The writer also reaches out to others, and if the result can't be speech, a conversation between two people, there is, I hope, another kind of exchange between him and someone else: the effort that has produced words on paper stirs a response in the reader—Pascal's 'motions of the heart.' "

—*Joan Bischoff*

Periodical Publications:

"Questions They Never Asked Me," *Esquire*, 88 (December 1977): 170-172ff.;

"Why I Live Where I Live," *Esquire*, 93 (April 1980): 35-37.

Interviews:

"Talking about Talking: An Interview with Walker Percy," *New Orleans Review*, 5 (May 1976): 13-18;

J. F. Baker, "PW Interviews: Walker Percy," *Publishers Weekly*, 211 (21 March 1977): 6-7.

References:

James Atlas, "Portrait of Mr. Percy," *New York Times Book Review*, 29 June 1980, pp. 1ff.;

Cleanth Brooks, "Walker Percy and Modern Gnosticism," *Southern Review*, 13 (Autumn 1977): 677-687;

Panthea Reid Broughton, ed., *The Art of Walker Percy: Stratagems for Being* (Baton Rouge: Louisiana State University Press, 1979);

Edward J. Cashin, "History as Mores: Walker Percy's *Lancelot*," *Georgia Review*, 31 (Winter 1977): 875-880;

Robert Coles, "Profiles: The Search," *New Yorker*, 54 (2 October 1978): 43-44ff.; 54 (9 October 1978): 52-54ff.;

Coles, *Walker Percy: An American Search* (Boston: Little, Brown, 1978);

Robert D. Daniel, "Walker Percy's *Lancelot*: Secular

Walker Percy

Raving and Religious Silence," *Southern Review*, 14 (Winter 1978): 186-194;

Constance Hall, "The Ladies in *The Last Gentleman*," *Notes on Mississippi Writers*, 11 (Spring 1978): 26-35;

Linda Whitney Hobson, "Walker Percy," *Horizon*, 23 (August 1980): 56-61;

Michael Kreyling, "*Crime and Punishment*: The Pattern beneath the Surface of Percy's *Lancelot*," *Notes on Mississippi Writers*, 11 (Spring 1978): 36-44;

Lewis A. Lawson, "The Gnostic Vision in *Lancelot*," *Renascence*, 32 (Autumn 1979): 52-64;

Lawson, "William Alexander Percy, Walker Percy, and the Apocalypse," *Modern Age*, 24 (Fall 1980): 396-406;

John Romano, "A Novel of Powerful Pleasures," *New York Times Book Review*, 29 June 1980, pp. 1ff.;

J. P. Telotte, "Walker Percy's Language of Creation," *Southern Quarterly*, 16 (January 1978): 105-116;

Telotte, "Walker Percy: A Pragmatic Approach," *Southern Studies*, 18 (Summer 1979): 217-230;

David L. Vanderwerken, "The Americanness of *The Moviegoer*," *Notes on Mississippi Writers*, 12 (Summer 1979): 40-53.

Katherine Anne Porter

(15 May 1890-18 September 1980)

The *DLB* entry on Katherine Anne Porter appears in *Dictionary of Literary Biography*, volume 4, *American Writers in Paris, 1920-1939* (1980), pp. 311-314.

Katherine Anne Porter, who died on 18 September 1980 at the age of ninety, is sometimes called a writer's writer. She consciously belonged to a central tradition of modern fiction whose masters were Flaubert, Turgenev, James, and Ford. There is really no name for this tradition unless we use Ford's term "the Impressionist novel," which is probably derived from James's formulation: "A novel is in its broadest definition a personal, a direct impression of life." For the Impressionist novelist (as for the Impressionist painter) the fully realized illusion, the finished work of art, is based on the assumption that a public reality is somehow accessible to a private vision. All of Flaubert's famous labors to achieve stylistic perfection were only meant to carry this assumption into practice. But the self-discipline that "brings off" the finished work of art is not easy; it is always being threatened by the indifferent or the restless. Miss Porter saw eye to eye with her great predecessors on these matters. Her successes were as hard-won as theirs.

Miss Porter can also be placed in a line of descent that is specifically American: the tradition of the beautifully made short story, which seems to have suited the American temperament ever since Poe made such considerable claims for it in his review of Hawthorne's *Twice-Told Tales* in 1842. She thus joins Poe himself, Hawthorne, Melville, James, Stephen Crane, and a dozen others, whose achievement stands very high even without the novels that most of them wrote. (This strong and continuous tradition of the short story is surely one of the things that distinguishes American fiction from British.) In 1941, introducing Eudora Welty's first book, *A Curtain of Green*, Miss Porter at least half-seriously warned of "a trap lying just ahead, and all short-story writers know what it is—The Novel." At that time she seemed to be as strict about the nature of her talent as Poe had been. But as we now know, she was already deeply involved in the short story that would not stop and that eventually became *Ship of Fools* (1962).

To describe Miss Porter in another way, she is usually located within a regional literary culture, the so-called Southern Renascence. A little older than her Southern friends (who included Caroline Gordon, Allen Tate, Andrew Lytle, Robert Penn Warren, and Cleanth Brooks), she caught up with them, as it were, with three brilliant short novels, "Old Mortality," "Pale Horse, Pale Rider," and "Noon Wine," which came out in the 1930s (two of them in the *Southern Review* edited by Brooks and Warren) and were published as a volume at the end of that decade. Before that she might have been thought of as a somewhat exotic figure, because her earlier stories, the best of them included in *Flowering Judas* (1930; enlarged edition, 1935), had a variety of settings and in most cases did not draw on her childhood in Texas. Most of her Southern friends had actually lived in Europe at one time or another and tended to judge their regional culture by European rather than by American standards. Indeed when they came to write their poems and novels they might project their own experience against the background of, say, France or England. Miss Porter's "much-loved second country" was Mexico. Although she lived in Europe, chiefly Germany and France, for several years, it never had the importance for her (or at least for her fiction) that Mexico continued to have. Mexico as she knew it was both "traditional" and revolutionary, and it offered her a way of realizing, at firsthand, the clashes of values that have occurred in so many places in our century. All of this comes out in the first scene of her first published story, "María Concepción" (1922), where the young peasant woman and the American archaeologist confront each other over the ruins of a buried city.

Miss Porter, however, did not have to go to Mexico to know about the archetypal patterns of behavior that often reveal themselves in the minutiae of social habits and gestures. In "Noon Wine," for instance, which is set on a small farm in South Texas around the turn of the century (the time and place of Miss Porter's childhood), the action is based to some extent on the code of behavior that Mr. and Mrs. Thompson would have thought "becoming" to a man and a woman of their station. Mr. Thompson, that is, simply does not believe that it is a man's duty to run a dairy and do certain other tasks. When Mr. Helton, the Swede from North Dakota, turns up one day and gradually restores the farm to a modest prosperity, that only reinforces Mr. Thompson's sense of his own dignity. Mrs. Thompson, on her side, has to struggle against her husband's inertia; and she has probably married beneath herself. There is in the circumstances a tension between the man

Katherine Anne Porter

and the woman that drains their psychic energy. What "brings off" the story so firmly is the point of view, which shifts back and forth from Mr. Thompson to his wife, in a slow rhythm that never stops until the final turn in the tragedy when he kills himself. This is the work of a master in the Impressionist tradition; the illusion is so effortlessly sustained that one has to study the story at length in order to realize what the author has done.

Katherine Anne Porter's sense of social relationships was extraordinary. Although she was not a modern equalitarian, she felt that every human being, however aimless or wicked, had a story that might be told. (It was probably some such idea that led her to put so much into *Ship of Fools*.) Many years ago, when I was driving her through the mountains in Virginia—she was already late for an appearance at Sweet Briar College—we had to stop for an interminable delay at a point where the road was being repaired. An old man with a wooden leg, who signaled the cars by waving a red cloth on a stick, hobbled over. Miss Porter, still elegant in her early sixties, rolled down the window and proceeded to talk to him for twenty minutes. I daresay she knew the story of his life very soon; most people would have ignored him. She was, so obviously, more open to experience than most of us. On another occasion when I was present with some others, she was introduced to Flannery O'Connor in the parlor at Andalusia Farm. By this time she was a legend, but too charming, too light in her conversational touch, to be a *grande dame*. She blessed the household with a glass of sherry and an old proverb in Spanish (which she thoughtfully translated); for a moment she brought something of her Mexico to Georgia. And then the established master, Miss Porter, turned to the young master, Miss O'Connor, who was a little shy, and started the evening off as an eighteenth-century musician might have started a Mozart divertimento; there was no need for a conductor.

—*Ashley Brown*

A TRIBUTE
from HOWARD BAKER

After fifty years I've made up my mind. My nomination for the best compact dramatic narrative of the species which we call the "short story" would be Katherine Anne Porter's "María Concepción." It happens to be her first published fiction (*Century Magazine*, 1922), and is also unusual in that it confines itself to events that happened in an archaic Mexican village, while Miss Porter herself was a journalist living in New York. I want to try to say how a seemingly "exotic" story about Indians can be as good as I am convinced this one is. To do that could furnish the key to our author's astounding genius: I use the story as a text for more general remarks.

We know that Katherine Anne Porter was born in the Eighteen-nineties on the Texas-Mexican border and that her family had become entangled materially in the erratic wars going on to the south. This explains something about her insight into the stubbornness of villagers clinging to their way of life in spite of violent intrusions—the theme on which the story hangs. Moreover, the surprising and arresting fact is that Miss Porter, in New York, was acknowledging Mexico as "My Familiar Country."

And we know too, that as a journalist with partisan views throbbing within her, she was politically eloquent about the oppression of hundreds of thousands of natives by "Mexican and American capitalists and the Church." When she was even younger, she had sat in the bell tower in a cathedral in the city of Mexico and watched street fighting, which she visualizes as bringing glory not to angels but to the beautiful unprized country natives. Which side is which in the fighting in the streets below and what she thinks the goals will turn out to be are impossible to decipher. All we do know is that she was partial to fairly commonplace intellectual, revolutionary views.

Very well. With these deeply seated deviant urgencies in her makeup as a young woman, she sits down somewhere and writes the story of María Concepción, a statuesque, church-married young wife, who stumbles onto the sight of the glittering young Don Juan to whom she is married, in the midst of an act of grossest infidelity. Juan immediately leaves her for the wars, taking his amorosa with him. María endures. Juan returns, and along with him his amorosa. María's first compulsion toward total vengeance narrows itself to his childlike camp companion, whom she murders and whose newborn child she takes for her own. When the barefooted police and the neighbors set out to investigate the murder, Juan and María, out of an instinct for self-preservation, are found eating food from the same bowl. All that which would be harmful to María is concealed under a shroud of impenetrable native faces. María is free. Only Juan has faint misgivings. He is condemned from now on, like most men, to the lot of daily labor and fidelity.

I recount this story in order to demonstrate that not one of the author's personal attitudes is visible in it. Not a hint of a political or a sociological or a psychological parti pris colors the account of the natives living in their own way in their own world. We enjoy the privilege of sharing firsthand in far from ordinary happenings, without a trace of editorial slanting.

Katherine Anne Porter wrote slowly, and only once at any great length. Looking back over all those carefully wrought, compact narratives, I seem to see in each a unique cast of characters who lived in their own highly individual way in their unique world, never shaped in the narration by the behavioral generalities which usually infiltrate our reports of the lives of others.

Miss Porter was explicit about her rule that the writer must detach himself from his subject matter. In D. H. Lawrence's *The Plumed Serpent* she finds Lawrence much too involved in his own preoccupations with a "terror of death and nausea of life, sexual egotism and fear, a bitter will to power and an aspiration after mystical apartness. . . ." to allow him to touch "the darkly burning Indian mystery."

Katherine Anne Porter

With the exception of passages in *The Ship of Fools*, her sacrifices of conventional loyalities and of all of the personal trappings normally put on by an artist, were consumed one by one on the altar of the creation of an art which is as purified as an art is ever likely to be. Of course other examples of the short story par excellence come to mind. James Joyce's "The Dead" is one. But I think all comparable pieces would share more or less noticeably in the sort of discipline to which Miss Porter submitted herself.

A TRIBUTE

from CLEANTH BROOKS

Katherine Anne Porter was many things: a sparkling conversationalist, a gracious hostess who was also an excellent cook, a warm friend, and, most important of all, a fine artist. In her art she was above all a perfectionist. She held back finishing works until she believed that she had done all that she could do to perfect them.

Her one novel, *Ship of Fools*, which she was over twenty years in writing, indicates her reluctance to send anything to the printer that she felt she needed to give more attention to. But her concern for perfection was most particularly borne in on me in the following episode.

She had sold a story to a magazine which could pay much, much more than could *The Southern Review* (which R. P. Warren and I were then editing). But when she discovered the cuts and changes that were demanded of her, she came to us and said in effect: I need the money very much and I know that you can pay only so much a word, but if you want it, I'll let you have it, for I don't want it pulled out of shape or cut and trimmed.

Of course, we said yes and *The Southern Review* printer set it up in our type—most of it, that is—from the galleys of the other magazine. It had gone that far toward publication before it was retrieved.

A TRIBUTE

from JANET LEWIS

My first sight of Katherine Anne Porter came many years after I had esteemed her as a friend through letters, and she was always marvellous as a letter writer. She had come to Stanford to teach, in a temporary capacity, because the academic powers did not feel themselves empowered to employ on an academic basis a writer who had not even finished high school. However, she was at Stanford, much admired and much loved, and she came to luncheon at our house in company with Wallie and Mary Stegner. I remember a small woman in a great green cloak, which may have been lined or partly lined with orange. She looked like the pictures she had sent us, snapshots from Mexico, the white hair, grey eyes far apart, features which photographed beautifully; and she was full of wit and charm, as in the letters. I think it was a rainy day. Our acquaintance began when Allen Tate recommended her as a contributor to *The Gyroscope*, which was the quarterly magazine published by my husband for one year. Howard Baker and Ruth Lockett were also on the editorial board, and Allen Tate adviser from the East. He recommended the work of Miss Porter very highly. I had read "The Jilting of Granny Weatherall" in a copy of *transition*, and admired it; I have grown to admire it even more with the passing of years and many rereadings. We were proud to publish "Theft" in *The Gyroscope*. I think it was not her third published story; before or after "Granny" and "María Concepción," there was another. But if not her third, it was her fourth, I believe, and she received no remuneration from *The Gyroscope*—none of the contributors were paid, and many deserved great sums. However, the correspondence which began then continued intermittently for many years. Even while she was at Stanford there were letters. Most of them have been destroyed, for which I am now sorry.

All her friends were much concerned, at the time of *The Gyroscope*, about her health. She had tuberculosis and no money, and either one is difficulty enough without the other. When *Flowering Judas* appeared there was a conspiracy among her friends to see that it had as many and as excellent reviews as could be contrived, and since enthusiasm for the book was great as well as sincere there was no problem there, so that *Flowering Judas* established her well in the literary sky. In fact, I seem to remember that Allen Tate's review was headed, "A New Star Rises."

She went to Mexico for her health, for less expensive living, for a multitude of reasons, many of which show clearly in her work. So there were letters from Mexico, and then from Paris, in the days "when the ground shook under our feet," as she wrote me. There was the Guggenheim Fellowship, and the new marriage. Eventually there was the time at Stanford.

She wanted to finish the novel. She had the theory that if she could just find herself a quiet spot for a few uninterrupted weeks, she could write the chapters that would pull it all together. She remembered how she had written "Pale Horse, Pale Rider," and "Noon Wine," at great speed, in an interval when nothing interfered. She found a house to rent at La Honda, which is a scattered sort of settlement in the Santa Cruz Mountains (the Coast Range) above Stanford. It is very beautiful because of the mountain trees, redwoods, madrones, tan oaks, and it is remote in more than miles. It is easily reached only by private car, although I think there is or was a bus, which went from Palo Alto to the Coast by way of La Honda. Friends tried to warn her that she would be isolated, that the weather would be cold, under the redwoods, and catching the wind from the sea. But this was just what she wanted—isolation in a world of beautiful trees and far vistas. The rains came, the roof of the woodsy cabin leaked, the stove smoked, the telephone went out, people were not inclined to drive the La Honda Road in bad weather—the road less trustworthy then than now. Katherine Anne sat up late reading *The White Goddess*, and feeling surrounded by the elemental air of myth, and took to writing letters. They were wonderful letters. The novel continued to be a problem. Eventually she moved to the Stanford campus, in a small but warm apartment behind the hillside garage of Mr. and Mrs. Ronald Hilton.

She had as much privacy there as she wanted or needed, and she said where else could she step outdoors and "lean against the smell of roses?"

I did not attend her classes, but I learned from some of those who did that even if she did no more than read aloud to them from Lady Gregory's diaries, she was a great experience for them. I did attend a reading of a part of the uncompleted novel. After a few comments she put on her glasses, and said, "I will now retire behind the written word." At least, I think I remember that correctly, and the gesture.

It was wonderful for me, after such a long acquaintance by mail, to have her actually present. And it is still wonderful to find her so present in her work. It is in the stories that I find her best; I have never made my peace with the novel. But the stories, almost without exception, still seem to me marvellous, in their strength, their skill, their delicacy and their warmth; and their elegance.

A TRIBUTE

from ANDREW LYTLE

First of all Miss Porter tells a good story, but always a story which concerns some instance of the insoluble but persistent concerns of the human predicament. Her words are usually of one or two syllables; the impact of them makes for a form moving and clear and dramatic. She fled from home, into her first marriage, both literally and metaphorically from the restraints of family life, symbolically from a society stricken by war and reconstruction to the second and third generations. She, like her heroine in "Old Mortality," remained her life long a romantic and a wanderer. This wandering, into Mexico, back and forth from Europe and the Northeast, gave her the necessary distance on her subject. Her view of it is Southern, in the sense that all action takes place somewhere, revealed through whatever manners and mores define that particular place. Such provinciality is necessary to literature. The mastery of her craft never allows her to debase an action by isolating the idiom of speech or a local custom from the humanity of the actors, as if the actors existed as examples of social history, seen by a foreigner for the first time. And when she uses symbols to concentrate meaning, as in "Rope" and "Magic," the symbols become flesh, that is concrete through the action. She has fled the family and the Roman Catholic church but not in her fiction. They are not her subject, but they are the occasion for and the form of her subject. Her particular kind of irony so disposes of them.

A TRIBUTE

from ROBERT PENN WARREN

In my view, the final importance of Katherine Anne Porter is not merely that she has written a number of fictions remarkable for both grace and strength, a number of fictions which have enlarged and deepened the nature of the story, both short and long, in our time, but that she has created an *oeuvre*—a body of work including fiction, essays, letters, and journals—that bears the stamp of a personality distinctive, delicately perceptive, keenly aware of the depth and darkness of human experience, delighted by the beauty of the world and the triumphs of human kindness and warmth, and thoroughly committed to a quest for meaning in the midst of the ironic complexities of man's lot.

—*Saturday Review* (December 1980)

William Styron

(11 June 1925-   )

The *DLB* entry on William Styron appears in *Dictionary of Literary Biography*, volume 2, *American Novelists Since World War II* (1978), pp. 460-475.

NEW BOOK: *Sophie's Choice* (New York: Random House, 1979; London: Cape, 1979).

In November 1979, at the annual meeting of the South Atlantic Modern Language Association in Atlanta, Georgia, William Styron read a short personal reminiscence which he had prepared especially for the occasion. The sketch was about his only previous visit to Atlanta, a trip that he had made in the winter of 1947 from Duke University, to compete for a Rhodes Scholarship. It was a humorous story in which he poked fun at himself as a young man and at the scholarly profession. He did not win the scholarship, and though he returned to Duke with some regret at his failure, he also felt a good bit of relief. For Styron knew that his destiny was to be a writer, and he sensed that a Rhodes Scholarship might have diverted him from that calling, temporarily if not permanently. Styron followed the reminiscence by reading from his recently published novel, *Sophie's Choice*, the section which had been published in *Esquire* and which opens the book, concerning Stingo's short employment at McGraw-Hill in New York City in 1947. Here, also, is a young man who knows he is destined to be a writer. And he, too, fails—fails as a reader for a large publishing house. But, again, the young man accepts his dismissal with a sense of relief, for he knows that now he can go about his proper business of writing books—not teaching, researching, or publishing them.

A comparison of these two stories is instructive: the first purports to be nonfiction, a sketch based on autobiographical fact; the second, fiction, about an imagined character named Stingo. Yet the first obviously has fictional elements. It is an episode remembered thirty-two years after the fact, and embellished for the sake of narrative interest. The second, as Styron has said, is based directly on his own experiences at McGraw-Hill in 1947. Furthermore, much of *Sophie's Choice* is derived from

Styron's experiences in New York during the late 1940s. Most of the characters are based on people Styron knew; and Stingo is hard at work on a first novel which is obviously Styron's first novel, *Lie Down In Darkness* (1951). Nevertheless, *Sophie's Choice* is fiction, and Stingo, for all his resemblance to the author, is a fictional character, not Styron himself. The question is raised, however, as to the distinction in Styron's work between fact and fiction, and, more importantly, why Styron has chosen to base his work so consistently on autobiographical and historical fact. *Lie Down In Darkness* is about a girl Styron knew and courted in his youth. *The Long March* (1953) is about an experience he had when he was called back into the marine corps in 1950. A good deal of *Set This House on Fire* (1960) is derived from his own autobiography, particularly his experiences in Italy in 1952-1953. *The Confessions of Nat Turner* (1967) is based on an actual historical event. The play *In the Clap Shack* (1973) draws on his military experience during World War II; and the novel on which he is presently working, "The Way of the Warrior," is obviously as autobiographical as *Sophie's Choice*.

Of course, one might answer the question by saying that all writers draw on their own experiences or historical record—some only transmute and hide it in their fiction more than others. But in Styron's case, this is not a satisfactory answer. For there are two tendencies in the progress of Styron's career that make the answering of the question crucial to an understanding of his work. First, there is the change from the detached third-person narrator of his first two novels to the first-person narrator of the last three (and the one he is working on now). Styron has said that he came to prefer the first-person narrator because it gives his fiction more immediacy. The second tendency has been to emphasize the fact in the later novels that they are based on real experience, either historical, as in the case of *The Confessions of Nat Turner*, or autobiographical, as in *Sophie's Choice* and "The Way of the Warrior." Our attention has been directed toward this tendency by Styron himself both in the fiction and in his public statements. It is obviously, then, a conscious strategy on his part.

Perhaps the best way to approach the question is to place it in the context of recent developments in the novel. The twentieth century has seen the laws of cause and effect as adequate explanations of the world, fall into disrepute. The reasons for this are numerous; but the main ones are the deterioration of traditional political and social structures; the historical horrors of modern wars—particularly the trench warfare of World War I, the extermination of the Jews by the Nazis, the bombing of Dresden, and of Hiroshima and Nagasaki, the war in Vietnam and the rise of terrorism—which seem to have no efficient causes; and the discovery of scientific indeterminacy, especially in the area of quantum mechanics. The novel has reacted to this situation in a number of ways: expressionism, the Dada movement, surrealism, the anti-novel—all basically retreats from objective reality as we have traditionally known it. For the artists of these movements, the objective world no longer has authenticity. Put simply: it no longer makes sense and therefore cannot be instructive. For them the only coherent world is the world of the individual mind. The most emphatic statement of this attitude was made by the German writer Gottfried Benn: "If this world is your reality, I want none of it. The only reality for me is the aesthetic sphere." Even writers who have continued to work in the realistic mode have been affected by these attitudes. They have often felt it necessary to indicate the fact that their fiction is indeed that—fiction—through the use of framing and distancing devices or by calling attention to the solipsistic nature of their visions.

Styron has resisted these tendencies. His particular use of the first-person narrator has been directed toward creating the illusion of reality—not toward calling the reader's attention to the fact that it is only an illusion. His use of history and autobiography has also been directed toward giving his stories credibility. By calling attention to their basis in real experience, he makes the reader believe in their authenticity; then, when he departs from the real into the realm of imaginative experience, he can carry his reader with him, still believing. This is certainly not a new artistic strategy: it is as old as storytelling itself. And we see the same kinds of strategies in Defoe, at the very beginning of the English tradition of the novel. But this does not mean that Styron is a reactionary, or that he has not been affected by modern experience as profoundly as his contemporaries. It does mean, however, that Styron has not turned away from the objective world as many of his contemporaries have. He still believes that the real world has meaning, that it is authentic, that it can be instructive.

One might ask, then, why Styron does not write historical and autobiographical nonfiction rather than novels. His answer (to Valarie Arms, in 1979) is that fact is too limiting. He insists on the necessity of the imagination's interaction with and transmutation of fact in the pursuit of understanding and truth. Thus Styron indicates not only the importance of the imagination in dealing with experience, but also the importance of the objective world in furnishing the evidence which directs the imagination toward truth—at a time when most are disparaging the

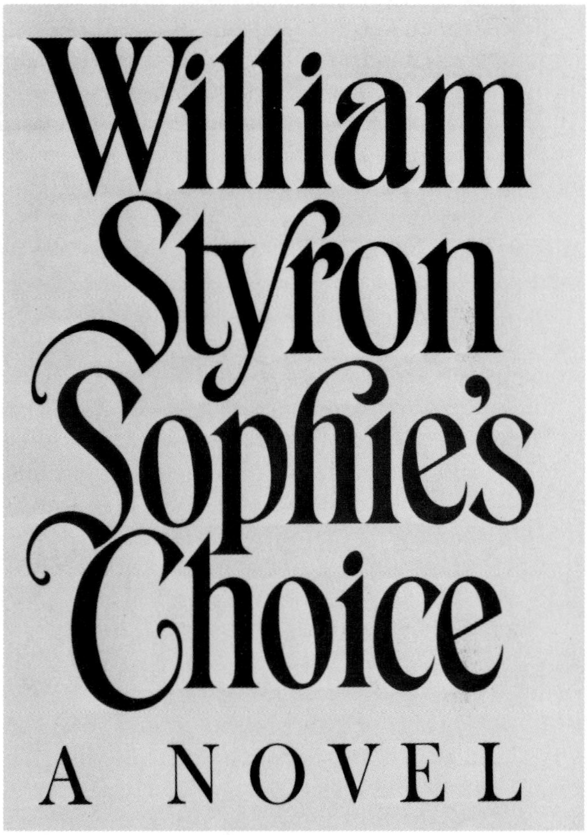

Dust jacket

objective world, because, for them, it is a meaningless chaos. As a traditional novelist, however, Styron has gone beyond his predecessors. Unlike the Southern regionalists, he has projected experience in national and cosmopolitan terms rather than provincial ones. He has consistently dealt with the problems which beset modern man—social and moral disintegration, the apparent absurdity of experience, the inexplicable evils of modern history. And unlike his realist forebears, he has rejected a deterministic view of the world, ruled by cause and effect, as an adequate explanation of existence. His public statements, his fiction, the epigraphs he has chosen to introduce his novels, from such writers as Thomas Browne, John Donne, Rainer Maria Rilke, and Theodore Roethke, all indicate that his attitude toward experience is religious rather than scientific. That is not to say that he believes in a traditional, institutionalized god. It seems that he does not. But he does seem to believe in some moral force, immanent rather than external, which directs and gives meaning to existence. Nowhere are these qualities more apparent than in his latest novel, *Sophie's Choice*.

Sophie's Choice appeared in the spring of 1979 to mixed reviews. Edith Milton, in *Yale Review*, found it "an ambiguous, masterful, and enormously satisfying novel." Paul Gray, the reviewer for *Time*, called it an impressive achievement. Philip Leon, in *Virginia Quarterly Review*, also found it masterful and impressive. In *Atlantic*, Benjamin DeMott said that although the book was serious to the core, it failed to take command of the reader: it was an "over-reaching blockbuster." John Gardner, in *New York Times Book Review*, stated that although it was in many ways a masterful and moving book, he was not persuaded by it: that the devices of the Southern Gothic novel were inappropriate to the treatment of the Holocaust. The anonymous reviewer for the *New Yorker* found it overwrought: its style and lectures reduced Sophie's story to theory. Alvin Rosenburg, in *Midstream*, stated that, from the Jewish point of view, Styron had written not so much a novel of the Holocaust, but a "spoof of the same."

Such diverse responses were to be expected for a book as complex as *Sophie's Choice*. The use of narrative suspension and the sheer length of the book make heavy demands on its readers, particularly those who want Styron to "get on with the story." Because the subject matter, the Holocaust, is one of the most horrifying and perplexing moral problems of modern history, it was inevitable that the novel evoke contradictory responses to Styron's treatment of it. The reaction by a number of blacks to his treatment of slavery in *The Confessions of Nat Turner* had led Styron to expect a similar reaction among Jews to *Sophie's Choice*. So far there has been no concerted attack on the novel (like that of *William Styron's Nat Turner: Ten Black Writers Respond* to the earlier book), but Rosenburg's review in *Midstream* is an example of the type of reaction Styron expected. To attack (or defend) Styron on the grounds of historical accuracy and interpretation, however, is beside the point. It is much like attacking Homer for the historical inaccuracy of his account of the Trojan War, or Shakespeare, for factual errors in his history plays. Although Styron researched the Holocaust as thoroughly as he thought necessary for his purposes, *Sophie's Choice* is a work of fiction and must be approached as such. Styron needed only to provide a credible account of one individual's experience of the Holocaust to satisfy the artistic demands of the story: whether or not it convinces us as a valid and moving projection of human experience is the question, not its historical accuracy.

First, one must see that despite its title, *Sophie's Choice* is Stingo's story, not Sophie's. The controlling vision is his, and all the strands of the novel are important because of their effect on him. He is the center: thus he provides the novel's structural coherence. Furthermore, it is an initiation story. Stingo is just out of college: his formal education is complete; now he must confront the world and come to terms with it. But if we see Stingo as an isolated individual, we miss the great importance of the novel. Stingo, besides being a believable and well-wrought fictional creation, is also representative of a whole generation of Americans. World War II had altered significantly the relationship of the United States to the rest of the world. It had become the world's major power. The lingering isolationist attitudes fostered by the Monroe Doctrine were effectively brought to an end, because the United States had assumed an international position of political and moral responsibility. The war also changed relationships within the country. It accelerated industrial and urban growth and promoted a new mobility of the population. As a consequence, regional differences began to disappear, and life all over the country became more uniform. American experience became national, rather than regional as it had largely been before the war. *Sophie's Choice* is about the period immediately following the war, and it captures in a vital way the process of change American attitudes had to undergo to reflect these new conditions.

From a historical literary point of view, this change is also evident. American literature has been, with few exceptions, a regional and provincial literature. This is especially true of Styron's own Southern literary heritage. Faulkner, as the culmination of that tradition, had indeed given universal significance to the regional experience, but his fiction remained regional to its very core. In important ways, *Sophie's Choice* is about the plight of the post-Faulknerian Southern writer. If he wants to carry the tradition beyond the point reached by his predecessors, he must deal with experience of a wider scope—he must come to terms with the new order of experience forced on (and invited by) Americans in the course of modern history. These are exactly the

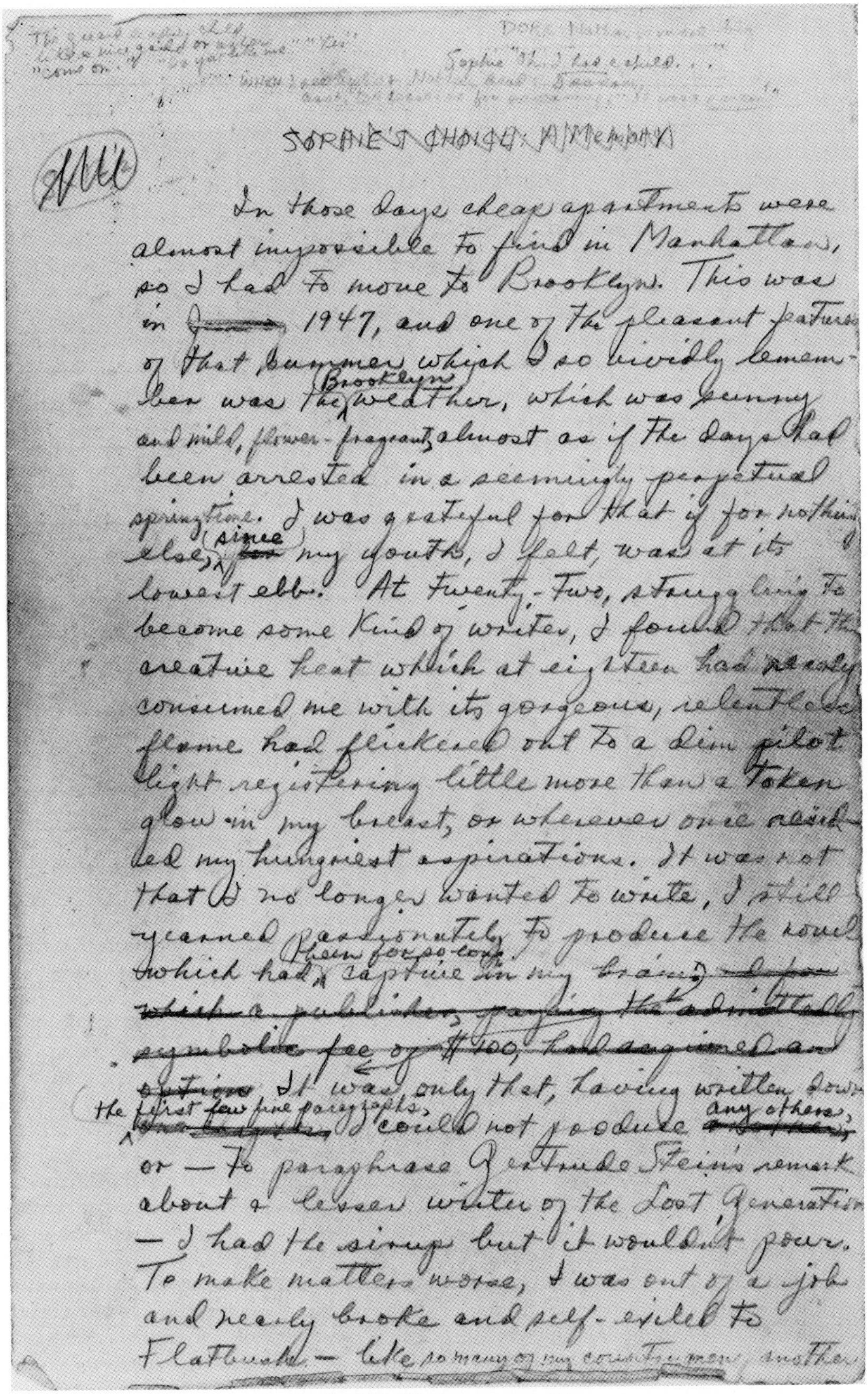

SOPHIE'S CHOICE: A MEMORY

In those days cheap apartments were almost impossible to find in Manhattan, so I had to move to Brooklyn. This was in 1947, and one of the pleasant features of that summer which I so vividly remember was the Brooklyn weather, which was sunny and mild, flower-fragrant, almost as if the days had been arrested in a seemingly perpetual springtime. I was grateful for that if for nothing else, since my youth, I felt, was at its lowest ebb. At twenty-two, struggling to become some kind of writer, I found that the creative heat which at eighteen had nearly consumed me with its gorgeous, relentless flame had flickered out to a dim pilot light registering little more than a token glow in my breast, or wherever once resided my hungriest aspirations. It was not that I no longer wanted to write, I still yearned passionately to produce the novel which had been for so long captive in my brain. ~~and for which a publisher, paying the admittedly symbolic fee of $100, had acquired an option.~~ It was only that, having written down the first few fine paragraphs, I could not produce any others, or — to paraphrase Gertrude Stein's remark about a lesser writer of the Lost Generation — I had the sirup but it wouldn't pour. To make matters worse, I was out of a job and nearly broke and self-exiled to Flatbush — like so many of my countrymen, another

Sophie's Choice, *manuscript*

kinds of problems Stingo faces and wrestles with in *Sophie's Choice*. By leaving the South and coming to New York, he literally chooses a national rather than the regional experience. By taking up residence among the Jews in Brooklyn, he metaphorically enters the international experience, since the Jews are the most extensive coherent cosmopolitan culture. And by confronting the Holocaust through Sophie, and through his reading on the subject, he attempts to understand one of the greatest moral problems of the modern world.

But Stingo has other problems to face as well—the personal ones of a young man entering the adult world. These are primarily social and sexual. His social education is manifested in his relationships with Farrell at McGraw-Hill, Nathan Landau, Sophie, Leslie Lapidus, and the other minor characters who inhabit the book. For Stingo it is primarily a matter of adjusting himself to a new social milieu with different attitudes from the one he had left in the South. His sexual education is determined by his encounters with the Jewish "princess" Leslie Lapidus, the "Southern belle" Mary Alice Grimball, and, most importantly, Sophie. Some reviewers and readers have objected to the heavy sexual emphasis of the novel as being irrelevant to its main concerns. But if we see Stingo as the central figure, they are certainly not irrelevant. His personal social and sexual problems make him come alive as a fictional creation. If Stingo's problems were only of a metaphysical and higher moral nature, his characterization would be incomplete—he would be a flat, theoretical character indeed. As Styron has pointed out, Stingo's masturbatory fantasies and sexual frustrations are just the kind that the sexual and emotional stinginess of the late 1940s and 1950s caused. Through Leslie and Mary Alice, Styron plants the novel solidly in the ground of its times. One must also see that the sexual, emotional, moral, and metaphysical concerns of the novel come together in Sophie. Thus the final consumation of Stingo's sexual drives by Sophie has a structural and metaphorical function. It is through Sophie's revelation of her experiences that Stingo is able to see the magnitude of evil represented by the Holocaust. Through Sophie's (and his own) relationship with the attractive but psychotic Nathan, Stingo learns firsthand about love, hate, and anguish. Since Sophie serves in this way as the vehicle through which Stingo learns about the world on a number of levels, it is appropriate that she initiate him into manhood by giving him his first complete sexual experience.

Besides the digressive sexual episodes concerning Leslie and Mary Alice, there is also the digression about the slave Artiste and the $5,500 bequest that resulted from his sale, part of which supports Stingo while he is working on his novel. To some this material has seemed irrelevant. But seen from Stingo's point of view, it is quite relevant. In dealing with the evil and guilt Sophie reveals in her conversations about her early life and her experiences at Auschwitz, Stingo must reach into his own personal and cultural past for an analogy to help him understand the things she tells him. The closest analogies he can find to the concentration camps and racial hatred of the Nazis are slavery and the whites' hatred of blacks he has witnessed in his own past. The stories of Artiste, of Nat Turner, of Bobby Weed, the modern victim of Southern racial hatred, all help him to understand the Holocaust. The analogies are not exact, but they are close. Moreover, Styron's psychology here is quite valid. Whenever humans encounter the new, they must draw analogies from their own experience to help them understand it. The gestalt furnished by the analogy is necessary before the particularities of the new can be studied and sorted.

It is interesting to note in this connection that Styron originally intended to make "Shadrack," which appeared in *Esquire* (November 1978), part of *Sophie's Choice*. The story establishes the narrator's personal contact with a black who had lived in slavery. But Styron decided that it did not belong—probably because its rather sentimental treatment was inappropriate to the tone of the novel. Also its inclusion would have given too much emphasis to the theme of slavery and, thus, reduced the weight of Sophie's ordeal.

Two other aspects of *Sophie's Choice* need comment here. The first is the characterization of Nathan, which some readers have criticized because the reasons for his "paranoid schizophrenia" are never adequately explained. They fail to see that that is precisely Styron's strategy. Nathan represents on an individual level the "paranoid schizophrenia" that can beset society at large. Nathan's disease is equivalent to that which led to Nazism in Germany. The German culture was intelligent and capable of great love and the creation of great beauty (as represented in the novel by their music)—but they proved also capable of the greatest evil. Nathan, likewise, is intelligent, capable of great love and the appreciation, if not the creation, of great beauty; but he is also capable of hatred, persecution, and destructive evil. Neither Nathan nor German history can be explained by laws of cause and effect. They are part of the inexplicable mystery of existence.

The other aspect that needs comment is the novel's title. It refers on one level to the choice given Sophie at Auschwitz between sending her son or her daughter to the gas chambers. On a more important level it refers to her choice to commit suicide with Nathan. But by extension it also refers to Stingo: he has the choice of whether to reject or accept life, whether to live or die. His symbolic rebirth at the end of the novel on the beach at Coney Island, where he emerges from the sand the children have covered him with while he slept, indicates his decision. He has looked into the face of the Gorgon of life through the mirror-shield of Sophie. He does not understand it, but he now knows its terms. He knows the depths of ugliness and horror and the exquisite heights of beauty and love. And he chooses to accept it: it is a choice available to all men. Thus, through the title and its implications Styron indicates his belief that man is a morally free creature: he is free to choose. He may choose to commit the most horrifying of evils; but he may also choose to work for greatest good. What he must not do is convince himself, as the German Commandant Höss does, that he has no choice. If he does, he has already committed himself to evil.

—*Keen Butterworth*

Periodical Publications:

FICTION:
"My Life as a Publisher," *Esquire*, 89 (14 March 1978): 71-79;
"Shadrack," *Esquire*, 90 (21 November 1978): 82-96.
NONFICTION:
"Auschwitz's Message," *New York Times*, 25 June 1974, p. 37;
"Race Is the Plague of Civilization: An Author's View," *U.S. News and World Report*, 88 (28 January 1980): 65-66;
"Almost a Rhodes Scholar: A Personal Reminiscence," *South Atlantic Bulletin*, 45 (May 1980): 1-6;
"In Praise of Vineyard Haven," *New York Times Magazine*, 15 June 1980, p. 30.

Interviews:

Genevieve Stuttaford, "William Styron," *Publishers Weekly*, 215 (21 May 1979): 10-11;
James Atlas, "A Talk with William Styron," *New York Times Book Review*, 27 May 1979, pp. 1, 18;
Valarie Meliotes Arms, "An Interview with William Styron," *Contemporary Literature*, 20 (Winter 1979): 1-12;
Hillary Mills, "William Styron," *Saturday Review* (September 1980): 46-50.

References:

Benjamin Demott, "Styron's Survivor: An Honest Witness," review of *Sophie's Choice*, *Atlantic*, 244 (July 1979): 77-79;
John Gardner, "A Novel of Evil," review of *Sophie's Choice*, *New York Times Book Review*, 27 May 1979, pp. 1, 16-17;
Paul Gray, "Riddle of a Violent Century," review of *Sophie's Choice*, *Time* (11 June 1979): 86-88;
Philip W. Leon, "A Vast Dehumanization," review of *Sophie's Choice*, *Virginia Quarterly Review*, 55 (Autumn 1979): 740-747;
Edith Milton, Review of *Sophie's Choice*, *Yale Review*, 69 (Autumn 1979): 89-103;
Review of *Sophie's Choice*, *New Yorker*, 55 (18 June 1979): 109-110;
Alvin H. Rosenfeld, "The Holocaust According to Styron," review of *Sophie's Choice*, *Midstream*, 25 (December 1979): 43-49;
Robert Towers, "Stingo's Story," review of *Sophie's Choice*, *New York Review of Books*, 26 (19 July 1979): 12, 14-16.

AN INTERVIEW *with WILLIAM STYRON*

DLB: You said at least ten years ago that you basically dislike writing. Has it grown easier in any way?

STYRON: I have mixed feelings about my own attitude toward it now. On certain levels it is easier. The mechanics of writing have become simpler. Having written so much enables one to write with a certain fluency that one did not have earlier on. However, I think the deeper and more obdurate parts of the active writing are still tough. Reconciling all the complexities of a work of fiction, or of any kind of narrative, is just as difficult as it ever was.

DLB: Do you attempt to read all that's been written about your work?

STYRON: No, I don't. In fact, with my most recent work, *Sophie's Choice*, I really didn't read very many of the reviews at all, pro or con. I find it counterproductive.

DLB: Much recent literary criticism seems to convey the impression that reading a book simply for the pleasure of an absorbing and well-told story is an unworthy pursuit. How much do you think readers and writers are affected by this kind of critical approach?

STYRON: I'm glad you asked that because it's a bothersome question and one that I react rather violently to. Academic criticism of the kind that is involved, among other things, in what they call postmodernism in literature, nouveau roman, and so on, I find very pernicious. And it's very hard to describe my reaction because it's the kind of criticism that hails writers whom I rather admire—John Barth, Thomas Pynchon, and Donald Barthelme—as being the writers it is worthwhile to read. But it embodies a parallel feeling that the kind of literature I and certain other contemporaries write is completely declasse. Plainly such a point of view does affect young and vulnerable readers, and I find that really bad news.

I don't want to sound like a reactionary. I'm not. I have the highest respect for the kind of experimentation that adds to the excitement of fiction. I feel that the great thing about fiction as an art is that it is so mercurial, so fluid, so various. One should be able to read fiction in any mode, asking only that it be intelligent, exciting, poetic, or whatever words you wish to apply to it. And I do think there's a strain of academic critical thought which has become blind to the real joys a good, straightforward narrative can provide.

DLB: Music is very much present in *Sophie's Choice*, as it is in some of your earlier fiction. Has it been a major influence on your work?

STYRON: Yes. I have an unprovable theory, but a strong theory, that most artists have to have a subsidiary art to support their own. Certain poets respond to visual art. For instance, E. E. Cummings was a very good painter and plainly derived a great deal of his talent from another aesthetic response. I know that there have been musicians who've been profoundly involved in literature, such as Berlioz. Music has been a very central fact of my life. I got it from both my mother and my father, who were not professional musicians but passionately devoted amateurs. I always had music in my life as a child and as I grew up. To this day I can't read a note, nor can I pick out a tune on the piano or guitar, but I respond intensely to music and I'm sure it has permeated my work—so much so that I can say with some confidence there would not be a writer by my name had there not existed Bach and Vivaldi and Mozart and Schumann and so on. It's intertwined in the rhythms of my work and my whole weltanschauung and my whole understanding of the natural world. Without it I would not be a writer.

DLB: Are movie plans firming up for *Sophie's Choice*?

STYRON: Yes. It's going very slowly, but I think it's going to be filmed this summer. I don't know anything about the casting except that they have cast for the heroine, Sophie, a Czechoslovakian actress named Magda Vasanyova, whom I saw in a screen test and was very captivated by.

DLB: Will you be involved in the actual making of the movie?

STYRON: No, I really have only a very informal advisory capacity and nothing at all direct in the making of the movie. I'm on very good terms with the director, Alan Pakula. He's doing the script himself, and he often talks to me about it, but I have no legal connections with it whatsoever. It's a friendly and informal thing, and I think he's going to make a reasonably good movie out of it.

DLB: You're working now on the novel that you abandoned to write *Sophie's Choice*. Would you like to comment on it?

STYRON: I would prefer only to say that it's a story about the Marine Corps during the Korean War, and it has to do with certain philosophical matters that I've developed in regard to what militarism means, what the military life is, what the soldier's life is. It's called "The Way of the Warrior." Beyond that I really don't want to go into much detail about it.

DLB: Do you think a lot of good fiction is going to be written in the near future?

STYRON: I'm rather optimistic because I do believe, in a way that I would not have believed even as recently as twenty years ago, that fiction is a very powerful and very widespread art form. I think the experience I've had with *Sophie's Choice* is a good example of what can happen when a work of fiction seizes a certain area of the popular imagination, and I'm not talking about just in this country but also abroad, where even in the Soviet Union it's going to be translated and have apparently a first edition of several hundred thousand copies. I'm saying this only because I believe it demonstrates a need for fiction. When you have an art form that works, there will always be artists coming along to meet the need, so I have high hopes for the future.

—*Jean W. Ross*

John Updike

(18 March 1932-   )

The *DLB* entries on John Updike appear in *Dictionary of Literary Biography*, volume 2, *American Novelists Since World War II* (1978), pp. 484-491, and *Dictionary of Literary Biography*, volume 5, *American Poets Since World War II, Part 2: L-Z* (1980), pp. 327-334.

NEW BOOKS: *The Coup* (New York: Knopf, 1978; London: Deutsch, 1979);

Sixteen Sonnets (Cambridge, Mass.: Halty Ferguson, 1979—250 numbered copies, signed);

Too Far to Go: The Maples Stories (New York: Fawcett Crest, 1979);

Three Illuminations in the Life of An American Author (New York: Targ Editions, 1979—350 numbered copies, signed);

Problems and Other Stories (New York: Knopf, 1979; London: Deutsch, 1980);

Talk from the Fifties (Northridge, Cal.: Lord John Press, 1979—300 numbered copies, signed);

The Chaste Planet (Worcester, Mass.: Metacom Press, 1980—300 numbered copies, signed);

Ego and Art in Walt Whitman (New York: Targ Editions, 1980—350 copies, signed).

Although editors of *Commentary* and disparagers of the *New Yorker* may grimace at the thought, John Updike became a major American author in the 1970s. In the jargon of reviewers and critics, Updike graduated from everyone's writer-to-watch in the 1960s to one of such stature that even John Cheever, the author with whom he is, perhaps unfairly, most often compared, called him "the most brilliant and versatile writer of his generation." Updike had four novels, two collections of short stories, two short-story cycles, one book of poems, one play, and one collection of essays published in the 1970s. The list varies depending upon how one counts *Bech: A Book* (1970) and *Too Far to Go: The Maples Stories* (1979), but by any reckoning it is an extraordinary amount of work, most of it excellent and all of it interesting. Impressive as the list is, it does not include Updike's limited signed publications, which are a bane to collectors and a boon to dealers.

Updike treats his productivity with amusement: "I think everyone would be relieved if I would stop writing. In a world over-supplied with books, why should I keep trying to produce one a year? . . . I write only because it's all I can think of to do." Yet the marvel is not that he writes so much but that his writing is so consistently brilliant. Even readers disappointed by *A Month of Sundays* (1975) and *Marry Me* (1976), surely his two weakest novels, appreciate the quality of the prose. Updike has had so much published that the critical responses to his work are commonplace: the gorgeous prose often overshadows the mundane content; the subject matter is limited to the nostalgia of memory and the domesticity of suburbia; he refuses to address the "big issues of our time." Thus his novel about Africa, *The Coup* (1978), caught most readers by surprise; yet the standard reaction to the book became, in time, another cliche: Updike has moved out of suburbia.

It was an inspired move. Africa has long been for Updike "an invitation to the imagination": "I've always been attracted to hidden corners." Drawing upon that strange land as "the emptiest part of the world I could think of," he made *The Coup* a novel with noticeable though not dramatic differences from his other fiction. The most obvious difference is that the land of Kush is a long way from the lawns of suburbia. In addition, *The Coup* has a comic tone sustained largely by the sardonic observations of the narrator, Colonel Ellellloû. Ellellloû describes Kush, for example, as a constitutional monarchy "with the constitution suspended and the monarch deposed." Among Kush's natural resources, which seem largely to be comprised of drought and desert, is what Ellellou calls "the ample treasury of diseases." Finally, the narrator's conscious manipulation of narrative voice is distinctive in the Updike canon. Colonel Hakim Felix Ellellou, the recently ousted president of Kush, tells of his presidency primarily in the third person even while he is very much aware of the first person who experiences the events. A narrator watching his own presence in the tale, he interrupts his story, for example, to comment on how his manuscript is blurred in places by a wet ring from a glass of Fanta.

Part of the comedy, then, results from Ellellou's distancing himself from himself with the device of third-person narration and yet relying on first person when convenient: "There are two selves: the one who acts, and the 'I' who experiences. This latter is passive even in a whirlwind of the former's making, passive and guiltless and astonished. The historical performer bearing the name Ellellou was no less mysterious to me than to the American press. . . ." The point is that Ellellou writes his story as much to find out who he is, to distinguish public mask from private man, as to explain the coup that forces him to take up his pen. He understands now that the "he" carried the "I" here and there, and that the "I" never knew why but submitted. As a result, the "I" suffers the effects of the "he's" actions. A man of disguises and anonymous travels throughout Kush, "his domicilic policy is apparently to be in no one place at any specific time." Even his languages are "clumsy masks" that "his thoughts must put on."

Ellellou is a mystical leader without pragmatic talent because he believes primarily in "the idea of Kush." Yet one of his problems is that his obsession with his country is but the other side of his distrust of the world which nurtures his determination to burn food offered by bungling America while his people go hungry. A true son of the Third World, he understands how gifts bring men who in turn bring oppression, but his hatred of America is comically undercut by the cliches of revolution in his speeches. In light of the childish rhetoric of the Iranian Revolution, Updike's portrait of the Islamic nationalist is especially interesting. America, for example, is "that fountainhead of obscenity and glut," but in Kush "the land itself is forgetful, an evaporating pan out of which all things human rise into blue invisibility."

The first meeting between Ellellou and a goodwill bureaucrat from America is simultaneously ludicrous and pointed. Updike's two-pronged satire

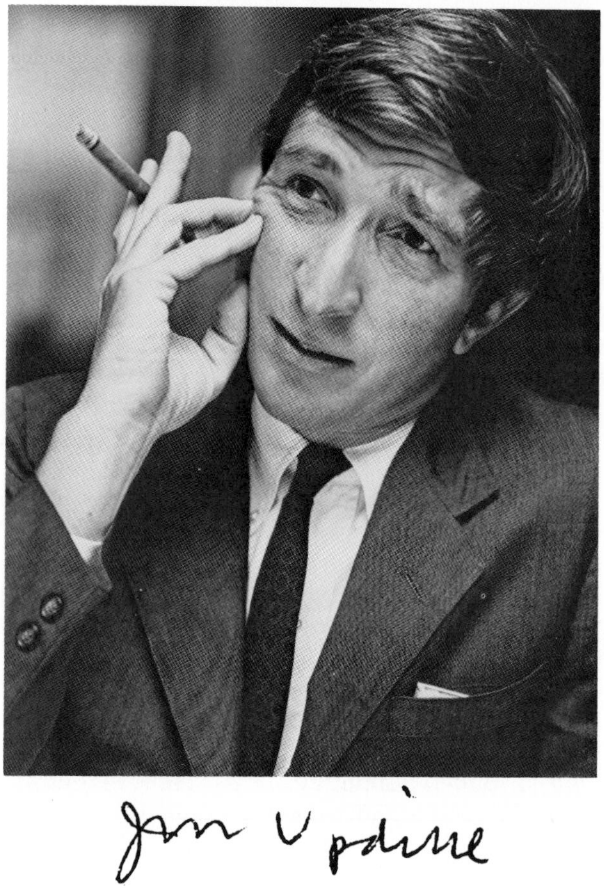

of the misguided American gift of a mountain of Trix cereal and potato chips to drought-stricken Kushites and of the indignant Ellellou, who burns both the junk food and the bureaucrat, is a comic set piece that underscores how America's mindless need to be loved and rigid Third World ideology clash while people starve. One is reminded of Updike's earlier story "I Am Dying, Egypt, Dying" (*Museums and Women*, 1972) with its portrait of the benign, rich American who cannot return the affection he seeks.

The comedy of this ideological sparring match depends upon the speech of the antagonists. Full of pop slang and bureaucratese, the American urges, "These cats are *starving*. The whole world knows it, you can see 'em starve on the six o'clock news every night. The American people want to help. We know this country's socialist and xenophobic." Ellellou's response is little better: "Offer your own blacks freedom before you pile boxes of carcinogenic trash on the holy soil of Kush!"

Updike's control of speech tones and language is so superb in *The Coup* that in one sense language itself is the hero of the novel. Style has always been a primary feature of his fiction, so much so that admirers praise him as a virtuoso while detractors damn him as a wordmonger. In a review of John O'Hara's letters (*New Yorker*, 6 November 1978), for example, Updike distinguishes his work from O'Hara's by his own love of language. Defining language as "a semi-opaque medium whose colors and connotations can be worked into a supernatural, supermimetic bliss," he criticizes O'Hara as "resolutely unmetaphorical, and language seldom led him with its own music deeper into the matter at hand." Style is such an important factor in *The Coup* that many reviewers judge the novel on the basis of their reactions to the language. Charles Truehart argues that Updike's "audacious command and assembly of words" permit him to "ripple" over weaknesses in the narrative. Harold Hayes agrees, claiming that Updike's considerable gift for language results in his "too blissfully" transcending the reality of Ellelloû. Yet Alastair Reid notes that "it is in language that Updike most clearly dramatizes his worlds in collision," and R. Z. Sheppard praises his "Nabokovian touches." This latter point is well made, for Updike pays homage to the master when he names a minor character with one of Nabokov's pseudonyms, Sirin.

Style is the triumph of *The Coup*, the primary means by which Updike makes fun not only of America's need to help despite its vexation by Vietnam and President Nixon but also indirectly of President Carter's fortune in peanuts. Typical of the comic tone is the following comment by one of Ellelloû's advisers when he learns that the national fad of dieting in America has caused a drop in the consumption of peanut butter and a corresponding increase in the exporting of peanuts: "Nothing more clearly advertises the American decline and coming collapse than this imperative need, contrary to all imperialist principles, to export raw materials." The laughter cuts both ways, for American peanuts on the open market threaten Kush's own crop of peanuts, which it must sell to purchase Czech dynamos. Updike understands that the intricacies of shifting political alliances often depend upon the supply of hardly strategic items like peanut oil, so he creates Ellelloû, an African revolutionary educated in America, a leader who despises the United States as a meddling superparanoid, to personify these contradictions which may be ridiculous but which are nevertheless lethal.

Longing to find a mystical cause for Kush's deprivation, Ellelloû travels the country only to collide with his Americanized side in a metropolis of MacDonald's and Coke. On his final journey through Kush, he stumbles into a surprise, a bustling, illegal city named for him. Drugstores sell deodorant ("God sees the soul; men smell the flesh."), women wear miniskirts and halters, and the people go western. Ready capital and comfort undermine Spartan tradition and myth. In this plastic town, with its commitment to upward mobility and declining quality, Ellelloû discovers that *he* is considered the curse on Kush. The coup achieved, he takes refuge as a short-order cook and parking attendant, searching the newspapers for news of himself, before accepting exile in France to write *The Coup*. The last lines reemphasize his dual narrative perspective: "He is writing his memoirs. No, I should put it more precisely: Colonel Ellelloû is rumored to be working on his memoirs."

The Coup is thus a comic fable of a revolution in a country that has nothing to revolutionize. It exposes the idiocies of Third World nationalism while it satirizes the United States as a country that may join the Third World in economic deprivation at a time when "the Arabs have all the capital, the Siberians and the Brazilians all the undeveloped resources, and the Chinese all the ideological zeal. . . ." Black Muslims, prejudiced whites, doublespeak bureaucrats, liberal college students, revolutionary Africans, dull Russians—all are targets for Updike's comic darts. His love for caricatures and parodies, for James Thurber and Max Beerbohm, once manifested in his boyhood desire to draw cartoons for the *New Yorker*, works itself out in *The Coup*.

The African adventure accomplished, Updike returns to suburbia with *Too Far To Go: The Maple Stories*, a collection of stories largely published before but now arranged to form a cycle of tales about Updike's nominees for the typical American marriage, Joan and Richard Maple. Of the seventeen stories collected here, nine were originally published in the *New Yorker*; seven more in *Harper's* ("Your Lover Just Called," "Eros Rampant," and "Sublimating"), *Weekend* ("Waiting Up"), the *New York Times Magazine* ("The Red-Herring Theory"), *Atlantic* ("Nakedness"), and *Playboy* ("Gesturing"); and one, "Divorcing: A Fragment," is published for the first time. Ten of the seventeen have been previously collected. A portrayal of contemporary domestic bewilderment, the Maples' dilemma was also presented by NBC on 12 March 1979 as "Too Far to Go," a television special directed by Robert Geller and starring Blythe Danner and Michael Moriarity.

As a unified cycle of tales, *Too Far to Go* focuses on a married couple struggling with the often hesitating but always insistent downhill glide

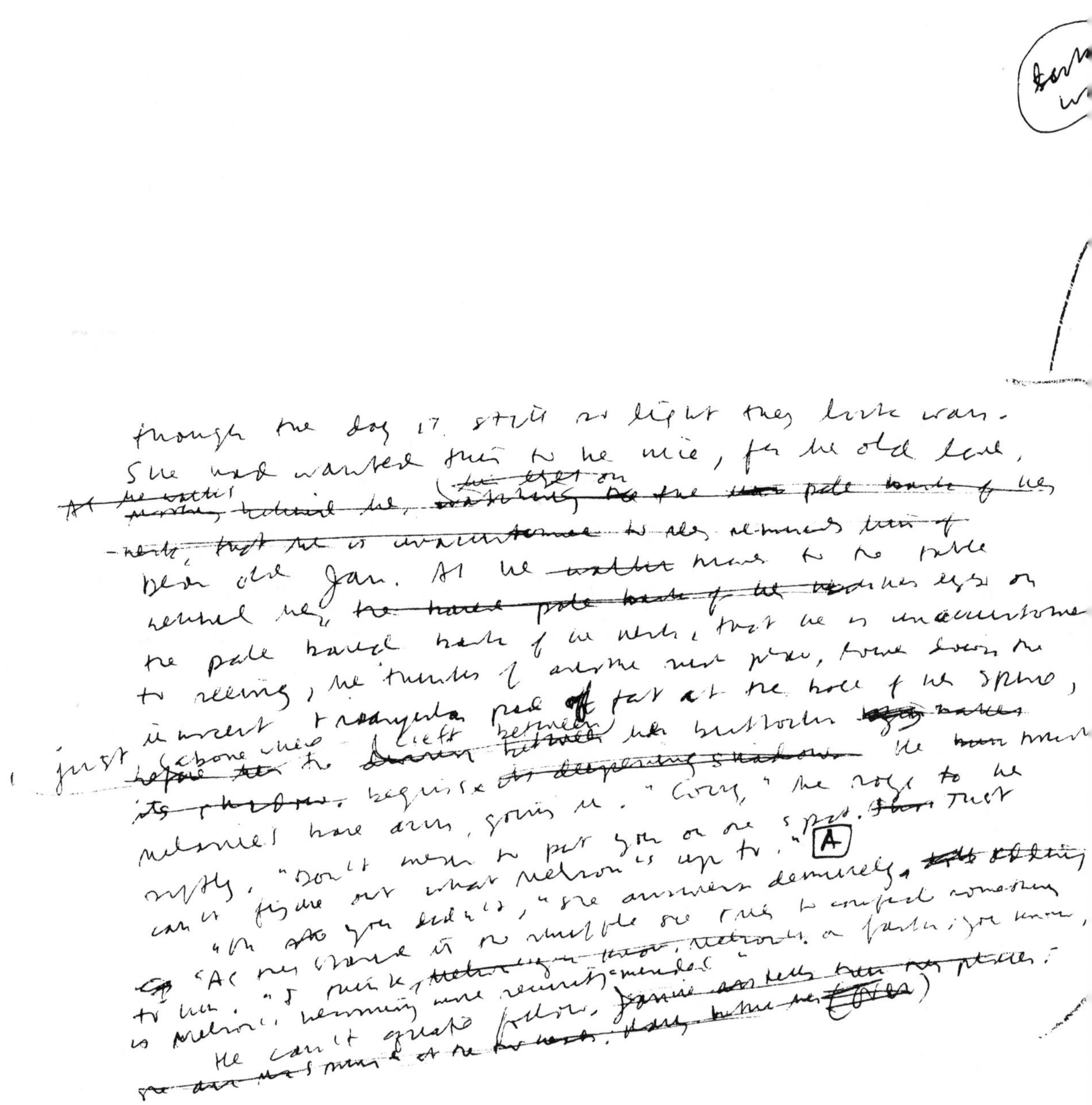

Manuscript pages from a novel in progress

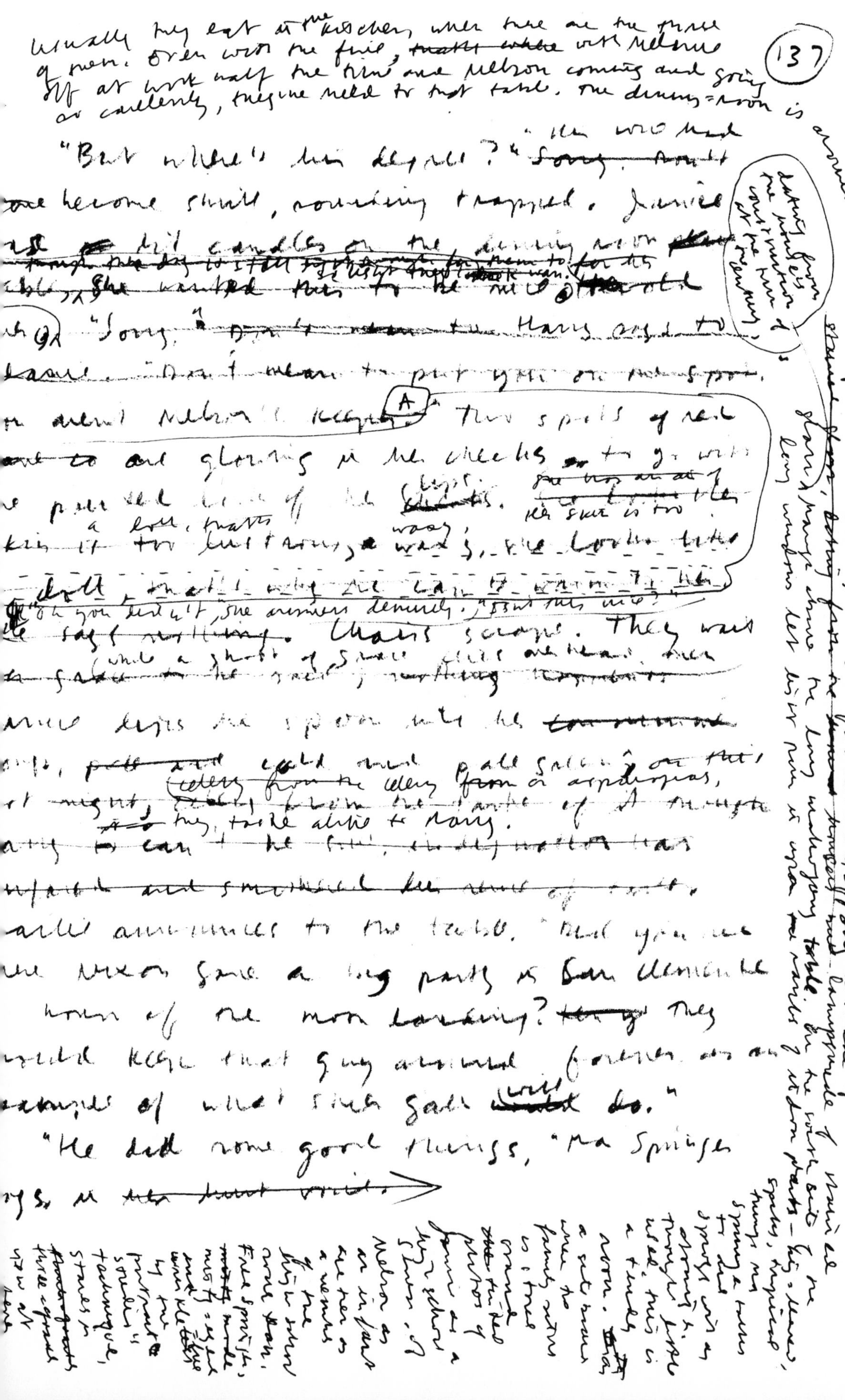
usually they eat at the kitchen, where there are the three of them. Even with the four, with Melanie off at work half the time and Nelson coming and going so carelessly, they've never needed to use that table. The dining-room is

137

"But where's his deposit?" "Sorry" ... voice become shrill, something trapped. Janice has lit candles on the dining room table ...

"Sorry," Harry says ...

... about Nelson's keeping. [A] Two spots of red ... glowing in her cheeks ... a bit, maybe ... her skirt is too ...

"Oh you didn't," she answers demurely. "But this ..."

Harry's scraps. They wait while a ghost of grace flits overhead, then ...

... cold and pale ...

... celery from the celery farm or asparagus, ... they taste alike to Harry.

... announces to the table, "Did you see the Nixon gave a big party in San Clemente in honor of the moon landing? They would keep that guy around forever as an example of what such a man will do."

"He did some good things," Ma Springer says ...

toward divorce. The prose is lucid, the details correct, and the emotion convincing and true. This well-educated, middle-class couple marry in the 1950s, raise children in the 1960s, and divorce in the 1970s, just as Updike published the first Maples story, "Snowing in Greenwich Village," in 1956 and the last one, "Here Come the Maples," in 1978. Although the Maples stories are not autobiography, the relationship between Updike's first marriage and these fictions is more than coincidental. Married to his first wife in 1953, separated from her in 1974, and married to his second in 1977, Updike has transformed the busy years of marriage into the alternative perspective of art. Not at all hesitant to base public fiction on private fact, he explains his extraordinary scrutiny of his own marriage: "In the author's mind it's always loving to try to get some qualities of a person into print—even if it doesn't seem flattering to the person." His first wife apparently agrees. Calling the Maples stories "gratifying," she says, "I've gotten used to being written about."

Too Far to Go chronicles the long decision to say good-bye. Neither husband nor wife acts hastily or melodramatically. Indeed, both resist the final parting despite Joan's despair and Richard's immaturity. When the moment of separation finally comes, a moment they now realize that they have been inching toward for two decades, they discover that their no-fault divorce case resembles their wedding many years ago when they were both young and lovely and when love was bright and new. In "Here Come the Maples," Richard recalls that "his wonder at the white creature trembling beside him" at the wedding ceremony so dazed him that he forgot to seal his vows with a kiss. Now, decades later, standing beside Joan while a judge grants the divorce, Richard is aware of the similarity between domestic ceremonies in church and court, and he does not make the same mistake again: "Joan and Richard stepped back from the bench in unison and stood side by side, uncertain of how to turn, until Richard at last remembered what to do; he kissed her."

This is the final sentence in *Too Far to Go*, and it sears the reader of the entire collection because the buildup of emotion has been insistent and intense. Yet Updike argues in the foreword that the stories should not be read solely as a meditation on sadness: "Though the Maples stories trace the decline and fall of a marriage, they also illumine a history in many ways happy, of growing children and a million mundane moments shared. That a marriage ends is less than ideal; but all things end under heaven, and if temporality is held to be invalidating, then nothing real succeeds. The moral of these stories is that all blessings are mixed. Also, that people are incorrigibly themselves." The motions of change, natural processes, mutability, and death are considerations that lift Updike's tales of the vicissitudes of marriage beyond another trite picture of family crisis. In the beautifully written "Plumbing," Richard senses the relationship between the relative permanence of plumbing pipes and the gradual losses of love that Updike speaks of in the foreword: "My time, his time. His eyes open wide in the unspeaking presence of corrosion and flow. We push out through the bulkhead; a blinding piece of sky slides into place above us, fitted with temporary, timeless clouds. All around us, we are outlasted."

Outlasted they are, despite twenty years of marriage and countless moments of love. As Richard knows, their unhappiness together seems "consecrated," yet they separate with tenderness. Many of Updike's sentences illuminate the baffling recesses of marriage, for his style glitters brightest in his short fiction. Of all the memorable prose, the following comment from "Wife—wooing" summarizes with grace and insight the wisdom gleaned from married life: "Courting a wife takes tenfold the strength of winning an ignorant girl." Richard, unhappily, lacks that strength.

In "The Music School" (*The Music School*, 1966), a story not collected here, Updike writes, "We are all pilgrims faltering toward divorce." Dickie, the Maples' oldest son, does not see why the pilgrimage is so inexorable. In the most moving scene in the book ("Separating"), he, now tearstained and fearstricken, asks his father the crucial question, "Why?" The query cuts Richard to the quick. Facing a darkness that is suddenly grim, he realizes that he has no answer: "*Why*. It was a whistle of wind in a crack, a knife thrust, a window thrown open on emptiness. The white face was gone, the darkness was featureless. Richard had forgotten why." Depicting that one lapse of memory, Updike dissects the breakdown of traditional values that seemed permanent in the 1950s and became baffling in the 1970s. Paul Theroux writes, "Updike is one of the few people around who has given subtle expression to what others have dismissed and cheapened by assuming it is a nightmare." The point is well taken. No American author is currently writing about the mystery of family with such patience and grace as John Updike.

Although "Separating" and "Here Come the Maples" are included in *Problems and Other Stories* (1979), the collection is not organized around a

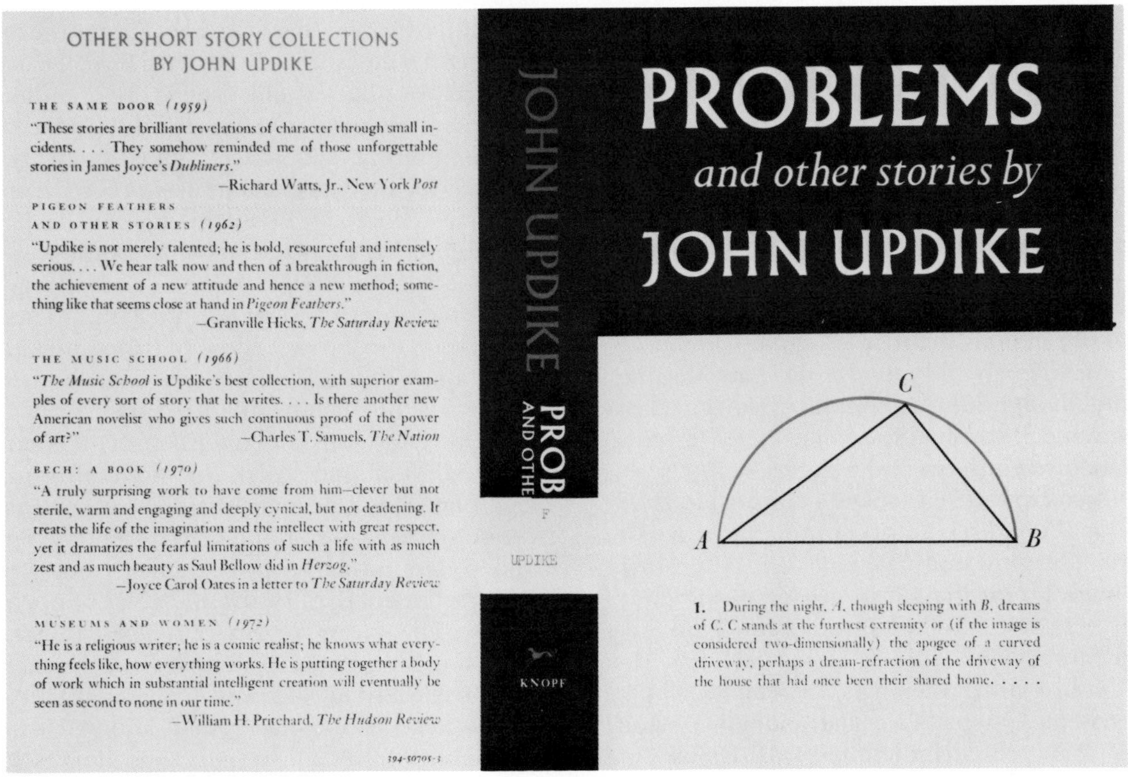

OTHER SHORT STORY COLLECTIONS
BY JOHN UPDIKE
THE SAME DOOR (1959)
"These stories are brilliant revelations of character through small incidents. . . . They somehow reminded me of those unforgettable stories in James Joyce's Dubliners."
–Richard Watts, Jr., New York Post
PIGEON FEATHERS
AND OTHER STORIES (1962)
"Updike is not merely talented; he is bold, resourceful and intensely serious. . . . We hear talk now and then of a breakthrough in fiction, the achievement of a new attitude and hence a new method; something like that seems close at hand in Pigeon Feathers."
–Granville Hicks, The Saturday Review
THE MUSIC SCHOOL (1966)
"The Music School is Updike's best collection, with superior examples of every sort of story that he writes. . . . Is there another new American novelist who gives such continuous proof of the power of art?"
–Charles T. Samuels, The Nation
BECH: A BOOK (1970)
"A truly surprising work to have come from him–clever but not sterile, warm and engaging and deeply cynical, but not deadening. It treats the life of the imagination and the intellect with great respect, yet it dramatizes the fearful limitations of such a life with as much zest and as much beauty as Saul Bellow did in Herzog."
–Joyce Carol Oates in a letter to The Saturday Review
MUSEUMS AND WOMEN (1972)
"He is a religious writer; he is a comic realist; he knows what everything feels like, how everything works. He is putting together a body of work which in substantial intelligent creation will eventually be seen as second to none in our time."
–William H. Pritchard, The Hudson Review
394-50705-3
JOHN UPDIKE
PROB
AND OTHE
UPDIKE
KNOPF
PROBLEMS
and other stories by
JOHN UPDIKE
C
A
B
1. During the night, A, though sleeping with B, dreams of C. C stands at the furthest extremity or (if the image is considered two-dimensionally) the apogee of a curved driveway, perhaps a dream-refraction of the driveway of the house that had once been their shared home. . . .

Dust jacket

single theme as are *Too Far to Go* and *Olinger Stories* (1964). Yet the title of the collection sets a key for the stories which, while not heard in every tale, directs the tone of most. *Problems* is largely a gathering of stories about domestic trauma. Teenaged sons criticize the rest of the family, daughters go away to live with red-bearded harpsichord makers, unhappy fathers forget why, and guilt creeps through suburbia.

Of the twenty-three stories gathered in *Problems*, seventeen were first published in the *New Yorker*. The others appeared in *Oui* ("Transaction"), *Audience* ("Minutes of the Last Meeting"), *Atlantic* ("Augustine's Concubine"), *Playboy* ("Nevada" and "The Faint"), and *Harper's* ("Believers"). Another, "From the Journal of a Leper," has also been published in a limited signed edition by Lord John Press (1978, 300 numbered copies). The stories were written from 1971 to 1978, a period of unsettling family conditions for Updike himself. Although the tales are not autobiography, the specter of domestic loss, of love moving forward from all sides toward a contact barely reached, hovers around most of them. It is not that love is denied but that it is difficult to sustain. Updike supplies a definition in "Love Song, for a Moog Synthesizer": "love must attach to what we cannot help—the involuntary, the telltale, the fatal. Otherwise, the reasonableness and the mercy that would make our lives decent and orderly would overpower love, crush it, root it out. . . ." These stories detail the problems suffered when the threats to love do not stay hidden behind the bedroom wall. As Updike writes in the author's note, "Seven years since my last short-story collection? There must have been problems. . . . the collection as a whole, with the curve of sad time it subtends, is dedicated lovingly" to his children.

The plunge to domestic problems takes place immediately, for in "Commercial," the first story, Updike contrasts the manufactured familial snugness of a television commercial for natural gas with the calm, unspoken, and finally hesitant familial tension of a suburban home. "Commercial" is vintage Updike in many ways. Nothing "happens": a husband, having watched the ad for natural gas late at night, shuffles and urinates, tosses and turns, tries to doze. Yet the reader knows that all is not well: the husband's fretfulness, the wife's sleepiness, the cold room. The little details are exact: the cat's need to go out, the noise of the hampster's wheel. The prose is exquisite: "The sharp bright wires of noise etched on darkness dull down into gray threads, an indistinct blanket." And the saving grace of comedy touches here and there: "GRANDMOTHERLINESS massages her from all sides, like the brushes of a car wash." Tone is finally all. In eight pages, Updike conveys the bewilderment of sadness, the bleakness of loss. The implied question is why can't the long years of the man's domestic life equal the thirty seconds of the commercial's ideal family? The particulars behind this question are not important, but the final word of the story is: "Nothing."

Other stories touch on the unspectacular but felt burden of religious belief in a secular community: the comic allegory "Minutes of the Last Meeting" and the thoughtful "Believers." "How to Love America and Leave It at the Same Time," a lyrical meditation reminiscent of the stories in *The Music School*, contrasts with Nabokov's satire of motelville in *Lolita*: "America is a vast conspiracy to make you happy." The most unusual stories are "Augustine's Concubine," a meditation in defense of the saint's mistress which recalls the less successful "Four Sides of One Story" (*The Music School*), and "The Man Who Loved Extinct Mammals," a comic tale of the relationships between love and extinction which echoes "The Baluchitherium" (*Museums and Women*) and which has in it the following metaphor, an example of Updike's sparkling language: "And the child's voice, so sensible and simple up to this point, generated a catch, tears, premonitions of eternal loss; the gaudy parade of eternal loss was about to turn the corner, cymbals clanging, trombones triumphant, and enter her mind."

But except for the two Maples stories, the finest tale in *Problems* is "The Gun Shop." With touches of *The Centaur* (1963), "Home" (*Pigeon Feathers*, 1962), and "Leaving Church Early" (*Tossing and Turning*, 1977), "The Gun Shop" is a story of fathers and sons filled with the gestures of domestic particulars that Updike at his best details with delicacy and care. In this portrait of generations, in which the unnecessary tension caused by a grandson's disappointment with a malfunctioning .22 rifle is eased into harmony, Updike shows the ambiguities of love that bind grandfather, son, grandson, and surrogate father into a moment of communication free of the embarrassment that close proximity always nurtures.

"The Gun Shop" is not a lyrical meditation as are, say, "Leaves" and "The Music School" (*The Music School*); that is, dialogue, characterization, and pacing carry the burden instead of meditative prose. Yet nuance takes the place of overt drama as Updike writes of the complications encountered when a country-bred but city-dwelling father brings his city-bred son back to the farmhouse of his parents. To the father, the farm is a field of memories and echoes, but to the son it is a promise of experience: he is always permitted to shoot the old Remington .22 following Thanksgiving dinner. Updike focuses on the contrasts between the ways fathers handle sons. Aware that his own tendency to respond to his son's distress with gentle irony is a reaction against his own father's embarrassing habit of good-humored acceptance, the father watches as the grandfather turns the boy's disappointment into the expectation of adventure. The grandfather knows just the man to fix the rifle.

Dutch the gunsmith is the hero of the tale, a man to be admired and loved, for although gruff and grimy and direct, he is an artist with machine tools, a country-bred man who can both repair the firing pin and communicate with a stranger's boy familiar with the language of skiing and golf but not of gun shops. The father is out of place in the shop. Rejecting the grandfather's life of blundering forays and unexpected breakdowns, he has made his life in Boston a model of propriety and caution. He says all the wrong things in the gun shop, makes all the wrong gestures. The grandfather makes most of the right ones. With the insight of a man who is open to the world, the grandfather knows that the grandson is like Dutch and that even the father should have had Dutch for a parent. The rare combination of love and skill emanates from the gunsmith. The story ends with the father remembering his childhood and the son firing the rifle. Pride and relief are heard in the father's final laugh. The irreconcilable tensions between generations of family will never completely dissolve, but for the moment communication offers its balm.

None of these touches is forced, for "The Gun Shop" is a story not of commentary but of reverberation. Nor does the father have an epiphany that promises to narrow the distance between his son and himself. His retort to his wife's comment that he is too hard on the boy shows that the lesson in the gun shop is observed but not absorbed: "My father was nice to me, and what did it get him?" Indeed, the final paragraph suggests that the son is on the verge of his own rebellion. But for the moment, at least, the family holds on, as it does in another story, "Son," where the boy is the family's "visitor" and "prisoner." Fathers always fail their children, who are always beautiful.

It is not at all outrageous to say that *Problems* will eventually be judged as one of the major collections of American short stories published in the twentieth century. John Romano supports this opinion: "*Problems and Other Stories* won't be surpassed by any collection of short fiction in the next year, and perhaps not in the next 10. Its satisfactions are profound, and the proper emotion is one of gratitude that such a splendid artistic intelligence has been brought to bear on some of the important afflictions of our times." Updike remains our foremost family chronicler because he understands that little incidents, grace notes as it were, make up the true drama of a home. The woman in "Nevada" who cries out "that it was nobody's *fault*, that there was nothing he could *do*, just let her *alone*" is a more convincing snapshot of a troubled wife than a dozen descriptions of women who survive on tranquilizers and thoughts of suicide. In this sense, *Problems* is a volume of middle age. Wives' accusations are "moralistic" reflexes, and husbands' responses are full of "predictable mockery." As Updike writes in "The Egg Race," "The stratum of middle age has its insignia, its clues, its distinguishing emotional artifacts." Unlike *The Same Door* (1959) and *Pigeon Feathers*, which focus on the nostalgia felt for a time left far behind with the dogwood tree and youth, this collection is closer to *Museums and Women*, which details the love that lingers after the marriage goes bad. Not every story is about family, and not every story is about loss, but the fact remains that *Problems* reemphasizes Updike's move from pastoral Olinger, Pennsylvania, to suburban Tarbox, Massachusetts. He took this step in his fiction a long time ago, of course. The difference is that whereas in *Museums and Women* he occasionally glances back over his shoulder at the tranquil, "voluptuous" 1950s, at a time "when everyone was pregnant," in *Problems* his stories document the plunge into middle age when wives and husbands finally separate, when children unexpectedly grow up, when "the soul grows calluses," and when guilt, oddly, both lacerates and soothes.

—*Donald J. Greiner*

Other:

Introduction to *Loving, Living, Party Going*, by Henry Green (New York: Penguin, 1978), pp. 7-15;

Introduction to *Sanatorium under the Sign of the Hourglass*, by Bruno Schulz (New York: Penguin, 1979), pp. xiii-xix;

Afterword to *Memoirs of Hecate County*, by Edmund Wilson (Boston: Nonpareil, 1980), pp. 449-459.

Periodical Publications:

"Through the Mid-Life Crisis with James Boswell, Esq.," *New Yorker* (6 February 1978): 102-110;

"Walt Whitman: Ego and Art," *New York Review of Books* (9 February 1978): 33-36;

"Pinter's Unproduced Proust Printed," *New Yorker* (20 February 1978): 129-133;

"Layers of Ambiguity," *New Yorker* (27 March 1978): 127-133;

"One Writer's Testimony," *National Review* (26 May 1978): 641;

"Advancing over Water," *New Yorker* (31 July 1978): 72-78;

"Tote That Quill," *New Yorker* (14 August 1978): 94-98;

"Czarist Shadows, Soviet Lilacs," *New Yorker* (11 September 1978): 147-158;

"Saddled with the World," *New Yorker* (23 October 1978): 176-182;

"The Doctor's Son," *New Yorker* (6 November 1978): 200-214;

"Fish Story," *New Yorker* (27 November 1978): 203-206;

"Green Green," *New Yorker* (1 January 1979): 58-64;

"Lem and Pym," *New Yorker* (26 February 1979): 115-121;

"To the Tram Halt Together," *New Yorker* (12 March 1979): 135-144;

"Un Pé Pourrie," *New Yorker* (21 May 1979): 141-144;

"The Cuckoo and the Rooster," *New Yorker* (11 June 1979): 156-161;

"Mixed Reports from the Interior," *New Yorker* (2 July 1979): 89-94;

"A Feast of Reason," *New Yorker* (30 July 1979): 85-88;

"Jake and Lolly Opt Out," *New Yorker* (20 August 1979): 97-102;

"Bruno Schulz, Hidden Genius," *New York Times Book Review*, 9 September 1979, pp. 1, 36-39;

"An Old-Fashioned Novel," *New Yorker* (24 December 1979): 95-98;

"From Fumie to Sony," *New Yorker* (14 January 1980): 94-102;

"The Bear Who Hated Life," *New Yorker* (25 February 1980): 127-134;

"Journeyers," *New Yorker* (10 March 1980): 150-159;

"A Cloud of Witnesses," *New Yorker* (7 April 1980): 143-149;

"Disaffection in Deutsch," *New Yorker* (21 April 1980): 130-142;

"Vignettes of Martha's Vineyard: Going Barefoot,"

New York Times Magazine, 15 June 1980, pp. 29-30;

"Imagining Things," *New Yorker* (23 June 1980): 94-101;

"Dark Smile, Devilish Saints," *New Yorker* (11 August 1980): 82-89.

References:

James Atlas, "John Updike Breaks Out of Suburbia," *New York Times Magazine*, 10 December 1978, pp. 60-76;

Harold Hayes, "Updike's African Dream," *Esquire* (19 December 1978): 27-29;

Alastair Reid, "Updike Country," *New Yorker* (25 December 1978): 65-69;

John Romano, "Updike's People," *New York Times Book Review*, 28 October 1979, pp. 1, 44-45;

R. Z. Sheppard, "White Mischief," *Time* (18 December 1978): 90;

Paul Theroux, "A Marriage of Mixed Blessings," *New York Times Book Review*, 8 April 1979, p. 34;

Charles Truehart, "Updike Fashions an African Mask," *Chronicle of Higher Education* (11 December 1978): R7-8.

Kurt Vonnegut, Jr.

(11 November 1922-   )

The *DLB* entries on Kurt Vonnegut, Jr., appear in *Dictionary of Literary Biography*, volume 2, *American Novelists Since World War II* (1978), pp. 493-508, and *Dictionary of Literary Biography*, volume 8, *Twentieth-Century American Science-Fiction Writers, Part 2: M-Z* (1981).

NEW BOOKS: *Jailbird* (New York: Delacorte/Seymour Lawrence, 1979; London: Cape, 1979);

Sun Moon Star, by Vonnegut and Ivan Chermayeff (New York: Harper & Row, 1980);

Palm Sunday (New York: Delacorte/Seymour Lawrence, forthcoming 1981).

Speaking of the problems of revitalizing himself as a writer, in a 1976 interview Kurt Vonnegut told Robert Short: "I think it's just Puritanism now that keeps me writing, as I simply . . . I don't know, whatever I was born to do I completed after I completed *Slaughterhouse-Five*. After that, I just had to start a new career somehow, you know. All I say is that I have a feeling of *completion* after that. . . . It's just something was finished when I finished that." This was just before the publication of *Slapstick* (in October 1976) and before work on a subsequent new novel which eventually emerged as *Jailbird*. The novel-in-progress called "Spit and Image," noted in *Dictionary of Literary Biography*, volume 2, appears to have been based on the story mentioned in *Jailbird* (about being in heaven with his father, who has chosen to spend eternity as a nine-year-old boy), but this plot line never matured as a finished novel. Recent years have been busy for Vonnegut; his literary career has been recharged, and he has undertaken a number of other activities.

The focus of Vonnegut's "new career" has been New York City, where he lives with his second wife, photographer Jill Krementz, whom he married in November 1979. He finds stimulation in the city, often enjoying its architectural treasures with an eye trained by his architect father. New York figures in *Jailbird* as much as Vonnegut's native Indiana does in some of his earlier books. With his literary reputation established, he has become something of a celebrity, a sought-after name. He made appearances in behalf of the 1980 presidential campaign of Rep. John Anderson, for instance, and his feature, "How to Write with Style," presented nationally in a magazine advertisement, was applauded by English teachers.

Even Vonnegut's doodles have undergone artistic growth. He calls his drawings "felt tip calligraphs." He told *Horizon* (October 1980), "The human face is the most interesting of all forms. So I've just made abstracts of all these faces. Because that's how we go through life, reading faces very quickly." He reports having sold one of his drawings for $850—"That was great. It was my first sale."—and held a one-man exhibition at the Margo Feiden Galleries in New York in October 1980.

One other venture saw a kind of return to Indiana—to the Rosewater County of *God Bless You, Mr. Rosewater* (1965). He presented the stage rights to this novel to his daughter Edith as a birthday present, and she produced a musical version of it. That this novel would lend itself to adaptation as a *musical* surprised many, but the outcome, with book, lyrics, and direction by Howard Ackman and music by Alan Menken, was delightful. With Frederick Coffin in the title role and Janie Sell as Sylvia, the play opened at the Entermedia Theatre, New York on 11 October 1979, to generally favorable reviews, but it had trouble attracting the kind of audiences that might have taken it to Broadway.

A different kind of New York performance was Vonnegut's delivering a Palm Sunday sermon at Saint Clement's Episcopal Church on 30 March 1980 (it was reprinted in the *Nation*, 19 April 1980). In it he described himself as "a Christ-worshipping agnostic" who is "enchanted by the Sermon on the Mount." He took as his text John 12, ending at "The poor you always have with you, but you do not always have me." This Vonnegut interprets as a divine black-humor joke "which allows Jesus to remain civil to Judas, but to chide him about his hypocrisy": "Judas, don't worry about it. There will still be plenty of poor people left after I'm gone." The Sermon on the Mount and worrying about the poor are both central to Vonnegut's newest novel.

Jailbird, published in 1979, superficially resembles a return to "mainstream Vonnegut," sharing more with the first five novels than with those which have followed *Slaughterhouse-Five* (1969). The novel, or its prologue, even begins with the announcement, "Yes—Kilgore Trout is back again." It echoes *God Bless You, Mr. Rosewater* in its heavy emphasis on economics and *Mother Night* (1962) in its prison-confession personal narration. In fact, however, its characteristics tie it to the later period and point toward a process of continuing evolution in Vonnegut's use of the novel form.

The prologue recalls a day in 1945 when Vonnegut, freshly returned from the European war, met with his father, his Uncle Alex, and a union officer named Powers Hapgood to discuss his finding work with a union. In 1927 Hapgood had led demonstrations at the executions of Nicola Sacco and Bartolomeo Vanzetti, anarchists who ended up being sent to the electric chair for crimes to which another man confessed. Sacco and Vanzetti are woven through the novel as symbols of the injustices inherent in our economic system, while Hapgood serves as the prototype for one of the novel's fictional characters, Kenneth Whistler, who affirms the Sermon on the Mount as the basis of an answering morality.

The second half of the prologue moves from the reality of actual history to the creation of a fictional reality as the premise of the novel. It tells the story of the McCones, a family of rich industrialists. Alexander McCone selects his chauffeur's son as a protege, offering him wealth, privilege, and a Harvard education. To fit the part, the boy's name is changed from Walter Stankiewicz to Walter Starbuck. He becomes the central character and narrator of the novel and the jailbird of the title.

While at Harvard, Starbuck turns toward socialism and the example of Kenneth Whistler and consequently loses McCone's patronage. His career as a government bureaucrat crumbles soon after he exposes his friend Leland Clewes to the House Committee on Un-American Activities as a former Communist. Years later, when he becomes President, former committee member Richard Nixon calls Starbuck to the White House to serve as Special Adviser on Youth Affairs. Subsequently a trunk stowed in Starbuck's subbasement office turns out to be filled with cash, and he goes to jail as a Watergate co-conspirator.

Although it is punctuated by constant flashbacks which relate the past, the plot begins with Starbuck's release from jail. His unpromising start as a free man is transformed by a fairy godmother—in a modern variant of the medieval knightly test of kindness to an ugly hag. A decrepit shopping-bag lady who befriends him on a New York street corner turns out to be Mary Kathleen O'Looney, a sweetheart from his Harvard days. More than that, Mary Kathleen in fact is Mrs. Jack Graham, reclusive owner of the RAMJAC Corporation, the largest conglomerate in the country. The reunion is short-lived as Mary Kathleen soon dies after a traffic accident, but for two years Walter manages to conceal her death and to direct RAMJAC. The discovery of what he has done sends Starbuck back to jail, where, at sixty-six, he writes the memoir that becomes this novel. RAMJAC, having been left by Mary Kathleen to the people of the United States, is dismantled by the government and sold off to foreign-owned or Mafia-controlled conglomerates.

As is typical of Vonnegut's novels, the mosaic of vignettes, jokes, sketches, and analyses supersedes the importance of a story line per se. Vonnegut observed this direction in his fiction in the 1976 interview with Robert Short: "There'll be more and more to complain about in my fiction. People will say it's not fiction any more, it's editorializing. And, you know, the stories are getting sketchier and sketchier and sketchier. But I like stories because they allow you to digress. I'm not capable of logic, really a paragraph to paragraph logic. And so the story form allows me to just make statements that I know intuitively are true. I can't begin to buttress with arguments." In part, as Vonnegut says, these novels are less narrative and more editorial in nature. Also, like the "nonfiction novel" (for example, Truman Capote's *In Cold Blood* or Norman Mailer's *Armies of the Night*), which creates a fiction out of a "real," historical event, his novels acknowledge the unreality of the factual and the inevitability of reality's being given artistic form in its recounting. At the same time, there is recognition of the fictiveness of fiction. Reader and writer both know that while a novel is being told as if it were reality it remains a fiction. Our era finds itself uncomfortable with artifice presented as reality, so the sculptor in metal may leave girders showing to reveal the true artistic medium. Vonnegut exposes authorial presence and acknowledges the fictiveness of his novels most dramatically by the inclusion of himself in *Slaughterhouse-Five*—"That was me"—and his direct involvement as character-author in *Breakfast of Champions*.

In those terms, *Jailbird* is an interesting development. It makes a curious blend of fact and fiction, of public realism and private imagination. It is almost like *Slaughterhouse-Five*, a story framed with an autobiographical introduction and conclusion. *Jailbird* begins factually, recalling a period in Vonnegut's own life, but the prologue then moves into an event—the "Cuyahoga Massacre"—which, while fictional, resembles historical events and does itself become a premise of the novel which follows. Similarly, at the end of the novel, an index lists both real and fictional characters without distinction. The novel between the prologue and the index ranges from the fanciful stories of Kilgore Trout to major historical events like the Nuremberg trials or Watergate.

The juxtaposition of these elements instructs. It emphasizes how some historical events are bizarre beyond imagining (truly fact stranger than fantasy), while the fantastic, no matter how far-fetched, may be the vehicle to Vonnegut's "editorializing" or making moral observation on the realities of daily existence. One example is the story of the planet Vicuna (named after an actual animal now threatened with extinction) where the people learn to extract time from their environment for use as a fuel, overindulge themselves, and literally run out of time as their planet disintegrates. The lesson for the fuel consumers of Earth could not be more obvious. So the documentary (the use of actual historical events and persons) and the fantastic (Trout-style stories, fanciful characters) interact as effectively here as they do in *Slaughterhouse-Five*.

The technique serves Vonnegut's themes well. In *Jailbird* the central theme concerns economics—the effects of an economic system on a nation and the individuals within. As elsewhere in

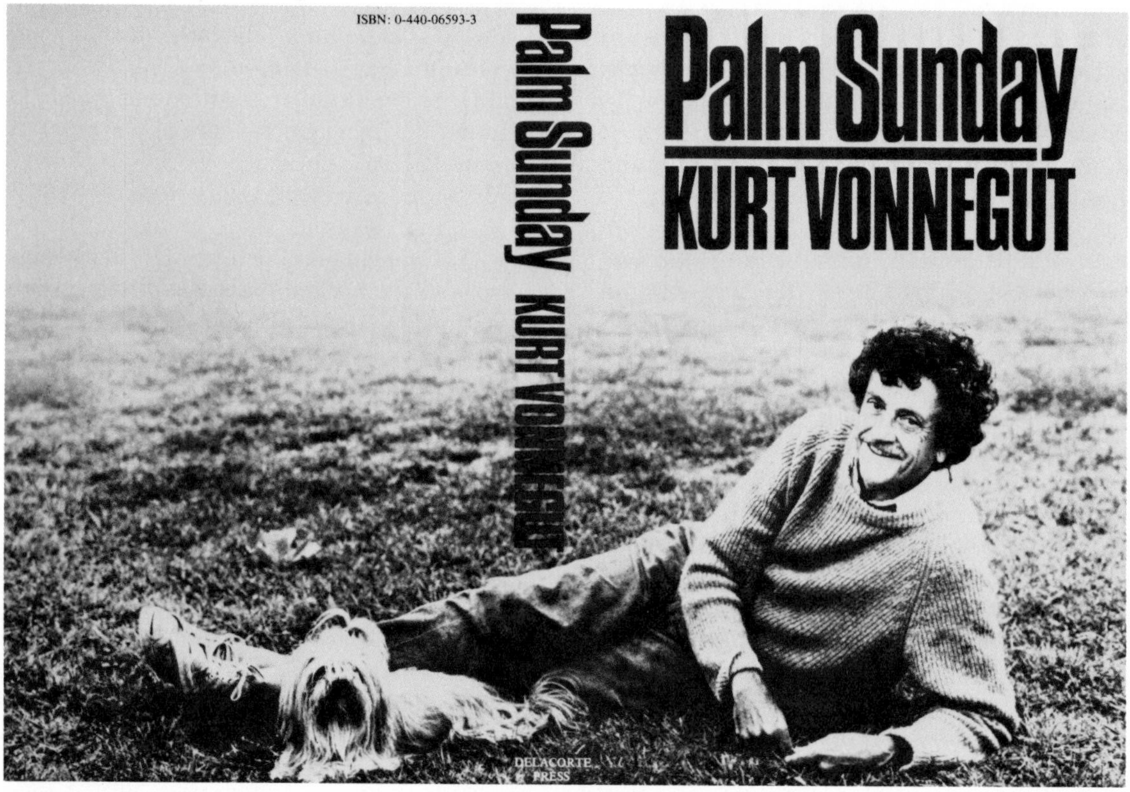

Dust jacket

his novels (especially *God Bless You, Mr. Rosewater*), he examines the politics and economics which precede and follow the Great Depression, that event which transformed the fortunes of his family and left a lasting impression on Vonnegut. All the documentary elements, like the Sacco and Vanzetti executions, authenticate the context the novel creates. Even the years are capitalized and characterized—"Nineteen-hundred and Twenty-nine wrecked the American economy"—like people who shape events and help fix the inexorability of life. The times themselves have personalities which we cannot escape, so that the 1930s can persuade Starbuck to embrace communism and the 1950s can persecute him for it.

Once again, Vonnegut's universe seems almost mechanistic and devoid of free will. The individual remains powerless in the face of uncontrollable forces, taking comfort from minor victories, like Starbuck's last consolation: "At least I don't smoke anymore." Mary Kathleen assembles the largest conglomerate, yet her attempt to redistribute wealth fails. Government and corporations alike seem fixed in their established courses, becoming part of an undeviating cosmos rather than human instruments to contend with it. People are left to face life as they might play a chess game, asking the questions *Jailbird*'s players taunt each other with: "Have you played this game before?" "Is this a trap?"

Yet Vonnegut does offer faint rays of hope, suggestions of alternative. His retrospective on the Depression is tinged with nostalgia because he believes that then there was a sense of brotherhood: unions were run by worker-idealists not Mafia goons, and communism, not yet discredited, had offered many hope. He shows that the Sermon on the Mount asserts values which, if embraced, could change things. It leads Powers Hapgood in real life and Kenneth Whistler in fiction to devote themselves to the aid of the unjustly deprived. These men put the ideals they gained from their Harvard educations to practice; most of the many other Harvard men in the book are "the brightest and best" who become servants to, or pawns of, the political and economic system.

Without reflection and change our society remains one where the pathetic shopping-bag lady coexists with the conglomerate. A central symbol in the book is that of the dining room of the Hotel Arapahoe, to which Walter goes during the Depression. Restaurant and hotel are under separate control; the hotel has become derelict while within it the restaurant glitters affluently. Again a Vonnegut fantasy "editorializes" on the cruel disparities of real life.

How does Watergate fit into this? Vonnegut has always been topical, and perhaps this story is in part a commentary on all the self-justifying books written by Watergate jailbirds. Starbuck, of course, does not try to justify himself even though he seems to have been, like so many of Vonnegut's protagonists, "a victim of a series of accidents." Even while Vonnegut obviously sees Watergate as a frightening aberration, *Jailbird* suggests it is almost inevitable in a system where governments, agencies, and politicians—like corporations, divisions, and company officers—seek endlessly expanded power without due regard for human welfare.

In the telling of this story, many familiar Vonnegut touches remain. Sex and romance do not fare well: Starbuck has a happy but short marriage and appears mostly on his own. Kindness to the unlovable, decency, and human compassion are affirmed. Like many of his fictional predecessors, Starbuck has an unusual size (tiny) and moments when he is threatened with craziness. And, as in *The Sirens of Titan, Cat's Cradle, God Bless You, Mr. Rosewater*, and elsewhere, there is a two-men-one-woman triangle, this time with Starbuck, Leland Clewes, and Mary Kathleen.

These familiar touches survive the continuing evolution in Vonnegut's fiction. Looking back at his first two novels from the last three we see that plot and narrative have declined in importance but that the moral and social commentaries have become overt and frequent. Whereas the early works made the fictional realistic, even lending plausibility to fantasy and science fiction, the newer novels set the two elements—the real and the fictive, the documentary and the fantastic—side by side. They are juxtaposed, not blended.

There are other changes in pattern, too. The later novels may end in dissolutions—Dwayne Hoover's rampage in *Breakfast of Champions*, heavy gravity's causing civilization to collapse in *Slapstick*, RAMJAC's fragmentation in *Jailbird*—but not the apocalyptic cataclysms that culminate in the Dresden fire-bombing of *Slaughterhouse-Five*. Similarly, the personal crisis or breakdown of the protagonist which accompanies the public one in earlier works is muted. *Jailbird* shows fewer signs of strain or despondency in its author than the previous two novels. It is a more outward-looking book, concerned with social interaction rather than with psychological struggle.

Since *Jailbird*, Vonnegut has written the text for a children's book called *Sun Moon Star*, published by Harper & Row in fall 1980. Accompanying the striking color illustrations by Ivan Chermayeff, it is a Christmas story recounting the first visual perceptions of the baby Creator of the Universe.

In addition, he has completed a book of essays, *Palm Sunday,* to be published by Delacorte/Seymour Lawrence Press in spring 1981. This book incorporates a number of previously published pieces, notably his self-interview for the *Paris Review,* his short story "The Big Space Fuck," and his Palm Sunday sermon as delivered at Saint Clement's in 1980. Contributions by other hands include "An Account of the Ancestry of Kurt Vonnegut, Jr.," by his uncle, John Rauch, two songs by the Statler Brothers, a letter by his daughter Nanette, and a speech by his great-grandfather, Clemens Vonnegut. These, along with many other letters, book reviews or introductions, speeches, and even a musical script, are linked together by what he calls "connective tissue." These commentaries seem a logical outgrowth of the conversational introductions to Vonnegut's later novels and read much like them. The book is Vonnegut's most complete autobiographical statement to date, revealing more of his life and background than anything previous, yet it is "complete" primarily in the breadth of topics on which it reveals his thinking. *Palm Sunday* is a treasure trove for Vonnegut devotees, but its humor and thoughtfulness, applied with characteristic freshness to so many aspects of contemporary life, should engage a wider audience.

—Peter J. Reed

References:

Charles B. Harris, *Contemporary American Novelists of the Absurd* (New Haven, Conn.: College and University Press, 1971), pp. 51-75;

Jerome Klinkowitz, "Kurt Vonnegut, Jr.," in his *Literary Disruptions: The Making of a Post-Contemporary American Fiction* (Urbana: University of Illinois Press, 1975), pp. 33-61;

James Lundquist, *Kurt Vonnegut* (New York: Ungar, 1977);

Clark Mayo, *Kurt Vonnegut: The Gospel from Outer Space* (San Bernardino, Cal.: Borgo Press, 1977);

Robert Short, *Something to Believe In: Is Kurt Vonnegut the Exorcist of Jesus Christ Superstar?* (New York: Harper & Row, 1976).

Robert Penn Warren

(24 April 1905-   )

The *DLB* entry on Robert Penn Warren appears in *Dictionary of Literary Biography,* volume 2, *American Novelists Since World War II* (1978), pp. 513-524.

NEW BOOKS: *Now and Then: Poems, 1976-1978* (New York: Random House, 1978);

Being Here: Poetry 1977-1980 (New York: Random House, 1980);

Robert Penn Warren Talking: Interviews, 1950-1978, ed. Floyd C. Watkins and John T. Hiers (New York: Random House, 1980).

RECENT AWARDS: Harriet Monroe Prize for Poetry, 1977; Pulitzer Prize for *Now and Then: Poems: 1976-1978,* 1979; Presidential Medal of Freedom, 1980; Common Wealth Award, 1980.

Robert Penn Warren is perhaps the greatest living literary figure in the United States. He is still active in the fields of criticism and poetry, and in both continues to be influential. On the whole, however, Warren appears to be most interested in poetry, an area of literary endeavor in which his preeminence remains unquestioned and continues to grow. Janis Starcs, for example, commenting on *Being Here* (in *Streets,* November 1980), remarks that Warren's poetry, despite shortcomings, is "preferable to the feeble navel-gazing so prevalent today." She concludes, "May he continue writing for many more years," a wish no doubt shared by all interested in the development of American poetry.

Being Here (1980) is intended by Warren to be a "shadowy" biography, something of a modern Seven Ages of Man. Whatever biographical significance one is tempted to read into the book, however, must be tempered by the realization that Warren is attempting to provide an overview of the human condition and to explicate, or mirror, the perplexities of existence in a world in which belief in God has faded. Warren characterizes himself as a "yearner," suggesting that although he does not believe in God, he does believe that man must work out his own code by which to interpret his life and the things around him, a belief expounded in several of his novels. In his view, man must come face to face with a reality stripped of both God's benign or malevolent intentions and the Romantic's pathetic fallacy.

Despite whatever difficulties man may face in his existence, Warren does not counsel despair or state that life is not worth living. Indeed, it is the recollection of life that is the impetus of Warren's book, and if the poems are not recollections in tranquility, they are not, on the other hand, the recollections of a man ignorant about life or of a pessimistic man who despairs of ever knowing. Certain things in this life are imponderable: "What tongue knows the name of Truth? Or Truth to come?" Warren asks in "What Is the Voice that Speaks?" He cannot answer this question but he knows how to approach the dilemma his lack of knowledge poses: "All we can do is strive to learn the cost of experience." It is essential, Warren asserts, to learn whatever answers one can.

A rich, complex irony has always been one of the distinguishing marks of Warren's writing, and *Being Here* exemplifies this aspect of his craft. Warren says in "Afterthought" that the idea underlying the whole book is, "As with question and answer, fiction may often be more deeply significant than fact." He continues, as an echo of Wallace Stevens: "Indeed, it may be said that our lives are our own supreme fiction." One of the ironies Warren repeatedly explores is why we remember what we do remember—and what to make of both the event remembered and its significance, if it has any at all. "Recollection in Upper Ontario, From Long Before," for example, opens with a question, "Why do I still wake up and not know?" The perplexity arises from an accident or murder (the poet is never sure which) he is presumed to have witnessed years before as a youth. Even now, he can hear the train whistle and see Mag and Zach struggling on the tracks. The only indisputable truth that has ever emerged from this incident was summed up years before by Zach: Warren at least had "enough sense / To haul-ass afore the durn coroner come." Despite the vividness of the incident in memory, the poet still cannot decide what to make of it, for the last line of the poem is, "Or what did I see?"

Whatever the function of nature in man's experience, Warren argues repeatedly that the natural world is not a sympathetic or reliable guide to interpreting human life and that man's affairs are a matter of indifference to the rest of creation. Only man's pride or ignorance allows him to impute to the natural world any concern with his comings and goings. In "Recollection in Upper Ontario, From Long Before," the owl and the loon figure prominently, but not as creatures who will help Warren interpret what he has seen and experienced by the railroad tracks. The loon "Bursts out laughing again at his worn-out / Joke," and the owl still repeats

> his same old gargle of question,
> The question he ought long back to have answered,
> But asks just for fun.
> Or to make your conscience ask if it's you who—*who-who*—
> Did whatever it was.

Having thus postulated that these voices of nature seem to probe man's affairs, Warren promptly corrects the impression he has created, for it is just his own mind making up their interest in man: "no owl speaks yet, no loon." The role of nature is just another joke man plays on himself. When the loon does finally cry, it merely awakens Warren from his dream, after which "Stars faded. That was all."

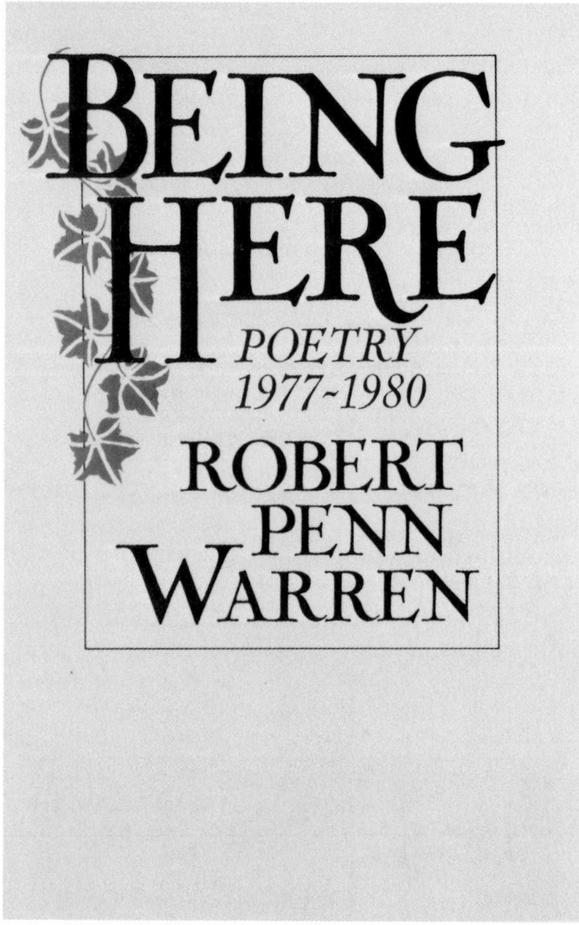

Dust jacket

Now and Then: Poems: 1976-1978 (1978) is organized around the dichotomy suggested by the title, with a section entitled "Nostalgic" and another, longer one entitled "Speculative." In a way, therefore, this simple dichotomy was a predecessor of the more complex, extended arrangement of *Being Here.* The epigraph to the volume is drawn, ironically, from the section of Isaiah which begins, "Sing unto the Lord a new song," and constitutes one of the Bible's more celebrated paeans to God. Though Warren does not believe in God, he believes in the joy of living, and these poems, despite the perplexities they sometimes show, are songs of joy at being alive. As he concludes in "American Portrait: Old Style," the first poem in the book:

> I am not dead yet, though in years,
> And the world's way is yet long to go,
> And I love the world even in my anger,
> And love is a hard thing to outgrow.

Though being alive may not always be easy and fun, Warren believes it is well worth the effort.

"Heart of the Backlog," the twenty-first poem of the second section, may suggest the theme of Wallace Stevens's "The Snow Man." Stevens argues in his poem, "One must have a mind of winter" to behold the "Nothing that is not there and the nothing that is." In "Heart of the Backlog," Warren argues that we must dispassionately consider the nature of time and human existence. In most ways, he says, we are like the vole, which

> has neither theology nor
> Aesthetic—not even what you may call
> Stoicism. . . .

And the vole, like everything else alive, dies, in its case caught in an owl's talons. Must we humans, therefore, constantly look apprehensively over our shoulders, listening for the "creak of wing-joint gigantic in distance"? Warren says that we must not, but rather we must live each day constantly looking forward, undisturbed by the ghosts and chimeras of metaphysics and religion. Warren has one piece of advice, "I beg you not to look back, in God's name."

In these two latest volumes of poetry, Warren is attempting to draw together poems which illuminate basic themes that have long been hallmarks of his personal philosophy. In arranging these poems, he combines a strong narrative force, a potent sense of irony, and a deep conviction that man must face the true nature of existence if he is ever to make sense out of life. That he should strive to arrange diverse poems around common themes is significant, for it represents a summing up and an attempt to order these numerous poems into a broad statement. These new arrangements are indicative of Warren's powerful urge to narrate, for in arranging these poems into sequences, he is attempting to tell the story not only of his personal concerns but also of the concerns which must engage the attentions of every man.

Robert Penn Warren Talking: Interviews 1950-1978 (1980) includes eighteen significant public and private interviews. Some of the larger context has been removed because the editors have edited out many of the comments of interviewers and other participants in panel discussions, but the volume offers valuable insights into Warren's growth as a writer, allowing the reader to meet Warren directly. As the editors, Floyd C. Watkins and John T. Hiers, point out, "The interviews of Red Warren reveal much of this man who is so concealed in his writings."

Of the eighteen interviews in the book, one of the most recent took place in 1978. The first is an

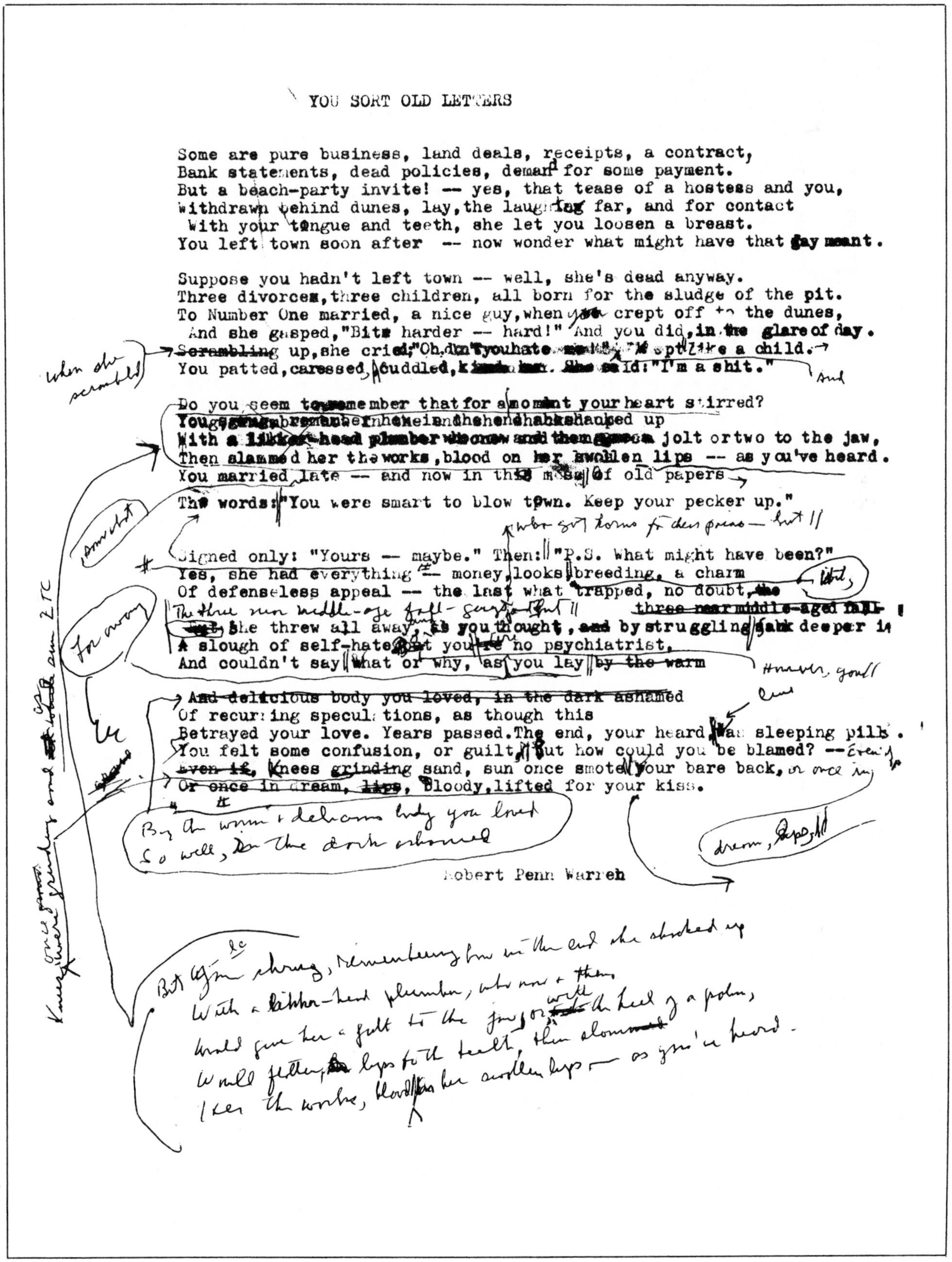
YOU SORT OLD LETTERS

Some are pure business, land deals, receipts, a contract,
Bank statements, dead policies, demand for some payment.
But a beach-party invite! — yes, that tease of a hostess and you,
Withdrawn behind dunes, lay, the laughing far, and for contact
With your tongue and teeth, she let you loosen a breast.
You left town soon after — now wonder what might have that day meant.

Suppose you hadn't left town — well, she's dead anyway.
Three divorces, three children, all born for the sludge of the pit.
To Number One married, a nice guy, when you crept off to the dunes,
And she gasped, "Bite harder — hard!" And you did, in the glare of day.
Scrambling up, she cried, "Oh, don't you hate me?" ... like a child.
You patted, caressed, cuddled, ... "I'm a shit."

Do you seem to remember that for a moment your heart stirred?
...
With a ... jolt or two to the jaw,
Then slammed her the works, blood on her swollen lips — as you've heard.
You married late — and now in this mess of old papers
The words: "You were smart to blow town. Keep your pecker up."

Signed only: "Yours — maybe." Then: "P.S. What might have been?"
Yes, she had everything — money, looks, breeding, a charm
Of defenseless appeal — the last what trapped, no doubt, the three near middle-aged fall-
... She threw all away, as you thought, and by struggling sank deeper in
A slough of self-hate. But you're no psychiatrist,
And couldn't say what or why, as you lay by the warm
And delicious body you loved, in the dark ashamed
Of recurring speculations, as though this
Betrayed your love. Years passed. The end, your heard, was sleeping pills.
You felt some confusion, or guilt, but how could you be blamed? —
Even if, knees grinding sand, sun once smote your bare back,
Or once in dream, lips, bloody, lifted for your kiss.

Robert Penn Warren

"You Sort Old Letters," revised typescript

unusual one with Warren and his wife, Eleanor Clark, herself a writer of distinction. The interview reveals something about the relationship between these two writers who have known and respected each other for nearly four decades. Warren admits that he rarely discusses his writing with his wife and that what discussion he does have of work in progress is "To taxi drivers, and anybody else. . . ." Indeed, he adds "And in late years I find myself talking less and less to anybody, or showing things." Warren and Clark also both reveal that they are disturbed by the decline of an appreciation of history in the modern world and by the increase of the feelings of rootlessness evident today. Warren firmly believes that art belongs to the "now," but to appreciate the present a sense of one's own history is essential. On the other hand, Warren does not believe that those who worry about the future, while ignoring the present, have much to offer, either. As he remarks, "I'll tell you one thing right now. The people who talked about the future of the world all the time never became writers." It is essential, he feels, that one develop a sense of his past and a sense of place, especially if one would become a writer.

Warren is now seventy-six, and his biography will almost surely be written sooner or later. It is problematic if Warren will ever participate in the production of such a document. As Watkins and Hiers remark, "At least as much as the shy Faulkner, Warren is repelled by the idea of a biography. His reticence seems to derive fundamentally from an inborn and constant self-effacement which has always revealed a genuine interest and concern with things outside the ego." Warren also fears that his biography might be used unskillfully as a background for interpreting his own life to the detriment of the interpretations applied to his poems. As he remarked in 1970 of critics who read poems as biography, "The poems have a much deeper and more immediate personal reference. This does not necessarily mean autobiography. I have been amused to see, in a few cases, critics using poems as a source of biographical material. What balls! It's very naive—for a professed critic, too." Thus, it does not seem likely that Warren's permission for a biography will be forthcoming, if for no other reason than his fear that such a document would detract from his own poetry.

—Everett C. Wilkie, Jr.

Other:

Katherine Anne Porter: A Collection of Critical Essays, edited by Warren (Englewood Cliffs, N.J.: Prentice-Hall, 1979).

New Entries

Jonathan Baumbach

(5 July 1933-)

SELECTED BOOKS: *The Landscape of Nightmare: Studies in the Contemporary American Novel* (New York: New York University Press, 1965; London: Owen, 1966);

A Man to Conjure With (New York: Random House, 1965; London: Gollancz, 1966);

What Comes Next (New York: Harper & Row, 1968);

Reruns (New York: Fiction Collective, 1974);

Babble (New York: Fiction Collective, 1976);

Chez Charlotte and Emily (New York: Fiction Collective, 1979);

The Return of Service (Urbana: University of Illinois Press, 1979).

Although Jonathan Baumbach's contributions to contemporary fiction and criticism have only recently begun to be widely acknowledged, his influence on the direction of recent American fiction as a writer, critic, professor, and editor has been considerable. Perhaps best known as an author of experimental novels and as a movie reviewer for *Partisan Review*, Baumbach was also the co-founder in 1974 of the Fiction Collective—a significant and innovative publishing venture.

Born in Brooklyn, New York, Baumbach was the son of Ida and Harold Baumbach, the American painter. After graduating from Brooklyn College with an A.B. in 1955, he attended Columbia University in 1955-1956, receiving an M.F.A. in 1956. At Columbia he worked primarily on writing plays, and his M.F.A. thesis, a play entitled *The One-Eyed Man is King*, was produced at Theater East in 1956. This play, which shows the influence of Ibsen, is of little surviving interest and anticipates Baumbach's later work only in its concern with form.

Having at this time no interest in getting a Ph.D., Baumbach, in effect, allowed himself to be drafted in 1956. He married Elinor Berkman in September of that year and they had a son, David, while Baumbach was in the army. Most of his army service (1956-1958) was at Fort Huachuca, Arizona, where he began writing stories. After his discharge, Baumbach accepted a teaching assistantship from Stanford University, where he focused his scholarly interests on contemporary American fiction. His dissertation, written in 1960 under Wallace Stegner and entitled "Theme of Guilt and Redemption in the Post-Second World War American Novel," examines eight novels, by Saul Bellow, Ralph Ellison, Bernard Malamud, Wright Morris, Flannery O'Connor, J. D. Salinger, William Styron, and Robert Penn Warren—the writers Baumbach felt to be the definitive figures of the postwar period. Holding that "to live in this world, to live consciously in this world in which madness daily passes for sanity is a kind of madness in itself." Baumbach explored each novel in terms of how it portrays the nightmarish conditions of contemporary society and how each individual protagonist attempts to carve his own niche, or openly rebels against these conditions. Baumbach reports, however, that what interested him about most of these works was their relation to Hawthorne's notion of romance, the way in which they make manifest the inner worlds and secret lives of their protagonists. This study, somewhat revised, was published in 1965 by New York University Press as *The Landscape of Nightmare: Studies in the Contemporary American Novel* and is an important early consideration of the direction American fiction took during the 1950s. It is also an acknowledgment of the literary parentage that Baumbach would never acknowledge again.

After receiving his Ph.D. in 1961, Baumbach accepted a position as an instructor of English at Ohio State University in Columbus; in 1964 he returned to the New York City area as an assistant professor at the University Heights Campus of New York University, where he became director of freshman English. Throughout this period, however, Baumbach's principle interest was writing rather than academics. Having lost interest in playwriting, he had from 1957 on been writing stories. (His first important story, "Code of Honor," published in the *Michigan Quarterly Review* in 1965, was written while Baumbach was in graduate school.) In 1961 he started work on his first novel, *A Man to Conjure With* (1965), which immediately established the shifting terrain of dream, memory, imagination, and public nightmare that his fiction would explore during the next fifteen years.

In most respects, *A Man to Conjure With* remains Baumbach's most conventional novel. Its protagonist, Peter Becker (the man to conjure with) is obsessed with restoring his marriage after a fourteen-year separation from his wife. Like most of the writers he considered in *The Landscape of Nightmare,* Baumbach examines the psychological responses of a sensitive outsider who feels himself adrift, cut off from those around him, unable to piece together the fragments of his life into a meaningful whole. Becker's need to summon up his past in imaginative reconstructions establishes a pattern evident in later Baumbach works, such as *What Comes Next* (1968) and *Chez Charlotte and Emily* (1979): since Baumbach's main characters cannot establish fulfilling and sustaining relationships with others or with a destructive, dehumanizing outer world, they tend to retreat inward to memory, dream, and imagination in order to conjure up a satisfying sense of self. As the novel moves back and forth in time and into and out of Becker's dreams (which in this novel are always clearly identified as such), *A Man to Conjure With* gradually establishes the nature of Becker's current crisis and his need to define a present sense of personal identity in terms of what he once was. As Baumbach explained in a 1973 interview with John Graham, "It's as if all the details will add up to a picture of himself. And then, he can look at himself as he was. He has the idea, perhaps, that the man he was at twenty is still somewhere there, all the potentiality that was there at twenty and forgotten and lost. To look at himself at twenty is to come back there and start again, to recoup what he's lost."

Perhaps the most significant aspect of *A Man to Conjure With* is Baumbach's use of Becker's dreams to help in defining his character. In a 1980 letter Baumbach commented that in this novel, "My particular concern was with the coded language of dreams and with rearranging the parts of a novel in order to discover new form; consequently I think the most interesting thing about *A Man to Conjure With* is its structure." Although his use of dreams to illustrate important aspects of personality is not employed as radically as it would be in later books—where little or no distinctions are made between his characters' "real worlds" and their dream worlds—the emphasis on both private and public fantasies in this first novel is a feature common to all of Baumbach's work. As critic Jerome Klinkowitz explains, Baumbach uses Peter's dreams not merely to provide psychological insights but also to explore the process of imaginative creation itself: "Baumbach's interest in the psychological . . . is more properly a concern with the liberated working of the imagination, not with clinical abnormality. He is not interested in a character's curious behavior except for the way it reveals itself in language; and then *the way,* the manner, the form is the important thing."

Baumbach's next novel, *What Comes Next,* was published in 1968, by which time he had had a second child, Nina, divorced his wife (in 1967), and moved back to his native Brooklyn to teach at Brooklyn College. (He married Georgia Brown in June 1969, and they have one child, Noah.) *What Comes Next* captures the violent, confusing, and emotionally charged spirit of the mid-1960s by fusing public and private nightmares. The novel's two main characters are Christopher Steiner—"a college student in the process of flipping out entirely," the dust jacket calls him—and Curtin Parks, a history professor who is impressed with Steiner's intellectual potential and is directing a tutorial for him. As the novel develops, Steiner begins to spy on Parks and Rosemary Byrd, a student with whom Parks is having an affair; meanwhile Steiner, who fails to distinguish between dream and reality, is trying to work out his private anxieties, desires, and obsessions. Steiner is unable to decide what to do with the freedom and responsibility his rebellious generation has demanded. The novel's opening words introduce this dilemma in a manner typical of the hallucinatory progress of Steiner's thinking: "My father passes. I am sinking in some gelatinous substance. 'What do you plan to do with your freedom?' he asks. *What can I do?* Up to my chin in the stuff. 'You can choose to stand or fall, Christopher, huh?' *But I'm falling, for God's sake.* A tooth wriggles loose. *It's a Fact. Can't you see that I'm falling?* 'It's your choice, son.' "

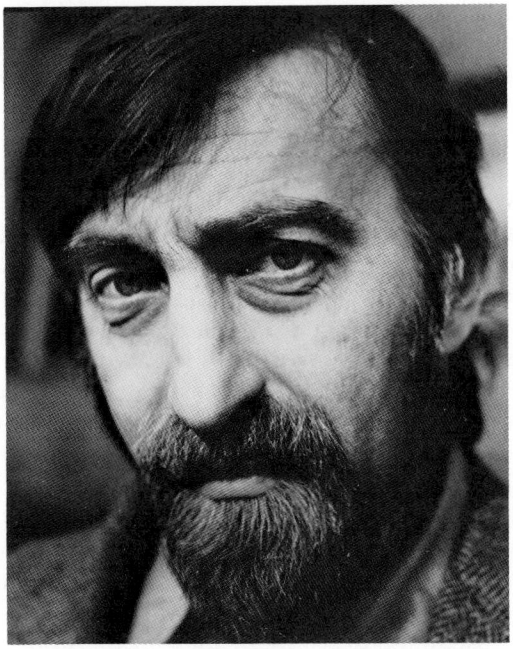

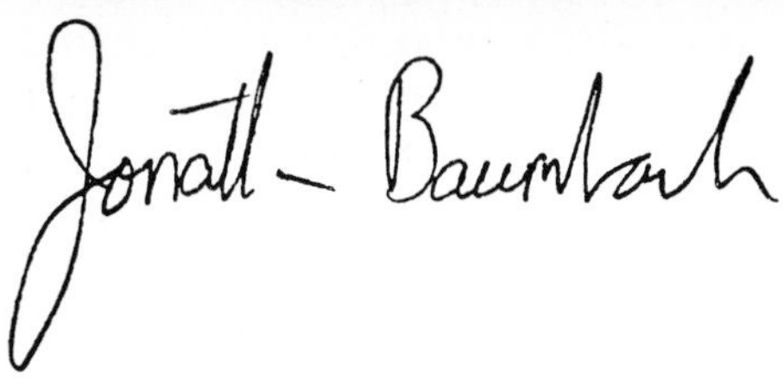

The atmosphere of *What Comes Next* is intense and confusing due to Baumbach's decision to allow Steiner's dreamlife to overlap utterly with his real world. The motifs and images of his dreams (*fantasies* may be closer to the appropriate term) reflect Steiner's sexual and identity crises; just as importantly, these fantasies also vividly reflect the nightmarish public realities that are swirling around Steiner and Parks. "Where is there to go?" asks the anguished Steiner at the outset of the novel, "Too much violence in the street. Sex, bombing, suffocation, rape. Too much madness." With such madness all around, Steiner retreats inward to a dreamworld where the different warring factions of his psyche engage each other. This inner realm, however, offers no respite from the brutality and insensitivity of the outside world. Although Steiner himself seems unable to distinguish between inner and outer realities, Baumbach has suggested to Graham that: "Though most people have felt that he is mad and he's certainly mad by conventional standards, it seems to me that his madness is relative sanity." This comment introduces an idea common to all of Baumbach's works—that of the healing, ordering, and restorative function of the imagination. In a world such as ours, Baumbach implies, the role of the imagination becomes central to the individual's attempts to establish some small corner of coherence and comfort, even if such a niche seems to others to be illusory or "mad."

During the early 1970s, Baumbach was not only writing fiction but also writing film criticism for *Partisan Review* (his first film reviews were published in 1956 in *Film Culture*), as well as directing undergraduate and graduate creative writing programs at Brooklyn College. While visiting in Europe during the summer of 1973, he also began thinking for the first time about organizing a novelists' cooperative as an outlet for nontraditional works and corresponded with Ronald Sukenick and Peter Spielberg about the possibility. Baumbach, of course, had had his own first two highly experimental novels published by prestigious New York publishers (Random House and Harper & Row); but he had also seen his works—and those of other innovative talents such as Sukenick, Steve Katz, and Robert Coover—being badly distributed, inadequately advertised by major publishers. More personally distressing, his own most recent novel, "Dreambook" (later to be retitled *Reruns*), was rejected thirty-two times between 1970 and 1973, and was also accepted three other times by editors only to be rejected by their superiors. The problem, as Baumbach saw it, was that publishing was beginning to change around 1968, moving by degrees from the influence of editors to the influence of accountants. As he bluntly put it in 1977: "By and large, accountants and computers are directing the publishing industry today and as a result it is run like a fast-food restaurant." Baumbach felt that with many major book publishers now being owned by large conglomerates, with independent bookstores giving way to national chains, and with the editors' attentions becoming more and more focused on marketing considerations, it was not surprising that the flood of talented, innovative writers emerging during the late 1960s and early 1970s was finding it difficult to get their works considered seriously by publishers. Baumbach, Spielberg, and Sukenick were soon joined in the discussion by other writers such as Steve Katz, Ray Federman, and B. H. Friedman, who were also interested in starting a "fiction collective." By October 1974 the first three Fiction Collective books were published to considerable fanfare and enthusiasm by the national media.

As organized by the original members, the Fiction Collective was established to be a cooperative outlet for nontraditional fiction. Writers would make all the business decisions and assist one another with all editorial work. Once a writer has a book accepted by the collective (a rotating board of members is set up to consider manuscripts individually), he pays for publication himself. (This has come to about $4000 for runs of 1200 hardcover and 1800 softcover copies, although grants have often been available to help defray this cost.) This money is considered to be a loan to the cooperative and is repaid to the writers from proceeds; after a book pays for itself—and to date most of the books have returned their original investment within about a year—the collective is allowed to keep the remaining profits (which have been minimal thus far) to help cover operating expenses. A writer will never get rich from the Fiction Collective's publication of his works, but Fiction Collective writers are able to ensure that their works are printed the way they want them, advertised honestly, and kept in print as long as the Fiction Collective remains in business. Indeed, the most important aspect of this system is precisely the fact that the writer retains complete control over his manuscript, even in such matters as the book's cover design. By using their collective energies and skills—and with the considerable assistance of Brooklyn College, used as a working base of operations—the collective has managed to eke out a precarious existence on the fringes of the publishing industry. The collective has published some thirty-four titles in the seven years of its existence; and although the quality of these works has varied, the collective's publications, when taken as a whole, represent an impressively wide range of innovative works, "All in all, probably the best list in town," Robert Coover commented in a recent interview. As Baumbach, Sukenick, Federman, and other vocal members have frequently noted, the collective does not view itself as competing with commercial publishers, but rather as doing what these other publishers cannot afford to do, given their financial pressures.

Baumbach's position from 1974-1978 as co-director of the collective's operations (with Peter Spielberg as the other director) required long, often frustrating hours of work trying to coordinate grant proposals, seeing to it that the manuscript readings were proceeding smoothly, and generally attempting to oversee the enormously complicated process of getting books accepted, proofread, printed, and distributed. This was a tremendous work load, much of it having to do with the thankless, time-consuming production end of bookmaking rather than with the artistic end. With considerable relief, Baumbach and Spielberg turned over the directorship of the collective's operations to Ray Federman and Carol Sturn Smith in 1978.

Despite his teaching load and the hours devoted to directing the collective's operations, Baumbach was also extremely busy writing fiction during the middle and late 1970s. He began to devote considerable energy to the creation of short fictional forms for the first time: from 1975 until 1979, he published over two dozen stories in various prestigious literary journals, including *The Iowa Review*, *TriQuarterly*, *Chicago Review*, *Anteus*, and occasionally in more popular publications such as *Esquire* and *The North American Review*. A few of these short fictions eventually surfaced as part of Baumbach's collagelike Fiction Collective novels, but twelve of the best of them were gathered in his first short-story collection, *The Return of Service*, which appeared as part of the University of Illinois Press's Short Fiction series in 1979. Although about half of the stories retain Baumbach's formal concern with unconventional, dreamlike narratives, there is also an interesting shift in approach which Baumbach described: "With some of the stories in *The Return of Service* I begin to deal (a starting over in a sense) with the discovery of language and the invention of narrative—that is, with imagination, with the process of imagining." The result is a remarkable diversity of formal strategies, themes, and voices in this collection—a diversity which displays Baumbach's talents for parody, wit, and narrative control. For example, his interest in verbal mimicry and parody—strongly evident in his fiction of the 1970s—is shown in "Neglected Masterpieces," a hilarious, Borgesian pseudoessay which examines a neglected masterpiece of epic melodrama; in "King Dong," a somewhat transformed version of the King Kong legend in which the latent sexual symbolism of the familiar myth is emphasized with amusing results; and in "Another Look at the Blackbird," in which Sam Spade tells the story of his first caper. It would be wrong, however, to view these stories as merely parodic; as with Coover and Barthelme—the two American writers with whom Baumbach can be most usefully compared—Baumbach obviously thinks of popular materials as a kind of mythmaking, with his stories transforming these already resonant materials into new myths, new perceptions. Despite the distancing and comic devices, Baumbach is also concerned with making his fiction affect the reader on an emotional level, even in his obvious satiric pieces. For example, in the collection's title story, a male narrator and his father play a Kafkaesque game of tennis whose progress gradually reveals certain insights into the narrator's relationship with his father and also metaphorically suggests the guilt, self-doubts, ambitions, and other key aspects of the narrator's personality. A strangely moving story, "Return of the Service" perfectly demonstrates Baumbach's ability to create a carefully controlled narrative structure which illuminates personal relationships as subtly and passionately as the traditional storyteller's realistic methods.

Baumbach's three Fiction Collective novels—*Reruns* (1974), *Babble* (1976) and *Chez Charlotte and Emily*—reflect his sustained interest in the imagination's role in shaping personality and its relationship to a world characterized by violence, insensitivity, and fragmentation. All three books explore the role of the media (especially cinema) in creating societal norms and the individual's notion of self. Baumbach has commented about his consistent fascination with films: "I've always been interested in film and have never given up the idea of directing a film. Film is dream, of course, which is the reason that we are often haunted by movies that seem from a literary standpoint hopelessly banal. Film images are dreamlike (atavistic, primordial), which is what every moviegoing child knows. The filmmakers I feel closest to are: Godard, Bresson, Antonioni, Chabrol, Rivette, the Truffaut of *Mississippi Mermaid,* the Polanski of *Cul de Sac,* the Hitchcock of *Vertigo,* the Hawks of *The Big Sleep,* Fritz Lang, Max Ophuls, Buñuel of *Belle de Jour.*" Feeling these kinds of affinities, it is not surprising that Baumbach often seeks out archetypes and patterns which apparently have spoken to our inner needs and desires—Dracula, Frankenstein, King Kong, sports mythologies—and then examines how individuals attempt to apply the mythic impulses contained within these motifs by redirecting the original pattern; such transformations have the effect of liberating the energy stored within these primordial images.

This approach is evident in the structure of *Reruns,* whose French edition has been rededicated to the major influence on it, Jean Luc Goddard. *Reruns* presents a life which has been literally transformed into thirty-three nights at a Cinémateque. These "reruns" are nightmarish, frantic, often violent episodes (somewhat reminiscent of Christopher Steiner's hallucinatory visions in *What Comes Next*) whose characters and events are generated from a wide variety of cultural cliches, fairy tales, stories, and movies—all of which symbolically reenact the pattern of a life. This is a world of terror, loneliness, and absurdity, populated by Walter Brennan, Dracula, and Goldilocks. The narrator confronts these haunting combinations of senseless violence, inexplicable loss, and utterly banal chatter, which are also analogues for his deepest anxieties and obsessions. As I commented in my analysis of *Reruns* in *Contemporary Literature,* "Baumbach's book succeeds because it is created out of the language and archetypes through which we respond to everyday life. Baumbach realizes, for example, that movies provide psychic dramas, and even the idiosyncratic language which the public appropriates for its own private purposes. . . . The issues which Baumbach raises in *Reruns* turn out to be at the center of many of the Fiction Collective's books: to what extent is our response to the world the product of our imagination? what is the value of our fictional constructs, and to what extent do our lives follow the patterns we have invented in our movies, books, or dreams?"

As with *Reruns,* Baumbach's next novel, *Babble,* effectively assembles a variety of our culture's stock fears, obsessions, and desires and recombines them for its own purposes—in this case, the presentation of a kind of surreal *Bildungsroman.* The "hero" of this novel is a three-year-old child who is portrayed experiencing all the trials and tribulations of youth, love, college, and old age. The baby's father, who narrates the book, also provides a series of anecdotes and stories told by the baby; these stories, appropriately enough, are apparently derived from fairy-tales, television, and comic books and contain their own childish concepts of morality and causality. Throughout the novel, Baumbach adheres fairly rigidly to the literary conventions commonly associated with the various stages of life through which the baby-hero is advancing; more crucially, *Babble* is utterly realistic in dealing with the language and fantasy of children, allowing Baumbach to investigate the process whereby language is discovered and narrative patterns are imposed. This peculiar but highly effective narrative approach often creates a delightful incongruity between familiar literary cliches and formulas and the comically trivialized "baby material" being forced into the conventions, as when the baby must at one point "scour the city for someone who will change his diaper without asking in return an excess of gratitude. He leaves a notice in the personals column of an underground newspaper: 'Groovey baby, Capricorn, interested in meaning of life, seeks mature couple for intimate exchange.' " Klinkowitz concludes that "Baumbach's intervention with the traditions of fiction has thrown them into sharper relief, reminding us that they are merely conventions, but also showing just how potent conventions are when the author uses them with a sense of self-conscious power."

Baumbach's most recently published novel, *Chez Charlotte and Emily,* is his most ambitious and successful work to date. Extending the structural methods of *Reruns* and *Babble, Chez Charlotte and Emily* is a collagelike work built out of various familiar cinematic and literary cliches. Although the book may initially appear to be a bewildering and chaotic jumble of violent and erotic adventures—adventures which complement and contradict each other in a timeless process which is "as dreamlike as reels of film," as the dust jacket states—the various plot elements are subtly interrelated fantasies composed by the book's two main characters, Joshua Quartz and his wife Genevieve. In the opening paragraph of the novel, it is revealed that Joshua and Genevieve are suffering through a marriage which has lost its vitality and passion. In order to bridge their barrier of isolation, Joshua begins to tell his silent wife the story of Francis Sinatra, a bookish man whose humdrum life with his wife and teenage daughter obliquely reflects Joshua's own situation. Francis, it seems, was one day swimming at a public beach at Cape Cod and was suddenly propelled out beyond his depth by the inscrutable tides; these tides do not drown him but carry him to a private cove, where he is rescued by two mysterious young women named Charlotte and Emily. Exhilarated by his new-found freedom, Francis decides to abandon his former life and adopt a new identity; soon he begins to tell Emily—who differs from Charlotte mainly in her interest in the past rather than in "the ever-changing here and now"—various fictions about his life which Emily takes for the truth. Indeed, we are told that, "as times wear on, he gets better and better at it, persuades himself of the actuality of what he has spontaneously imagined." Francis's involvement with these mental rehearsals of "the screenplay of the life he has imagined" gradually evolves into an obsessive means of reshaping his past—and, consequently, his present—into a more pleasing and satisfying pattern. His fictitious past and his equally bizarre present life are constantly compared by means of simile and metaphor to the plots of movies and books; often even the substance of his life is highly reminiscent of spy movies, soap operas, gothic horror stories, and romantic melodramas. It is strongly hinted, in fact, that the entire episode of Francis's near-drowning and subsequent rescue is a fictional projection of his inner needs and desires. (This suspicion is partially confirmed late in the novel when it is said that "The entire narrative has taken place in Francis' imagination. When he returns to shore, . . . pitting his strength against the exertions of the tide, barely two hours have elapsed." This variation, however, like all others in the novel, is contradicted by other interpretations.

Naturally the reader must be constantly aware that it is Joshua who is telling Genevieve the story of Francis's real (or imagined) adventures; and as with Francis's apparent motives in retelling fictional versions of his past and present, it seems that Joshua is inventing Francis's story as a means of opening up communication channels with his wife. Soon Genevieve is telling her own stories which variously intersect and diverge from Joshua's account. Because all these stories are evidently metaphorical reflections of inner tensions, desires, and personality traits, the tales inevitably revolve around domestic intrigues, love triangles, psychic and occasionally physical violence, and all manner of erotic encounters. "Matters work themselves out in metaphor," says Genevieve at one point, and thus it is that through the agency of imagination and metaphor that Joshua and Genevieve perpetuate themselves and their relationship, make love, and communicate.

Chez Charlotte and Emily is typical of all of Baumbach's fiction in depicting a world in which, as Joshua says, "Everything tends to be a lie" and "Nothing is reliable." Like many other postmodern writers, Baumbach's focus is not so much on the ambiguous, destructive, entropic "outer world" as it is on the resources of the imagination in coping with this reality. The imagination for Baumbach, however, is not really a retreat or a place of idealized beauty and harmony—as it was viewed by the great modernists—but is instead a realm where man can freely manipulate the components of his experience (which is produced as much by symbols and media-produced substitutions as it is by the so-called real world) into structures of utility, order, and possibly even beauty. The imagination, then, provides a kind of communication link between man, the world, and others; so long as the process of imagination remains flexible and open within limited bounds, one can define his very nature. Convinced, as he told John Graham, that "the conventional novel, for me, anyway, is on its way to a dead end," Jonathan Baumbach has been busily engaged in "trying to get at the way things are in a way that no one has ever seen them before." In his role as fiction writer and as

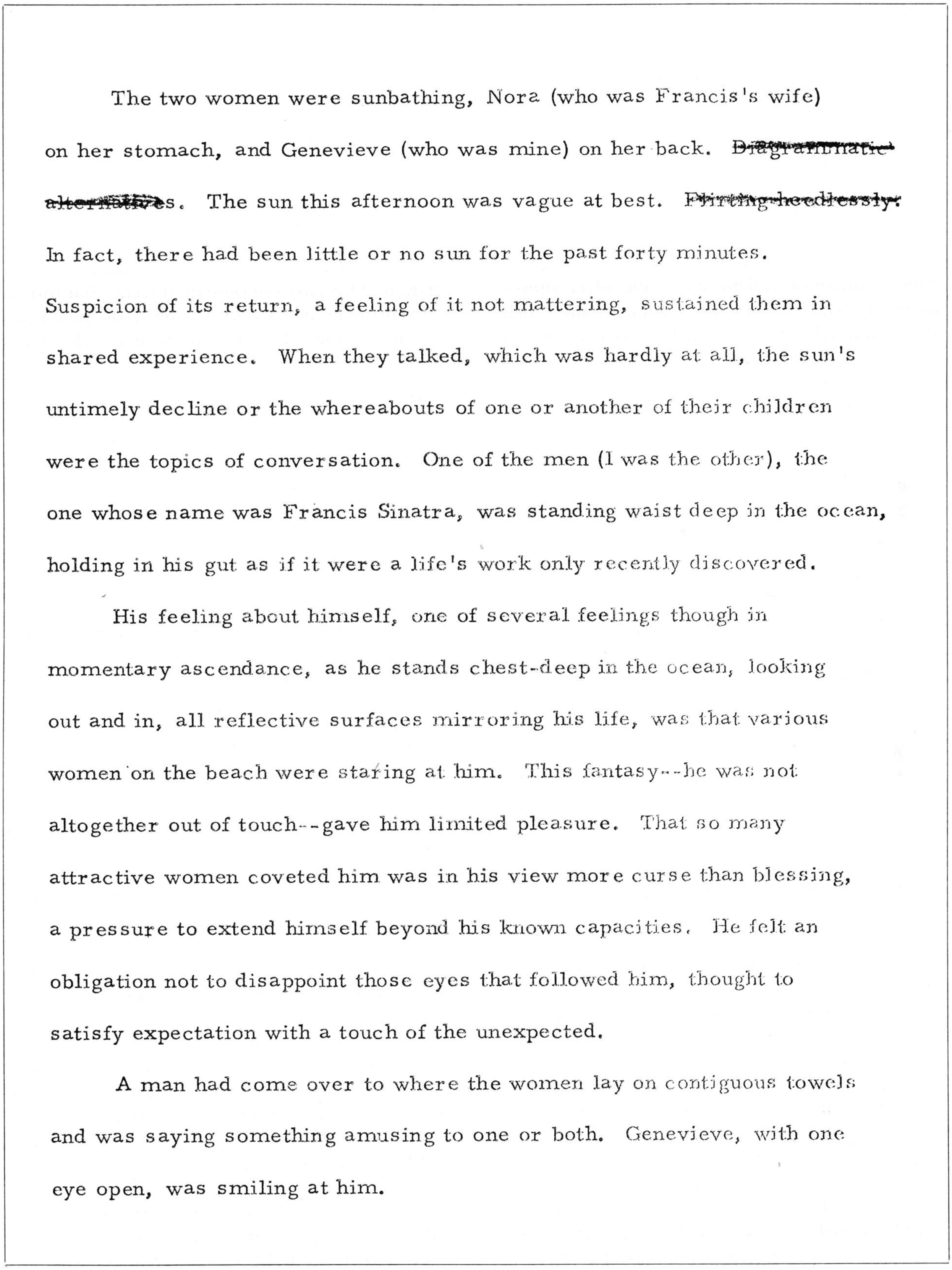

The two women were sunbathing, Nora (who was Francis's wife) on her stomach, and Genevieve (who was mine) on her back. ~~Diagrammatic alternative~~s. The sun this afternoon was vague at best. ~~Flirting heedlessly.~~ In fact, there had been little or no sun for the past forty minutes. Suspicion of its return, a feeling of it not mattering, sustained them in shared experience. When they talked, which was hardly at all, the sun's untimely decline or the whereabouts of one or another of their children were the topics of conversation. One of the men (I was the other), the one whose name was Francis Sinatra, was standing waist deep in the ocean, holding in his gut as if it were a life's work only recently discovered.

His feeling about himself, one of several feelings though in momentary ascendance, as he stands chest-deep in the ocean, looking out and in, all reflective surfaces mirroring his life, was that various women on the beach were staring at him. This fantasy--he was not altogether out of touch--gave him limited pleasure. That so many attractive women coveted him was in his view more curse than blessing, a pressure to extend himself beyond his known capacities. He felt an obligation not to disappoint those eyes that followed him, thought to satisfy expectation with a touch of the unexpected.

A man had come over to where the women lay on contiguous towels and was saying something amusing to one or both. Genevieve, with one eye open, was smiling at him.

Chez Charlotte and Emily, *revised typescript*

one of the organizers and guiding spirits of the Fiction Collective, Baumbach has not only presented his own vision of the way things are but has created an opportunity for others to do so as well.

—*Larry McCaffery*

Play:

The One-Eyed Man is King, New York, Theater East, March 1956.

Other:

Moderns and Contemporaries, edited by Baumbach and Arthur Edelstein (New York: Random House, 1968);

Writers as Teachers/Teachers as Writers, edited by Baumbach (New York: Holt, Rinehart & Winston, 1970);

Statements 2, New Fiction, edited by Baumbach and Peter Spielberg (New York: Fiction Collective, 1977).

Periodical Publications:

FICTION:

"Code of Honor," *Michigan Quarterly Review* (Summer 1965): 166-173;

"You Your Enemy," *Epoch* (Fall 1970): 57-75;

"Crossed in Love by Her Eyes," *Esquire*, April 1975;

"Spooky in Florida," *Chicago Review*, 26, no. 4 (1975), 46-62;

"The Frozen Yak Fields of Alaska," *TriQuarterly*, Spring 1976;

"Passion?" *The North American Review*, Spring 1978;

"Whatever Happened to Dr. Malone," *Iowa Review*, Fall 1978.

NONFICTION:

"Nightmare of a Native Son: Ralph Ellison's *Invisible Man*," *Critique*, 6 (Spring 1963): 48-65;

"The Economy of Love: The Novels of Bernard Malamud," *The Kenyon Review*, Summer 1963, pp. 438-457;

"The Saint as a Young Man: a Reappraisal of *The Catcher in the Rye*," *Modern Language Quarterly*, December 1964, pp. 461-473;

"A Personal History of the Fiction Collective," *TriQuarterly*, Fall 1978;

"Apocalypse Now and Then," *New York Arts Journal*, November 1979.

References:

John Graham, *The Writer's Voice: Conversations with Contemporary Writers* (New York: Morrow, 1973), pp. 214-220;

Jerome Klinkowitz, *The Life of Fiction* (Urbana: University of Illinois Press, 1977), pp. 129-139;

Larry McCaffery, "The Fiction Collective," *Contemporary Literature*, 19 (Winter 1978): 99-115;

McCaffery, "The Fiction Collective: An Innovative Alternative," *Chicago Review*, 30 (Autumn 1978): 107-126.

Peter S. Beagle
(20 April 1939-)

BOOKS: *A Fine and Private Place* (New York: Viking, 1960; London: Frederick Muller, 1960);

I See by My Outfit (New York: Viking, 1965; London: Frederick Muller, 1966);

The Last Unicorn (New York: Viking, 1968; London & New York: Ballantine, 1971);

The California Feeling, text by Beagle, photos by Michael Bry and Ansel Adams (Garden City: Doubleday, 1969);

Lila the Werewolf (Santa Barbara, Cal.: Capra Press, 1974);

American Denim: a New Folk Art, text by Beagle, photos by Baron Wolman and the Denim Artists (New York: Abrams, 1975);

The Lady and her Tiger, by Beagle and Pat Derby (New York: Dutton, 1976);

The Fantasy Worlds of Peter Beagle (New York: Viking, 1978);

The Garden of Earthly Delights, text by Beagle, paintings by Hieronymus Bosch (Los Angeles: Rosebud Books, 1981).

Quality rather than quantity has characterized Peter S. Beagle's twenty-five-year career as a fiction writer. After having published only one story, "Telephone Call" (1956), at seventeen in *Seventeen*, he brought out his critically praised first novel, *A Fine and Private Place*, in 1960 at the age of twenty-one. Two stories and eight years later he produced his masterwork to date, *The Last Unicorn* (1968), already a text in college courses and the subject of several scholarly treatments. Since then the only fiction he has published is the novella *Lila the Werewolf* (1974), although a third novel is in progress. Because all the longer works and one of the stories belong to the genre of fantasy, his publisher,

Viking, has been able to package virtually his complete fictional works in one volume, *The Fantasy Worlds of Peter Beagle* (1978).

This list of Beagle's fiction, however, is misleading as an index to the author's literary output, for Beagle has always supported himself primarily through his writing. His fiction is surpassed in quantity by nonfiction magazine journalism, travel books, texts for art and photography books, introductions to the fiction and poetry of other authors, screenplays, and teleplays. He candidly admits to undertaking many of these projects merely for the money. Yet almost all of them display the same intense, lyrical style and reflect the same concerns as his fiction. Those concerns are, primarily, the proximity of the fantastic to the mundane in everyday experience and the power of love to give value to the otherwise transient, meaningless, and vulnerable condition of being human. And because much of the nonfiction is autobiographical, and even confessional, in nature, it increases one's understanding of the fiction. The symbiosis between literary and commercial writing is just one of a series of complementary relationships that are the hallmark of Beagle's art and life.

Peter Soyer Beagle was born in New York City, one of two sons of teachers in the city schools, Simon and Rebecca Soyer Beagle. He grew up in a Jewish neighborhood in the Bronx. Reading, talking about books, and spinning tales were encouraged in the home: "I grew up in a family of story-tellers; my grandfather wrote fairy stories in Hebrew, and I read a lot of fantasy on my own. Nobody said fairy tales weren't all right." These early experiences have also inclined Beagle to enjoy and to emulate the kind of stories that benefit from being read aloud. (He would later substitute reading aloud to his children for the television set the family did not own.) Overweight and asthmatic, he felt "different" and isolated outside his home. Reading, and creating fantasy worlds, became his escape.

Another passion from childhood that fills Beagle's novels is his love of animals, a love that flourished despite severe asthmatic allergies to them. Having outgrown his allergies, he currently has seventeen pets of several domestic and exotic species and has owned over one hundred in his lifetime. "For myself, I have always wanted fur, ever since I saw and touched my first cat. (I have also wanted to be a cat since that day, but that is definitely another matter)," he writes in his commentary for the folk-art photo book *American Denim*. Indeed, the merging of human and animal frequently occurs in his fiction (perhaps an understandable preoccupation in a man named Beagle). There are the curmudgeonly talking raven and pseudointellectual squirrel in *A Fine and Private Place* and the many articulate beasts in *The Last Unicorn*. The unicorn temporarily becomes a young girl, and the young girl Lila of *Lila the Werewolf* from time to time turns into a wolf. In Beagle's poem "Stable of Dragons" (1960), the narrator keeps a barn full of dragons and mates with one of them, hoping for a fine son with "sharp teeth."

After graduating from the Bronx High School of Science in 1955, Beagle attended the University of Pittsburgh, where he studied creative writing under Edwin Peterson and received his B.A. in 1959. At Pittsburgh he completed his first novel, *A Fine and Private Place*, which would be published in 1960. There followed a year of living in Paris and traveling in Europe, the success of *A Fine and Private Place*, and a Wallace Stegner Creative Writing Fellowship to Stanford for the 1960-1961 academic year. At twenty-one Beagle had established himself as a rising talent in American fiction.

A Fine and Private Place shows few signs of being written by a nineteen-year-old. Its tone is bittersweet and reflective. The youngest of the main characters is twenty-nine, and the protagonist, Jonathan Rebeck, is fifty-three and convincingly middle-aged. He also happens to have lived for nineteen years inside a large mausoleum in the Yorkchester cemetery. A druggist who owned an old-fashioned neighborhood pharmacy, he had taken pity on the unhappiness of his customers and let them persuade him to concoct herbal potions that they hoped would help them find love or "make their children well or make their husbands stop drinking." He had become "a witch doctor, a witch doctor in New York. . . . I was their prophet, a prophet fallen on evil days, perhaps, but not without honor." But the potions worked only sporadically, business dropped off, and Rebeck went bankrupt. Depressed at the sight of the chain drugstore that had then taken over his building, its ads promising magical happiness by means of patent remedies, he got drunk; he woke up after dark to find himself locked in the cemetery. As the novel opens, he has never passed outside the gates in all the years since that time.

Rebeck is fed, as befits a prophet, by a tough-talking, cynical raven, who flies in daily, weighted down with bolognas and other delicatessen treats. The bird also provides books and has assembled a chess set piece by piece. The raven does not perform these tasks out of any sense that Rebeck is somehow of the elect; to ravens even Elijah was merely "an old man with a dirty beard." It is just that "Ravens bring things to people. We're like that. It's our nature. We don't like it. We'd much rather be eagles, or swans, or even one of those moronic robins, but we're ravens and there you are. Ravens don't feel right without somebody to bring things to, and when we do find somebody we realize what a silly business it was in the first place."

During his years in the graveyard Rebeck has also become able to see and speak with the ghosts of his dead neighbors. According to Beagle's conception, ghosts retain, in an incorporeal form, as much of their living selves as they choose to remember for as long as they have the ability to remember. They can wander at will through the cemetery in which they are buried but cannot go beyond its gates. But they are like pockets with holes in them; inevitably too many memories slip through and they must retire to eternal rest in their graves. Rebeck eases their transition from one world to the other and so finds among the dead the opportunity he craves to be of use to others, an opportunity the living world denied him.

The particular early summer day on which the novel begins brings two new ghostly inhabitants, Michael Morgan and Laura Durand, and a living visitor, Gertrude Klapper. As the plot develops, the two spirits find with each other a love they never knew in life, and a similar bond of affection develops between Rebeck and Mrs. Klapper. Together the three newcomers will lead Rebeck back out into the world again.

While alive, Laura, the character with whom Beagle most closely identified at the time of the novel's composition, had been an embittered young woman, never finding love and despising her own plainness. Michael, a college history professor, rages against his early death by poison, supposedly administered by his wife Sandra. Mrs. Klapper is the Bronx Jewish widow of the estimable Morris Klapper, to whose memory she remains almost obsessively devoted. The three have come spiritually to dead ends, and all three have deceived themselves as to the cause of their emotional stagnation. With Rebeck acting as catalyst, they come eventually to realize that they have run from life, love, and happiness. Laura had only imagined herself unlovable and unattractive; her own mental barriers had created her alienation. Mrs. Klapper's marriage was not as idyllic as she remembers it; she has used Morris's memory as an excuse to resign herself to the grandmotherly, neurotic existence of the neighborhood *yentas*, constantly calling herself "old woman" when she is just in her early forties.

But the crucial revelation concerns Michael. The raven, following Sandra's murder trial in the papers, reports her exoneration with the discovery that Michael had committed suicide and arranged the evidence to implicate his wife in his death. He had blamed her for their loveless marriage, which made life boring and meaningless to him. This fact is, understandably, the first thing he has forgotten after dying, but the raven's report brings it devastatingly back to him: "The chase is over. The Morgan-hunt is over. I know what I am. I am everything I feared in life, everything I hated in other people, falseness and brutality and mindless arrogance. And I have to drag them with me, wherever I am dragged, because they are part of me, skin and skeleton. I can never hide from them again."

The results of the trial have more concrete results for Michael than simply providing self-enlightenment. As a Catholic suicide, he can no longer rest in consecrated ground. Workmen come to disinter his body and move it to Mount Merrill cemetery, sundering him from his newfound love Laura. She pleads with Rebeck to get his friend Campos, one of the Yorkchester workers who can also see ghosts, and together move her coffin to Mount Merrill in his truck. But Rebeck, terrified at the thought of leaving the cemetery, refuses. "The animals outside are rapidly becoming the animals inside. I'm sorry, Jonathan," she tells him. It looks as though he will once more fail, in their hour of greatest need, those he has tried to help, and thus see his graveyard sanctuary turn as bitter as the outside world he fled.

To the rescue, however, comes the hitherto unmet spirit of Morris Klapper. When Rebeck encounters him by accident and confesses that he can hardly tell anymore whether he is alive or dead, Klapper sternly enunciates an ultimatum: "I tell you that you are a living man and that you have deceived yourself. For a man there is no choice between worlds. There never was. . . . Die, if you choose. Die, and you and I will sit together and talk about friendship." Then Rebeck hears Gertrude calling him and, following the biblical injunction, chooses life. (That Gertrude never sees the ghosts, and Rebeck knows he will never tell her about them, further identifies her as a life-force for him.) They move Laura's casket so that she can be with Michael all the days of their death, and, as the sun comes up, Rebeck goes home with Mrs. Klapper for breakfast.

A Fine and Private Place could easily lapse into the incredible or the sentimental, but Beagle skillfully avoids both pitfalls. Careful detailing makes Rebeck's long survival in the cemetery plausible. The ghosts' otherness is brought out subtly and effectively, as when Michael reaches up reflexively with incorporeal arms to catch a sandwich the raven has dropped "and then lowered them and held them behind his back." Beagle also balances two different dialogue styles so that humor comes in any time pathos threatens to occur. Rebeck and the ghosts, existing in a contemplative realm detached from action, speak in a lyrical, reflective manner that is counterpointed by the vulgar colloquialisms of the raven and the Yiddish-accented common sense of Gertrude Klapper.

The message of the novel is that any time spent living is never wasted. As the famous ironic couplet of Andrew Marvell's that gives the book its title states: "The grave's a fine and private place / But none, I think, do there embrace." Although life is frequently painful and sad, with no transcendent, lasting significance, to run from it, particularly when there is the slimmest hope of finding love, is folly. Contact among living things is what Beagle values above all, as he says in his text for *American Denim*:

> I am for voices—human voices, however ugly, as distinguished from the ones on the radio and in the fourth-class envelopes. I am for familiarity, whatever it breeds; for anything that undermines our terrible gift for dehumanizing one another, for turning the Other Side into movie evil—motiveless, loving nothing, never telling jokes, never crying. I am for anything that says anything in a human voice . . . I am for talking, whatever form it takes. I am for voices.

Like *A Fine and Private Place*, Beagle's 1963 story "Come, Lady Death" is a tale of the supernatural, dealing with the attitudes of the living toward death and the dead toward life. A fable set in eighteenth-century England, it concerns Flora, Lady Neville, a haughty, aged, aristocratic giver of fashionable balls, who suddenly begins to find everything in life, including her own parties, dull. To alleviate her boredom, she decides to invite Death to her next entertainment, heartlessly sending the invitation via her hairdresser, whose child is dying. Death arrives in the person of a young, delicate, pretty girl. The story examines the contrasting reactions of various human types—the military man, the poet, the young lovers, the fashionable beauty—to the concept of death and juxtaposes these to their unanimous personal attraction to Lady Death. When all beg her not to leave them at dawn, she eagerly agrees to become mortal once more and pass on her unpleasant duties to one of the company, just as the duties had once been passed to her. After considering them all, she chooses Lady Neville, who, weary of being human and seeing life as meaningless, is perfectly suited to the role: "Death has a heart, but it is forever an empty heart, and I think, Lady Neville, that your heart is like a dry riverbed, like a seashell."

Aside from some satire of aristocratic etiquette, as Lady Neville and her friends worry over the proper title with which to address Death and assure themselves that Death must live at a fashionable address, the story has little of Beagle's whimsical humor. Its message is simple, and similar to that of *A Fine and Private Place*: to sink into ennui (Michael Morgan was also bored with existence) and to perceive too clearly the ultimate futility of living is fatal to body and soul.

Although Beagle had lived temporarily in Pittsburgh, Paris, and California and traveled steadily since 1956, New York was still his home when this European story was written. The Bronx is a powerful presence in his fiction. He had lived near the cemetery portrayed in *A Fine and Private Place*, and the capaciousness of the mausoleums provided the germ for his creation of Rebeck's odd hermitage. His 1966 magazine story "My Daughter's Name Is Sarah," about a loving father's inability to shield his daughter from the pains of growing up, likewise has a Bronx setting; and Lila the werewolf has an overprotective Bronx mother. But in 1964 Beagle moved across the continent to marry Californian Enid Nordeen and to settle permanently in California. He also legally took on the role of father to her three children, Vicki, Kalisa, and Daniel. Although he had been an urban dweller for most of his life, he moved into a cabin with few conveniences in the mountains outside Santa Cruz.

Beagle made the transition in an unusual manner. Shortly before the marriage he and his New York artist friend Phil Sigunick journeyed from the Bronx to San Francisco on their motor scooters Jenny and Couchette. Beagle described the odyssey in his second book, *I See by My Outfit* (1965). With guitars in tow for impromptu concerts, the two friends, when they are not worrying about scooter breakdowns and how cold a May they have picked to travel in, envision themselves as wandering minstrels on a knightly quest (Paladin is their favorite television hero): " 'It's like *The Lord of the Rings,*' I say. *The Lord of the Rings* is a fantastic odyssey written by J. R. R. Tolkien, and it forms part of our private Gospels, along with *The Once and Future King*, the songs of George Brassens, the world of Pogo, and a few other strangenesses. 'The beginning of the journey,' I say, 'the first night on the road to Mordor. This could be Bree, I guess, the edge of the wild country. What could Ann Arbor be?' "

I See by My Outfit reveals another of the balanced opposites in Beagle's life. He grew up during the 1950s, but his attitudes and affinities—Tolkien, harmony with nature, wearing a beard, singing to guitar accompaniment, valuing the eccentric individual—are all of the 1960s. When Tolkien's works became the object of a college cult during that era, Beagle served as a leading U.S. spokesman for them. He wrote an introduction for the Ballantine paperback *The Tolkien Reader* and later contributed to the screenplay of the Ralph Bakshi animated film of *The Lord of the Rings*. Beagle is highly critical of the paranoid conformity and denial of individualism of the 1950s, and he writes bitterly of his adolescence during such a depersonalizing period. Yet he was born about ten years too early to join the counterculture with that fanatic youthful zeal that marked the true radical child of the 1960s. Radicalism itself is too violent and intolerant to fit into Beagle's gentle, flexible perspective on life. It is instructive to compare the motor scooter journey in *I See by My Outfit* to another fictional cross-country bike trip made just five years later in the film *Easy Rider*. Respectable citizens see the bearded Beagle and Phil as "beatniks," not "hippies." They are artists and musicians, not drug dealers. They diffuse a touchy situation with some policemen by showing their thick folders of traveler's checks. And Beagle first sold accounts of the trip to *Holiday* magazine.

Having personally experienced this Tolkienesque cross-country quest may have contributed to Beagle's trying a different kind of fantasy in his next novel, *The Last Unicorn*. While both *A Fine and Private Place* and "Come, Lady Death" are supernatural fantasies, this novel is a mythopoeic fantasy, patterned on the heroic quest romance. It involves a long and arduous journey toward a goal rather than having a basically static action within a confined space as in the two former works. Because Beagle had been a vocal Tolkien advocate and had acknowledged the influence of many mythopoeic writers, critics rushed to make comparisons. They mentioned Tolkien and Lewis Carroll most frequently, but the names of James Branch Cabell and Robert Nathan (to whom the book is dedicated) also surfaced in reviews. Louis Untermeyer proclaimed that "Lewis Carroll, Hans Christian Andersen, both Grimm brothers, Bulfinch and Malory must have been looking over Beagle's shoulder and smiling approvingly while he wrote."

One should, however, distinguish between Beagle's evocation of the works of such writers and any actual attempt to emulate them. On the one hand *The Last Unicorn* is a traditional quest romance about the attempt of the last free unicorn on earth to find and liberate her fellow creatures from their imprisonment by King Haggard and his fearsome Red Bull. It is a tale that arouses strong emotions of fear, joy, and sadness. On the other hand, it is simultaneously a loving and funny parody of all the conventions of the quest romance, Beagle's most complex balancing act.

As in all his works the characters are avid readers, with literary allusions ever ready on their lips, just as they are also singers with a song ever ready on their lips. (In both respects they reflect the preoccupations of their creator.) Schmendrick can divert the attention of the unicorn's jailer by asking him to solve the insoluble Carrollian riddle "Why is a raven like a writing desk?" He can quickly grasp the essentials of unfamiliar situations because he knows all the mythic archetypes: "Haven't you ever been in a fairy tale before? . . . The hero has to make a prophecy come true, and the villain is the one who has to stop him—though in another kind of story, it's more often the other way around. And a hero has to be in trouble from the moment of his birth, or he's not a real hero. It's a great relief to find out about Prince Lir. I've been waiting for this tale to turn up a leading man." Captain Cully and his ragtag band of outlaws, a poor imitation of Robin Hood and his merry men, compose ballads about themselves that they hope will be included in the Child collection. And Prince Lir defines true heroism as "knowing the order of things":

> The swineherd cannot already be wed to the princess when he embarks on his adventures, nor can the boy knock on the witch's door when she is away on vacation. . . . Quests may not simply be abandoned; prophecies may not be left to rot like unpicked fruit; unicorns may go unrescued for a long time, but not forever. The happy ending cannot come in the middle of the story.

Although the novel contains much more action than his first, its plot is less complex. The unicorn, hearing from passing hunters that unicorns are no longer seen in the world, leaves her magic wood in search of her vanished fellows. She is set on the right road by an eclectic butterfly full of literature, songs, and popular culture who goes from Shakespeare to twentieth-century commercials and Broadway musical lyrics at the flap of a wing. In between quotations he manages to tell her, "You can find your people if you are brave. They passed down all the roads long ago, and the Red Bull ran close behind them and covered their footprints."

But before she can decipher his riddle she is captured by the evil witch Mommy Fortuna, whose Midnight Carnival promises "Creatures of night, brought to light." There she meets Schmendrick (whose name is Yiddish for a Caspar Milquetoast, a no-account, immature person who cannot succeed but thinks he can), a magician so incompetent that his teacher Nikos felt he must be destined for eventual greatness. Nikos has accordingly cast a spell that has made Schmendrick stop aging until the day he comes into his power.

Schmendrick knows the way to the realm of King Haggard, whom Mommy Fortuna has named as the master of the Red Bull. After they escape from the witch and are joined by Molly Grue, Captain Cully's wench, and the magician has managed sufficient tricks to keep them in provisions and out of trouble, they reach the town of Hagsgate. The town trembles under a curse: it is doomed to fall when Haggard's castle falls, a deed one born of Hagsgate will accomplish. Hagsgate has consequently denied itself children, and the one infant born there in the past twenty years was abandoned in the town square in a blizzard. Rescued and adopted by the childless King Haggard, he is Prince Lir, the "hero" of the fairy tale.

Leaving Hagsgate, the trio encounter the Bull. The fear he engenders overwhelms the unicorn, and he nearly succeeds in driving her into the waves where the other unicorns are imprisoned. Schmendrick forestalls disaster by summoning up his erratic magic and transforming her into a pale, mortal girl, the Lady Amalthea. The three gain admittance to Haggard's household, where Schmendrick assumes the post of court magician, and Lir and the former unicorn fall in love. Here the central conflict of the novel arises. Should Schmendrick permit the Lady Amalthea to remain human, forget her former existence, marry the Prince, and be happy, but leave the world bereft of unicorns? It is the gentle Lir, who has made himself into a Malory-style hero for love of the Lady, who decides that the sacrifice must be made. Advised by a cat, they find the secret path leading to the Bull's lair and prepare for the unicorn to confront him.

For a moment it appears that Schmendrick will not have the power to reverse the transformation. When he sees Lir foolishly standing before the Bull, sword raised, "about to be trampled flat," to keep him from reaching Amalthea, "wonder and love and great sorrow shook Schmendrick the Magician then, and came together inside him and filled him until he felt himself brimming and flowing with something that was none of these." Having come into his greatness at last, he returns the Lady to her unicorn's shape. She still, however, cannot resist the Bull until Lir, running between them, is gored and killed. Then the unicorn's anger and sorrow overcome her fear. She turns on the Bull, drives him out to sea, frees the unicorns, who stream out of the water to repopulate the world, and restores Prince Lir to life with her healing horn. The castle melts away, and Haggard falls to his death with a laugh "as though he had expected it," for "very little ever surprised King Haggard."

The ending is both happy and sad. Lir loses his love but is established as the local heroic ruler, to whom all damsels in distress will flock. The unicorn regains her immortal form, but her time as a mortal has stained her with regret and sorrow usually foreign to such creatures. Molly and Schmendrick are heartbroken when the unicorn leaves them, but they set off together down her road on the way to their "own strange and wonderful destiny . . . out of this story and into another."

The Last Unicorn has many links with Beagle's previous work. As in *A Fine and Private Place* there are two young lovers whose time together is fleeting and an older, eccentric pair who settle into a long-term companionship. The commonsensical Molly, who handles the housework and corrects Lir's spelling in his romantic ballads, is especially reminiscent of Gertrude Klapper. Haggard is that familiar Beagle figure, the person for whom all life has turned into boredom, for whom there is no longer beauty, wonder, or surprise.

More importantly, the novel further explores the relationship between mortality and immortality, living in or out of time, primarily through the complementary experiences of Schmendrick, whose period of immortality interrupts his mortal career, and the unicorn, for whom a period as a mortal human intrudes upon her eternal enchanted existence. (Don P. Norford demonstrates that the imagery of the moon, the tides, and of emptiness and fullness in the book relates also to this theme.) Beagle once more prefers temporality to eternity, for the very briefness and vulnerability of life make it precious and engender the love and compassion that are the sources of all true magic in the novel. As Schmendrick observes: "Whatever can die is beautiful—more beautiful than a unicorn, who lives forever, and who is the most beautiful creature in the world."

Critics agree, however, that this theme is secondary; the main theme of the novel concerns the death of imagination in the world. People look at the unicorn and see only a white mare. They only respond to the sham wonder produced by Mommy Fortuna's evil magic, as she makes a poor spider appear to be an Arachne, a mangy dog, a Cerberus. The wasteland that is restored in the novel is specifically a land wasted by a lack of wonder, and it is the artist, whom Schmendrick is frequently seen to symbolize, who assists in resupplying that want.

Although *Lila the Werewolf* was not commercially published until 1974, its composition dates from roughly the same period as that of *The Last Unicorn*. It is the least typical of Beagle's works, lacking his lyrical style and any character who, like the Lady Amalthea, Sarah, and Laura Durand, is vulnerably innocent in the Blakean sense. (It does deal with the concept of "disguise, camouflage, shape-changers" that has always fascinated Beagle and with the appearance of the fantastic in the midst of the mundane.) The story seems in general to criticize those temporary sexual liaisons that have replaced committed love in much of urban America. The latest live-in girl friend of the protagonist, Farrell, has, like most of her predecessors, neurotic sexual hangups and regularly visits an analyst. What makes Lila Braun distinctive, however, is that her neurosis manifests itself as lycanthropy so that she turns into a wolf at the full of the moon. For the most part the story is a tongue-in-cheek account of how Farrell learns to take this peculiarity for granted, as has Lila's gorgon of a mother and as will her future husband, a Stanford research psychologist: "He's proud of it—He thinks it's wonderful! It's his field."

But the incident that destroys Lila and Farrell's relationship is presented in a different and rather disturbing manner. One month Lila goes into heat during her transformation. After leading a pack of stray male dogs on an all-night orgy throughout Manhattan, she gets her needed quota of fresh blood by seducing and devouring several of the pampered household pets of Farrell's neighbors. When the Eastern European building supervisor, who knows a werewolf when he sees one, raises his gun to fire a silver bullet at her, Farrell, appalled by Lila's massacre, does nothing to stop him. (She is saved only by the dawn, which turns her back into a woman.) The misogyny that seems to underlie this episode, particularly the equation of female sexuality with bloodlust—"Since I hit puberty. First day, cramps; the second day, this"—is puzzling in an author who portrays romantic relationships in a lyrical fashion and excels in creating sensitive, nonstereotypical female characters. Beagle himself admits that since a critic pointed out the implications of the story to him, "it continues to make me a bit nervous these days, and I don't know what I think of it anymore."

For the past decade Beagle's creative output has been solely comprised of journalism, introductory essays, and scripts. Yet he has in no way "sold out" or produced hack work. Every piece is well crafted and related to the preoccupations of his fiction and to his personal values. His one screenplay that did not adapt Tolkien's work or his own is for a film, *The Dove*, that follows a Beagle-style journey, Robin Graham's solo sailing trip around the world. His teleplay for the series *Apple's Way*, "The Zoo," is all about animals; he coauthored *The Lady and Her Tiger*, the memoirs of a friend, animal trainer Pat Derby. He has introduced collections of the works of

121

though I suppose my delight should be mitigated by the near-certainty that, as I write, the navigator of the freighter in question is off in Gulag. But it couldn't have happened to a nicer country.

I had a friend called Carl, who used to sail with us ~~constantly~~ [regularly]. He was a shipmate of exact, entirely unfocussed, intelligence. If you gave him a line and told him on no account to ~~drop~~ [release] it, he would hold on to it even if his maiden aunt fell overboard [& he alone could -- at the price of temporarily releasing the line, toss her a life preserver.] ~~rather than drop it~~ -- boy-stood-on-the-burning-deck stuff. Once, coming down Buzzards Bay, after an entire night on the helm, I gave him a course of 260° and asked him to hold it while I snatched a couple of hours' sleep. It was midafternoon, bright as Hollywood Bowl, when I was awakened by the unmistakable shock of [yacht-]running-smack-into-rocks. I bounded up to the cockpit and found us aground. The rocks we had hit were not submerged. They rose six feet above the water. I had made a terrible mistake. My instructions to Carl should have been: "Follow a course of 260 degrees until you see a rock. When you see that rock, go 240 degrees until you have passed the rock. Then go [back] to 260 degrees."

Well, this here Russian navigator was using plotting sheets, sailing from the Baltic to the Gulf of Mexico. Plotting sheets are squares of paper marked with horizontal lines, each one representing one degree of latitude. You draw in the vertical lines, representing the meridians of longitude, -- spacing them apart to correspond to the distance between meridians at those particular latitudes: as simple as applying your divider to the little ~~code~~ [graph] printed at the bottom right hand corner of every plotting sheet. What this does is save you thousands of charts of empty stretches of ocean, which after all you don't need.

Provided there isn't an obstruction in the area.

"Knight of Ghosts and Shadows," revised typescript for a work in progress

favorite writers Robert Nathan, Avram Davidson, and Edgar Pangborn. A 1969 book, *The California Feeling*, explores the many facets of life in his adopted state. Even such a dubious sounding piece as "Kids and Kinkajous: special blessings of growing up with animals" in *Today's Health* concludes in pure Beagle fashion: "Lizard and louse, man and tiger, we are all here together, barely alive in the dark, clinging to the earth and trying to stay warm. Either we all have souls, or none of us do."

The only major alteration in Beagle's life during the past fifteen years has been his divorce from Enid Beagle in July 1980. He best describes his current situation himself: "I live on five acres just outside Watsonville, California, in company with my son Daniel, three dogs, six cats, one goat, one kinkajou, one ferret, one bushbaby, four turtles, and a lot of books and records. And four old guitars. I am currently working on a novel [tentatively titled "Knight of Ghosts and Shadows"], doing occasional scriptwriting and consulting, and singing in a French restaurant in Santa Cruz every Saturday night. I go to a lot of old movies, and I'm nuts about baseball, jazz, George Brassens, Chet Atkins, Cleo Laine and the poetry of Colleen McElroy."

Peter Beagle has pursued an extremely consistent career. His first novel was unusually accomplished and he has maintained an impressive level of quality in all his subsequent writings. He has regularly explored the intersections between ordinary life and the unexpected fantasy that he sees hidden just beneath that ordinary surface. He has always affirmed the value of life, "the magic," Raymond Olderman says, "of being human." No reader of even the most peripheral Beagle prose has any cause for disappointment, except perhaps, that he has not written more.

—*Ina Rae Hark*

Screenplays:

The Dove (Paramount, 1974), by Beagle and Adam Kennedy;

The Lord of the Rings (Fantasy Films, 1978), by Beagle and Chris Conkling;

The Last Unicorn (Marble Arch/Rankin-Bass, 1981).

Television Script:

"The Zoo," *Apple's Way* (CBS, 1974).

Other:

The Tolkien Reader, introduction by Beagle (New York: Ballantine, 1966);

J. R. R. Tolkien, *The Lord of the Rings*, introduction by Beagle (New York: Ballantine, 1973);

T. Scott and C. Wayburn, eds., *In the Ocean Wind*, introduction by Beagle (Felton, Cal.: Glenwood Press, 1973);

Robert Nathan, *Evening Song*, introduction by Beagle (San Francisco: Capra Press, 1973);

Michael Kurland, ed., *The Best of Avram Davidson*, introduction by Beagle (Garden City: Doubleday, 1979);

Edgar Pangborn, *The Atlantean Nights' Entertainment*, introduction by Beagle (Berkeley, Cal.: Pennyfarthing Press, 1981).

Periodical Publications:

"Telephone Call," *Seventeen* (May 1956);

"Stable of Dragons," *Texas Quarterly*, 3 (Fall 1960): 24-26;

"Come, Lady Death," *Atlantic*, 212 (September 1963): 46-53;

"Goodbye to the Bronx," *Holiday*, 36 (December 1964): 96-97;

"Wayward Reader," *Holiday*, 37 (June 1965): 35-38;

"My Last Heroes," *Holiday*, 38 (August 1965): 8ff.;

"My Daughter's Name Is Sarah," *Ladies' Home Journal*, 83 (February 1966): 62-63, 106-107;

"Tolkien's Magic Ring," *Holiday*, 39 (June 1966): 128, 130, 133-134;

"John Barth: Long Reach, Near Miss," *Holiday*, 40 (September 1966): 131-132;

"On Being the Man of the House," *Saturday Evening Post*, 239 (31 December 1966): 70;

"D. H. Lawrence in Taos," *Holiday*, 42 (September 1967): 44-45;

"Cockfight," *Saturday Evening Post*, 241 (24 August 1968): 28-29;

"Kids and Kinkajous," *Today's Health*, 52 (October 1974): 44-47;

"Maya's Christmas," *Today's Health*, 53 (December 1975): 46-49;

"Spot," *Harper's*, 252 (March 1976): 10.

References:

Benedict Kiely, "American Wandering Minstrel: Peter S. Beagle and *The Last Unicorn*," *Hollins Critic*, 5 (April 1968): 1-12;

Don Parry Norford, "Reality and Illusion in Peter Beagle's *The Last Unicorn*," *Critique*, 19 (1977): 93-104;

Raymond Olderman, "Out of the Wasteland: Peter S. Beagle, *The Last Unicorn*," in *Beyond the Wasteland: a Study of the American Novel in the Nineteen-Sixties* (New Haven: Yale University Press, 1972);

David Van Becker, "Time, Space and Consciousness in the Fantasy of Peter S. Beagle," *San Jose Studies*, 1 (1975): 52-61.

Dee Brown

(28 February 1908-)

BOOKS: *Wave High the Banner* (Philadelphia: Macrae Smith, 1942);

Fighting Indians of the West, by Brown and Martin F. Schmitt (New York & London: Scribners, 1948);

Trail Driving Days, by Brown and Schmitt (New York & London: Scribners, 1952);

Grierson's Raid (Urbana: University of Illinois Press, 1954);

The Settlers' West, by Brown and Schmitt (New York & London: Scribners, 1955);

Yellowhorse (Boston: Houghton Mifflin, 1956);

Cavalry Scout (New York: Permabooks, 1958);

The Gentle Tamers: Women of the Old Wild West (New York: Putnam's, 1958; London: Barrie & Jenkins, 1973);

The Bold Cavaliers: Morgan's Second Kentucky Cavalry Raiders (Philadelphia: Lippincott, 1959);

They Went Thataway (New York: Putnam's, 1960);

Fort Phil Kearny: An American Saga (New York: Putnam's, 1962); republished as *The Fetterman Massacre* (London: Barrie & Jenkins, 1972);

The Galvanized Yankees (Urbana: University of Illinois Press, 1963);

The Girl From Fort Wicked (Garden City: Doubleday, 1964);

Showdown at Little Big Horn (New York: Putnam's, 1964);

The Year of the Century: 1876 (New York: Scribners, 1966);

Action at Beecher Island (Garden City: Doubleday, 1967);

Bury My Heart at Wounded Knee: An Indian History of the American West (New York: Holt, Rinehart & Winston, 1970; London: Barrie & Jenkins, 1971); republished as *Wounded Knee: An Indian History of the American West*, adapted for children by Amy Erlich (New York: Holt, Rinehart & Winston, 1974; London: Chatto & Windus, 1978);

Andrew Jackson and the Battle of New Orleans (New York: Putnam's, 1972);

Tales of the Warrior Ants (New York: Putnam's, 1973);

The Westerners (New York: Holt, Rinehart & Winston, 1974; London: Joseph, 1974);

Hear That Lonesome Whistle Blow: Railroads in the West (New York: Holt, Rinehart & Winston, 1977; London: Chatto & Windus, 1977);

Teepee Tales of the American Indians (New York: Holt, Rinehart & Winston, 1979);

Creek Mary's Blood (New York: Holt, Rinehart & Winston, 1980).

Dee Brown is the author of *Bury My Heart at Wounded Knee: An Indian History of the American West* and of eleven other carefully documented volumes of history generally about the American frontier or the Civil War. Writing primarily for a popular audience, he typically adopts a simple prose style, tells his larger stories through sketches of individuals and groups, and enlivens his narratives with information and anecdotes taken from the memoirs, letters, and diaries of participants in the events he treats. He has also written fiction and books for children.

Born in Alberta, Louisiana, to Daniel Alexander and Lulu Crawford Brown, Dee Alexander Brown grew up in Ouachita County, Arkansas. After attending Arkansas State Teachers College, he obtained a B.S. in library science from George Washington University in 1937 and an M.L.S. degree from the University of Illinois in 1952. He married Sara Baird Stroud in 1934, and they had two children. For most of his career, Brown reconciled the demands of research and writing with his professional duties as a librarian. He worked in the Washington, D.C., area as a library assistant for the U.S. Department of Agriculture from 1934 to 1942 and, after serving in the army, as a technical librarian for the U.S. Department of War from 1945 to 1948. He then went to work as librarian of agriculture for the College of Agriculture at the University of Illinois, Urbana, from 1948 until his retirement in 1972. From 1956 through 1958 Brown edited the journal *Agricultural History*. He currently lives in Little Rock, Arkansas.

Brown's first book was a novel, *Wave High the Banner* (1942), based on episodes in the life of Davy Crockett. Several years after its publication, while searching the National Archives for military pictures, he and his colleague Martin F. Schmitt began collecting and annotating the photographs of the Old West which were to become the basis for their three pictorial histories of the frontier. The first book of this highly praised series, *Fighting Indians of the West* (1948), is made up of pictures of battlefields and battles—as well as pictures of white soldiers, Indian warriors, and chiefs—all taken during the Indian wars, from the 1862 Sioux War in Minnesota to the time of Sitting Bull's death at Pine Ridge in 1890. Its sequel, *Trail Driving Days* (1952), documents in picture and text the various phases of the annual cattle drives from Texas and across the Plains in the years between 1865 and 1890 and offers glimpses of life on the ranches, in the towns along the cattle trails, and on the open range. The final volume, *The Settlers' West* (1955), with a running commentary that includes the words of the actual settlers, gives a rapid visual history of successive cycles of migration and settlement in many areas of the West from the early 1840s to the start of the twentieth century.

Turning his attention from the frontier to military history and using as his sources nineteenth-century newspaper accounts, unpublished autobiographies, and personal papers, Brown wrote two books about Civil War raiders, making his protagonists take on individuality and color. Cast in a diary form, *Grierson's Raid* (1954) is a lively narrative about the cavalry exploits of Benjamin Harrison Grierson, who in the spring of 1863, in order to disrupt rail and telegraph communications in Confederate territory, led a brigade of wild-riding Union horsemen on a six-hundred-mile raid from La Grange, Tennessee, to Baton Rouge, Louisiana. Similarly, *The Bold Cavaliers: Morgan's Second Kentucky Cavalry Raiders* (1959) recounts the adventures of an intrepid band of Confederate soldiers from Kentucky, who under the leadership of John Hunt Morgan battled and skirmished in many states from 1861 to 1865.

It was with *The Gentle Tamers: Women of the Old Wild West* (1958), an entertaining and factual introduction to the part women played in the shaping of the American West, that Brown first achieved popular success. Drawing on a rich store of diaries, letters, published and unpublished accounts, he recreated the lives of more than two dozen women who traveled westward between 1850 and 1890, grouping them in chapters that consider them in such guises as settlers, army wives, missionaries, schoolteachers, adventuresses, courtesans, and entertainers. His gallery includes informative portraits of well-known people such as Calamity Jane, Lola Montez, and Elizabeth Custer, but he is at his best when dealing with less famous women, whom he mainly presents through excerpts from their letters and diaries. Throughout, he goes beyond the stereotype of the pioneer woman as a "face hidden in a sunbonnet" and shows that the women who went West, aware that they were involved in an epic venture, faced the dangers and hardships of frontier life with wit, courage, ingenuity, and endurance. Despite its hodgepodge nature, the book is thought provoking and engaging.

Military duty on the frontier during the Indian wars is the subject of both *Fort Phil Kearny: An American Saga* (1962) and *The Galvanized Yankees* (1963). In *Fort Phil Kearny* the author narrates, month-by-month, the incidents which led up to the Fetterman Massacre of 21 December 1866, the culmination of a guerilla war the Indians had waged to oppose the federal government's decision to link the gold-mining towns of the Dakota Territories to the East with roads that would spoil the last hunting grounds left to them. On that day, near Fort Phil Kearny, Wyoming, a group of Sioux, Cheyenne, and Arapaho warriors ambushed a party of soldiers under the command of Capt. William Fetterman and killed all eighty-two of its members. Through a balanced presentation of the facts and events surrounding this massacre, Brown manages to communicate a sense of the tragedy of all the Indian wars. *The Galvanized Yankees* tells the little-known story of the approximately 6,000 Confederate soldiers who, taken prisoner during the Civil War, were enlisted in the U.S. Volunteers in 1865 and 1866 and sent to deal with Indian uprisings on the Plains and in the Far West. This study, though of interest for its accurate and exhaustive information about the activities of each of the six regiments of Galvanized Yankees, lacks a unifying principle and fails to investigate the psychology of the converted Rebels and the implications of civil strife.

Along with a detailed description of the International Exposition held at Fairmount Park in Philadelphia in 1876 to celebrate the centennial of the Declaration of Independence, in *The Year of the Century: 1876* (1966) Brown tries to offer a kaleidoscopic view of the social, political, and cultural atmosphere of the United States in the decade following the Civil War. He touches on topics such as the Reconstruction, political frauds, labor unrest, religious revivals, women's rebellions, Indian wars, mythmaking in the West, and debates about the future of the black population. Successful in evoking the confident and exuberant spirit of 1876 and in providing a fast-reading and often amusing series of vignettes and character sketches, Brown is, however, as several reviewers complained, sometimes very imprecise in his interpretations of specific events.

Meticulously researched, original in its approach, and ardently told, *Bury My Heart at Wounded Knee: An Indian History of the American West* (1970) deservedly received both popular and critical acclaim. In this important contribution to frontier

history, Brown gives an eloquent and moving account of the fate of the roughly 300,000 Indians—survivors of more than a century of white man's wars and diseases—who were living in the United States in 1860 and who over the next thirty years struggled hopelessly to protect their land and their independence from the threats posed by the expanding white population which pressed in on them from both the East and the Pacific Coast. Each chapter focuses on a different Indian tribe and, after outlining the reasons why the whites wanted the territory, provides a compact chronological report of the conflicts, events, and betrayals which sooner or later forced the Indians to abandon their land. Some of the episodes chronicled are the long walk of the Navahos, the flight of the Nez Percés, the wars of the Kiowas to save the buffalo and of the Teton Sioux to resist invasion of the Black Hills, the Battle of Little Big Horn, and the massacre of Cheyenne and Arapaho at Sand Creek. The concluding chapter deals with the symbolic end of Indian freedom, the Battle of Wounded Knee, during which more than two hundred of the representatives of various tribes who had gathered to perform the ghost dance were attacked and killed by soldiers who feared that they were starting another uprising.

As Brown unfolds the tragedies which befell the Indians he judiciously refrains from moralizing; nor does he need to. From his factual reconstruction of the events, based on treaty council documents and on transcriptions of the words of leaders such as Red Cloud, Crazy Horse, Geronimo, Sitting Bull, and Chief Joseph, it becomes clear that the frontier was the home of richly diverse native peoples whose civilization and culture were systematically destroyed by the white newcomers.

The ruthlessness with which the West was won is also emphasized in *The Westerners* (1974) and *Hear That Lonesome Whistle Blow: Railroads in the West* (1977). Unlike many books of its kind, *The Westerners,* a panoramic history of the West from Hispanic days until the start of the twentieth century, stresses exploitation—of the Indians, of the land, and of its natural resources. A few chapters of this beautifully illustrated volume present white men who loved the frontier in its natural state and approached it respectfully in search of knowledge, but most are about individuals whose primary motivation for going west was either ambition or greed. In *Hear That Lonesome Whistle Blow* the author traces the stages of the construction of the Union Pacific-Central Pacific Railroad and examines the hold the railroads had on the imagination, the politics, and the economy of the United States during the second half of the nineteenth century. Both an engaging reconstruction of the drama surrounding the advent of the iron horse and a case against the railroads, this study focuses on the wonders and woes of early travel, the hard times of the Irish and Chinese laborers, the struggles of the Plains Indians to keep the trains from cutting through their hunting grounds, and the heedlessness of so many of the men who planned, built, financed, and attempted to control the railway network. While most reviewers praised the author for his open indictment of the excesses and corruption which the roads fostered, others objected that because of his constant emphasis on shoddy deeds, Brown tended to underestimate the complexity of the events and the epic nature of the undertaking.

During his career Brown has occasionally returned to the writing of fiction. *They Went Thataway* (1960), the only one of his works with a modern setting, spoofs government inefficiency in tracking down threats to national security, while *Yellowhorse* (1956), *Cavalry Scout* (1958), *The Girl From Fort Wicked* (1964), and *Action at Beecher Island* (1967) are standard westerns enriched by his

Chankpe' opi wakpala — Sioux name for Wounded Knee

I. ~~INTRODUCTION~~

1.

It began with ~~Cristoforo Colombo~~ Christopher Columbus who gave the People the name Indios. Those Europeans, the white men, spoke in different dialects and some pronounced the word Indien or Indianer, or Indian. Peaux-rouges or redskins came later. As was the custom of the People when receiving strangers, the Tainos on the island of San Salvador generously presented Columbus and his men with gifts and treated them with honor.

"So tractable, so peaceable, are these people," Columbus wrote to the King and Queen of Spain,"that I swear to your Majesties there is not in the world a better nation. They love their neighbors as themselves, and their discourse is ever sweet and gentle, and accompanied with a smile; and though it is true that they are naked, yet their manners are decorous and praiseworthy."

All this, of course, was taken as a sign of weakness, if not heathenism, and Columbus being a righteous European was convinced the People should be "made to work, sow and do all that is necessary and to adopt our ways." Over the next four centuries (1492-1890) several million Europeans and their descendants undertook to enforce the ~~adoption of~~ their ways upon the People of the New World.

Columbus kidnapped ten of his friendly Taino hosts and carried them off to Spain where they could be introduced to the white man's ways. One of them died soon after arriving there, but not before he was baptized a Christian. The Spaniards were so pleased that they had made it possible for the first Indian to enter Heaven, ~~and~~ they hastened to spread the good news throughout the West Indies.

The Tainos and other Arawak people did not resist conversion to the Europeans' religion, but they did resist strongly when hordes of these bearded strangers began scouring their islands in search of gold and precious stones.

Bury My Heart At Wounded Knee, *revised typescript*

extensive knowledge of frontier history. His most ambitious novel is *Creek Mary's Blood* (1980), the saga of an Indian family from the time of the Revolution to the beginning of this century. A fictionalized history in microcosm of the dispossession and destruction of the American Indians, it follows Creek Mary and her descendants from Georgia and the Trail of Tears out to the Plains, where they get involved in Red Cloud's War and fight at Little Big Horn, before most of them are massacred at Wounded Knee. The bitter story of their lives is told in retrospect in 1905 by Creek Mary's aging grandson Dane; interspersed with his first-person account are third-person omniscient chapters about events relating to the Indians in the nineteenth century. In this absorbing historical romance Brown skillfully blends fact with fiction but falters in his attempt to confer on his characters an authentic Indian perspective.

Viewing history as the interaction of many dynamic and prosaic factors, in fairly orthodox regional studies as well as in openly critical accounts, Dee Brown has, over the years, examined nearly every chapter in the saga of the westward movement. His best work, generally based on original documents, has portrayed the destruction of ancient Indian cultures and investigated other aspects of the toll exacted by the nation's western expansion. Though sometimes criticized for not attending to all the complexities of the events he treats, he has always been recognized as a tireless researcher and a gifted raconteur who narrates his stories in an informative and entertaining manner.

—*Winifred Farrant Bevilacqua*

Other:

Pawnee, Blackfoot and Cheyenne, edited by Brown (New York: Scribners, 1961);

Rural America Series, edited by Brown (Wilmington, Del.: Scholarly Resources, 1973).

Periodical Publications:

"The Settlement of the Great Plains," *American History Illustrated*, 9 (June 1974): 4-11;

"The Day of the Longhorns," *American History Illustrated*, 9 (January 1975): 4-9;

"The Day of the Buffalo," *American History Illustrated*, 11 (July 1976): 4-7;

"Pony Express," *American History Illustrated*, 11 (November 1976): 4-7;

"Perspectives on the Past," *American History Illustrated*, 14 (June 1979): 14-18;

"Geronimo," *American History Illustrated*, 15 (June 1980): 12-21; 15 (July 1980): 26-35.

William F. Buckley, Jr.

(24 November 1925-   )

BOOKS: *God and Man at Yale: The Superstitions of "Academic Freedom"* (Chicago: Regnery, 1951);

McCarthy and His Enemies: The Record and its Meaning (with L. Brent Bozell) (Chicago: Regnery, 1954);

Up from Liberalism (New York: McDowell Obolensky, 1959);

Rumbles Left and Right: A Book About Troublesome People and Ideas (New York: Putnam, 1962);

The Unmaking of a Mayor (New York: Viking, 1966);

The Jeweler's Eye (New York: Putnam's, 1968);

The Governor Listeth (New York: Putnam's, 1970);

Quotations from Chairman Bill: The Best of William F. Buckley, Jr., compiled by David Franke (New Rochelle, N.Y.: Arlington House, 1970);

Cruising Speed (New York: Putnam's, 1971);

Inveighing We Will Go (New York: Putnam's, 1972);

Four Reforms—A Guide for the Seventies (New York: Putnam's, 1973);

United Nations Journal: A Delegate's Odyssey (New York: Putnam's, 1974);

Execution Eve and Other Contemporary Ballads (New York: Putnam's, 1975);

Airborne: A Sentimental Journey (New York: Macmillan, 1976);

Saving the Queen (Garden City: Doubleday, 1976; London: W. H. Allen, 1976);

A Hymnal: The Controversial Arts (New York: Putnam's, 1978);

Stained Glass (Garden City: Doubleday, 1978; London: Penguin, 1979);

Who's on First (Garden City: Doubleday, 1980).

William F. Buckley, Jr., has earned a reputation over the past three decades as one of the most articulate, provocative, and entertaining spokesmen for American conservatism. His influence is exercised in a dazzling variety of media: he is editor, founder, and sole stockholder of the *National Review*, the nation's largest conservative journal, with a current circulation of about 100,000; his syndicated column, "On the Right," appears three times a week in over 300 newspapers across the country; his television show, "Firing Line," has been broadcast weekly since 1966 on commercial television stations and has been aired by the Public Broadcasting Service; and he is the author or editor of more than twenty books, ranging from political and social commentary to books on sailing and spy novels. Buckley has regularly contributed essays and articles to many American publications, and he makes frequent appearances as a lecturer or debater. Numerous awards and honorary degrees testify to his abilities as a journalist and interviewer. In addition to his ongoing activities as a publicist, Buckley has also engaged in politics more directly: he was the Conservative party candidate in the New York mayoral race in 1965, in which he was defeated by John Lindsay, but received a substantial 13.4% of the total vote; and in 1973 he was appointed a member of the United States delegation to the United Nations General Assembly.

Throughout his career Buckley has stood, in the name of "radical conservatism," against what he has seen as the prevailing ideology of liberalism, arguing staunchly, and at times eloquently, for a return to what he regards as the basic values of the past: for the promulgation of "truth" and increased human freedom, as against religious "secularism" and political or economic "collectivism." Although an ardent Republican, Buckley has often taken independent stands on specific issues. For example, he disagreed with Ronald Reagan's opposition to the Panama Canal Treaty. Now, following Reagan's election, Buckley is no longer "conservatism's one-man band," but finds himself fairly in the mainstream of the "new conservatism," as one of the acknowledged champions of American conservative thought.

William Frank Buckley, Jr., was born in New York City, the sixth of ten children born to William Buckley, Sr., a Texas lawyer and oil millionaire, and Aloise Steiner Buckley. In a 1968 *Esquire* article, Dan Wakefield wrote of this close-knit clan: "The Buckley family history describes the full circle of a class [*sic*] American pattern in the span of only four generations: great-grandfather Buckley left Ireland after feuding with the Orangemen and came to the New World; one of his sons, John, went west and became the sheriff of Duval County, Texas; one of the sheriff's sons, William, struck oil; William's sons went to Yale." One might add that the first immigrant Buckley had feuded not only with Orangemen (he later took a Catholic wife, and his children were raised Catholic) but with a fellow Protestant, whose skull he is said to have split with a plowshare. Nor did the elder Buckley strike oil at home, by drilling; he struck Mexican wealth through daring financial speculations in oil and real estate, until he was asked to leave the country by presidential order in 1919, whereupon he turned his attention to Venezuelan oil. At the time of his death in 1958, the net worth of the Buckley empire, with holdings in seven countries, was estimated at about $100,000,000.

William F. Buckley, Jr., began to display his gadfly talents early: at the age of six, he wrote an indignant letter to the king of England demanding the repayment of British war debts. Buckley was educated in England and France, and he also received private tutoring. At St. John's Beaumont, the "Catholic Eton" in Old Windsor, England, which he entered at the age of ten, he approached the president of the school two days after his arrival to complain of its shortcomings (the results were not recorded, but Beaumont is probably a prototype for "Greyburn," the British public school where a somewhat older Blackford Oakes, Buckley's spy hero, spends a lively semester). When he was fifteen, Buckley received a letter from his father admonishing him "to learn to be more moderate in the expression of your views and try to express them in a way that would give as little offense as possible to your friends." Yet this pattern of protest was repeated, with appropriate variations, at Millbrook School, New York, from which Buckley graduated in 1943, and again when he was drafted into the army in 1944 as a private in the infantry (he was discharged with the rank of second lieutenant in 1946).

Buckley entered Yale in 1946 and immediately began addressing long critical letters to the *Yale Daily News* over such issues as the basic course requirements or the policies of university charities. He rose to become one of the most famous—or infamous—of all the editors of the *News*, the oldest college daily, and he turned its editorial pages into a widely read and hotly disputed campus sensation. According to the dust jacket copy on his first book, he was labeled "the most dangerous undergraduate Yale has seen in years"; he was also named Undergraduate of the Year, delivered the Class Day oration, and graduated in 1950 with honors in political science, economics, and history.

Buckley had studied at the University of Mexico in 1943 and had taught Spanish while at Yale. After graduation, he returned to Mexico to work briefly for the Central Intelligence Agency, a period of his life about which he continues to maintain a professional reticence. He has admitted, however, that his supervisor in Mexico, the only one of his contacts whose real name he knew, was Howard Hunt. Buckley married Patricia Austin Taylor of Vancouver, B. C., on July 6, 1950. Their only child, Christopher Taylor Buckley, was born in 1952.

Buckley's first major work, *God and Man at Yale: The Superstitions of "Academic Freedom,"* was published in 1951 and created an immediate sensation among both critics and readers. Because this work established a pattern repeated in many of Buckley's later works, it is worth examining in some detail. Buckley proclaims his credo in the foreword: "I myself believe that the duel between Christianity and atheism is the most important in the world. I further believe that the struggle between individualism and collectivism is the same struggle reproduced on another level." The subsequent argument of *God and Man at Yale* may be summarized as follows: the faculties of private universities such as Yale are responsible to their trustees, who in turn are responsible to the alumni whose contributions keep them in business; and the nature of this responsibility is such that the faculty have an obligation to support and transmit the values of those on whom they are financially dependent. Buckley's ideal university is not so much a place for developing research methods—methods for investigating or seeking "truth"—as a place for the indoctrination and refinement of acknowledged truths. As he says, "The cause of truth must be championed, and it must be championed dynamically." Buckley defines his cardinal truths: "Let us say that Christianity *may not be truth,* but that in the eyes of Christians it is at least the *nearest thing to unrevealed* and *perhaps inapprehensible ultimate truth* [italics his]. . . . Individualism, we are entitled to say, is, if not truth, the nearest thing we have to truth, no closer thing to truth in the field of social relations having appeared on the horizon." Thus the faculty are obliged, in Buckley's view, to espouse Christianity and individualism, or at least not actively to oppose them. But the faculty at Yale is doing just the contrary; and much of Buckley's book is devoted to a lengthy catalogue of specific examples of "anti-Christian" utterances by teachers and administrators, and of "collectivism" in basic textbooks (Paul A. Samuelson's *Economics* is one of the worst offenders). Having named names and supplied an appendix listing all the universities where the textbooks he abhors are being taught, Buckley comes to a somewhat disingenuous conclusion: "I shall not say, then, what specific professors should be discharged, but I will say some ought to be discharged."

Buckley thus supports laissez-faire economics while staunchly opposing laissez-faire education. He regards "academic freedom" as a dangerous superstition, since education can never be value free: one inevitably imparts some values in teaching, so they had better be what he considers the right ones, Christian and individualistic. Buckley never explains why he considers Christianity and individualism the "nearest thing we have to truth," and he assumes for the purposes of his argument that a simple majority of Yale's alumni share his values. Buckley also fails to explore the impact of his suggested reforms on Yale's non-Christian or sociologically minded faculty and student body; he remains content that "*no freedom has been abridged so long as he* [the offending professor] *is at liberty to quit his job.*"

Buckley's polemical style is that of a tough debater, skillfully defining issues to his own best advantage so as to build a compelling logical case on debatable first principles. He is also a master of close textual analysis, examining clauses and reconstructing emphases with an advocate's attention to useful nuance and future profit. In a reference to Buckley's 1965 mayoral campaign, Norman Mailer described debating as "a highly difficult but very low art since it depends on being scrupulously dishonest. You fix facts with fancy and throw the suspicion of fancy on the other man's facts. Nobody in America is better at this than William B. . . ." Mary McCarthy expressed a similar view as a guest on "Firing Line," when she told Buckley, "Don't ascribe positions to me and then attack them." One of the more flagrant examples of such strategic ascription occurs in *God and Man at Yale,* where Buckley attributes to his opponents his own view of the university as a training camp for crusading gladiators: "The school is conceived as an extension of the arena in which battle is done, whereas, more properly, the teaching part of a college is the practice field on which the gladiators of the future are taught to use their weapons, are briefed in the wiles and strategems of the enemy, and are inspired with the virtue of their cause in anticipation of the day when they will step forward and join in the struggle against error." This blend of crusader's fervor and cold-warrior's fear is characteristic of Buckley's bellicose style—a style which, if out of fashion during the 1960s, now appears to be again in the ascendant (and one singularly appropriate for Buckley's most recent works, three spy novels which take place in the grim postwar climate of the 1950s).

Those who are charmed by Buckley's style often speak of his having mellowed with time, but the written record reveals, on the contrary, a striking consistency in both style and subject matter. As Buckley's biographer, C. L. Markmann, has noted: "Virtually every major position held by Buckley and supported by his associates today was first taken and enunciated during his years at Yale, often in terms that have altered hardly at all with time." In 1967, sixteen years after the publication of *God and Man at Yale,* Buckley made an unsuccessful bid for a post in the Yale Corporation; and he sent his son Christopher to Yale.

If Yale provided one powerfully benignant influence on Buckley's career, another, equally durable, was supplied by his sense of the injustices of the so-called McCarthy Era—injustices practiced not against blacklisted artists and former fellow travelers, but, Buckley felt, by liberal ideologues and historians against McCarthy himself and the House Un-American Activities Committee. Buckley's second book, *McCarthy and His Enemies: The Record and its Meaning* (written with his brother-in-law, L. Brent Bozell) was no less provocative than his first.

In a later preface added in 1961, Buckley described it as "the single serious book on McCarthy." Published in 1954, the year the Senate passed a resolution condemning McCarthy for misconduct, *McCarthy and His Enemies* is an attempt to exonerate McCarthy. While admitting that certain of McCarthy's "exaggerations" are "deplorable," Buckley and Bozell conclude that, in the war with communism, McCarthyism is "a weapon in the American arsenal," and that "as long as McCarthyism fixes its goal with its present precision, it is a movement around which men of good will and stern morality can close ranks." The authors are appalled by the tendency of liberals to apologize for McCarthy abroad, and they offer instead the following response to European critics: "America is simple. America understands pro-Communism, and she understands anti-Communism; but she is bewildered by 'non-Communism.' You may call this stolidity on her part, a sign of dogmatism, of ignorance, of absolutism. Call it what you will. It is there. And McCarthyism reflects it."

The theme of McCarthyism is also developed in Buckley's later work. In 1963 he edited a collection of essays entitled *The Committee and Its Critics: A Calm Review of the House Committee on Un-American Activities.* Here, as before, Buckley's

Magazine cover

terrain was carefully chosen: as he says in his own introductory contribution, "This book does not attempt to evaluate the performance of the members or staff of the Committee." It concerns itself rather with the Committee's right to exist, and with various (generally favorable) appreciations of its work. Buckley dedicated the collection to the widow of his friend Whittaker Chambers, who died in 1961, and some of whose letters were published in 1970 in a volume Buckley edited entitled *Odyssey of a Friend: Whittaker Chambers' Letters to William F. Buckley, Jr., 1954-1961.*

Following his book on McCarthy, the next major event of Buckley's career was the founding of the *National Review* in 1955. Buckley's own view of history is evident in the publisher's statement introducing the first issue, a rallying cry on behalf of the politically insulted and injured: "Radical conservatives in this country have an interesting time of it, for when they are not being suppressed or mutilated by the Liberals, they are being ignored or humiliated by a great many of those on the well-fed Right, whose ignorance and amorality have never been exaggerated for the same reason that one cannot exaggerate infinity." The magazine's "Credenda," printed on the following page, echo the language of *God and Man at Yale*: "The profound crisis of our era is, in essence, the conflict between the Social Engineers, who seek to adjust mankind to conform with scientific utopias, and the disciples of Truth, who defend the organic moral order." The *National Review* has been largely a Buckley family operation, employing both family money, to make up yearly deficits, and family members such as Buckley's sister Priscilla, who has served as associate editor and managing editor since leaving the CIA to join the staff in 1957. Regular contributors have included theoretical conservatives like James Burnham and Russell Kirk, and conservative ex-liberals such as Willmoore Kendall and Max Eastman. Buckley also assembled a wide variety of aspiring and talented young writers, helping launch the careers of such authors and columnists as Renata Adler, Joan Didion, John Leonard, and Garry Wills. According to George H. Nash, "*National Review* will be seen as central, of crucial importance to the development of the conservative intellectual movement." The very least one can say is that Buckley, through the *National Review*, has been an articulate spokesman for the idea of a conservative intellectual movement.

Since 1955, most of Buckley's political articles, editorials, and lectures have been collected in several books: *Rumbles Left and Right* (1962); *The Jeweler's Eye* (1968); *The Governor Listeth* (1970); *Inveighing*

We Will Go (1972); *Execution Eve and Other Contemporary Ballads* (1975); and *A Hymnal: The Controversial Arts* (1978). In addition, David Franke compiled a selection of Buckley's comments and quips and had them published in 1970 as *Quotations from Chairman Bill: The Best of William F. Buckley, Jr.*—alluding with his title not only to Chairman Mao, but also to Buckley's positions on the *Yale Daily News* and the *National Review*.

Following the debater's adage that the best defense is a strong offense, Buckley expresses his conservatism most frequently as meticulously offensive antiliberalism. He brilliantly and tirelessly exposes what he considers the intolerance and hypocrisy of liberals; and when objections are voiced against conservative abuses, Buckley instinctively counters with a comparable example or two from the liberal camp, as though, in the great battle for truth against error, objectionable practices were somehow capable of neutralizing one another's effects in a Balance of Error.

The more positive aspects of Buckley's political philosophy have been presented in *Up from Liberalism* (1959), with a foreword by John Dos Passos (and, in a later edition, an introduction by Barry Goldwater), which again is largely devoted to the exposure of liberal foibles; in *Did You Ever See a Dream Walking?: American Conservative Thought in the Twentieth Century* (1970), which Buckley edited and which he has described as his textbook; in *Four Reforms—A Guide for the Seventies* (1973), which argues for radical-conservative reforms in the areas of welfare, taxation, education, and crime (including the repeal of the Fifth Amendment "as currently interpreted"); and in the opening essay in *The Jeweler's Eye* entitled "Notes toward an empirical definition of conservatism." The basic themes of reverence for established "truth" and the call for a crusade against "errors" recur throughout these texts. Buckley's nearest asymptotic approach to a straight definition of conservatism is the following statement from *Up from Liberalism*: "Conservatism is the tacit acknowledgement that all that is finally important in human experience is behind us; that the crucial explorations have been undertaken, and that it is given to man to know what are the great truths that emerged from them. Whatever is to come cannot outweigh the importance to man of what has gone before. . . . Certain problems have been disposed of. Certain questions are closed: and with reference to that fact the conservative orders his life and, to the extent he is called upon by the circumstances to do so, the life of the community." Even here, a strategic vagueness prevails: *which* truths have answered *which* questions once and for all? How can we know already what will prove to be *finally* important in human experience? This definition might be reduced to nothing more than a declaration of the individual's inalienable right to his own prejudices; yet on this foundation Buckley claims the right to influence his community even to a drastic degree: "If it is right that a single man is prepared to die for a just cause, it is arguably right that an entire civilisation be prepared to die for a just cause." But who is to decide the justice of the cause? This is a weighty question, and it is regrettable that Buckley, while arguing for a vast array of specific social and political reforms, never explicitly traces the links between his tacitly acknowledged truths and their overt practical applications. Which truths from the past are the "true" ones, and how does Buckley know? To ask these questions is to cross over from political debate to epistemological theory; yet if the truth should prove to be incommunicable after all, save in a muted, equivocal form, then Buckley's Yale professors would also prove to have been wiser than he realized in the exercise of their academic freedom. It appears that Buckley, against the advice of his adversary friend John Kenneth Galbraith that he get himself to a university, prefers to remain argumentative and superficial.

This argumentative superficiality is characteristic of Buckley's account of his 1965 New York mayoral campaign, *The Unmaking of a Mayor* (1966), which he is said to regard as his single best work. It is again an attempt to set the record straight, to explore and explain the use of the media as a political instrument, citing numerous instances of selective quotation and inflammatory journalism. Although he received only 13.4% of the final vote, Buckley regards his candidacy as a success, because, while he never seriously hoped to win, his candidacy served to unite and establish the Conservative party as a political force to be reckoned with. New Yorkers were quick to respond to Buckley's cleverness, and several of his witty quips have become minor classics: when asked what he would do if elected, Buckley replied, "Demand a recount"; and when asked how many votes he expected to receive, conservatively speaking, he answered, "Conservatively speaking—one." Thus it was difficult to gauge the final seriousness of Buckley's merry campaign; Norman Mailer hailed it as "High Camp," and coined an apt metaphor for the ambiguities of Buckley's style: "If he had been elected, New York would have had a robber bridegroom for a mayor."

In 1966 Buckley began broadcasting his weekly television show, *Firing Line*, whose guests over the years have included Muhammed Ali, Jimmy Carter, Allen Dulles, Daniel Ellsberg, Valery Giscard d'Estaing, Billy Graham, Hugh Hefner, Henry Kissinger, Timothy Leary, Clare Boothe Luce, Groucho Marx, Richard Nixon, Ronald Reagan, Norman Thomas, and George Wallace. Buckley's unique conversational style—replete with delectably sesquipedalian asseverations—has long been familiar to the viewing public; he uses as many Latinisms in his speech as he does italics in his prose: he is probably the only personality in the American media who actually says "i.e.". Garry Wills has described his "English way of groping elegantly for a word and stuttering to a climax." Buckley often appears to get the best of his guests, charming them with what he calls his "disconcerting sea of teeth" while keeping them on the defensive. Markmann quotes the following advice from one anonymous veteran of such encounters: "Basically, his method of debating is to throw in a comment totally irrelevant to the subject being debated, trying to take the opponent off on a tangent, and then to follow that comment with a question to the adversary on still another subject. . . . He's extremely glib, and able to deal with a large number of subjects, making witty and biting comments on a great many different issues. He is not capable of delving in any depth into any single issue. So, as a debating tactic, it is a good idea to ignore his random sallies and stick to the particular subject of the debate and lead him as far into it as possible, because he quickly gets out of his depth. He does not have the facility to debate effectively under those circumstances, and he'll fall back on name-calling. . . ." (Perhaps the most notorious example of such public name-calling occurred when Buckley and Gore Vidal were invited together to comment on the Democratic National Convention in Chicago in 1968, which ended in an edifying exchange of epithets such as "crypto Nazi" and "queer"; Buckley's version of the encounter and the ensuing lawsuits is set forth at some length in *The Governor Listeth.*)

In 1973, President Richard Nixon appointed Buckley a public member of the United States delegation (under Ambassador John Scali) to the 28th United Nations General Assembly. Buckley's activities are chronicled in *United Nations Journal: A Delegate's Odyssey* (1974). He was assigned to the Third Committee, dealing with issues of human rights, where he was annoyed and saddened by his own delegation's bureaucratic commitment to avoiding "disharmony," and by the "moral hypocrisy" involved in adapting questions of principle, such as the Universal Declaration of Human Rights, to the pragmatic demands of politics (for example, avoiding references to freedom of emigration so as not to offend the Arabs and Russians during the Arab-Israeli War). Buckley noted that "it has become the habit of the United Nations increasingly to ignore major affronts upon the dignity of mankind while going on endlessly about relatively minor affronts, and to engross itself in economic approaches different from our own, in search of material progress." Toward the close of the sessions, Buckley was invited to a party in honor of Roger Baldwin, the liberal founder of the American Civil Liberties Union, and he commented that "there was more devotion to human freedom in that living room than I had seen in three months with the Human Rights Committee of the United Nations." He concluded that "the United Nations is the most concentrated assault on moral reality in the history of free institutions."

Buckley employed a similar day-to-day documentary style in two other works: *Cruising Speed* (1971), a personal record of one week in the life of the publisher of the *National Review* (the week beginning November 30, 1970), which has been described as Buckley's "most nearly self-examining book"; and in *Airborne: A Sentimental Journey* (1976), a detailed account of a transatlantic sailing voyage Buckley made with his family and friends.

His three most recent works have been in a fictional mode: the spy novel. Buckley's hero, Blackford Oakes, is a 1951 Yale classmate (Davenport College, like Buckley) whose brash Yankee charm and "obtrusive good looks" get him into places the merely intelligent would never manage to penetrate. Buckley has said that the descriptions of Oakes's induction into the CIA faithfully reproduce his own experiences; and—to use a Buckleyism—one is "entitled to suppose" that the descriptions of Oakes's early sorrows at Greyburn College may owe something to Buckley's own time at Beaumont. Oakes is humiliated at Greyburn, where he is given a bare-bottom thrashing by the headmaster as punishment for having drawn on the blackboard an illustrated conjugation of the Latin verb *mingere* (to piss), but also as a more general reward for his rude colonial manners. Oakes leaves the school in angry disgrace, stung especially by the headmaster's smug taunt after the beating: *"Courtesy of Great Britain, sir."* Much of the first part of the novel is taken up with Oakes's background and training, until finally he is sent to London on a spectacular first mission. It appears that secret American information, shared only with the British prime minister, is regularly getting into the wrong hands; and Oakes's task is to

page 56

"Mosaic," Farrell said automatically. Then Julie Tanikawa walked by Piglet's and Farrell got up and went after her without a word, bumping into tables.

He followed her for a moment without calling, not to make sure of her - since he had willed her to Havelock and Parnell Street, and to this spring moment, he certainly ought to know whether it was Julie or not - but only to watch her walk. A deep relief came over him to see Julie's legs switching along Parnell: the curious sigh of rightness that cats and apples and rain stirred in him. Oh, that was it. I should have known it was time again.

"Akiko Tanikawa," he said in the whining beggar's voice of a Kabuki demon. "You wear short dresses and do not go to the ritual baths. You have broken faith with the eight million gods of Shinto. The footless dead will come to you when the grasses sleep and bitch in your ear."

Julie turned when he spoke her name; blinked, dropped her handbag, smiled like water breaking in the moonlight, and ran silently into his arms. She almost knocked him off his feet - Julie was a strong girl, and quite as tall as Farrell - and that was right too, that was the only tradition they had ever had time to establish, unless you counted their habit of meeting one another in strange places, always unprepared. Farrell had thought often in the last ten years - though never

"Atlantic High," typescript for a work in progress

mingle with the highest circles of British society to trace the source of the leak. He starts at the top, literally charming the pants off Queen Caroline (an image altogether in keeping with the sophomoric glee Buckley feels at uncovering phallic double entendres in the language of undercover penetration and exploiting them to the hilt). When the queen summons Oakes to her bed, he does his duty—and then whispers in her royal ear, "*Courtesy of the United States, ma'am.*" Oakes quickly discovers that the queen herself is the conduit through which the secret information is being unwittingly conveyed from her faithful prime minister to her first cousin and childhood friend, the villainous Viscount Peregrine Kirk. Oakes's challenge is thus to put Perry Kirk out of commission while preserving the reputation of the queen, and he achieves this in a manner fully consonant with the unwritten rules of cold-war chivalry.

Buckley's second spy novel, *Stained Glass* (1978), is set in West Germany in 1952, and tells the story of a brutal murder committed by Oakes and other CIA agents (though Oakes does not himself push the button). Oakes and his cohorts join forces with the KGB to assassinate Count Axel Wintergrin, a popular German candidate for chancellor (a nobleman, a man of taste, another of Queen Caroline's cousins) on the very eve of his election victory, since Wintergrin represents a bellicose Reunification party prepared to go to war if necessary to liberate East Germany, and thereby possibly provoke a third world war. The moral squalor of the tale is compounded by Oakes's cover as an engineer engaged in restoring the bomb damaged cathedral of St. Anselm adjoining the count's palace. A machine designed to compare the colors of fragments of stained glass is rigged to serve as the murder weapon. Yet Oakes apparently has no choice. Orders are orders, even when given by self-avowed "ambiguists" such as Buckley's Allen Dulles. After the successful accomplishment of the murder, Oakes, speaking to his lovely KGB counterpart, Erika, pays their victim the following tribute: " 'He was the finest man I ever knew,' Blackford said. And then, hoarsely, 'If there's anybody left like him, we must meet again to . . . eliminate him.' " The Americans remain to complete the restoration of the cathedral—the least they can do, really—and the story concludes with Oakes and Dulles sharing a handshake, in agreement over Dulles's admission that although the assassination was based on dubious projections later thought to be false, nevertheless the act was justifiable. As Dulles tells Oakes, " 'I *don't* believe the lesson to draw is that we *must not* act because, in acting, we may *prove* to be wrong. And *I* know'—his eyes turned to meet Blackford's—*'that you know that Axel Wintergrin thought so too!'* " Thus the victim is rehabilitated after the fact as *willing*, as having himself sanctioned the rules of the game from which he is eliminated, since all the players agree that a just cause justifies unjust methods (the end justifies the means).

It is almost as though the line Oakes delivers early in the third novel to his faithful American fiancee, Sally, is not altogether in jest: "If you're as good looking as I am, people don't mind being killed by you—it's just that simple." This third novel, *Who's on First* (1980), follows the second chronologically, covering the period from the Hungarian revolution of 1956 to the launching of the first sputnik in October 1957. Two plots are interwoven, one dealing with the Hungarian events, including the execution of one of Oakes's friends before his very eyes, and the other with the space race, the competition to "get on first." Most of the novel takes place in Paris, where Oakes participates in a CIA-staged kidnapping of a Soviet scientist and his wife, in order to learn from them information crucial to the U.S. space effort. Everything works, except that Oakes's old KGB enemies recognize him in a chance snapshot, so the scientist and his wife are imprisoned on their return to the Soviet Union. The resolution of the novel hinges on Oakes's decision (in quasi-disobedience of his superiors for the first time) to *allow* the Russians to get on first, in return for the lives of the scientist and his wife, who are permitted to emigrate.

The tendentious history retold in these novels, including frequent informal conversations between Dean Acheson and Allen Dulles, is in many respects a particular illustration of the virtues of Christian individualism and gladiatorial bravado espoused by Buckley throughout his career. History is made in these works by individual cavaliers for personal as well as patriotic reasons. Buckley's years of practice as a political polemicist are not without effect on his novelistic style. His penchant for long words of Latin origin occasionally results in cumbersome comedy ("She was silent, but prehensile"). Buckley also invents participial adverbs suggesting the concessions of a debater ("concededly," "acknowledgedly").

The Oakes novels are also filled with little jokes, self-referential gags, and elegantly vulgar snatches of college humor, all of which help the reader not to take the stories too seriously. Some are Yale inside jokes, such as giving a retired atomic scientist at Yale the name Rene Wallack, a play on the name of literary critic and longtime Yale professor Rene Wellek. The name of the kidnapped Russian scientist in *Who's on First,* Viktor Kapitsa, may also be an oblique reference to the physicist Pyotr Kapitza, who was invited to return to his native land from England in 1934, and was never again permitted to leave. In *Stained Glass,* Buckley also pokes fun at his own new persona as spy novelist, caricaturing himself in the person of old Razzia, a writer "whose mannerisms were widely known, and widely caricatured, because of his depressing ubiquity: he was a syndicated columnist, a television host, an author, editor of his own magazine, and had now announced he would also write novels!" Buckley's characters read not only old Razzia, but also James Burnham and Buckley himself; and the top KGB official in Europe, Boris Bolgin, is an avid reader of *National Review* (it makes him feel so "funny-sad"). Some critics and reviewers have felt that such witty allusions are the most interesting feature of Buckley's novels. As in other areas of Buckley's activity, the reader may wonder just how seriously these novels should be taken: read as historical fiction, they are implausible; neither do Oakes's cold war high jinks succeed as popular entertainment.

Buckley currently divides his time between the offices of the *National Review* on New York's East Thirty-fifth Street and at least three other residences: the family estate of Great Elm in Sharon, Connecticut, which his father purchased in 1922; another estate in Camden, South Carolina, called Kamschatka, now the primary residence of his widowed mother; and Chateau Rougemont, in a village near Gstaad, Switzerland. He enjoys skiing, sailing, and music, and is an accomplished harpsichordist.

Buckley has been consistently faithful to the basic tenets of his "radical conservatism," however vaguely defined: upholding Christian values and the sovereignty of the consumer in the free market, while steadfastly defending the realm against the dragons of collectivism, communism, secularism, and the search for meaningful new moral options. Some of his critics try to dismiss this position as a thin screen for the defense of privilege and exclusivism; and it is true that in Buckley's particular case, the "us/them" style of right-wing anticommunism merges smoothly with the clubroom suavity of a professional Ivy Leaguer. Yet, with few exceptions, even Buckley's most perfervid ideological opponents appreciate his wit, bravado, and intelligence: while abhorring the Buckley substance, they applaud the Buckley style.

Buckley said as long ago as 1967 that his own favorite presidential ticket would consist of Ronald Reagan and Jacob Javits; and now that his wish has come half true, and Buckley is no longer in the embattled ranks of a "suppressed and mutilated" opposition, it will be interesting to see how he adapts himself to his role as an ideologue of incumbency. Reagan is a fan of the *National Review,* and Buckley's gray eminence may well influence the course of Reagan administration policy.

William Buckley's flickering tongue and flashing wit have challenged a generation to remember the old truths while searching for the new, to abhor hypocrisy and to value logic, and to join in the worldwide struggle for human rights and human freedom. He continues to remind his readers of the potential discrepancy between high-sounding theory and human practice. As he wrote in a speech he was not allowed to deliver at the United Nations: "The world is divided not between those who say they do not believe in torture and those who say that they do believe in torture. Rather it is divided between those who practice torture and those who do not practice torture. Indeed, the world is divided not between those who say they believe in human rights and those who say they do not believe in human rights, but between those who grant human beings human rights and those who do not grant human beings human rights." In such a divided world, William Buckley's voice rings loud and clear.

—*Gene M. Moore*

Other:

Racing at Sea, edited with contributions by Buckley (New York: Van Nostrand, 1959);

The Committee and Its Critics: A Calm Review of the House Committee on Un-American Activities, edited, with a contribution, by Buckley (Chicago: Regnery, 1963);

Odyssey of a Friend: Whittaker Chambers' Letters to William F. Buckley, Jr., 1954-1961, ed. Buckley (New York: Putnam's, 1970);

Did You Ever See a Dream Walking?: American Conservative Thought in the Twentieth Century, ed. Buckley (Indianapolis & New York: Bobbs-Merrill, 1970).

References:

Interview, *Playboy,* 17 (May 1970): 75-88, 180-193;

Charles Lam Markmann, *The Buckleys: A Family Examined* (New York: Morrow, 1973);

Robert W. Merry, "Buckley at 50: Lively Warrior,

Deadly Wit," *National Observer,* 29 November 1975, p. 24;
"Sniper," *Time* (3 November 1967): 70-80;
Dan Wakefield, "William F. Buckley, Jr.: Portrait of a Complainer," *Esquire,* 55 (January 1961): 49-52;
Garry Wills, "Buckley, Buckley, Bow Wow Wow," *Esquire,* 69 (January 1968): 72-76, 155, 158-159.

Frederick Buechner

(11 July 1926-)

BOOKS: *A Long Day's Dying* (New York: Knopf, 1950; London: Chatto & Windus, 1951);
The Seasons' Difference (New York: Knopf, 1952; London: Chatto & Windus, 1952);
The Return of Ansel Gibbs (New York: Knopf, 1958; London: Chatto & Windus, 1958);
The Final Beast (New York: Atheneum, 1965; London: Chatto & Windus, 1965);
The Magnificent Defeat (New York: Seabury Press, 1966; London: Chatto & Windus, 1967);
The Hungering Dark (New York: Seabury Press, 1969);
The Entrance to Porlock (New York: Atheneum, 1970; London: Chatto & Windus, 1970);
The Alphabet of Grace (New York: Seabury Press, 1970);
Lion Country (New York: Atheneum, 1971; London: Chatto & Windus, 1971);
Open Heart (New York: Atheneum, 1972; London: Chatto & Windus, 1971);
Wishful Thinking: A Theological ABC (New York, Evanston, San Francisco & London: Harper & Row, 1973; London: Collins, 1973);
Love Feast (New York: Atheneum, 1974; London: Chatto & Windus, 1975);
The Faces of Jesus (New York: Simon & Schuster, 1974);
Telling the Truth: The Gospel as Tragedy, Comedy and Fairy Tale (San Francisco: Harper & Row, 1977);
Treasure Hunt (New York: Atheneum, 1977; Chatto & Windus, 1978);
Peculiar Treasures: A Biblical Who's Who (San Francisco: Harper & Row, 1979);
The Book of Bebb (New York: Atheneum, 1979);
Godric (New York: Atheneum, 1980).

In *After the Lost Generation,* published in 1951, John W. Aldridge presents an extended analysis of the young Frederick Buechner and his first novel, *A Long Day's Dying* (1950). Although he compares Buechner to more established writers such as Henry James, Irwin Shaw, James Jones, and Truman Capote, Aldridge finds little to praise in *A Long Day's Dying* except the poetic "high" style and confesses, "About Buechner it is still too early to tell." Nevertheless, the perceptive Aldridge had given the novel critical attention and had heralded the literary career of one of the most promising contemporary authors.

A native of New York City, Carl Frederick Buechner began his career as a novelist following two years in the army and graduation from Princeton University in 1948. Concurrent with his early writings, he taught English at Lawrenceville, New Jersey (1948-1953); attended Union Theological Seminary, teaching creative writing at New York University during the summers; and served as head of the employment clinic, East Harlem Protestant Parish (1954-1958). In 1958, he received his Bachelor of Divinity degree from Union Theological Seminary and was ordained a Presbyterian minister. For the next nine years, he served as chairman of the religion department and school minister at Phillips Exeter Academy. With increasing success as a writer, Buechner became an itinerant preacher and teacher and now lives in Vermont with his wife, Judith, and their three children.

In his writings, Buechner is preacher, philosopher, and educator—all roles dedicated to discovering truth and conveying it to others. He is equally adept at writing fiction and nonfiction, which complement one another. The nonfiction, devoted solely to matters of faith, makes extraordinary use of the techniques of the creative artist; and, conversely, the fiction is built largely upon the same religious concepts and beliefs expressed in the nonfiction.

The narratives are primarily character studies concerned with man's efforts to discover the reality that underlies the human situation. Buechner presents each of his central characters at a crucial period in his life—a time when he is questioning principles and beliefs, when he is being personally tested, when he has an opportunity to make an important movement. The resulting character portrayal is often a psychological study handled by means of the meditation and introspection that distinguish Buechner's narratives. The external world is usually of little concern, and topical references are seldom included.

Concerning his approach to writing, Buechner explains, in *Telling the Truth: The Gospel as Tragedy, Comedy and Fairy Tale* (1977), that "truth in the sense of fullness, of the way things are, can at best be only pointed to by the language of poetry—of metaphor, image, symbol." Consequently, he writes in a highly poetic style which occasionally becomes so pronounced as to obscure the thought being conveyed.

Written when Buechner was twenty-three years old, *A Long Day's Dying* is a study of love and human relationships that concentrates on the interrelated lives of a restricted number of characters. The motivating factor is a sexual relationship between Elizabeth Poor, who sees herself as "an old princess enjoying her last lover," and Paul Steitler, an attractive but cynical English instructor. The repercussions of this relationship are immediately felt; primarily affected are Elizabeth's two admirers, the novelist/scholar George Motley and the sensitive, obese Tristram Bone. In an effort to silence Paul concerning their affair, Elizabeth falsely accuses the young instructor of having a homosexual relationship with her son Leander.

Employing a theme to which he would often return in his later novels, Buechner presents a perceptive study of the absence of meaningful human relations. Because they are essentially superficial, existing relationships are readily violated when the affair of Elizabeth and Paul unleashes a destructive force. However, a positive reaction comes from the same source, with the characters gaining a degree of honesty and freedom as well as greater understanding.

The work proves an ambitious undertaking, but one frequently marked by weaknesses in execution. The psychological approach is more realistically employed than by most authors, and Buechner's prose style complements this approach. Extensive use is made of symbolism, imagery, and allusion throughout the novel. The primary motifs are furnished by the classical myths of the unicorn and of Philomela. Individually, the numerous devices are effectively employed; collectively, they sometimes fail to mesh, therefore blurring purpose and movement in the total work. However, despite its unevenness, *A Long Day's Dying* is a novel of value; more importantly, it is a harbinger of literary greatness soon to be realized.

Written during his theological studies, *The Seasons' Difference* (1952) combines Buechner's knowledge of and interest in religious belief with his imaginative expression. Again, if not totally satisfying, the result was at least promising, and religion has continued to be an important part of all his subsequent works.

Frederick Buechner

The novel is set during the summer season at an estate of the idle rich. It is a time of merriment—of swimming and sunbathing, croquet, and cocktails. A disruptive force is introduced into this world devoted to escape through idle pleasures when Peter Cowley, the tutor for the children, reports that he has had a mystical experience. The precise nature of the vision is never made clear; but, as a result, Peter is convinced that there is a God and that He cares for mankind very much. Later, Cowley leads the adult members of the group back to the scene of his own reawakening. He is fired by his belief that the world is faced with "the destructions and despairs of unbelief," that people are "overeducated, ineffectual, and faithless," and that the only way to bring the world to Christ is through miracles. However, the only miracle taking place at this time is a mock one staged by the children. Cowley now realizes that the words and example of Christ are sufficient as inspiration and guidance. Diametrically opposed to him and his belief is Richard Lundrigan, an intelligent, self-sufficient person who stresses rationality. The conflict over faith that ensues is one that mars the merriment and spoils the summer for all concerned.

The Seasons' Difference poses the question of whether the fear of being deceived by one's hope for salvation is not better than the alternative—the abject loneliness of the totally rational man. At the end of the novel, most of the characters are still trying to escape the problem of belief with which they have been confronted—and to escape their empty lives. Nothing is fully resolved: ambiguity prevails in reference to the two basic positions, the needed change or movement, and the method by which it might be accomplished. Answers are not simple and not suddenly arrived at.

The novel contains very little action or plot. Instead, the content is a mixture of parables, sermon-like passages, and indirect commentary on society, the nature of man, the state of belief, and contrasting philosophies and approaches to life. This material is handled primarily through the use of dialogue and interior monologue. Also, to give dimension and scope to the life-view presented, Buechner brings forth numerous effective symbols and images. For example, life is viewed as a circus in which man is seen in extreme conditions. Similarly, a game motif is employed for much the same purpose.

The resulting novel is a haunting one. A deceptive simplicity marks the treatment of the most profound subject, the question of faith. This study is heightened through an effective use of indirection. The symbols and motifs impress but confuse; beautifully stated, they nevertheless evade the full grasp of the reader. Presumably, this protean nature was intended by Buechner.

In *The Return of Ansel Gibbs* (1958), Buechner shifts to the topical subject of politics. Returning to New York after a two-year hiatus in Montana, the brilliant and genteel Ansel Gibbs is scheduled to appear before a Senate committee for a confirmation hearing on his appointment to the President's Cabinet. He immediately encounters strong opposition from antiintellectual forces in the Senate, is made aware of obligations to relatives and friends, finds the spectre of his past life hovering over him, and begins to have self-doubts about his qualifications. Much of the novel that follows consists of the conflict between Gibbs, the ultimate human animal, and Senator Farwell, the right-wing leader of the opposition to his appointment.

As he is scrutinized and tested by others and his life becomes increasingly complex, Gibbs searches for the truth beneath his fluency and for the real person behind his urbanity. With the past returning to impinge upon the present, which in turn is forming his future, he reassesses his values and priorities; in the process, he discovers some harsh realities about himself and goes through a period of great self-doubt. The novel traces Gibbs's journey from indifference to negation to dedication before he can be said to have finally returned.

Imposing great restrictions on time, setting, and cast of characters; offering a very limited plot and scant action; and employing only a few of the symbols and images that distinguish his other works, Buechner presents a penetrating study of several issues and problems still relevant in today's society. Although it evidences some problems in control and occasionally offers action and ideas that defy full comprehension, *The Return of Ansel Gibbs* is a polished, engrossing narrative. Its author was a deserving recipient of the Richard and Hinda Rosenthal Award.

Following his ordination in 1958, Buechner alternated between fictional and nonfictional writings. For example, while serving as minister and chairman of the religion department at Phillips Exeter Academy, he wrote two volumes of meditations as well as his fourth novel, *The Final Beast* (1965). Despite its seeming simplicity and greater use of specificity, the novel proves to be a highly complex study brilliantly executed. The prologue is taken from Stephen Crane's *The Black Riders*, a poem that refers to the ancient beasts of darkness: guilt, sin, and desire. At the opening, Buechner casts his reader in the middle of a half-told narrative and rapidly introduces him to a small-town congregation and its young minister, Theodore Nicolet. All are confused, unfulfilled, and pursued by these ancient beasts. The town of Myron and its citizenry are sorely in need of salvation.

Much of the novel employs the journey motif. As the narrative begins, Rooney Vail, a wealthy member of the congregation, has traveled to a distant town to seek the aid of a faith healer, and Nicolet has followed. However, he is destined to take a longer journey, back into his family history to discover his father. As a symbolic action, Nicolet's trip is a journey to faith and results in his becoming a true priest.

The Final Beast is also a recounting of the

celebration of Pentecost. Throughout his trip, Nicolet is preparing his sermon for the occasion. In the early stages he has a vision of Pentecost; at his father's house he prays for help and experiences a revelation; and, following his delivery of the sermon, a tragic fire cauterizes the ills of the community and leads to an atmosphere and attitude of hope. With the celebration of Pentecost, the triangle of life has been completed with the Holy Ghost at the apex. The last of the beasts that haunt the characters has been confronted and defeated.

The unfolding of the narrative is a masterful weaving of a religious tapestry containing multiple strands. As usual, the progression is on two levels of perception, a recording of restricted actions on the conscious level and a moving backward and forward in visions, dreams, and memory pieces. The emerging scene is a confirmation of faith. In a world of sin and guilt, confused directions, and perverted relationships, the characters are not defeated; instead, they move to a state of joy.

Five years later, in *The Entrance to Porlock* (1970), Buechner employs a theme and motif bearing strong resemblance to those in *The Final Beast*. Here, however, he substitutes the family unit for the congregation. In the later novel, the quest motif is used to record a crucial day in the lives of the Ringkoping family. They are living inverted, unnatural lives and heading toward a destruction largely of their own making. The literal quest is to give away the Ringkoping mountain land to Hans Strasser, who maintains a home for the mentally retarded. The metaphorical quest is for self-discovery to be facilitated by moving back to a more elemental life. Each character has lost something that is needed to make life worthwhile; each is trying to escape from something that must be confronted before life can be a meaningful experience.

On their journey, the members of the family move back in time to key periods in their lives. Then, at the village, under the benevolent and inspired Hans Strasser's guidance, their primary movements—from ignorance to knowledge, blindness to sight, death to life—are begun. The movement of each character is expressed in symbolic terms; for example, Peter Ringkoping, the patriarch, frequently has the vision of lifting up a loose corner of the sky and discovering the unknown; ironically, his vision of the unknown obscures the needed vision, that of faith. The characters learn that salvation is to be attained through others.

As in the earlier novels, the story is told on two levels of consciousness—the real world and the dream world. Through a constant use of reveries, Buechner presents the fears, frustrations, weaknesses, and hopes of each of the characters. In doing so, he attains a quality of realism that other writers have seldom managed. There is no distinct line drawn between the waking and the dreaming, between the external and the internal worlds.

Interspersed with his fictional writings of the late 1960s and throughout the 1970s are various nonfictional works. Beginning with *The Magnificent Defeat* (1966), a collection of Presbyterian sermons, Buechner continued to produce nonfiction devoted largely to religious concerns. However, the succeeding volumes were essentially nonsectarian in their content. In these works, the elements of faith—including biblical characters, actions, and concepts—are presented in commonplace terms; conversely, the common things and experiences in life are elevated in the light of belief. The view is consistently fresh, clear, and infectiously enthusiastic.

The Alphabet of Grace is representative of Buechner's nonfictional statements. Originally delivered at Harvard University as the William Belden Noble Lectures in 1969, and published the following year, the book contains Buechner's reflections on the ordinary experiences of daily life. They demonstrate both a deep appreciation of the commonplace and an awareness of the metaphysical. Buechner's most direct autobiographical statement, *The Alphabet of Grace* contains commentary on his writings as well as his faith. Concerning the former, he identifies several experiences from his own life that became part of his novels, and he frequently offers the same concepts and analogies that appear in his fiction. In reference to his faith, he presents "The occasional, obscure glimmering through of grace. The muffled presence of the holy. The images, always broken, partial, ambiguous of Christ." Concerning his life, he speaks of personal longings, loves, and grievances. Then, noting that what he says about himself is also relevant to much of the human race, Buechner comments on the common needs of man (especially the need to find renewal and to live life fully) and the mysteries confronting all people.

Also written in 1969, *The Hungering Dark* contains essentially the same kind of material, although not expressed in the same subjective terms. It is a book of thirteen loosely related meditations advocating the rebirth of religious spirit in today's world and emphasizing the need to search for one's true self and for the oneness of mankind. Although it recognizes the guilt of man and the darkness in which he lives, *The Hungering Dark* offers a lesson of faith and hope. The book is an effort to help show the way to salvation—at least to offer encouragement. The highly abstract content is simplified through the use of illustrative narratives and practical application and is imbued with a powerful spirit. The style is marked by striking phrasings and extensive use of figurative language.

In 1973, Buechner produced his own particular kind of religious lexicon. *Wishful Thinking: A Theological ABC* attempts to redefine and revitalize familiar religious terms. Its purpose is to clear up many common misconceptions, to correct both over-simplification and over-complication, to state the ideas in concrete modern terms, and to use simple and ordinary language to express the complex and marvelous. The brief entries consist of a highly effective combination of anecdotes, analogies, commonsense explanations and analyses, well-chosen quotes from Scripture, and supporting views from other authorities. The fresh and witty writing style ranges from the employment of slang and colloquialisms to the use of expressions marked by purity and precision. For example, he offers this definition of *agnostic*: "An agnostic is somebody who doesn't know for sure whether there is really a God. . . . There are some agnostics who don't know simply because they've never taken pains to try to find out—like the bear who didn't know what was on the other side of the mountain. There are other agnostics who have taken many pains. They have climed [*sic*] over the mountain and what do you think they saw? Only the other side of the mountain. At least that was all they could be sure of. The faint glimmer on the far horizon could have been just Disneyland."

In a later reference to *Wishful Thinking*, Buechner explains: "I tried to shake a little of the dust off a lot of moth-eaten religious words and put some color back into their cheeks." In admirably accomplishing this objective, he proves not to be overawed by his subject or task; however, he clearly demonstrates wonderment and respect, along with a firm faith, throughout the book.

Having updated biblical terminology in *Wishful Thinking*, Buechner later did the same for characters in *Peculiar Treasures: A Biblical Who's Who* (1979). He attempted to put life into the characters and to humanize them without robbing them of any dignity, strength, or effectiveness as guides. Also, in an effort to relate the material as directly as possible to the present age, Buechner "transposed scenes from ancient Israel to more familiar settings" and "paraphrased passages or translated them into contemporary Americanese." In this modernization, he again made extensive use of slang terms, colloquialisms, and present-day parallels. The resulting camp treatment of the material would seem to be too flippant, too modish for most readers. In addition, the book lacks the polish and appeal of *Wishful Thinking*—the beautiful poetic expression often found there, the striking and highly original utterances.

Buechner's finest work linking his roles of minister and novelist is *Telling the Truth: The Gospel as Tragedy, Comedy and Fairy Tale.* As the Henry Ward Beecher Lecturer at Yale University in the spring of 1977, he presented these four lectures on preaching to those preparing for the ministry. In addition to their inspirational and informative message to that audience, these lectures offer significant keys to the understanding of the author's own fictional works and also present a perceptive view of the creative process.

In *Telling the Truth*, Buechner contends that a message must be directed not only to the audience's intellect, but also to the inner person, that part where dreams originate, "where thoughts mean less than images, elucidation less than evocation." He further explains that the language of poetry is the language of truth. Therefore, the words of the Bible are viewed as poetry, with image and symbol, sound and rhythm, and passion, because poetry "transcends all other language in its power to open doors of the heart."

Buechner explains that, in the revelation of truth, tragedy presents man as a sinner, comedy shows that man is loved anyway, and the fairy tale reveals that man has extraordinary things happen to him. He emphasizes that a preacher must deal with the naked man as well as the larger social problems. In other words, he must deal with tragedy. Likewise, the creative artists "preach the word of human tragedy, . . . the word that God has overcome the dark world—the word of divine comedy." In dealing with "the gospel as comedy," Buechner shows that laughter is an adversary of darkness, an antidote. When the darkness of tragedy and the light of comedy meet, "the gospel of fairy tale" results. The characters are transformed into that which reflects them at their best, a light breaks into the world, and the reader catches a glimpse of joy and realizes the triumph of hope. It is a fabulous tale that should be told in such manner as to stretch the imagination and strain credulity.

Although somewhat flawed by repetition and vagueness, the first two chapters of *Telling the Truth* are brilliant—a sparkling mixture of penetrating thought and effective examples. They offer worthwhile reading for students of literature as well as those concerned with philosophy and religion. However, the last two chapters offer little in the way of additional theory, consisting primarily of examples.

With the publication of the novel *Lion Country* in 1971, Buechner unknowingly began a project that, along with his nonfiction, would demand his application throughout much of the 1970s and would yield three additional novels. He got the basic inspiration from "a news story about a man who was in trouble with the law for running some sort of religious diploma mill and had done time for something else even more baroque in the past." Beginning what he termed the greatest romance of his life, Buechner felt a personal involvement which drove him to complete the first of the four novels in only about six to eight weeks.

The value of *Lion Country* is found primarily in its restricted cast of highly memorable characters. Antonio Parr, the narrator, is an average person who moves from his humdrum life and his conservative friends and relatives into an entirely different world. Frequented by a host of eccentric characters, this world is dominated by the personality of the incredible Leo Bebb. Distinguished by a rebellious eye, Bebb is an evangelist and faith healer. Other characters that would continue to play major roles in the tetralogy are Bebb's wife, Lucille, a heavy drinker with a butcher shop image; his adopted daughter, Sharon, a willowy carnivore with a bootleg smile; and his associate, Brownie, a Christian who has literally been born again.

The narrative in *Lion Country* is less calculated than in the previous works, and there is an obvious shift to the comic voice. Buechner now makes extensive use of satire aimed primarily at certain aspects of religion, church, and divines. However, this change is not as radical as it might seem. Although his earlier works, both fiction and nonfiction, were essentially serious studies, rooted in faith, they also made generous use of wit and humor. Correspondingly, beneath the comic grotesqueries of *Lion Country* is much serious commentary.

Lion Country reads much like the first installment in a serialized soap opera. It offers a slowly unfolding story that gives the impression that more is happening than is actually the case, and the highly episodic narrative presents many overstated scenes and overdrawn characters. Although ambivalence and indirection are still evidenced, this narrative does offer much use of concrete details, images, and facts. Also, Buechner clarifies and enriches many points by means of allusions. Parallels are drawn between the primary material and the Bible, opera, fairy tales, radio shows, television, movies, and various art forms. Nevertheless, beneath this factual surface is still the same basic grappling with issues that by nature must remain ambiguous. In *Lion Country*, these issues are introduced through the use of symbols and motifs that are then sustained throughout the tetralogy.

Buechner has explained that, when he began writing *Lion Country*, he did not have a clear idea of where he was going. However, it soon became evident to him that it was not going to work to make Leo Bebb the villain; likewise, it was soon obvious that Antonio Parr would undergo a character reversal. Ordained by mail, Parr journeys to Armadillo, Florida, for the purpose of writing an expose of a religious diploma mill, Gospel Faith College. Prepared to ridicule and condemn the evangelical head of the sponsoring Church of Holy Love, Leo Bebb, Parr finds him to be a good and sincere person. In the upside-down world of Armadillo, Parr soon becomes vitally and personally involved with Bebb, his family and followers, and their religious work. His movement is the search for self and a meaningful life; the process is the cultivating of his potential for growth in terms of emotions, experiences, and relationships. He escapes from a self-imposed imprisonment and moves to at least modified freedom in lion country. Through his own kind of literary evangelism, Buechner exhorts man not to fear life or try to escape from it. Instead, he encourages him to become truly alive: to know, develop, and reveal his full potential and thereby make living the meaningful experience it was intended to be.

As Buechner explains, the characters refused to let the narrative end with *Lion Country*; and, therefore, *Open Heart* (1972) resumes the religious parody a few years later. The first part of the sequel is set near Houston, Texas, where Bebb had earlier taken his revivalist troupe and, under the patronage of a "Cherokee Croesus," established his second Church of Holy Love. Soon thereafter, having done his work in the Southwest as well as the South, Bebb is ready to move north, where history is being made and where money and power are centered. Also, it is there, Bebb explains, that the fighting is thickest: "And the great whore is in the North too . . . holding a golden cup in her hand full of the abominations and filthiness of her fornications."

The traveling religious sideshow now moves to a location near New York City, where Bebb establishes his totally new church, Open Heart. He plans to perform his own kind of open-heart surgery. However, attendance is poor at the revival meetings in the North, and Bebb soon feels a lack of purpose and freedom. Admitting that Open Heart has not panned out, he turns his attention to the younger generation. Noting that youth are using drugs, giving in to fleshly desires, and becoming fed up with everything, the evangelist plans "to bring the gospel of Jesus straight to the Pepsi generation" and "to lead them out for Beulah Land."

In *Open Heart*, Buechner continues to add to his fine cast of seriocomic characters, including several Indians and Gertrude Conover, a rich theosophist from Princeton. Also, increased emphasis is now placed on the belief in both a prior and a future existence and on a need to avoid "spiritual hemorrhoids." The author's handling of both character and concept has now become more direct and earthy.

Presenting the next episode in his comic strip, the next reel in his home movie, Buechner soon resurrects the same characters with essentially the same basic problems and gives them a new setting in *Love Feast* (1974). The first half of this novel lacks the clear lines of movement usually found in Buechner's works. As the characters seem to be groping for direction and purpose, the author is also struggling. At the opening, he works at forming the transition, retelling several events that happened in the previous volume; then he seems to struggle to resuscitate the characters, to move them from the stasis into which they have lapsed.

When Buechner moves to the first "love feast," the narrative again becomes effective. The congregation at this feast, held on Thanksgiving in Princeton, ranges from teenyboppers to long-haired pot-smokers to blue-haired dowagers. In his message to the feasters, Bebb speaks directly from his heart to the needs of the congregation and elicits a highly emotional confession from Nancy Oglethorpe. Having finally opened a heart to Jesus, Bebb is now immersed in the Pepsi generation and "poised to evangelize Princeton, New Jersey, to set up the Supper of the Lamb in the groves of academe." This extended scene alone makes *Love Feast* the best of the Bebb books. Brilliantly conceived, it offers fine comic material and yet touches the emotions in a deep and meaningful way.

The rest of the novel is anticlimactic. Bebb and his followers are eventually locked out of Alexander Hall and denied the right to save souls on the Princeton campus. The last act of the love feasters is a march on Nassau Hall followed by a sacramental orgy. At the end of the novel, a funeral service is being held for Bebb in a potato field north of Princeton. The evangelist and an old friend have died in a fiery plane crash when buzzing a parade down Nassau Street at the Princeton reunion. Therefore, the work closes on what seems a very definite note of finality, as if Buechner intended to rid himself of Bebb forever.

After letting the character rest for three years, Buechner returns to his "love letter" in 1977 with *Treasure Hunt*. Although the roly-poly evangelist does not participate directly in the action, his presence is felt throughout the novel. On a cassette recording, he explains that he is leaving his old home in Poinsett, South Carolina, to Sharon and that he wants Antonio "to do something nice with that old place . . . to do it for Jesus." About a year after his death, the entourage goes to Poinsett "for Bebb and Jesus."

The messy finale to the tetralogy takes place in the mad, mad world of Poinsett. In the potpourri called *Treasure Hunt*, the scene is a mixture of carnival, asylum, horror movie, and bad science fiction; the new characters are grotesque; and the content now ranges from the ridiculous to the serious to the pathetic. The narrative clears up several of the major mysteries in the tetralogy. Only the question of Leo Bebb's possible reincarnation remains. The reader, as well as the central characters, has a strong but unconfirmed suspicion that the evangelist has returned to earth as Jimmy Bob Luby, a blind one-year-old son of food-stamp parents living in Poinsett. Therefore, the last glimpse of Leo Bebb may be found in the haunting and hilarious image of a little boy who is distinguished by his predilection for Milky Ways and his consistently filled rubber pants.

Despite its gimmickry, *Treasure Hunt* does present vital concerns. For example, it offers a serious study of the way to faith and the demand which it makes on the believer. The associated religious conflict is presented through the use of obvious contrasts, especially the contrast between Leo Bebb and his twin brother, Babe. Most importantly, the novel presents the journey of life, which usually takes the form of man's search for self and for that crucial element missing in his life. Man's condition is symbolized by repeated uses of the triangle, and his movement by use of the circle. The characters learn to live with the duality of the triangle and the repetition of the circle.

Revised and published as a single volume in 1979, *The Book of Bebb* frequently becomes repetitive in an effort to give unity, cohesion, and continuity to the total narrative. Direction and purpose are especially weak in the last two books; here, the narrative tends to move in various

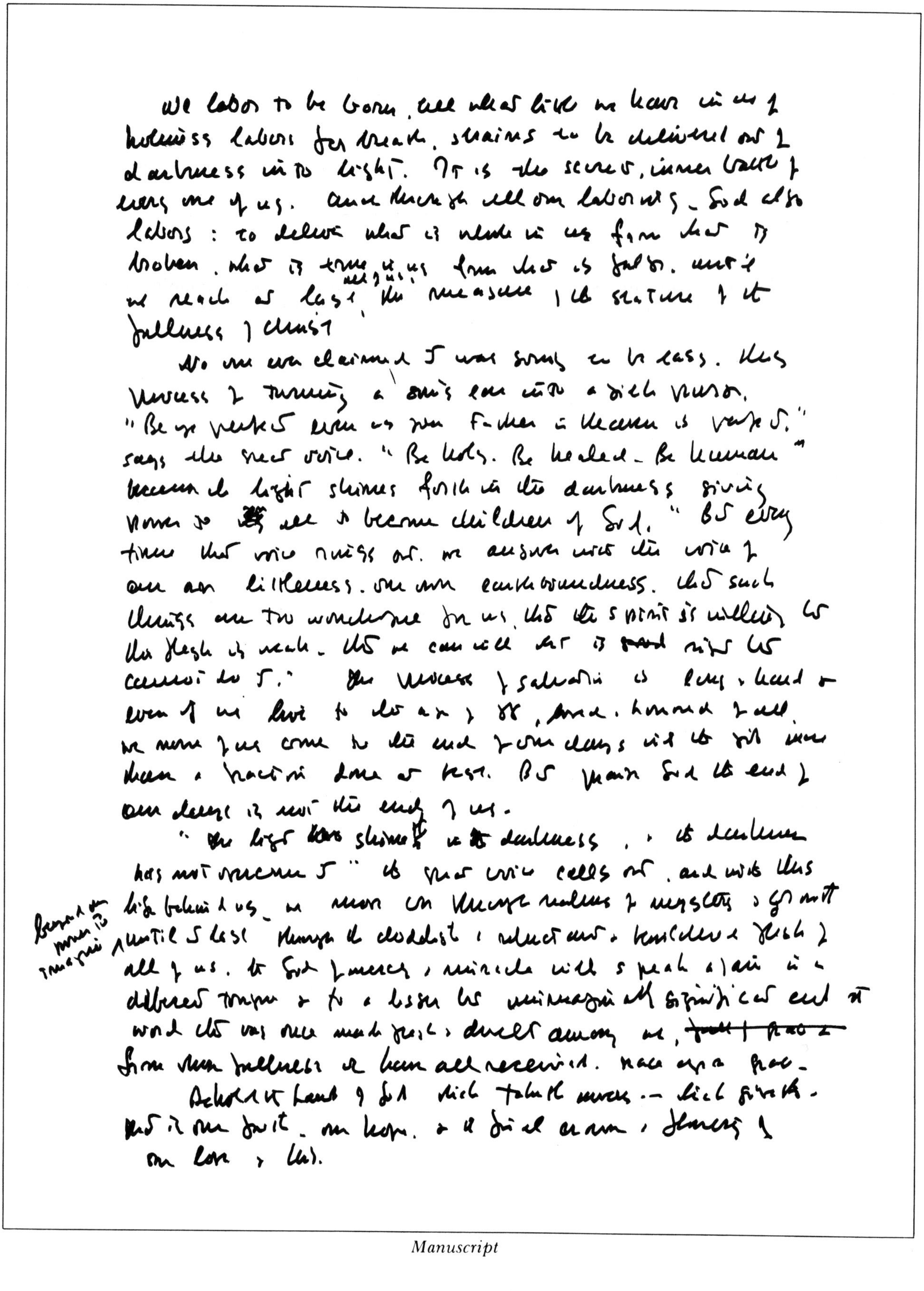
We labor to be born, all what little we have in us of holiness labors for breath, strains to be delivered out of darkness into light. It is the secret, inner battle of every one of us. And through all our laboring, God also labors: to deliver what is whole in us from what is broken, what is true in us from what is false, until we reach at last the measure of the stature of the fulness of Christ.

No one ever claimed it was going to be easy. This process of turning a sow's ear into a silk purse. "Be ye perfect even as your Father in heaven is perfect," says the great voice. "Be holy. Be healed. Be human" because the light shines forth in the darkness giving power to ~~all~~ all to become children of God. But every time that voice rings out, we answer with the voice of our own littleness, our own earthboundedness. That such things are too wonderful for us, that the spirit is willing but the flesh is weak. That we can will what is ~~good~~ right but cannot do it." The process of salvation is long and hard and every one of us has to do a lot of it, and, humanly speaking, we none of us come to the end of our days with more than a fraction done at best. But praise God the end of our days is not the end of us.

"The light ~~has~~ shines in ~~the~~ darkness, and the darkness has not overcome it" the great voice calls out, and with this life behind us we move on through realms of mystery and growth until at last [beyond our power to imagine] through the cloddish and reluctant and knuckleheaded flesh of all of us the God of mercy and miracle will speak again in a different tongue and to a lesser but unimaginably significant end the word that was once made flesh and dwelt among us, ~~full of grace~~ from whose fullness we have all received, grace upon grace.

Behold the Lamb of God which taketh away — which giveth — that is our faith, our hope, and the final answer and fulness of our love and life.

Manuscript

directions looking for a past or future thread. Also, the work becomes increasingly dependent on gimmicks. Conversely, the strength of *The Book of Bebb* is found in the masterful blending of disparate elements, the handling of the comic spirit, and the use of the psychological approach. Also, the reader's personal involvement in the narrative is outstanding.

Demonstrating great versatility, Buechner's latest novel, *Godric* (1980), is a moral allegory set in medieval England. Using documented historical data, he presents the story of a son of Anglo Saxon peasants who moves from a life of sin to salvation and sainthood. Marked by miraculous occurrences and spiritual encounters, his journey takes him to Jerusalem, where he experiences rebirth and dedicates himself to Jesus. Having chosen spiritual over earthly love, Godric lives a life of austerity, charity, miraculous works, and worship. As he nears the end of his 105 years, the title character presents his life primarily in retrospect, and it is recorded to glorify God's name and to afford others an example of a good life.

While fleshing out the historical account of Godric's life with fine imagination, Buechner effectively presents the human dimensions of the character and also gives an aura of greatness to the man. Especially noteworthy are the author's projection of the mind of Godric and his ability to draw the reader into that mind during both the character's period of sinful living and his later hermitic life.

Godric demonstrates much of the lustiness in both language and content that had entered Buechner's work with *The Book of Bebb*. Also, although not as obvious as in the tetralogy, humor is still present, and the religious theme obviously is still the dominant one. In this novel, Buechner demonstrates artistry in the simplicity and purity of his narrative expression, the careful structuring of the material and handling of movement and pace, and the fine control over the degree of emotional intensity demanded of the reader. Evidencing a full grasp and appreciation of his subject, the minister/novelist here gives proof of a rich talent that has matured.

In his numerous and varied writings, Buechner has made extensive and effective use of the symbols and images of his faith, the tools and techniques of his profession, the sincerity of his belief, and the hope engendered by his humanity. These writings are distinguished by an insistence on belief that is essentially nonsectarian, a vagueness of statement that is dictated by the nature of the content, a blending of elements that seemingly should not work but does, and an elusive form of the psychological that is appreciated for its realism.

Early appraisals of Buechner's work have proved accurate. After producing ten novels and seven volumes of nonfictional writings, he has demonstrated his right to be listed among such contemporary writers as Mailer, Ellison, Updike, and Barth. Although his literary appeal has been primarily to the intelligentsia, he is now widely recognized as a brilliant, inspirational writer and an original voice.

—*Max L. Autrey*

References:

John W. Aldridge, *After the Lost Generation: A Critical Study of the Writers of Two Wars* (New York: McGraw-Hill, 1951), pp. 219-230;

Ihab Hassan, *Radical Innocence: Studies in the Contemporary American Novel* (Princeton: Princeton University Press, 1961), pp. 153-161.

C. J. Cherryh

(1 September 1942-   )

BOOKS: *Gate of Ivrel* (New York: DAW Books, 1976);

Brothers of Earth (Garden City: Doubleday, 1976);

Hunter of Worlds (Garden City: Doubleday, 1977);

Well of Shiuan (New York: DAW Books, 1978);

The Faded Sun: Kesrith (Garden City: Doubleday, 1978);

The Faded Sun: Shon'Jir (Garden City: Doubleday, 1978);

The Fires of Azeroth (New York: DAW Books, 1979);

Hestia (New York: DAW Books, 1979);

The Faded Sun: Kutath (New York: DAW Books, 1979);

The Green Gods, with N. C. Henneberg (New York: DAW Books, 1980);

Serpent's Reach (New York: DAW Books, 1980);

Downbelow Station (New York: DAW Books, 1981).

Carolyn Janice Cherry, writing under the pseudonym C. J. Cherryh, is rapidly building a reputation as a prolific, versatile, and inventive science-fiction writer. Her novels include two trilogies, the "sword and sorcery" Morgaine series, and the Faded Sun trilogy, an extended study of an alien race. The first volume of the Morgaine series earned Cherryh the J. C. Campbell award for "Best New Writer of the Year" in 1977; the first volumes of the Faded Sun trilogy were nominated for Nebula and Hugo awards.

In Cherryh's varied works two themes recur: the theme of absolute power, especially when such power is held by a woman, and the theme of culture as a force shaping the whole of life. It is in the convergence of these themes, perhaps, that Cherryh's unique contribution to science fiction can be located. Since the days of the movie *Flash Gordon*, with its imperial villains, science fiction writers have been interested in the possibilities of autocratic societies. Cherryh, however, is one of the few writers who has presented such societies sympathetically, without taking the viewpoint of a rebel or an alienated outsider. Furthermore, interests in power have generally not, in science fiction, been combined with interests in culture: "space opera," with its starship battles and elaborate technological schemes, is often opposed to the more reflective "anthropological science fiction" which portrays alien social structures, family relations, and rituals. Cherryh, however, tells stories in which very powerful characters are situated in extremely complex cultures.

Cherryh's background has prepared her to handle such themes, if only by indirection. Born in Saint Louis, Cherryh moved to Lawton, Oklahoma, where she watched *Flash Gordon* serials and read and reread the two volumes of science fiction in the Lawton public library. During her adolescence, having decided to write professionally, Cherryh

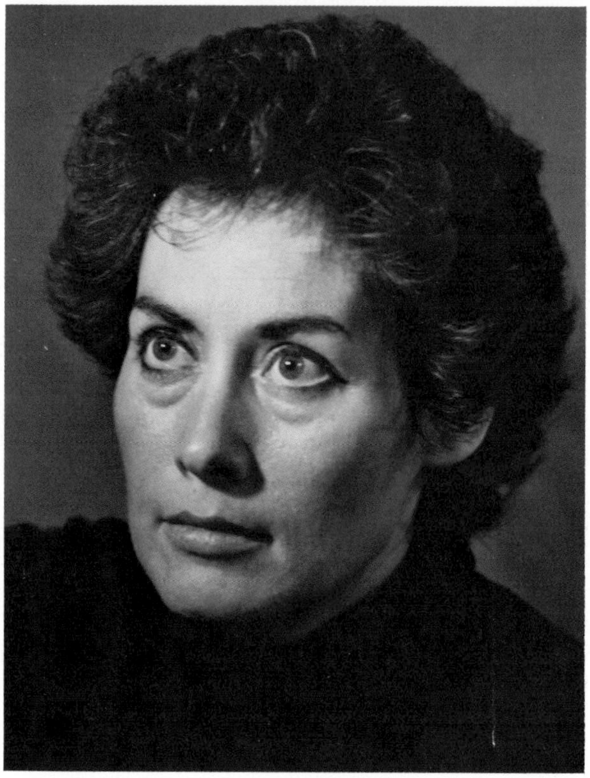

C. J. Cherryh

produced a novel a year. She also prepared herself for a more conventional career, taking a B.A. in Latin from Oklahoma University and an M.A. in classics from Johns Hopkins. This preparation gave her both a means of livelihood—she taught Latin and ancient history in the public schools of Oklahoma City for eleven years—and an absorbing interest in the ancient cultures of the Mediterranean. This interest has been nourished by extensive travel, including one journey in which Cherryh retraced the route of Caesar's British campaign. Such imperial figures as Caesar and Alexander, in fact, have absorbed Cherryh's interest: she was once interviewed sitting next to a bust of Julius Caesar.

While teaching in Oklahoma City, Cherryh continued her practice of producing a novel a year. She also developed her talent as a painter, using her own paintings for story ideas. "I look at what comes out and then try to figure out what might have created the situation I have painted," she says. One such painting, a shadowy figure standing by a castle door, was the seed of Cherryh's first published novel, *Gate of Ivrel* (1976), which was issued by DAW, a small house with a reputation for discovering new writers, especially in the field of fantasy. With the publication of *Gate of Ivrel,* Cherryh became a full-time writer.

Gate of Ivrel, the first volume of the Morgaine trilogy, is a "sword and sorcery" novel, a story of adventure and the supernatural. A band of a hundred humans sets out to close the gates built by the alien *qhal,* who use them to travel through time and space, destabilizing the human worlds. Armed with a sword that can destroy gates, the humans search for a master gate that will enable them to close the whole system. The band meets with misfortune and opposition, and by the book's end only the sword-wielding Morgaine is left alive.

Morgaine is the first of Cherryh's women rulers; she is, however, a rather conventional character, the stock enchantress of the "sword and sorcery" novel. Her sword, with its opalescent glimmerings and its soul-destroying power, is one of the dangerous weapons that have been part of the stock in trade of fantasy writers since Tolkien. However, Morgaine's character is not limited to stock qualities. Silver haired and elusive, like the *qhal* she opposes, Morgaine is a disaster for any world she visits, since closing the gates is almost as disruptive as leaving them open. Thus, although Cherryh relied heavily on the conventions of her genre in this first published effort, her inventive skills were already evident.

Gate of Ivrel was enormously successful: not only did Cherryh earn the Campbell award, but the novel's first printing sold very rapidly. It was soon followed by the second volume of the Morgaine trilogy, *Well of Shiuan* (1978). This novel recounts Morgain's struggle to close the gate on a world that is slowly drowning in its own oceans. She is aided only by Vanye, her *ilin,* a bond servant without rights or honor, reduced to that status as penalty for killing his brother. Her enemy is Vanye's cousin Roh, who has perhaps been taken over by an exceptionally wily *qhal.* The setting of this novel, with its interminable rainstorms and frequent floods, is especially effective. The novel ends with the hordes of Shiuan escaping from their doomed planet just before Morgaine closes its gate.

The series ends with *The Fires of Azeroth* (1979), in which Morgaine fights a final battle for the master gate against both the original *qhal* and the hordes of Shiuan.

While the last volumes of the Morgaine trilogy were still in press, Cherryh published one of her best-developed novels, *Hunter of Worlds* (1977), and began her second series, the Faded Sun trilogy. *Hunter of Worlds* is a linguistic tour de force: three separate languages appear in the text, each with a distinct grammar and a specific history. These languages are creations of the three alien races of the novel—the *iduve,* a predatory, competitive and pack-oriented race who, not surprisingly, hold power on the starship *Ashanome,* which is the setting for the novel; the artistic and collaborative Kallia, and a technically skilled, hierarchical race who figure in the novel's denouement. The protagonist and narrator of the novel, Aiela Lyaillueue, is a Kallian who is abducted by the *iduve,* and joined telepathically to the *iduve*'s servant Chaike and to a degraded and enslaved human. In the first part of the

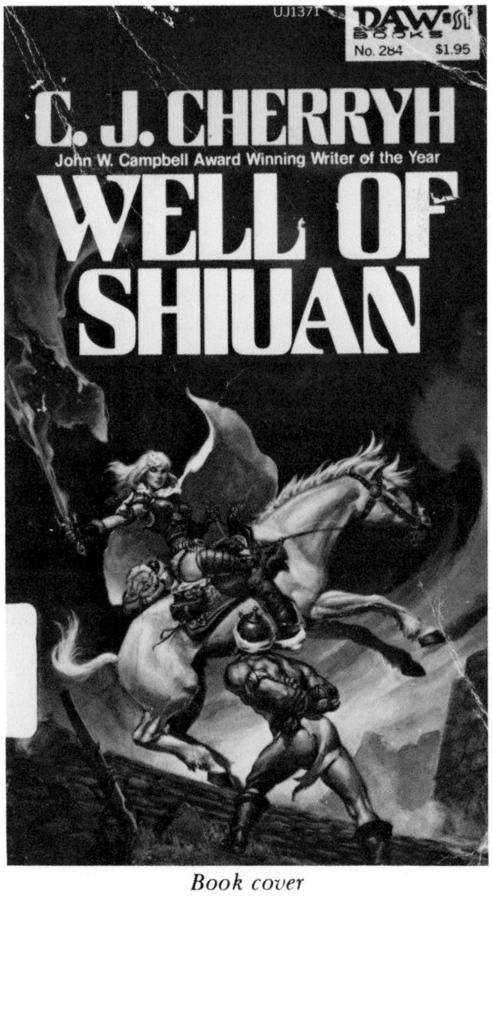

Book cover

novel, Aiela learns to see the *iduve* as members of a complex society, bound by their own ethics and norms, rather than simply as a race of bloodthirsty conquerors. Cherryh seems to have used the biological model of the wolf pack in imagining the *iduve,* and she had invested these characters, especially their leader, Chimele, with a dangerous allure, indicated by frequent comparisons with social carnivores.

The second half of *Hunter of Worlds,* however, is somewhat less successful. The focus of the novel shifts from the relations among the species on the *Ashanome* to the duel between Chimele and the outlaw *iduve* Tejef. The plot is highly compressed, not always clear, and sometimes arbitrary in its development: the author's interest seems to be absorbed in the cultures she has developed rather than in the machinery of connecting incidents.

It is in the Faded Sun trilogy that the central themes of Cherryh's science fiction—the woman in power and the centrality of culture—have been most fully deployed. The woman in power in these three novels is Melein, the *she'pan* (the mother and absolute ruler of the *mri,* a race of mercenaries). In this series, Cherryh concentrates on the relationships among Melein, Niun, a young *mri* warrior, and Sten Duncan, a human soldier who becomes enmeshed in their affairs. The overall action of the trilogy describes the destruction, on Kesrith, of all but a remnant of the *mri*; the journey of Melein, Niun, and Duncan to the original *mri* homeworld, Kutath; and their reclamation of that planet. Most of the story is told from the point of view of Duncan, who eventually becomes a *mri* warrior.

The *she'pan* is perhaps the most interesting of Cherryh's women in power because of the ambiguity of her position. Among the *mri,* whose society is strictly separated into warrior, priestly, and childrearing castes, the *she'pan* is at once high priestess, ruler, and mother; she is held in both awe and affection. But Melein has lost all of her people except for her brother Niun. Her exalted status, thus, has a bitter and almost elegiac quality. This melancholy becomes intense in the second volume of the trilogy, which concerns the voyage through the *Shon'jir,* the interstellar "between." Duncan has been sent on this voyage with the *mri,* and the ship that he shares with Niun and Melein is slowly transformed into an archaic, tribal *mri* dwelling, with traditional inscriptions, burning incense, and ritualized sacred spaces. Melein, lost and confused, rules this mad ship absolutely, by fiat, whim, and affection, as the three voyagers watch a procession of destroyed planets that had employed the *mri* in their

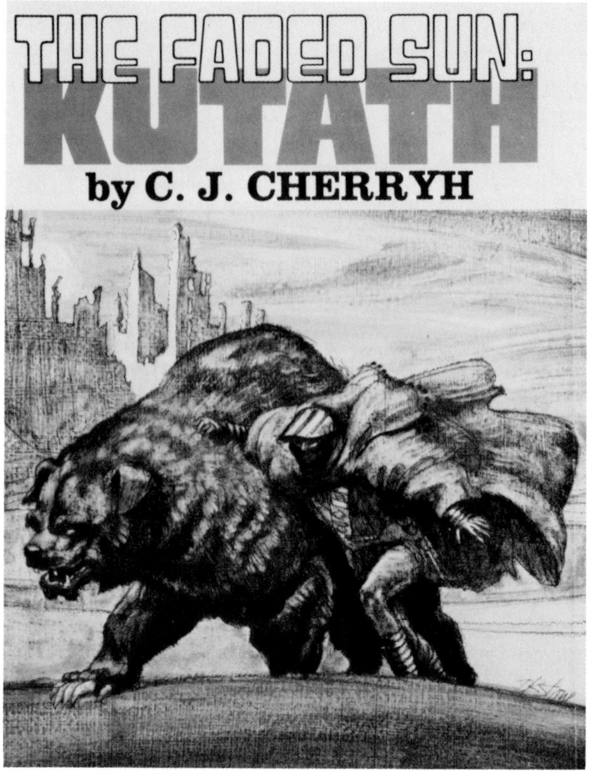

Dust jacket

wars, and wonder what they will find on the original homeworld.

It is through Duncan [illegible]hat Cherryh's second theme, the theme of culture, is most fully realized. Duncan and Niun are analog[illegible] figures: both of them are bred for war and know [illegible]r occupation. When the *mri* are callously des[illegible]n Kesrith, however, Duncan holds himself [illegible]ble and becomes obsessed with the two surviv[illegible] he is allowed to take them back to their ho[illegible]e hopes this futile gesture will at least prev[illegible] destruction of the race. But when Melein r[illegible] no *tsi'mri* (not *mri,* not a person) can join th[illegible] the home planet, Duncan surprises himsel[illegible] agreeing to become one of them. His acculturation [illegible] a painful process: he hates the *dus,* the huge telepathic beasts that follow the *mri*; making interstellar jumps *mri* fashion, without drugs, sickens and disorients him; and he finds their languages impenetrable. Duncan finds that he does not know who he is, or why he has agreed to this mad journey, or how it will end. He finally comes to terms with *mri* culture, however, by playing *sho'nai,* a game played by throwing wands or weapons in intricate patterns. *Sho'nai* symbolizes *mri* acceptance of chance and contingency, their fatalism, and their interest in skill, trickery, and prowess. Through the game, Duncan learns to absorb the *mri* culture. It is entirely believable when he later replies to a human's accusation of desertion by saying: "I was set aboard a *mri* ship to learn them. I was thrown away. The *she'pan* gathered me up again."

In the final volume of the trilogy, *The Faded Sun: Kutath* (1979), Cherryh joins two levels of action. On Kutath, Melein establishes herself as the ruler of the nomadic tribes of desert *mri* who have survived on that homeworld. Above the surface of the planet, the fate of the *mri* is decided by rivalries between the humans and the *regul,* who had employed the *mri,* and then massacred them on Kesrith. Duncan, who is now linked to both the *mri* and the humans, negotiates an alliance between them. His integration into *mri* culture provides the humans with a reliable guide to the aliens' intentions and permits them to learn from this ascetic culture. At the end of the novel, Duncan stays on Kutath, where Melein has established a unified and renewed *mri* culture.

The Faded Sun trilogy demonstrated Cherryh's mastery of the "alien anthropology" genre of science fiction. The first volume was especially popular, having been serialized in *Galaxy* magazine with Cherryh's own illustrations. Both *The Faded Sun: Kesrith* (1978) and *The Faded Sun: Shon'Jir* (1978) were nominated for Hugo and Nebula awards.

Cherryh's first novel since the Faded Sun trilogy repeated many of the elements of the trilogy in a concentrated form. Analogous to *Hunter of Worlds* in its compactness and its choice of challenging material, *Serpent's Reach* (1980) features an alien race modeled on the social insects. Again, the novel involves a very powerful woman, Raen. Raen is a member of the Families, who control all commerce in the Serpent's Reach, the isolated space colonies near Hydrus. The novel is told from Raen's point of view; her power is matched by the complexity of her position. She is a member of a very powerful social group, but within the Family Raen is isolated and in danger of assassination. She survives only by developing a special relationship with the *majat,* the insect people. Her precarious position is symbolized by her skill at *sej,* a game of rapid losses and gains, and of intense ritualized competition.

Cherryh's latest novel, *Downbelow Station* (1981), once again invokes the theme of empire. Pell's Station is the key link between the Company, an earth-based commercial empire, and the rebel Union of offworld planets; the novel concerns the struggle for control of the station. Like many of Cherryh's other novels, *Downbelow Station* includes multiple species of aliens; however, its orientation seems to be more technical than that of Cherryh's other work.

When questioned about her working habits, Cherryh once said that she always has a novel in hand: "I don't like to go to bed without a book, or something, in progress in the house. . . . even if it is two or three o'clock in the morning when I finish a novel, I always try to type, at the very least, the first line of the next one." Such unrelenting progress has characterized Cherryh's work so far. Her novels have steadily become more complex, more challenging, more skillful in evoking a mood. She has demonstrated, not only control of an exceptional range of genres within science fiction, but the ability to write novels that renew and transform their generic frames.

—*Susan Wells*

Other:

"Dream Stone," in *Amazons,* ed. Jessic Amanda Salmonson (New York: DAW, 1980), pp. 16-56.

Laurie Colwin

(14 June 1944-   )

BOOKS: *Passion and Affect* (New York: Viking, 1974); republished as *Dangerous French Mistress and Other Stories* (London: Chatto & Windus, 1975);

Shine On, Bright and Dangerous Object (New York: Viking, 1975; London: Chatto & Windus, 1976);

Happy All The Time (New York: Knopf, 1978; London: Chatto & Windus, 1979);

The Lone Pilgrim (New York: Knopf, 1981; London: Collins, 1981).

By limiting themselves to a specific place, characters of a single class, and situations of a predictable sort, some novelists risk charges of imaginative smallness. In all four of Laurie Colwin's books, surface has triumphed over depth and over variety of characterization, but such is the novelist's choice, not her limitation. Colwin has established herself as an anatomist of sanguinity in an age when unhappy families and desperate social lives have become the norm in fiction. Her world is that of comfortable, *New Yorker*ish people, talented, reasonable, attractive, and emotionally stable, who have money (or at least are not struggling for it) and who work as professors, philanthropists, cartographers, museum curators, or at other acceptably genteel professions. Only recently has Colwin begun investigating the less pleasant aspects of life. In her early work there is no sense of gritty social reality, no feeling for the turbulence of city life or national politics, little investigation of a deeper world of angst and despair. The reader is in a circumscribed reality.

It is like the world of Jane Austen (a novelist with whom it is instructive to compare Colwin). Like Austen's, Colwin's world depends on manners and morals, love and marriage: she charts the emotional growth of mostly sane individuals from solitude to mating or community. The very audacity of the title of her second novel, *Happy All The Time* (1978), suggests not so much breathless optimism as the fulfillment of dreams in a fairy tale, which only our resolute determination to fight has prevented us from realizing. Colwin takes seriously, without ever saying so, E. M. Forster's dictum, "Only connect." The connections are assumed as important in the tea-tabling, Austenish opening sentences of the novel: "Guido Morris and Vincent Cardworthy were third cousins. No one remembered which Morris had married which Cardworthy, and no one cared except at large family gatherings when this topic was introduced and subjected to the benign opinions of all." "Benign" adds the right touch of satire, ironic but not severe.

Colwin was born in New York City, grew up in Chicago and Philadelphia, and then returned to her native city for college and employment. She has strayed very little from its paths, although several of her stories have New England or midwestern settings. She focuses on the lives of smart, successful professionals in a city which makes privacy difficult and therefore very precious. Indeed, it is privacy, with its dangers and its attractiveness, which is Colwin's main theme, and which underlies the niceness of her characters' lives. Only privacy allows for the sanctity and integrity of the individual; and whether it is disrupted by the unknown, or the goofy, usually in the form of love, it is the central gift to which her characters aspire or cling.

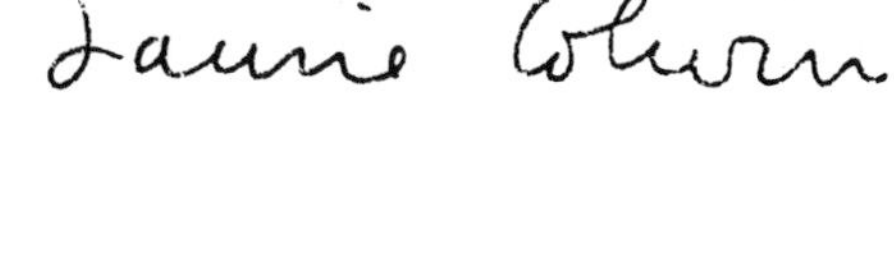

Thus, in the opening story of *Passion and Affect* (1974) ("Animal Behavior"), set in the Museum of Natural History, we watch Roddy Phelps, a controlled and orderly man, whose life has been invaded by Mary Leibnitz, a woman with a high sense of personal dignity which does not preclude occasional eccentricities of diction or behavior (she is the first avatar of the classic Colwin heroine, of whom the finest example is Misty Berkowitz in *Happy All The Time*). Roddy Phelps takes afternoon naps, and is upset when he learns that Mary Leibnitz has been watching him: "I don't like my privacy invaded." In "A Road in Indiana," Patricia Burr, the distressed wife of a college professor, finds herself in the grip of what her husband calls "emotional sloppiness," and her one cherished posession, a country/western record album, becomes the symbol of her private life and the single thing she takes with her as she drives the car out of town at the end of the story. In *The Lone Pilgrim* (1981), a second collection of short stories, another faculty wife, Ann Speizer, never tells her husband that she has been continually stoned on marijuana since they first met, until, at the end, she turns him on as well ("The Achieve of, The Mastery of the Thing"). Best of all, the earlier story "Wet," (*Passion and Affect*) about another transplanted academic couple, presents a husband who is terrified to learn accidentally that his wife Lucy, who he knows is an avid swimmer, has been swimming every day, in the depths of winter, without telling him: "The fact that she had gone swimming every day since they had come to Chicago and had never said a word about it left him speechless . . . How could he not know such an elementary fact about his own wife?" What Carl cannot understand is that Lucy's secret is neither a deliberate attempt to keep something from him, nor an unusual effort to sabotage his sanity. He comes to accept the status quo in the story's last line: "What grieved him was simply a fact: every day of her life she would be at some point damp, then drying, and for one solid time, wet."

Gestures like Lucy's swimming pinpoint Colwin's attempt to answer a single metaphysical question, even in seemingly "light" fiction: can order, and our definitions of it, be expanded to include eddies of disruption and disorder? For into the lives of these characters, arranged for comfort and organized according to domestic and personal artfulness, some tumultuous derangement bursts forth. Usually, the force controlling the hurricane is love: in "The Elite Viewer," Greenie Frenzel, as odd as her name, invades Benno Moran's life while his wife is away; Phillip Hartman (in "Dangerous French Mistress"), one of Colwin's "intellectual sensualists," feels his world crumbling when Lilly Gilette disturbs his library shelves: "My life, which had a comfortable, likable, productive shape to it, had incorporated something—someone—I didn't understand." At times, the tables are turned: in "Children, Dogs, and Desperate Men," Elizabeth Bayard "wanted a life that was clear and straightforward, that made sense. George was like a tornado, or a random act of God."

These obsessions with order or privacy are sometimes easy to overlook, especially in stories where the main character is rich, self-reliant, easily bored, and slightly nasty, like Jane Catherine Jacoby in "Imelda," whose title character is a South American servant with a private life of her own. Jane Catherine is one of Colwin's prototypes, a marginal juvenile delinquent who poses no real threat: "Most difficult to contend with was that Jane Catherine could not be threatened. She had been born smart, which was bad enough, but worse, she seemed to have been born wise." This precocious adolescent, no soppy, simpering girl, will turn out fine, especially because of the harmless eccentricities of her teenaged rebellion.

Elizabeth ("Ollie") Bax's growth from madcappery to emotional well-being and reasonable adulthood at the belated age of twenty-seven is the main concern of Colwin's first novel, *Shine On, Bright and Dangerous Object* (1975), a work slightly longer than it should be, but one which shows the author widening her themes and deepening her characters. Widowed after a blissful five-year marriage when her daredevil husband is drowned off the Maine coast in a sailing accident, Ollie must learn to take adult emotional risks, to balance passion and propriety, to remain true to herself but to expand her personal arrangements at the same time. Ollie (like Misty Berkowitz in Colwin's next novel) is a Jew who marries into high WASP society, and therefore a woman always conscious of being something of an outsider. The Baxes are stereotypical Yankees, without shows of affection. Either they lead an impoverished inner life, or else it is so turbulent as to defy articulation. Merida Bax, Ollie's mother-in-law, is always civil and efficient ("there was not an ounce of sentiment in her, and she doted on nothing she owned . . . Merida's emotional spectrum ran from the polite to the concerned. Warmth didn't filter through her prism."). Both of her sons receive an abundance of attention but a minimum of affection, and the expected result is a kind of emotional dislocation.

Sam Bax is the bright and dangerous comet in Ollie's life, a risky type who inspires an adolescent girl who "believed that if you loved, you loved uncritically." He allows Ollie to have it two ways at once (like those precocious but harmlessly delinquent adolescents in the earlier stories): "To have your rebel be second in his class, to marry your rebel, to have your rebel make law review buttered both sides of the bread and coated it with strawberry jam. What a life it was." But the life was doomed, not only by the hero's fortuitous death, but because, as Colwin's fiction recognizes, certain kinds of fairy-tale romances are not possible. Ollie's brother-in-law Patrick wisely informs her that Sam's early death has spared the pain of eventual divorce, a shocking fact but one which she comes to accept as true. The second inevitability is the coming together of Ollie and Patrick, the older, more circumspect Bax ("He was private not because he was remote, but because he was cautious"), who seems initially less available than Sam but turns out to be finer because his apparent privacy disguises a deeper dignity which his brother lacked. Patrick and Ollie, two hermits, learn to stick together, much to her confusion: "There is terror and there is joy and there is something that can be either; it takes you out of your own skin." This literally "ecstatic" condition is distinguished from the wacky, fearless, and fleet excitement of life with Sam and his motorcycle, because it gives the heroine "a glut of usable riches." At the novel's end, after a summer separation from Patrick at a New England music colony, Ollie returns, knowing that her commitment has been strengthened.

Absence makes the heart grow fonder because it toughens and hones it. Colwin's characters are committed to the inner life that must remain sacred and dignified, which is why so many of them have secrets, make seemingly irrational or headstrong moves, or simply disappear to get a perspective on their lives. Ecstasy is often balanced by a simple act of moving to a point on the periphery so as to observe the center with greater clarity. Both daily life and what Ollie terms "the secret life of things" demand formal and artful arranging, the control of passion which will nevertheless not stifle a rational sensibility.

In *Happy All The Time,* the dangers of isolation wrung from privacy, and the pains of coupling, in spite of gregarious sociability, are more deeply plumbed. The four central characters, who appeared in vignettes in *Passion and Affect,* are Holly Sturgis, "a strong domestic sensualist" of enormous talent but little achievement, with a passion for order ("She has not opted for neatness: it had been thrust upon her by nature"); the two men of the opening paragraph, who are cousins and best friends ("Guido was elegant, lithe, and sensual; Vincent was casual, springy, and game"); and Misty Berkowitz, never quite sure how she is to fit into a world in which, she is convinced, happiness is not quite possible, or at least not deserved, and never to be trusted. Her growing acceptance of sanguinity validates the easier graces of the other three characters.

Misty thinks that the twentieth century is not the great age of happy futures. "There are happy futures for some," says Vincent hopefully. "You and your debutante fantasies," she replies. The woman who calls herself the scourge of God, fit only for Attila the Hun, the nascent socialist whom rich people sicken, has a crustiness gradually softened by her love for Vincent. "Love turns you into mush," she thinks, but her frazzlement, a coming to terms with feelings she has denied or repressed, humanizes her at last. For fear of being hurt, as is even Holly, Misty is wary of the heart's uncertainties. Guido thinks of Holly, whom he meets and marries early in the novel, as a city-state, strong, well-defended, and self-sufficient, but she requires periodic retreats as strategies for garnering her strength, husbanding her emotions, and preparing for the future. Her need for distance, in the form of escape, is interpreted by her husband as a threat to their well-ordered lives, but instead it enriches that order by keeping it flexible.

In a different way, Misty deliberately takes it upon herself to give Vincent a hard time during their courtship; her tactic makes it possible for her to resolve what she calls the war between her character and personality, the latter of which is a conscious creation, a seashell housing a very soft animal. She convinces herself that she is interested in ultimate values like passion and honor, but she also learns to polish the rough edges of her personality through her contact with the more elegant Holly. Misty discovers that ordinary people may be vouchsafed limited perfection. As Misty comes to accept happiness, the reader realizes that Colwin has deliberately chosen an idealized arena for her characters which cannot be mistaken for the real world. Misty is incredulous that the two families get along so well when she and Vincent plan their marriage: "In the real world, Misty knew, people like Walter Cardworthy and Fritz Berkowitz waged social warfare . . . She did not believe that life left you alone to be happy in this world."

Happy All The Time may end a chapter in Colwin's creative life; already, in *The Lone Pilgrim,*

-243-

as Easter Sunday. They were an old, [redacted] old Jewish family of the sort that is more identifiably old American than Jewish. They gathered at Passover but not at Chanuka and they went to synagogue twice a year on the two high holy days. On Yom Kippur they did not fast but had family lunch in the afternoon.

They had their Thanksgiving turkey, Easter ham, Christmas goose and Passover capon off English Victorian plates. Their silver was old Danish. They liked great big ~~cut~~ crystal glasses and ~~cut~~ crystal wine glasses. Proper wine glasses seemed precious and rather <u>arriviste</u> to them.

On an early spring day, Polly sat in [redacted] a big leather chair [redacted] in [redacted] her father's study. The Solo-Millers had a duplex apartment the study of which was on the second floor. Polly [redacted] could faintly hear the sound of her children Pete, [redacted] six, and Dee-Dee, [redacted] four, downstairs annoying their father and grandfather. The Sunday paper was on Polly's lap. She had skimmed its contents and was now staring out the window, past the big china bowl of paperwhite narcissis that Wendy had set on a table in the corner. She was finishing her coffee and waiting until it was the right time to call her best beloved. Polly was having an affair with a man her own age, a painter by the name of Lincoln Bennett. She dialed his number, let it ring once, hung up, and dialed again. It was her signal. He picked up instantly.

"Family Happiness," revised typescript

we can hear new notes. "The Boyish Lover" presents a self-depriver who will not allow himself happiness; "A Girl Skating" and "Delia's Father" explore the mysterious gap between adults and children, and the more mysterious crossing from childhood into maturity; "A Mythological Subject" treats but never resolves an adulterous love affair ("Of all the terrible things in life, living with a divided heart is the most difficult for an honorable person"). When Colwin entitles one piece "An Old-Fashioned Story," in which the heroine ends up with the man whom, as an adolescent, she detested, we know she means "An Old-Fashioned Colwin Story."

Colwin's audience has been mindful of the new tones in her work. A survey of the critical responses to her four books shows that reviewers have gradually taken her more seriously as her reputation has increased and her work deepened. At the beginning of her career she was accepted as another author of "women's magazine" stories because some of the stories first appeared in *Redbook*, *Mademoiselle*, and *Cosmopolitan*. Others, however, appeared in more specialized, "literary" journals, and she came to seem like a writer who had perfected a formula for a *New Yorker* story. By the time of the second novel, observers such as John Leonard and Maxine Kumin were willing to take a deeper look, and with the publication of *The Lone Pilgrim*, the title story of which was included in the 1976 O. Henry Award Collection, Joyce Carol Oates added her approval in an omnibus review in the *New York Times*.

Most writers, as they veer into middle age or creative maturity, whichever comes first, enter a crisis period. It was to this that Keats referred when he mentioned those "dark passages" which he was hopeful of exploring in poems which were, tragically, never to be written. Colwin has entered a new room in the mansion of many apartments (to continue Keats's image). Already we have seen how the novelist of cheerfulness has embarked on an investigation of melancholy, the troublesome trials of the heart, and those uncertainties which are bound to make being happy all the time much less of a possibility.

—*Willard Spiegelman*

Alfred Corn

(14 August 1943-)

BOOKS: *All Roads at Once* (New York: Viking, 1976);

A Call in the Midst of the Crowd (New York: Viking, 1978);

The Various Light (New York: Viking, 1980).

Alfred Corn's first volume of poetry was hailed by the poet John Ashbery as "a brilliant beginning." Two more collections of soft-voiced lyrics have appeared since then, and the critic Harold Bloom has written of Corn that "his aesthetic prospects are remarkable, even in this crowded time."

Alfred DeWitt Corn III was born in Bainbridge, Georgia, to A. D. and Grace Lahey Corn, the third of three children. He spent his childhood and youth in Valdosta, a setting he evokes at the end of *The Various Light* (1980) in his autobiographical poem, "The Outdoor Amphitheater." Corn attended Emory University, graduating with a B.A. in French in 1965. He continued his studies at Columbia University, receiving his M.A. in 1967 with a thesis on the French poet Henri Michaux. He spent the following year as a Fulbright Fellow in Paris, beginning research for what was to have been his doctoral dissertation, a comparative study of the works of Albert Camus and Herman Melville which he never completed. In 1967 he married Ann Jones. They were divorced in 1971.

After returning from Paris, Corn worked in New York City as an associate editor for *University Review* and as a staff writer for the Da Capo Press. He began writing fiction, but turned to poetry after 1970 and began to publish his poems in numerous magazines and periodicals, including the *American Review*, the *Nation*, the *New Yorker*, *Poem*, *Poetry*, and *Saturday Review*. He was awarded an Ingram Merrill Foundation grant in 1974, and the following year he received *Poetry*'s George Dillon Memorial Prize. More recently, he received *Poetry*'s Blumenthal Prize in 1977, and an award from the National Endowment for the Arts for 1979-1980.

All Roads at Once, Corn's first volume of poems, appeared in 1976, dedicated to his ex-wife and containing many poems that had previously appeared in periodicals. The thirty-six poems in this collection were described by J. D. McClatchy in the *Nation* as "contingency plans to counter the hazards of overdetermined or undermining circumstance." Some of the poems are suggested by a specific locale, in New York City or at the seashore, in Oregon or Paris; others reflect on works of art or literature, Chinese porcelains or Charles Darwin's *The Voyage of the Beagle*. Yet they all attempt to achieve a kind of "infinity effect," an opening of the poet's awareness to encompass the multiplicity and mutability of his own experience.

Alfred Corn

Corn's poems frequently begin with a descriptive slice of life, with closely observed sights and sounds which are casually displayed and examined before finally being brought into larger symbolic focus, near the end of the poem, in an open-ended rhetorical question. Sometimes this abstract expansion takes the form of a grim joke, as in "What Sea Urchins Eat," one of the more metaphorically solid of Corn's offerings. Another typical example of this pattern occurs in "Measuring a Rooftop in the Cast-Iron District," where the heat and tarpaper-stickiness of roof-measuring serve as background to a leisurely catalogue of elements of cityscape; although the "chrome needle" of the Empire State Building "identifies the city," an Italian Romanesque church suggests that "we could be in Lucca, almost." The poet's eye descends from chimneys and water tanks to the street, where "someone throws garbage into a parked dumpster." Then, in the final stanza, the poet at last springs his question:

> What's struggling to be said in these
> inharmonious
> surroundings? Why is it their not adding up,
> American randomness takes on dimension?

The closing line turns the poem into a Whitmanesque celebration, a sensitive study in ashcan socialist realism: "Work, Art, Industry, all around us."

Corn lived in New York City for eleven years, from 1965 to 1976, and he pays poetic homage to the city in his second collection, *A Call in the Midst of the Crowd* (1978), which consists of eleven short poems in addition to the long title work, a "Poem in Four Parts on New York City" that occupies most of this volume and attempts to render the city in all its historical depth and colorful contemporary breadth. The four parts correspond with the four seasons, and are further subdivided into twenty-seven individual poems interspersed with quotations from sources as disparate as de Tocqueville and Billie Holliday, Henry James and the *New York Times*. Each of the four sections also includes a poem about one of the four classical elements—earth, water, fire, and air—treated in relation to a specific seasonal aspect of the city.

The poems are uneven in quality, ranging from the scrupulous platitudes of one unfortunate experiment in prose, "Bike Ride," to more ambitious attempts to capture the vivid quiddity of city life. One is struck by the triviality of many of Corn's citations, passing references which, taken singly, hardly seem to merit attention as epigraphs, yet which, as they accumulate, do manage to convey a sense of the normalcy of the New Yorker's view of his daily routine. This routine is the immediate occasion of one poem, "Nine to Five." Here the petty aggravations of a bureaucratic workday—of mechanistic circulation among radios, elevators, clocks—are worked into the texture of the poem itself, where the breaks between lines of blank verse occur as arbitrary interruptions of the poet's half-developed statements, stopping and starting as fitfully as city traffic:

> From your window tarpaper rooftops blacken
> And silver under a grainy fallout
> Of gusting sleet. There is no sun, there
> Never has been. Personnel across the street
> Just like you, clock-watchers all . . .

ALCAICS: REMEMBERING MYKINAI   Reconstr

Guides urged us, praised us up to the Lion Gate, its
Carved lintel "brought from twenty or possibly
   Two hundred miles away" and wedged in
   Place by the gods or a tyrant's hybris.

High up, the fallen muscular citadel,   modeled & smoothed like
Great blocks the winds had ~~sculpted~~ and ~~rounded~~, the
   Hard flesh of some remembered Argive--
   Vengeful Orestes, the seed of Pelops?

Nearby, the beehive tomb lay, an underground
Dome sunk in gloom. Its resonance chilled us, as
   Trapped flies, whose droning stunned the eardrum,
   Sluggishly spiraled above our comments.

Stones, stone, the life they hewed; and the self a dark
Construct, both tomb and citadel. Why will a
   Dead hour, when change breeds mishap, rise to
   Strike us, metallic and harsh as noonday?

Rocks, thyme, the ~~sun~~ wind-scorched Peloponnese--to which
Years stretch blank kilometers back. But those
   Strong measures taken, steps our feet took,
   Echo through ruins like yours, Mykinai.

in mute ?

"Remembering Mykinai," revised typescript

Here the heavy stresses are laid like stumbling blocks in the reader's path; all thoughts are afterthoughts; and the motto of the whole echoes this devastating banality: *"Kill time; but don't seem to."*

Some reviewers found the general structure of *A Call in the Midst of the Crowd* distracting, complaining that there was "too much commentary" (Michael Wood in the *New York Review of Books*), or that Corn had written "a sort of commonplace book" that "seems to possess no distinctive voice of its own" (Joyce Carol Oates in the *New Republic*); but others were quick to praise particular poems and to appreciate Corn's wit and fluency. And, while some readers felt that Corn's lyric impulse was "almost defeated by unyielding city surfaces" (C. Molesworth in the *New York Times Book Review*), others could point to brilliant lyrical flashes, often—and typically—attempting to enfold myriad impressions in a single pellucid image:

> Plural, countless, sand falls in a silken stream,
> The sound unreturning except as wind or rain
> Trembling through fictive summer leaves.

Corn himself responds to the division among his critics with quiet confidence: "I think I'm the kind of poet who provokes controversy."

In his third volume, *The Various Light,* Corn returns to more rigorous formal structures, to greater regularity of rhyme and meter. One classic example of this occurs in "Tanagra," a post-Keatsian blank-verse sonnet to a Greek figurine, where he seems deliberately to weaken his own effects by his plays on words, as in the first quatrain:

> Hellenic times so slight as you a ware
> Foreknew how it was that laws like gravity's
> Had immersed your stance in streamlike drapery
> And fixed your earthen gaze on Theban stars.

Striving for his "infinity effect," Corn employs temporal inversions as intimations of timelessness: Hellenic times (and/or the figurine) foreknew how something *had* happened; and later the Tanagra is perceived as a "Memento of future but still classic terrors, / The darkening pull down perpetuity." In a final inversion, the figure is viewed as if from within: "A single column, capital your head / That bears the pondered weight of what we are." Elsewhere in this collection, Corn maintains and develops his characteristic low-key meditative diction and his choice of homely, symbolic subjects: grass, New England townscapes, the changing seasons. Elegiac tributes to Wallace Stevens and Robert Lowell are also included.

In addition to his poetry, Corn has also published numerous review articles in such periodicals as *Parnassus,* the *Yale Review,* and the *Hudson Review,* discussing the works of writers and poets ranging from Andrey Bely and Eugenio Montale to Howard Nemerov and Karl Shapiro. He has also held several teaching positions, including a visiting lectureship at Yale from 1977 to 1979. New Haven has been his home since 1976, and he is currently employed as an assistant professor at Connecticut College, where he teaches creative writing, both fiction and poetry. He also enjoys biking, swimming, and music.

Alfred Corn has been compared favorably with contemporary poets like James Merrill and John Ashbery, and the "meditative" impulse in his work has often been noted. His homespun style seems to hover dangerously between common speech and commonplace thought, between the typical and the banal. Yet, as Richard Howard has observed, "there is an extremity, even a kind of heroism, in Corn's insistence that the poem be realized on its own terms, without much conceptual meddling on the poet's part." In the sequence of Corn's three volumes, it is possible to detect an increasing mastery of poetic modes, an increasing confidence in his own "voice," although the poet's fundamental impulses—to record his wonder at the "various light," and to seek the unstable essence of experience "in the midst of the crowd" by taking "all roads at once"—remain unchanged. As for the future, one might simply reaffirm the wish with which "The Outdoor Amphitheater" closes: "that this stage be not the last; / And that the performance move on from strength to strength."

—Gene M. Moore

References:

Richard Howard, "Art or Knack?" *Poetry,* 129 (January 1977): 226-228;

Stephen Yenser, "Recent Poetry: Six Poets," *Yale Review,* 68 (October 1978): 90-93.

George Cuomo
(10 October 1929-)

BOOKS: *Becoming a Better Reader* (New York: Holt, Rinehart & Winston, 1960);
Jack Be Nimble (Garden City: Doubleday, 1963);
Bright Day, Dark Runner (Garden City: Doubleday, 1964);
Among Thieves (Garden City: Doubleday, 1968; London: Hodder & Stoughton, 1969);
Sing, Choirs of Angels (Garden City: Doubleday, 1969);
The Hero's Great Great Great Great Great Grandson (New York: Atheneum, 1971);
Geronimo and the Girl Next Door (Shawnee Mission, Kans.: Bookmark Press, 1974);
Pieces from a Small Bomb (Garden City: Doubleday, 1976);
Becoming a Better Reader and Writer (New York: Harper & Row, 1978).

George Cuomo is a novelist and short-story writer in the tradition of "masculine" novelists who are more intent on characters, action, and theme than their own personal quirks, on the story rather than the act of writing. He is an objective writer, not an introspective one, and his characters do not all sound like their creator. Cuomo searches for the plausible links between what they do and say and what they are, so far as they are knowable. Sometimes they are not, and even their opaqueness becomes a character trait rather than a comment on epistemology. Cuomo's realistic technique sets the difference between him and such contemporaries as John Barth, Thomas Pynchon, and John Hawkes. They are preoccupied with how they "know" the world and the degree to which their language can or should stand for reality. Cuomo looks at the world about him through familiar perspectives and tells stories about what he sees.

Most of Cuomo's short stories and all of his novels deal with tradition in some way. One of the most vivid memories of his Depression childhood was of his father's inability "to put bread on the table," to find and hold a job. This personal failure, repeated throughout the 1930s, becomes in Cuomo's fiction a test not only of his father and the family, but of the whole American tradition. Most of Cuomo's work explores the strains that circumstances put upon America and Americans, and the past that Americans of the present stand upon.

Cuomo constantly draws from his own experiences for the settings and subjects of his fiction, but none except his latest, scheduled for publication in 1982, is distinctly autobiographical. In this novel Cuomo writes about his family and the place in which he grew up. That place was the Bronx, where he was born in 1929 to parents of differing backgrounds. His father, John Joseph Cuomo, was a second-generation Italian-American. Cuomo remembers his grandmother Cuomo as a small shriveled thing wrapped in a black shawl, nodding her head but speaking little because she knew little English. His aunts and uncles, who lived nearby, visited the Cuomos' flat frequently, and their conversations were generously laced with Italian. Cuomo's mother, Lillian Vogt Cuomo, was from a German Catholic family, from northern rather than southern Europe. That her parents were considerably better off than the Cuomos seemed to cause no friction, however. Cuomo visited his maternal grandparents' compulsively neat bourgeois household fairly often, and later noted the differences between the middle-class Americanism of his mother's parents and his Italian relatives' tight circle of peasant-family loyalty.

The atmosphere of Cuomo's childhood was financially deprived, at least relative to the standards of the post-World War II period in which his own children grew up. His older sister, with whom he had established his closest relationship as a small child, died of polio in the early 1930s, when Cuomo was about five. His father sought jobs where he could, but he had little success. There was simply no steady work to be had. Yet, unlike other American novelists, Cuomo did not become critical of America or its values because of his Depression experience. His line is through Whitman, Dreiser, and Steinbeck rather than Twain, Hemingway, or Fitzgerald—not unconditionally approving, but not rejecting either.

Although Cuomo always liked to write, he came to "literature" late. At the age of ten he had his own small printing press and put out his own newspaper. But his family had little interest in art and literature. His father read newspapers voraciously, but for practical reasons, for information, to keep up with the world. The serious activity of the world, he believed, was work—especially mechanical work that produced something solid, like a bridge, or a door, or a piano. When Cuomo was accepted into Peter Stuyvesant High School in Manhattan, an academically superior school that emphasized science and mathematics, he seemed to be launched on a career in science or engineering. He entered Tufts University as an engineering major at the recommendation of one of his math teachers, but before the first semester was over, he knew that he would never be an engineer, for instead of studying for his science courses, he had taken to reading novels. By the second semester he had changed his major to English. His family was more puzzled than alarmed or angry. What did an English major do for a living?

Cuomo received his B.A. from Tufts in 1952, and worked in the advertising and public relations department of a manufacturing firm in New York in 1953-1954. In 1954 he married Sylvia Epstein. They now have five children. Cuomo then did graduate work at Indiana University, receiving an M.A. in creative writing in 1955.

At one point when he was a young man, Cuomo also worked in a large New York department store, and years later he employed this setting for most of the stories in *Sing, Choirs of Angels* (1969). After he completed his M.A., he went to work as an instructor of English at the University of Arizona in Tucson, where he taught from 1956 to 1961. During these years, Cuomo drew on his campus experiences to write his first book, a short, entertaining novel called *Jack Be Nimble* (1963), in which a cynical but attractive young student/con man wheels and deals in the activities of his college's big-time football team.

In 1961, Cuomo moved to the University of Victoria, in Victoria, British Columbia, and there completed a book he had begun in Tucson, *Bright Day, Dark Runner* (1964). In Judas Iscariot LeBlanche, the novel's narrator/protagonist, Cuomo created one of his best character types: the middle-aged, or old, man who refuses to give up. "Nobility is all," says LeBlanche. "Man does not become less than man through tragedy, through failure, through defeat. Man becomes less than man through shirkery." Oliver Wendell Garvey in *The Hero's Great Great Great Great Great Grandson* (1971) and Jerome Tinney in *Pieces from a Small Bomb* (1976) are similar characters with similar views.

The dialectic between hardship and failure versus strength and survival plays throughout Cuomo's fiction, and he deals with it most effectively in *Bright Day, Dark Runner*, a big, robust story whose framework is constructed out of the conflict between the dark tragedy of LeBlanche's past and the comedy of the present. It is a story about fathers and sons, malingering and forgiveness, rancor and revenge, acted out on a large stage, and whose characters, like Fielding's, are both realistic and larger than life. LeBlanche, the most exuberant and vital of them, takes seriously his role as head chef of the Cape Cod resort restaurant The Mariner. Cooking well, even better than well, is his way of surviving three devastating losses in his life—his mother, who died bearing him; his father, who rejected LeBlanche as an infant and, blaming him for his mother's death gave him the name Judas Iscariot; and his beloved deaf wife, whom his father kills in a senile rage. To escape the pain of these losses, LeBlanche drifts through the army, then from one job to another, from one resort to another, where it is always summer and sunlight, anchored only by his devotion to his culinary art. The novel becomes a kind of parable of the cook as artist and the role art can have in one's life.

LeBlanche deals with his past by giving his son to his wife's stern sister to avoid blighting that life as his father had blighted his, and he continues to hate his father. He has never laid down the burden of these pains, which need to be put to rest. Even at fifty-four LeBlanche has not learned how to forgive, and that has kept him from coming to terms with his past. He is even caught up by his friend Phil Manchester in a scheme that would do harm to one of the resort's guests simply because the two men think he deserves to be hurt. And LeBlanche's whole somber past threads darkly through the brighter present of the resort's holiday atmosphere. In that light, LeBlanche finally confronts the memory of his father because of a series of crazy coincidences and appropriately outrageous discoveries. Through his son, who comes to the resort not knowing that LeBlanche is his father, an ignorance that LeBlanche at first shares, he learns to forgive his own father and achieve peace for himself.

LeBlanche has had much to overcome in his life, but being the prototypical Cuomo character, he maintains a world view that is both cynical and good-natured, and he articulates that view with an eighteenth-century penchant for the well-modulated sentence that is both self-mocking and gently satirical. For example, after having laid to rest the ghosts of his past and decided that he has a future even at his age, he reflects: "As we all know, my namesake, who has contributed so uniquely to the peculiar flavor and substance of my life, chose to end his by hanging himself on a blood-red tree. I, however, do not so choose, and hope I haven't unreasonably encouraged your expectations along that line, only now to disappoint you. But I'm no longer the suicidal type. My sense of the ridiculous saves me. And what with the parsimony of my diet, the rigor of my constitution, and the serenity of my spirit, I expect to live to a full and foolish old age. I have barely, I feel, begun to get my feet planted."

Bright Day, Dark Runner has all the ingredients Cuomo likes in a story—wide, sweeping action that covers both distance and time; characters who act with vitality and gusto; a seasoning of mystery and suspense; and a unity of form and theme. He has not quite repeated the success of that novel. Talking about it, he suggests why so many writers' work seems to decline from their first efforts. "I didn't have any problems with any of those characters," he says of *Bright Day, Dark Runner,* "like sitting down and saying, 'What should they do now and what is their background and what should I say?'—it just came very naturally." As "you build up a certain number of publications you start getting much more self-conscious about repeating yourself or doing the same thing again, doing the same kind of character."

Fear of repeating oneself leads to a depletion of the artistic store. Yet, Cuomo's books, which vary greatly in character and situation, show no signs of his losing his inventiveness. What has tended to take over in Cuomo's writing since *Bright Day, Dark Runner,* though, is the exploration of current social issues and concerns replacing his natural inclination to observe his characters closely and let them act out their own stories. Occasionally one gets the feeling that Cuomo is contriving actions and characters to serve his themes rather than drawing the themes from his characters' actions. This division between character and theme is a serious flaw, but, paradoxically, one of the interesting things about Cuomo is this very concern with the issues that face Americans. In any case, the three novels since *Bright Day, Dark Runner* show that literary and social themes have come more and more to dominate Cuomo's attention.

Among Thieves (1968), written in Victoria, is a prison novel set in a desert town like Tucson, although the idea for the novel came from a brief newspaper article Cuomo read in a Canadian paper. *Among Thieves* raises the question of how men behave as prisoners and how the public and its representatives regard prisoners. It pits the liberal psychologist, Dr. Samuel "Flash" Fleishman, who seeks more permissiveness, against the traditional old-timer who *knows* that severity is the only thing criminals understand. Cuomo also suggests that many of the prisoners, like two-time loser Mel Simmons, feel better off in prison, and want to be punished, as if they unconsciously desire justice. *Among Thieves* might have been a better novel had its sociological content not been quite so conspicuous. One wonders whether the reader is more touched by the characters' emotions or instructed by the author's sociology. Fleishman can speak on a television interview show of "recidivism," statistics, and the average IQ of prison inmates, but he later lapses into densely emotional language describing his inadvertent witnessing of a drugstore robbery: "I simply can't do justice to what I felt, to what I saw in this man's eyes, the unearthly fusion of terror . . . and defiance, and pride, and abject humiliation, and a kind of electric alertness, and confusion, and anguish, and determination, and about ten other things."

In 1965 Cuomo went to teach at California State College (now California State University) in Hayward, where he began work on *The Hero's Great Great Great Great Great Grandson,* in which a young American working for a cash register company finds himself transferred to Victoria and thinks to discover there a new and heroic life. This novel also seems to grow out of a theme rather than the peculiarities of character, as Cuomo asks questions about our relationship with our ancestors and how the past figures in the present. The typical modern male, he suggests, is a businessman. Is there anything left for him to conquer similar to the great

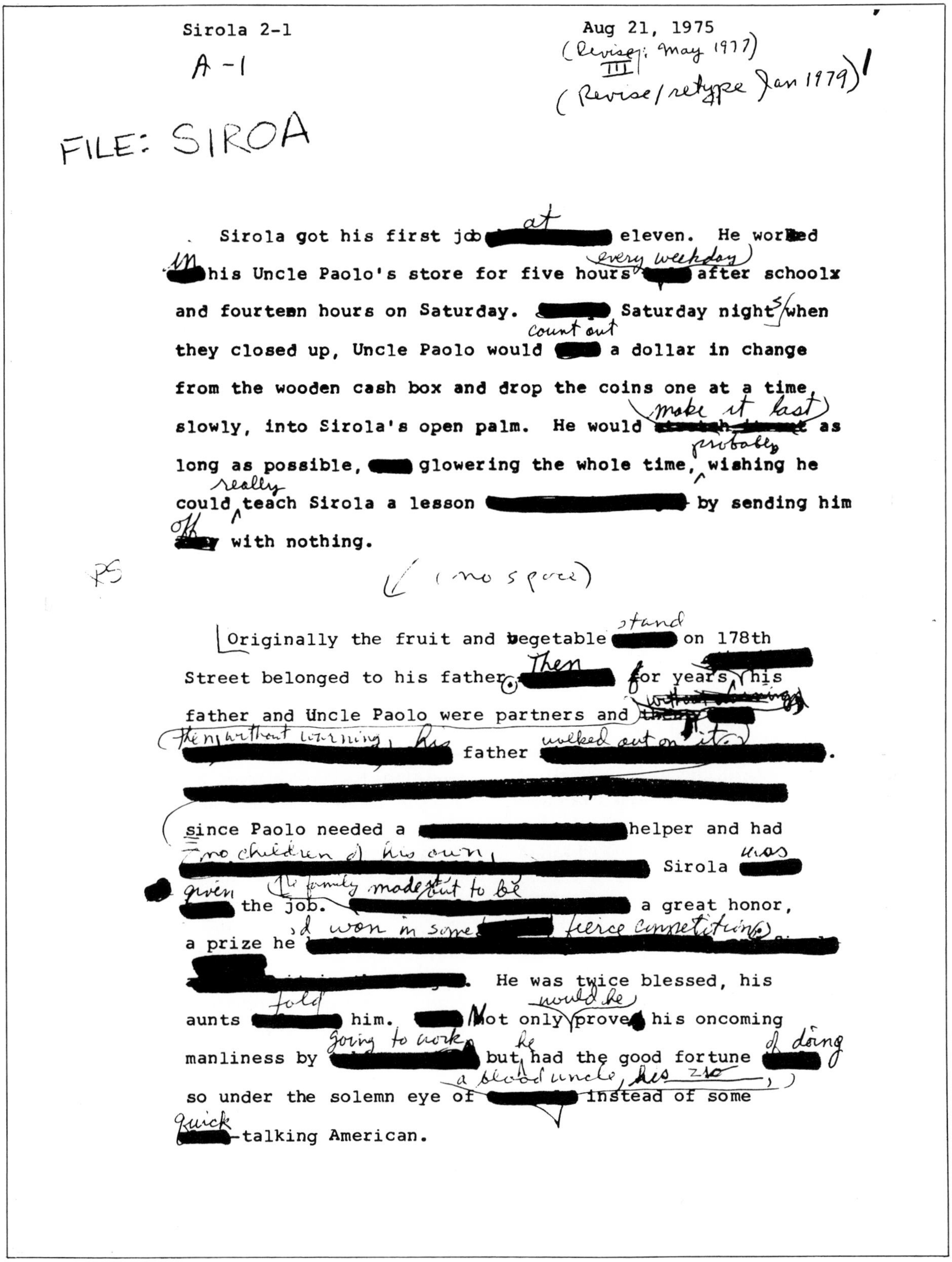

Sirola 2-1 Aug 21, 1975

A-1 (Revise; May 1977) III

(Revise/retype Jan 1979) I

FILE: SIROA

Sirola got his first job at [redacted] eleven. He worked in [redacted] his Uncle Paolo's store for five hours every weekday [redacted] after schoolx and fourteen hours on Saturday. [redacted] Saturday nights when they closed up, Uncle Paolo would count out [redacted] a dollar in change from the wooden cash box and drop the coins one at a time, slowly, into Sirola's open palm. He would make it last [redacted] as long as possible, [redacted] glowering the whole time, probably wishing he could really teach Sirola a lesson [redacted] by sending him off [redacted] with nothing.

PS (no space)

Originally the fruit and vegetable stand [redacted] on 178th Street belonged to his father. Then [redacted] for years his father and Uncle Paolo were partners and then without warning his [redacted] father walked out on it [redacted]. [redacted] since Paolo needed a [redacted] helper and had no children of his own, [redacted] Sirola was given [redacted] the job. The family made it out to be [redacted] a great honor, a prize he'd won in some [redacted] fierce competition [redacted]. He was twice blessed, his aunts told [redacted] him. [redacted] Not only would he prove his oncoming manliness by going to work [redacted] but he had the good fortune of doing [redacted] so under the solemn eye of a blood uncle, his zio, [redacted] instead of some quick [redacted]-talking American.

Revised typescript for a work in progress

frontiers traversed by Daniel Boone and Daniel Falconer, the great great great great great grandfather in the novel? Does the attraction that the North American continent held out to adventuresome Europeans of the 1730s remain real in the western Canadian territories that are yet to be tamed and put to making a profit? Byron Falconer, the "hero's" great great great great great grandson in the twentieth century, must try to answer these questions for himself. In doing so, he falls into the middle of the contest between the old-fashioned, individual entrepreneur and the newfangled accountant who watches only the bottom line. In the end, after an abortive trek into the Canadian wilderness, simulating a journey into his ancestor's past, Byron realizes that he cannot repeat the exploits of the eighteenth-century frontiersman in a world of tall buildings filled with computers, but that he should not be expected to, either.

In 1973 Cuomo went to the University of Massachusetts, where he still teaches English and creative writing and where he completed his last published novel, *Pieces from a Small Bomb* (1976), set in a university town similar to Berkeley, California, in the same area as Hayward. Although it is probably his least successful novel, *Pieces from a Small Bomb* is an excellent example of the skill with which Cuomo conceptualizes his novels and orchestrates his complex plot threads, weaving the lives of his characters into surprising and unexpected patterns, whose implications become clear only when the reader completes the work. The design of the action is masterful, precisely expressing the point that he wants to make—that the rebellions of the 1960s and early 1970s brought unlikely people together in implausible relationships. When a bomb explodes outside a barbershop in a university town on the West Coast, the reader is projected into the lives of a rebellious black community worker, his black ex-convict friend, a black politician on the take, a shady Jewish entrepreneur who survived the Nazi death camps, an attractive female socialite, and old white Anglo-Saxon Jerome Tinney. Cuomo brings these characters together in a meaningful pattern, clearing up mysteries in surprising ways and revealing identities at just the right time. It is a satirical but affectionate comment upon a highly political time, dramatizing the personal jealousies and petty struggles that lie behind events of the 1960s and early 1970s.

As in his earlier fiction, Cuomo asks how one deals with hardship and failure, the disappointment of expectations. In this case, how does a man in his seventies figuratively gather up the pieces of a small bomb; where does such an incident fit into the American continuum? These questions are as much about America as they are about individual characters in the world of the novel, and Cuomo answers them like a modified Whitman, a gut-deep, radical, democratic conservative who, in spite of everything, still believes in the great American myths about hard work, determination, and the heroism of the common man. (Politically Cuomo has always been a New Deal or Kennedy liberal.) He asserts against the failures of the American Dream a loyalty to the best images of America.

The conviction that cements nearly all of Cuomo's fiction and gives him enduring value as an American writer is that unimportant people can achieve their triumphs, however minor. Their victories are not unalloyed; a tradeoff has to be made. And the victories are usually of acceptance rather than dominance. But victories they are, of characters over themselves and circumstances, of self-understanding and self-discovery. Such victories usually come about through a reinforcement of the values that link us to the past. Old Jerome Tinney, in his journey through the pages of *Pieces from a Small Bomb*, observes the confused fumblings of people who profess to know, the rise and fall of new ideologies, and the misting over of new truths by the smoke of modernity. He sticks to his old certainties—loyalty, tenacity, and courtesy. He walks off the novel's stage "without any of the easy winners, maybe, but not fool enough, not by a longshot, to start playing fast and loose with the kinds of truth that had gotten him this far."

Few reviewers have allowed Cuomo's affirmation of traditional values to move them very much, and on the whole they have not been enthusiastic about Cuomo's fiction, though comments have varied widely. Only two of his novels, *Bright Day, Dark Runner* and *Among Thieves*, have been widely noticed. The latter was a Literary Guild selection for 1968. Similarly, the academic community has not paid the attention to Cuomo that it has to some of his contemporaries. Those who do praise his work appreciate his ear for language and his structural skills. They praise the very quality that leads some reviewers to spurn his work as derivative and imitative, the vivid realism of his characters and the photographic detail of his descriptions. No real critical consensus has been reached on Cuomo, but when it is, one of the major attributes of his work will be recognized as a tough, open-eyed optimism.

Cuomo is a social man, one who enjoys conversation, although he does not surrender information about his emotional life easily, whether in his fiction or his talk. Nor is he an introspective man who retreats into his study to contemplate his nature. Warm, open, and gently honest in his criticism, not sharp-tongued or iconoclastic himself, he gets along well with bright, sharp-tongued iconoclasts. Because his master's degree was in creative writing rather than literature, he feels somewhat deferential toward colleagues whose formal education in the critical study of literature was more extensive than his. What he says about the most influential ones reflects his own genuine humility. While at Arizona, he writes, "I met regularly with two other guys to discuss each other's poetry, and both were a hell of a lot smarter and better educated (Ph.D.'s) than me, and I learned a lot." Of John Peter, whom he met at Victoria, Cuomo writes, "John too was incredibly intelligent and educated, a South African who went to Cambridge, is (and was when I met him) a distinguished and well known critic, with books on Milton and medieval poetry and many articles in *Scrutiny*." Cuomo always expects more of himself than of others. He works hard and regularly, not writing rapidly but with great care. He is surely one of the few writers in existence who can do three things at once: consult with a student, listen to the ball game on the radio (turned low), and retain the material he wanted to write down when the student interrupted him.

Cuomo has more books to write, and his place is not yet firmly set in American fiction. When it is, he will be linked with the realists who criticize Americans but also love them.

—*Jerry H. Bryant*

Plays:

Hobbies and Ambitions, Vancouver, Vancouver Little Theater, 1962;

Jack Be Nimble, by Cuomo and Richard Matthews, San Rafael, California Shakespeare Festival, 1968; New York, Juilliard School of Drama Tryout Group, 1970.

Periodical Publications:

"Of Children and Idiots," *Nation,* 184 (1 June 1957): 482-484;

"How Fast Should A Person Read?," *Saturday Review* (21 April 1962): 13-14;

"Everything Is A Character," *Writer* (February 1970): 15-16;

"History and Nightmare, Two Versions," *California Quarterly,* no. 2 (Summer 1972): 80-92.

References:

Jerry H. Bryant, "The Fiction of George Cuomo," *Arizona Quarterly,* 30 (Autumn 1974): 253-272;

Rose Basile Green, "George Cuomo," in her *The Italian-American Novel* (Rutherford, N.J.: Fairleigh Dickinson University Press, 1974);

John Peter, "The Self-Effacement of the Novelist," *Malahat Review,* no. 8 (October 1968): 119-128.

Annie Dillard

(30 April 1945-   )

BOOKS: *Tickets for a Prayer Wheel* (Columbia: University of Missouri Press, 1974);
Pilgrim at Tinker Creek (New York: Harper's Magazine Press, 1974; London: Pan, 1976);
Holy the Firm (New York: Harper & Row, 1977).

An essayist, poet, and fiction writer, Annie Dillard is best known for her first full-length book, *Pilgrim at Tinker Creek* (1974), which won her the 1975 Pulitzer Prize for General Nonfiction when she was twenty-nine. Published earlier in 1974 was a small book of her poems, *Tickets for a Prayer Wheel,* which received much less critical attention. In 1977 she produced *Holy the Firm,* a brief, highly charged book of nonfiction exploring more directly the religious and metaphysical questions which underlie her first two books. *Holy the Firm* also was highly acclaimed, and like *Pilgrim at Tinker Creek,* sections from it have been widely anthologized in texts for aspiring writers. In addition Dillard has served as contributing editor for *Harper's* since 1974 and has written many essays, short stories, and poems.

Born to Frank and Pam Doak in Pittsburgh, Pennsylvania, Annie Dillard grew up in an affluent world of country clubs and private girls' schools, where she began writing poetry and fiction in high school. Eventually she enrolled in a writing program at Hollins College in Roanoke, Virginia, where she was elected to Phi Beta Kappa and received a B.A. (1967) and an M.A. (1968), both in English. In 1965, while still a student at Hollins, she married writer R. H. W. Dillard, her teacher. She reads widely in such diverse fields as theology, philosophy, physical sciences, anthropology, and literature; critics have praised the accuracy of her scientific knowledge, especially as it is revealed in *Pilgrim at Tinker Creek* and in her many essays on the natural world.

Her first book, *Tickets for a Prayer Wheel,* collected some previously unpublished poems along with many which had appeared earlier in magazines. The poems portray human characters and employ themes of human love and desire; however, the main impetus behind the poems is strongly religious. Dillard writes of the intricacy and detail of nature, the changing lights of consciousness, the mystery of time's relation to eternity, the futility of asking questions about God, and ultimately, through all the poems, the poet's urgent longing for a God who is hidden. Finally, according to the poet, the union of a human with God depends as much on God's action as on the human's, and when the divine presence acts upon her, the poet says, "I rang a hundred prayers of praise." The final poem, "Tickets for a Prayer Wheel," is considered by Dillard to be her best; it contains the refrain to be heard later in *Holy the Firm*: "who will teach us to pray?" The poems also employ images which appear in *Pilgrim at Tinker Creek,* such as the trees on fire and the depiction of the poet as a bell rung by God. But the images in the poems are more varied, more frequent, and more complex than in her prose. They occasionally border on the macabre, revealing the power of her imagination and her eye for precise detail. The structures of individual poems are complex and there are many links between poems. *Tickets for a Prayer Wheel* was praised by the few critics who reviewed it, but it was overshadowed by the dazzling reception of *Pilgrim at Tinker Creek.*

Dillard herself was surprised by the publishing world's overwhelming recognition of *Pilgrim at*

Annie Dillard

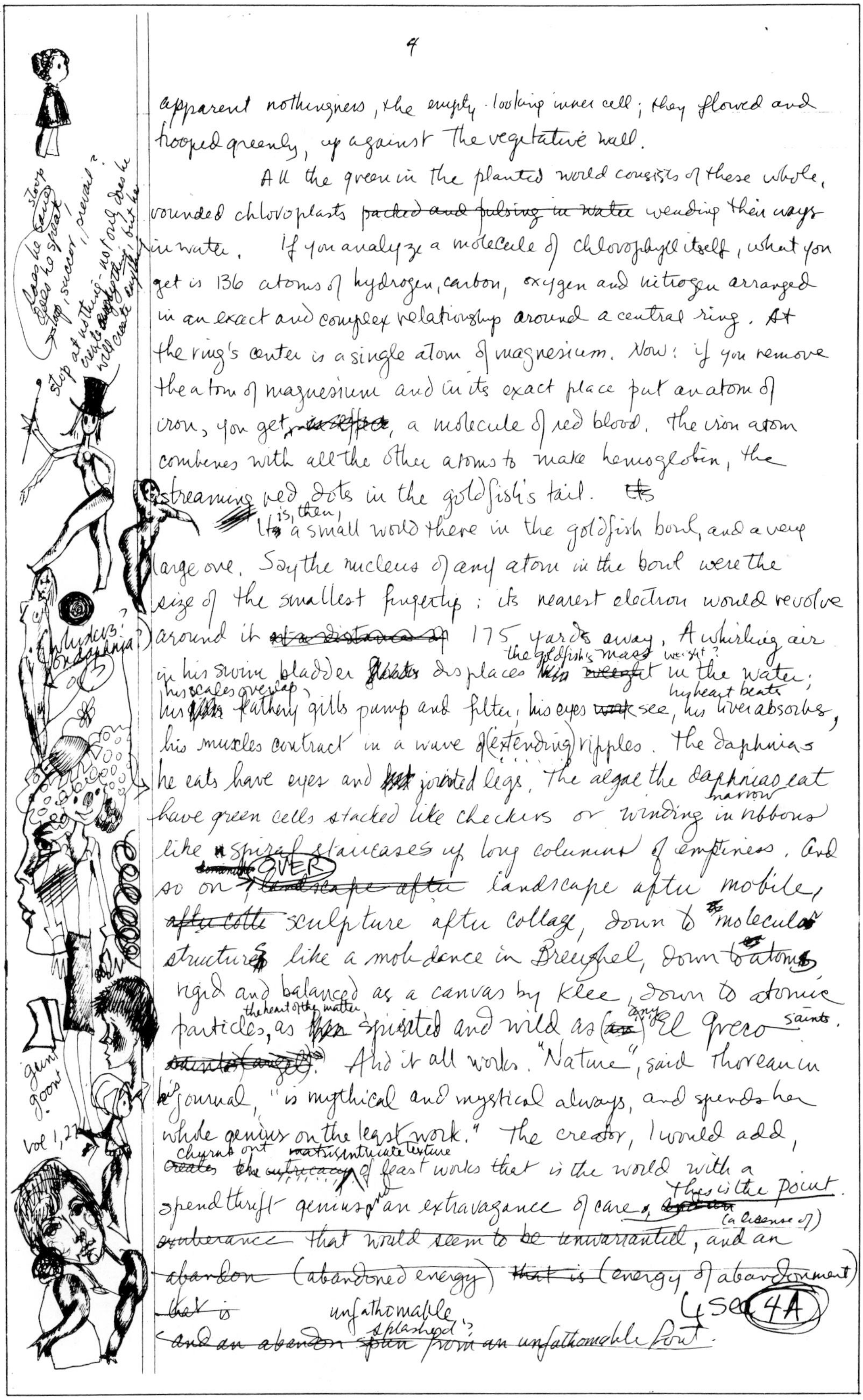

4

apparent nothingness, the empty-looking inner cell; they flowed and hooped greenly, up against the vegetative wall.

All the green in the planted world consists of these whole, rounded chloroplasts ~~packed and pulsing in water~~ wending their ways in water. If you analyze a molecule of chlorophyll itself, what you get is 136 atoms of hydrogen, carbon, oxygen and nitrogen arranged in an exact and complex relationship around a central ring. At the ring's center is a single atom of magnesium. Now: if you remove the atom of magnesium and in its exact place put an atom of iron, you get, ~~in effect~~, a molecule of red blood. The iron atom combines with all the other atoms to make hemoglobin, the streaming red dots in the goldfish's tail.

It ~~is~~ is, then, a small world there in the goldfish bowl, and a very large one. Say the nucleus of any atom in the bowl were the size of the smallest fingertip: its nearest electron would revolve around it ~~at a distance of~~ 175 yards away. A whirling air in his swim bladder ~~floats~~ displaces ~~his weight~~ the goldfish's mass weight? in the water; his scales overlap, his ~~flat~~ feathery gills pump and filter, his eyes ~~wat~~ see, his heart beats; his liver absorbs, his muscles contract in a wave of (extending) ripples. The daphnias he eats have eyes and ~~feet~~ jointed legs. The algae the daphnias eat have green cells stacked like checkers or winding in narrow ribbons like ~~a~~ spiral staircases up long columns of emptiness. And so on ~~landscape after~~ OVER landscape after mobile, ~~after colle~~ sculpture after collage, down to molecular structures like a mob dance in Breughel, down to atoms rigid and balanced as a canvas by Klee, down to atomic particles, as ~~these~~ the heart of the matter, spirited and wild as (~~an~~ any) El Greco saints. ~~saints (angels)~~ And it all works. "Nature", said Thoreau in his journal, "is mythical and mystical always, and spends her whole genius on the least work." The creator, I would add, ~~creates the intricacy~~ churns out ^ the intricate texture of least works that is the world with a spendthrift genius and an extravagance of care. ~~, ...~~ This is the point. ~~exuberance that would seem to be unwarranted~~, and an ~~abandon~~ (abandoned energy) ~~that is~~ (energy of abandonment) (a license of) ~~that is~~ 4 see 4A

~~and an abandon~~ ~~spun~~ splashed? ~~from an unfathomable font~~ unfathomable

Pilgrim at Tinker Creek, *manuscript*

Tinker Creek. The book grew out of notes she wrote during 1972 while living on Tinker Creek in the Roanoke Valley of Virginia. For a year, as she gathered material, she says she read voraciously, took walks, and "did nothing." But those daily walks and her reading of naturalists, anthropologists, physicists, and biologists were recorded in detail; when she did begin to write, she worked for eight months, seven days a week, up to fifteen and sixteen hours a day in a library carrel, recording her insights and observations from 1,103 index cards. She sent the first chapter to a New York agent who successfully placed it with *Harper's* magazine. Almost immediately the following chapters of *Pilgrim at Tinker Creek* were snapped up by *Harper's* and other magazines; the completed book was a Book-of-the-Month Club main selection, and in October 1973, Dillard was invited to become a contributing editor of *Harper's*.

Pilgrim at Tinker Creek has been categorized as a nature study, although it might just as accurately be labeled "poetic-religious essays," for it powerfully blends scientific facts, theological musings, and strong visual images. Dillard writes of everyday natural phenomena, and these details of nature form the core of the book. For example, she writes vividly of the 228 muscles in the head of a caterpillar, the capillaries in the tail of a goldfish, and the billions of microorganisms in a cubic inch of topsoil. But more than an objective description of these phenomena, the book is, in her words, "what Thoreau called 'a meteorological journal of the mind.' " It is a book about consciousness—her consciousness (and human consciousness) in relation to time, the universe, and God. In these deeply personal essays Dillard focuses closely on fragments of nature, tries to sense their relation to the Whole, and ultimately, through them feels God's connection with the world. She demonstrates how a careful and attentive observer can see something extraordinary in a common occurence as she moves from observation, to reflection, to praise. She is a seeker, a pilgrim in the religious sense of the word.

There are no real characters in the book other than the author/observer, and no plot. The book follows the progression of seasons in the valley beginning in January and ending the following December, but the real structure is only loosely tied to chronology. Instead in each chapter the author's observation of some concrete physical event becomes the point of departure for an informal essay encompassing bits of remembered stories, odd scientific facts, and philosophical questions. The central philosophical question of each essay connects with the next and the next, increasing the intensity of the pilgrim's spiritual quest.

In the first essay, for example, the narrator graphically recalls the horrifying death she observed as a giant water bug sucked the insides from a living frog, an incident which becomes a recurring metaphor for nature's predations upon itself; she wonders about the significance of such occurrences, whether the world is running crazily on its own or whether it is sustained by a caring creator. Yet she also reveals in this and the next chapter that she has had moments of mystic vision when she has encountered the divine in nature, sensing its grandeur manifested in the commonplace: "One day I was walking along Tinker Creek thinking of nothing at all and I saw the tree with the lights in it. I saw the backyard cedar where the mourning doves roost charged and transfigured, each cell buzzing with flame." She finds it difficult to reconcile her mystic encounters with the apparently senseless horrors of nature; therefore she goes to nature seeking, as she says, "not an explanation but a picture." She wants to see all of reality as fully and consciously as she can. Dillard's writing about nature is never saccharine or sentimental, but always clear and toughminded, because of this basic tension between its grandeur and its horror.

The second chapter explores the difficulties of seeing with accuracy and understanding, and throughout the middle chapters Dillard describes more fully the results of her seeing: she provides a detailed picture of nature's minute and intricate beauty, its rich texture and power. She displays her grounding in scientific fact and her own keen powers of observation in a style that is dense and poetic, with a tone that is tinged with awe. For her, the intricacy, multiplicity, and texture of the world form "a beauty inexhaustible in its complexity," and as always, she extends this realization into its theological implications, for this beauty, she says, "trains me to the wild and extravagant nature of the spirit I seek."

But this is not to say that nature all fits together like clockwork, for in the second half of the book, after a devastating flood and the height of summer growth, Dillard begins to explore more intensively the other half of the tension that was present throughout, the idea that the natural world is full of horrors, senseless pain, and death, as well as fecundity. Observing that while humans value the individual supremely, nature values him not a whit, Dillard insists on asking the difficult questions and facing the whole picture, not just focusing on the pretty parts of nature.

Finally she concludes that her emotions need some calming, calling her reservations "mere squeamishness." She says in effect that there are no answers to the questions of pain and death; they must simply be accepted as part of "the thorny beauty of the real," part of the way it is: "That something is everywhere and always amiss is part of the very stuff of creation." Beauty and death, she says, are two branches of the same creek, and it is impossible for humans to decide that one more than the other reveals the meaning of existence. Although some critics found it logically inconsistent for Dillard to praise a world which often seems senseless and chaotic to her, nearly all acclaimed her powers of description; they commented especially on the brilliance and preciseness of her prose and the freshness of her perceptions.

When *Pilgrim at Tinker Creek* won the Pulitzer Prize and became a best-seller, Dillard's success brought her many offers to make appearances, give readings, and even write filmscripts, but she declined most offers in an effort to maintain the privacy and energy necessary for serious writing. During one summer she traveled to the Galapagos Islands for *Harper's*, where she wrote a long essay discussing the interplay between freedom and evolutionary necessity. For this essay, "Innocence in the Galapagos," she won the New York Presswomen's Award for Excellence in 1975. She also traveled and wrote several columns for the journal of the Wilderness Society, the *Living Wilderness*, between 1974 and 1976.

When her nine-year marriage ended in 1974, Annie Dillard moved to the Pacific Northwest to become scholar-in-residence at Western Washington University at Bellingham. There she taught creative writing and poetry, and began work on *Holy the Firm*, published in 1977.

In *Holy the Firm* Dillard again struggles with the problem of pain, but she is more explicitly concerned with the metaphysical aspects of pain than she was in *Pilgrim at Tinker Creek*. She is also more concerned with philosophical discussions about time, reality, and the will of God. Although the book is only seventy-five pages long and covers the events of only three days, it took her fifteen months to write. Its language is highly condensed and poetic, and its narrative framework is built from a complex set of internal elements which interrelate and recur in the reflexive manner of a complicated poem. The book is perhaps more self-consciously artistic than *Pilgrim at Tinker Creek*. Although *Holy the Firm* was highly praised by reviewers, some considered it less penetrable than its predecessor.

Set near Puget Sound where the author was living at the time, the book contains three parts, which, according to Dillard, refer to the Creation, Fall, and Redemption. The first section, "Newborn and Salted," praises each day as a god, meaning that each day has its own unique holiness and that what the human mind can perceive about its events is certainly not the complete picture. The central event of the first section is the death of a moth caught in a candle flame: its body becomes a wick "like a hollow saint, like a flame-faced virgin gone to God." The moth's immolation becomes one of the central images of the book, suggesting at first that God flames through the commonplace, with additional meanings added later. The second part, "God's Tooth," focuses on seven-year-old Julie Norwich, the narrator's alter ego in a way, who survives a plane crash which burns off her face. "Has God a hand in this?" the narrator asks, as she temporarily despairs of God's connection with the world. She struggles also with the possibility that the world is illusion, and with questions of epistemology, wondering if she can really know even her own experience. In part three, "Holy the Firm," she continues to try to reconcile human suffering with the idea of a merciful God, asking what purpose such suffering can serve. "Do we need blind men stumbling about, and little flame-faced children, to remind us what God can—and will—do?" The answer is essentially the same one offered in *Pilgrim at Tinker Creek*: such events remind us that God does not have to answer to us, "that we are created, *created*, sojourners in a land we did not make" and that "we are most deeply asleep at the switch when we fancy we control any switches at all." The image of the flame here begins to include strong associations between sacrifice and self-immolation. She arrives at acceptance once again and affirms her faith that God is connected to the world. The notion of God as the ground of all being helps the narrator experience again the mystic unity of all things, and she feels again the artist's nunlike dedication to serve as God's visionary through her art and her life. "Held, held fast by love in the world like the moth in wax, your life a wick, your head on fire with prayer, held utterly, outside and in, you sleep alone, if you call that alone, you cry God."

Although some reviewers quibbled about the metaphysics of the book and chided Dillard for not fully answering the questions she raised, most agreed with Frederick Buechner, who welcomed it as "a rare and precious book, . . . a book of great richness,

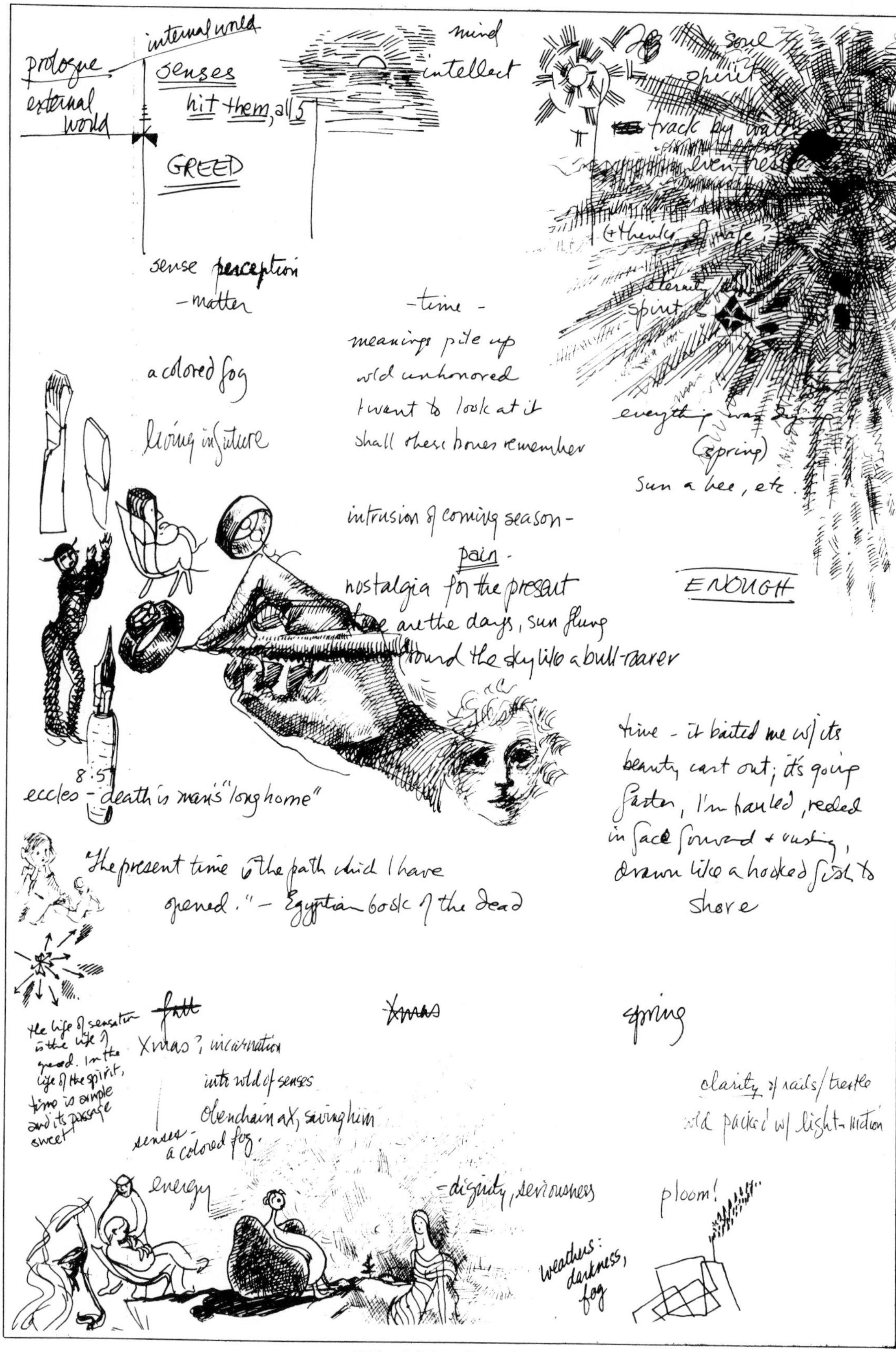

"The Living," outline

beauty, and power." Many readers were affected by its spiritual message (for example, one man wrote her that he changed his profession after reading the book) and Dillard received letters from persons who perceived her as a saint or prophet. She urgently denies such claims, asserting as she did in the book itself that no one lives a saintly life, including her, but that some people simply describe their visions well. *Holy the Firm* has been widely reprinted and a dramatic version has been performed by Atlanta's Imaginary Theatre.

Dillard's many essays and poems, written throughout her career, describe her essentially spiritual vision. Her subjects include the role of the artist, the artistic process, evolution, and wildlife—all discussed in the larger context of her philosophical concerns. Her one long piece of fiction, "The Living," which appeared in *Harper's* (1978), also deals with human consciousness and awareness of time and death. Set in 1905, the story concerns Clare, an easygoing and unreflective man who teaches high-school shop near Northern Puget Sound. When one of his ex-students announces that he plans someday to kill him, Clare becomes intensely conscious for the first time of his own mortality. Dillard traces the changes in Clare's life and his consciousness with great psychological acuity, as the story builds to his final realization of his place in time and his unity with the eternal. This gripping story displays Dillard's talent for physical description once again, but it also reveals more fully than any of her previous works her powerful gift for narrative and for psychological description.

Annie Dillard has been acclaimed not only as an inspiring writer but also as a stimulating intellectual. She reads widely and questions boldly as she ponders the role of the artist in the modern world; her works continue to reflect humanity's concern with the eternal. Despite her continuing production of essays and poems, recent interviews indicate Dillard's growing interest in the writing of fiction. Since 1979 she has been Distinguished Visiting Professor at Wesleyan University in Connecticut where she is at work on a book of personal narratives and a book called "Fiction and the World's Meaning." During the summer 1981 Centennial of the Boston Symphony Orchestra, the orchestra will perform *The Tree With Lights In It*, a symphony by Sir Arthur Tippett based on *Pilgrim at Tinker Creek*.

—*Nancy Lucas*

Periodical Publications:

FICTION:

"A Christmas Story," *Harper's*, 252 (January 1976): 58;

"Five Sketches," *North American Review*, 260 (Spring 1978): 50-51;

"The Living," *Harper's*, 257 (November 1978): 45-64.

NONFICTION:

"Artists of the Beautiful," *Living Wilderness*, 38 (Winter 1974-1975): 62-63;

"Innocence in the Galapagos," *Harper's*, 250 (May 1975): 74-82;

"The Deer at Providencia," *Living Wilderness*, 39 (Spring 1975): 46-47;

"A Field of Silence," *Atlantic Monthly*, 241 (February 1978): 74-76;

"Is Art All There Is?," *Harper's*, 261 (August 1980): 61-66;

"Teaching a Stone to Talk," *Atlantic Monthly*, 247 (February 1981): 36-39.

Interviews:

Michael Burnett, "An Interview with Annie Dillard," *Fairhaven Review* (Bellingham, Wash.: Fairhaven College Publications, 1978);

Anonymous, "A Face Aflame," *Christianity Today*, 22 (5 May 1978): 14-19.

References:

Frederick Buechner, "Island Journal," *New York Times Book Review*, 25 September 1977, pp. 12, 40;

Hayden Carruth, "Attractions and Dangers of Nostalgia," *Virginia Quarterly Review*, 50 (Autumn 1974): 637-640;

Mike Major, "Annie Dillard, Pilgrim of the Absolute," *America*, 138 (6 May 1978): 363-364;

Patricia Ward, "Annie Dillard's Way of Seeing," *Christianity Today*, 22 (5 May 1978): 30-31;

Eudora Welty, "Review of *Pilgrim at Tinker Creek*, *New York Times Book Review*, 24 March 1974, pp. 4-5;

Eleanor B. Wymard, "A New Existential Voice: For Annie Dillard the World is an Epiphany," *Commonweal*, 102 (24 October 1975): 495-496.

John Gregory Dunne

(25 May 1932-)

BOOKS: *Delano: The Story of the California Grape Strike* (New York: Farrar, Straus & Giroux, 1967; revised, 1971);

The Studio (New York: Farrar, Straus & Giroux, 1969);

Vegas: A Memoir of a Dark Season (New York: Random House, 1974; London: Quartet, 1974);

True Confessions (New York: Dutton, 1977; London: Weidenfeld & Nicolson, 1978);

Quintana & Friends (New York: Dutton, 1978).

John Gregory Dunne, journalist, novelist, and screenwriter, is one of America's most versatile writers. He is among the most highly regarded of the school of participatory reporters usually called New Journalists who evolved in the 1960s. His nonfiction—*Delano, The Studio, Vegas,* and *Quintana & Friends*—has been praised for its sharply satirical slant and for the vitality of a usually spare style, and *True Confessions* is a rarity: a powerful and funny first novel which has both won critical praise and become a best-seller.

Dunne was born in Hartford, Connecticut, the fifth of the six children of Dr. Richard Edwin and Dorothy Burns Dunne. A 1954 graduate of Princeton with an A.B. in English, Dunne spent two years in the army and brief periods with an industrial advertising agency and a trade magazine in New York before joining *Time.* In his five years as writer and editor there, he developed disdain for the assembly-line techniques of newsmagazines. He met novelist Joan Didion, then an editor at *Vogue,* in 1958, and they were married 30 January 1964, moving to Los Angeles shortly afterward. They now live in Trancas, California, north of Malibu, with their adopted daughter Quintana Roo Dunne, born in 1966. In addition to five books and three screenplays, Dunne has written articles, essays, and reviews for such magazines as *National Review,* the *New Republic, New York, Holiday,* and *Atlantic Monthly.* From 1967 to 1969, he and Didion collaborated on a column, "Points West," in the *Saturday Evening Post,* and he wrote another column, "The Coast," for *Esquire* during 1976-1977.

Delano: The Story of the California Grape Strike (1967) describes Cesar Chavez's initial efforts to establish his National Farm Workers' Association among the nonunionized, mostly Mexican-American farm workers in California's Great Central Valley. The NFWA's strike against grape growers in the Delano, California, area began in the fall of 1965 and was continuing when Dunne's book appeared. (After the strike ended in 1970, an updated edition was published.) Dunne depicts the economic and social history of the region, Chavez's background, the efforts of priests and civil rights workers to help the laborers, and conflicts between the NFWA and unions from the AFL-CIO and the Teamsters. Dunne is objective about all these matters, trying to be fair to all parties: "In both camps there was a morbid fascination with what the other side was thinking and doing, and at times I felt almost like a Red Cross emissary passing between the lines under a flag of truce with parcels of quite meaningless information."

Reviewers were generally appreciative of Dunne's efforts. In the *New York Times Book Review,* Gladwin Hill called it "an exceptionally incisive report on the anatomy of the strike; a colorful, perceptive examination of its impact on the community; and an analysis of actions of both employers and labor so realistic as to make it important reading for current students of economics and public policy." Robert Coles writing in *Book World* called it "a quiet, well-written book that avoids rhetoric and the easy gratification of polemics in order to tell a story, and tell it fairly, coherently and with a appropriate touch of irony." The most common complaint of the dissenters was, surprisingly, about Dunne's impartiality. Martin Duberman complained in the *New Republic* that "Dunne's 'objectivity' sometimes serves as an easy way of avoiding the rigors of interpretation; he settles for presenting all available points of view instead of trying to discover where, amongst them, the truth might lie. In failing to adjudicate, he dilutes his own viewpoint: though his sympathy with the strikers is clear, his willingness to admit considerable contrary—and often specious—argument ends by maximizing the 'anguish' of the growers."

In his introduction to *Quintana & Friends* (1978), Dunne defines and defends his objective approach to reporting, a method which evolved because of a lifelong stammer, which led him to express himself in writing, and because of his distrust of the "standard programmed answers" reporters usually elicit from their questions: "What I do is hang around. Become part of the furniture. An end table in someone's life. It is the art of the scavenger: set a scene, establish a mood, get the speech patterns right. What matters is that the subject bites his nails, what matters is that he wears brown shoes with a blue suit, what matters is the egg stain on his tie, the Reader's Digest Condensed Books on the shelves, the copy of *Playboy* with the centerfold torn out." This approach is perhaps more suitable for the subjects of *The Studio* and *Vegas*, subjects given more to humor, irony, and absurdity than the emotional issues of *Delano*.

John Gregory Dunne

The Studio (1969) is an account of the year Dunne spent hanging around Twentieth Century-Fox, a movie company recently rescued from potential collapse by the enormous profits brought in by *The Sound of Music* (1965), a trend the studio hoped to continue by producing more big-budget "family" musicals—*Star!* (1968), *Dr. Doolittle* (1967), *Hello, Dolly!* (1969),—all destined to be critical and financial failures. Dunne's purpose was "to see how some of the people there got along, got ahead, fell behind, stayed in place, and, above all, fabricated the myth."

Dunne employs his objective approach most successfully in *The Studio*, creating a wickedly funny portrait of allegedly grown people playing childish, egotistical games. He does not have to underscore the absurdities his subjects commit; he allows them to hang themselves with their own words. For example, Paul Monash, producer of *Butch Cassidy and the Sundance Kid* and the *Peyton Place* television series, feels guilty about his success and wants admiration for participating in peace marches and worrying about Watts: "Maybe I should write a book. I'd like to take a year off and do a book on the Detroit riots. Of course, there wouldn't be any motion picture rights for something like a book on the riots. But it will give me the feeling of accomplishing something. Maybe I will. A friend of mine got $175,000 paperback for a book he wrote."

Much of *The Studio* is devoted to preparations for the release of *Dr. Doolittle*, an $18-million production. The chapter in which the producer, director, studio executives, and various girl friends and flunkies go to Minneapolis for the first sneak preview is the high point of the book. A publicist "approached the task as if it were—and indeed he seemed to equate it with—the annual pilgrimage of the English royal family from Buckingham Palace to Balmoral." After the audience fails to respond, the theater owner explains, "You've got to realize that this was a typically sophisticated Friday night Minneapolis audience." The producer desperately wants to hear something encouraging from the powerful, but all he gets is "You've got yourself a picture, Arthur. It's all up there on the screen." Dunne and the reader are amused by how everyone eventually writes off *Dr. Doolittle* after several drastic attempts to save it and then blithely moves on to perpetrating more misguided disasters upon the public.

The Studio received an enthusiastic reception. In *Newsweek*, Paul D. Zimmerman wrote, "The real contribution of Dunne's book lies in its nicely honed portrait of the Hollywood ethos, that gothic mix of greed, hypocrisy, shrewd calculation, mad hoopla and boundless optimism that shapes American films and, through them, much of the sensibility of the American public." Albert Bermel, in *The New Leader*, doubted if any writer since Nathanael West had "taken Hollywood apart . . . quite so mercilessly and served up as many cruel laughs." *The Studio* ranks at the top of the short line of good behind-the-scenes views of Hollywood such as Lillian Ross's *Picture* (1952) and Paul Mayersburg's *Hollywood: The Haunted House* (1967). It should continue to be read not just as an examination of the inner workings of Hollywood and big business but as a hilarious expose of the fallibility of the powerful who think they are in touch with the public's needs.

Dunne's usual objectivity is modified in *Vegas: A Memoir of a Dark Season* (1974), an alternately funny and sad combination of satirical reportage, confessional memoir, and novel. In a preface Dunne calls it "a fiction which recalls a time both real and imagined." The impetus for the book came as Dunne developed an irrational fear of death when he turned thirty-five and began aimlessly driving California's freeways in search of peace (much like the heroine of his wife's *Play It As It Lays*). After seeing a sign suggesting that motorists "VISIT LAS VEGAS BEFORE YOUR NUMBERS UP," he decided to seek therapy among "the Snopses of the free-enterprise system": "It seemed the perfect place to spend that summer, a paradigm of anti-life. . . . there were days when I told myself that through the travail of others I might come to grips with myself, that I might, as it were, find absolution through voyeurism. Those were the good days."

Dunne focuses on his relationships with three pseudonymous characters who appear to be composite portraits of the many Las Vegas "types" he met. Artha Ging is a prostitute who is studying to be a beautician, writes poems in imitation of Sara Teasdale, and keeps detailed records of the services she provides her clients. Buster Mano is a Midwestern policeman turned private investigator who reads Martin Luther because of their shared constipation: "His lower intestine was a Dunkirk always waiting to be evacuated and Buster kept up-to-the-minute status reports on the departure readiness of his bowels." Jackie Kasey is a comedian who warms up audiences for Frank Sinatra and Elvis Presley; he makes $10,000 a week for his lounge act but is depressed at remaining only a "semi-name." Dunne devotes the most time to Kasey because he identifies with him: "Watching a comic flailing against an indifferent audience seemed a refraction of my own depression. Vegas has a way of coopting burned-out cases; there is a sense that failed expectations are the mean, the norm." Dunne fails, however, to make Kasey as colorful, as complex, as human as the other two. Buster Mano, especially, is more consistently interesting: "He was a man without illusions. He expected the worst and the worst did not mean much. He viewed life, his own especially, as a hopeless patchwork of small strategies and minor betrayals." Like Dunne in much of his work, Mano is "a connoisseur of failure."

Vegas is far from being as depressing as it might have been because of Dunne's delight in the absurd and the constant joy he takes in writing for its own sake, as with a parody of tough-guy style in a Buster Mano section: "She looked like Frances Langford, right out of the big-band era, a lot of blonde hair piled on top of her head, big wedgies, thirty-five years old on a good day. She looked like she had spent a lifetime meeting guys in Vegas or Miami Beach or Louisville for the Derby. But there were lines around the eyes now and there weren't going to be many more post times at Churchill Downs." The confessional sections are also treated humorously for the most part; far from asking for self-pity, Dunne views himself with as much ironic distance as he does the other characters. Especially funny is the lengthy account of how he finally yielded his virginity to a New York prostitute four days before he turned twenty-one. Since hearing about her in prep school, he had longed to visit this legend who specialized in Ivy League boys; she turned out to have "a square stocky figure and a face like a gravel pit."

The critical response to *Vegas* was mixed. In the *New York Times Book Review*, Jonathan Yardley wrote, "No one, not even Hunter Thompson, has depicted Las Vegas more tellingly" but complained that "Dunne injects himself into the book more than really seems warranted." Bruce Cook praised Dunne in the *New Republic* for making "his hell a thing of beauty, or, a very peculiar sort of beauty," but like many reviewers, he had difficulty classifying *Vegas*: "As a novel, as a memoir it is unsatisfactory. But as a piece of writing, it is superb."

One review of *True Confessions* (1977) opens, "We might have known he'd do something like this," and Dunne's first novel is the irreverent, scatological, parodying treatment of sex, violence, guilt, and pop-cultured America that readers of *The Studio* and *Vegas* would expect. In fact, many of the characters and events are embellishments of those in *Vegas*. The novel examines the relationship between two brothers, a Los Angeles cop and a priest, as the former tries to solve the murder of a prostitute found cut in half just after World War II. Dunne has admitted in an interview that he is writing as much about the Catholic community in the Hartford of his childhood as he is about Los Angeles.

Tom Spellacy is an ex-boxer with an institutionalized wife who talks to imaginary saints, a pregnant mistress, and a shady past as a onetime bagman for Jewish-Mexican gangster Jack Armstrong. His work as a homicide lieutenant provides some order in his life: "He was not certain of many things anymore, but he was sure of one thing: he was a very good cop. Maybe not always honest, but always thorough. He liked the trivial detail work of an investigation." Des Spellacy, four years younger

72-H/

"He's got a place in ~~Lauderdale~~ [Balboa] now, I hear, the last guy."

"And one in ~~Havana,"~~ [Ensenada,"] Crotty said. "He come out of it all right. Two houses and he beats the rap. Tears the shit out of being chief, though, getting indicted like that, even you beat it."

The waiter brought two more Carta Blancas. Crotty ordered chiles rellenos and enchiladas verdes for the two of them. When the waiter left, he leaned across the table and said softly, almost as if he were afraid of being heard, "What do you think of Morty Davis' chances?"

He thinks I'm afraid Morty's going to get rid of me, Tom Spellacy thought suddenly. [He doesn't know] ~~I~~t's no worse than Des saving my ass.

"He's ~~[illegible]~~ ~~A~~ saint, actually," [Tom Spellacy said.] "Twenty-two cents he's got in the bank, Morty, and a hole in his shoes. He's either dumb or honest, he's so poor, and honest is the one I'd pick. And he never looked the other way when the last guy had both his dukes in the tambourine."

Crotty leaned back and smiled. That reassuring conspiratorial smile. That you've-got-nothing-to-worry-about-Morty-Davis[']smile.

"Not a chance. He blew the whistle on the last guy. The last time they rewarded a guy for blowing the whistle, they had white blackbirds. The sun rose in the west that day, too. Sure they want somebody honest, but they want somebody knows how to play ball, too, the Commissioners."

He knew that Crotty was right. Morty Davis never looked the other way. That could be dangerous. He was suddenly angry. The last guy indicted, poor John Dempsey's brains splashed all over a wall, Morty Davis out in the cold because he was honest. And not a finger laid on Jack Amsterdam. The paymaster. [Now] ~~T~~he civic benefactor. [And] Des Spellacy's golf partner. [Not a man to forget the finger off (?)] ~~I wonder if he even knows I used to work for him. Probably not.~~ There ~~were too many~~ [just too many] layers between Jack

PICK UP PAGE 72-I/

True Confessions, *revised typescript*

than Tom, is a war hero known in the press as the "Parachuting Padre." As his cardinal's chancellor, Des becomes a consummate manipulator of wealthy parishioners: "He could run General Motors, the Cardinal thought. An Irish Medici, that one." He plots to succeed the cardinal but is not certain he wants the job. Des has also awarded $17 million in building contracts to Jack Armstrong but wants to get him out of church business because of suspicions about his using the church in his rackets. Tom discovers that the murder victim was involved in one of Armstrong's schemes and tries to implicate him in the murder. By doing so, Tom ruins Des's career.

One of Dunne's major successes in *True Confessions*, as with his previous books, is the verisimilitude of his subject matter. He convinces the reader that the worlds of Irish-American policemen and priests must be like this. The effectiveness of his milieu is aided by the vividness of his dozens of minor characters, including a fat cop who buys Sidney Greenstreet's suits from Warner Brothers and a fifty-one-year-old nun who mistakes her menopause for pregnancy since she does not know how women get pregnant. The novel is most notable for Dunne's complex portrait of Tom and Des and their growing awareness of the ambiguities of good and evil, of their own natures: "He sometimes wondered how much he really liked Des. It was as if he was always waiting for you to stumble, and after you did, it proved some kind of point that only he could understand. Until he found the opportunity to use it. He was like a cop that way. Maybe that was it. They understood each other too well." Twenty-eight years later, the dying Des tries to explain how he has regained some sense of his humanity by serving at a run-down church in the desert, how Tom has unintentionally provided his "salvation": "You made me remember something I forgot. Or tried to forget is more like it. You and me, we were always just a couple of harps."

True Confessions was praised by most of its reviewers as a highly intelligent entertainment and character study, drawing comparisons to the works of Dashiell Hammett, Raymond Chandler, Ross Macdonald, George V. Higgins, and Graham Greene. Christopher Lehmann-Haupt said in the *New York Times* that Dunne "seems at last to have written the book he was born to write"; and in the *Times Literary Supplement*, Anthony Bailey wrote, "*True Confessions* has a muscle-bound, dirty-talking strength which suggests that Mr. Dunne . . . has it in him to write a first-rate Irish-American novel." Judith Rascoe, in *Harper's*, called it "one of those novels in which all the elements fit together so aptly and simply and apparently naturally that it seems, like vodka and orange juice, a truly inspired combination." However, *True Confessions* also solicited more strongly negative commentary than any of Dunne's other books, primarily because of his emphasis on earthy humor. James G. Murray called Dunne a "smart-ass one-liner" in *The Critic*, and Maureen Howard complained about the "sodden barroom humor" in the *Hudson Review*: "Outside of Lenny Bruce records this novel must take the prize for the use of ethnic slurs."

Quintana & Friends (1978) is an uneven collection of thirty-three magazine articles Dunne selected from among the seventy-five he had written. The selections include reviews, character sketches, and essays about Dunne, his family, and his friends. The most frequent subject is California; he writes in the introduction, "if there is a single thread in this book it is the confrontation of the transplanted Easterner with the culture of the contemporary West." Typical of the articles is "Eureka!," in which he tries to show how the flaws of the West Coast can be interpreted as being virtues: "The absence of past and structure is basic to the allure of Los Angeles. It deepens the sense of self-reliance, it fosters the idea of freedom, or at least the illusion of it."

The most interesting and entertaining of the selections are those about Hollywood, especially "Gone Hollywood" and "Tinsel" which deal with Dunne and Didion's adventures as screenwriters. Dunne uses his out-of-the-mouths-of-fools method again as when they try to interest a studio executive in F. Scott Fitzgerald's *Tender Is the Night*. After reading a five-page synopsis written in 1945, he says, "I would gather that what interests you about this property is the glamour and glitter of the Edwardian age." Dunne explains why they continue writing movies given such people to deal with: "We do it because we like the action, even playing against a heavy deck, and because writing screenplays . . . is a lot of fun. The possibilities are infinite; it is only the probabilities that are finite."

These two articles imply that Dunn and Didion have co-written several screenplays, but they have received screen credit only three times: *Panic in Needle Park* (1971), *Play It As It Lays* (1972), and *True Confessions* (1981). Both *Panic in Needle Park*, based on James Mills's 1966 novel about New York heroin addicts, and *Play It As It Lays*, adapted from Didion's 1970 portrait of Hollywood ennui and psychosis, were critical and commercial failures. Reviewers and audiences found their characters unpleasant and unsympathetic. The Dunnes' most famous non-credit is for the 1976 remake of *A Star Is*

Born. At least fourteen other writers worked on the script before it finally reached the screen with director Frank Pierson listed as the screenwriter. Dunne writes amusingly about their fifteen-month labor on that film in "Gone Hollywood."

Dunne is an interesting writer because of the liveliness of his style, the vividness of his settings, the colorfulness of his characters—both real and imagined—and his devastating senses of humor, irony, and absurdity. One hopes that he will find subjects in addition to California, show business, Catholicism, and people who live on the fringes of society to write so well about.

—*Michael Adams*

Screenplays:

Panic in Needle Park, by Dunne and Joan Didion, Twentieth Century-Fox, 1971;

Play It As It Lays, by Dunne and Didion, Universal, 1972;

True Confessions, by Dunne and Didion, United Artists, 1981.

References:

John Lahr, "Entrepreneurs of Anxiety," *Horizon,* 24 (January 1981): 36-39;

Herbert Mitgang, "Publishing: Going to Moscow Book Fair," *New York Times,* 2 September 1977, III: 19.

Raymond Federman

(15 May 1928-)

BOOKS: *Journey to Chaos: Samuel Beckett's Early Fiction* (Los Angeles & Berkeley: University of California Press, 1965);

Among the Beasts/Parmi les Monstres (Paris: Editions Millas-Martin, 1967);

Double or Nothing (Chicago: Swallow Press, 1971);

Amer Eldorado (Paris: Editions Stock, 1974);

Me Too (Reno: The Westcoast Poetry Press, 1975);

Take It or Leave It (New York: The Fiction Collective, 1976);

The Voice in the Closet/La Voix dans le cabinet Debarras (Madison: Coda Press, 1979);

The Twofold Vibration (Bloomington: Indiana University Press, forthcoming).

Raymond Federman is one of the leaders of the American literary avant-garde, and, as a novelist, essayist, critic, teacher, and lecturer both in the United States and abroad, he has worked to define the new fiction (or "surfiction," as he has termed it) and to analyze the issues raised by the fundamental changes the novel has undergone in the twentieth century. Federman's own novels are unique examples of what he means by surfiction. Building on the work of Joyce, Céline, Beckett, and other twentieth-century masters, his fictions are fascinating constructs that combine a brilliant style, unorthodox typography, and a masterful new approach to the development of characters and literary structure. Unlike the traditional novel, these works are not intended to be representations of events; they are events in their own right, language events that reflect on their own mode of becoming and that, in effect, critique themselves. These are fictions that betray themselves as fictions, stories that declare themselves to be untrue even as they are told. Through his novels, Federman questions the very nature of fiction, the fiction writer, and the reality that the writer's language is supposed to represent.

Federman's novels have developed from two sources: the writings of Samuel Beckett and the extraordinary events of the author's own life. Federman is a well-known critic of Beckett's writings, and his first book, *Journey to Chaos* (1965), is an appreciative analysis of the Irish writer's early fiction. He has also contributed essays on Beckett to anthologies and journals, and he serves as an honorary trustee of the Samuel Beckett Society. His debt to Beckett is enormous, because Federman has followed through on the implications of Beckett's *Molloy* (1955), *Malone Dies* (1956), *The Unnamable* (1958), and *How It Is* (1964), just as Beckett pursued the implications of James Joyce's *Ulysses* and *Finnegans Wake.* For Federman Beckett demonstrated that it was possible to write novels without the traditional concepts of character, plot, and chronological structure, that fiction could be based on the idea of a disembodied voice speaking itself into existence. Federman's fictive voices are uniquely his own, but they are the descendants of Beckett's named and nameless characters, because they *are* only insofar as they speak, and, for the most part, what they say is that they are speaking.

The author's experiences provide the subject

matter for his novels, and yet it is inappropriate to categorize Federman as an autobiographer because his entire enterprise questions the very possibility of accurately remembering and recording the events of one's life. According to Federman, a life consists of the stories one creates after the fact; therefore, it is a fiction. Thus, in telling the various stories of his own life, he admittedly embellishes the details, changes the facts completely, contradicts himself, or tells his stories as if they had been told to him by someone else. His life as recounted in the novels is not true,

but Federman admits that he is lying, and this is the paradox of his fiction, for the liar who confesses his lies in the process of lying is telling the truth.

In the novels, the author fictionalizes his life, and yet Federman's works are based on his own experiences. He was born in Paris in 1928 and came to the United States shortly after World War II. At that time, he knew almost no English. He lived in Detroit until 1951, when he was drafted, and served in Asia until 1954. Federman became an American citizen in 1953, and, after his term in the army, he attended Columbia University, taking a B.A. degree there in 1957 and an M.A. in 1959. In 1963, he received his Ph.D. from the University of California at Los Angeles, and, since 1964, he has lectured in English and comparative literature as a faculty member of the State University of New York at Buffalo. He is an exciting teacher and a man of almost limitless energy who inspires others with his own passionate love for literature. Federman enjoys laughing and making others laugh, and, as a natural storyteller, he is capable of spinning tall tales for hours in his rich, thick French accent. Every event is exciting to him, from a literary discussion to a Buffalo Bills football game, from a new novel by a writer he loves to the jazz music that is always playing in his home, in his car, even in his office while he works. At every moment, he lives his life fully and completely, and this passion for living is at the very roots of his writing.

Federman is totally bilingual, and, though he has published works in both his native and his adopted tongue, his best-known novels were written originally in English. Like his mentor and longtime friend, Samuel Beckett, an Irishman who writes in French, Federman uses a language that is not his by birth.

One cannot understand Raymond Federman's life and work, however, without knowledge of the crucial event which he has recounted again and again, directly and indirectly, in every one of his novels. Federman is a Jew, and, in the summer of 1942, the gestapo came to his family home in Paris. Before the German soldiers entered the apartment, however, his parents hid young Raymond in a closet, and, while he crouched there in the darkness, his mother, his father, and his two sisters were taken away to die in the camps.

This experience is central to Federman's fiction; repeatedly he has tried to understand the significance of this "rebirth" and to come to terms with the fact that he survived the Holocaust while his family and so many other European Jews did not. The story is told for the first time in a poem contained in a bilingual collection, *Among the Beasts/Parmi les Monstres*, that was published in Paris in 1967, and many of the subsequent tellings are based on the imagery of this early work. In effect, this first verbalization of the crucial event has become even more significant to Federman than the event itself, and each subsequent writing of the story is actually a rewriting of that original text. Federman's writings never reach the truth of his experience, as he knows all too well, for his accounts of that event are never more than words and words about words.

The central event is in the background of

Federman's first novel, *Double or Nothing* (1971), the story of a young French immigrant who comes to America after he loses his family in the German death camps. Actually, it is misleading to say that this is the story of *Double or Nothing*, though it is the fulcrum of the work. In fact, there are four levels to this extremely complex novel. The story of the boy's arrival in America is being told by an author-to-be who is planning to write a novel based on the boy's experiences. This writer is leading a double life, for he is trying to plan how he will tell the story of the boy, and he is also planning to get a rented room, supply it with all that he will need to stay there for a year, and use that time to write his novel. Though *Double or Nothing* is "about" the boy, it is, at another level, the writer's story, a collection of his lists, calculations, and thoughts about what he will need in his room as well as notes for his soon-to-be written fiction.

The nameless writer is the voice of *Double or Nothing*, and he tells two stories simultaneously, the boy's and his own; often these two narrative levels become hopelessly mixed. When the young immigrant begins to tell of his arrival in New York in the first person, the writer adds his own comments in parentheses, disrupting the *what* of the story with the *how* of the writing: "We got off the subway at 185th Street (just like that). I remember that quite clearly (in the first person). Quite vividly (with a lot of adverbs). It was a very warm, humid, and sticky day (and lots of adjectives and commas). Or was it 210th Street (and a great deal of confusion and indecision)? By then the suitcase was getting quite heavy (and lots of realism too). Particularly as we (myself: BORIS, and my uncle: DAVID) went up the stairs into the streets."

There is every indication that the writer is also a French immigrant and that he also lost his family to the Holocaust, but he insists that the projected novel about the boy is not autobiographical. Still, at times, he suggests that the story of the boy is true, that it was told to him by a real person, though he tries to conceal the truth by refusing to use the young man's real name and by calling him Jacques, Robert, Boris, etc., at various points in the narrative. At other times, however, the writer contradicts himself by insisting that the boy's story is not true, that the character and his tale are products of the imagination. For the reader, there is no way of telling truth from fiction, if, in fact, there is any truth here at all.

The reader might be tempted to identify Federman as the writer in *Double or Nothing* except for the fact that there is a third voice involved in the narrative, the voice of the recorder who never speaks about himself but who is telling the story of the writer, thus indicating that the writer and his creation, the boy, are equally fictive. But Federman is not the recorder either. A fourth voice is introduced in a footnote, the voice of the one who is orchestrating the various levels of *Double or Nothing* and whose existence is implied by the text. Of course, once this fourth person appears in the fiction, a fifth person is implied, that is, the person who records the existence of the fourth. The fifth person, in turn, implies a sixth, and so on. In short, there is a potentially infinite regression of narrative voices which can never reach the reality of Federman or his life.

Double or Nothing begins with an introduction that tells the entire "story" of the novel in the opening pages. The reader who only wants to know what the book is about need go no further. *Double or Nothing* exists not for the sake of the story that is told but for the *how* of the telling. The novel is a typographical tour de force; each page is a complete visual unit, and this visual aspect contributes to the telling by making the language both a conceptual and a concrete event. By drawing on his own experiences and by following through on the implications of Beckett's concept of the narrative voice, Federman has created a highly original work which establishes the themes of his later novels.

Humor is one of Federman's key tools, and *Double or Nothing* makes fun of the novel as a literary form and of the actual process of writing fiction. The style is frantic and purposely paradoxical, and often the reader laughs not so much at the antics of the characters as at his own confusion in the face of this convoluted text. The later books are also funny, though at times, given his subject matter, Federman's humor is very black indeed. Like Louis-Ferdinand Céline, Federman believes that, in the face of absurd horror, laughter is the only possible response, and this dark laughter is an integral element in the works which follow *Double or Nothing*. Published in 1971 by Swallow Press of Chicago, *Double or Nothing* was awarded the Frances Steloff Prize for that year.

Take It or Leave It appeared in 1976 under the imprint of the Fiction Collective, an innovative publishing company for which Federman served as codirector in 1979-1980. This work is an extended version in English (though not a translation) of *Amer Eldorado*, a novel written originally in French and published in Paris in 1974. Like *Double or Nothing*, *Take It or Leave It* is again the product of many voices. This text is an "exaggerated second-hand tale," according to the note on the title page,

I

In matters such as these there's much food for thought undoubtedly. That's the point. Another guy would say little food but that's his business But there is no point For if the room costs 8 bucks a week

8 dollars

If the room costs twelve dollars a week then it'll have to be noodles. Noodles then it is. Imagine that. For 8 bucks - 10 even - I could have had something better. A little piece of meat here and there. Can meat of course. It's better than nothing. But 12 dollars a week. That's 52 times 12. That's 624 bucks. Imagine that just for a room. But the room is important. A room with a large window. With a view. Who gives a damn about the garbage cans. No, a view on the street. I think. ~~I should have looked.~~ So many rooms all over. ~~In Detroit, Chicago, L.A., Frisco, etc.~~ Many without views. But this time it's different. 12 bucks for a room. 10 ~~even~~, that's what I thought it would be. I was paying 5 last time I was here. Ok, ~~it was three years, maybe four years ago~~. 52 times 10 makes 520. 520 dollars. That makes a difference. But the room is important. Not just a room to sleep in, to take craps, to jerk off, to hide, to feel sorry for yourself, etc. A room with a meaning. A working room. ~~You might~~ say. A romm to work in. Yes, that's what it is. And a piece of blue sky once in a while, out of the window. Yes, the room is important. Particularly in cases like these. Unbelievable. So many shit-holes in ~~my~~ life. This one will be paradise. I just hope the fuck there are no ~~cockroaches~~ in this one. I hate those filthy things. And rats even worse. I hate ~~those damn bastards~~. Rats with long trailing tails. At night you dream they come to nibble your ears. ~~Disgusting~~. Gives me the creeps. For 12 bucks. [illegible] You should get something better than for 8 or even 10. ~~I don't~~ care about the furniture. As long as there is a table. ~~And there is~~ one. A working table. A table to work on. The wall paper is important too. So many crummy wall papers all over. Uninteresting wall paper, shitty wall paper. Or sometimes no even any wall paper. But this ~~one is not bad~~. Horses all over. I think. Yes, looks like flying horses. It could help in rough days. Moments of panic. I'll bet that by the time I'm out of there I'll know exactly how many horses there are flying all over. Though in some places I'll have to put them toge-

Double or Nothing, *revised typescript*

which, at the outset, places the work at two removes from whatever one might want to think of as the reality beyond words. A tale is not an event in the extralinguistic world, and an exaggerated secondhand tale lacks even the questionable accuracy and immediacy of an eyewitness account. Here, the secondary teller must remember and put into words the remembering and the putting-into-words of the original teller, and so the tale itself is immediately suspect and open to error throughout.

The tale is quite simple. A young French immigrant who came to America after the death of his family in World War II is drafted into the U.S. Army and requests a transfer to the Korean theater to get out of the 82nd Airborne Division. The transfer comes through, and Frenchy has thirty days to get from Fort Bragg, North Carolina, to California, where he will meet his ship. He decides to go by car, in his own Buick Special, and see America, but, because of a bureaucratic error, his papers and the money he needs to make the trip are sent off to Camp Drum in upstate New York. He must get there himself, must make the drive north from the Carolinas to New York before he can begin his journey west.

This tale, full of false starts, digressions, repetitions, and contradictions, is told by a nameless voice that is addressing a faceless and almost voiceless audience. Like the writer and the young immigrant in *Double or Nothing*, the narrator of *Take It or Leave It* and Frenchy have much in common, so much in fact that one is tempted to think of them as the same person, though the teller insists that they are not:

> But in case you guys get confused in the course
> of this twin recitation with the me and the he
>   & the I and the He
>   & the me now and the he then
>   & the he past and the me present (he past in
>   the hole me present on the platform
> let me make it quite clear once and for all
> lest WE forget it (here & there & everywhere)
> I am here (alone)
>   He is there (together we are)
> as one are we not / multiple though
> single / I + He = WE or WE - I = HE
> pluralized in our singularity
>   me telling him
>   him telling me   etc.

Unlike the writer in *Double or Nothing*, who seems to be making up the story of Boris as he goes along, this narrator insists that the tale he tells is not his own but one that was told to him by Frenchy while they sat together at some time in the past under a tree or at the edge of a precipice or somewhere else.

The narrator is not the only voice in this novel. Though the fictive listeners in the audience do not speak intelligibly, the teller understands their questions, comments, and interruptions and tries his best to respond to them. There are also literary critics-in-residence in the text who comment on the very work which gives them their being. And there are others. Still, Frenchy and the teller are the focal points of the text. Frenchy, the original teller of the tale, is the one whose story is told by the narrator of *Take It or Leave It*, but this secondhand teller is told as well. Without *Take It or Leave It*, he would not and could not exist. Like the voices of *Double or Nothing*, the teller is both the producer and the product of the text.

Take It or Leave It is a text which constitutes, contradicts, and erases itself, as it constitutes, contradicts, and erases the voices which it produces and by which it is produced. The reading of the text leaves no remainder. In canceling itself, the novel refuses to serve as the story of Frenchy, the teller, or Federman himself, if a *story* is a coherent sequence of actual, remembered, or imagined events. The novel is, rather, the sum of its own words. *Take It or Leave It* is purely fiction.

The Voice in the Closet/La Voix dans le cabinet Débarras was published in 1979 in a bilingual edition which also includes "Echos á Raymond Federman," French novelist Maurice Roche's unique response to these texts. This work addresses the crucial event of Federman's life directly, and it marks a turning point in his writings, because, for the first time, the name "federman" actually appears in the fiction. The author joins Boris, Frenchy, and the other characters of his novels; his name becomes purposely fictive.

The form of *The Voice in the Closet* is incredibly strict: twenty pages, eighteen lines per page, sixty-eight characters (letters and spaces) per line. This form creates enclosed boxes of words which reflect, on the visual level, the claustrophobic narrative. Within these tight restrictions, only the essential can remain. There is no place for a story, and in fact there is none. There is only a voice, the voice of a boy who hides in a closet while his family is taken off to the camps by a troop of German soldiers. This voice speaks from its hiding place to someone named federman, the writer who has tried and failed again and again to tell the truth about the boy and his devastating experience.

The voice wants to tell the truth at last, the truth

that the writer has never been able to reach. The boy in the closet wants to create himself "in my own voice at last a beginning after so many detours relentless false justifications in the margins more to come in my own words now that I may speak say I the real story from the other side extricated from inside roles reversed . . ." Unfortunately, like federman, the voice also fails to find the proper beginning for a story that is terrible beyond words. Instead, it stumbles and falters, accuses its creator, and returns again and again to the images of the poem in which the story was attempted for the first time. *The Voice in the Closet* never reaches the truth; it remains a fiction.

This strange and disturbing text repeats all the themes of Federman's earlier novels in a marvelously concise form. There is the narrative voice which speaks itself into existence, seemingly without the need of an author. There is the betrayal of the fictivity of language, of the inability of words to capture the meaning of a man's life. There is the search for the truth of memory, a truth which never seems to materialize. And there is the convoluted, multileveled narrative which critiques itself and cancels itself at the same time.

Still, *The Voice in the Closet* is very different from *Double or Nothing* and *Take It or Leave It* because, while Boris and Frenchy are characters whose stories are told by others, the boy in the closet tries to seize the narrative power for himself. His attempt to reverse the roles of writer and character still fails to get at a truth that is somewhere beyond words, but *The Voice in the Closet* points to an interesting shift in Federman's fiction. In this brief work, it almost seems that Federman has turned *Double or Nothing* and *Take It or Leave It* inside out.

The English version of *The Voice in the Closet* is part of another novel, *The Twofold Vibration*, which, at the time of this writing, is awaiting publication by Indiana University Press. This work is a new departure for Federman; the typography is more orthodox and the style is more controlled than in the earlier works, and here there is a clearly recognizable story. Still, Federman's characteristic themes are present, and the crucial event is central to the narrative.

In *The Twofold Vibration*, Federman is a character, the first-person narrator, but he is not alone. He shares the narrative voice with two others: Namredef (his mirror image) and Moinous (me/we). Together, they tell the story of their friend, the old man, who, like his three tellers and like the real Raymond Federman, is a bilingual French immigrant and a survivor of the Holocaust. He is also a writer, and, within the context of *The Twofold Vibration*, *The Voice in the Closet* is presented as his work.

The old man's story is a not-yet, a tale out of time (the subtitle for the novel is "an extemporaneous novel"). It is almost midnight, 31 December 1999, and, at the coming of the millenium, the old man is to be deported from earth to the space colonies. His friends are trying to find out why he is being deported and to save him if possible. They are also trying to tell his story, and, in the process, they digress into his past and tell about his affair with Jane Fonda, his spectacular win at the Travemünde Casino, his literary efforts, and so forth. They are trying to explain their unnamed friend completely, usually by repeating what he has said about himself, and in the attempt they also say something about themselves. But the who and the why of the old man continually escape them, as the old man seems continually to escape himself and his own story.

Namredef and Moinous are the investigators, and Federman is the recorder, the orchestrator of the text. This Federman sits in his room at his desk and records the reports, observations, and reminiscences of Moinous and Namredef, making his own contributions along the way. He is the explainer, the teller of the tellings of his two conarrators. He is, apparently, the one who puts the words on paper.

And yet, once again, the Federman of the novel is not Federman the author of *The Twofold Vibration* because the first Federman is a fictional character while the second is not. Or is he? Federman would claim that his life *is* a fiction, a story which is part truth, part lie, full of digressions, repetitions, alterations, and invented details and transitions. The events of the author's life are the sources for his novels, and yet Federman understands that writing cannot expose the truth and meaning of those events. The writing of fiction is simply another event in its own right, not an answer to the author's life but another part of it.

Federman's novels have received praise from critics in the United States and abroad, and his writings have been translated into German, Polish, Spanish, Italian, Japanese, Hungarian, and Portuguese. By coming to terms with the fiction of Samuel Beckett and by pushing Beckett's concepts of the novel to their limits through the use of incidents from his own life, Federman has produced an impressive and challenging body of work that is uniquely his own. Even now, younger fiction writers throughout the world understand that, if the novel is to continue to develop and grow, they must come to terms with the work of Raymond Federman.

—*Welch D. Everman*

Other:

F. J. Temple, *Postal Cards,* translated by Federman (Santa Barbara, Cal.: Noel Young Editions, 1964);

Yvonne Caroutch, *Temporary Landscapes,* edited and translated by Federman (Venice, Italy: Mica Editions, Stamperia de Venezia, 1965);

Samuel Beckett: His Works and his Critics, coauthored by Federman and John Fletcher (Los Angeles & Berkeley: University of California Press, 1970);

Cinq Nouvelles Nouvelles, edited by Federman (New York: Appleton-Century-Crofts, 1970; New York: Irvington, 1975);

Surfiction: Fiction Now and Tomorrow, edited by Federman (Chicago: Swallow Press, 1975);

Samuel Beckett: Cahier de l'Herne, coedited by Federman and Thomas Bishop (Paris: Editions de l'Herne, 1976);

Samuel Beckett: The Critical Heritage, coedited by Federman and Lawrence Graver (London: Routledge and Kegan Paul, Ltd., 1979).

Interviews:

"Sperimentalismo tra Francia e America," *Uomini E Libri,* 50 (Fall 1974): 26-29;

"The New Innovative Fiction (A Dialogue with Ronald Sukenick)," *Antaeus,* 20 (Winter 1976): 138-149;

"Interview about New Fiction in America," *Le Figaro Littéraire* (15 June 1976);

"Tri(y)log (A Conversation about New Fiction with Mas'ud Zavarzadeh and Joseph Hynes)," *Chicago Review,* 28 (Fall 1976): 93-109;

"Interview: Part I and Part II," *Cream City Review,* 4 (Spring 1979): 16-21; 5 (Winter 1979): 76-88;

"Federman: An Interview," *Phoebe,* 10 (Fall 1980): 37-39.

Robert Fitzgerald

(12 October 1910-)

BOOKS: *Poems* (New York: Arrow Editions, 1935);

A Wreath for the Sea (New York: New Directions, 1943);

In the Rose of Time (New York: New Directions, 1956);

Spring Shade (New York: New Directions, 1971).

Robert Stuart Fitzgerald was born in Geneva, New York, but moved to Springfield, Illinois, with his family when he was an infant and spent his childhood there. His early interest in writing was encouraged by Vachel Lindsay, who returned to Springfield in 1928. Fitzgerald attended Choate School in Connecticut in 1928-1929, where he studied under Dudley Fitts, with whom he later collaborated on translations. In fall 1929 he entered Harvard and won *Poetry* magazine's Midland Author's Prize for a group of poems that he had submitted to the magazine at Lindsay's suggestion. By then he was at Trinity College, Cambridge, studying philosophy and classical languages. He returned to Harvard and graduated in 1933, the year T. S. Eliot was giving the Norton lectures there. Eliot accepted two of Fitzgerald's poems for his London literary quarterly, the *Criterion.* After graduation Fitzgerald worked as a business reporter for the *New York Herald Tribune,* leaving that job in 1935. He spent the summer of 1935 at the MacDowell Colony in Peterborough, New Hampshire, where he put together his first book of poems and worked with Fitts on a translation of *Alcestis* (1936). From 1936 to 1940 he worked for *Time* in several departments: art, books, business, and financial news. Resigning in 1940, he went to Santa Fe, New Mexico, where he completed his translation of *Oedipus at Colonus* (1941) and his second book of poems, *A Wreath for the Sea* (1943). He returned to *Time,* working as writer and editor until 1943, when he received a commission in the navy to serve on the staff of the Commander-in-Chief of Pacific Ocean Areas, first at Pearl Harbor and then on Guam. Fitzgerald married Eleanor Green in 1935; they were divorced in 1946. Baptized and brought up Roman Catholic, he had left the faith before he was twenty-five but returned to the Catholic Church in 1946. He married Sarah Morgan in 1947; they had six children. In 1948-1949

he was poetry reviewer for the *New Republic*. Between 1946 and 1953, Fitzgerald taught at Sarah Lawrence College, Princeton, and Indiana University. He received a Guggenheim Fellowship in 1952, and in 1953 he and his family moved to Italy, where they made their primary home for several years. Fitzgerald has also taught at Notre Dame (1957), the University of Washington (1961), and Mount Holyoke College (1964); he has been Nicholas Boylston professor at Harvard since 1965. Between 1956 and 1974 he published two more collections of poetry and translations of *The Odyssey* (1961) and *The Iliad* (1974). He is at present working on a translation of *The Aeneid*. Fitzgerald lives in Connecticut but still spends time at his farmhouse in Italy. He and his wife are now separated.

Among the honors and awards Fitzgerald has received are the Guggenheim Fellowship, 1952 and 1971; the Shelley Memorial Award, 1955; a Ford Foundation grant in creative writing, 1959; the Bollingen Poetry Translation Prize, 1961, for *The Odyssey*; the Landon Translation Award, 1976, for *The Iliad*; the Ingram Merrill Literature Award, 1978; and the Williams-Derwood Award in recognition of his life's work as a poet and translator, 1981.

Robert Fitzgerald is probably best known for his translations. In an interview by Edwin Honig he has given some insights into his attitude toward the art of translation. He believes that the impetus to translate comes as "one finds in poems and language some quality one appropriates for oneself and wishes to reproduce. . . . Something seems unusually piercing, living, handsome, in another language, and since English is yours, you wish it to be there too." Fitzgerald speaks of having had to memorize six or seven hundred lines of Greek when he was in the Classical Club production of Sophocles' *Philoctetes* at Harvard. He feels that the experience made the language come nearer to being a living one for him and led to the "overpowering sense that justice had not been done to the poetry of Sophocles." Fitzgerald translates directly from the original because he does not want "any mediation" through other translations.

Of his translations in collaboration with Fitts, the first, *Alcestis*, has been praised as spirited and sensitive. Reactions to *Antigone* (1939) are generally enthusiastic, though some critics feel that the passion and sublimity of the original are at times sacrificed in making it clear and credible in English. Others especially admire the naturalness and vitality of the translation, and most comment on the superb lyrics. The brilliance of their collaboration, a happy combination of Fitts's wit and Fitzgerald's lyricism, is also recognized in *Oedipus Rex* (1949).

Fitzgerald has received high praise for his other translations. His *Oedipus at Colonus* has been called sparkling, smooth, and natural. Reviewers speak especially of his remarkable flexibility and fine sense of cadence. In his translations of *The Odyssey* and *The Iliad*, he succeeds in finding a rhythm and level of diction that make us feel the beauty of the original. He is recognized for his fine balance between freedom and literal translation, his true ear for Homer, his grasp of the voice and role of each character, and his sensuous sharpness of descriptive detail. In discussing Fitzgerald's translation of *The Odyssey*, George Steiner expresses the opinion that Fitzgerald is "taking his place beside Chapman and Pope in the unbroken lineage of English Homeric translations. In many respects he excels them." Steiner compares Fitzgerald with several other translators and praises him for avoiding "obtrusive singularities" and for developing "a mode which is at once neutral and modern, lyric yet full of technical resource. . . . Written in a flexible blank verse, Fitzgerald's narrative moves with such ease of tread

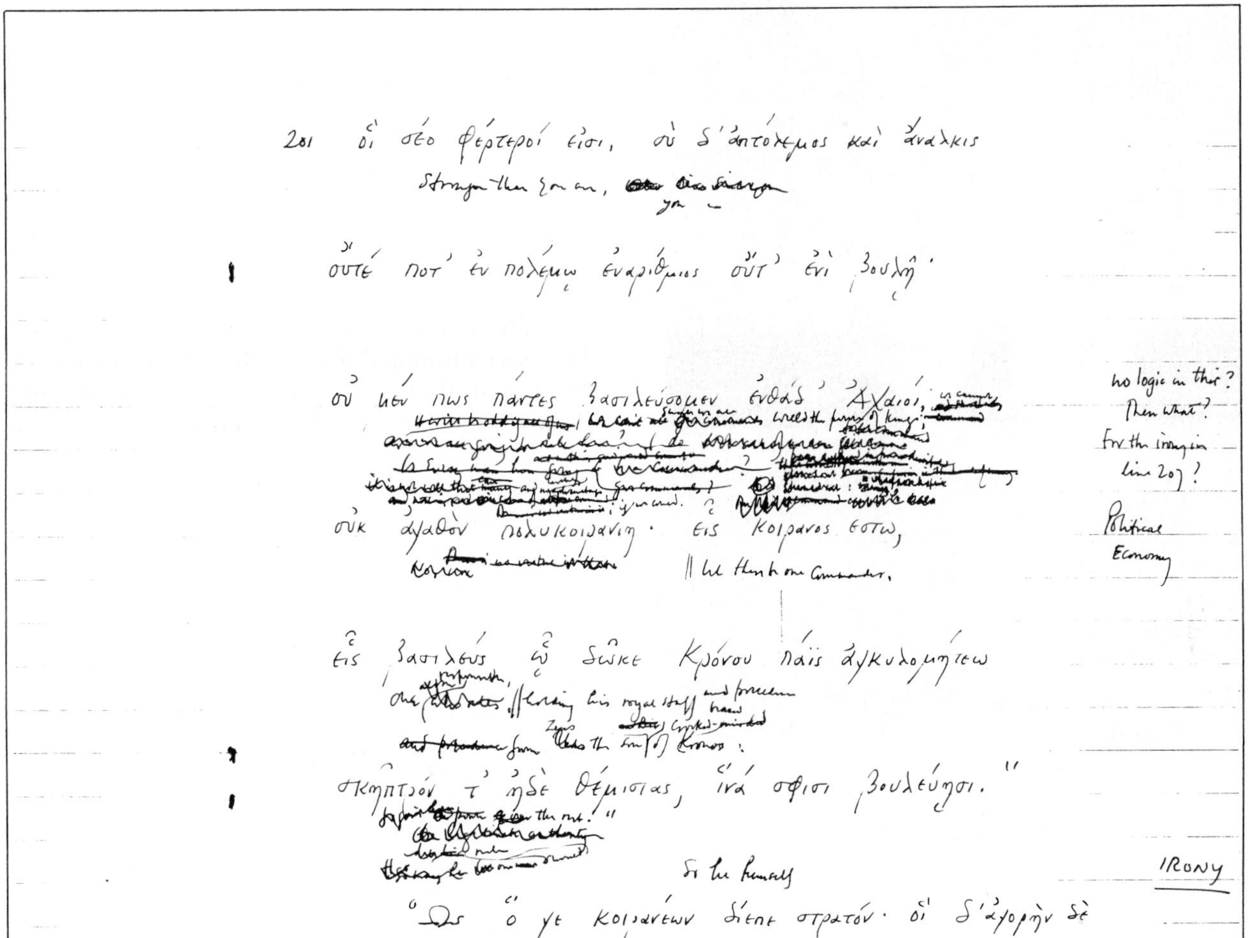
201 οἳ σέο φέρτεροί εἰσι, σὺ δ' ἀπτόλεμος καὶ ἄναλκις
Stronger than you are,
you
οὔτε ποτ' ἐν πολέμῳ ἐναρίθμιος οὔτ' ἐνὶ βουλῇ·
οὐ μέν πως πάντες βασιλεύσομεν ἐνθάδ' Ἀχαιοί·
no logic in this? Then what? For the irony in line 207?
οὐκ ἀγαθὸν πολυκοιρανίη· εἷς κοίρανος ἔστω,
|| let there be one Commander,
Political Economy
εἷς βασιλεύς, ᾧ δῶκε Κρόνου πάϊς ἀγκυλομήτεω
throne his royal staff and precedence
Zeus crooked-minded
Kronos:
σκῆπτρόν τ' ἠδὲ θέμιστας, ἵνα σφίσι βουλεύῃσι."
the rest!"
So he himself
IRONY
Ὣς ὅ γε κοιρανέων δίεπε στρατόν· οἱ δ' ἀγορὴν δὲ
took his commanding way through all the army:
αὖτις ἐπεσσεύοντο νεῶν ἄπο καὶ κλισιάων
and back and the assembly ground
they poured from
from ships and huts, with a rushing roar,
ἠχῇ, ὡς ὅτε κῦμα πολυφλοίσβοιο θαλάσσης
as when a big wave from the seething
two noises
αἰγιαλῷ μεγάλῳ βρέμεται, σμαραγεῖ δέ τε πόντος.
sea upon a long shore thunders and the deep
of shore resounds

Iliad, *first-draft manuscript*

that we often forget the sheer virtuosity of the artisan." Fitzgerald has also translated extensively in Latin and French, with the same assurance and graceful control. He has included a few translations in his latest volume of poetry, a selection which illustrates his sensitivity, range, and impeccable scholarship. We may look forward to the same high quality in his forthcoming translation of *The Aeneid*.

Fitzgerald's reputation for excellence as a translator is surely deserved, but it has regrettably tended to overshadow his recognition as a poet. *Poems*, Fitzgerald's first collection of poetry, was published in 1935. At twenty-five he had already developed a fine command of form and phrase and mastery of patterns of sound. The form and tone of each poem is beautifully realized; however, the overall tone of the collection is somewhat lacking in variety. We can feel Eliot's influence in this volume, in both technique and philosophy. Fitzgerald seems to have a natural affinity of mind with Eliot, based in the strong historical sense. Fitzgerald's essay "The Place of Form," gives some indication of his intense interest in the complex questions of form and reveals the breadth of his vision as he relates ideas of Aristotle, Saint Thomas Aquinas, Saint Augustine, Coleridge, Valéry, Einstein, and others. His sure and frequent use of classical allusions in his poems, often in juxtaposition with images of modern life, reminds one of both Eliot and Pound; but the poems lack the nervous, shifting rhythms of modern life counterpointed with the more classical tones—the combination which brought such vitality to much of their poetry.

Echoes, especially of Eliot, are so strong in some of these poems that they become distracting, as in these lines from "For the Others":

They will come to my house, to the street's end
In the tedious season,
Naming the dry leaf and the wind at morning
Bearing death.

....

Birds
Sing in the dark trees at the world's end
In the evening of time. The bearded men
Stand there among the horses. Musicians play.

And there are valleys in the mountains
And women cutting the hay, and carrying it
In under warm rain.

In Fitzgerald's later work, many echoes from modern poets are clearly deliberate, used for a kind of resonance off of which he can play. But in these early poems it is not clear how conscious the echoes are; at times they seem imitative rather than instrumental. The Frostian voice in "Winter Night," for instance, is obtrusive, even though Fitzgerald somehow makes the poem assuredly his own.

The grey day left the dusk in doubt.
Now it is dark.
Nightfall and no stars are out,
But this black wind will set its mark
Like anger on the souls that stir
From chimney side or sepulcher.

From hill to pasture moans the snow.
The farms hug tight
Their shaking ribs against the blow.
There is no mercy in this night
Nor scruple to its wrath. The dead
Sleep light this wind being overhead.

Another short poem, "Phrase," illustrates many of Fitzgerald's strengths, and some of his limitations, in this collection.

Sorrowful love passes from transparencies
to transparencies of bitter starlight
between antiquities and antiquities so simply

as in evening a soft bird flies down
and rests on a white railing under leaves

Love thinks in this quietness of falling
leaves birds or rain from the hushes
of summer clouds through luminous centuries

Touch unconsolable love the hands of your ancestors

Though lovely, the poem tends to drift into abstraction and become lost in sound. This personal, yet somehow distanced, objective voice is more moving when there is a kind of excitement in the language, as in these lines from "Himeros":

The locust sobs in the leaves. Her dusty hair
My love has now let fall upon the sun's
Stream. Beyond pale trestles
Flows evening: darkness and earth-drift.
Under a shard of moon the locust sings,
Mourning holocausts of summer.

And these from the strong poem "Elegy":

What should you know at last when spirit's
Spun from you, bobbin of bone, ghostbody in
the sun?
Enumerate your keen, wind-feathered
Moods up-tossed and patterned in swift
weather
With colors of shirts and flowers;

A Wreath for the Sea has more longer poems, more Latinate titles, and a few interspersed translations. The translations blend smoothly with Fitzgerald's original poems; both show remarkable control and modulation of his lyrical gift. His passages from Virgil's "First Georgic," for example, never lapse in verbal expression or decorum. His taste remains classical in tone and precision, in translations and original poetry. Lines such as the following from "Georgic" reflect the grace and skill of his own poetry:

The happy sailors load the prow with garlands.
Then is the time to gather acorns and
Laurel berries and the bloodred myrtle,
To lay your traps for cranes and snares for buck,
To hit the fallow deer with twisted slingshots,
And track the long-eared hare—
When snow is deep, and ice is on the rivers.

Many of the poems in this collection show Fitzgerald's kinship with the Southern Fugitive Poets: his interest in form, classicism, and the gentlemanly, scholarly tone. These lines from "Souls Lake," for instance, remind one of both Allen Tate and Donald Davidson in diction and theme:

The evergreen shadow and the pale magnolia
Stripping slowly to the air of May
Stood still in the night of the honey trees,
At rest above a star pool with my friends,
Beside that grove most fit for elegies,
I made my phrase to out-enchant the night.

The epithalamion, the hush were due,
For I had fasted and gone blind to see
What night might be beyond our passages;
Those stars so chevalier in fearful heaven
Could not but lay their steel aside and come
With a grave glitter into my low room.

And echoes of John Crowe Ransom's wit and use of rhyme to undercut sentimentality can be heard in several of the poems, especially in the translation of Villon's "Ballade des Pendus." In these lines we have a rich mixture of the original, of Ransom's "Captain Carpenter," and Fitzgerald's own voice:

The rain has drubbed us in his cold laundry,
The sun has parched us blacker than a crow,
And kites have made each eye a cavity
And torn our beards and eyebrows even so.
There is no resting place where we may go,
But here or there, just as the wind may blow,
We dangle at his pleasure to and fro.

But overall the collection seems to lack a strong center, the kind of coordinating theme or direction that was stimulated in the Fugitive group. One feels that Fitzgerald's poems come deeply out of himself, but the scope and manner sometimes limit them. Lyrical, eternal, and objective rather than immediate and personal, some of the poems seem somewhat cold and lacking in enthusiasm.

In several of the poems Fitzgerald deals with aspects of modern life in an interesting way. In "Cobb Would Have Caught It," for instance, through controlled free verse he attempts to make modern atmosphere and mood work through more traditional form. He combines colloquialism and formal diction, as in these lines:

Talk it up, boys, a little practice.

Coming in stubby and fast, the baseman
Gathers a grounder in fat green grass,
Picks it up stinging and clipped as wit
Into the leather: a swinging step
Wings it deadeye down to first.
Smack. Oh, attaboy, attyoldboy.

It is well done, an effective poem, but the point finally becomes a kind of disillusionment. Fitzgerald works with colloquialism but not so much with speech rhythms, as we can imagine William Carlos Williams doing with this subject. Fitzgerald does not really seem interested in working with the patterns of American speech that can catch the vitality and enthusiasm of American life. In "The Shore of Life," he plays off of the mood of Eliot in "The Waste Land" with the overt echo in the opening lines: "I came then to the city of my brethren. / Not Carthage, not Alexandria, not London"; and later, "Not Athens, Alexandria, Vienna or London." This gives his more positive picture of New York a resonance that intensifies the contrast—and, perhaps, a turn away from despair. But here, too, there is no attempt to catch the special rhythms of the speech and life of the city. The effect, rather, is of seeing the city through a mythic mood and context.

The fine poem "Animula," free verse with an underlying sense of form and beautiful control of the lines, shows Fitzgerald's characteristic delicacy and precision. The poem is deeply moving as it reconstructs the magic world of a childhood winter. A personal voice emerges through sensory details; the abstract takes on emotional significance through images such as, "A pretty woman toweling my cheek / Would lay it close to hers; drier and warmer"; and "Powdery sugar in a cut glass and silver / Shaker might be held, massy and lovely, / With such cool facets, like so much of winter." This more personal voice increases as Fitzgerald continues to develop as a poet.

The last few poems in the collection evoke the sense of a world disorder. They are reminiscent of Auden's poems of the 1930s, visions of Europe—violence, refugees, the coming of war. In Fitzgerald's "Sympathy of Peoples" the combination of close details and a detached long distance vision raises the poem above simple protest and anger. He uses the figure of the man with binoculars in a manner somewhat similar to Auden's use of the airman or the mountain climber as a kind of allegoric figure of the man who sees history.

> You may discern through binoculars
> A long line of the shawled and frozen,
> Moving yet motionless, as if those
> Were populations whom the sun failed
> And the malicious moon enchanted
> To wander and be still forever
> The prey or wolves and bestial mazes.

It is a powerful poem, specific yet transcending the specific through historical perspective. Fitzgerald never loses touch with what he is trying to say in the midst of these beautifully precise lines and long sentences; he sustains the sense of immediacy while he extends the vision.

In the Rose of Time (1956) is a selection of poems from the two earlier volumes, with fifteen new poems in the final section. Fitzgerald maintains his many strengths throughout the volume, and in some of the later poems he speaks in a fresh new tone of personal warmth and joy. This tone is especially noticeable in poems dealing with children. For example, "Lightness in Autumn" is a delightful poem in which Fitzgerald seems to be playing off echoes of Frost's "Stopping by Woods on a Snowy Evening" with a lightening of tone:

> I reckon how the wind behaves
> And rake them lightly into waves
> And rake the waves upon a pile,
> Then stop my raking for a while.
>
> The sun is down, the air is blue,
> And soon the fingers will be, too,
> But there are children to appease
> With ducking in those leafy seas.

And the lovely poem "Spring Shade," which furnishes the title for his next volume, movingly evokes the presence of the child through sensory images. Here the celebration of innocence is delicately combined with recognition of its transience by "the man of memory in his iron chair." As Ransom does in "Bells for John Whiteside's Daughter" and "Janet Waking," Fitzgerald expresses a strong, bitter-sweet feeling without sentimentality in "Spring Shade":

> The April winds rise, and the willow whips
> Lash one another's green in rinsing light.
> The dream eludes the waking finger tips.
>
> . . . .
>
> A girl in watered blue, as he conceives,
> And shy from study on the garden grass,
> Turned a great page of sunprint and new leaves,
>
> Closing the volume. You may leave the class,
> The Teacher seemed to say. And he was Dunce.
> Now all the colored crayons break, alas,
>
> And all the daffodils blow back at once.

Spring Shade (1971) brings together poetry from Fitzgerald's previous collections, a number of more recent poems, and selections from his translations. In many of the later poems the personal sense comes through as he deals more with what Lionel Trilling calls "the recalcitrant stuff of life." A poem such as "Errantry," for example, does not seem distanced by intellectual considerations. The feeling of immediacy of experience is captured through sense impressions and humor. Fitzgerald achieves a tone of real affection for the child, with no tinge of sentimentality and no sacrifice of form—terza rima is masterfully handled:

> Hot on the smudgy toes of both his feet.
> Rages of Infancy! How he could cry!
> But man's attempt he loves and will repeat,

Robert Fitzgerald

Surging and teetering, with impassioned eye,
To reach the wildwood lilac shade, and enter
Under the Persian leaves where kittens lie,

Green-eyed, bedizened, at the dappled center.

In a number of other poems, too, wit combines with a sense of tenderness in the relationship with a child. These lines from "Figlio Maggiore" illustrate how effectively Fitzgerald can use mixed diction and semihumorous rhyme while maintaining authentic grace and tone.

Twitched in her belly, or he raised a fist,
and came and cried. O red and meager baby,
umbilical, priapic, knobby,
mashed and wrinkled like an old pugilist.

. . . .

Of iodine-scented rock pure undersea,
fronded, astir, awaited our explorer.
Noon. With a small tentacled horror
draped on his tines he swam ashore in glee.

Perhaps through his family and his return to Catholicism, Fitzgerald has discovered a center from which he extends the personal into the historical more naturally and movingly. For example, the epiphany in "July in Indiana" comes convincingly out of the fine sensory images of particulars.

Evening came, will come with lucid stillness
printed by the distinct cricket
and, far off, by the freight cars' coupling clank.

A warm full moon will rise
out of the mothering dust, out of the dry corn
land.

Some of these later poems have a special quality that seems to come out of Fitzgerald's personal faith. Especially fine is "Metaphysical." A sunset becomes the metaphor for a seizing of light, a leap of faith in acceptance of the grandeur of the moment that cannot last.

Rays of his mercy are besought.
To magnetize my speck of thought.
Elated let the evening fall,
Abysmal be the golden day;
The ravaged carcass far away
Be supple in the life of all.

Fitzgerald has also written a number of pieces which reveal his skill and versatility in prose. His essay "The Place of Form" proves his ability to express complex ideas in a clear and interesting manner. "Some Details of Scene and Action in *The Odyssey*" shows his excitement in reliving some of the steps of the journey of Odysseus and his joy in personal investigation of details related to his translation. His long memoir which introduces *The Collected Short Prose of James Agee* (which Fitzgerald also edited) gives fresh and valuable insights into Agee's personality and work. Most recently, Fitzgerald has had several fine sketches in the *New Yorker*. These too are memoirs, here of his own boyhood and adolescence. These pieces are lively, moving, and filled with gentle humor. "Light From the Bay Windows," for instance, brings to life the tender moments of communion of the young boy and his invalid father. Fitzgerald's prose shows his characteristic control of form and tone in a variety of modes.

Fitzgerald's major achievements have been his own poetry and his translations. During the decades when contemporary taste turned toward confessional poetry and open form, he continued to write formal verse. At present, there are indications of a return to acceptance of formal poetry as one important mode. We may hope that Fitzgerald will receive the recognition he deserves as a lyric poet of authentic grace who combines a sense of history and world view with personal vision.

—*Anne Newman*

Other:

"Some Details of Scene and Action in *The Odyssey*," in *Yearbook of Comparative and General Literature* (Bloomington: Indiana University Press, 1962);

"A Memoir," in *The Collected Short Prose of James Agee*, edited by Fitzgerald (Boston: Houghton Mifflin, 1968);

"The Place of Form," in *The Rarer Action*, ed. Alan Cheuse and Richard Koffler (New Brunswick, N.J.: Rutgers University Press, 1970);

"Conversations with Translators III: Robert Fitzgerald and Christopher Middleton," interview with Edwin Honig, *Modern Language Notes*, 91 (December 1976): 1572-1602;

"Light From the Bay Windows," *New Yorker*, 54 (18 December 1978): 36-40.

Translations:

Euripides, *Alcestis*, by Fitzgerald and Dudley Fitts (New York: Harcourt, Brace, 1936);

Sophocles, *Antigone*, by Fitzgerald and Fitts (New York: Harcourt, Brace, 1939);

Sophocles, *Oedipus at Colonus* (New York: Harcourt, Brace, 1941; London: Faber & Faber, 1957);

Sophocles, *Oedipus Rex*, by Fitzgerald and Fitts (New York: Harcourt, Brace, 1949; London: Faber & Faber, 1949);

Homer, *The Odyssey* (Garden City: Doubleday, 1961; London: Heinemann, 1962);

Homer, *The Iliad* (Garden City: Doubleday, 1974).

References:

Reuben Brower, "A Poet's Odyssey," in *Mirror on Mirror* (Cambridge: Harvard University Press, 1974);

Dorothy Nyren, ed., *A Library of Literary Criticism: Modern American Literature* (New York: Ungar, 1960);

George Steiner, "Two Translations," in *Language and Silence* (New York: Atheneum, 1967).

Thomas Flanagan

(5 November 1923-   )

BOOKS: *The Irish Novelists: 1800-1850* (New York & London: Columbia University Press, 1959);

The Year of the French (New York: Holt, Rinehart & Winston, 1979; London: Macmillan, 1979).

Thomas James Bonner Flanagan, a scholar of Irish literature and cultural history, recently won wide acclaim for his historical novel, *The Year of the French* (1979), concerning the Irish uprising of 1798. His other contributions to his field of study include a book, *The Irish Novelists: 1800-1850* (1959), and several articles published in scholarly journals.

Flanagan was born in Greenwich, Connecticut. After serving in the United States Army during World War II, he graduated from Amherst College with a B.A. in 1946 and received his M.A. and Ph.D. degrees in English literature from Columbia University in 1948 and 1958 respectively. He married in 1949 and has two daughters. He taught English literature at Columbia University from 1952 until 1960 and then at the University of California at Berkeley from 1960 to 1976, serving as department chairman from 1973 until 1976. He is currently teaching English at the State University of New York at Stony Brook.

Flanagan's fascination with Irish history and literature springs from a strong Irish background. Both of his grandfathers belonged to the Irish Republican Brotherhood before immigrating with their families to the United States in the nineteenth century. Flanagan describes himself as having "a real sense of place," having been "immersed in Ireland for most of my life." He visits his "second home" often and has spent his summers there for the past ten years.

Flanagan's critical work demonstrates his thorough knowledge of Irish history and literature. *The Irish Novelists: 1800-1850*, is an intensive treatment of the works and careers of five Irish novelists of the early nineteenth century: Maria Edgeworth, Lady Morgan, John Banim, Gerald Griffin, and William Carleton. Flanagan's selection of these five novelists is based on their deep involvement with the Irish scene and their ability to reflect the changing pressures of Irish life. He traces their literary sources in the chaotic fragmentation that characterizes Irish history and culture—the variety of classes, creeds, loyalties, and aspirations that are embodied in the rise and fall of the Protestant nation, the reemergence of Celtic Ireland, and the vivid transformation of Irish life during the first half of the nineteenth century. Confronted with such confusion, the Irish novelists tended to write for an English readership, emphasizing questions of race, creed, and nationality rather than social choice and personal morality, the great issues of European fiction. Positive critical reaction to *The Irish Novelists* emphasized Flanagan's compelling writing style and his skill in literary criticism. A reviewer for *Library Journal* specifically praised the book's contribution to a clearer "understanding of the milieu from which Yeats and Joyce sprang."

In an article published in the *Kenyon Review* (1966), entitled "The Big House of Ross-Drishane," Flanagan uses quotations from the fiction of Edith Somerville and Violet Martin to contrast the culture symbolized by the Irish manor house with that of Irish cabin life. He documents the slow passing of that social order, from the 1890s until about 1920, as the Irish economy changed and the landlords left.

In "Yeats, Joyce, and the Matter of Ireland," published in *Critical Inquiry* (1975), Flanagan considers the different ways in which the two authors came to understand their roles as Irish writers. Yeats led an Irish literary revival which emphasized the ancient legends of Ireland. Joyce was the chief rebel against this approach; his aesthetic principles were shaped partially by his resistance to traditional assumptions and modes of expression. Struggling to free himself from the past, he detested Yeats's involvement with primitive Ireland. Joyce felt the poet should be aloof from society; he saw nationalism and the Church as opponents to imaginative freedom, and he condemned Yeats for adapting to these pressures in attempting to found an Irish movement in literature and drama.

Thomas Flanagan

Flanagan reached a larger readership with *The Year of the French*, a novel of epic proportions. The story is built around a true episode in Irish history, the French invasion of remote County Mayo in support of local insurgents in the summer of 1798 and the ill-fated Irish rebellion against British rule which followed it. The factual account of 1798 is documented in Thomas Pakenham's *The Year of Liberty* (1969). Other sources, according to critic Denis Donoghue in the *New York Times Review of Books*, include *The Croppy* (1828) by John Banim, and *The Memoirs of Richard Lovell Edgeworth*, completed after Edgeworth's death by his daughter Maria and published in 1820. The rebellion actually began in the south, in the counties of Wexford, Carlow, and Kilkenny; the peasants, led by the gentlemen republicans in Wolfe Tone's United Irish Movement, were routed by British army regulars and bands of loyalist yeomanry. Rebellion next broke out in the north, where the insurgents were quickly put down, their disorganization a product of the distrust between Catholic and Protestant rebels. Flanagan's story begins at this point, concerning itself with the second half of the rebellion.

A brief prologue is set in the tavern of a northern coastal town at twilight, where poet and schoolmaster Owen MacCarthy is being urged by several poor farm laborers to write a threatening letter to an Irish landlord who has taken some farmland for pasture, thus robbing his tenants of their homes. The dialogue in this scene is given authenticity by Flanagan's careful approximation of the spoken and written language of the time. A dramatic change of pace to straight narrative in the following section introduces several of the book's main characters.

The story is told through the eyes of five contemporary witnesses: a minister of the Church of Ireland, a young English aide to General Cornwallis, an Irish schoolmaster, a landowner and solicitor member of the Society of United Irishmen, and the solicitor's English wife. The huge cast of characters includes representatives from all segments of the Irish population—an itinerant schoolmaster (a character based on a number of insurrectionist poets of the time) who cannot make up his mind whether or not to become involved in the conflict, a gentleman farmer who fights in the rebel army, a peasant farmer who organizes the rebellious peasantry, a member of the Society of United Irishmen who serves as an officer in the French army, and a landlord who commands the local yeomanry. Some of the characters are historical: Cornwallis, the British general; Humbert, the French general; Wolfe Tone, Dublin barrister and emissary from the Society of United Irishmen to the French Directory; Richard Lovell Edgeworth, Irish landlord and member of Parliament; and Dennis Browne, High Sheriff of Mayo. George and John Moore are part of the same family that produced the novelist George Moore; and Ellen Treacy, daughter of an Irish landlord, is based on one of Flanagan's grandmothers.

Interweaving the five personal accounts, Flanagan builds tension and intrigue from the first letter of warning sent by the agrarian "Whiteboy" terrorists to an Irish landlord, through the efforts of Wolfe Tone in Paris to get a commitment of French troops to aid in the rebellion, to the actual landing of those troops on the shores of Ireland. From there the insurrection gathers momentum as the combined French troops and Irish rebels easily defeat the British forces in several surprise attacks. Ultimately, however, the superior numbers of Cornwallis's British troops overwhelm the rebels, surrounding them in a lonely bog area in the Irish midlands. The French surrender immediately and are escorted to Dublin before being repatriated. The Irish surrender is not accepted; instead they are driven into a bog where they are bayoneted to death.

Flanagan's rich descriptive skill is evident throughout the book, especially in frequent, almost lyrical, passages about the Irish countryside: "But it was the landscape itself which I came in time to find unbearably oppressive, that very landscape which once had seemed to me endowed with a magical power and beauty. The River Moy, which formed one boundary of the estate, flowed dull and sluggish towards Killala and the sea, and the red bog which stretched westwards was desolate and sombre. The low hills, upon which cottiers crouched in their misery, were formless and mute of meaning. And above all arched the immense Irish sky, at times bright as porcelain, but often sunless and heavy, terrifying in its ability to drain all human definition from the earth and water beneath it. It was a landscape which hugged dark and unfathomable secrets before which I stood alien and unprotected."

The author's intimate knowledge of Irish terrain is also demonstrated in MacCarthy's cross-country flight as he deserts the rebel troops and in the detailed account of the climactic battle at Ballinamuck. The battles, as well as other scenes of violence, are vividly rendered, giving a clear impression of the fear and danger which pervade the atmosphere: "MacCarthy walked shivering from tavern to tavern, looking for the farmer who had promised him a ride back to Killala. Lobsterback soldiers wandered up to the barracks in threes and fours, arms wound around the necks of comrades. Boiled lobsters, red dragons of the sea, walking upright, high helmets like briny plates of shell. At the top of Castlebar High Street, in the yard formed by the joining of barracks and gaol, three bodies hung from the gibbet, tar-coated and weighted down with chains. Worst of all deaths. A lure for the flies of summer. MacCarthy crossed himself and hurried past them."

The reader not well-versed in Irish history will benefit from Flanagan's insertion of historical background at pertinent intervals. As Cornwallis and his troops move across Ireland to ambush the French, Flanagan recounts the part played by various landmarks in earlier Irish conflicts.

The Year of the French has been praised as "the finest historical novel by an American to appear in more than a decade . . . a permanent contribution to the new, demythologized history of Ireland," and "a novel of major significance" which "deserves every major literary prize." Critical response has been highly complimentary, with only a few reservations. Peter S. Prescott in *Newsweek* responded appreciatively to the sheer ambition in Flanagan's attempt to "recreate, from barroom to manor hall, the entire intellectual and emotional climate of the time," while Hubert de Santana in *MacLeans* chided Flanagan for trying to "write a sort of Hibernian *War and Peace*."

A few critics were put off by Flanagan's style, calling his narrative "ponderous," "a bore," "slow going," piling "detail upon detail until characters and events are buried under a mountain of words." Yet others were impressed by "his device of splitting his story between third-and-first-person narrations" and "weaving an account of great events from a patchwork of contemporary observations." Denis Donoghue expressed the opinion that "the uses of impersonal narrative, different points of view and style, the voice of history (spoken) through a particular character keep the reader sensitive to the proportions of ignorance and knowledge in any account of an experience. . . . there is a loss of immediacy . . . our interest is not allowed to focus on a character as distinct from his role in the story as a whole. There is a gain in depth and resonance of characters; when we meet them they have already been changed by their experience. . . . Impartiality is achieved by admitting to the narrative several different forms of partiality."

Dust jacket

Other reviewers also have noted Flanagan's impartial handling of the varied characters and their complex motivations. *Publishers Weekly* commented: "Flanagan's special gift is his intuitive understanding that in Ireland . . . nothing is black and white. Doomed romantics, well-intentioned landowners, desperate peasants, drunken poets, decent men on both sides, and the women who suffer because of what happens to the men—these are Flanagan's people." Despite their conflicting motivations, many of the Catholic and Protestant Irish were united briefly during what they called "the year of the French," and they did so, according to Flanagan, because they recognized "that they shared a common economic destiny. The conflict never has been a religious one except insofar as religion became a badge. The problem of the Irish today is still one of identity, what makes a man an Irishman as apart from English."

The Year of the French was a main selection of the Book-of-the-Month Club. It had a first printing of 50,000 copies, with rights sold in England and France, and an eight-part television series based on the book is being planned. In an interview by *Publishers Weekly*, Flanagan is described as "a quiet man who still cannot quite believe what has happened to him and who admits to the Irish superstition that when good things seem on the way you pretend otherwise so as not to tempt fate." Flanagan tells how he began writing his book: "I actually started to write the novel in a very strange way in my office in Berkeley one day, writing in longhand on blue memo paper, and keeping going almost as if in a trance. I began with what is still the first scene in the prologue, in the pub and along the coast road. I wrote the whole first draft with incredible happiness. . . . I already knew the period very well and I knew a lot of the Irish folk legends about 'the men of the West,' and their uprising contained a grain of truth. The only trouble was in deciding which was the right grain. Afterwards I made charts to make sure the dates were right, and it took me about two months to realize that I didn't have to footnote everything in the novel. Most of the research I had to do dealt with British and French military records."

Flanagan is now at work on a second novel. Tentatively titled "Unexamined Lives," it is a study of city and country life in Ireland during the Fenian days, from the 1860s to the 1890s, ending with the fall of Parnell. The characters are so totally ruled by their commitment to a cause that they never have time to examine their personal lives. Flanagan seems destined to make a major contribution to the literature about Ireland and to an understanding of the Irish literary culture. Considering the problems in Ireland today, and the resulting interest in and need for enlightenment about that unique country, future work from Flanagan should be highly welcomed.

—*Elizabeth Werth Oakman*

Periodical Publications:

"The Big House of Ross-Drishane," *Kenyon Review*, 28 (January 1966): 54-78;

"Frank O'Connor, 1903-1966," *Kenyon Review*, 28 (September 1966): 439-455;

"Rebellion and Style: John Mitchel and the Jail Journal," *Irish University Review*, 1 (Autumn 1970): 1-29;

"Yeats, Joyce, and the Matter of Ireland," *Critical Inquiry*, 2 (Autumn 1975): 43-67.

Other:

Benedict Kiely, *State of Ireland*, introduction by Flanagan (Boston: Godine, 1980).

Reference:

Interview with Thomas Flanagan, *Publishers Weekly*, 215 (14 May 1979): 114-115.

Nancy Hale

(6 May 1908-)

BOOKS: *The Young Die Good* (New York: Scribners, 1932);

Never Any More (New York: Scribners, 1934);

The Earliest Dreams (New York: Scribners, 1936; London: Dickson & Davies, 1937);

The Prodigal Women (New York: Scribners, 1942);

Between the Dark and the Daylight (New York: Scribners, 1943);

The Sign of Jonah (New York: Scribners, 1950; London: Heinemann, 1951);

The Empress's Ring (New York: Scribners, 1955);

Heaven and Hardpan Farm (New York: Scribners, 1957);

A New England Girlhood (Boston & Toronto: Little, Brown, 1958; London: Gollancz, 1958);

Dear Beast (Boston & Toronto: Little, Brown, 1959; London: Macmillan, 1960);

The Pattern of Perfection (Boston & Toronto: Little, Brown, 1960; London: Macmillan, 1961);

The Realities of Fiction (Boston & Toronto: Little, Brown, 1962; London: Macmillan, 1963);

Black Summer (Boston & Toronto: Little, Brown, 1963; London: Gollancz, 1964);

The Life in the Studio (Boston & Toronto: Little, Brown, 1969);

Secrets (New York: Coward, McCann & Geoghegan, 1971);

Mary Cassatt (Garden City: Doubleday, 1975);

The Night of the Hurricane (New York: Coward, McCann & Geoghegan, 1978).

After she was graduated from the Winsor School in Boston in 1926, Nancy Hale set out to be a painter like her parents. Her father, Philip L. Hale, had showed two paintings in the epoch-making 1913 Armory Show and was also a distinguished critic and teacher of art. Her mother, Lilian Westcott Hale, was one of the most talented portrait painters of her generation. At the Boston Museum of Fine Arts, Nancy Hale enrolled in life-drawing classes to study formally what she had been studying informally for years as the only child of two fiercely dedicated artists. There is no doubt that this early training in close observation of form, color, texture, the fall of light on objects, and subtle changes in human posture, gesture, and facial expression would enrich the nineteen books of fiction and nonfiction she was to write over the next fifty years.

When Nancy Hale was barely twenty she married Taylor Hardin, a Virginian she had met at a dance in Boston, and moved with him to New York City where she had managed to get a job at *Vogue* on the basis of some drawings she brought to the interview. "I was hired to work in the Art Department," she says, "but I never got there." Instead she spent the first few weeks huddled in a corner of the chief fashion editor's office. Then she was sent to a glassed-in cubicle to work as assistant to the editor of *Vogue*'s etiquette column, and eventually she was put to work in the bullpen writing text and snappy captions, a job that suited her fine since writing was as much in her blood as painting. Her grandfather, the writer and Unitarian clergyman Edward Everett Hale, was as famous for his essays and stories, especially *The Man Without a Country* (1863), as he was for his sermons. One of her great-aunts, Lucretia Hale, wrote *The Peterkin Papers* (1880) and another, Harriet Beecher Stowe, *Uncle Tom's Cabin* (1852).

When Nancy Hale was not quite eight years old, she asked to be given a printing press for her birthday, astonishing her mother, but not her father, who explained that most Hale children ask for printing presses at some point in their childhoods. The whole family—male and female members alike—had been involved in writing for and publishing newspapers, particularly the *Boston Daily Advertiser*, since the beginning of the nineteenth century. As soon as Nancy Hale got her printing press she began to put out a family newspaper called the *Society Cat* "at wildly irregular intervals." By the time she was eleven, she sought a wider audience by submitting a story to the *Boston Herald,* with a letter explaining that "my purpose is remuneration," thus expressing her determination even then to be considered a professional in the field.

By 1933 she had moved from *Vogue* to *Vanity Fair,* where she was assistant editor, and in her spare time had written numerous short stories, as well as a first novel, *The Young Die Good* (1932), a lively, up-to-the-minute satire of the attitudes and antics of New York's smart set. Its heroine is an appealing but absurdly naive working girl, a younger sister to the flapper, determined to seize her share of glamour, fun, and sexual freedom without a moment's thought to how long her health, or her money, or her whole society, in fact—already plunged into the Depression and threatened with the growing power of the Fascists—will last.

Today, when Nancy Hale recalls the ten years she lived and worked in New York City, holding down full-time jobs first at *Vogue* (1928-1932), then at *Vanity Fair* (1933-1934), and then at the *New York Times* (1935) as its first woman reporter, all the while writing fiction at night, she has little sympathy for writers who complain that they cannot find the time to write. "If you really are a writer, you will somehow *make* the time to write," she says, though she admits she did not get much sleep during that period. After the birth of her son, Mark Hardin, in 1930, she would come home from a full day at the office, play with the baby for a while, then get dressed and go out for the evening with her husband. "It was only after we got back from whatever party we had been to that I would set up my typewriter on a table in the living room and work on fiction until two or maybe three in the morning."

The strain was even greater one winter when she did not have a full-time job. By this time (1934-1935) Taylor Hardin was living in Virginia; she had lost her job at *Vanity Fair* and was trying to support herself and her son solely on her earnings as a free-lance writer. "You can't imagine how relieved I was to get that job at the *New York Times* and a regular paycheck. The first thing I did was rush out and buy a raincoat so I would look like the reporters in the movies."

Already Nancy Hale had received considerable recognition as a fiction writer. Almost immediately magazines like *American Mercury, Harper's Harper's Bazaar, McCall's,* and the *New Yorker* had begun to publish her sensuous, yet understated, deftly crafted stories. In 1933 she had won an O. Henry Award for "To the Invader," a short-short story which recreates the musty atmosphere of an old Virginia house and the anguish of a Northern-born bride as her husband's relatives react, with fanatical interest, to the news that she is bearing a child who will carry on their line. On a level much deeper than any North-South conflict, the girl is forced to come to terms with the fact that she can never regain her original integrity.

Three years later Scribners republished the story with fourteen others in *The Earliest Dreams* (1936), a collection which contains some of Nancy Hale's most poetic stories. With a skill that is often dazzling in its swiftness and precision, the author manages to recreate in these stories the world—both physical and psychological—that her characters inhabit. She often accomplishes this feat in a single sentence—through a striking image, a deft description of a texture, scent, or sound, or fragments of dialogue that seem fresh from life.

In 1934, Scribners had published Nancy Hale's second novel, *Never Any More,* a neatly constructed tale of three sixteen-year-old girls forced to spend several weeks together on an island in Maine because their mothers once were friends. Already the young author shows remarkable skill in rendering subtle shifts in the moods, thoughts, and feelings of the three girls, who are as fundamentally different as any girls could be. It foreshadows the skill she would display in the more complex and extended study of three very different women that forms the basis of her major novel, *The Prodigal Women* (1942).

Maxwell Perkins, the legendary editor at Scribners, was an early admirer and stalwart supporter of Nancy Hale. He met her when she first came to New York City in 1928 and ten years later confessed to their mutual friend, Elizabeth Lemmon, that he had instantly recognized in her a writer of unusual talent: "I thought she could write before she had written—like you Virginians think a colt could run when he could barely stand. So I watched her and got us to publish her when she couldn't sell. Now she has a great name in the magazines, but she hasn't sold for us. So I want to be vindicated."

When *The Prodigal Women* came out in 1942, Maxwell Perkins was vindicated with a vengeance. Overnight the book became a best-seller—possibly because it dramatized, with unflinching candor, the psychological cost of being a woman of that time, inclined to spend her spirit much too prodigally in love relationships. In this huge, ambitious, and at times unwieldy novel, Nancy Hale's gift for portraying widely differentiated characters is given full rein. The result is a fictional world as richly populated as Thackeray's *Vanity Fair* and dominated by three fascinating women who work out their destinies through their relationships with men.

The first is Leda March, an introverted Bostonian, as bitter as she is beautiful and brilliant, because she cannot forgive or forget anybody who has ever hurt her. Ultimately, Leda prevails in a narrow sense; at least, she finds a safe retreat in her rich imagination, her love for solitude, and her indestructible selfishness.

The second is Maizie Jekyll, a dependent Southern belle who is driven into madness by the shock of being transplanted from the warmth of a small town in Virginia to the coldness of Boston and by the overwhelming ego of the artist she traps into a marriage that destroys them both.

The third and finally the most triumphant character is Maizie's younger sister, Betsy, a loving, loyal extrovert who is so busy living—for a while pursuing a career in fashion which she values mainly as a base for romantic adventures and abandons gladly when she falls in love—she cannot be bothered to nurse grudges or waste time in introspection. Her marriage to a man potentially more destructive than Maizie's husband is redeemed by the durability of the kind of love that drives her; it is a mindless, sensual, Earth Mother instinct so attuned to the rhythms of the natural world that it does not even hear the shrill voice of the ego.

Through these three radically different women, Nancy Hale dramatizes three responses to the age-old problem of being a woman—of trying to establish a separate identity and if possible acquire a modicum of power, yet still fulfill that vague, transcendent, biological pull into motherhood and its ensuing complications. It is the problem the New Feminists would be analyzing endlessly some thirty years after *The Prodigal Women* came out.

The book was an immense success—more than two million copies of it had been sold by the time it was republished in paperback by Avon in 1981—and no one took more pleasure in its success than Maxwell Perkins. In 1942 he wrote the author: "from the very beginning, I believed in you and said so, and while I don't believe that sales are in themselves a proof, they are the only proof and the irrefutable proof to a lot of people to whom I have to say things—booksellers and such."

The Prodigal Women was the hardest book for Nancy Hale to write. For more than five years she worked on, and sometimes agonized over, the manuscript, which turned out to be more than 700 printed pages. By 1937 she had written two-thirds of it, but a series of interruptions in her personal life—the birth of her second son, William Wertenbaker, in 1938, the dissolution of her second marriage to writer Charles Wertenbaker, whom she had married in 1937, and a nervous breakdown at that time—delayed the finishing of the final third until 1942. As late as November 1941 Perkins was reassuring her: "You cannot worry me about your novel. I remember so well the quality of all that I saw of it, and I know that you have a rich and sensitive mind and memory. . . . I, myself, feel certain that it will end very well indeed, if you can endure the struggle."

The fact that Nancy Hale not only endured, but triumphed was a source of deep satisfaction to Perkins, who said: "I think your book is really much bigger and better than even the best reviewers realized. It tells much that never was before revealed. And the business of literature is to reveal life. Not, of course, in just the realistic sense, for it is done by the poets too, and in fact what underlies your writing is a poet." When Scribners published another collection of her stories, *Between the Dark and the Daylight* (1943), the following year, Nancy Hale dedicated the book to Maxwell Perkins. Most of the stories here, as in the earlier collection, are set in the present—some in fact already deal with situations caused by World War II, but a few are memoirs in which the author looks back to her childhood and recreates atmospheres and emotions. At the same time she looks forward, technically, to a form of autobiographical essay which she would perfect in her maturity and publish in *A New England Girlhood, The Life in the Studio,* and *Secrets.* This type of memoir is so intensely imagined, so carefully shaped, and so precisely worded that, when it is successful, it amounts to an extended prose poem.

Eudora Welty, in reviewing the twenty-one stories in *Between the Dark and the Daylight* for the *New York Times,* indicated a strong preference for the stories of childhood, which she described as "the real stories in the book, the fountains of the others." The spirit of the adult stories she found to be "tense and antagonistic—against one sex or the other, some section or other of the country, some social class or race, or even, in several of the light sketches, against some mannerism." She then added, "Miss Hale says easily and well what she wants to say, as usual, and for this reason any group of her stories has that special interest which attends good writing. Cruelty, which is in some of the stories, has interest as well as tenderness, but one feels that it does not tell as much in the end. The stories of childhood go through a door which the other stories halt before and find locked."

In an interview conducted at the height of the success of *The Prodigal Women,* just before the publication of *Between the Dark and the Daylight,* the thirty-four-year-old Nancy Hale was already musing about the new direction her talent seemed to be taking: "I feel as though I had dozens of novels still to write and all kinds of stories. The only difficulty is that I most want to write, it seems, about things that happened before I was twenty-five." Then she goes on to express a fear that she may be "just drawing on the life—the life that I really and

Nancy Hale

fully lived—before I wrote much. Well, you can't draw on that forever. One reason there are so many one-book authors is that they used up the living years in one book." As it turned out, her fear was unfounded. Nancy Hale's imagination was able to keep responding to and fashioning new (although more carefully restricted) fiction from the experiences that came to her as an adult, while it was also making rich use of her childhood.

The year 1942 was an unusually lucky one for Nancy Hale, not only because of the success of *The Prodigal Women,* but more important personally because in March of that year she married Fredson Thayer Bowers, a professor of English at the University of Virginia. In the months preceding Pearl Harbor, he had been trained secretly as a cryptographer and was soon transferred with his new family from Charlottesville to Washington to oversee a group deciphering codes in the navy department. After the war the Bowers moved back to Charlottesville, where they have remained ever since, though they go to New England every year to spend the summer on Cape Ann.

During the next three decades, Nancy Hale adapted to the relatively quiet life of a small academic community and continued to write not only novels, short stories, and what she calls "autobiographical fiction" but also a biography and a book for children. She also edited *New England Discovery* (1963), an anthology representing 300 years of New England writing.

The decade of the 1950s was probably the most productive of Nancy Hale's literary life. Her first novel of the decade, *The Sign of Jonah* (1950), provides "an encyclopedic and consistently amusing report" on "the dizzy Twenties and the dazzling Thirties," according to one reviewer. It is initially set in the South which the author had come to know as an adult, while the novel after that, *Heaven and Hardpan Farm* (1957), is set in a bucolic modern sanatorium. Its irresistibly funny yet touching episodes involve the women patients and the gentle doctor, a Jungian with an ebullient sense of humor, who takes care of them. Throughout this book, which is one of Nancy Hale's finest and most daring, she manages to maintain a tone that is full of laughter yet always compassionate, never condescending toward the fragile neurotics struggling to find those secrets in the inner world that will give them the strength to return to and survive in the outer one. Her third novel of the 1950s, *Dear Beast* (1959), is a comedy of manners based on the conflict between a clever woman writer from Vermont and her smugly Southern husband. In addition to these three novels, Nancy Hale collected twenty-four stories and semi-autobiographical memoirs in *The Empress's Ring* (1955). Though they vary widely in mood, tone, and setting, almost all of them share with the title story a narrator sifting through memories of the past for insights to illuminate the present and the future.

In an unusual announcement at the front of *The Empress's Ring,* the author tries to make a distinction between the kinds of stories she is writing: "The pieces in this collection called THE COPELY-PLAZA and THE FIRST DAY OF SCHOOL, although some of their details are fictional, are founded upon fact and are autobiographical; all other stories (including those written in the first person), although some of their details may be factual, are works of fiction."

Three years later in the introduction to her "most autobiographical work," *A New England Girlhood* (1958), she further explains "the protean uses to which I have put the past," maintaining that "after Proust and Joyce, after Freud and Jung," the modern author can no longer view the past as "something which will stay firmly behind," as her grandfather Edward Everett Hale viewed it when he wrote *A New England Boyhood* (1893). Today, Nancy Hale explains, "the boundaries [that separate past, present, and future] are down, the whole territory is seen to be one, with time only the self caught in the act of measuring itself against passing events. . . .

"My pieces . . . are intended less to be about the real and ascertainable past than about my memory of it; and memory, as a mode of thinking, tends to burst spontaneously into fantasy at every turn. Some of the events in the stories are true to fact, some not."

A whole generation of readers of the *New Yorker* came to feel that they were intimate friends of Nancy Hale's, or more accurately of Nancy Hale's imagination, since almost all of the sketches in *A New England Girlhood* and the stories in *The Empress's Ring* and *The Pattern of Perfection* (1960) appeared originally in that magazine. In fact, during one year in the 1950s, Nancy Hale had more pieces of fiction in the *New Yorker* than any other writer.

In 1958 she was awarded the Benjamin Franklin special citation for the short story; in 1969 the Henry H. Bellamann Foundation Award for literature, and in 1974 the Sarah Josepha Hale Award. From 1957 to 1965 she lectured on the short story at Bread Loaf Writer's Conference and published some of these lectures in *The Realities of Fiction* (1962). During the next year, 1963, she produced a novel, *Black Summer* (about a seven-year-old Southern boy's confrontation with the austere attitudes of New

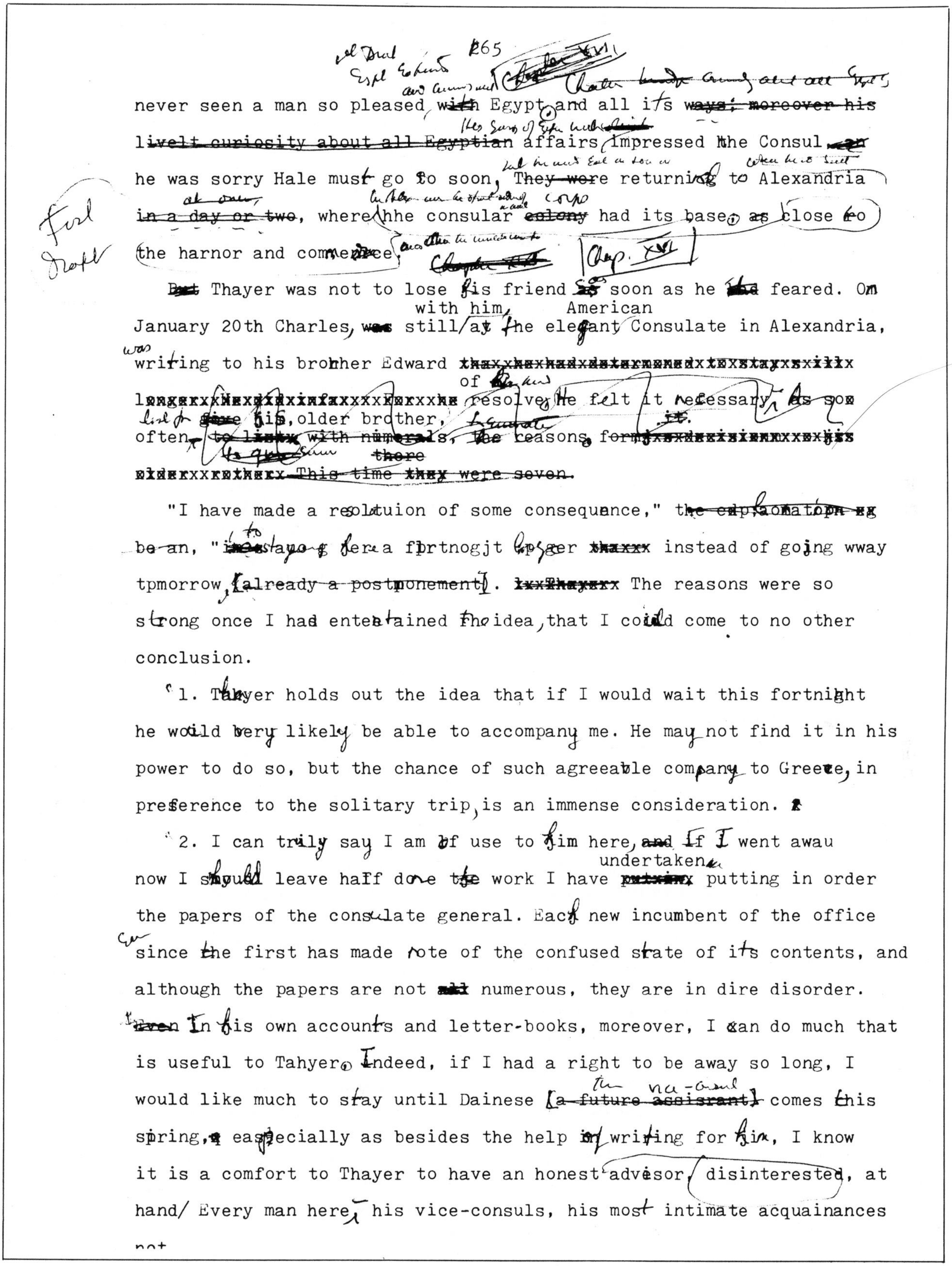

265

never seen a man so pleased with Egypt and all its ways; moreover his livelt curiosity about all Egyptian affairs impressed the Consul. He was sorry Hale must go so soon. They were returning to Alexandria in a day or two, where the consular colony had its base, as close to the harnor and commerce.

But Thayer was not to lose his friend so soon as he had feared. On January 20th Charles, with him, was still at the elegant American Consulate in Alexandria, writing to his brother Edward of resolve. He felt it necessary, as so often, to list his reasons. This time they were seven.

"I have made a resolution of some consequence," be an, "to stay here a fortnight longer instead of going away tomorrow [already a postponement]. The reasons were so strong once I had entertained the idea, that I could come to no other conclusion.

1. Thayer holds out the idea that if I would wait this fortnight he would very likely be able to accompany me. He may not find it in his power to do so, but the chance of such agreeable company to Greece, in preference to the solitary trip, is an immense consideration.

2. I can truly say I am of use to him here, and if I went away now I should leave half done the work I have undertaken putting in order the papers of the consulate general. Each new incumbent of the office since the first has made note of the confused state of its contents, and although the papers are not numerous, they are in dire disorder. In his own accounts and letter-books, moreover, I can do much that is useful to Thayer. Indeed, if I had a right to be away so long, I would like much to stay until Dainese [a future assistant] comes this spring, especially as besides the help of writing for him, I know it is a comfort to Thayer to have an honest advisor, disinterested, at hand. Every man here, his vice-consuls, his most intimate acquainances not

Working typescript for a novel in progress

England), and *New England Discovery, A Personal View*.

After the death of her mother in 1963, she began to clear out the objects in her mother's studio on Cape Ann and to write about the feelings this activity engendered. Before she knew it, Nancy Hale was engaged in a series of affectionate, but unflinchingly honest, reminiscences of the artists she grew up among—her mother, her father, and her aunt. Most of them appeared separately in the *New Yorker* before she gathered them into *The Life in the Studio* (1969). This masterful collection of familiar essays opens with a list of objects she found lying around the studio, a list which extends over three printed pages and ensnares the reader—sensually and intellectually—in the artists' world. The reader then proceeds to stroll through the past with the middle-aged author, stumbling unexpectedly upon hitherto hidden truths, "secrets" that the author did not know she knew.

A few years later, when she gathered together some semiautobiographical sketches about her childhood and adolescent adventures with the children next door, she actually called the book *Secrets* (1971). What John Coleman has written about this book would apply equally well to most of her work: "There is far more to *Secrets* than the narrative. For in her story, Miss Hale deals directly or obliquely with many matters; the difference between appearance and reality; between imagination and fact, social and racial discrimination, the individual and the group . . . [making this a book that] is both light and somber, easy and difficult, but above all . . . the work of a writer who has a special feeling for the conflict between the world within and the world without and who knows that we must learn to live with both worlds if we are to survive."

Because of her extraordinary understanding of the inner world of artists and of women, and so, particularly, of artists who are also women, Hale was commissioned by Doubleday to write a full-scale biography of the American painter Mary Cassatt. The resulting book, *Mary Cassatt*, was an immense undertaking in a genre new to her which consumed four years in research and writing before the book was published in 1975.

Immediately afterward, she went to work in another new genre, writing a children's book, *The Night of the Hurricane* (1978). Again she found the task "surprisingly difficult," this time because her audience was so demanding. "Children don't give a hair for effect," she explains. "They only demand that a story be absolutely true emotionally." For the past four years, Nancy Hale has been busy working in yet another genre, a blend of fact and fantasy which she calls "a novel in history," based loosely on the life and letters of her great-uncle, Charles Hale, a newspaper editor who served as U.S. Consul General to Egypt in the 1860s.

As one looks back over Nancy Hale's long and varied career as a writer, it is difficult to determine exactly where she has made her greatest contribution. It may be in her penetrating portraits of women who may seem calm, and even satisfied, but beneath the surface are struggling to retain their self-esteem and individuality; or it may be in her extension of the autobiographical essay into realms of fantasy and psychological analysis possible only in a post-Jungian age; but probably it is in her mastery of the short-short story, which, at its best, is brilliant.

In Charlottesville, Virginia, the local newspaper dedicated its 1980 arts supplement to Nancy Hale, enumerating the many contributions she has made to that community: among them serving as a visiting Phi Beta Kappa scholar and as a moving force in the creation of the Virginia Center for the Creative Arts. She was also the first woman ever invited to give the graduation address at the University of Virginia. The fact that a so-called Yankee (Hale has written one of her most trenchant essays on the Southerner's misuse of this specific term and often says, "I only wish I were one") could earn such an outpouring of affection from a Southern community is a tribute to the fact that she is an expert at reconciling differences in her life, as well as in her art. The contrasts among the manners and the values of the Bostonians she grew up with, the New Yorkers she spent her young adulthood with, and the Virginians she has settled down to live with is a source of continuous amusement to Nancy Hale.

As a satirist, she is more akin to Jane Austen than to Jonathan Swift, for instance, or even to Mary McCarthy, her contemporary, because she accepts the people, even the most foolish ones, she writes about and also because she deliberately narrows her focus to individuals (from roughly the same ethnic, economic, and educational background) in conflict with each other and with themselves. In order to maintain the sharpness of this focus she has had to exclude the more generalized sociopolitical concerns (including feminism) with which so many of the writers of her time have been concerned. Nancy Hale was trained from childhood by her painter parents to "look hard" and directly at specific objects, individuals, and scenes. As a result, she has become an extraordinarily keen observer of the minute differences in gesture, manners, speech patterns, and attitudes that individuals in specific social situations display. Through her art she is able to share her delight in all these differences, capturing them first in dialogue or deft description, then illuminating them with that carefully controlled irony that has earned her the title of "classicist" in the portrayal of contemporary manners.

—*Anne Hobson Freeman*

Plays:

The Best of Everything, Charlottesville, Virginia Players, Minor Hall Theater, University of Virginia, 7 May 1952;

Somewhere She Dances, Charlottesville, Virginia Players, Minor Hall Theater, University of Virginia, 13 May 1953.

Other:

New England Discovery: A Personal View, edited with introduction and commentary by Nancy Hale (New York: Coward-McCann, 1963);

Joe McCarthy, ed., *New England,* introduction by Nancy Hale (New York: Time-Life Library of America, 1967);

"Who Needs No Introduction," in *A Book for Boston,* ed. Llewellyn Howland and Isabelle Storey (Boston: Godine, 1980), pp. 39-44.

Periodical Publications:

FICTION:

"Sunday Lunch," *New Yorker,* 41 (8 May 1965): 44-49;

"The Most Elegant Dining Room in Europe," *New Yorker,* 42 (17 September 1966): 55-64;

"The Interior," *Virginia Quarterly Review,* 56 (Spring 1980): 234-243.

NONFICTION:

"Child Training at Harvard," *New Yorker,* 33 (15 February 1958): 28-30;

"Poor Man's War Between the States," *New Yorker,* 37 (25 March 1961): 34-37;

"A Gift from the Shops," *New Yorker,* 37 (11 November 1961): 48-51;

"A Ceremony of Innocence," *Virginia Quarterly Review,* 52 (Summer 1976): 389-399;

"The Real Thing," *Virginia Quarterly Review,* 59 (Spring 1979): 275-283.

References:

Ruthe Battestin, "Dedication, Nancy Hale," in *Our Community & the Arts, Charlottesville Daily Progress,* 23 September 1980, pp. 6-7;

A. Scott Berg, *Max Perkins, Editor of Genius* (New York: Dutton), pp. 206, 402-403, 413;

John C. Coleman, Unsigned review of *Secrets, Virginia Quarterly Review,* 47 (Summer 1970): xcvii;

Robert van Gelder, "Nancy Hale . . . An Analyzer of the Feminine," in his *Writers and Writing* (New York: Scribners, 1946), pp. 330-333;

Doug Kamholz, "Writing Careers for Charlottesville Couple are a Natural," *Charlottesville Daily Progress,* 18 November 1979, pp. E1, E8;

The Letters of Maxwell Perkins, ed. John Hall Wheelock (New York: Scribners, 1979), pp. 126-127, 191, 209-210;

Eudora Welty, "Women and Children," review of *Between the Dark and the Daylight, New York Times Book Review,* 2 May 1943, p. 8;

Ned Wilcox, "Hale and Bowers: A Marriage of Two Minds," *University of Virginia Cavalier Daily,* 18 November 1979, p. 3.

Papers:

The largest collection of Nancy Hale's papers is in the Smith College Library.

Diane Johnson

(28 April 1934-)

BOOKS: *Fair Game* (New York: Harcourt, Brace & World, 1965);

Loving Hands at Home (New York: Harcourt, Brace & World, 1968; London: Heinemann, 1969);

Burning (New York: Harcourt, Brace, Jovanovich, 1971);

Lesser Lives (New York: Knopf, 1972; London: Heinemann, 1973);

The Shadow Knows (New York: Knopf, 1974; London: Bodley Head, 1975);

Lying Low (New York: Knopf, 1978).

Although women are focal characters in her five novels and one biographical book published to date, Diane Johnson is not a narrowly feminist writer. True, her protagonists do contend with often nightmarish versions of the conventional enemies of women's liberation—manipulative or ineffectual husbands and lovers, suffocatingly demanding families and friends, and such unyielding institutional bureaucracies as welfare agencies, police and immigration departments, and the legal system. Yet woman's struggles against repressive social forces are, in these works, clearly secondary to her conflicts within herself. The typical Johnsonian protagonist is intelligent, sensitive, restless, and confused about her own desires and purposes. Her uncertainties about how to manage either the complex self or the complex outer world provide the substance of her story. What emerges, then, in Johnson's fiction and biography are not stock feminist heroines but instead fully developed characters whose perplexed, often funny, and always compelling quests for understanding testify to their creator's wisdom and artistry as a writer.

The daughter of Dolph and Frances Elder Lain, Diane Johnson was born in Moline, Illinois. She attended Stephens College in Columbia, Missouri, from 1951 to 1953, and in July 1953 married B. Lamar Johnson, Jr., with whom she had four children: Kevin, Darcy, Amanda, and Simon. She earned her B.A. (1957) from the University of Utah and her M.A. (1966) and Ph.D. (1968) from the University of California at Los Angeles. In May 1968 she married John Frederic Murray, a professor of medicine at Berkeley. Johnson has, since 1968, taught fiction writing and nineteenth-century British literature at the University of California at Davis. Among her awards are a grant from the Woodrow Wilson Foundation in 1965, an American Association of University Women grant in 1968, a National Book Award nomination for *Lesser Lives* (1972) in 1973, a Guggenheim Fellowship in 1977-1978, and a Rosenthal Foundation Award for *Lying Low* (1978) in 1979. In addition to her six books, Johnson has written critical essays for such publications as the *New York Review of Books* and the *New York Times Book Review*, has collaborated with Stanley Kubrick on the filmscript for *The Shining* (1980), and is working on a biography of Dashiell Hammett.

Johnson's first novel, *Fair Game* (1965), shares with its immediate successors a comic tone, a California setting, and a central female character who is uncertain about how to conduct her life. Dabney Wilhelm initially believes that she can successfully balance her roles as prospective wife-mother-homemaker, as owner and clothing designer for a children's boutique, and as writer of charming allegories similar to her already moderately successful *Mister Wister's Clocks*. Yet she soon finds herself involved in a kind of love pentagon which makes her and her plans "fair game" for four different men: her wealthy fiance Charles Earse, a handsome young Dynamic Space Corporation executive who wishes Dabney to dedicate herself exclusively to marriage and family; the middle-aged, half-Japanese Emerson Kado, author of *Excrescence* and other banned classics, who no longer writes but who sees in Dabney a source of inspiration and a perfect protegee; Parker Peterson, a failed poet and academic and dissatisfied Dynamic Space engineer, who wants Dabney to provide him with a real purpose in life; and Marcus Stein, a psychiatrist who preaches sexual freedom through short-term vital relationships and who views commitment to himself as the only road to Dabney's liberation. Each of these men correctly perceives the impossible nature of Dabney's complicated balancing act, yet each also errs in trying to mold her to fulfill his own individual needs. Thus, in regarding her as fair game for their self-centered desires, the four men themselves become fair game, both for the heroine and for her creator.

Because she is conveyed primarily through the male figures' speculations about her, Dabney is not so fully nor so intimately drawn as Johnson's later protagonists. However, her essential problem clearly foreshadows theirs. Confused about who she is and what she wants to become, Dabney describes herself the mop and thinks that maybe he'll be out in time to get a couple of weeks of duck hunting in. When he has finished sweeping and mopping the floor some of the boys come in and throw cigarettes ~~xxxxx~~ butts down on ~~him, drop their butts~~ and laugh, and Hammett curses them and ~~fusses~~ again with the broom. This is a ritual, the litter and the curses. The boys like Hammett and he likes them. Hillbillies, mostly from West Virginia and Tennessee.

~~Fxxxxxxxxx~~ The ~~hillbillies~~ kind of like prison; some of them say they never had it so good, better than home, the food was better and there was enough of it, and in prison they teach you to read and write if you can't. There was a committee, Hammett and Fred Field served on it, to help teach the new ~~ones~~ how to use the toilets and the showers. It shocked Fred Field to think that there were American men who didn't know how to use indoor toilets; this even shocked Hammett , and he had seen everything. ~~It did something to justify one's radical politics.~~

Hammett didn't do any preaching in the prison, not to men who half of them didn't even know what they were in there for, crossing the state line with a twelve-year old and it was just cousin Sally, or a little corn liquior, hell. Hammett spoke plainly ~~to them~~ - it made Fred nervous sometimes, when Hammett would say "what do you murderers know," ~~or something like that, you never knew when~~ he'd say it to someone unbalanced: after all this was a prison, and things happen. ~~Sometimes~~ Hammett ~~would~~ try a little consciousness-raising, ~~but~~ it never got very far. "It's not that I'm prejudiced," ~~axxxxxxxxxz~~ ~~xxxxxxxxxx~~ the kid from South Carolina put it, "because I've got no reason to dislike niggers, but I just hate 'em."

There were no black ~~pxxxxx~~s in this prison, and Dr. Alphaeus Hunton, who had been sentenced along with Hammett & Field,

Biography of Dashiell Hammett, *revised typescript for a work in progress* as "crawling after mirages" and "susceptible," both to others' manipulations and to her own contradictory desires. She thus variously welcomes and resists the safe marriage to the conventional Charles, is alternately attracted to and repelled by the exotic Mr. Kado, and simultaneously entices and rebuffs the romantic adventurers Parker and Marcus. Near the end of the novel, with her suitors brought together in a bizarre party scene, Dabney seems to recognize the nature of her problem as she declares, "None of you loves me. You just want me to *be* something to you. Well, I haven't been sure what I *am*, so I suppose I have no right to complain." Yet her apparent realization that she, not others, must take charge of her destiny is forced by events over which she has no real control, and both the language and the vehicle for her final defiant gesture—toward "wholeness, a sense of what is real, and the courage to act"—are provided by a fifth man, a poet/critic described by Dabney as "the Lennie Bernstein of letters." Thus it appears that the young woman, still confused about her own identity and still uncertain about what she should do, seeks at least temporary refuge in the arms of yet another potentially manipulative man.

Fair Game is polished, sophisticated social comedy. The male characters are thoroughly developed, and although they often become satiric targets as they attempt to work their wills on the heroine, they are also rather sympathetically treated. Yet it is Dabney, precariously searching for a vision of herself and her role in the world, who finally commands the reader's attention, if only as an early, still somewhat fragmentary embodiment of the Johnsonian woman to come in the later fiction.

That woman is perhaps most appealingly rendered in Karen Fry, the protagonist/narrator of *Loving Hands at Home* (1968). At the center of the novel lies the question posed to Karen by free-spirited art patroness Paris Pratt: "Whether or not it is possible to be happy in this world." The question is a difficult one for the protagonist to answer affirmatively, bound as she is by the double chains of a tyrannical domestic code and a vulnerable psyche. Karen has married into a Mormon family which adheres to the principle that men and women have differing, clearly defined roles to play. Father Fry and two of his sons—Mahonri and Garth, Karen's husband—are successful professional men who expect their worlds at home to be orderly, comfortable, and essentially undemanding. Mother Fry and two of her daughters-in-law invest domestic accomplishments with "a mystical significance

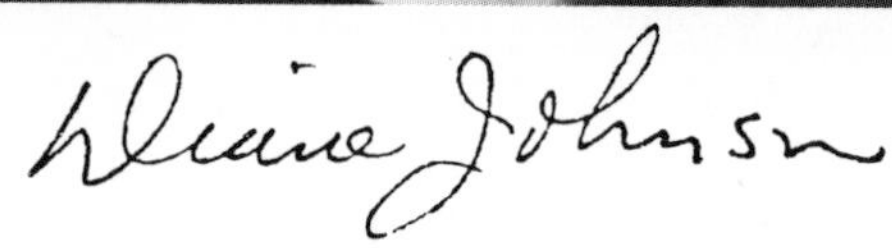

related to femininity and the life force." Only Karen and the third Fry son, Sebastian, seem uncomfortable operating within these sexual stereotypes, Sebastian because his job as Paris Pratt's secretary/art curator is regarded by his family as not quite respectable and Karen because she is inept at the tasks required by her prescribed role. Her messy house, her fallen cakes, her rumpled husband and children, and her non-Mormonism turn her into a pariah to be freshly humiliated at each Sunday family dinner.

Karen is beset not only by the stultifying Fry domestic code but also by more difficult and interesting personal problems. Filled with vague longings for a life which is "courageous, eager, and enjoying," Karen is so confused about who she is and what she wants that she initially cannot define, much less pursue, the elements of that better life. Instead, in the early parts of her narrative, she merely buries herself in her secret life of searching out unusual jobs which she knows she will never take and in spinning romantic fantasies about her childhood friend Alma, another outcast. Furthermore, when Paris Pratt devises a stratagem that throws Karen into direct confrontation with the Frys and with her own confusions, she reflexively takes flight with her two children. But because she has no clear vision of herself, she is unprepared to cope with the harsh, perverse, terrifying outside world, in which not even her fantasy of Alma is allowed to survive, and she returns home.

During a final hilariously devastating family dinner, the protagonist fully perceives the depth of her own and others' sufferings. Both delighted and appalled by the shocking revelations of her in-laws, Karen literally and, on this occasion, resolutely drops out of the family a second time. In the novel's final scene she concedes that life in the outside world is as lonesome, terrifying, boring, and arduous as she had found it to be on her first flight; moreover, she confesses that she is still uncertain about who she is or what she will ultimately do. Yet she declares, "I am not running, nor am I waiting. I am reorganizing. The good weather will not last much longer." Karen Fry thus emerges as one of the truly successful Johnsonian women. Although she realizes that she can never fully untangle the mysteries of either the complex world or the complex self, she courageously continues her quest for understanding and purpose.

Loving Hands at Home is wonderful domestic comedy. Though the members of the Fry family, particularly the males and Mother Fry, are somewhat broadly drawn, they do remain recognizable human beings. Furthermore, the family dinner scenes capture all the dangerous ambiguities of that often sentimentalized American institution. The real triumph of the novel, however, is Karen, stumblingly but bravely moving toward self-knowledge and self-reliance.

Johnson's third novel, *Burning* (1971), focuses on a single day in the lives of a conventionally liberal couple, Barney and Bingo Edwards, who are thrust by the removal of their hedge into the bizarre world of their next-door neighbors: psychiatrist Hal Harris, his wife Irene, and several of the doctor's patients. Harris, through his drug-and-sex therapy and his near catatonic behavior, has become an irritant to his beautiful, shallow wife and a kind of cult leader to his patients, particularly Max Gartman, an addicted counterculture welfare mother, and Noel Fish, a pathetic junkie. Harris and his circle manage to entangle the well-intentioned Edwardses in a web of disastrous events, and both Edwardses are plunged into encounters with other demented institutional representatives—the handsome, libidinous fireman Geoffrey Nichols; ludicrously persistent drug agents; and constantly predatory policemen. Barney and Bingo's long day culminates, almost mercifully, in the holocaust of the Bel Air fire.

Burning is on one level a biting satire of Southern California commitments, life-styles, and institutions. On another level, however, the novel functions as an incisive analysis of a marriage in trouble. Although they treat one another with unabated compassion and understanding, both Barney and Bingo have begun to feel bored with their relationship. As he makes love to her, Barney wishes that his wife were more beautiful, more stupid, and more passive—a direct attack on Bingo's self-definition as a plain but intelligent and assertive woman. As she endures the traumas of her day, Bingo wishes that Barney were more handsome, more virile, and more aggressive. Even more important, the protagonists view themselves as pathetic. During one of his encounters with Max and her friend, Barney remarks, "In many ways I am a failure as a man." During her errand of mercy for Max, Bingo, who has already decided that her messy house symbolizes her messy mind and life, tends to believe the welfare department's assessment of her as cold, inadequate, hateful, fearful, and isolated. Yet the Edwardses manage to conceal their tortured feelings about themselves until they unexpectedly participate in a weird, late-night, fire-threatened group therapy session at the Harrises' home. Shattered both by their revelations and by the fire, Barney and Bingo come to a reconciliation, but it is fraught with the ambiguities of their shared final words, "Terrible, terrible. What will we do?"

A brilliant satire, *Burning* also succeeds in terms of its character development. Since he shares with Bingo those qualities of intelligence, sensitivity, and self-questioning that the novelist sometimes tends to reserve for her female protagonists, Barney emerges as one of Johnson's best male figures. However, the Edwardses are not as appealing as many of the writer's other characters, possibly because they are so coolly scrutinized and because their personal problems appear so insurmountable. Yet two such confused, vulnerable, and terrified beings seem to deserve more compassion from their creator.

Lesser Lives is a biographical account of Mary Ellen Peacock Nicolls Meredith, daughter of Thomas Love Peacock and first wife of George Meredith. Mary Ellen left Meredith after seven years of marriage and then began an affair with the painter Henry Wallis, by whom she bore a son. In *Lesser Lives*, Johnson contends that Mary Ellen was, in fact, a courageous rebel against repressive Victorian conceptions of ideal womanhood. The author views her protagonist as the spiritual daughter of such educated, independent, sexually liberated women of the eighteenth and early nineteenth centuries as Mary Wollstonecraft and Mary Shelley. Johnson also believes that both Mary Ellen's actual life and Meredith's fictionalized portrait of her in *Modern Love* and in his novels make her a prototype for twentieth-century women and their concerns.

Johnson draws her most interesting interpretations of her subject from the works of Peacock and Meredith and from Mary Ellen's own *Extracts*, a revealing collection of pieces that she copied from various authors. Johnson argues that literary works can be used to illuminate the lives of their writers since those writers' most intense relationships influence the works' subject matter and themes; she concedes, however, that drawing historical lives from fictional sources "can be more easily justified on artistic grounds than as sound biographical methodology." Yet, Johnson maintains, the responsible biographer or critic when analyzing an author's fiction "must perform an empathetic (fictional) act," especially if earlier biographers have recorded "factual error" or have employed "a really unreliable sensibility" in analyzing the life in question. The earliest accounts of the Merediths, Johnson believes, erred in both ways, accepting as facts the myths that Mary Ellen abandoned her son to flee with Wallis, that Wallis in turn abandoned her following their elopement, that Peacock refused to see either Mary Ellen or her illegitimate baby after her return to England, and that she died alone and intensely unhappy because of her unconventional actions. These myths, the biographer contends, merely conform to Victorian conceptions of what *should* happen to an adultress. They result, too, she declares, from the fact that a "lesser life" had seriously embarrassed "a major life or two."

By analyzing works of the two important writers involved in Mary Ellen's life and by calling upon her own knowledge of the Victorian period, Johnson counterbalances the errors of previous biographers through her inclusion of materials that she believes to be consistent with psychological and historical probabilities. If this methodology does not produce conventional biography, it does generate interesting, seemingly valid portraits of the major literary figures Peacock and Meredith, of the lesser-known but compelling central character Mary Ellen, and of such other "lesser" but fascinating subjects as Mary Ellen's daughter, Edith Nicolls, who wrote an early biography of Peacock, compiled several popular cookbooks, founded a cooking school, and was ultimately named a Member of the British Empire.

The greatest fault of *Lesser Lives* is an occasional archness in style which seems inappropriately reductive both to the story and to its characters. Of the legacy of Mary Ellen's long-suffering adopted sister May, for example, the biographer comments, "It is certain that . . . the Upsdill boys thought it swell of Aunt May, who had been so lucky in the world, to do so well by them," and of Mary Ellen's lover, Johnson writes, "We shall pause here to introduce Henry. He is about to let himself in for a whole lot of trouble." Yet these stylistic liberties do not fatally mar the portrayals of an authentic Victorian rebel and her world.

Johnson's fifth book, *The Shadow Knows* (1974), focuses on one week in the life of a young divorcee who resides in a North Sacramento housing project with her four small children and her black housekeeper Ev and who believes herself the target of numerous terrifying assaults, among them threatening phone calls, a mutilated and defiled front door, a vomit-splattered windshield and slashed tires, a strangled cat, and a ghastly Vietnam atrocity picture. Determined to ferret out her potential murderer, the protagonist/narrator finds herself surrounded by suspects—her bitter former husband Gavin Hexam, her married lover Andrew Mason, her insane former maid Osella, her friend and confidante Bess, a contingent of black men connected to either Ev or Osella, a skeptical police investigator whom the protagonist envisions as the Famous Inspector, and, perhaps most horrifying, a nameless stranger, the embodiment of pointless impersonal mayhem. Through its handling of plot and its presentation of a multitude of troubled, potentially dangerous characters, *The Shadow Knows* operates on one level as a fine thriller.

On another level the novel functions as an extraordinary examination of the complexities in a woman who abandons her "safe" life to pursue one that is "reckless and riddled with mistakes." As a rebel against traditional middle-class assumptions and values, the narrator/protagonist surprisingly reveals none of her personal history preceding her marriage to Gavin, not even her proper name; she is simply N. Hexam whose essential identity can be forged only through confrontations with her complicated self and with the mysterious outside world. In her attempts to create a fresh, true identity unconfined by the usual social and familial influences, N. must penetrate the evils which lurk in the hearts of men, even in her own heart, in order to find her "way in the dark." Thus, she has not only to uncover her potential murderer but also to deal with her own considerable problems and confusions—her partial responsibility for the failure of her marriage, her possible role in precipitating Osella's madness, her motivations in her affair with Andrew, her uncertainties about her relationship with Bess, her ambivalent attitude toward the abortion she is trying to induce, her rationale in pursuing a graduate degree in linguistics when easier and more practical professions are available to her. Because the pressures upon her are so great, the possibility arises that N.'s terrors are powerful projections of her own sense of guilt and confusion rather than appropriate responses to the malevolent acts of an outside aggressor.

Whatever the case, *The Shadow Knows* is perhaps the best of Johnson's novels, both in terms of its action and theme and in terms of its portrayal of a very complex and compelling heroine. At a key moment in her narrative, N. encounters a grotesquely beautiful vision of the "superfemale," a vision which causes her to muse, "Potentiality is what that strange sight must represent, . . . human potentiality, and this is rather inspiring as well as terrifying. Terrifying as well as inspiring . . . " In this statement, the protagonist seems to define both the nature of her own character and the central theme of her narrative—that in struggling toward some realization of human potentiality, the individual must relentlessly probe the ambiguities, terrifying and inspiring, within herself and within the world surrounding her. From this requirement there can be no escape, yet the fulfillment of this requirement guarantees no final and certain answers. Because they so perfectly embody this vision of the human experience and of the modern world, N. and her story emerge as the most subtle and interesting of the novelist's creations.

Set in a Sacramento Valley university town, *Lying Low*, the most recent of Johnson's books, concerns three women in crises. Sixty-year-old Theodora Wait, who, with her photographer brother Anton, owns the rambling house in which much of the novel's action occurs, is engaged in a painful retrospective on her own character and career. The Waits' two female boarders are faced by even more pressing problems. Ouida Sensa, a young Brazilian immigrant, fears that she may be unjustly deported, and Marybeth Howe, a 1960s student radical hiding under an assumed name, constantly expects to be betrayed to the police. During the four days covered by the novel, these women are compelled by outside forces to scrutinize closely the principles by which they have lived and to make decisions and take actions that threaten their very existences. The book's title perhaps suggests the basic ambiguity in these women's situations: they can no longer afford the luxury or endure the pain of "lying low," but in forging new commitments, in engaging themselves with the other lives and dangerous events confronting them, they risk being "laid low" permanently.

Johnson allows her omniscient narrator to slip in and out of the minds of the women so that each character reveals her own principles and uncertainties while also commenting, reliably or not, upon those of the other residents. Theo, for example, who has during her sixty years dedicated herself to ballet, is often "ashamed of having cared about art and order, of not having wanted a messy life." She consequently admires Marybeth's commitment to radical political beliefs, beliefs which, ironically, the exhausted underground fugitive can herself scarcely remember. Moreover, neither Marybeth nor Theo can fully comprehend the difficulties of Ouida's life, caught as she is between Portuguese and English, between her disparate visions of the United States as promised land and as possible agent of her destruction, and between her mystical religious conceptions of order and her everyday perceptions of disorder. These figures in crises afford Johnson yet another opportunity to define and evaluate the terrifying and inspiring potentialities in modern women.

Because it focuses upon three very diverse central characters, *Lying Low* has a broader scope than Johnson's earlier fiction. Yet once again the work's primary power lies in the rich portraits of each woman struggling toward some sort of understanding of herself and her world. If the novel has a weakness, it is in the conclusion which covertly suggests that societal injustices, not individual confusions and ambiguities, are primarily responsible for the heroines' difficulties and ultimate fates. Such a conclusion seems to undercut the central focus and thrust of the work. Yet the remarkably complex and varied female characters who populate *Lying Low* make it Johnson's most ambitious novel to date.

The fiction and biography of Diane Johnson have received little sustained critical attention. Individual books have been reviewed in various periodicals, but no evaluation of the works as a whole has appeared since Marjorie Ryan's 1974 essay on *Fair Game, Loving Hands at Home,* and *Burning*. Reviewers unanimously praise the writer's polished, graceful prose style. Many critics, however, have tended to overemphasize the comic or satiric elements in Johnson's work, currents that dominate the first three books but which are less pronounced in the final three. At least one commentator has, in addition, accused the author of indulging in a mild anti-male prejudice. Furthermore, some reviewers have commented unfavorably upon the highly ambiguous conclusions of Johnson's novels, though the lack of a clear resolution in her fiction is consistent with the characters and their problems. Indeed, the writer's central theme, treated with ever-increasing seriousness in her work, is the difficulty of perceiving and acting upon one's own complicated nature. Heroines who embody the ambiguities of the human character are the hallmarks of Diane Johnson's art.

—Judith S. Baughman

Screenplay:

The Shining, by Johnson and Stanley Kubrick, Hawk Production Company, 1980.

Reference:

Marjorie Ryan, "The Novels of Diane Johnson," *Critique*, 16 (1974): 53-63.

Stephen King
(12 September 1947-)

BOOKS: *Carrie* (Garden City: Doubleday, 1974; London: New English Library, 1974);
'Salem's Lot (Garden City: Doubleday, 1975; London: New English Library, 1976);
The Shining (Garden City: Doubleday, 1977; London: New English Library, 1978);
Night Shift (Garden City: Doubleday, 1977; London: New English Library, 1978);
The Stand (Garden City: Doubleday, 1978);
The Dead Zone (New York: Viking, 1979; London: Macdonald & Jane's, 1979);
Firestarter (New York: Viking, 1980);
Danse Macabre (New York: Everest, 1981).

Each night when Stephen King gets into bed, he makes certain his legs are under the blankets before the lights go out. "The thing under my bed waiting to grab my ankle isn't real," he acknowledges. "I know that, and I also know that if I'm careful to keep my foot under the covers, it will never be able to grab my ankle."

King was born in Portland, Maine. He began writing during his undergraduate years at the University of Maine at Orono (where he obtained a Teaching Certificate and a B.A. in English), and sold his first pieces for thirty-five dollars each to *Startling Mystery Stories*. Even then he had the power to terrify: a story he published in the student literary magazine continues to horrify a classmate who remembers it. Judging from the popularity of his books—some 22 million copies of his books were in print by the end of 1980—King's readership must enjoy the terrifying and the gruesome, even though some seem almost embarrassed to admit it: "People who write me often begin by saying, 'I suppose you will think I'm strange, but I really liked 'Salem's Lot.' "

In a way, King is less concerned with the events of his fiction than with the fear these events produce in his characters. For him, all fear moves us toward the comprehension of death, and he sees a parallel between fear and sexual desire: "As we become capable of having sexual relationships, our interest in those relationships awakens. . . . As we become aware of our own unavoidable termination, we become aware of the fear-emotion." King's growth as a writer can in part be measured by his progress as he develops a rhetoric of fear.

Physical descriptions of fear occur frequently in King's novels, and it seems that he intends to catalogue all possible responses to it. Some people scream; some perspire; others wet or soil themselves. Still others experience a mouth-wetting, metallic taste. These descriptions, which have increased in number and quality as King has gained control of his craft, force the reader more deeply into the world of the novel. It is difficult not to taste the cool tanginess of an old penny on the tongue after reading a passage such as the following: "But still: the fear.

"It rose suddenly, emotion overspilling logic and the bright Formica reason of the cerebrum, filling her mouth with a taste like black copper."

Fear, as King is fond of pointing out, originates in a part of the brain that developed earlier in man's evolution than the part of the brain responsible for thought. When activated, this ancient part of the brain stem, "so similar in physical construction to the brain of the alligator," interferes with the activity of the cerebrum and rapidly makes rational thought impossible. "Fear is blind," King writes, and "makes a stealthy ruin of the thinking process."

Although his novels and stories vary widely in subject and even technique, a common pattern underlies many of them. King reads avidly, both fiction and nonfiction, and often the germ of a work can be traced to a scientifically plausible idea that King then manipulates to reveal its possible logical and emotional consequences. The idea may be as simple as a "what if." The novel *The Stand*, for example, poses the question: what if one of the already-extant germ warfare research facilities accidentally released a potent and contagious virus? Or, as in *Firestarter*, it may be as complex as wondering whether two adults who acquired parapsychic powers through a government drug experiment would pass these powers on to their offspring. Whatever the source, however, King feels that his first task as a writer is to be a storyteller. "For me the idea of writing always came after the idea of creating an event. Love of the word wasn't first. It was second."

Before becoming a full-time writer, King taught high-school English and worked summers in an industrial laundromat. He married Tabitha Spruce in 1971. In 1973, they lived in a trailer, where King wrote in a tiny boiler room on a child's desk he propped on his knees. Times were hard: "We didn't have enough money for gas most of the time. We'd had the phone removed." A first novel had not sold. Then Doubleday bought the rights to *Carrie*, a novel he wrote after wondering what kind of children would be produced by a strange woman he had seen while working at the laundromat. The advance was $2,500. The paperback rights were sold for $400,000, and King was on his way to becoming one of the most widely read novelists writing today.

For a first novel, *Carrie* (1974) reveals some surprising strengths. The portrait of Carrie White, a young woman with telekinetic powers, is deftly done, and her relationship with her demented, fundamentalist mother is convincingly brought to life in King's prose. King carefully avoids sentimentalizing Carrie, who is the pariah of her high school. Although his descriptions of the town and the events leading up to Carrie's revenge on Prom Night are good, the reader may be confused by his device of presenting pieces of the story in the form of a report prepared by a commission investigating the Prom Night events some time in the future. A similar technique used to add depth to other characters (most notably Sue Snell, whose boyfriend Tommy Ross asks Carrie to the prom and precipitates the story's apocalyptic end) is less confusing, but appears rather mechanical. At relevant points in the text King introduces passages from a book titled *My Name Is Susan Snell*, written sometime in the unspecified future of the novel.

In spite of their strengths, however, the characters and setting of *Carrie* seem on the whole to exist more as conveniences for telling the story than as interests in their own right. Dialogue often sounds stiff, and some insights in the novel are beyond the capacity of the eighteen-year-olds to whom they are attributed. Even Carrie at times diminishes in depth and importance, becoming a mere vehicle for her telekinetic powers and thus a less sympathetic character. As a result, the reader may take a perverse satisfaction in watching her classmates taunt her with cries of "PER-iod" and "Plug it *up*" when her menses begin while she is showering after gym class one day. The teasing only exacerbates the fact that

Carrie does not know what is happening to her.

King wrote his second novel, *'Salem's Lot* (1975), while teaching high-school English in Herman, Maine. The idea for the book occurred when he was reading Bram Stoker's *Dracula* with his class and his wife asked if he could imagine Count Dracula living in Herman. King could, and the result was this novel about a local boy, Ben Mears, who grows up in "the Lot," moves away and becomes a successful writer, then returns to write a novel about the town. Although the book is long and often confusing, the difficulty with perspective and time reference which plagued *Carrie* is resolved here by having Ben Mears as a focus for the story. The novel begins with Mears and a small boy who is not his son living in Los Zapatos, Mexico. Each day Mears scans the newspapers for any story about 'Salem's Lot, and the boy visits the town priest frequently. Something terrible—it is not clear exactly what—happened to Mears and the boy (who, we later learn, is Mark Petrie) in 'Salem's Lot, and they fled to Mexico. This first section ends when Ben and Mark decide to return to the town.

The novel then jumps backward in time to Ben's first visit to the town after becoming successful as a writer. He is drawn to the Lot by childhood memories of a particular house, the sort many small towns have, rumored to be haunted because of strange happenings that have taken place in it. As a boy, Mears had a vivid experience in the Marsten house that remains locked in his memory and that, since the death of his wife Miranda in a motorcycle accident two years before, has returned to trouble his dreams. As the initiation into a club he wanted very badly to join, he was dared to enter the Marsten house and take something. Inside, he mounted the dusty stairs to the attic room where Hubie Marsten, the last inhabitant, reputedly had hanged himself after murdering his wife. When the young Ben opened the door to this room, he confronted a scene that impressed itself on his memory as hotly and permanently as a solar eclipse can burn the retina: "Hubie was hanging there, and his face wasn't black at all. It was green. The eyes were puffed shut. His hands were livid . . . ghastly. And then he opened his eyes." Twenty-four years later, Ben Mears remembers the scene as though it were last night's nightmare. So he returns to 'Salem's Lot to write a novel about the house, hoping to lay the memory to rest.

'Salem's Lot differs from *Carrie* in that it presents a number of characters the reader comes to care a good deal about. Mears falls in love with a young woman, Susan Norton, who has a B.A. from Boston University and dreams of leaving the Lot; he makes the acquaintance of a teacher in the town high school, Matt Burke, whose talents exceed his station. Mark Petrie, a precocious boy of twelve, is a resourceful and fascinating character whose manner of besting the school bully endears him to the reader from the novel's beginning. Still another character, Father Callahan, presents one of the most interesting studies in King's fiction and introduces a new theme in King's work: the problem of evil.

At fifty-three, Father Callahan finds himself world-weary and bored almost soulless by the dullness and triviality of the people whose sins he absolves. His church, with its "ritualistic acknowledgement of evil, . . . bearing down all petty sins on its endless shuttle to heaven," leaves him feeling "that there was no Evil in the world at all but only evil—or perhaps (evil)." He pines for a challenge—a battle rather than the "skirmishes of vague resolution" he finds himself fighting—and finding none turns to the comforts of the bottle and the club (Associated Catholic Priests of the Bottle and Knights of the Cutty Sark). Despite his flaws, his drinking, his palsied spirit, Father Callahan is granted his wish to "slug it out toe to toe with EVIL": as champion of God he comes to face the dark powers in the person of Barlow, the vampire.

Barlow is drawn to 'Salem's Lot in part because of the Marsten house. During his long lifetime he has known many evil places and evil people, and while Hubie Marsten lived he and Barlow corresponded. Marsten burned the letters before he killed himself. Now Barlow's emissary is a walking skeleton named Slaker, whose job is to prepare the way for Barlow; on that account he comes to the Lot one hot July day and purchases the Marsten house and the Village Washtub, a long-defunct laundromat on Jointner Avenue, for one dollar and the deed to some property in the middle of a shopping-center development. Larry Crockett, the real estate agent who sells Slaker the house and the building, is the first in a series of King characters, usually businessmen, who inadvertently do evil by letting their business sense overthrow their moral scruples. Crockett makes a "killing" on the deal, and is more or less directly responsible for Barlow's presence in the Lot. A vampire, the reader recalls, must be invited to enter a house.

More than just the Marsten house or Larry Crockett brings Barlow to 'Salem's Lot, however. King's portrait of the town and its people reveals a moral lassitude that evil may find inviting: "There's little good in sedentary small towns. Mostly indifference spiced with an occasional vapid evil—or worse, a conscious one." At times King appears almost Faulknerian in his insistence on the connection between evil and the town. The townspeople know the infidelities, the perversions, the child abuse more terrible for its mild infrequency. But there are things secret and more terrible known only to the town and the growing darkness around it.

After some bizarre preparations (the slaying of a black dog with white tufts of fur above each eye, the sacrifice of a child) Barlow is established in 'Salem's Lot. People begin to disappear. Ben, Matt, Susan, and Mark band together to combat a situation they cannot quite believe real; they enlist Father Callahan. King ably produces a growing anxiety by manipulating the reader's feelings for these main characters. For instance, when Susan and Mark pay a late afternoon visit to the Marsten house, the reader is swept onto a roller coaster of fear by this detailed description of Susan's responses: "All the thought processes, the act of conversation itself, were overshadowed by a more fundamental voice screaming danger! danger! in words that were not words at all. Her heartbeat and respiration were up, yet her skin was cold with the capillary-dilating effect of adrenaline. . . ."

In many respects, *'Salem's Lot* shows King at his best. The story is engaging, the characters appealing and memorable. His use of the rhetoric of fear is resourceful, even ingenious at times, and the presentation of evil as something vital, dynamic, and very real adds a note of Manichean poignancy to the struggle between Barlow and the tiny group of humans who know him for what he is. Ben Mears tells Susan Norton in *'Salem's Lot* that he wants to write a novel "about the recurrent power of evil." King has written the novel his fictional author might have written.

With some of the money he made from his first two novels, King took his family on a trip to Colorado. The peculiar solitude of a resort hotel there on the last day of the summer season gave him the germ of a story about a resort hotel called the Overlook. That story became *The Shining*, a novel published in 1977.

Like the Marsten house in *'Salem's Lot*, the Overlook in *The Shining* is a building with a colorful past. Erected in the first decade of the twentieth century, the Overlook had had five owners by the time it closed in 1936. It sat abandoned for some years and finally was reopened by Horace Derwent in 1945 after a million-dollar renovation. Derwent sold the hotel in 1954, then repurchased it in 1963 using a fictitious land-development corporation as a front, and the Overlook became an exclusive retreat for the Mafia. In 1967 a gangland-style shooting took place at the hotel; in 1970, its ownership changed hands again. The first winter, the new management installed a man and his family to make small repairs, heat rooms on a rotating basis, and minimize the wintertime damage in general. The man, Grady, murdered his wife and two daughters, then committed suicide. Cabin fever, the authorities concluded. But there were some who thought differently. The hotel, they said, had a powerful spirit, an evil one.

The plot of *The Shining* is set a few years after the triple murder/suicide. Jack Torrance, a down-on-his-luck writer with a history of drinking problems, applies for the job of winter caretaker. Because of the steepness and narrowness of the passes leading to the Overlook it is accessible only by snow machine or helicopter from mid-October to late April, and Torrance feels that this isolation might provide him with the stability and incentive he needs to finish a play he has been working on for some time. Despite his reservations—Grady had also been a drunk—the hotel manager agrees to hire Torrance. With his wife Wendy and son Danny (another of King's psychically gifted children, as in *Carrie*, and *Firestarter*, 1980), Torrance goes up to the Overlook in early October.

While *The Shining* is in many ways a classic horror tale, King has given it some decidedly modern twists. The portrait of the Torrances' marriage, with its soaring and plummeting and the tension brought on by Torrance's drinking, rivals any in contemporary fiction. In fact, psychology plays almost as big a role in this novel as the supernatural. When eventually Jack succumbs to the spirit of the place, and stalks Danny and Wendy in the long halls of the hotel with a roque mallet in his hand, his madness seems an extension of his character rather than demonic possession. When the novel finally settles—somewhat heavily—on a supernatural interpretation, this in no way dimishes the fine study of Jack's deterioration.

The Shining drew King his first wide acclaim, and also his first sharp criticism. Major objections focused on the mixing of classic horror elements with name-brand pop culture and psychology, and King's "inelegant" style. But if King is sometimes less than glib, he shows in *The Shining* the beginnings of a style wholly his own. His predilection for approximate alliteration ("The elevator clanked to a stop below them, at lobby level.") and exotic punctuation (!! FALSE FACES !! NOT REAL !!) can be cloying, but on the whole his prose serves its purpose well. And the use of brand names, popular songs, and other accoutrements of modern culture can be seen as part of King's strategy for making the bizarre seem familiar, possible, actual.

Night Shift (1977), King's next book, is a collection of short stories, many of which first appeared in magazines. Their collection here provides an opportunity to study King's development as a writer. Some of the stories show King working out his novels. "Jerusalem's Lot" and "One for the Road," for example, both concern 'Salem's Lot. Some stories imitate Poe ("Graveyard Shift," "Jerusalem's Lot"), and a few are reminiscent of Kate Wilhelm's or the best of social-science fiction. "Strawberry Spring," "Quitter's, Inc.," and "Children of the Corn" are especially fine. King's work experiences, during high school and his undergraduate years, in places as various as a knitting mill and a laundromat, combine with his childhood phobias (which King says quickly take root and are never completely overcome) and storytelling ability to produce a fine anthology. At his best King is simply himself, and when he loses consciousness of himself as a writer—the way the old tale-teller around the campfire occasionally will—he can be outstanding. Further anthologies of his fine short stories may be anticipated; King is prolific and writes daily.

King's next novel, *The Stand* (1978), is his most ambitious (and longest—the Signet paperback runs more than 800 pages), most complex, and perhaps best book. In it, King returns to the episodic structure he used in *'Salem's Lot*. The plot is easily traceable: a germ-warfare research facility run by the U.S. Army develops a potent and deadly virus. Security is tight: the airtight laboratory below the California desert is monitored by a closed-circuit camera from a watchpoint some miles distant. On paper the system is foolproof. Any loose virus triggers an alarm at the watchpoint and all exits from the laboratory are sealed. But one day the light flashes and the precautions fail. A man escapes the laboratory, takes his wife and daughter, and flees eastward in a car. With them travels a disease more deadly than the plague. Capable of rapid and unpredictable mutation, the virus is immune to both the body's disease defenses and all antibiotics. Confronted with a threatening substance, the virus simply changes chemistry. Anything strong enough to kill it will destroy the organism it infests. Worst of all, the disease is 99.4 percent communicable. Two weeks after the man leaves the facility hidden in the desert, most of the world's population is dead or dying.

Those who are still alive begin to experience two strange dreams. One features a threatening figure whose face is never seen; it produces great anxiety in the dreamer. The other dream is of an old, old woman, face as wrinkled as dark muslin, who invites the dreamer to "Come see me. Anytime" at her farm in Nebraska. King shifts his narrative across the country, New England to the Midwest, New York to Oklahoma, focusing on little bands of survivors in each place. Once again, he carefully creates characters the reader either cares about or is very interested in.

What makes *The Stand* different from other post-apocalypse novels (such as *Dahlgren, Dune, Daybreak 2250*) is that King separates the survivors into two distinct groups. Those who follow the dream of the faceless dark man head west for Las Vegas. Those who follow the dream of the old woman, Mother Abagail, travel first to her farm in Nebraska, then south and west to Boulder, Colorado. The people of Las Vegas, led by the dark man—a necromancer, wizard, and servant of evil—plan to organize their forces and, while the rest of the country is still in chaos, conquer the North American continent. The people of Boulder, guided by Mother Abagail and a council of elected peers, hope to reestablish democratic principles of liberty and equal opportunity for the survivors of the epidemic. Mother Abagail, slight and a bit feeble with her 108 years, is reminiscent of Father Callahan in *'Salem's Lot*—a servant of God weak in her humanity. Her presence in the novel moves it beyond a fascinating study in speculative fiction; it becomes the second chapter in King's novelistic study of evil.

Most of the people who come to Boulder hold the modern view of evil. Like Father Callahan, Mother Abagail recognizes how harmful such a view can be: "There wasn't really any Satan, that was their Gospel. There was evil, and it probably came from original sin, but it was in all of us. . . . Yes, that had a good modern sound to it; the trouble with it was that it wasn't true. And if Nick were allowed to go on thinking that, the dark man would eat him for dinner." Her view of evil, which is Manichean, brings her to a new view of God too. Committed to his service in spirit, she recognizes that he is a great and terrible God: "Every man or woman who loves Him, they hate Him too, because He's a hard God, a jealous God, He Is, what He *Is*, and in this world He's apt to repay service with pain while those who do evil ride over the roads in Cadillac cars. Even the joy of serving him is a bitter joy."

The survivors of the epidemic thus confront a

difficult situation, one familiar to readers of Tolkien, Charles Williams, and C. S. Lewis. The dark man, while frightening, promises to reward faithful servants with wealth and power, the currency of this world. Mother Abagail promises only that those who follow God choose the narrow and rock-strewn road, and may only increase their suffering by serving him: a difficult choice indeed for people who have grown up believing God to be a kindly grandfather and Satan a kind of unrestrained id.

But many of the people who choose to go to Boulder love democracy if not God, and elect to stay in that city. At the first town meeting, the Bill of Rights to the U.S. Constitution is ratified, and committees are formed to remove the bodies of disease victims and restore electricity and other services. Meanwhile, across the mountains in Las Vegas, the dark man organizes his forces. Anyone with military training rises quickly in the hierarchy. Pilots and weapons experts receive special privileges, and a network of secret police guarantees that everyone else follows instructions. Mother Abagail warns the citizens of her New Jerusalem that they cannot ignore the dark man or simply wish him away. Neither, however, can they hope to defeat him in open combat, since he has attracted many people with military and technical training and possesses jet fighters and helicopters, perhaps even tanks. She insists they must look to God and seek his plan for their deliverance.

King's employment of a deus ex machina in no way diminishes the novel. As it turns out, Mother Abagail is right: what weak attempts the people of Boulder do make to battle the evil in Las Vegas fail rather pathetically. Only after swallowing enormous pride do the people realize that the way to beat the dark man is to submit to God. The band of four that God commands Mother Abagail to send to Las Vegas meets an uneasy end, but when things look darkest, God intervenes to set things right. Whether or not the reader accepts Mother Abagail's doctrine, it is difficult to be unmoved by the story of the tiny group that marches straight into the enemy's hand and, despite its destruction, triumphs.

"Not the potter but the potter's clay": Mother Abagail's words echo through the last third of *The Stand*. King does not profess to be a religious man, but in an age when most people believe evil to be the result of illness or error, King writes novels (especially *'Salem's Lot* and *The Stand*) showing evil in its darker and more ancient vitality.

King remembers being an avid movie fan as a child, and confesses to sitting through *The Creature from the Black Lagoon* five times in a single day. "And I still see things cinematically," he adds. "I write down everything I see. It seems like a movie to me, and I write that way." Critics have noted the cinematic qualities in King's fiction, and he has also written screenplays for *The Shining* (although Stanley Kubrick decided to write his own for the 1980 movie version of the novel) and *The Stand*, and is collaborating on the screenplay for a film tentatively titled "Creep Show."

This cinematic quality is again evident in King's fifth novel, *The Dead Zone* (1979). Christopher Lehmann-Haupt comments in his review that when he had finished this novel, he found himself replaying scenes in his mind the way one will after a movie. King, he writes, "makes it easy and fun and, above all, frightening to believe in John Smith" (the protagonist). *The Dead Zone* is set in Maine. As a boy, John Smith had suffered a bad fall on a frozen pond but experienced no immediate aftereffects. By 1970, when he graduates from college, he has forgotten the fall entirely. In Cleaves Mills, where he has taken a job teaching high school, he meets Sarah Bracknell, another teacher there. The action of the novel begins when John and Sarah drive to Esty in Sarah's car to attend the county fair.

At the fair, they succumb to the lure of a huckster and purchase a ticket to play the Wheel of Fortune. "Turn dimes into dollars," the carny yells. John has an incredible run of luck in the game; he seems to know in advance where the wheel will stop, and ends the evening some five hundred dollars ahead. The joy of winning is somewhat tempered by the fact that Sarah gets ill, presumably from one of the notorious hot dogs they had eaten at the fair. Although they had planned to spend the night together—their first—John drives Sarah home and gets a cab for himself. On the way to John's place, the cab collides with a car racing in the wrong lane. The driver is killed outright; John plunges through the windshield, ripping the meter out with his left leg as he goes. The impact leaves him with a severe concussion, and he remains in a coma for more than four years.

When John awakens from his long sleep, he notices many changes. Convinced that John would never rewaken, Sarah has married a law student. John's mother, who was always possessed by a tendency toward religious mania (a scenario familiar to readers of *Carrie*), has become more immersed in her beliefs, and has even spent one summer on a farm in Vermont waiting for flying saucers to appear bearing God's emissaries. The biggest change of all is in John himself: he finds that he can learn things about another person just by touching him. The doctors believe that John survived the accident partly because the fall he suffered as a boy destroyed a small portion of his brain. Somehow this injury, which was discovered when they x-rayed his skull, "taught" his brain to survive trauma; how this teaching took place is a mystery, as is John's ability to know things about people simply by touching them.

King does a fine job of presenting John in all his perplexed complexity. The guilt John feels when his mother suffers a fatal stroke while watching a newscast about his powers; his puzzlement at her final reminder that he is "not the potter but the potter's clay," and her charge to "heed the still, small voice when it comes" to tell him his duty; the anger and sense of betrayal he feels toward Sarah—these emotions are poignant and human. When Sarah comes to visit John and they consummate the relationship they had begun so much earlier, King achieves a balance between bathos and true emotion that dazzles and deeply touches the reader. John and Sarah agree that they have been cheated but that their only course is to part, without fruitless speculation about what might have been.

If King had ended the story at this point, contenting himself with telling the story of John's readjustment to life, *The Dead Zone* could have been a tightly constructed, powerful novel. Instead he takes up a story that might well have been a second novel. The opening chapters of *The Dead Zone* contain several passages about an unscrupulous salesman named Greg Stillson. These passages originally seem totally unconnected to John's story, and as a consequence are paid little attention by the reader. The last third of the novel, however, is devoted to developing the connection between Stillson, who has become a Huey Long type of politician, and John. Stillson wins a U.S. Senate seat from New Hamspire on a platform composed of such absurdities as shooting all pollution into space. His campaign staff and bodyguards are ex-motorcycle toughs, and his campaign runs roughshod over anyone who gets in the way. John develops a fascination with Stillson and begins keeping a scrapbook on him. The fascination grows to obsession, and John travels to a Stillson rally to see the man in person. At the rally, John positions himself along Stillson's route and shakes his hand as he passes. The vision that overcomes John following that contact is one of the strongest and most unpleasant he can remember: Stillson will become an American Hitler and will involve the world in nuclear war.

Convinced that God has called him to stop Stillson, John sinks deeper into his obsession. His mother's last words recur like the echo of a nightmare. His brain begins to bleed from an old wound, as the doctors had feared it might, and he knows he has only a short time to live. He is tormented by the question "If you could jump into a time machine and go back to 1932, would you kill Hitler?" After considering the alternatives, he determines to kill Stillson. The rest of the novel presents the working out of his plan.

The Dead Zone succeeds in making the reader take John Smith and his obsession seriously; America's record of attempted and successful assassinations makes a story from the viewpoint of an assassin doubly provocative, but it deserves separate treatment from the story of John and Sarah. The attempt to combine two equally interesting stories makes *The Dead Zone* a loose and sometimes confusing novel.

Charlene McGee (Charlie), the protagonist of King's most recently published novel, *Firestarter*, is a little girl who can start fires with her mind. Her parents, Andy McGee and Vicky Tomlinson McGee, have taken part in a government drug experiment that caused nine of its twelve subjects to die—some through suicide—or go insane. As a result of the drug Vicky is mildly telekinetic and Andy can, by mentally "pushing," exert his will over others through a kind of hypnosis. The novel's plot traces the efforts of a government intelligence agency, The Shop, to capture Charlie and test her powers.

King portrays The Shop agents in *Firestarter* as nasty and brutish for the most part. Many are sadistic; some are insane. One, a horribly-maimed, full-blooded Indian, looks deeply into the eyes of every person he kills in his capacity as hit man, hoping to see in someone else's eyes the reflection of what it will be like to die. He is convinced that Charlie can teach him how to die, and the story of his fascination with her and his attempts to win her confidence adds a particularly chilling episode to this quietly gruesome novel.

In his other novels, King exhibits to a lesser extent a distrust of science (as when all the hard technicians in *The Stand* gravitate toward Las Vegas), but in *Firestarter* his suspicion is overt. The continuous inability of scientists in the novel to evaluate accurately or to estimate such things as the potency of the drug, the extent of Andy and Vicky McGee's powers, and the force and range of Charlie's pyrotechnics makes a strong statement about the author's feelings.

Firestarter is neither so rich nor compelling a novel as *'Salem's Lot, The Shining*, or *The Stand*,

58

Just before Tad's bedtime, he and Vic sat on the back stoop. Vic had beer. Tad had milk.

"Daddy?"

"What?"

"I wish you didn't have to go away next week."

"I'll be back."

Yeah, but--"

Tad was looking down, struggling with tears. Vic put a hand on his neck.

"But what, big guy?"

"Who's gonna say the words that keep the monster out of the closet? Mommy doesn't know them! Only you know them!"

Now the tears spilled over and ran down Tad's face.

"Is that all?" Vic asked.

The Monster-Words (Vic had originally dubbed them the Monster-Catechism, but Tad had trouble with that word, so it had been shortened) had come about in late spring, when Tad began to be afflicted with bad dreams and night-fears. There was something in his closet, he said; sometimes at night his closet door would swing open and he would see it in there, something with yellow eyes that wanted to eat him up. Donna had thought it might have been some bad fallout from Maurice Sendak's book, *Where the Wild Things Are*. Vic had wondered aloud to Roger (but not to Donna) if maybe Tad had picked up a garbled account of the mass murders that had taken place in Castle Rock, and decided that the murderer --who had become a kind of town boogeyman--was alive and well in his closet. Roger said he supposed it was possible; with kids, *anything* was possible.

And Donna herself had begun to get a little spooked after a couple of weeks of this; she told Vic one morning in a kind of laughing, nervous way that things in Tad's closet sometimes appeared moved around. Well, Tad did it, Vic had responded. You don't understand, Donna said. He doesn't go back there anymore, Vic...never. He's scared to. And she had added that sometimes it seemed to her that the closet actually smelled bad after Tad's bouts of nightmare followed

Cujo, *corrected typescript*

but like King's other good work it succeeds in creating characters the reader cares about. Charlie McGee touches the reader especially because of her inability to understand everything that happens to her. The power she possesses terrifies her (partly because she cannot fully control it, partly because she so enjoys using it), and she finds it hard to accept the necessity of acting, using her power in situations she does not fully comprehend. The story of her learning to act makes for good reading.

King now lives in Center Lowell, Maine, with his wife and three children. Despite his considerable output—seven novels, a non-fiction study of horror tales, an anthology of short stories, and three screenplays—his work exhibits versatility. His recurrent themes—fear and evil in their many faces, the gray areas of human experience where the possible becomes actual and the improbable becomes real—should provide him still more room to grow. His ability to create sympathetic and compelling characters, apparent even in *Carrie*, could continue to serve him well and insure at least his popular success in any fictional task he undertakes. Whether or not he develops, with time, a style uniquely his own, he will be remembered as a writer who peeked into the corners of his mind and wrote accurately about what he saw there. Today, when much of the world has convinced itself, by daylight at least, that the scratching at the windowpane is that and nothing more, King's voice cries at the darkness.

—*Mark Harris*

Periodical Publications:

FICTION:

"Suffer the Little Children," *Cavalier* (February 1972);

"The Cat From Hell," *Cavalier* (June 1977);

"The Night of the Tiger," *Fantasy and Science Fiction* (February 1978);

"Man With a Belly," *Cavalier* (December 1978);

"The Crate," *Gallery* (July 1979);

"Monkey," *Gallery* (November 1980);

"The Wedding Gig,"*Ellery Queen's Mystery Magazine* (December 1980).

NONFICTION:

"The Fright Report," *Oui* (January 1978): 76;

"The Horrors of '79," *Rolling Stone*, 307 (27 December 1979-10 January 1980): 17-20;

"A Pilgrim's Progress," *American Bookseller* (January 1980);

"How I Became a Brand Name," *Adelina* (February 1980);

"Why We Crave Horror Movies," *Playboy*, 28 (January 1981).

Interviews:

John F. Baker, "Stephen King," *Publisher's Weekly*, 211 (17 January 1977): 12-13;

Frank Sleeper, "Stephen King Makes Millions by Scaring Hell out of 3 Million Readers,"*People*, 7 (7 March 1977): 61-62;

Mel Allen, "Witches and Aspirin," *Writer's Digest*, 5 (June 1977): 26;

Carol Lawson, "Behind the Best Sellers," *New York Times Book Review*, 23 September 1979, p. 42;

William Wilson, "Riding the Crest of the Horror Wave," *New York Times Magazine*, 11 May 1980, pp. 42-43;

"A Mild Down-Easter Discovers Terror is the Ticket," *People*, 14 (29 December 1980-5 January 1981): 53-54.

Maxine Hong Kingston

(27 October 1940-   )

BOOKS: *The Woman Warrior: Memoirs of a Girlhood Among Ghosts* (New York: Knopf, 1976; London: Lane, 1977);
China Men (New York: Knopf, 1980).

An American writer born of Chinese immigrant parents, Maxine Hong Kingston blends myth, legend, history, and autobiography into a genre of her own invention. She is the author of two books, both of which span two continents and several generations. The first, *The Woman Warrior: Memoirs of a Girlhood Among Ghosts* (1976), is a personal work, an effort to reconcile American and Chinese female identities. Its companion volume, *China Men* (1980), attempts a broader synthesis, dealing with male Chinese "sojourners" in North America and Hawaii, but it is inextricably tied to the autobiographical interests of *The Woman Warrior*. For their insight and art both books have earned high praise from critics. *The Woman Warrior* won the National Book Critics Circle Award for nonfiction in 1976, and three years later *Time* rated it among the top ten nonfiction works of the decade. Recent reviews of *China Men* indicate that it may fare as well and that Kingston is on her way to recognition as a major American writer.

Biographical fact suggests that Maxine Hong Kingston was long ago destined to retrace her ancestral past in life as well as art. She was conceived in New York, where her father made his first American home and where her mother joined him after her arrival at Ellis Island in 1939. But she was born in California where her father's father had sojourned three times, somehow establishing Hong claims to U.S. citizenship in the years when it was possible to do so. Named by her father for a blond American, a lucky lady gamester in the gambling house where he worked, Maxine Hong grew up in Stockton's Chinatown, conscious at a very young age of conflicting cultural allegiances. After she received an A.B. from Berkeley in 1962 and returned in 1964-1965 to earn a teaching certificate, she taught English and mathematics in Hayward, California, during 1965-1967. In 1967 she, her husband, Earll Kingston, whom she married on 23 November 1962, and her son, Joseph, moved to Hawaii, the place her ancestors called the "Sandalwood Mountains," where two of her great-grandfathers had hacked sugarcane farms out of wilderness. She held various high-school and college teaching positions in and around Honolulu and eventually gave up teaching after the success of her first book. She continues to reside in Hawaii, halfway between the two cultures which have rent her spirit and inspired her art. Shortly before the publication of *China Men*, a Honolulu Buddhist sect claimed her as an official "Living Treasure of Hawaii" in a ceremony at Honpa Hongwanji Temple. Whether or not she will ever go to ancestral China, "a country that may not be there at all . . . I having made it up," she does not know.

The sources for both Kingston's books are tales she heard from her family and other Stockton Chinese "story-talkers" in her youth. For the material of *The Woman Warrior*, the story-talker was primarily Kingston's mother, Brave Orchid, who intended her stories as lessons "to grow up on." Simple structures, "powered by Necessity," they stimulated Kingston's mind to embroider detail upon them. Especially appealing were the tales of heroines and swordswomen, for the prosy realities of daily life brought Chinese-American girls too many epithets like "stink pig." In fact, a woman in China could grow up to be a slave or a wife. In legend, she could also turn into a warrior. *The Woman Warrior* weaves fact and legend into a continuous reality.

The story of one woman, either mythical or real, dominates each of the five parts of this narrative, which is plotless in the conventional sense. In the second section, "White Tigers," and the fifth, "A Song for a Barbarian Reed Pipe," the central figure is Kingston herself. She identifies herself in each case with a lengendary warrior woman. In "White Tigers" Kingston tells of Brave Orchid's song about a female hero named Fa Mu Lan and repeats her childhood fantasy of herself as swordswoman, warrior, and avenger. The story of her training reads like poetry; that of her march against the warlords and emperor, like romance. Then Kingston's return to actuality at the end of "White Tigers"—"My American life has been such a disappointment"—plunges the story into irony. Suddenly, the only possible victories are A's on report cards, and the only possible battles are between slum toughs. But the fantasy swordswoman who went to war with a village's grievances carved into her flesh is not irrelevant. An inspired synthesis blends myth and irony to create a new realism: "The swordswoman and I are not so dissimilar. . . . What we have in common are the words at our backs. The ideographs for *revenge* are 'report a crime' and 'report to five families.' The reporting is the vengeance—not the beheading, not the gutting, but the words. And I have so many words—'chink' words and 'gook' words too—that they do not fit on my skin."

The structure of "A Song for a Barbarian Reed Pipe" is just the reverse. It begins with the actual and then proceeds to the lengendary before it resolves into another and final synthesis. Difficulties with English, which their parents had not taught them, and with American conventions of tone and gesture apparently kept Maxine Hong and her younger sister silent at school for years. Except for reading lessons whispered or squeaked aloud, they talked only to other Chinese children. Years later, talking still made Maxine Hong anxious. Bus drivers, sales clerks, and telephones all provoked a constricted throat and her "pressed duck voice." So did the young Chinese men whom her parents brought home as potential husbands for their daughters. So did an unsuccessful effort to confess 207 fears, guilts, and angers to her mother, an effort which ended in Maxine's departure from home. She could not, it seems, communicate in either the Chinese or the "demon" (white) world.

Appended to "A Song for a Barbarian Reed Pipe" is an account of a legendary warrior poetess, Ts'ai Yung. She was born to a Chinese scholar and, as a young woman, seized by barbarian nomads from the south. As a captive wife to one of the chieftains and a soldier besides, she spent twelve years with the marauders before she was ransomed and returned to her father. During her captivity, she bore two half-barbarian children. She attempted to teach them Chinese, but they laughed and mocked her in cruel imitation. Then one night Ts'ai Yung sang a high clear song above the haunting melodies of the barbarian flutes. The words were Chinese, but her children did not laugh, and the barbarians understood the sadness and anger of the song in spite of its alien language. When she returned to China, she took her songs with her, and several of these, including "Eighteen Stanzas for a Barbarian Reed Pipe," China adopted for its own. If Kingston is a swordswoman "reporting a crime," she is also an exiled poetess with a song for barbarians and Chinese alike.

The first, third, and fourth parts of *Woman Warrior* record stories of three Chinese women relatives in the generation directly preceding Kingston's own. The book opens with the tale of an aunt in China, her father's sister, whose name is never revealed to her nieces and nephews in America. "No Name" aunt cursed the family by bearing an illegitimate child. On the same day she delivered her baby, the villagers destroyed the family compound, and she committed "spite-suicide" with her baby in the family well. Brave Orchid supplied the bare facts

Maxine Hong Kingston

of the tale, but her daughter must conjure up additional details on her own. Did her aunt indulge in romance or lust in a world which did not recognize women's rights to either? Or was she forced by some man who then himself organized the raid upon her household? Did she carry the baby into the well because it was also a female? Deliberately forgotten by her family, "No Name" aunt has an avenger in the niece, who, fifty years later, devotes "pages of paper to her, though not origamied into houses and clothes."

"At the Western Palace," part four, presents the pitiful account of Moon Orchid, another aunt on Kingston's mother's side. Fragile, timid, and a little silly, she was convinced by her sister to come to California in her old age to confront the husband who left her in China thirty years before. He now enjoyed a successful medical practice and a new, young wife. He rejected Moon Orchid, though he continued to support her financially as he had all along. Shamed and traumatized, Moon Orchid became a paranoid schizophrenic and died shortly thereafter. Hers is one story which Brave Orchid does not have to repeat for her children. Live witnesses to its injustice, "Brave Orchid's daughters decided fiercely that they would never let men be unfaithful to them."

"Shaman," part three, explores Brave Orchid's own life during the long interval between her husband's departure for the "Gold Mountain" of America in 1924 and her reunion with him in New York in 1940. Of the three women of her generation whose stories are told in this book, she is the most heroic. Alone after her husband left China and her two toddler-aged children died, Brave Orchid traveled to the capital of Kwangtung to study medicine at the To Keung School of Midwifery. Two years later she returned to the countryside with certifications in surgery, gynecology, dermatology, midwifery, pediatrics, ophthalmology, nursing, and bandaging. By mingling ancient magic with modern medicine and by accepting only those patients whom she knew would recover, Brave Orchid became rich and respected, enjoying an unusual status among Chinese women, a fact which was not lost on her first American daughter when she heard it years later.

In her mid-forties, Brave Orchid sacrificed both money and position to come to America and begin life all over. She worked as a servant, laundress, and fruit picker and became the mother of five more children. She is the life force of the family, particularly during periods of misfortune: "Her energy slammed Baba [Kingston's father] back into his chair. She took care of everything; he did not have a reason to get up." When some readers of *Woman Warrior* expressed doubts as to whether Brave Orchid is "truly that large in real life," Kingston responded, "I calmed her down for the book. She is even larger than that."

The Woman Warrior and *China Men* were originally conceived as one work. Both mix myth, legend, and history. Both also read like reconciliations with the past: the first with female ancestors, the second with their male counterparts. Kingston's mother dominates the first book; her father, the second. In both books, additional characters flesh out the social, political, and cultural history Kingston introduces. But there are differences between the two books.

As a source of "talk-story," Kingston's father proved far more taciturn than her mother. Early in *China Men,* there is an emotional apostrophe to Kingston's father: "Father, I have seen you lighthearted. . . . But usually you did not play. You were angry. You scared us. Every day we listened to you swear. 'Dog vomit. . . . Stink pig. Mother's cunt.' Obscenities. . . . Worse than the swearing and the nightly screams were your silences when you punished us by not talking. . . . You say with the few words and the silences: No stories, No past. No China. . . . You fix yourself in the present, but I want to hear the stories about the rest of your life, the Chinese stories. I want to know what makes you scream and curse, and what you're thinking about when you say nothing, and why when you do talk, you talk differently from Mother. . . . I'll tell you what I suppose from your silences and few words, and you can tell me that I'm mistaken. You'll just have to speak up with the real stories if I've got you wrong." But then, the narration becomes more impersonal and objective as Kingston constructs a more comprehensive and painstaking history than appears in *The Woman Warrior,* a strong factual basis for her interpretation of Chinese-American masculinity. This heavier emphasis on historical fact is coupled with a broader compass of characters (each of four generations is represented by several individuals).

Kingston is confident in her exploration of masculine experience, and throughout her careful chronicles, her imagination elaborates according to familiar patterns from *The Woman Warrior.* Just as "No Name" aunt's fate is repeated in several variations in the first work, so is Kingston's father's story in *China Men.* In the book, there are five different versions of how he entered the United States, a fact of which she is "proud." The underlying assumption is that imaginative repetitions and transformations will approach a more significant truth than will the mere compilation of fact. Of her technique in *China Men,* she argues: "This kind of writing is an emotional process as well as an artistic one. The form of what I write forces me through a series of emotions. . . . Most literary forms are not artificial. They reflect patterns of the human heart."

Aside from brief interludes of straight myth and history, *China Men* presents a series of fictionalized biographies of male ancestors. Two of these are based on Kingston's father's experience. He appears first in "The Father from China," a father Kingston never knew because his story ends with the swindle which deprived him of his laundry in New York shortly before her birth. In China, he was the youngest of four sons. His mother decided at his birth that he would become a scholar instead of a

The couple who should have sent them messages through the cooks who also knew

men from other sheds gathered

73

because it showed a willingness to work. But this week, they like 'yes job' and 'Yes money' because you wouldn't be taking jobs away from white workers." The men groaned, 'Some help." These workers were indeed priceless, bringeng news, telling wich immigrant demons could be bribed and for how much, telling what a relative ahead said so that the brother or uncle would answer consistently, slipping them notes from them. Put this with former paragraph on food, put all toghet wirht mother section?

During the legal father's stay, he was let out of the Wooden House once, he circled the yard as far as the fence, where there were guards in uniform. A guard threw him a ball and said, motioning, "Play ball. Go ahead. Play with it," as if he were a boy and could play. Even the boys didn't play. "Who can be that lighthearted?" A couple of men did throw the ball back and forth, nothing else to do. "We'd better start learning American customs," they said. Leave out?

He was now eligible to vote whether or not to spend money on a ball. They could throw it over the crowd. He votes no. He loves picture. He voted for a record.

Put w/ 1st conclud 69

Jesus Demons entered the barracks and sat right on the beds to pester them. They had white faces but Chinese words came out of their mouths.) They talked about ow they were old China hands and how much they respected Chinese. "I am not Chinese, I am a Gold Mountain Man," themen said, the legal father heard, impressing him very much. However, a few listened to them; the women listened to hem, The women nodding as they walked about the yard with the Jesus Demons. It was like the women to be so women believed anything. "Would help us land if we converted?" the men asked the Jesus Demons, who did not give a clear yes, so only fools converted. At least in China, converts got a western eduction, free clothes, food, a job, a place to live, a free burial. These Island missionaries left grisly cards with pictures of a demon nailed to a cross, proably a warning about what happened to you if you didn't convert. Chinese crucified people too, bhtey were not nailed like this but tied to the wood and grrrtoted. IN china, thre were pictues of soldiers eating the meat of Christians; it looked like drumstics tattooed "West."

Compare to Ch. 2

The horror of these kids of death added to the fear that was already in the Wooden House.

Everyday men were called out one by one at various intervals. The legal father kept himslf looking presentable, kempt. Some of these ... as they could,

wait til 75 — after all the little incidents on pg 74 (death)

China Men, *revised typescript*

laborer. His father (in defiance of all Chinese convention) was weary of sons and attempted to exchange him for a neighbor's daughter. Sometime in his adolescence he scored high enough on the Imperial Examinations to be appointed village teacher to a pack of unruly boys, but years of waste and abuse in the village school taught him to yearn with other Chinese men for the "Gold Mountain." So he abandoned his post and sailed to the United States. The Father from China was a blessed creature, a mother's favorite, an ideal specimen of Chinese masculine beauty and brains among a village of manual laborers. Fortune favored him in America also, for a while. In New York he discovered friends, fancy clothes, movies, dancing, and unprecedented freedom; he became a dandy.

It was only with the arrival of Brave Orchid and then the birth of their babies that his fortunes turned. For a period in California, he was reduced to poverty, humiliation, and depression. This is a man Kingston remembers well, and in the fourth biography, "The American Father," the same delicacy which gained him success in China contributed to his failure in America. It is difficult to integrate these two fathers, so between their stories Kingston reaches back to grandfathers and great-grandfathers whose histories provide a context in which to better understand her father's own.

According to the second section of ancestral biography, "Great Grandfather of the Sandalwood Mountains," two great-grandfathers left China in the early 1850s to make their fortunes planting sugar cane in Hawaii. They were seduced into going there by the promise of high pay and the proximity of Hawaii to the "Gold Mountain." The "Sandalwood Mountain" was beautiful, and fruit was plentiful, but the "white demons" exploited and tyrannized the Chinese laborers, who fell ill, turned to opium, spent the money they were to send home, or forgot their families altogether. Both great-grandfathers, Bak Goong and Bak Sook Goong, returned to China, but they were unusual. More frequently, men settled permanently in Hawaii or traveled to the "Gold Mountain" in time for the end of the gold rush.

Neither did Ah Goong, the grandfather who once tried to exchange his son for a daughter, forget his Chinese family. In "Grandfather of the Sierra Nevada Mountains" Kingston tells how he sojourned three times in the United States. During the first of these trips, he helped build the California railroad, tunneling through mountain rock with picks, axes, and crude explosives. Accidents, strikes, and American xenophobia made this work a dangerous business. By the time the railroad was finished, Ah Goong had to hide, for the roundup and expulsion of Chinese had begun. His contribution to America seems to have impressed his Chinese descendents even if it was lost on Americans: "Grandfather left a railroad for his message: We had to go somewhere difficult. Ride a train. Go somewhere important. In case of danger, the train was ready for us." During his third trip to America, Ah Goong became a bum. His family had to borrow to recall him to China. He was the family "Fleaman," but he was also the family claim to the United States. His presence in the San Francisco earthquake and fire of 1906 earned him the right to claim that the document granting him citizenship had been burned in the fire. He secured the Hong family citizenship before it was too late.

"The Making of More Americans" describes a miscellaneous collection of additional male relatives from Kingston's grandfather's generation to the present. They include two of Ah Goong's younger brothers who settled in California, establishing the family ancestral ground in Stockton; one of their grandsons, Mad Sao, who interrupted an apparently sane and prosperous life in America one day to guide his mother's ghost back to her Chinese grave; Kau Goong, another grandfather, a pirate and murderer, who babysat for Kingston's younger sister in his old age; Uncle Bun, who talked only of wheat germ and Communism until he returned to China to become a Communist; and finally, a stepuncle, a ruined Hong Kong entrepreneur who married the widow of an uncle stoned by the Communists in China. It is women from whom Kingston gathered the stories of these men's lives, and about her sources, she concludes: "I would never be able to talk with them; I have no stories of equal pain."

The pain that most impresses is, after all, that of her own father, to whom Kingston returns in "The American Father," which begins with memories of "father places." How better to understand a silent man than by the space he commands: a dirt cellar with a bottomless well, the "opening to the inside of the world"; an attic smelling of pigeon feathers, an "extravagance of empty space"; and the hidden gambling house where he worked illegally to support his family. But "The American Father" is also a story of exploitation at the hands of a villager from home and a story of unemployment and depression. It is a story of a wife's recriminations: "You're shy. You're lazy. . . . You piece of liver," and the story of a daughter's attempt to rescue him by sending in a Charles Atlas body-building coupon from a comic book. Finally, miraculously, it is also the story of a man who wakes from a trance to ransom his self-respect. Nearly a half-century after The Father from China leaves one house, one family, and one career in China, The American Father attained their equivalents in America.

China Men is brought full circle with the close of "The American Father," but Kingston's own generation is yet to be represented in "The Brother in Vietnam." Kingston's younger brother was the first immediate family member to serve in the United States military. A pacifist and a teacher, he refused advanced training that would have qualified him as a pilot, spy, or interrogator. He survived his navy tour in Vietnam without "having to kill or be killed."

On leave in Hong Kong, this brother began a search for relatives out of the same mysterious past that he shares with his sister. After the war, he planned to return to look further and to ride into China for the other relatives there. Like Kingston he is ambivalent about his search: the relatives will be poor; they will have no manners; they will look like his family; they will need his strength. He will not find his past at all, or if he does, it will devour him. At the least, he thinks, it will disappoint him.

Perhaps the book itself is the best return to China. Kingston describes *China Men* as a "claiming of America," a sort of vindication of all the Chinese who helped build America but who were rewarded with abuse and neglect. She is still an avenger "reporting crimes." But perhaps, like Mad Sao, she is also guiding Chinese ghosts to their graves.

Just after the publication of *China Men*, Kingston acknowledged an end to her Chinese material: "I don't have any more stories saved up. . . . I am facing a blank, but I feel good about it. . . . I am going to make something out of nothing, which is the greatest creativity." She is now writing a novel set in 1963 in California, a novel with "modern" characters who have "forgotten or never knew their mythology and history." It is a new experiment in style and structure also, an effort "to make beautiful literature without the aid of Chinese metaphors."

Any attempt to evaluate Maxine Hong Kingston's career now would be premature. Only five years have passed since Kingston entered the national literary scene. Her work has been well received by critics, and the personal silence which once got mistaken for a low I.Q. seems only to have heightened public appreciation of her literary eloquence. John Leonard, who first reviewed *The Woman Warrior* in the *New York Times*, was nearly as moved by the unobtrusiveness of the author as he was overwhelmed by the book: "Those rumbles you hear on the horizon are the big guns of autumn lining up, the howitzers of Vonnegut and Updike and Cheever and Mailer, the books that will be making loud noises for the next several months. But listen: this week a remarkable book has been quietly published; it is one of the best I've read in years." He went on to describe the work as "dizzying, elemental, a poem turned into a sword." William McPherson, in the *Washington Post*, found it to be "strange, sometimes savagely terrifying . . . and extraordinary." Jane Kramer, in the *New York Times*, judged it "a brilliant memoir."

Critical reception of *China Men* has about matched that of *The Woman Warrior*. Mary Gordon called it "a triumph of the highest order, of imagination, of language, of moral perception." But some reviewers have faulted its unconnected interludes of myth and history, passages which would have been integrated into the narrative line in *The Woman Warrior*.

Regarding both works, Kingston has been criticized for tampering with Chinese myths, in particular, and for misrepresenting Chinese experience, in general. In her new book, Kingston is likely to escape these flaws, if they are such, since there will be no Chinese consciousness, no Chinese metaphor. Perhaps something will be lost in the exchange, for so far Chinese consciousness and Chinese metaphor number among Kingston's most valuable gifts. Just as likely, however, Kingston will create another original form, so compelling that comparisons will seem irrelevant.

—*Susan Currier*

Periodical Publications:

"Literature for a Scientific Age: Lorenz' King Solomon's Ring," *English Journal*, 62 (January 1973): 30-32;

"Duck Boy," *New York Times*, 12 June 1977, VII: 54-58;

"Reservations About China," *Ms.*, 7 (October 1978): 67-68;

"San Francisco's Chinatown," *American Heritage*, 30 (December 1978): 35-47;

"The Making of More Americans," *New Yorker*, 55 (11 February 1980): 34-58;

"China Men," *Redbook*, 155 (July 1980): 161-176.

Interviews:

Susan Brownmiller, "Susan Brownmiller Talks with Maxine Hong Kingston," *Mademoiselle*, 83 (March 1977): 148ff.;

Timothy Pfaff, "Talk with Mrs. Kingston," *New York Times Book Review*, 15 June 1980, p. 1ff.

References:

Mary Gordon, "Mythic History," *New York Times Book Review*, 15 June 1980, p. 1ff.;
Jane Kramer, "The Woman Warrior," *New York Times Book Review*, 7 November 1976, p. 1ff.;
Timothy Pfaff, "Whispers of a Literary Explorer," *Horizon*, 23 (July 1980): 58-63.

Louis L'Amour
(1908?-)

SELECTED BOOKS: *Smoke From This Altar* (Oklahoma City: Lusk, 1939);
Hopalong Cassidy and the Rustlers of West Fork, as Tex Burns (Garden City: Doubleday, 1951);
Hopalong Cassidy and the Trail to Seven Pines, as Tex Burns (Garden City: Doubleday, 1951);
Hondo (New York: Gold Medal, 1953; London: Muller, 1954);
Showdown at Yellow Butte, as Jim Mayo (New York: Ace, 1953; London: Tandem, 1972);
Utah Blaine (New York: Gold Medal, 1954);
Kilkenny (New York: Ace, 1954; London: Tandem, 1972);
Heller With a Gun (New York: Gold Medal, 1955; London: Gold Lion, 1973);
The Burning Hills (New York: Jason, 1956; London: Hammond, 1965);
The Tall Stranger (New York: Gold Medal, 1957; London: Gold Lion, 1973);
Sitka (New York: Hawthorn, 1957; London: Corgi, 1973);
Flint (New York: Bantam, 1960; London: Transworld, 1961);
The Daybreakers (New York: Bantam, 1960; London: Hammond, 1964);
Sackett (New York: Bantam, 1961; London: Hammond, 1964);
Shalako (New York: Bantam, 1962; London: Hale, 1976);
Lando (New York: Bantam, 1962);
Catlow (New York: Bantam, 1963; London: Hale, 1976);
Hanging Woman Creek (New York: Bantam, 1964; London: Hale, 1976);
Mojave Crossing (New York: Bantam, 1964; London: Hale, 1976);
The Sackett Brand (New York: Bantam, 1965; London: Transworld, 1965);
Mustang Man (New York: Bantam, 1966; London: Hale, 1978);
The Sky-Liners (New York: Bantam, 1967);
Down the Long Hills (New York: Bantam, 1968; London: Corgi, 1968);
The Lonely Men (New York: Bantam, 1969; London: Corgi, 1973);
Treasure Mountain (New York: Bantam, 1969; London: Corgi, 1973);
Galloway (New York: Bantam, 1970; London: Corgi, 1970);
North to the Rails (New York: Bantam, 1971; London: Corgi, 1971);
Ride the Dark Trail (New York: Bantam, 1972; London: Corgi, 1972);
The Californios (New York: Saturday Review Press, 1974; London: Corgi, 1975);
Sackett's Land (New York: Saturday Review Press, 1974; London: Corgi, 1975);
Over on the Dry Side (New York: Saturday Review Press, 1975; London: Corgi, 1976);
Rivers West (New York: Saturday Review Press, 1975; London: Corgi, 1976);
The Man from the Broken Hills (New York: Bantam, 1975; London: Corgi, 1976);
The Rider of Lost Creek (New York: Bantam, 1976; London: Corgi, 1976);
To the Far Blue Mountains (New York: Dutton, 1976; London: Corgi, 1977);
Borden Chantry (New York: Bantam, 1977; London: Corgi, 1978);
Fair Blows the Wind (New York: Dutton, 1978);
Mountain Valley War (New York: Bantam, 1978);
Bendigo Shafter (New York: Dutton, 1979; London: Corgi, 1980);
The Strong Shall Live (New York: Bantam, 1980; London: Corgi, 1980);
The Warrior's Path (New York: Bantam, 1980);
Lonely on the Mountain (New York: Bantam, 1980);
Yondering (New York: Bantam, 1980);
Comstock Lode (New York: Bantam, 1981).

Louis L'Amour, author of more than seventy-five novels about life in frontier America, is one of the best-selling fiction writers of all time. In 1979 alone, Bantam Books, one of his paperback publishers, shipped 7,820,000 copies of L'Amour titles; and in June 1980, *Yondering*, a collection of the author's early short stories, was published simultaneously in paperback and hardcover editions by Bantam to celebrate one hundred million copies of L'Amour books in print around the world. The latter figure includes translations in Swedish, Norwegian, Danish, Italian, Greek, Dutch, French, Portuguese, Japanese, and Serbo-Croatian. In addition, L'Amour has written some four hundred published short stories and has had more than thirty of his works turned into motion pictures, including *Hondo* (1953), *Shalako* (1962), *The Burning Hills* (1956), and *Catlow* (1963). The nature of his fame is such that a profile of his life and works has been shown twice on CBS television's *60 Minutes*, and his name figures prominently in a 1980 country-and-western hit record, "The Last Cowboy Song."

The man who has achieved such phenomenal popular success and personal fame was born Louis Dearborn LaMoore in Jamestown, North Dakota, about the year 1908. (L'Amour prefers not to discuss his age, which he feels is not the measure of a man so much as his experiences, knowledge, and accomplishments.) He was the youngest son of Emily Dearborn and Louis Charles LaMoore. The elder LaMoore sold farm machinery and was a veterinarian in the Dakotas until the 1920s, when an agricultural depression forced the family to move on.

Even as a child, L'Amour was a storyteller, beginning his career before he went to school. He would draw pictures of cowboys and Indians, cut them out, and act out stories with them. As he grew older, he thought that he could write professionally, but it was a long time before he tried to sell his work or found any success in the literary marketplace. Instead, after his family left the Dakotas, L'Amour, at the age of fifteen, dropped out of school and began a life of wandering that was to take him literally around the world and to give him material for many of the stories he was to write later.

At first, L'Amour moved south and west, working at any job he could find. He worked as a roustabout in a circus, as a lumberjack, and as a miner in hard-rock mines for copper, silver, gold, zinc, and lead. In the latter jobs, he became proficient with the shovel and sledgehammer. On another job, he helped an old trapper skin 925 dead cattle for a Texas rancher. The old man told L'Amour of his being kidnapped by Indians as a child, riding with the great war chiefs, and fighting the white man. From the trapper's tales L'Amour got the ideas for many later stories and novels.

After riding freights from El Paso to the Gulf of Mexico, L'Amour went to sea, traveling first to the West Indies, then to Europe. The life of the merchant seaman seems to have appealed to him, and he worked his way to San Pedro, California, where, at the age of seventeen, he shipped for the Orient, eventually putting in at such ports as Shanghai, Singapore, Hong Kong, Yokohama, and Borneo. During this time, he is said to have fought for Chiang Kai-shek, and further adventures followed. According to one story, it was in Macao that L'Amour had the first great stroke of luck in his life. Overhearing some men discussing their plans for recovery of $50,000 from a sunken ship, L'Amour decided to try for the money himself. He got it before the others, and at the age of nineteen he used the money to go to Paris and try the bohemian life. From Paris he traveled by bicycle to Marseilles, later going to Italy and Hungary, and returning to the United States only when the money ran out.

Although L'Amour's early life sounds romantic, almost idyllic, such was not the case. Money and jobs were not always easy to come by, and there were times when he missed meals and slept in lumber piles with newspapers wrapped under his coat for warmth. Too, L'Amour was often involved in fights, both in and out of the ring. At one time he fought professionally in preliminary events; of fifty-nine fights in his career, he lost five times.

After years of wandering, L'Amour was reunited with his parents in Oklahoma City in the late 1930s, and it was at that time that he began his writing career. He did not meet with instant success, receiving more than 200 rejection slips before he learned what he believes to be the secret of telling stories: beginning in the middle of the action to get the reader involved. His first sales of stories, articles, and poetry were to such magazines as Rob Wagner's *Script*. (A number of the early stories are reprinted in *Yondering*; along with the autobiographical introductions provided by L'Amour, these stories offer interesting insights into the author's early career and his ideas about writing.) L'Amour's first published book was a volume of poetry printed by the Lusk Publishing Company of Oklahoma City in 1939. The title was *Smoke from this Altar*.

L'Amour's literary life had hardly begun when it was interrupted by World War II, in which he served in Europe as an officer in the Tank Destroyer and Transportation Corps. During the war, L'Amour would pass the time by telling other

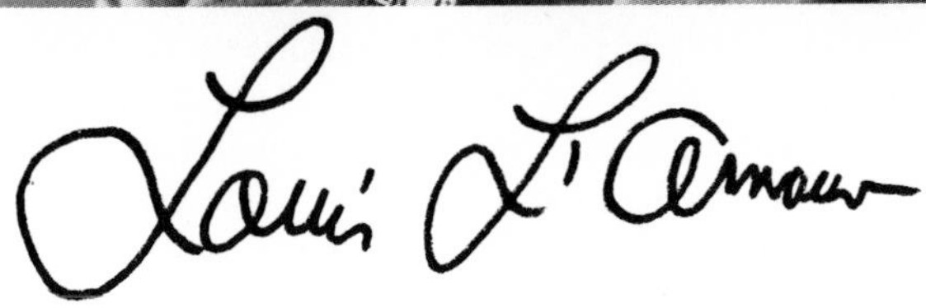

soldiers some of the tales he had picked up on his travels. Their response encouraged him, and in the late 1940s he began submitting his work to the numerous pulp magazines still extant. Soon, he was selling to all sorts of markets; his work appeared in such magazines as *Detective Tales, G-Men Detective, Popular Sports, Thrilling Adventures, Giant Western, Popular Western, Sky Fighters, Thrilling Western,* and *Rio Kid Western.* By the early 1950s, L'Amour was selling to the better-paying slick magazines such as *Collier's* and the *Saturday Evening Post.*

L'Amour sold more stories to the Western pulps than to those of other genres, and it was on Westerns that he began to concentrate. His first published novel was a result of his work for one of the Western magazines. Better Publications introduced *Hopalong Cassidy's Western Magazine* in 1950, and it was L'Amour, writing as "Tex Burns," who did the lead novel for the first issue. The title of the novel was *Hopalong Cassidy and the Rustlers of West Fork* (1951). This was followed by another Tex Burns novel, *Hopalong Cassidy and the Trail to Seven Pines* (1951), in the second issue, after which the magazine folded.

The failure of the magazine did not affect the popularity of the Cassidy stories, however, and in 1951 Doubleday published both the Tex Burns novels in hardcover and followed them with two others written under the same pseudonym. It seems likely that in such contract writing L'Amour would have been somewhat artistically restricted. While he might have been allowed to introduce new characters, major characters (such as Cassidy) would have had to remain true to the originals as developed by their creator, Clarence E. Mulford, and as they had evolved over the years in the movies featuring Bill Boyd. It is even possible that L'Amour merely fleshed out Mulford's original story ideas rather than developing his own, although the basic plot of *Hopalong Cassidy and the Trail to Seven Pines,* which deals with an attempt by unscrupulous men to gain control of a ranch held legally by others, is one that L'Amour used frequently in his early work.

By the early 1950s many pulp magazines had ceased publication; some never recovered from the paper restrictions of World War II, and the new popularity of original novels in the paperback format drew readers and authors from the pulps. It was in the field of paperback originals that L'Amour was to find his huge success, beginning with the publication in 1953 of a novel that he had expanded from a *Collier's* short story. The book was *Hondo,* and it was published by Fawcett under its Gold Medal imprint. The book's cover featured a comment by John Wayne, "Best western I have ever read," and Wayne starred in the 1954 three-dimensional movie version of the book, along with Geraldine Page, Ward Bond, and James Arness. (Page was nominated for an Academy Award for her work in the film.)

In *Hondo* the main character, Hondo Lane, meets a young woman and her son who live alone on a small ranch in Indian territory. The conflict with the Indians is the main plot of the story, and the developing love of Lane and the woman forms the subplot. Hondo Lane is typical of the strong, tough, competent men who are fast with their fists or a gun and who fear nothing. L'Amour makes no apologies for writing of such men, even though some say that we live in the age of the antihero. "When the hero is gone," says L'Amour in the introduction to *Yondering,* "man himself will be gone, for the hero is our future, our destiny."

As a novel, *Hondo* shows all L'Amour's strengths. It is a swiftly told story with touches of sharp, effective violence. It demonstrates L'Amour's understanding (owing to careful research) of frontier life, the Indians, and nature. As in all L'Amour's books, the Indians are treated with respect. Hondo Lane is made into a man of complex emotions, gentle toward the woman and her son, savage toward his enemies, respectful of those deserving respect. Lane never kills unnecessarily, but he has no pity for those who through weakness or stupidity bring on their own deaths.

The theme of *Hondo,* and of most of the novels which L'Amour has written since, is best expressed by L'Amour himself in the title of his 1980 short-story collection, *The Strong Shall Live*. The frontier demanded strength of body and strength of character. Those who have both are the survivors in L'Amour's novels. Those who lack either are not likely to last long.

Following *Hondo,* L'Amour wrote a number of paperback novels for both Gold Medal and for Ace Books. Two of the Ace novels, *Showdown at Yellow Butte* and *Utah Blaine* (1954), were originally published under one of L'Amour's pulp pseudonyms, Jim Mayo, but both have since been published under the author's own name, the name with which all his subsequent books have been branded. Of the early novels, with the exception of *Hondo,* perhaps the most interesting is *Heller with a Gun* (1955, filmed as *Heller in Pink Tights,* 1960), in which King Mabry protects a wandering theatrical group from bitter weather, Indians, and outlaws. Also notable is *Sitka* (1957), published by Appleton in hardcover, a historical novel about the purchase of Alaska. In 1956 L'Amour married Katherine Elizabeth Adams; they have one child.

It was in 1960 that Bantam Books published *The Daybreakers,* the first novel in what was to become the Sackett Series. L'Amour now envisions a series of about forty books in which he will depict three hundred years of life on the frontier (1600-1900) through the interconnected lives of three fictional families: the Sacketts, the Chantrys, and the Talons. He had, by the end of 1980, spent most of his time with the Sacketts, who have appeared as major characters in sixteen novels and as minor characters in several others. (Ethan Sackett is one of the mentors of the title character in *Bendigo Shafter,* 1979; Tyrel Sackett shows up briefly to claim the body of his brother Joe, a murder victim in *Borden Chantry,* 1977.) L'Amour may have had none of this in mind when he wrote *The Daybreakers,* for the series has not been written or published in chronological order. In fact, after Bantam began numbering the books in the series, L'Amour wrote *The Warrior's Path* (1980), which at the time of its appearance had to be numbered 15; it is actually the third book in order of events.

Dust jacket

The Sackett family has two branches, the Clinch Mountain Sacketts (including Tell, Tyrel, and Orrin), and the Cumberland Gap Sacketts (including Flagan, Galloway, and Nolan). The former are hardworking, law-abiding citizens. The latter are prone to engage in escapades on the shady side of the law, although they share basically the same ideals as their more upright cousins. The wide appeal of the series (which formed the basis for a television mini-series in 1979) seems to be related to the feeling of solidarity shared by all the members of the Sackett clan. When one member gets into trouble of any kind, whether his wife has been murdered (*The Lonely Men,* 1969) or whether he is unable to deliver the cattle he has promised to a desperate town (*Lonely on the Mountain,* 1980), the others will come to his aid, no matter what the obstacles.

The adventures of the Talons and the Chantrys have not yet been chronicled as extensively as those of the Sacketts, but part of the early Talon history is revealed in *Rivers West* (1975), and Milo Sackett, who is the product of a Talon-Sackett marriage, appears in *The Man from the Broken Hills* (1975). The Chantry saga is developed in such books as *North to the Rails* (1971), *Over on the Dry Side* (1975), *Borden Chantry*, and *Fair Blows the Wind* (1978). Another character of whom L'Amour seems fond is Lance Kilkenny; and although there are no announced plans to include him in the family series, L'Amour has written three books about him. The first was published in 1954 and titled *Kilkenny*; it gives a number of hints about the title character's past, which was detailed in two novels, *The Rider of Lost Creek* (1976) and *Mountain Valley War* (1978), both based on earlier magazine stories.

Aside from the panorama that L'Amour is developing in his novels of intertwined family histories, books worthy of mention include *Catlow*, a story of two strong men on opposite sides of the law, notable for its good-humored, tall-tale quality; *Flint* (1960), a hardboiled story of concealed identity; *Down the Long Hills* (1968), which was awarded the Western Writers of America Award in 1969, about a seven-year-old boy and a three-year-old girl who must survive and find the boy's father after all the other members of their wagon train are massacred; *The Californios* (1974), a gentle fantasy; and *Bendigo Shafter*, one of L'Amour's longest works, in which he develops a wider gallery of frontier characters than usual. *Comstock Lode*, a 400-page historical novel, was published in hardcover and trade paperback editions by Bantam in February 1981.

Despite L'Amour's huge popular and commercial success, his books have received little critical attention. Often, they are not even reviewed by major publications. This is a disappointment to the author, who believes that Westerns should be taken more seriously by critics, but he says in the introduction to *Yondering* that he does not write for the critics. Instead, he tells his stories "for the people who do the work of the world, . . . for the people who do." These are the people who buy and read L'Amour's work, and his standing with them is likely to remain high, in spite of critical indifference.

Any critic who studies L'Amour, however, would no doubt notice his gift for first-person narration. Indeed, he claims to edit his stories so that they sound as if they were being spoken by a storyteller; but he also says that he does not revise his work, that his first draft is also his last draft, and that he can write a book in three weeks. It is this "one draft only" quality which has become noticeable in some of L'Amour's later work. Some books switch from first-person to third-person narration, not only in separate chapters but sometimes on the same page. This is particularly confusing in the ending of *Lonely on the Mountain*, where, on the last two pages, the narration slips from first to third person so suddenly that the reader is taken aback and must reread to find out what has caused him to be diverted. The drama of the book's climax is lessened considerably by this lapse.

Even Irwyn Applebaum, Western editor at Bantam Books, admits that L'Amour's work may be lacking in literary quality. He emphasizes, however, that a better storyteller is nowhere to be found. He might have added that in addition to his gift for straightforward yarn spinning, L'Amour grounds his work in solid research which gives it an authenticity that the works of other writers in the genre sometimes lack. L'Amour has read widely in diaries and histories of the periods about which he writes; he has also traveled extensively in the West. His accuracy about historical matters, combined with a strong narrative, certainly provides entertainment if not enlightenment.

Perhaps L'Amour himself should be allowed the last word on the importance of literary quality in the work of a popular writer. In *Bendigo Shafter*, the young hero is quite fond of reading and in fact has become a writer himself before the story's end. In one scene another man remarks on Bendigo's reading and tells him how lucky he is that he has been able to read good books and that later the West will be flooded with books of negligible worth. Bendigo replies, "I'd find something to learn in any of it . . . for even a man who writes trash has to think, to select, to try to write as well as he can." Louis L'Amour has thought about the American frontier, selected the details of its life and its people that seem significant to him, and written of it as well as he can. His work is far from being trash, and it has entertained millions. It is a good thing to have done.

—*Bill Crider*

References:

Brad Darrach, "Out of the Pages," *People* (9 June 1975): 64-66;

Arturo F. Gonzalez, "Louis L'Amour: Writing Tall in the Western Saddle," *Writer's Digest* (July 1980): 93-98;

John D. Nesbitt, "Louis L'Amour's Pseudonymous Works," *Paperback Quarterly* (Fall 1980): 3-6;

Susan Price-Root, "Driving Through the Old West, L'Amour's Novels Are Road Maps," *US* (25 July 1978): 28-29;

Fred C. Whitledge, ed., *The Hitching Rail*, no. 4, Louis L'Amour bibliography issue (February 1973).

Ross Lockridge, Jr.
(25 April 1914-6 March 1948)

BOOK: *Raintree County* (New York: Houghton Mifflin, 1948; London: MacDonald, 1949).

The tragedy occurred more than three decades ago, but the suicide of Ross Lockridge, Jr., continues to echo through informed discussions about contemporary American fiction. What, the initiated reader wonders, might the author of *Raintree County* have contributed not only to American literature but also to the genre of fiction following the stunning achievement of his only novel? Would he have weathered the curious combination of clamor and glory that swirls around the gifted young novelist with a major success, and then moved on to make his mark as a respected artist of an enduring canon? Or would he have gone the route of countless other successful beginners and given way to the hoopla—to the approval and applause, to the checks and contracts—and written a series of books that failed to measure up to the standards of the initial breakthrough? These queries are, of course, forever moot, for Lockridge killed himself two months after the publication of his masterpiece. Thus the question that subsumes all of the others about him is "why?"

To speculate about the answer is to consider that mass neurosis known as the American Dream. The story has a familiar ring to it: The dream consumes the dreamer, and the fall from grace occurs. What is puzzling about the history of *Raintree County* is that Lockridge's all-American hero, John Wickliff Shawnessy, survives with his epic unwritten but his dreams intact, while Lockridge found himself with a masterpiece completed but his dreams in disarray.

His association with his fictional dreamer is so close that speculation about the suicide unfortunately often overshadows discussions of the novel. Published on 5 January 1948 to reviews that John Leggett, Lockridge's "unauthorized" biographer, describes as having "a prominence and profusion that is no longer seen," *Raintree County* remains a curio of contemporary American literature. Its current status—admired but not read—is baffling when one considers that *Raintree County* had a widespread pre-publicity campaign, that it won the coveted MGM award of $150,000 for movie rights and the resulting publicity, that by March 1948 it was the number-one best-seller in the country, that Howard Mumford Jones saluted it in the *Saturday Review of Literature* as marking "the end of a long slump in American fiction," and that it occasionally appears on lists that name the best American novels since World War II. Yet, as of this writing, only five critical essays and two notes join Leggett's *Ross and Tom: Two American Tragedies* (1974, a study of Lockridge and novelist Tom Heggen) as the published scholarship on the novel.

Ross Lockridge

Perhaps Lockridge himself feared the silence after the cheering stopped. Born in Bloomington, Indiana, and growing up in the heart of the country, he first announced his ambition to write a great American novel while a student at Indiana University from 1931 to 1935. (He graduated summa cum laude and was elected to Phi Beta Kappa.) His father introduced him to family and local myths as well as to national history, and Lockridge became intrigued by the life of his grandfather, John Wesley Shockley. The echoes of the real Shockley in the fictional John Wickliff Shawnessy are even more apparent when one realizes that "Seth Twigs," the grandfather's newspaper pseudonym, is the same name Lockridge assigned to Shawnessy's backwoods "reporter." Apparently suspecting, like Shawnessy, that his family was illegitimately descended from Thomas Carlyle, Lockridge looked for continuity in local myths and formulated his idea of the quest for the golden raintree while researching the history of Robert Owen's nineteenth-century social experiment, New Harmony. But although he was a brilliant student, renowned for his memory and for his achievement of earning the highest grade average in the history of Indiana University, Lockridge feared the specter of failure.

It is not at all outrageous to suggest that the hot flash of success and the subsequent plunge to despair that Lockridge suffered were transposed to the character of John Wickliff Shawnessy in an attempt to exorcise the fear. But Shawnessy remains a man of the middle while his creator felt the scorch of the extremes. For despite attraction to the American Dream and confidence in his own creative genius, Lockridge strove to accomplish more for fear of achieving less. His obsession to be the best took concrete form when he decided to be an author.

According to Leggett, Lockridge's first plan to write a novel about his Indiana family went nowhere. Abandoning the project in 1938, he began an epic poem titled "The Dream of the Flesh of Iron." The unpublished poem is unavailable to the public, but it is the forerunner of *Raintree County* because the sensitive, Everyamerican hero seeks the meaning of his country in the guise of a beautiful woman. When the dream girl eludes the dreamer, he discovers that the quest alone has meaning. From the little that is known about this unpublished epic poem, two points are significant. First, by 1940, Lockridge had completed the germ of the unconsummated love that adds such poignancy and despair to *Raintree County*, the story of what would become Shawnessy's courtship of Nell Gaither. More important, it seems, Lockridge realized that the American dreamer always fails in his quest. Few would insist that he foresaw personal disillusionment at this point in his life, but for the purposes of his writing he understood how the glorious dreams and deeds that he gave his fictional counterpart would be forever unfulfilled. The contrast between Lockridge's own confidence and the mood of defeat in the poem is not only startling but also prophetic when one has the advantage of hindsight.

By December 1940, Lockridge, then a graduate student at Harvard, had completed 400 typed pages of "The Dream of the Flesh of Iron." Unapologetic about his aspirations, he submitted the epic to Houghton Mifflin in February 1941. It was promptly rejected. Shelving the typescript with his confidence still intact, he immediately began writing the novel that would earn him wealth and fame. The ordeal of composition took six years.

Unfortunately, the task devoured his strength. Attracted to the structure of James Joyce's *Ulysses*, the lyricism of Thomas Wolfe's *Look Homeward, Angel*, Thomas Mann's descriptions of a shattered culture, and the unusual transitions between historical moments in D. W. Griffith's *Intolerance* and Orson Welles's *Citizen Kane*, Lockridge learned how to set his novel during a single day (4 July 1892) and still unite dream sequences and the literal histories of nineteenth-century America, Indiana, and the Shockley family. He confidently stated his goal: to write "the first real representation of the American culture in fiction." Significantly, John Wickliff Shawnessy has the same plan. Earning his living by teaching at Simmons College (1941-1945) in Boston, Lockridge once scrapped a 2,000-page rough draft and began anew. The final draft, which was submitted to Houghton Mifflin as "The Riddle of Raintree County" on 24 April 1946, contained 600,000 words, weighed twenty pounds, and took his wife eighteen months to type.

Although he seemed entirely certain the novel would be the masterpiece many critics have judged it to be, the tension between confidence and fear of failure apparently began to stretch to unbearable lengths following the submission to Houghton Mifflin. Lockridge entered a period of unsettling highs and lows that ended with his suicide. Outwardly, he exuded confidence. Not only did he reject an offer to serialize parts of the novel in *Ladies Home Journal* because he wanted *Raintree County* to be published in one piece, but he also took the extraordinary step of flooding the Houghton Mifflin offices with letters of advice about how to publicize the book. Leggett notes that he even wrote to editor Dorothy Hillyer, "It will be talked about, written about, and read, read, read!"

The truth is that his judgment was correct. The irony is that behind the show of confidence lurked the shadow of failure that had nagged him all along. Too much of his spirit had gone into *Raintree County*, and he found that he could neither let it go without directing the entire publication process nor smooth the rough edges without giving rein to his doubts. His revisions became compulsive. Awaiting publication, he tried and failed to begin a new novel. His emotional difficulties were diagnosed as paranoia, and he endured a series of shock treatments. Perhaps the saddest sign of his breakdown was the list of rules he drew up in the hope of regaining his balance and discipline. Leggett reports that the first rule was to forget *Raintree County*: "I should exclude it from my thoughts or, if I think of it at all, simply pick it up and read one of the optimistic 'sweet' parts." But nothing worked. The novel had exhausted him. On 6 March 1948, two months after the publication of his great book, Ross Lockridge, Jr., drove his new Kaiser into the garage, locked the door, and switched on the engine to die.

Why? No one knows the answer, but Leggett has a point when he speculates that Lockridge was plagued by the "bitch goddess" of success to which American authors seem peculiarly vulnerable. Another possible answer is the suggestion that Lockridge's faith in his novel amounted to an idealism that could not withstand the impact of the practical decisions to revise the manuscript. But the most acceptable answer may come from the close relationship between Lockridge and Shawnessy in which the author recognized in his fictional hero a similar spirit-draining dilemma: well-founded confidence challenged by unexpected doubt.

John Wickliff Shawnessy never considers suicide to be the way out of the dilemma; indeed, at the end of this long novel (1,066 published pages), he returns home with his dreams still beckoning, having parried a series of verbal thrusts from his attractive yet cynical alter ego, Jerusalem Webster Stiles. But now in his fifties, he has not completed the glorious epic with which he has been tinkering for thirty years, his tale "of a man's days on the breast of the land," and the reader knows he never will. The similarity between author and character spotlights the irony, and Lockridge undoubtedly saw his tragedy in these lines from the end of *Raintree County*: "Make way, make way for the Hero of Raintree County! His victory is not in consummations but in quests!" Both men stop short of the laurel crown, but Shawnessy stumbles homeward with his "great fair dream" still intact. Now, more than three decades after the suicide, one wonders if in consummating his own dream Lockridge consumed himself. The quest was all.

Even the reviews of *Raintree County* exacerbated Lockridge's sense of success tainted by failure. Ecstatic praise from such commentators as Howard Mumford Jones, James Hilton, and Charles Lee was tempered by attacks from M. P. Corcoran and Hamilton Basso. Published while Lockridge was near mental collapse, the negative reviews, especially those that accused him of moral laxity and "rank obscenity," exaggerated his own doubts. He was so worried, for example, about his parents' reactions to the descriptions of Nell's nakedness and Susanna's scarred breasts that he feared the book's appearance in Bloomington.

The point is that Lockridge suffered puritan pangs of guilt and that he gave Shawnessy the same moral twinges. Apparently, Shawnessy is the man Lockridge wished to be, the passionate artist who dreams a masterpiece but never completes the task. But that predicament would also be intolerable, for Lockridge realized that his hero's unfinished epic has the taint of failure. Trapped between consummation and quest, between a flawed creation and the obsession to create, both men missed the goal. The primary difference is that Shawnessy holds the golden ideal in sight because his guilt can be absorbed in the privacy of his lyrical dreams. Lockridge could not do the same once he delivered his typescript to the publisher, for his visions became public when he attributed them to his fictional hero.

No better illustration can be found than the dust jacket and map that Lockridge drew for the novel. Glanced at hastily, the jacket shows the shape of the county. Looked at a second time, the jacket outlines a reclining nude female with hills for breasts and a tributary of the Shawmucky River flowing between

Dust jacket

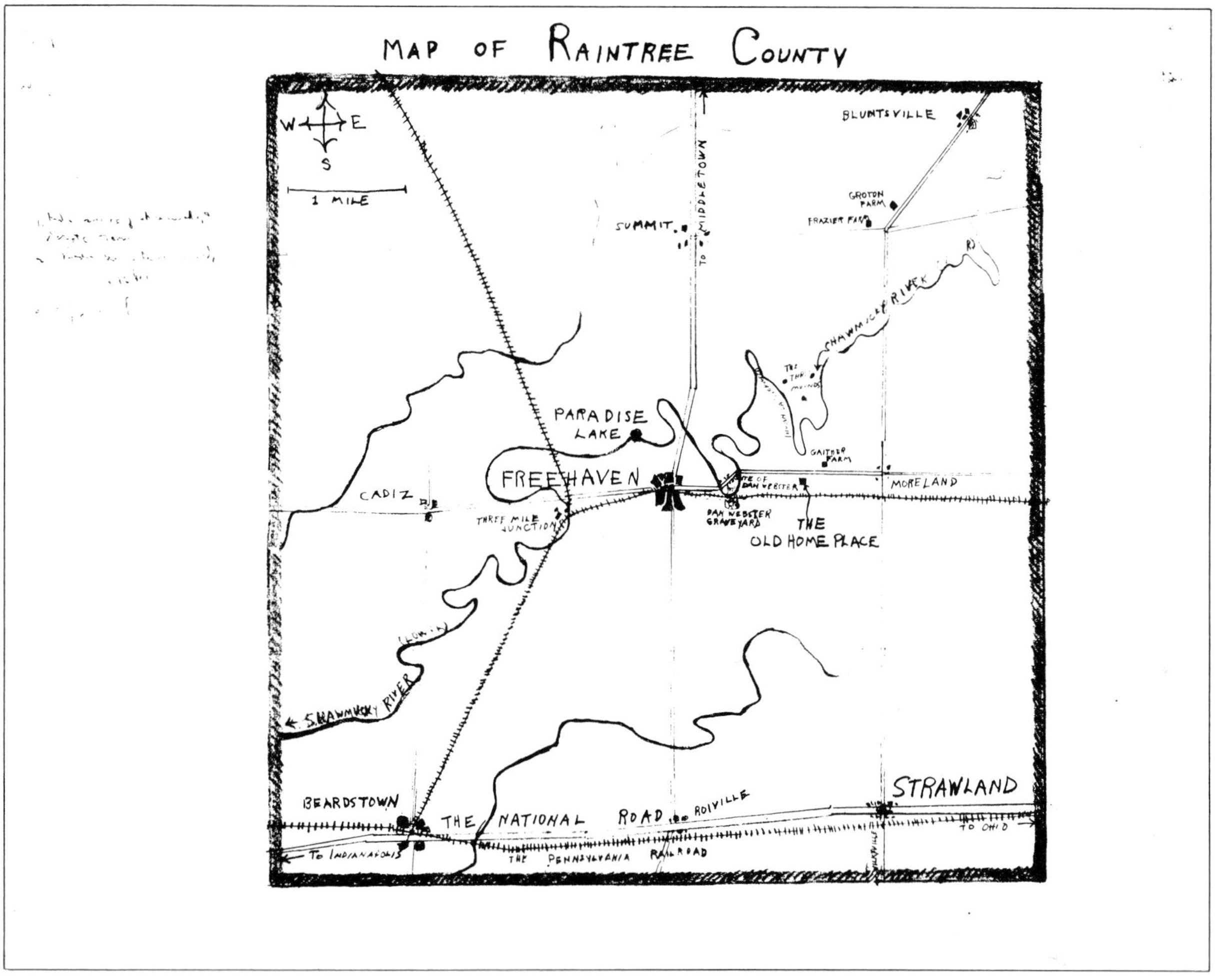

Map of Raintree County, early version

her legs to the genitals. Just as symbolic is the map of the county that Lockridge placed opposite the title page. The Shawmucky, the river of life, flows toward both Lake Paradise and the Great Swamp, and the feminine curves near the townships of Mount Pleasant and Summit point toward the town of Climax. Reading with the dust jacket and map in mind, one soon realizes that John Shawnessy's pursuit of the ideal America is wrapped up in the temptations of sexual intercourse. Apprehensive about moral censure, Lockridge nevertheless explicitly identifies his hero's quest with the map: "He was certain that in the pattern of its lines and letters this map contained the answer to the old conundrum of his life in Raintree County. . . . With a feeling suspended between erotic hunger and intellectual curiosity, he looked for the young woman."

Lockridge uses the sexual allusions consciously when he suggests that Shawnessy associates the glory of America as a garden of Eden with the mysteries of sexuality: "The two were always colliding with each other as Mr. Shawnessy went his ritual way through conversations and thorough-fares, and mr. shawnessy carried on his eternal vagabondage through a vast reserve of memories and dreams. . . . It was clearly the whim of mr. shawnessy to prepare a naked woman on the stone slab in the Post Office, but it was Mr. Shawnessy who timidly asked for a newspaper, trying his best to adapt himself and his puritan conscience to the bizarre world of his twin."

Unlike his creator, however, Shawnessy does not question his union of sexuality and idealism to the point of self-doubt. He feels guilty, for example, when he is stunned while watching Nell Gaither swim nude in the Shawmucky, but he easily merges his guilt with his idealization of her as a goddess. A similar guilt looms when he romps with Southern belle Susanna Drake beside the same river, but even though her beautiful, scar-marred breasts signal both her own dissolution and that of America in the

Civil War, he neutralizes the guilt by marrying her. Later, he dodges an invitation from actress Laura Golden to enter her secret bedroom. And finally, now a middle-aged husband to someone other than Nell or Susanna, he shrinks from the public while turning the pages of a pirated history of Raintree County in search of nude drawings. The implications are shattering to the dreamer: his vision of the goddess recedes the older he gets or the faster he pursues it. Married to a good but hardly awe-inspiring woman half his age, John Wickliff Shawnessy discovers that he is left with not Nell's naked beauty to shape his dream but only the rumor of nude drawings to fire his curiosity.

Professor Jerusalem Webster Stiles nevertheless hints that John Wickliff Shawnessy successfully finds his heritage and his future in the sexually suggestive map, and that thus Shawnessy fulfills his destiny as both creator and preserver of the American Dream. As a final gesture of homage and farewell, the professor traces in smoke the letters *JWS* which, when swirled by the wind, take the shape of the Shawmucky River on the map. Ross Lockridge yearned for the same identification with America, but one continues to wonder about the motive he assigns to the professor's gesture. Possessing the same intitials, the professor is clearly the dark side of Shawnessy's questing innocence, a cynical counterbalance to the believer in never-ending possibilities and golden days. Shawnessy may need Stiles because the mentor forces the pupil to defend his faith in the quest, but Stiles, for all his wit and charm, is nevertheless associated with the devil. Journalist, urban, and promiscuous where Shawnessy is poet, rural, and monogamous, Stiles believes as fervently in his cynicism as Shawnessy does in his dreams.

The professor's gesture may thus be suspect, as Lockridge no doubt knew. Showing his dexterity by carving the initials *JWS* backward in the smoke so that they are easily identified by his pupil, Stiles may indeed be celebrating the battered but still searching hero. But recalling that *JWS* are also the professor's initials, one wonders if Stiles is playing his final cynical trump, revealing to Shawnessy that the hero's unfinished epic and unfulfilled quest are noble but useless relics of an America long past, worth no more in the post-Civil War era than initials fading away in the darkness and the gloom.

Lockridge, of course, created these negative implications, and he knew readers would understand that Shawnessy's dreams are tarnished by incompleteness. Pushing himself for six years to fashion an ideal American hero who epitomizes his own aspirations for the nation, he could not fail to note the negative side of his own hopefulness when the hero stops short of the goal. The ironic dilemma is that John Wickliff Shawnessy must leave forever incomplete the grand myth of the nation because the country itself never fulfills its promise. Shaping his lyricism in the relative innocence of antebellum America, he discovers that his vision no longer speaks to the realities of slavery, war, and urban squalor. The sickening purge of the national conscience by the bloodshed of the Civil War sullies both the dreamer and his dream. Thus Shawnessy's inability to complete his epic suggests America's failure to meet its potential. When Shawnessy turns from Laura Golden and the city to return home to Indiana and the land, he finds, to his sorrow and Lockridge's, not Nell beside the river but trains upon the earth.

Yet to say that Shawnessy must leave his myth incomplete is not to dismiss the suggestion that he is also culpable, as Lockridge undoubtedly realized. Irony and failure dog his life as much as love and promise glorify it. The reader understands, even if Shawnessy does not, that he makes the wrong choice time after time. When a young man, for example, he refuses to trek down the Great National Road to the alluring West, despite the beckoning of its call and the symbolism of its presence through the center of the county. He never consummates his love for Nell, the personification of America's lovely potential, giving himself instead to the scarred Susanna, to the still beautiful but grievously flawed nation. Worse, when Susanna collapses in madness with the onslaught of fratricide and war, Shawnessy enlists in the Union army and thus loses his second chance with Nell. Finally, after the war, he marries a woman half his age and turns his back on the city where the new, albeit less glorious, America will have to build its future out of the horror of blood and smoke. No one who cares about America's perpetual falls from grace can fail to feel the pathos of these questions in the novel: "Was this the Union they had hammered out ringing on the forge of Battle? Was this the Raintree County of which Johnny Shawnessy had intended to become the hero?" The answer, unfortunately, for both Shawnessy and Lockridge is yes and no: yes, because disastrous choices blurred the vision and ruined the country; no, because for many Americans the dream will never die. Shawnessy can accept the paradox; Lockridge could not.

John Wickliff Shawnessy fails because he refuses to change with his country. Yet his heroism lies in his refusal, for he sings not of consummation but of quest. If Shawnessy repudiates the professor's cynicism; if, even in the defeats of middle age, he insists on shaping the legend of his life "by a myth of homecoming and a myth of resurrection," Lockridge was not as sure. Wanting to believe as he voiced his vision, he could not believe when he completed his novel. Too many of his doubts surfaced in his fictional hero, and too much of his confidence seeped away when realities did not square with dreams. If one censures John Shawnessy even as one praises him, one knows that Lockridge deserves the same.

Lockridge's suicide was a stunning blow to American literature. The pathos is that he apparently tried but failed to exorcise during the writing of *Raintree County* the threats to his once pervasive confidence. Unable to finish his epic, John Shawnessy finds a measure of success—he refuses to abandon his dream. Ross Lockridge was not as lucky. He suspected that in completing his masterpiece he had compromised his vision. One can only read *Raintree County* and regret the loss of what his continued presence and writing might have offered to the spiritual life of the nation—a sense of creation, a story, an ever expanding hope.

—*Donald J. Greiner*

References:

Joseph L. Blotner, "*Raintree County* Revisited," *Western Humanities Review*, 10 (Winter 1956): 57-64;

Delia Clarke, "*Raintree County*: Psychological, Symbolism, Archetype, and Myth," *Thoth*, 11 (Fall 1970): 31-39;

Lawrence J. Dessner, "Value in Popular Fiction: The Case of *Raintree County*," *Junction*, 1, no. 3 (1973): 147-152;

Donald J. Greiner, "Ross Lockridge and the Tragedy of *Raintree County*," *Critique: Studies in Modern Fiction*, 20 (April 1979): 51-63;

Howard Mumford Jones, Review of *Raintree County*, *Saturday Review of Literature*, 31 (3 January 1948): 9;

John Leggett, *Ross and Tom: Two American Tragedies* (New York: Simon & Schuster, 1974);

Boyd Litzinger, "Mythmaking in America: 'The Great Stone Face' and *Raintree County*, " *Tennessee Studies in Literature*, 8 (1963): 81-84;

Leonard Lutwack, "*Raintree County* and the Epicising Poet in American Fiction," *Ball State University Forum*, 13 (Winter 1972): 14-28;

Gerald C. Nemanic, "Ross Lockridge, *Raintree County*, and the Epic of Iron," *MidAmerica*, 2 (1975): 35-46.

Phillip Lopate

(16 November 1943-)

BOOKS: *In Coyoacan* (New York: Swollen Magpie Press, 1971);

The Eyes Don't Always Want to Stay Open: Poems and a Japanese Tale (New York: Sun, 1972);

Being With Children (Garden City: Doubleday, 1975);

The Daily Round: New Poems (New York: Sun, 1976);

Confessions of Summer (Garden City: Doubleday, 1979);

Bachelorhood (Boston: Little, Brown, forthcoming 1981).

Phillip Lopate is concerned primarily with the psychology of the human personality and the mental process through which people handle emotional pain. He is particularly adept at offering well-observed descriptions of persons in poignant situations. Lopate has experimented with a wide range of genres, including poetry, the novel, the short story, and the essay, and he has been prominently published, though he has not garnered wide attention outside New York City.

Lopate was born and raised in New York City in a lower middle-class family. His father, Albert, was an "auto-didactic intellectual" whose love of books created respect for a reflective approach to life. His mother, Frances, fostered his interest in music and psychology. Lopate's attraction to literature appeared early, as he edited his high school literary magazine, *Caravan*, during his senior year at Eastern District High in Brooklyn. Although he began work at Columbia University in a prelaw program, he eventually majored in English and minored in art history, taking a B.A. in 1964. In his senior year, he edited the *Columbia Review* and was president of the Jazz Club and the Filmmakers of Columbia. During his last year at Columbia, he married Carol

Bergman, who encouraged him to write full time. They used money from wedding presents to finance a year in Morocco and Spain—primarily Nerja and Madrid—where he began work on a novel, "Best Friends," that was never published. He and his wife were divorced in 1969.

Beginning in 1968 Lopate supported himself by teaching creative writing in the public schools. In 1971 he created and supervised the Arts Team Project at P.S. 75 in Manhattan under the auspices of the Teachers and Writers Collaborative, of which he is a board member. In this program, which provided material for his description of "P.S. 90" in *Being With Children* (1975), he has worked with grade-school children on creative efforts in such media as poetry, film, and plays; the program he supervised touched on all forms of creativity, including art, music, dance, film, video, theater, radio, and writing. He completed a Ph.D. in English education in 1979 at Union Graduate School and, after ten years with the Poets-In-The-School Program, left New York City to join the writing program in the English department at the University of Houston as an associate professor.

Lopate has won a variety of awards, including the Christopher Medal (1975) for *Being With Children*, a New York Creative Artists' Public Service grant (1977), an NEA Literary Fellowship (1978-1979), and the Distinguished Service Award from the Educational Press Association (1980) for the Best Educational Feature. His poetry has been published or reprinted in more than 100 journals and his work has frequently been anthologized. He has directed a film, *The Casserole Dish*, with Rudy Burckhardt, acted in the plays *The Bingo* and *Philoctetes*, and danced with the Good Dance Company.

Lopate says he finds childhood to be an "endless source of interest" for both his writing and teaching, noting that "certain sufferings, a certain sense of humiliation at times forced me to wake up and to understand my environment. . . . I think that I was jarred from a kind of revery early on, because I tended to be as a child somewhat of a daydreamer. It was these jarring experiences that really woke me up and gave me a self."

Writers who have influenced him most are Dostoevski, Céline, Chekhov, Cesare Pavese, Lionel Trilling, Rilke, Flaubert, Charles Lamb, Randall Jarrell, and Charles Reznikoff. "What interests me," he has said, "are the personality problems, largesses, layers of rationalization, class background, speech patterns, sexual tropisms that make up a single person. . . . I don't consider myself an experimentalist . . . but a very traditional writer with a psychological bent. . . . I hate this modern emphasis on bodiless, neutral narrators, Inferno surrealism, stripped-bare syntax masquerading as punctilious craftsmanship, and the infuriatingly overused present indicative mode. . . . I have to go back to what I love, to what first drew me to novels and prose: 1) that it gave you a world; 2) that it did that in the voice of a lively, worldly person you wanted to know."

In Coyoacan (1971), Lopate's first book, is a family saga novella about a German immigrant family that runs a small glassmaking business in Mexico between the 1930s and 1968, the year of the Mexican University student riots. Lopate traces the family history from Senor Kalcus, an exile, to his great-grandchildren but characterizes only the middle two generations in depth: he concentrates on Lily, the Kalcus daughter who takes over the operation of the business; her husband, Hermann Rauss; and their children, Claire and Geraldo. This novella details life in a traditional, respectable bourgeois family that is proud of its simple accomplishments but torn by the pressures of modern life and the conflict between modern values and Latin family traditions.

Lopate's deliberately simple style contributes to a quaint, engaging tone that evokes a sense of Mexican life and values. The pace is slow and quiet. This is an experimental work in which Lopate, influenced by Gertrude Stein's "singsong childlike narrator" in *Three Lives*, uses a narrator who "hinted at and then undercut" the "pathological tendencies . . . of this family which used Geraldo as a scapegoat, with his complete complicity." Lopate's narrator was repeatedly "going up to this family's dynamics and then shying away, out of 'niceness' or blindness or social smoothing over." Lopate was also "interested in using a tricky sense of scale, telling a family saga a la *Buddenbrooks* in 60-odd pages, and 'wasting' two of those pages on a . . . character who will never appear again. It was meant to mimic the way stories are told within a family circle: the 'focus' always deviates in such situations."

Lopate's experiment in plotting and characterization caused him to relate events involving a panoply of minor, shadowy characters who engage the reader's attention momentarily but who are not significant in the main story line. Likewise with the characterization, some of the detail about Lily, Hermann, Claire, and Geraldo is effective; at other times, though, characters are introduced and dropped with abandon or they are undeveloped.

Phillip Lopate

In Coyoacan is an interesting experiment; ultimately, though, problems with control over the ironic distance mar the work. In this novella, Lopate's nascent ability to handle tone and character is visible, as are his sensitivity and perceptive insights. The experimental plotting, however, does not indicate the potential that he will demonstrate in *Confessions of Summer* (1979) to shape a sharply focused narrative sequence.

The Eyes Don't Always Want to Stay Open (1972), Lopate's first collection of poetry, is a much more controlled work than *In Coyoacan*, containing five notable poems and a Japanese fairy tale in prose. Lopate does not use rhyme and is not especially concerned with form. This book consists mostly of psychological poetry—occasional arresting narrative sequences and lyrical descriptions of people and situations.

In the first poem, "Snowball Journal," Lopate offers a richly detailed description of how a couple vacationing in Vermont interact. "In the Time" creates haunting, almost tormenting temporal images. "1949" (reprinted as "Home Run Thighs") vividly evokes the aura of movie starlets in another era. "Split Ends" uses graphic detail from daily life, some a bit repulsive, some evoking painful childhood moments, to indicate that valuable love relationships must set aside romantic ideals in order to provide what individuals really need. The prose fairy tale, "How the Cloudy Lake Was Formed," provides an example of Lopate's ability to evoke significantly different moods. "Satin Doll," an elegy for George Soto (one of Lopate's students who "fell off a roof in East Harlem") reveals the two voices in Lopate's poetry to which Rochelle Ratner refers when she says: "He speaks of love with all honesty, lyricism, even eroticism. But then there always have to be the other poems . . . to cover up . . . confirm his own self image. . . . Perhaps it's the combination of two voices, often within the same poem, that make his work really exciting." The poem concerns Lopate's sense of loss at George's death and his questions about why such an event took place; equally significant, though, is his concentration on the interrelation between the living and the dead. The combination of toughness and sensitivity stands out most graphically when Lopate writes, in the guise of a macho street kid:

> dead people are   disgusting
> they just want attention
> . . . .
> but mostly dead people are unreal
> . . . .
> jive antique wax works with no sweat
> no hearts no blackheads no favorite groups no
> erections.

Lopate juxtaposes this crude perspective with his own anguish abut the awful bruise on George's face and about his own feelings—reluctant intimacy with the dead:

> My guts are churning
> you're trying to make me feel bad
> but I won't fall for that
> I'll look away
> I keep looking
> this shock is like perfume.

Through this combination of voices Lopate is able to draw close to the problems and the pain of slum kids by maintaining some emotional perspective through the "tough" voice.

When *Being With Children* was published in 1975, Lopate achieved national prominence in education circles (125 reviews and more than four dozen interviews), but the book is not strictly about education. An account of Lopate's experience with the Poets-In-The-School Program in New York City, the book has five sections: a general description of who Lopate is and why the Teachers and Writers Collaborative was established; detail on how Lopate dealt with the adults who were involved in the program directly or indirectly; a narrative account of Lopate's efforts to stage *West Side Story*; seven ideas (literary lesson plans) for stimulating the urge to write; and diverse comments on relations between teachers and their students. Lopate's topic, children and the poet's relation to them, influenced many educators because the book presents sensible suggestions about how to inspire young writers, but Lopate refers to it as a "disguised novel." In fact, the dominant tone and the formal structure derive from the sensibility of a poet, with scholarly elements arising in only a few instances (for example, "Balkanization of Children's Writing").

The tone in *Being With Children* becomes literary because of three elements: Lopate repeatedly uses narrative to make his point; he inserts personal comments, replete with a healthy willingness to sing his own praises and to confess his limitations ("I was curious to see how they would solve the problem of filmed flying in technical terms. Personally, I had no idea how to do it"); and he creates a narrative voice that reveals his own character. The most salient of these literary elements—narrative—surfaces in the form of Lopate's presentation: he frequently tells stories, in many forms, in order to make the impression he desires. He opens the book with a "tour" of the school rather than a factual description of P.S. 90. He relates a "Cautionary Tale" about the quest for foundation support. He shares his diaries with the readers. He draws portraits of students in order to elicit indirect lessons about teaching creative writing, but in doing so he renders strikingly incisive character sketches. Most tellingly, one fourth of the book is devoted to "The Big Show," a tale about Lopate's experiences in staging *West Side Story*. If in the process of reading "The Big Show" a teacher learns a great deal about how to relate to children, this effect is incidental to the "drama" of staging a grade-school theatrical production. A vignette involving Gene, one of his young actors, illustrates the point. The first afternoon performance had already taken place; Lopate and cast were frantically preparing for the more important evening performance (parents would be present) when the following exchange took place: " 'Leave those curtains alone!' I shouted.

"Gene pulled me over to a quiet corner backstage.

" 'Come 'ere; I want to talk to you.'

" 'What is it?' I bent down to Gene. He came no higher than my stomach.

" 'I want to ask you something.'

" 'Ask me,' I said tiredly.

" 'I'll do anything you say. I'll sing loud, I'll face the audience, but we've got to make a deal.'

" 'What's the deal?' He seemed to be stalling before saying it, and I was in no mood to play guessing games. 'Come on, tell me.'

" 'Just cool down! You're way too nervous.'

" 'Right.' I put my arm around him. I laughed. I kissed him. He was taking care of me. The kid saw right through me and he understood me and he was giving me his protection. It made me secure as nothing else could have." Such scenes are as literary as they are "educational."

The critical response to this book in education circles was so positive that Lopate found himself in danger of becoming an "education expert," a label he resists because he thinks of himself primarily as an artist. Praising Lopate's "rare ability to accept reality as a starting point for his work," Anne Martin in the *Harvard Education Review* treated the book primarily as an educator's handbook, but she alluded to the literary/psychological elements when she wrote: "On a much deeper level it is a thoughtful, touchingly honest examination of . . . the relationships between people who struggle constantly to reach one another in spite of all obstacles to communication." Myra Cohen Livingston argued in *Psychology Today* that this is a book "only a poet, who believes feeling is at the heart of poetry, could write." Referring to *Being With Children* as a "very special and important book," Vivian Gornick noted in the *New York Times Book Review* that "the heart of the book is Lopate himself: Lopate and his kids." She also added that through this work "the story of P.S. 90" unfolds. *Library Journal* commented that this book is "beautifully written, compassionate yet unsentimental. . . . The essential virtue, however, is reading a poet who writes movingly of what it's truly like to be with children."

The poetry in Lopate's next book, *The Daily Round* (1976), like that in *The Eyes Don't Always Want to Stay Open*, consists primarily of narratives and tightly controlled images of food, people, or situations. *The Daily Round* is a stronger collection because the narratives are more compelling, the images sharper, the insights more arresting, and the intensity more sustained. It contains four topical sections: "Not Sadness, Which Is Always There"; "Childhood, Boyhood, Youth"; "The Singles"; and "Meditations." Six of the poems in this collection merit individual attention.

"Indigestible," the first poem, effectively combines strong narrative and psychological insight about the distance between a man on the verge of insanity who is described as "pre-suicidal" and other people. This man wishes to set himself apart from the ordinary person because of the intensity with which he experiences life's pain. Lopate intends to be both sympathetic and ironic about this man's sense that he is more "alive" than others.

On the surface, "Numbness," an example of Lopate's growing ability to sustain a lyrical moment, concerns his problem of writing poetry when he is unenthusiastic. A more fundamental problem emerges when he examines two elements of his personality, asking, "Is the neutral state a cover for unhappiness / Or do I make myself impatient and unhappy / To avoid my basic nature, which is passive and low-key?" This poem is striking because its topic transcends a modern preoccupation with literature about ordinary people and ordinary lives to ask whether poets can create effective poetry out of ordinary emotions, without "professional liveliness." The work is also engaging because of Lopate's disarming willingness to indicate that his basic nature may not fit the ideal of the emotionally charged artistic personality.

In "Film Noir" Lopate conveys in only forty-five lines a taut story of murderous lovers and indicates character, background, and the nature of the love relationships in the story. In "It's Painful Getting Letters," Lopate discusses how difficult it is for the stronger party in a lopsided relationship to establish a comfortable distance from his correspondent, as mail arrives "from those / you love only a little, and who / think you're their best friend." Lopate precisely evokes the discomfort and guilt in such relationships as the disparity between friends grows:

> They write you four page laments and you
> return one, three months later
> full of hasty regrets.
> You would love to love them completely
> . . . .
> but as you watch them flounder
> in blandness and self-pity
> . . . .
> you can't escape the thought that they can do
> nothing for you.

"Allende" is a political poem that presents an objection to the Marxist leader's decision to take his own life. Lopate successfully avoids the quandary surrounding most "socialist realism"—the deadening abstraction—by directing a dramatic, narrative monologue to the dead Allende. The conversational flavor of the poem—direct and therefore powerful—hits the reader in the opening lines and remains as Lopate with his "street-wise" voice cuts through the usual cant after a death: "In 200 years they won't remember me, Salvador / And they won't remember you, so let's skip the part about / He will live with us forever." The disagreement with Allende's decision goes beyond philosophical issues to an emotional level that, once again, causes this political poem to work as art: Lopate experiences despair about the future, as he admits reluctantly that "it looks as if they have got us by the balls / These faces in the street, how can they take power / How can they rule?"

"The Truth That Hurts," an autobiographical poem, is the most outstanding work in *The Daily Round.* Bits and pieces of detail from Lopate's life lead into highly perceptive comments about his own character as he relates to those he loves and attempts to create healthy defense mechanisms and, at the same time, desirable intimacy with others. This is confessional poetry at its best because it avoids becoming mired in problems that are of interest to no one other than the poet and assumes a requisite measure of universality. In this poem, as so often, narrative serves Lopate well. A former girl friend slices through the lyrical narrator's elaborate defense mechanism to observe that despite his intense desire for love and adoration, he is incapable of reciprocating: "Oh—you're incredibly supportive / But that supportiveness is the expression / Of your guilt for not being able to love them." As the bright, defense-bound interlocutor twists deftly to avoid being skewered by this woman's rapier, she pursues him relentlessly about the distance he maintains between himself and others, until the climax, after he has admitted to being defensive, at which point she scores her last hit: "My final point is that you qualify everything! / Your favorite way of countering criticism / Is to say: 'Well to some extent yes, not always.' / That's how you deaden the truth that hurts." Concerning the power of this poem, Lopate has noted: "I don't want to hurt people . . . but I'm interested in bringing them to that moment of cringing slightly, where they recognize themselves. I want that shock of recognition to occur."

The Daily Round has received mostly positive response from reviewers. Hayden Carruth in the *New York Times Book Review* said that the poems passed the acid test: "They work. They move us." Stephen Vincent in the *San Francisco Review of Books* worried about Lopate's detached intelligence but praised his wit, his willingness to lay out his experiences before the reader, and his "almost demonic love of story," leading Vincent to conclude that this "is a terribly important book." *Library Journal* was also positive about the poems: "All, in their various approaches, are representative of the best in poetry."

Confessions of Summer, Lopate's first full-length published novel, depicts a trio of characters involved in a tormenting love triangle: Eric, the narrator; Jack, his best friend for the past ten years; and Marie, a troubled, beautiful woman who loves both men. Lopate is more interested in why these individuals become embroiled in the triangle and how they handle their pain than in the details of their love affairs. The opening gambit between Eric Eisner and Jack Bogarde, bright Columbia University graduates in their twenties, sets an intellectual atmosphere in which the two friends pursue a discussion of euthanasia, with Jack needling Eric about not accounting for feelings and actual experience with such controversial issues. The discussion of openly having two lovers begins once Eric falls in love with Marie. Eric is unable to foresee the problems until they inundate him and he cannot deal with the issue on an emotional level, making the mistake of believing that if he can accept the idea of sharing Marie, he must be able to cope with it emotionally. Eric and Jack exchange the intellectual arguments for an "open" relationship overtly, so that initially *Confessions of Summer* appears to advocate a liberal attitude toward love and sexual relations. Eventually, though, Lopate argues against that philosophy when Eric, having decided to renounce his love for Marie, repeatedly returns to her and finds himself "caught in the destructive power of a love stronger than myself." Lopate suggests that this novel "shows people projecting a greater flexibility intellectually than they have emotionally, so that intellectually they are always aware that they are behaving somewhat immaturely or that they should be doing something else, but they just can't transfer what they know, cognitively, into action."

Lopate's investigation of why "open" relationships almost always fail leads him to the twin problems of guilt and taboos. From the outset, Eric assumes that he should not become involved with Marie if he wishes to retain his friendship with Jack,

I.

It was a period of my life I am not particularly proud of. It happened before the era of accomplishment. I had not yet become the hero of my life, nor was I even its villain. I was twenty-six, a graduate of a prestige college, believing that I was meant to lead and not take orders--a belief which in no way was shared by those who employed me. Powerlessness gave life a peculiarly iodized taste, like mercurochrome: it seemed to me that before I could enjoy to the full a sunset, a love affair, drunken nights, the so-called pleasures of youth, I would have to get this taste of powerlessness out of my mouth.

I remember it was the first of July when I returned to New York, to the city where I had grown up, after two years of trying to leave it.

I remember ~~I came back to New York in~~ it being July, because it was a time when everyone with any sense was ~~escaping.~~ leaving. The air was close and listless and white. A hot wind blew into my mouth. Sweat-soaked travellers waiting by the taxi stand at the airline terminal gulped for oxygen.

I relaxed in the back seat of the cab, with my bags beside me. I had adjusted already. One look at the gunmetal bridges and the warehouses and factories brought me back; I knew I was returning to myself. It was a landscape as convincing and stoically familiar as sadness itself.

Confessions of Summer, *revised typescript*

but he capitulates to his emotions anyway. As he does so, he experiences so much guilt that he never fully enjoys his experience with Marie; instead it becomes a sweet torture. Lopate does not insist that guilt in such situations is inevitable, but he notes that he "is a great respecter of taboos and things like that. Basically the [book's] position . . . is that taboos have their place. . . . Maybe not everybody is interested in transcendence."

The process through which Eric learns about the legitimacy of taboos leads, in turn, to a discovery of the disparity between intellectual and emotional maturity as Eric learns that growth is painfully, frustratingly slow. Lopate suggests that "people can't talk about themselves definitively when they are thirty years old. . . . We're in a kind of culture where people assume that they can leap to maturity. Actually you get into a pattern when you have to repeat the same mistake a hundred times." Lopate's concern with the slowness of the learning process is a key to understanding the second and third sections of the book. Halfway through the novel, Eric realizes that he must remove himself from Marie's influence, but though he tries repeatedly, he finds it very difficult to renounce this destructive relationship. In a recent interview, Lopate said he hopes that "At a certain point the objective reader leaves the side of the narrator [Eric] and starts to become this judge and says: 'No, you idiot, you can't be doing this [repeating the same mistake over and over].' But if the objective reader will look into his or her soul, that reader will realize that it has happened to him in real life also." By the time that Eric leaves Marie permanently, the reader is disaffected with him.

The critical reception of the novel has been mixed. Joyce Carol Oates in *Mademoiselle* praised the story as a "darker and more intelligent imagining of some of the concerns of Woody Allen's *Manhattan*." Joseph McLellan in the *Washington Post* wrote that "the details behind this brusque summary are intricate and subtle: deceptions (beginning with self-deceptions), hesitations, ambiguities, terrible weaknesses and tiny, catastrophic flaws in the way good people perceive and react to one another." He concluded that Lopate "approaches his time-worn subject with acute perceptions and mastery of style." Kirkus Review Service offered a mixed evaluation: the book is "too long, too unvaried, and occasionally embarrassing; but the single point—how a casual mistake can turn into a major life dilemma—is pressed hard enough to make a strong impression." Praise in the *Library Journal* review was guarded but clear: "This is a narrowly focused but promising first novel; Lopate's exploration of the classic triangle is unpretentious, intelligent, and occasionally lyrical." The reviewer in *Publishers Weekly*, who missed Lopate's deliberate attempt to make Eric an unlikeable character, was not so kind: "Unfortunately, no matter how frequently Lopate praises his characters, they seem a rather unexceptional lot who offer little more than adolescent perceptions. . . . Lopate also tries to make them likeable, but instead they strike us as selfish and childish in their convoluted affair."

In his next book, *Journal of a Living Experiment* (1979), Lopate has edited a "documentary history of the first ten years of Teachers and Writers Collaborative," consisting of a collection of diaries, interviews, statements of purpose for the organization, recorded impressions, analytical essays, samples of student writing and art, narrative histories and recollections by staff members and luminaries such as Anne Sexton and Muriel Rukeyser. Lopate's contributions, in addition to his work as editor, include three interviews and introductory essays for each of the four sections.

Between 1971, when his novella *In Coyoacan* was published, and 1980, Lopate has progressed significantly in his mastery of different literary forms. He likes the challenge of working in more than one genre and considers himself "still in a kind of apprenticeship." His present challenge, as he notes, is the novel: he would like to concentrate on a "large, third-person novel" he says. He would also like to work on developing more compassion and "more understanding of 'the Other.' " His most recent book, *Bachelorhood* (forthcoming 1981), is a collection of personal essays, in the tradition of Lamb and Hazlitt.

Lopate has already written some significant poetry and in *Confessions of Summer* has produced a good novel. It remains to be seen how much he will accomplish as he emerges from his self-styled apprenticeship.

—Richard Ziegfeld

Other:

The Effects of Preschool Education on the Cognitive Development of Disadvantaged Children, by Lopate and Roslyn O'Brien (Urbana: University of Illinois Press, 1968);

"Remembering Lionel Trilling," *American Review*, 25, ed. Theodore Solataroff (New York: Bantam, 1976), pp. 148-178;

Journal of a Living Experiment: Documentary History of the First Ten Years of Teachers and

Writers Collaborative, edited with commentary by Lopate (New York: Teachers and Writers, 1979).

Periodical Publications:

POETRY:

"Evolution," "Visage of Hate," *Caravan* (1958): 33-34;

"A Special Case," *World,* no. 11 (April 1968);

"Judex Avenging Rosa Luxembourg," *First Issue,* 2 (Summer/Fall, 1968);

"Spring Offensive," *Columbia Review* (1969): 24;

"The Bad Girl," "Watching You," *Right On,* no. 5 (1970): 14-15;

"To the King of the Wild West Rodeo Circuit (I Actually Knew Him)," *Roy Rogers,* 1 (1970);

"Nosferatu," "Instructions for Dope," "Ode to Submariner," *New York Times 2* (March 1971);

"The Germans," *Telephone,* no. 6 (Spring 1972);

"Untitled Poem," *Mulberry,* 1 (November 1972): 43;

"The Chestnut," "The National Elections," *Z,* 1 (1972): 9, 14;

"December," *New York Times 4* (Winter 1972-1973);

"The Little Magazines Keep Coming," *Little Magazine,* 7 (Fall 1973): 26-28;

"The Community Organizer's Wife," *Liberation* (May/June 1974): 31;

"The Monster's Friends," *Onyx,* 10 (Spring 1975): 71;

"The Scream," *New York Arts Journal* (September/November 1975): 18;

"My Mouth," "Laziness," "The Gary Who Loved Schubert," "The Bright Spot Luncheonette," "Love Freely Chosen," "What's Left in the Pot at the End of the Day?," *Blue Pig,* special Lopate issue, 22 (Fall 1975);

"The Sketch Group," "Angels and Snow," *Waluna: The Soho Review* (Winter 1976): 33-36;

"Brie and Coke," *Little Magazine,* 10 (Spring/Summer 1976): 75;

"The Hour After Finishing," "Critique," "Las Chuletas De La Frontera (which translates: Frontier Cutlets)," *Chouteau Review* (Summer 1977): 23-25;

"A Free Ride, New York," *Mother Jones* (September/October 1977): 12;

"Secrets, Rehearsals," *Response* (Winter 1978-1979): 78-81;

"Venetian Silences," *Sun* (Winter 1979-1980): 1-7;

"Regrets," "The Unexpected Failure," *Lost Glove* (Spring 1980): 4-5.

FICTION:

"The Party," *Caravan* (1960): 30-33;

"The Virtue Problem," *Columbia Review* (1962): 22-30;

"Eli's Story," *Censored Review* (April 1963): 3-18; republished in *Columbia Review* (Spring 1963): 44-60;

"The Disciple," *Columbia Review* (Spring 1964);

"Basic Facts Leading to an Analysis," *Columbia Review* (1969): 12-13;

"The Purple Necklace," *World,* no. 16 (June 1969);

"Page From the Diary of an Omniscient Narrator," *Center,* no. 3 (April 1972): 61;

"Athens Afternoon with Black Cows," *Center,* no. 5 (September 1973): 47;

"Chamber Music Evening," *Paris Review,* no. 56 (1974): 63-89.

References:

Vivian Gornick, Review of *Being with Children, New York Times Book Review,* 2 November 1975, pp. 8, 28, 30;

Anne Martin, Review of *Being with Children, Harvard Educational Review,* 46 (May 1976): 267-272;

Joseph McLellan, Review of *Confessions of Summer, Washington Post Book World,* 16 July 1979;

Stephen Vincent, Review of *The Daily Round, San Francisco Review of Books,* September 1976, pp. 24-26.

William Maxwell

(16 August 1908-)

BOOKS: *Bright Center of Heaven* (New York & London: Harper, 1934);

They Came Like Swallows (New York: Harper, 1937; London: Joseph, 1937);

The Folded Leaf (New York: Harper, 1945; London: Faber & Faber, 1946);

The Heavenly Tenants (New York: Harper, 1946);

Time Will Darken It (New York: Harper, 1948; London: Faber & Faber, 1949);

Stories by Maxwell, Jean Stafford, John Cheever, and Daniel Fuchs (New York: Farrar, Straus & Cudahy, 1956; London: Gollancz, 1957);

The Chateau (New York: Knopf, 1961);

The Old Man at the Railroad Crossing and Other Tales (New York: Knopf, 1966);

Ancestors (New York: Knopf, 1971);

Over By the River and Other Stories (New York: Knopf, 1977);

So Long, See You Tomorrow (New York: Knopf, 1980).

Since the publication of his first novel, *Bright Center of Heaven* (1934), more than forty-five years ago, William Maxwell has written six novels, more than fifty short stories, a nonfiction study, *Ancestors* (1971), and a short book for children entitled *The Heavenly Tenants* (1946). Although his fiction is set in many parts of this country and in France, Maxwell is most comfortable when he is writing about life in the Midwest. In a recent *Publishers Weekly* interview he said: "I think it's an unconscious choice of scene. Writers don't really choose their material. I've lived in New York since 1936, and I've written an ocean of short stories about New York, but I would never feel at ease with it in a novel. New York is so big, I wouldn't know how to come at it. In general, there is something about the Midwest, something that claims my imagination."

He was born on 16 August 1908 in Lincoln in downstate Illinois. His parents were Eva Blinn Maxwell and William Keepers Maxwell, a fire insurance salesman who traveled extensively throughout Illinois. Maxwell was a solitary child, noncompetitive in sports, content to read a book or play alone in the old house where he spent the first ten years of his life. He was unusually close to his mother. Many of his books, including *They Came Like Swallows* (1937), *The Folded Leaf* (1945), and *So Long, See You Tomorrow* (1980), are testimony to their loving relationship. When she died in the Spanish influenza epidemic of 1918-1919, he was only ten. "It happened too suddenly, with no warning, and we none of us could believe it or bear it. My father's face turned the color of ashes and stayed that way a whole year. The nightmare went on and on. He did all a man can do in those circumstances; he kept the family together. But he could not make what had happened not have happened, and the beautiful, imaginative, protected world of my childhood was swept away."

The next four years were marked by many changes, including his father's decision to remarry. In *So Long, See You Tomorrow,* in part a memoir, Maxwell recalled the time: "A year or two before this, at the Country Club on a summer day, wandering idly near the caddie house, I came upon a sight I didn't understand. I thought at first it was some new kind of animal. Then I retreated in horror. What I was looking at was a snake in the act of swallowing a frog that was too large and wouldn't go down. Neither would the idea that another woman was not only going to sit in my mother's place at the dinner table, but also take her place in my father's heart."

When Maxwell was fourteen, his father received a promotion that took the family from Lincoln to the Near North Side of Chicago. There he was enrolled in the Nicholas Senn High School, where although he was lonely, he enjoyed the fact that to be recognized it was not necessary, as it had been back home, to play a sport. At Senn, he found teachers who encouraged him in music and literature. In the summertime he often spent part of his vacation on a farm near Portage, Wisconsin, where he met Zona Gale, the poet and novelist. Shortly after the publication of his fourth novel, *Time Will Darken It,* in 1948, he recalled how she had furthered his interest in literature: "I am only beginning to understand how much in the way of literary taste and craftsmanship I received from her."

After graduating from high school, he went on to obtain a B.A. degree in 1930 at the University of Illinois. He received a number of awards in college, among them a scholarship for graduate work at Harvard University, where he received an M.A. in 1931. After his year in Cambridge, he returned to teach at the University of Illinois for two years. In 1936, after the publication of his first novel, he joined the staff of the *New Yorker*, where his first assignment was in the art department. Later he was transferred to the fiction department where he learned to edit on his own: "Wolcott Gibbs gave me a story to edit, and I really didn't know what to do, so I just cut out what I didn't like."

He stayed on at the *New Yorker* for nearly forty years, where he edited short stories for such writers as John Cheever, Irwin Shaw, and John O'Hara. On occasion, he found himself in a predicament, as in 1960 with John O'Hara, whose work had not appeared in the *New Yorker* for several years. O'Hara suggested that Maxwell read three of his novellas and consider them for publication, and, Maxwell remembers, "The first two I was reasonably sure the *New Yorker* would not want to publish, and, very much wishing I had not got myself into such a tight situation, I started to read the third, which was 'Imagine Kissing Pete,' and thought it was a masterpiece, and that the *New Yorker* would want it."

From the outset Maxwell decided to read other people's work only on a part-time basis because he thought it was important to use the rest of his time for his own writing. In 1952 when William Shawn became editor of the *New Yorker*, Maxwell was selected as one of seven fiction experts: "All of us had our own authors, and we all consulted with one another. There was great freedom. You can imagine how pleasant that was." In 1977, he retired from the magazine. He lives with his wife, the former Emily Gilman Noyes, whom he married on 17 May 1945, in a spacious apartment on New York's Upper East Side. Their two children are now grown.

Bright Center of Heaven (1934) was published two years before Maxwell began work at the *New Yorker*. It is a warm, touching comedy filled with delicate character delineations, in which Maxwell also demonstrates his skill in capturing the mood of place, in this case rural Wisconsin. The story is about a kindhearted and gracious, if impractical, woman named Mrs. West, whose farm, Meadowlands, is doing so poorly that she takes in an assorted group of twelve boarders to supplement her income. Mrs. West makes the mistake of inviting a black lecturer for a guest appearance. His arrival disrupts the otherwise peaceful setting at Meadowlands.

Although this novel is not considered one of Maxwell's best, it was viewed by the critics as a promising beginning for the twenty-six-year-old writer. Theodore Purdy, Jr., writing in the *Saturday Review of Literature*, called the book "An admirable satiric comedy, bittersweet in flavor, yet always humorous" and added that it "exhibits few of the weaknesses present in most recent efforts by American writers to achieve subtlety and a graciously detached viewpoint in dealing with human relationships."

Maxwell's second novel, *They Came Like Swallows* (1937), won the Friends of American Writers award and was a Book-of-the-Month Club selection. The story is set in a small town in downstate Illinois and revolves around the Morisons, an ordinary middle-class family, during the closing days of World War I, in November 1918. The dominant figure in the family is Elizabeth, the mother, who is loved and adored by her two sons and husband.

There is a somber note to much of Maxwell's writing that is particularly evident in *They Came Like Swallows*. The father, for example, is drawn as a distant and cold figure. He makes no effort to talk with his sons and communicates by reading out loud dull portions of the daily newspaper at the breakfast table. When Elizabeth is taken to Decatur to give birth to her third child, her two boys are placed under the care of their domineering Aunt Clara, who does not allow them to touch anything in her house or to play like normal youngsters.

Tragedy strikes when the influenza Elizabeth had contracted before going to the hospital becomes double pneumonia. The strain is too much, and she dies. Now that his wife is gone, the father, bereft of hope and happiness, concedes that raising his two sons is more than he is able to do. He will send them away to live with their Aunt Clara. But this dismal fate is stopped by the intervention of Irene, Elizabeth's sister and a favorite of the boys, who volunteers to move into the house and take on the responsibility of raising the children.

One of the chief merits of the book is Maxwell's keen insight into the world of children. Much of the story is presented from the points of view of Bunny, age eight, and Robert, age thirteen. Amy Loveman, writing in the *Saturday Review of Literature*, praised Maxwell's talent: "To recapture the elusive wistfulness of youth, to reconstruct its fears and confusions, the fleeting poignancy of its pain and ecstasy of its joy, and to present them unalloyed by the exaggerations of memory needs a singular clarity of insight and emotion. Mr. Maxwell's book is one of those rare tales in which childhood is reflected in the simplicity and intensity of its own experience."

Fifteen-year-old Lymie Peters in *The Folded Leaf*, Maxwell's third and best known novel, bears some temperamental resemblance to the quiet and withdrawn Bunny in *They Came Like Swallows*. The setting of *The Folded Leaf* changes as Lymie moves from a small town in downstate Illinois to Chicago with his father, and later to a college town in Indiana. After the death of Mrs. Peters, Lymie's father sells the family house in their small town and takes his son to Chicago, where they live in rundown hotels and cheap furnished apartments. Mr. Peters, bereaved over the loss of his wife, sees no point to life. In Chicago he starts to drink too much, consorts with prostitutes, and finds no interest in his work.

The central theme of the story is the friendship that develops between Lymie and Spud Latham. Like his friend, Spud feels uprooted from his home in Wisconsin and out of place in a large city. Unlike Lymie, however, Spud is self-confident, athletic, and has no trouble making friends. For Lymie, Spud and his family offer security and comfort. One of the most touching scenes in the novel occurs when Lymie is invited to his friend's apartment for dinner. The Lathams live in cramped quarters and have decorated their rooms in obvious bad taste. None of this matters to Lymie, however, because this warm and kind family succeeds in softening the pain of his mother's death and the move away from his first home.

At college, jealousy and misunderstanding over a girl whom both boys love cause a rift in their friendship. Lymie, heartsick over the break with Spud, attempts suicide by cutting his wrists. One of his friends finds him lying on the bathroom floor and calls for an ambulance. Lymie's father comes to the side of his son, who is recovering slowly in a hospital room. He is more distraught over the absence of a farewell note addressed to him than he is over whether Lymie will recover.

Maxwell's style is simple and sparse, and he avoids lapsing into sentimentality, an easy pitfall in a novel of this kind. More than one critic has noted the author's ability not only to recreate the longings, joys, and sorrows of adolescence, but also to evoke the mood of Midwestern America in the 1920s. There are many scenes in the book, including college dances and a fraternity initiation ceremony, which memorably depict the era. But close to the heart of the story is loneliness. Although Lymie can no longer love his father, the real source of his loneliness is the death of his mother. She has been dead for eight years by the time Lymie is in college; neither father nor son has been happy since then. Lymie can still remember his mother's voice, the clothes she wore, and the feeling he had when she was present in the room.

The ending of *The Folded Leaf* is the least convincing part of the book. As Lymie gathers his strength in the hospital, he tells his father that he will put this dreadful episode behind him. He seems to have learned a great deal from his mistake and won a new independence, but the reader has not been shown how he has gained this maturity in such a short time. Yet this weakness does not overshadow the otherwise high quality of this carefully written and moving novel.

The Heavenly Tenants (1946) is a short book of less than sixty pages written for a younger audience. Accompanying the story are three double-page drawings by Ilonka Karasz, who is best known for her *New Yorker* covers. The book foreshadows a literary form that Maxwell later would use frequently in his stories for adults: a story which is a blend of Aesop's fables and the fairy tales of the brothers Grimm. In *The Heavenly Tenants* the Marvell family, who live on a farm in Wisconsin, are packing their suitcases in preparation for a visit to the children's grandmother in Virginia. Before departing, Mr. Marvell takes his children outside to look at the constellations of the zodiac that appear in the spring sky. Gazing up at the dark sky, the children listen, entranced with their father's story about the arrangement of the stars in animal shapes. The next morning the family leaves for Virginia, and while it is away, strange things happen at their old farmhouse. A bright, glowing light permeates the grounds and house, a glow that persists even at night. Neighbors from all around come to see a weathervane replaced by a shining golden lion, and in the pasture stand a milk-white bull, a ram, and a goat—animals that never belonged to the Marvells. At grandmother's house, Mr. Marvell searches through his telescope for the constellation of the crab, but always in vain. The heavenly tenants had taken their own vacation.

Maxwell's simple and controlled style, by now a trademark, are evident throughout this short narrative. The *Saturday Review of Literature* praised this quality and admired the way in which it encouraged young readers to suspend their disbelief: "Nothing is obvious, much is implied. The stars are in the sky. But no imaginative child will hesitate in his belief that the signs of the zodiac came down and spent three weeks at the Marvell farm."

Time Will Darken It (1948) is Maxwell's only novel set before the outbreak of World War I. The year is 1912 and the place is a tree-lined street in the small town of Draperville, Illinois. The story is narrow in scope, covering six months in the lives of Austin King, a young lawyer, his pregnant wife Martha, and their four-year-old daughter Abbey.

Most of the novel revolves around an inadvertent mistake of Austin's. In order to repay a social obligation contracted long ago by his now deceased father, he has invited some nearly forgotten relatives for a visit. Mr. and Mrs. Potter and their two children, Randolph and Nora, have come up from Mississippi for an extended stay. As the narrator points out, "For most people, having company for more than three or four days is a serious mistake, the equivalent to sawing a large hole in the roof and leaving all the doors and windows open in the middle of winter." When the novel opens, Martha King is lying on her bed in tears, moaning over the recent arrival of her husband's relatives.

During the Potter's stay Nora, an independent-minded young woman bored by life in the Deep South, falls in love with her cousin Austin. When her parents and brother finally decide to return home she remains behind. To be closer to her cousin she studies law in his office until local gossip threatens Austin's marriage and his legal career. In the end, following a serious accident, Nora's parents return to Draperville and take their daughter back home to Mississippi.

Maxwell's gift for capturing the mood of time and place is evident throughout this novel. In summer when school is out, children look for the ice-cream wagon and once in a while see a caravan of gypsies ride by at dusk. On Sundays, families hitch up the horse to the surrey and ride out into the country through fields of wheat and corn. At parties, men talk with other men about politics and business while women babble among themselves about magazine recipes and childhood illnesses. Only the young and old are free of the confines of these separate worlds and act "as ambassadors" and keep "open the lines of communication between the sexes."

Even the lesser characters in the novel come alive because of Maxwell's ear for dialogue. The conversations between the black cook and her twelve-year-old daughter, Abbey's imaginary conversations with her dolls while the grownups talk on "serious" subjects, and signs of senility in old Mr. Ellis, who cannot quite remember the end of his story, all seem to be authentic recordings of pre-World War I conversations.

Time Will Darken It is not as well known as some of Maxwell's other novels, but it has their charm and nostalgic tone. The author provides an interesting contrast between the more settled times of Midwestern life prior to the outbreak of war and the dramatic changes introduced in the early 1920s. Writing in the *New York Times Book Review*, Richard Sullivan noted, "There is a sense of responsibility in Mr. Maxwell's writing. . . .Reading it one feels that its elements—its people and place and time—have been permanently, faithfully rendered."

In *The Chateau* (1961) a young American couple, Harold and Barbara Rhodes, visit France in 1948 and spend a large part of their stay as paying guests at the chateau of Madame Vienot. Although they are not completely naive, there is "in their faces, something immature. . . ." With an openness born of their Midwestern upbringing, Harold reaches out too easily to people: "It never seems to occur to him that there is a limit to the number of close friendships anyone can directly and faithfully accommodate." In their expectation of an easy understanding of France and the people they meet there, Harold and Barbara suffer the disappointments of "second meetings that aren't always successful, and third meetings that are even less satisfactory." What little plot underlies *The Chateau* consists mainly of such encounters and sometimes tries the reader's patience by its slowness, but the characters are well delineated through the subtleties of their interactions. Certain scenes convey vivid impressions of Paris and the chateau country, and there is an acute sense of the lingering effects of World War II. A. W. Phinney said of the book in the *Christian Science Monitor* that "it does not achieve the over-all muted intensity of 'The Folded Leaf' "; but in a *New Yorker* review Naomi Bliven called it "a large-scale work whose smallest details are beautifully made."

In *The Old Man At the Railroad Crossing and Other Tales* (1966), a collection of twenty-nine stories, each no more than a few pages in length, Maxwell develops the literary form he introduced in his children's book *The Heavenly Tenants*. There are tales about kings and queens, deep forests, wise old men, princesses, and talking birds. In the tradition of Hans Christian Andersen's and the Grimms' fairy tales, Maxwell is doing more than telling a story simply and directly. Each story has a moral. In his introduction to the collection Maxwell tells how some of the stories came to him: "I would sit with my head bent over the typewriter waiting to see what was going to come out of it. The first sentence was usually a surprise to me. From the first sentence everything else followed. A person I didn't know anything about and had never known in real life—a man who had no enemies, a girl who doesn't know whether to listen to her heart or her mind, a woman who never draws breath except to complain, an old man afraid of falling—stepped from the wings and began to act out something I must not interrupt or interfere with, but only be a witness to. . . ."

176

now included in Logan County, in 1837, and built the first jail in Logan County. Mr. and Mrs. Gillett have eight children--Emma (wife of [redacted] Hon. R.J. Oglesby, Governor of Illinois, Grace (wife of D.T. Littler of Springfield), Nina, Amy, Kate (wife of James Hill, of Chester, Illinois), Jessie, John, and Charlotte. The family are members of the Episcopal church at Springfield."

~~How vast the holdings of John D. Gillett were the historian apparently felt that it would~~ [redacted] ~~in poor taste to say.~~ I have seen a photograph of ~~him~~ John D. Gillett, taken when he was well along in years. He has ~~with~~ a white beard shaped like the cow-catcher of a steam locomotive, a flower in his buttonhole, and the look of a bouncy man--as if nothing in the world was more conducive to cheerfulness than [redacted] amassing [redacted] a large fortune.

His death gave rise to a Balzacian novel. ~~which I used to hear my elders discussing when I was much too young to care about money except in relation to cracker-jack and ice cream cones.~~ An elderly ~~A family~~ friend has recounted to me the broad outline of this immensely complicated story, and the rest I found in a newspaper clipping in my Grandmother Maxwell's scrapbook. It seems that John D. Gillett left his widow a lifetime interest in 3800 acres of land, valued at $380,000, and personal property worth $100,000. At the time of the lawsuit, she also was dead, and her share of the estate was owned by the heirs in common, who had not been able to come to an agreement as to how it should be divided.

In devising his land to his children, the old man gave his only son, John P. Gillett, a double portion, and one of the sisters had willed her share to him, so, with what was coming to him from his mother, he ended up owning seven-sixteenths of the original estate. He made a will in which he left the bulk of his [redacted] property to Miss Jessie Gillett, my Grandfather Maxwell's client. Later, he added a codicil in which the property was left to

Ancestors, *revised typescript*

The title story, placed at the end of the collection, is about a very old man who is still able to operate the gates of a railroad crossing. All he can say to passers-by is "Rejoice." Those who are ambitious for power and money do not even hear him, the polite are embarrassed for him, and children tease the old man. But one gray-haired old woman stops to listen and finds meaning in his exclamation. This collection of fables was only the beginning of Maxwell's writing in this genre. In the future many similar stories appeared in the pages of the *New Yorker*.

In *Ancestors* (1971), Maxwell departs from the novel and the short story to venture into nonfiction, writing a history of his forebears on both his father's and mother's sides. Instead of creating fictional characters, which he has been doing since his first novel was published in 1934, he now is re-creating the real Maxwells: the Blinns, Englands, Higginses, and Harringtons who make up his family tree. These people immigrated to American shores early in the eighteenth century from Scotland through Ireland to Pennsylvania, and from England to Virginia. From there, they pushed westward through the wilderness and over the Appalachian Mountains until they reached Midwestern America.

The story of Maxwell's own ancestors begins in Lincoln, Illinois. Peering into the past, Maxwell adheres to his own historical methods: "I know that it is possible to consider history wholly in the context of ideas, but that isn't the way my mind works. I have to get out an imaginary telescope and fiddle with the lens until I see something that interests me, preferably something small and unimportant." In short, history should be treated in miniature, on the level of individuals. Maxwell's description of his grandfather's leaving Ohio in 1866 and traveling on foot to reach central Illinois, a distance of 600 miles, illustrates the merit of his method: "The National Road was used by a steady stream of two-wheeled carts, Conestoga wagons, farm wagons, men on horseback, men on foot, men driving cattle, hogs, horses, and mules. Now choking on clouds of dust, now with his new shoes caked with mud, my grandfather moved among them." Maxwell has taken a few bits and pieces of undisputed fact about his forebears and from that has woven them into a broader tapestry that encompasses the experience of tens of thousands of other people on the frontier. Pamela Marsh, writing in the *Christian Science Monitor,* has accurately summed up Maxwell's achievement: "Tiny human details that have lingered on in old documents or long memories will give most readers a clearer sense of how the United States developed than a shelfful of history texts could ever do."

Over by the River and Other Stories (1977) collects twelve short stories written from 1941 through 1976; nine of these originally appeared in the *New Yorker.* Only four of the stories are set against the Midwestern background of Maxwell's early novels and *Ancestors,* and Nicholas Delbanco, writing in the *New York Times Book Review,* commented, "Strangely, the author's persona seems least at home in . . . his 'hometown' stories; the elegiac mode appears a touch too pat." Two other stories are about Americans traveling in France, baffled, as are the Rhodeses in *The Chateau,* at the country's failure to fit their preconceptions. In the title story, a family living in Manhattan holds fast to one another to create a protective environment within the larger setting of the city, but they nevertheless experience individual loneliness and fear. Five other stories are also set in or around New York City.

Although *So Long, See You Tomorrow* (1980) is called a novel, at least half of the book is a personal memoir. In the first part Maxwell recalls an unhappy period during his adolescence. The latter half is a fictionalized account of a friend's tragedy.

In the memoir section, Maxwell relied not only on his memory, which he admits is rusty about events that occurred nearly sixty years ago, but also on information from a stepcousin and the Illinois State Historical Library. The events of this memoir happened between 1918 and 1921 in the small, cozy town of Lincoln, Illinois, beginning with the death of Maxwell's mother when he was ten and ending with the sale of his parents' house and the family's move to Chicago. Throughout this part of the book Maxwell's eye for detail and his ability to bring an era to life are evident. It was a time when fashion and morals were undergoing rapid and dramatic change. Maxwell can still remember going out with his father and mother for Sunday rides in the family horse and buggy, a weekly ritual that continued until he was six years old. By the early 1920s, the automobile had become commonplace, women wore skirts above their knees, and attitudes toward sex had changed.

The second part of the book is Maxwell's attempt to recreate and thereby understand the tragic story of a farm boy named Cletus Smith. As boys, Maxwell and Cletus played together and were becoming close friends when quite suddenly Cletus was taken out of school. It was soon clear why. His parents had been in the midst of a divorce, and Cletus's father in a fit of rage had murdered his wife's lover and then committed suicide. Maxwell thought he would never see Cletus again. Then by accident their paths crossed again. One day, after the Maxwell's move to Chicago, young Maxwell was walking along a corridor in his large city high school and saw Cletus approaching from the other direction. He walked by his friend without saying a word. His failure to acknowledge Cletus, with even a simple hello, has troubled Maxwell all these years. *So Long, See You Tomorrow* was Maxwell's "roundabout futile way of making amends." The overall effect of the book, especially the memoir, is sharp and moving. The descriptions of Maxwell's love for his mother and the impact her death had on him and his father are memorable.

Even though he has been writing for a period of nearly fifty years, stretching from the 1930s into the 1980s, the name of William Maxwell remains unfamiliar to the general reader. But despite his relative obscurity fellow writers such as Naomi Bliven, Joyce Carol Oates, and V. S. Pritchett have long recognized his talent as a writer, especially noting his ability to recapture the sense of time and place in the post-World War I small-town life of the Midwest. It is for this gift that he will be remembered.

—*Walter W. Ross*

References:

Matthew J. Bruccoli, *The O'Hara Concern: A Biography of John O'Hara* (New York: Random House, 1975), pp. 261-262;

Bruccoli, *Selected Letters of John O'Hara* (New York: Random House, 1978);

Brendan Gill, *Here at the New Yorker* (New York: Random House, 1975), pp. 162-163, 278;

"Interview with William Maxwell," *Publishers Weekly*, 216 (10 December 1979): pp. 8-9.

Michael Mewshaw
(19 February 1943-   )

BOOKS: *Man in Motion* (New York: Random House, 1970);

Waking Slow (New York: Random House, 1972; London: Constable, 1973);

The Toll (New York: Random House, 1974; London: Bodley Head, 1974);

Earthly Bread (New York: Random House, 1976; London: Secker & Warburg, 1977);

Land Without Shadow (Garden City: Doubleday, 1979);

Life for Death (Garden City: Doubleday, 1980; London: Cape, forthcoming 1981).

Michael Mewshaw has written five novels, one book of nonfiction, and several hundred articles and reviews for a variety of periodicals and newspapers. Critics and authors, including Graham Greene, William Styron, and Robert Penn Warren, have repeatedly praised Mewshaw's descriptive skills, his inventiveness, and his strong narrative pacing, as well as his thoughtful examination of contemporary social issues.

Born in Washington, D.C., son of John Francis and Mary Helen Mewshaw, Mewshaw grew up in East Riverdale, Maryland. He graduated magna cum laude with a B.A. from the University of Maryland in 1965, after having been editor of the campus literary magazine and a member of several honor societies, including Phi Beta Kappa. He received his M.A. from the University of Virginia in 1966 and continued working on his Ph.D. until 1968. At that time Mewshaw interrupted his graduate school career to spend eighteen months in France on a Fulbright fellowship in creative writing. Accompanied to Europe by his wife Linda, Mewshaw developed a penchant for travel, which has become a lifelong hobby. During his trip, which Mewshaw considers a turning point in his life, he finished and sold his first novel, *Man in Motion*.

Published by Random House in 1970, *Man in Motion* recounts the adventures of Walker Hawley, a young would-be writer who, having authored one short story in college, is stewing in his literary juices while feeling trapped by his family responsibilities. Following the unexpected death of his stepfather, Walker renounces his ties to home and to his college girl friend and aims his sports car for California, accompanied by a tall blonde rider named Lila Caine, who seems the fulfillment of Walker's youthful dreams. A detour to Mexico allows Mewshaw to display his considerable talent for black humor as Walker discovers that unlimited sex, drink, and freedom are not all they are rumored to be. Ultimately losing both car and Lila, Walker returns to his girl friend and familial obligations as the novel ends, having learned that sometimes one can—

and, indeed, should—go home again.

At the end of his Fulbright, Mewshaw returned to the States and completed his Ph.D. in English under a Du Pont Doctoral Fellowship. During that period, he taught at the University of Virginia and at the Hollins Conference in Creative Writing; he was also the William Rainey Fellow at the Bread Loaf Writers' Conference. After graduation Mewshaw accepted a position as an assistant professor of English at the University of Massachusetts, where he taught creative writing and modern fiction. Declining an offer to join Stanford University's fiction workshop on a Wallace Stegner Fellowship, Mewshaw left the country again for two years of travel in Europe, the Middle East, and North Africa.

In 1972, Random House published his second novel, *Waking Slow,* whose story traces the trials of a young man and his girl friend who move to California to await the birth of her illegitimate child by another man. With vivid and painfully comic clarity Mewshaw captures the young man's growing entanglements with shady loan companies and corrupt employment agencies as well as the quiet desperation of lives counted out on sliced fingers at franchise restaurants. Although as a whole the novel is uneven, the confusions and disappointments of young love set against the vulgar California skyline are sharply drawn. Graham Greene, whose work has influenced Mewshaw, described the novel as "one of the best black comedies I have read in years," and Anthony Burgess praised it as "a true picture of America today. . . . Such solid construction, such fluency, such totally credible characterization make this a very memorable novel."

During his two years abroad Mewshaw worked on his third novel, *The Toll,* published in 1974. With this novel, which is perhaps his best, Mewshaw departed from the darkly humorous style and autobiographical tone of his previous work. *The Toll* is at once a novel of adventure and of ideas, a story which dramatizes the tragic consequences of the naive, adolescent fantasies of revolution and political violence popular in the 1960s. The protagonist, Ted Kuyler, is a soldier of misfortune, a veteran of Korea, Vietnam, and Nigeria, who at thirty-nine is "searching for his first win." His dreams of retirement to an island paradise lead him to join five young hippie Americans who falsely promise nonexistent cash for his help in springing one of their friends locked securely in a small-town Moroccan jail for possession of hash and an unregistered pistol. Complicating the plot are the group's leader, Polo, a fiery pseudorevolutionary whose fury over public indignities masks a deeper personal rage over his own inadequacies, and "Burt," the young woman with whom Kuyler falls in love. The rivalry between Kuyler and Polo escalates, and the jailbreak scheme quickly leads from bribery and deceit to betrayal and murder.

Michael Mewshaw

Mewshaw's remarkable sense of place is at its best in this novel as he describes the Moroccan market stalls with their waist-high walls of dates, buckets of olives bobbing in brine, and stacks of sweets surrounded by bees drunk on sugar, benignly blowing like yellow feathers in the wind. In a meat market "hundreds of cow and goat carcasses swung on chains from overhead beams as butchers in gory aprons chopped them into slabs with giant cleavers. Though the animals had been recently slaughtered, the flesh was dark, the bones blue-tinted, the fat a rancid yellow. Tossed onto metal trays, the internal organs oozed and bubbled in their own fluids like submarine creatures.

"At a couple of stalls camel heads hung from rusty hooks. Skinned down to the purpling meat and muscle, they still had their eyes and appeared perfectly serene, as though they weren't aware that their bodies had been severed. Below them, like dusty, rundown shoes outside a mosque, their feet stood in neat lines—calloused pads, bracelets of hair, and, extending to the shattered knees, slick pink joints of bone." Market vendors also become distinct: here a man doing a brisk business from a table littered with false teeth; there a woman protecting useless stacks of discarded foreign magazines as if they were priceless icons; still another woman wallowing "in old underwear and shreds of linen" fingers her rags in a feeble but proud assertion of ownership. Hundreds of such memorable—and often brutal—scenes of Moroccan life give *The Toll* its rich visual texture as the accelerating pace of events hurls the characters toward an inescapable fate. The last portion of the novel details Kuyler and Burt's desperate flight to Algeria, during which they are terrorized by Moroccan authorities, parched by the desert, and stripped of their illusions. As the couple struggles across the sand guiltily dragging a dying companion, the reader feels the couple's exhaustion, fear, and despair perhaps more intensely than in any American fiction since Mailer's *The Naked and the Dead.*

In 1973 Mewshaw accepted a position at the University of Texas at Austin, where he is currently an associate professor of English. At that time he began writing articles and book reviews for various journals and newspapers; over the years his essays have included such diverse subjects as the talents of Graham Greene, the last years of James Jones, the difficulties facing first novelists, the inequities of copyright laws, and the efforts of small presses to rescue the short story. In 1974, with a grant from the National Endowment for the Arts, Mewshaw finished his fourth novel, *Earthly Bread* (1976). Described by one critic as a "seriocomical morality tale," *Earthly Bread* concerns the kidnapping and attempted deprogramming of a young Jesus freak. Father Tony Amico, a fat, spiritually troubled priest transferred to Austin, Texas, finds himself mediator between Noland Meadlow, the tough, professional deprogrammer, and "Tiagatha," whose parents will tolerate almost any youthful inanity but religious zealotry. The serious spiritual debates following the kidnapping take place in a south Texas whorehouse motel, whose sleazy atmosphere and co-owners once again reveal Mewshaw's exceptional descriptive skills. Billie, the female partner, is Mewshaw's most entertaining secondary character: a former fat lady in the circus who lost both weight and, consequently, her job, she spends her time popping cans of Pearl beer for breakfast and raising armadillos for flowerpots under the stifling, too-humid-to-breathe Texas sun. But pervading the comedy is Mewshaw's deep concern over deprogramming's violation of civil liberties and his sincere plea for religious tolerance in an increasingly dehumanized world. Mewshaw returned to these concerns in a 1976 essay for the *Chronicle of Higher Education* called "Irrational Behavior or Evangelical Zeal?" in which he again argues that despite any disapproval we may have, we have no right to interfere with someone's religious choice. Mewshaw asks, "Why have 'born again' Christians been singled out? . . . How would the public respond if a Protestant pulled his son out of a seminary and kept him incommunicado until he gave up his vocation? . . . if a Catholic dragged his daughter from a convent?"

Dust jacket

Mewshaw spent 1975-1976 in Italy and Africa working on his fifth novel, *Land Without Shadow,* selected by the *New York Times Book Review* in 1979 as one of the year's best works of fiction. Set in the Sahel region of Africa, where a drought and famine decimated the Taureg tribe in 1973-1974, the novel again illustrates Mewshaw's ability to combine successfully an adventure story with questions of moral responsibility. Jack Cordell, a recently divorced, unsuccessful painter, is talked into becoming art director of a cheap film project under the direction of a boyhood friend. Once on location in a desert nation called Maliteta, Cordell discovers a land of poverty, disease, and social unrest, where entire tribes of people are literally starving to death from lack of care. With one of the film's stars, Cordell becomes part of a plot to attract world attention to the famine, a scheme which goes awry and results in still more destruction and the revelation of a cover-up by both local and American officials. By juxtaposing the spoiled Hollywood film crew and the starving locals, Mewshaw is able to make his points easily and without preaching. The clatter of the crew's hotel trash cans—scavenged routinely each night by the hungry—echoes powerfully throughout the novel like the death knell it is.

Mewshaw took another leave of absence from the University of Texas in 1977 to become writer-in-residence at the American Academy in Rome. In an essay in the *Nation* in 1978 he summed up the importance of travel to his work: "Personally I would prefer to go to places where at first I don't speak the language or know anybody, where I easily lose my direction and have no delusions that I'm in control. Feeling disoriented, even frightened, I find myself awake, alive, in ways I never would have at home. All my senses suddenly alert, I can hear again, smell, see—and afterward, if I'm lucky, I can write."

But in his most recent work—his first book of nonfiction—Mewshaw turned not toward strange foreign lands as before, but to his past. *Life for Death,* published in 1980, is the story of Wayne Dresbach, Mewshaw's childhood friend, who at fifteen killed his socially prominent parents early one January morning in 1961. Given a one-day trial, Dresbach, virtually abandoned both by relatives and law officials, was convicted in twelve minutes and sentenced to life in prison. Over fifteen years later Mewshaw's interviews and thorough, sometimes frustrating investigation revealed the truth behind the murders, as a tale of child abuse, alcoholism, sadism, and bizarre sexual experimentation emerged. Unlike Capote in *In Cold Blood,* Mewshaw is an active participant in this story; he was, in fact, the first person to learn of the crime. The unselfish commitment of Mewshaw's entire family to helping the young Dresbach throughout the nightmare of his arrest, trial, and imprisonment gives the book a personal intensity lacking in other documentaries of this sort. Once more, Mewshaw's powers of description not only enable him to recreate the tragic series of events leading to the murders but also to dramatize accurately and expose the facade of propriety surrounding the case—a facade which silenced witnesses and cost an abused child twenty years of his life.

Peter Straub, author of *Ghost Story,* reviewed the book this way: "There have been many documentary books about crime but I cannot think of one as gripping. When you are through reading it, it stays in the mind for weeks with the power of a nightmare. . . . It is not just crafty and involving but a moving and brave account of a terrible moral crime." Not all readers were as pleased, however. Wayne Dresbach's brother Lee, who was also in the house at the time of the shootings, unsuccessfully sued Doubleday for libel and invasion of privacy.

With the possible exception of *Earthly Bread,* which some readers found too didactic, Mewshaw's latest books have been exciting, vivid, and thought-provoking. Despite a market replete with lightweight novels of the supernatural or of the historical romance variety, Mewshaw, to his credit, has repeatedly selected serious, controversial subjects which present complex questions of moral responsibility and ethical choice, and he has frequently found himself challenging currently popular positions, be they on revolution in the 1960s or deprogramming in the 1970s. Having received a grant from the Guggenheim Foundation, Mewshaw is spending the 1981-1982 academic year traveling in Italy and Spain with his wife and two small sons while working on a new book about people caught up in the turmoil of political assassination. If his new novel continues in the tradition of *The Toll* and *Land Without Shadow,* it should certainly add to his growing reputation as a talented writer who successfully confronts important moral issues in quick-paced, suspenseful stories set against precisely realized backdrops.

—*Jean Wyrick*

Other:

"Reviews Are Stranger Than Fiction," in *Intro 9, Close to Home,* edited by Mewshaw and George Garrett (Austin: Hendel & Reinke, 1978).

Periodical Publications:

"Irrational Behavior or Evangelical Zeal?," *Chronicle of Higher Education,* 18 October 1976, p. 32;

"The Staying Power and the Glory," *Nation,* 224 (16 April 1977): 469-472;

"James Jones, Another Side," *Nation,* 226 (8 April 1978): 406-407;

"Is Anybody Home?," *Nation,* 226 (3 June 1978): 673-675.

Interview:

John Graham, Interview with Michael Mewshaw, in *The Writer's Voice: Conversations with Contemporary Writers,* ed. George Garrett (New York: Morrow, 1973).

Willie Morris

(29 November 1934-

BOOKS: *North Toward Home* (Boston: Houghton Mifflin, 1967);
Yazoo: Integration in a Deep-Southern Town (New York: Harper's Magazine Press, 1971);
Good Old Boy: A Delta Boyhood (New York: Harper & Row, 1971; London: Deutsch, 1974);
The Last of the Southern Girls (New York: Knopf, 1973; London: Deutsch, 1974);
James Jones: A Friendship (Garden City: Doubleday, 1978).

Willie Morris, journalist, essayist, novelist, is a writer whose life and work are inseparable. Not only is most of Morris's writing about himself, but it is also about how his experience reflects a larger regional and national experience.

At the age of thirty-two, Morris recounted the first three formative stages of his life in his autobiographical work *North Toward Home* (1967), which received virtually unanimous critical praise for its forthright depiction of the emotional and intellectual struggles of growing up. The *Times Literary Supplement* termed the memoir "a dialectic between heart and reason . . . as finely poised as a scholastic dispute." The first section of the book describes his boyhood in the South, and how that region shaped his awareness and consciousness. Born in Jackson, Mississippi, the son of Henry Rae and Marion Weaks Morris, he grew up with a strong sense of family and place. A transplanted Tennessean who ran a gas station, Morris's father was "*country* in the way that he was tuned to its rhythms and its cycles." His mother's family, though not very wealthy, had impressive roots, tracing its origins to the Harpers of Harper's Ferry and counting among its number several former state politicians of high rank. An only child, Morris nonetheless had close ties with his grandmother, grandfather, and two eccentric great-aunts. From his family Morris developed an intense feeling for the past and the land.

From the age of six, Morris's home was the Mississippi Delta town of Yazoo City, "close to growing plants, to the earth, to nature's wilder moods." The place was prone to oppressive heat, seasonal flooding, and occasional tornadoes. The town itself gave the appearance of being settled, yet raw; gracious old houses on tree-lined streets stood a block away from dilapidated shacks. The drab main street formed the major highway through town, and few outsiders willingly lingered in that provincial spot. Here Morris grew up temporarily subverting his intelligence and sensitivity to the code demanded by this environment. He and his friends challenged oppressive authority by playing cruel practical jokes on teachers, ministers, and the ladies of the town. One of their favorite targets was Miss Abbott, who taught fourth grade and boasted that she had read no book through but the Bible. "You lived to believe her," Morris writes, "and to rue the day she got hold of that book." Fire-and-brimstone sermons and diatribes against sex were a routine part of his religious training, and repeated exposure to slide lectures on the Holy Land led thirteen-year-old Morris to vow never to go there "no matter what the inducements or how exceptional the circumstances."

Morris points out the contradictory impulses which such an atmosphere fostered, a curious combination of courtliness and violence. Nowhere

was this schizophrenia more evident than in the attitude toward the blacks, whom the whites regarded as "ours, to do with as we wished." Yet Morris and his friends were intrigued by the inhabitants of shantytown, perhaps simply because they represented a different way of life. The only other links to a larger world were baseball and the war; Morris followed the progress of both avidly. At the age of fourteen, he got his first journalistic experience doing editorial writing for his high-school newspaper. Later he became a part-time disc jockey, news analyst, and sports announcer for the local radio station, which broadcast from studios "high above the Taylor and Roberts Feed and Seed Store, in downtown Yazoo City." Yet his mind "sought some unknown awakening," and with his father's encouragement, at seventeen he left Yazoo and its dreams of success to enter the University of Texas at Austin.

The move to Texas marked the beginning of Morris's second stage of growth. The western "expansiveness" and "liberality of spirit" which he found there contrasted sharply with the world he left behind. Austin itself was "brisk, burgeoning, metropolitan," and the university, raw and unformed, yet enormous in size and wealth, was poised for better things. So was Morris as he stood awe-stricken before the thirty-story "Tower" and read the inscription on the edifice: "Ye Shall Know the Truth and the Truth Shall Make You Free." In this environment he became aware of the importance of books and ideas, and began to develop his own opinions and values.

Morris refined both his ideas and his writing style in weekly columns for the *Daily Texan*, regarded as one of the best student newspapers in the country. In his senior year, he became its editor, and his outspoken editorials, especially those dealing with the state's "twin deities," the oil and gas industries, brought down the wrath of the board of regents. He quickly learned that "a student editor in Texas could blaspheme the Holy Spirit and the Apostle Paul, but irreverence stopped at the well-head." Morris's lofty journalistic ideals were put to the test when the newspaper was threatened with censorship. In the struggle that followed, Morris defended his position and the university administration reluctantly backed down. Of the newspaper and the tradition which it upheld, Morris was unabashedly proud: "In its finest moments, and they had been often, the *Daily Texan* had defended the spirit of a free university even when the University of Texas itself was unable or unwilling to do so, and in these periods it had reached an eloquence and displayed a courage that would have challenged the mature profession."

As a result of his journalistic experience, Morris developed a keen understanding of Texas power and politics and a journalistic reputation which would later serve him well. He graduated from the University of Texas in 1956 with a B.A. and a Rhodes Scholarship, and spent the next four years at New College, Oxford University. Returning home for his father's funeral in 1958, he married his college sweetheart, Celia Ann Buchan, and the next year their only son, David Rae, was born. In 1959 Morris received a B.A. degree in modern history and in 1960 an M.A. from Oxford.

That same year he was invited back to Texas to edit the *Texas Observer*, a liberal weekly newspaper which concentrated on political and social concerns. Under the editorship of Ronnie Dugger, it had grown in reputation and influence and had a small but steady circulation. Morris saw the diversity and change which Texas embodied as a microcosm for the entire country and its problems. He envisioned the *Observer* as "something of a literary undertaking" and aimed at the best in political writing and investigative journalism. Through his daily contact with the state legislature, Morris became acutely aware of the wide divergence between the state's wealth and its commitment to social programs. Its senators and representatives were largely white, Anglo-Saxon, Protestant, and politically conservative, though the state itself was characterized by both ethnic and social diversity. At a special address to a joint session, he was astounded to hear a preacher assure the assembly that "Jesus upheld the profit motive." Morris came to know everyone from reactionaries and racists with "heavy, red-faced meanness" written on every feature to individuals like Rep. Bob Eckhardt of Houston and Maury Maverick, Jr., who fought often unpopular political battles for civil liberties and social reform. He followed political campaigns across the state, and his travels renewed his sense of Texas as a place both "expansive and volatile." Ultimately the pressures of writing and managing a weekly newspaper almost singlehandedly became overwhelming, and in 1963 Morris resigned after three years as editor. Of the first two stages in his life, he wrote, "Mississippi would lurk forever in the heart; Texas was where I reached maturity."

After a brief stint in graduate school in English at Stanford University, Morris headed to New York to look for a job. Aided by his journalistic background and a long-standing friendship with John Fischer, editor-in-chief at *Harper's*, Morris was spared the usual struggle of the newcomer to make it in what he called the "Big Cave." Fischer offered him an editorial position shortly after his arrival and Morris embarked on a new and challenging experience, yet one which required a great amount of personal adjustment. Attuned as he was to place, Morris was especially cognizant of the callousness, violence, and isolation of New York, a city which "lived frenetically in the present." He wondered especially "about the children, growing up with no local *belonging*, no feel for place or of generations gone," an experience so different from his own. Here personal ties were superficial and transient; people regarded each other as "friends" if they lunched once or twice a year. This was especially true of the New York literary establishment, which he described as a "harsh, cliquish, nervous world." Against this backdrop, Morris developed a heightened awareness of his own past and how it had shaped him, an influence he vowed not to sacrifice because it was unfashionable.

In 1965 Morris became executive editor of *Harper's* and immediately began to put into practice his plan for establishing it as a truly *national* magazine, one which would encourage "the most daring and imaginative and inventive of our writers, scholars, and journalists—to help give the country some feel of itself and what it was becoming." The work of such new contributors as Larry King and William Styron infused vitality into a journal that had become pedestrian, stuffy, and uninspired. In keeping with *Harper's* new emphasis on social concerns, an entire 1965 issue dealt with the problems of Morris's native South, especially the still controversial area of civil rights. Among the contributors were William Styron, C. Vann Woodward, Walker Percy, and Whitney M. Young. The same year *Harper's* published these essays as a book, *The South Today: 100 Years After Appomattox*, edited with an introduction by Morris.

In 1967 Morris became editor-in-chief of *Harper's* at the age of thirty-two. He was the eighth individual to hold that post and the youngest in the magazine's long and distinguished history. That same year, his memoir *North Toward Home* was published and won the Houghton Mifflin Literary Award and the Carr P. Collins nonfiction award. He continued to recruit for *Harper's* such talent as David Halberstam, Marshall Frady, and John Corry, and began to excerpt lengthy sections from such works as Styron's *The Confessions of Nat Turner* and Norman Mailer's *The Armies of the Night*. Under Morris's leadership the magazine boosted its circulation and developed a reputation for lively and provocative journalism.

However successful otherwise, Morris did find himself enmeshed in an internal struggle with William S. Blair, the magazine's president, over economics and philosophy. To ensure the caliber of work he wanted, Morris paid salaries of up to $25,000 a year to contributing editors. Individual articles were worth no less than $1,000 each. Though initially regarded as a warranted expense, such practices fell into managerial disfavor when profits began to slip in 1969. Morris's use of such controversial essays as Mailer's "The Prisoner of Sex" prompted an ideological showdown. Morris viewed the conflict between what he termed "the money men against the literary men" as irresolvable, and in March of 1971 he resigned as editor, taking with him a large portion of his loyal and sympathetic staff. He has since concentrated on his own writing.

During his last two years at *Harper's*, Morris wrote *Yazoo: Integration in a Deep-Southern Town* (1971), which describes the impact of the 1969 U.S. Supreme Court desegregation order on his hometown. The work won widespread critical praise for its unique blending of personal history and social reporting. Responding to an elemental urge, Morris returned after twenty years to "the place which shaped me for better or worse, into the creature I now am . . . ." The changes in his own life, including a failed marriage, seemed almost to compel him to make this pilgrimage. In Yazoo he found things superficially the same but fundamentally different. Physically the town had changed little, and certain streets and houses triggered a Proustian shock of recognition. There was still a sign advertising a "color bar," and blacks still went to their own schools. Like much of the South, Mississippi had sidestepped the Brown decision for fifteen years; the recent compliance order from the Supreme Court was the result of that evasion. What the town had failed to do willingly, however, it now seemed determined to carry out with grace. In a series of interviews conducted during several visits, Morris presents the emotional ambivalence and changing attitudes of the town's blacks and whites, adults and children alike, toward this new challenge. He introduces a state senator, a newspaper editor, a black priest, a supermarket owner, a basketball coach, and a civil rights worker; though their motivation and enthusiasm may vary, each is dedicated to making desegregation work. In Morris's view, "An immense facade was beginning to crack, barely perceptible at first, but to a writer and son of Mississippi, it was the little things which were gradually enclosing and symbolizing the promise and magnitude of what might be taking place here." With sometimes wavering faith and guarded optimism, the people of Yazoo were united in their commitment to have their town serve as an example of what could be accomplished with dedication and perseverance. For Morris personally, the return home helped to resolve his own ambivalent attitude toward his past and allowed him to view the present with a new perspective. In the *New York Times Book Review*, Dan Wakefield wrote: "In the deepest sense we all live in Yazoo. Mr. Morris's triumph is that he has made us understand that."

Good Old Boy: A Delta Boyhood (1971), for which Morris received the Texas Institute of Letters' Steck-Vaughn Award, was written to communicate his experience of growing up in the South to his own son, David, whose youth was spent in Manhattan. According to Thomas H. Stahel in *America* magazine, the memoir is delightful reading "for anyone who appreciates reminiscences vividly remembered and lovingly recounted." Here he elaborates on many of the episodes in *North Toward Home* and introduces a number of new anecdotes as well. Again the emphasis is on place. So deeply attached was he to his hometown that even when Morris went away to college, he was called "Yazoo." He writes evocatively of the country and people he knew there. Bubba Barrier, Spit McGee, Billy Rhodes, and Rivers Applewhite are restored to their youthful selves and join Morris and his favorite dog, Skip, in a variety of humorous, imaginative, and sometimes reckless exploits. There are the usual small-town stories of witches, ghosts, and graveyards, but an actual encounter with Amazonian Indian kidnappers in a deserted mansion outdoes the best fictional tale of adventure. Along with the happy memories, Morris recalls the claustrophobic restlessness and yearning that often possessed him: "I sat on a curb on Grand Avenue with the most dreadful feeling of being caught forever by time—trapped there always in my scrawny and helpless condition. *I'm ready, I'm ready,* I kept thinking to myself." Though ultimately he was compelled to leave, Morris feels bound to pass on to others the feeling that once lived "in the heart of a young and vulnerable boy, an allegiance and a love for one small place."

In *The Last of the Southern Girls* (1973), Morris's first attempt at writing fiction, he moves too far from both his emotional home and his creative

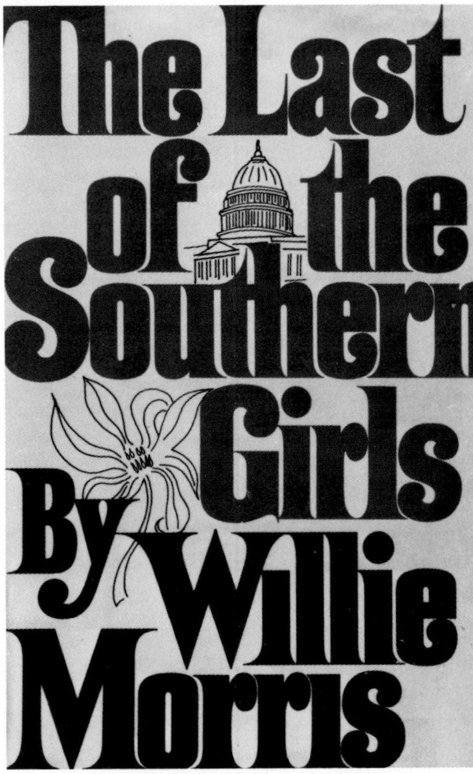

Dust jacket

milieu in the judgment of most critics. In a typical response, D. Keith Mano wrote that he was "not much persuaded by Morris's descriptions," which he terms "unexceptionable and unexceptional." Set in Washington, D.C., in the 1960s, the novel traces the social rise and fall of Carol Templeton Hollywell, a transplanted Southern belle who practices her charms on a receptive but fickle audience. By temperament and training, she is ideally suited to the part she chooses to play: "Her whole life, the grace and ease and the good-natured badinage, seemed to have prepared her for it, sprang from the soil of her birth. It had been so easy. She had learned a very important secret: *they were starved for a beautiful irreverent woman.*" Unfortunately, Morris is not as adept at creating fictional characters as he is at recreating actual ones. The reader learns of Carol's social triumphs and is occasionally allowed to see her in action. Yet her highly touted wit and supposedly novel frankness must be accepted on faith because they are never evident. In a round of social activities which includes a White House party, Carol Templeton captivates a host of unbelievably provincial journalists, political aides, and statesmen, all of whom have never seen her like before. The people she encounters, whether friends or lovers, are indistinguishable from each other. Carol's two confidantes, Elaine Rossiter and Jennie Grand, seem intended to serve as her foils, and they are never fully realized as characters. Carol's male conquests are equally undeveloped, though they do share a common characteristic: they are all her inferiors. She is aware of this natural superiority; yet she inexplicably marries one of them, a vacuous but wealthy industrialist.

Not until the scene shifts to Carol's home turf of DeSoto, Arkansas, does the novel become less static. In the familiar Southern setting, Morris evokes the land and the people he knows best—those elemental folk whose faith resides "in God, the river, next year's crops, the strange benevolence of nature, and the Democratic party." Carol is a product of this ethos, "a child of the place and the moment," and her native imagination, independence, and determination are illustrated in numerous childhood incidents, many of them borrowed from Morris's own experiences in *North Toward Home* and *Good Old Boy*. Like Morris, she is aware of the past as a living presence. Such figures as Hernando de Soto, whose bones supposedly lay buried outside town, the extinct Amazonian Indians, who once lived in the area, and her illustrious Civil War ancestors are all part of this consciousness. Here also she is shaped into a Southern belle. Elected "Most Beautiful, Most Popular and Best Dressed, only barely missing the coveted Most Versatile which she would get the following year," Carol's talents and ambitions are formed early.

However, when the action returns to the present, the narrative becomes discursive. After her fall from social favor and her failed marriage, Carol retreats to reassess her life and goals. While still in this limbo, she is drawn into a relationship with Jack Winter, a Southern congressman. Winter is decidedly the best of the men she has encountered, an honest politician who has heeded the warning of his best friend, a "Negro poet" from Mobile, "never to turn his back on seed stores, feed stores, and courthouse squares." A trip he and Carol take through the historic countryside of Virginia, stopping to talk in the local bars, serves to demonstrate that Winter is indeed a man of his word. As they walk together through the streets of a small town, the two are acutely aware of being bound by a common heritage and a shared vision. Indeed the relationship seems almost ideal. Winter behaves admirably throughout the affair; their precocious children from former marriages get along well. Quite suddenly, however, Carol begins to suspect that she has been "slumming" with Winter, though her reasoning is never explained. When he is defeated after a brutal statewide campaign, Carol's suspicions are confirmed: "He had let her down. *He was a loser*. Out of all these despairing thoughts, whirling within her like dervishes, she resolved that she must somehow leave him." When Winter proposes to her, Carol realizes that she is his superior and that she can never link her destiny to his. Once again her uniqueness must be taken on faith. Indeed Morris asks the reader to accept her as an original at the same time that he presents her as the last of a type. Though the conclusion is never really prepared for, the novel ends with Carol on the verge of some quasi-existential awakening as she returns again to that "national waystation," Washington, D.C.

Morris's most recent work, *James Jones: A Friendship* (1978), was harshly judged by a number of critics for its lack of objectivity, but it is not intended to be a biography, rather "the illumination of a friend." In it he describes his relationship with Jones, his neighbor on Long Island, during the last years of that writer's life. In the process he also tells something of his own life and work since his resignation from *Harper's* in 1971. Morris's attitude toward Jones is one of boyish admiration, if not awe. Such blatant hero worship is surprising in a man of Morris's experience and accomplishment. Yet while this quality is always present, it is seldom excessive. Morris does try to convey a personal sense of Jones, and he is generally successful.

He says of Jones that "the man and his work were all of a piece." Actually the adventurous, violent world which Jones depicted in such novels as *From Here to Eternity* and *Some Came Running* did not seem to suit his temperament and was far removed from his own experience after the war. Though he was given to occasional outbursts of vulgar language, his character was almost benign. Morris describes him as "an old-fashioned man," "deeply loving and tender." A disciplined and dedicated writer, he had none of the eccentricities to which the creative are sometimes prone. To Morris, he was "the sanest man I ever knew." Happily married to a beautiful and talented woman, he was a devoted father to his two children. Before settling on Long Island, the Joneses had spent fifteen productive years living in Paris, with a house on the Seine and the company of numerous friends.

In his relationship with Morris, Jones is a quietly indulgent father figure. When Morris overreacts to a *New York Times* review of *A Southern Album* (1975), for which he has written an introductory essay, Jones teasingly helps him to put the experience in perspective. Together they enjoy

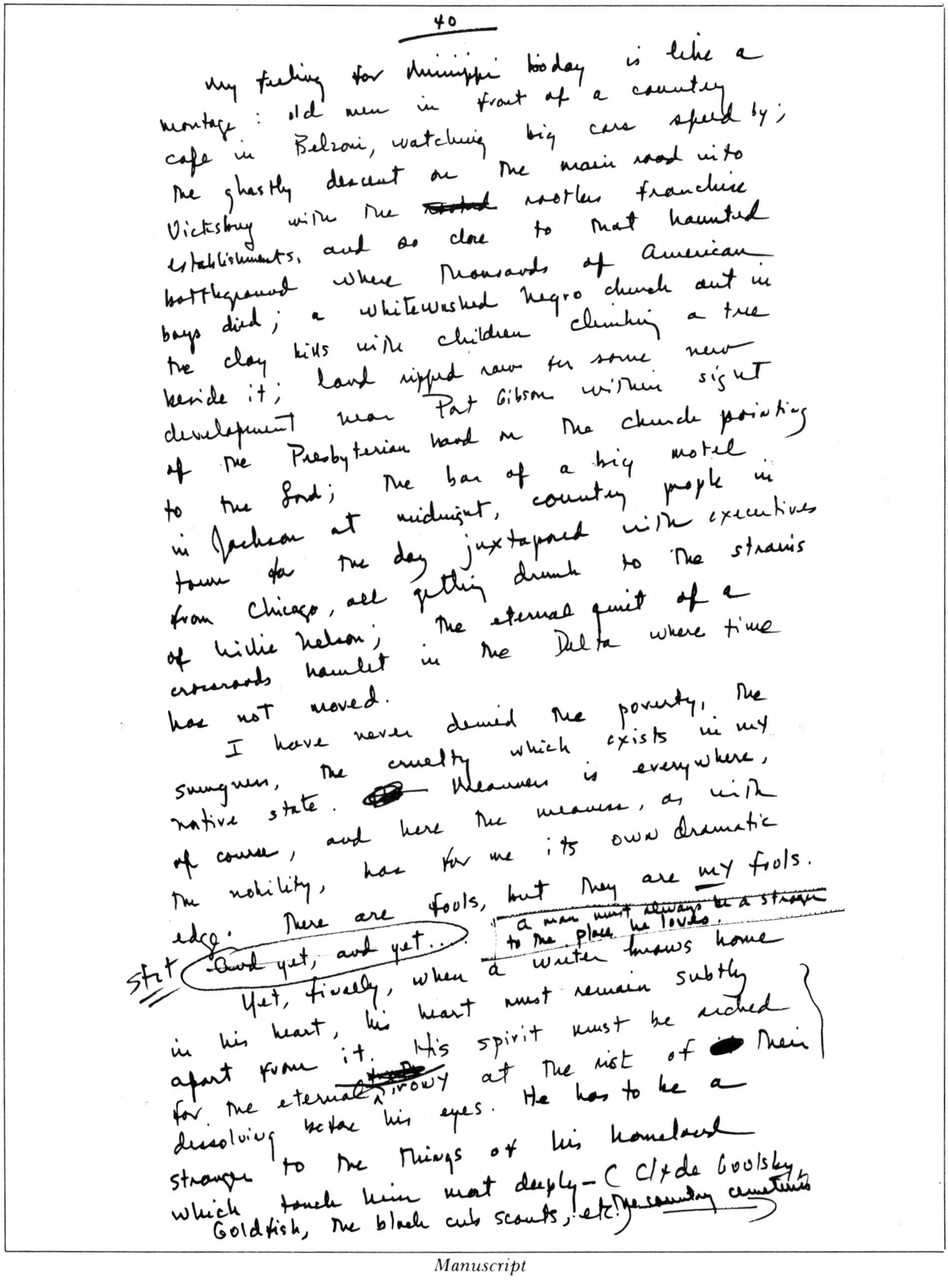

40

My feeling for Mississippi today is like a montage: old men in front of a country cafe in Belzoni, watching big cars speed by; the ghastly descent on the main road into Vicksburg with the ~~[illegible]~~ rootless franchise establishments, and so close to that haunted battleground where thousands of American boys died; a whitewashed Negro church out in the clay hills with children climbing a tree beside it; land ripped raw for some new development near Pat Gibson within sight of the Presbyterian hand on the church pointing to the Lord; the bar of a big motel in Jackson at midnight, country people in town for the day juxtaposed with executives from Chicago, all getting drunk to the strains of Willie Nelson; the eternal quiet of a crossroads hamlet in the Delta where time has not moved.

I have never denied the poverty, the smugness, the cruelty which exists in my native state. [illegible] Meanness is everywhere, of course, and here the meanness, as with the nobility, has for me its own dramatic edge. There are fools, but they are my fools. And yet, and yet... stet ~~a man must always be a stranger~~ to the place he loves.

Yet, finally, when a writer knows home in his heart, his heart must remain subtly apart from it. His spirit must be arched for the eternal ~~[illegible]~~ irony at the rot of [illegible] them dissolving before his eyes. He has to be a stranger to the things of his homeland which touch him most deeply—(Clyde Goolsby, Goldfish, the black cub scouts, etc! the country cemeteries)

Manuscript

the rural landscape of rolling potato fields and the small town of Bridgehampton, where they lunch and drink with the locals and play baseball for the Golden Nematodes. With their sons they make a pilgrimage to the battlefields and countryside of Virginia where Morris tries to imbue in Jones his own sense of a Southern past. At other times he attributes attitudes and feelings to Jones which are decidedly his own, so determined is he to forge a connection between them. Obviously sensitive to his friend's need, Jones accepts an invitation to watch *Gone With the Wind* on television because "I want to see it at the same time that damned Willie Morris from Mississippi does." In the opening pages of the book, Jones goes looking for Morris with the news that his mother has died, then invites him back to his farmhouse, Chateau Spud. In the final pages, Morris returns from his mother's funeral to sit at Jones's deathbed where he helps him to tape a few passages of an unfinished novel—like the others, a war story. Again Morris emphasizes the kinship between their experiences: ". . . the Army was, in truth, his Yoknapatawpha County; like Faulkner, he could not get away from it even when he wanted to." In his own writing as well, Morris continues to demonstrate that "unless we are fools and seek more than we bargain for, we always come back to what we are."

—*Joan Bobbitt*

Other:

The South Today: 100 Years After Appomattox, edited with an introduction by Morris (New York: Harper & Row, 1965);

Irwin Glusker, ed., *A Southern Album*, narrative by Morris (Birmingham, Ala.: Oxmoor House, 1975).

References:

"Coup at *Harper's*," *Newsweek*, 77 (15 March 1971): 64;

E. Z. Friedenberg, Review of *North Toward Home*, *New York Review of Books*, 9 (December 1967): 3;

D. Keith Mano, Review of *The Last of the Southern Girls*, *New York Times Book Review*, 20 May 1973, p. 7;

Review of *North Toward Home*, *Times Literary Supplement*, 12 September 1968, p. 985;

Review of *North Toward Home*, *Virginia Quarterly Review*, 44 (Spring 1968): lxii;

Mitchell Ross, Review of *James Jones*, *New Republic*, 179 (25 November 1978): 37;

Thomas H. Stahel, Review of *Good Old Boy*, *America*, 126 (25 May 1972): 324-325;

Dan Wakefield, Review of *Yazoo*, *New York Times Book Review*, 16 May 1971, p. 42.

Frances Newman

(13 September 1883-28 October 1928)

BOOKS: *The Hard-Boiled Virgin* (New York: Boni & Liveright, 1926; London: Secker, 1927);

Dead Lovers are Faithful Lovers (New York: Boni & Liveright, 1928; London: Secker, 1928).

Until recent republications of her work, Frances Newman's sole claim to literary fame seemed to be the fact that *The Hard-Boiled Virgin* was once "banned in Boston." Genteel readers of the time recoiled from the bold, experimental writing of a woman who had, in effect, exceeded the prerogatives of a lady in polite society. Moreover, the author had defied both the customs and moral sentiments of her native South by writing what she claimed was the first novel ever written by a woman that told the truth about women.

Frances Newman was born in Atlanta in 1883 (some sources cite 1888), the fifth and last child of Captain William Truslow Newman and Frances Percy Alexander Newman. The Newmans were eminent in Georgia politics and society and bestowed upon their children all of the advantages of wealth and prestige. Frances Newman attended private schools and watched with ambivalent envy as her sisters made their debuts. She was unquestionably a product of the caste against which she later rebelled.

A plain and intensely intellectual girl, Newman liked to reminisce that she spent most of her youth reading books in her father's massive library. She wrote a novel when she was ten years old, but was so ridiculed by the adults who discovered her secret that she suppressed her budding literary ambitions for many years. As her semiautobiographical first novel makes clear, she spent her adolescent years trying to "fit in" as a proper Southern lady. Ultimately, the obligations of proper Southern ladies proved too restrictive for this free spirit.

Newman's father was a city attorney and later a

district federal judge. Her mother claimed direct descent from the founder of Knoxville. Mrs. Newman's family traced their roots to a group of English and Scottish pioneers who had originally settled in what is now Tennessee. The Alexanders moved to Atlanta directly after the Civil War and quickly became a part of that city's gentility. Such people as the Newmans and the Alexanders did not send their children to public schools, and Frances Newman was duly enrolled in private institutions in Atlanta, New York, and Washington, D.C. Although her education seems to have been sporadic during these years, Newman absorbed information quickly and knew how to apply it. As she matured, she decided to specialize in library science, an "acceptable" occupation for a young lady of the age. She studied librarianship at Agnes Scott College in Decatur, Georgia, the University of Tennessee, and the library school of Atlanta's Carnegie Library.

In 1913 Newman accepted a library post at the Florida State College for Women in Tallahassee, a position she held for one year. From 1914 to 1922 she worked in the cataloguing and circulation departments of the Atlanta Carnegie Library. This assignment must have rekindled her literary interests, for in 1923 she left the library for Paris, where she studied literature at the Sorbonne and began translating materials she would include in *The Short Story's Mutations* (1924). It should be noted that Newman was still a voracious reader and fluent by this time in many languages.

Upon her return to the United States, Newman accepted an offer from the Georgia Institute of Technology in Atlanta, where, except for occasional leaves of absence, she would remain until the end of her life. Previously, at Carnegie Library, she had begun to write caustic book reviews for that library's bulletin as well as miscellaneous pieces of literary journalism for the *Atlanta Constitution*, Emily Clark's Richmond little magazine, the *Reviewer*, and various New York papers. The incisive, penetrating wit of her reviews attracted the attention of James Branch Cabell and H. L. Mencken, who directly encouraged her to pursue her writing. At this point in her life, Newman had apparently resigned herself to an aberrant life-style; she openly defied the norms of society with her unusual sartorial habits (she dressed in shades of purple) and her acquisition of many casual lovers, some half her age. The painful conflict between prescribed code and eccentric impulse had once weighed heavily upon her conscience, as her semiautobiographical novels reveal, but now she no longer cared what people thought.

In 1924 Newman produced her first book, a fascinating but bizarre study and history of the short story as a genre. The book also contains an anthology of stories arranged in chronological order, and her selections reveal that she admired fiction exhibiting mannered style and psychological subtlety of plot—the two most distinctive features of her own work. Newman's critical commentary in this book, *The Short Story's Mutations*, is highly personalized, even impressionistic, but nevertheless full of valuable and interesting insights. It was precisely her unorthodox views and her complex and convoluted prose style that captured the attention of the literary world.

Newman also had her first work of fiction published in 1924, a short story called "Rachel and Her Children." This story, which appeared in Mencken's *American Mercury*, won an O. Henry Memorial Award. By 1925, she was being invited to submit pieces to the *Saturday Review*, the *New York Herald Tribune*, and other notable publications. In 1926 she took up temporary residence at the MacDowell Colony for writers and artists in Peterborough, New Hampshire, and there finished the final draft of *The Hard-Boiled Virgin*, published later that year by Boni & Liveright.

The Hard-Boiled Virgin is uncompromisingly experimental. The story of a woman named Katharine Faraday who gradually throws off the yoke of social and sexual oppression, the novel has

Frances Newman

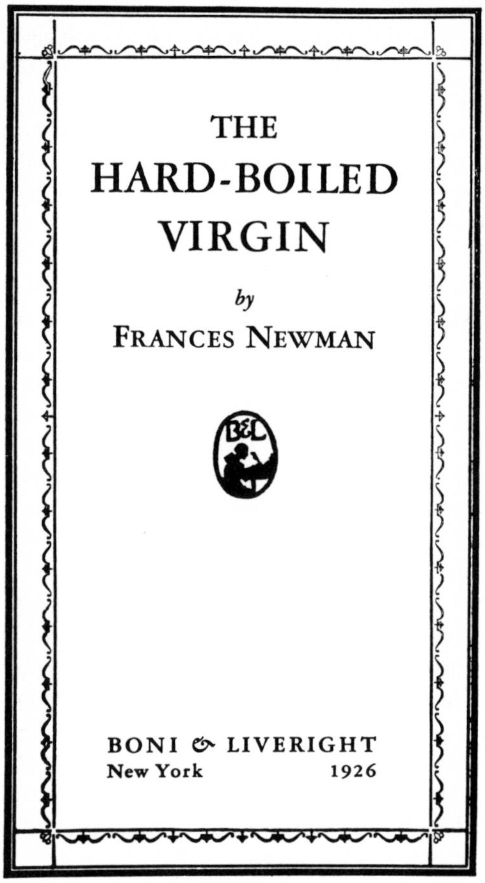
THE
HARD-BOILED
VIRGIN
by
FRANCES NEWMAN
BONI & LIVERIGHT
New York 1926

Title page

virtually no plot. Its prose style, characterized by the same difficult sentence structure Newman used in *The Short Story's Mutations*, has repelled some commentators and delighted others. Newman's intention was to record the unfolding of her heroine's state of mind in a daring new form of stream of consciousness, but whether she succeeds is a matter of dispute. At any rate, Katharine (a thinly disguised Newman) finally manages to come to terms with both herself and the numerous men who cause her so much anguish. Katharine's answer to the plight of the intellectual woman in chauvinistic society seems to be pursuing a career and independence. While she does not reject sex, she recoils from motherhood and, eventually, the prospect of marriage itself. *The Hard-Boiled Virgin* offended the prevailing social sensibility because it threatened the foundations of that sensibility: women were not *supposed* to think such thoughts.

In 1927 Newman was back at MacDowell Colony working on her second novel, *Dead Lovers are Faithful Lovers*, which appeared the following year. If *The Hard-Boiled Virgin* had examined the fate of solitary women in society, this new book took a closer look at the state of married women. Its heroine, Evelyn Dodge, bases her entire identity on the all-consuming passion she feels for her husband, an attractive business executive. Ironically, Evelyn's husband dies before she has a chance to discover that he was about to leave her for another woman. Thus the absorbing love that becomes enshrined in her memory is just a sacred illusion. In this second novel Newman duplicated the stylistic peculiarities that she had developed in *The Hard-Boiled Virgin*; in fact, the two books are nearly identical stylistically.

In 1928 Newman returned to Europe to work on a new project, what she described as a "history of sophistication." But she developed a mysterious eye ailment which almost completely incapacitated her. She returned to the United States to consult specialists in Philadelphia and New York, but they were unable to diagnose her troubles. While in New York, Newman collapsed in her apartment and was found unconscious by a friend. Reports on the cause of her untimely death vary, but an autopsy revealed that she had suffered brain hemorrhaging attributable to an aneurysm. Newman's last published work was a translation of Laforgue which appeared posthumously in 1928 as *Six Moral Tales from Jules Laforgue*. A volume of her letters, edited by Hansell Baugh and published in 1929, essentially completed the collected works of Frances Newman.

Although Newman received critical praise from a number of influential writers during the 1920s, her work quickly disappeared from the public purview. If she has been rediscovered, as critic Anne Firor Scott maintains, it is because readers have come to realize that her insights were far ahead of their time and that her controversial prose may indeed be the only medium through which these insights could have been transmitted. Generally, however, it can be concluded that Newman's accomplishment, while enormously sophisticated, was minor. She simply did not have the time to develop into the major writer she might have become with increasing confidence and greater experience.

—Louis Gallo

Other:

The Short Stories Mutations from Petronius to Paul Morand, edited and translated, with commentary, by Newman (New York: Huebsch, 1924);

Six Moral Tales from Jules Laforgue, edited and translated by Newman (New York: Liveright, 1928).

Periodical Publication:

"Rachel and Her Children," *American Mercury*, 2 (May 1924): 92-96.

Letters:

Frances Newman's Letters, ed. Hansell Baugh (New York: Liveright, 1929).

References:

James Branch Cabell, *Some of Us* (New York: McBride, 1921);

Robert Drake, "Frances Newman: Fabulist of Decadence," *Georgia Review*, 14 (Winter 1960): 389-398.

Josefina Niggli

(13 July 1910-)

BOOKS: *Mexican Silhouettes* (Hidalgo, Nuevo León, Mexico: Privately printed, 1928; revised edition, San Antonio: Silhouette Press, 1931);

Mexican Folk Plays (Chapel Hill: University of North Carolina Press, 1938);

Mexican Village (Chapel Hill: University of North Carolina Press, 1945);

Pointers on Playwriting (Boston: The Writer, Inc., 1945);

Pointers on Radio Writing (Boston: The Writer, Inc., 1946);

Step Down, Elder Brother (New York: Rinehart, 1947);

A Miracle for Mexico (Greenwich: New York Graphic Society, 1964);

New Pointers on Playwriting (Boston: The Writer, Inc., 1967).

Josefina Niggli has made a notable contribution to American drama and prose with her portraits of the humorously traditional but, at times, tragic lives of the people of northern Mexico. Unlike the usually too picturesque sketch of the Mexican so prevalent in American literature, or the frequently pathetic view in films and television, Niggli's work combines a deep understanding of the Mexican personality with a sure knowledge of custom and folkways.

Born in Monterrey, Mexico, in the year of the great Mexican Revolution of 1910, Niggli grew up in two worlds. Her father was a Texan who had gone to work for the Mexican railroad in 1893. By the time his daughter and only child was born, he had become the manager of a cement plant in Hidalgo, a small town near Monterrey. Her mother, a Virginian named Goldie Morgan Niggli, was a concert violinist. "Little Niggli," as the family called Josefina, was sent out of Mexico in 1913 to escape the turmoil of the Revolution; thus, her formative years were divided between Monterrey and San Antonio, Texas.

Until she went to Main Avenue High School in San Antonio, Niggli was taught by her mother. Moreover, she frequently studied on her own, because her mother had a burst eardrum and could not tolerate much noise. This unconventional schooling eventually served her in good stead, albeit in a strange way. She states that when, in 1925 at the age of fifteen, she went to Incarnate Word College in San Antonio, a professor, impressed by the gaps in her knowledge, told her he had never had a student with such a totally blank mind. He instructed her teachers not to let her take notes in class, saying that what she did not remember would not be of any use to her. As a result of this training, Niggli developed a keen memory, and she was later able to write extensively about Mexico without having to do much research. As another result of her nontraditional schooling, Niggli was not, as she laughingly commented, "contaminated by American institutions." Her outlook remained fresh and unspoiled by ideology.

Niggli began writing poems and short stories at an early age. Many were published in various magazines, such as *Mexican Life* and the *Ladies' Home Journal*. Her parents and teachers provided forceful encouragement, sometimes when Niggli herself was less than enthusiastic. She relates that one of the nuns at Incarnate Word, Sister Mary Clement, locked her in a room and would not let her come out until she had written a piece for the *Ladies' Home Journal* Short Story Contest. A few weeks later, when Niggli received a piece of correspondence from the magazine, she threw it in the wastepaper basket, thinking it an advertisement. Her mother noticed it and retrieved it. Niggli had won the second prize in the contest.

Her family continued to encourage her to write. In 1928 her father had her poems printed privately under the title *Mexican Silhouettes*. He took the books to an English-language bookstore in Mexico City and persuaded the owner to display them. They all sold immediately, and in 1931 a revised edition was published in San Antonio. This early success was followed by Niggli's winning the National Catholic College Poetry Contest.

During the late 1920s and early 1930s in San Antonio, she wrote for KTSA Radio. This experience gave her the opportunity to produce some serial cliff-hangers which were very popular with local audiences. After receiving her B.A. in 1931, Niggli became involved in an activity on which she would focus her energies for many years to come: she studied playwriting under Coates Gwynne, the director of the San Antonio Little Theatre. After Gwynne told her mother that he thought Josefina should be a playwright, Niggli decided to study this craft at the University of North Carolina at Chapel Hill. The decision, she says, was based on climate: she did not want to live any place where it snowed. Fortunately the Carolina Playmakers and Prof. Frederick Koch were made to order for her talents and interests. Two of the Playmakers who exerted a special influence on Niggli during this period were playwrights Paul Green and Betty Smith.

In 1935, the year Niggli went to Chapel Hill, the most creative period of her playwriting career began. She became an active participant in the Carolina Playmakers, acting, designing costumes, directing, and most important, writing. The folk-oriented, regional plays which were being produced provided a forum for Niggli's special background. In the next few years her most successful dramatic works, the Mexican folk comedies, were produced: *Tooth or Shave* in 1935, *The Red Velvet Goat*, and *Sunday Costs Five Pesos*, both in 1936. She wrote historical plays set in Mexico, including *The Cry of Dolores* in 1935 and *Soldadera* and *Azteca* in 1936. Two full-length plays, *The Fair God* and *Singing Valley*, were also written and produced in 1936.

The folk comedies reveal Niggli at her best. Brimming with conflict, these plays present Mexican village life with robust good humor. The characters are spirited, their simple lives briefly upset by greed, pride, or the desire to appear better than their neighbors. The desire for status is at the heart of the farcical *Tooth or Shave* in which two married couples clash over their concern for appearances. Anselmo, the simpleminded barber/toothpuller, manipulated by his wily neighbor, Tomás the carpenter, hands over the ten pesos his wife has been saving for her grand funeral. Tomás blackmails Anselmo by convincing him that the entire village will believe he is a coward merely because he does not want to have his head sawed off. Parallel to this conflict is the one between their wives, one of whom boasts of the lovely funeral she will someday enjoy, and the other who has ten pesos for a phonograph which will be the envy of the entire village. The conflict is resolved when Anselmo and his wife, whose money has actually paid for the phonograph, get it. Peace is restored, at least for the time being. In these small villages one's standing may be determined by a seemingly petty possession, such as a goat or a phonograph, and in a village where no one is truly wealthy, pride may be a person's only treasure.

Niggli's most performed play is *Sunday Costs Five Pesos*. Here, the love between a wood-carver and a village girl is disrupted by jealousy. When she sends him away in anger and then wants him back, she pretends to have jumped down a well. The play's title comes from another jealous confrontation: two young women engage in a rousing fight which carries a five-peso fine on Sundays. The resolution is hastened, and the lovers are reunited.

Deceit usually complicates the action of Niggli's folk plays. Irony runs rampant, as the quick-witted and willful try to achieve their ends. The richness of Niggli's folk comedies derives from the multiple complications of love, pride, deceit, willfulness, and tradition. But without Niggli's gift for plot, dialogue, and characterization, her one-act comedies would be merely picturesque. Her technical skill and an unfailing intuition for "what works" in the theater keeps her comedies fresh and funny a generation after they were written.

During these years of intense creativity, Niggli wrote a group of historical plays about Mexico. *The Fair God* and *The Cry of Dolores* were produced by the Playmakers, but not published. These two works demonstrate a different side of a playwright who is whimsical and lyrical in the comedies.

Another historical play, *Azteca*, was a rather daring effort on Niggli's part to represent the atmosphere and ritual of the Earth Mother Temple in ancient Tenochtitlán (Mexico City). Thwarted passions inspire the plot, while lyrical language captures the cadences of ancient ritual. Set more than 100 years before the conquest of Mexico by Cortés, the tragedy conveys authentically the atmosphere and human passions of a time difficult to reconstruct.

Also staged by the Carolina Playmakers in the 1935-1936 season was *Soldadera*, in which Niggli played a role. One of three Niggli plays treating the revolution of 1910, *Soldadera* was included in Margaret Mayorga's *The Best One-Act Plays of 1937*. In the introduction to the play, Mayorga calls Niggli "one of the few writers on the Revolutionary subject who does not outdo herself. She does not forget that, though war is said to be waged for causes, it is human beings who do the fighting, thinking their individual thoughts the while, and sometimes acting in original ways." Niggli's *Soldadera* is distinguished by her uniformly fair treatment of characters. The women soldiers who played a vital role in the war are not sanctified. Rather they are, in turn, heroic, selfish, vengeful, and self-sacrificing. They illustrate the mixed emotions of those involved in a cause.

Another Niggli play of the Revolution, *This Is Villa*, was included in Mayorga's *The Best One-Act Plays of 1938*. In its depiction of the most famous figure of the time, *This Is Villa* is effective drama. Pancho Villa emerges as the man of many contradictions that he was: cruel, tender, violent, generous, vulgar, ingenious. While *Soldadera* focuses on the suffering heroism of the women who helped to win the Revolution and explores their reasons, both personal and ideological, for participating in it, *This Is Villa* concentrates on character revelation. The dialogue has the authentic ring of Mexican speech, moving swiftly from the picturesque to the coarse. *This Is Villa* presents various types of people involved in the Revolution: a philosophical professor; the killer, Fierro, whose name in Spanish means "iron"; the loyal and innocent Antonio, "who has no place in the chaos of Revolution." Niggli uses the one-act form economically to explore the complicated subject of war, the inevitable opposites of violence and pacifism, idealism and realism. She avoids obvious resolution. For example, Antonio feels profound loyalty to his chief, Villa; thus, when the great leader accidentally kills the young boy's fiancee on their wedding day, Antonio can neither kill Villa for revenge, nor continue as his follower, and chooses to kill himself.

Niggli's writing is informed by a desire for realism. By her own account, her knowledge of the Revolution came primarily from friends who told her stories about Villa and the *soldaderas*. She had no desire to create a revolutionary myth, but rather to elucidate this moment of history in a dramatic form.

Niggli's thesis for her M.A. degree was a full-length play produced by the Playmakers in 1936. *Singing Valley* contains the germ of *Mexican Village* (1945), which also deals with the pain of separation and longing. The principal character of *Singing Valley* is a father who brings his son and daughter back to the valley of his birth, the Santa Catarina. The children have spent all their lives in the United States, and their attitudes toward Mexico are at odds. The son finds charm and sincerity in the villagers of the remote valley, while the daughter sees only boring lives and backwardness. In the course of the play, however, she discovers her American friends' shallowness and finally accepts the people of the "singing valley." It is a comedy of the pain of homecoming and the call of one's heritage, but Niggli's black-and-white treatment of life in the United States versus life in a Mexican village is a bit heavy-handed. When she returned to these themes later in *Mexican Village*, she handled them much more skillfully.

Niggli enjoyed many successes during the 1930s. In addition to the enthusiastic receptions given her folk plays, some of which were published in *One-Act Play Magazine*, she received two Rockefeller Foundation fellowships in playwriting (1935-1936 and 1937-1938). During the late 1930s she returned to Mexico and worked in the theater there, at one point serving as stage manager to Rodolfo Usigli, directing head of the Theatre of the National University of Mexico and a well-known dramatist, who was staging a one-act play by fellow Mexican playwright Xavier Villarrutia. Usigli admired Niggli's work and wrote a foreword to her *Mexican*

Manuscript page from new novel, work-title: THE RED AMAPOLA dealing with the first appearance of what is now Comunism in Mexico in 1872. Josefina Niggli

-126-

So this was the Grand Hotel in Laredo. Miniature palms in huge green tubs were scattered comfortable wicker armchairs and small tables. The red tiled floor glistened as did the mahogany reception counter where doña Brigida, with Pola standing quietly behind her, was talking to the señor Rives himself, a plump man in a pale blue linen suit. He waxxaax said about the public diligence to Monterrey, "It leave early to take advantage of the predawn coolness, especially if the norther comes."

"The norther?" snapped doña Brigida, "What do you mean, 'the norther'?"

"The cold wids of the Texas panhandle that come sweeping down ..."

"Saintedxgodxxxdo "Yes, 7yes, I remember," do;a Brigida said fretfully. "I remember. Sainted God even the weather is barberic."

She said this to Pola. But the girl was not listening. She was looking at a photograph hanging above the senor Rives head. It showed a muscular man standing by a velvet covered table black bowler. He looked like a dandy, his gray trousers creasing properly at the ankles and his vest, fastened with two buttons, a bit too small for his thick chest. His small head, with the thick military mustache and short cropped hair was pure Indian. This same photogra½h had been in the Texas newspaper yesterday. Pola caught her breath. What was a picture of Porfirio Diza doing in this respectable holtel? The paper said that President Juarez Lerdo had ordered his arrest.

Noticing her attention on the picture, the senor Rives turned quickly, gasped, and flipped the picture over to show the other side: a portrait of President Lerdo seated beside a table, his hand resting on a draped national flag.

"A thousand pzrdons," the senor Rives babbled. :Yesterday we had ten prominent Porfiristas as guests. After they left... I, a good citizen, very loyal...forgot to turn the picture."

Doña B4rigida drew herself erect. Pola recognized her expression. From that moment the senor Rives would no longer exist. The hotel would remain, yes, as it was necessary But the man would vanish as a leaf vanishes into the twilight.

"Red Amapola," revised typescript for a work in progress

Folk Plays, which was published by the University of North Carolina Press in 1938. He lauded her artful forging of Mexican character and drama, regretting that she did not write in Spanish for Mexican audiences because there was a need in Mexico for good folk drama that was neither overly picturesque nor vulgar.

In 1938 Niggli received another award, this time the Fellowship of the Bureau of New Plays, which allowed her to live in New York and attend the theater frequently. In 1939 she returned to Chapel Hill, serving as script editor for the radio division of the Playmakers.

In the early 1940s another former Carolina Playmaker and friend, Betty Smith, asked Niggli to write a play for a collection she was compiling, *Twenty Prize-Winning Non-Royalty One-Act Plays* (1943). Smith wanted Niggli's name to help promote the book, and Niggli wrote *The Ring of General Macías*, to which Smith awarded a fabricated honor, "Prize-winning drama, Inter-Isle Play Contest, Great Britain." With this play, Niggli returned to the theme of the Revolution, again painting it tragically. In this work, however, she centers on the honor of a family fighting against the Revolution. The wife of General Macías, a federal soldier, learns of her imprisoned husband's cowardice. She seals his doom by poisoning two revolutionary soldiers, but this act demonstrates her love for her husband because, by precipitating his death, she saves his honor.

Smith called on Niggli again when she was looking for plays to include in an anthology of plays for all-female casts. Niggli obliged by turning out *Miracle at Blaise* (1942), her only non-Mexican play. She chose a subject everyone would be interested in, the war raging in Europe. Set in France, *Miracle at Blaise* deals with the French resistance and an American woman's spiritual redemption through charity. The play was produced frequently during World War II and for many years after. Niggli began to pursue other interests and unfortunately never wrote another play.

Her connection with the University of North Carolina continued during World War II. Many of the male instructors were at war, and the university, which had previously employed only men, had to hire some women to teach. Niggli gave classes in English and drama, and during this time wrote what was to become her most successful work—ironically a novel, not a play.

For *Mexican Folk Plays* in 1938, Niggli had compiled an appendix on Mexican costume. The University of North Carolina Press editor was so delighted with her descriptions that he urged her to write a nonfiction book on Mexico. But when she began the project in the early 1940s, her storytelling skills led her to write *Mexican Village*. Writing from five to nine o'clock every morning before classes, and revising on Sundays, she created *Mexican Village*. The book that the author thought no one would read received magnificent reviews. According to Niggli, Clifton Fadiman proclaimed it "a classic" and it remained in print until 1978. It was translated into several European and Oriental languages and had a paperback printing. The novel received the Mayflower Cup Award in 1946 for the best book written by a North Carolinian during the previous year, an award usually given to a work of nonfiction.

The reason for *Mexican Village*'s success is undoubtedly Niggli's ability to tell a good story well. But the life she infused into the book because of her understanding of the people, their customs, personalities, dress, and language, make it a book to learn from as well as enjoy. One reviewer called *Mexican Village* a remarkable achievement because one could understand so much about Mexico from a single book. The same could still be said today. While reviewers in 1945 remarked that the book seemed a bit idyllic and romanticized, all agreed that Niggli's skillful storytelling makes the characters and settings seem alive. Mildred Adams of the *New York Times* pointed out a noteworthy aspect of Niggli's work: "Many things make this volume memorable in the modern spate of tales about Mexico. Not the least is the fact that it has no axe to grind, it demands no ideological bias on the part of the reader."

Mexican Village has been called both a novel and a collection of tales. Although the stories follow separate plot lines, the same characters appear thoughout the work, making it seem that the protagonist is actually the whole village, an idea which is also suggested by the title. The first and last chapters deal with the same character and serve as a framing device for the various stories. The physical movement of the book also helps support the relationship among the stories: the first tale takes place at the quarry, on the outskirts of Hidalgo; then the stories move from the lowliest parts of the town to the wealthiest. Each story bears as title a street or section of the town.

The individual tales have warmth, charm, irony, laughter, and sometimes tragedy. The element of trickery often observed in the folk plays is frequently present and surprises abound. In depicting the human comedy of life in the Sabinas Valley, of which Hidalgo is a part, the action concerns itself with courtship, marriage, death, family relations, and local entertainment such as cockfighting. Niggli employs Mexican folklore in *Mexican Village* as a means of bringing the people to life. The book is filled with legends, traditions, superstitions, and proverbs of the folk it describes. Witchcraft is a part of Catholic Hidalgo's life, a combination which persists in Mexico. The Latino's love of proverbs is exploited, as this device shapes the town's vision of reality and roots it in traditional beliefs.

The framing stories create a tension that helps to hold the tales together, as they explore the feelings of Bob Webster, a half-American and half-Mexican "outlander" who is torn between staying in and leaving the village, as he struggles with the difficulties of mixed heritage.

Webster goes to Hidalgo planning to stay only a year, but the tapestry of rural Mexican life gradually enfolds him, making him a part of its design. Webster becomes an important man in the village, one of its leaders, largely because of his irreverent attitude toward traditional ways. While he eventually feels at home in Hidalgo, his refusal to follow tradition blindly, coupled with a patient thoughtfulness, makes him a maverick respected by the entire town. Finally, at the end of a decade, Webster's assimilation is complete. He takes his mother's name, Ortega, and spurns the Anglo identity of the father who had never recognized his illegitimate son. Webster's redemption is a cultural reintegration of two heritages, presaging, in Ray Paredes's words, "the contemporary Chicano spirit." While Niggli does not consider herself a Chicana or even a Mexican-American, she believes that she opened the door for them in literature.

Much of Niggli's appeal as a writer lies in her skillful fictional use of people she has known or met, and she remembers that Mexicans who thought they were in the book "were after me with long guns." Actually she based characters only on people who were already dead. So many people were stopping in a little town near Monterrey to ask if it were "the" town that a restaurant owner erected a large sign that bluntly asserted: "No. This is not the right town."

In the same year *Mexican Village* was published, Niggli produced a book that brought together her theatrical experience and craftsmanship. Betty Smith had been asked to do a book on playwriting, but, as she was busy with other projects, she suggested her old friend Josefina Niggli. The resulting *Pointers on Playwriting* (1945) was very successful. It is well-organized, clear, and straightforward. Since it does not assume professional experience on the part of the reader, it is eminently practical. Niggli was asked to revise it in 1967, and the book has been widely used in schools. In 1946 Niggli attempted to repeat this success with *Pointers on Radio Writing*, which she now calls the worst book ever written on the subject. It was never revised nor reprinted.

Niggli produced her second novel, *Step Down, Elder Brother*, in 1947. It became a Book-of-the-Month Club selection and enjoyed highly favorable reviews. Some reviewers found fault with the pace, which slows down considerably at times, or said that the love story was saccharine, and some were disappointed that it was not another *Mexican Village*. But Niggli's evocation of the modern industrial city of Monterrey was applauded, and the book was successful. Niggli calls her second novel a more important book than *Mexican Village* because of its treatment of the rise of the lower middle class in Mexico. She believes that *Step Down, Elder Brother* was the first novel to deal with this theme.

As is always true of Niggli's drama and fiction, *Step Down, Elder Brother* is brimming with conflict and action. Domingo Vázquez de Anda, the principal character, experiences the turmoil of being caught between his own desires and the force of tradition. Pushed by his family into a career he does not want, engaged to a woman he does not love, Domingo is the elder son of an old, distinguished Monterrey family. His younger brother and sisters rebel, some more openly than others, against the dictates of tradition, while life in Mexico changes all about them. Domingo's love for another woman, his devotion to his younger brother, and the dynamic life of the city give shape to the conflicts. In contrast to Domingo's family, Mateo Chapa represents the new forces in society, trying to make their way into the middle class. Not only does he begin to take part in important business interests, but he actually marries into the Vázquez de Anda family. He, more than any other character, suggests the city of Monterrey in energetic, capitalist expansion.

Niggli's intelligence as a writer enables her to depict the complexity of the issues she treats. While the old Monterrey is idealistic, it is stiflingly traditional; the new Monterrey is energetically aggressive, but it can be pedestrian and too practical. Mateo's assertion that "I am a practical man. For me every peso contains 100 centavos," is inimical to the thinking of the more poetic Domingo, who, nevertheless, realizes that the old ways are changing. This change is reflected in his comment on two old men who take great pleasure in their conversations and friendships: "I shall be sorry to see their

Josefina Niggli and her dogs

generation disappear. We'll never have another that is so—innocent."

In 1948 Niggli went to Hollywood where she worked on various movie scripts. With a gift for exposition and a commonsense approach to plot, she was called on to work on parts of many movies. Her major effort was a collaboration with Norman Foster on a screenplay of *Mexican Village*. Entitled *Sombrero*, the film came out in 1953. It was panned by the critics who found the stories garbled and lumped together disjointedly. It was an unfortunate end, for the tales could have made a lively and authentic picture of Mexico. The *New York Times* movie critic found only one element of the movie, which had been filmed in Mexico, worthy of praise: the technicolor photography.

Niggli was awarded another fellowship in 1950 which enabled her to spend time at the Abbey Theatre in Dublin. She observed all rehearsals and acted in one performance. It was a fruitful period, matched by a similar one in 1955 when she attended the Old Vic School in Bristol. Niggli learned valuable lessons from the English actors and directors, which stood her in good stead for her next job.

Western Carolina University hired her to teach English and drama in 1956 and she headed the department of drama until her retirement in 1975. Her teaching career was the fulfillment of a lifelong desire. Students clamored to get into her classes, and many took drama classes just for the experience of working with her. A strict but affectionate relationship with her students as well as her unfailing professionalism and love of theater have kept many of them close to her years after they left the university.

During her career at Western Carolina University, Niggli wrote her third and last novel, *A Miracle for Mexico* (1964). The classification of this work as a book for juveniles probably ruined sales. Nevertheless, it was well received. She was considered for the Hawthorne Prize but, ironically, it was decided that the book was too mature for very young people.

A Miracle for Mexico exhibits the fine storytelling skills of Niggli's previous prose works. Set in 1531, the book relates the tumultuous emergence of Mexico after the Spanish conquest. The principal character, Martín Aguilar, smarts under the restrictions and scorn imposed upon him because he is a mestizo, albeit a noble one, in a society where Spaniards and Creoles rule. The novel deals with the theme of alienation.

The racial difference between the young Aguilar, born of don José de Aguilar and a mother from a Mayan royal house in Yucatán, and his Creole schoolmates immediately sets him apart, as does the treatment he receives from certain members of the new aristocracy of Mexico who spurn him for his mixed blood. Martín describes himself as "half Indian, half Spaniard, and half nothing." But his teacher, a friar, opens his eyes to his role in the New World. He recognizes that Martín is one of a new race, the new Mexico, the mestizo. The struggle of the protagonist of *Mexican Village* to slake the "nostalgia of the blood" is born in the conflict of the protagonist of *A Miracle for Mexico* in sixteenth-century New Spain.

The theme of racial conflict is developed parallel to the principal action of the novel, which is centered around the appearance of the Virgin of Guadalupe during the sixteenth century, the miracle referred to in the title. The miracle of Guadalupe tied the Indian in a religious bond to his conquerors, but it also gave the native Mexican a renewed sense of worth, as the Virgin chose to reveal herself to an Indian, not a Spaniard. *A Miracle for Mexico* is the best fictional account of the miracle of Guadalupe and is exceptionally informative about the era of the conquest.

In her early poems and stories, her plays of the

1930s and 1940s, and her novels, Niggli strives to open the eyes of North America to the richness of Mexico. Many Americans have written about Mexico, but Niggli does so without a trace of condescension. If her characters sometimes seem romanticized, it is because she penetrates the romantic heart of the Mexican. Her response to Usigli's lament that she did not write her plays in Spanish is confident: "The United States needed the folk drama more than Mexico. I wanted people to know the wonderful world south of the border and that there was something besides Europe." Her battle for recognition continues, but Niggli, by simply writing about what she knows best, has contributed a lively authenticity to our reading about Mexico. This contribution is marked by the fact that her one-act plays continue to be performed throughout the English-speaking world. In a way, Niggli never left Mexico; her distance from it has given her the perspective enjoyed by so many writers who have to leave home in order to find it.

—Paula W. Shirley

Screenplay:

Sombrero, by Niggli and Norman Foster, MGM, 1953.

Other:

Soldadera, in *The Best One-Act Plays of 1937,* ed. Margaret Mayorga (New York: Dodd, Mead, 1938);

This Is Villa, in *The Best One-Act Plays of 1938,* ed. Mayorga (New York: Dodd, Mead, 1939);

Miracle at Blaise, in *25 Non-Royalty One-Act Plays for All-Girl Casts,* ed. Betty Smith (New York: Greenburg, 1942);

The Ring of General Macias, in *20 Prize-Winning Non-Royalty One-Act Plays,* ed. Smith (New York: Greenburg, 1943);

This Bull Ate Nutmeg, in *Plays Without Footlights,* ed. Esther E. Galbraith (New York: Harcourt, Brace, 1945);

Singing Valley, in *Adventures in Playmaking: Four Plays by Carolina Playmakers,* ed. John W. Parker (Chapel Hill: University of North Carolina Press, 1968).

Periodical Publications:

"Salt in the Air," *Collier's,* 120 (11 October 1947): 14-15;

"Proportion in Writing," *Writer,* 66 (Summer 1953): 300-301.

References:

Raymond Paredes, "The Evolution of Chicano Literature," *MELUS,* 5 (Summer 1978): 71-110;

Walter Spearman, *The Carolina Playmakers: The First Fifty Years* (Chapel Hill: University of North Carolina Press, 1970), p. 71;

Rodolfo Usigli, Foreword to *Mexican Folk Plays* (Chapel Hill: University of North Carolina Press, 1938), pp. xv-xx.

Tim O'Brien

(1 October 1946-)

BOOKS: *If I Die in a Combat Zone, Box Me Up and Ship Me Home* (New York: Delacorte/Seymour Lawrence, 1973; London: Calder & Boyars, 1973; revised edition, New York: Delacorte/Seymour Lawrence, 1979);

Northern Lights (New York: Delacorte/Seymour Lawrence, 1975; London: Calder & Boyars, 1975);

Going After Cacciato (New York: Delacorte/Seymour Lawrence, 1978; London: Cape, 1978).

Tim O'Brien was drawn into a career as a novelist principally by the trauma of his experiences as a soldier in the Vietnam War. Vietnam seems to have produced in O'Brien a depth of feeling none of his other experiences had ever afforded. O'Brien has thus become a sensitive interpreter of basic elements in the American character and psyche—the nature of courage, the roles of violence and war, the meaning of perseverance. Although he sometimes draws heavily on previous novelists who have approached these same topics, O'Brien's point of view is thoroughly contemporary, and he offers valuable insights into the modern dilemmas posed by these issues.

William Timothy O'Brien was born in Austin, Minnesota, the son of William T. O'Brien, an insurance salesman, and Ava E. Schultz O'Brien, a schoolteacher. When he was ten, the family moved to Worthington, Minnesota, several hundred miles to the west of his birthplace. After graduation from high school, O'Brien matriculated at Macalester

College in Saint Paul, Minnesota, from which he graduated summa cum laude in 1968 with a B.A. degree in political science. While at Macalester, which achieved a reputation as a radical school during the Vietnam era, O'Brien became student body president his senior year and, according to a 1980 article in the college's newspaper, "did much to change Macalester's traditional ways, and help to plant the seeds that formed Macalester's radical reputation." He pressed for permission for twenty-one-year-olds to possess alcoholic beverages in dorms, the elimination of mandatory curfews for women, and a provision to allow coeds to close their doors while entertaining male guests in their rooms during open-house hours. He also advocated reform of the grading system and the development of dorm libraries. Despite his agitation for what were then radical ideals and practices, O'Brien did not consider himself a hippie, and many of his proposed reforms seem to have arisen from discontent with what he considered unfair social discrimination and unsound educational policy. During his college career, O'Brien also found time to write, completing a novel during a summer program in Czechoslovakia. It remains unpublished.

Immediately following graduation, O'Brien was drafted into the U.S. Army, and despite personal reasons for wishing to avoid military service, he went anyway, generally because of social considerations—tradition, obligation, consideration for his parents, and fear of being ostracized. In *If I Die in a Combat Zone* (1973), O'Brien characterizes his decision as a "sleepwalking default." O'Brien ended up fighting in Vietnam and was awarded a Purple Heart after he received a shrapnel wound near My Lai. He was promoted to sergeant during his service with the 198th Infantry Brigade.

After his discharge from the army in March 1970, O'Brien went to Harvard as a graduate student in government. During the summers of 1971 and 1972, he was an intern at the *Washington Post*, and he took a leave of absence from Harvard to serve as a national affairs reporter for the *Post* during the 1973-1974 academic year. He returned to Harvard in the fall of 1974 and studied there until the spring of 1976, when he left to pursue a full-time career as a novelist.

O'Brien has emerged as a respected writer on the subject of war and human courage, topics around which his three books revolve. He has received awards from the National Endowment for the Arts, the Massachusetts Arts and Humanities Foundation, and the Bread Loaf Writers' Conference. Chapters from *Going After Cacciato* were O. Henry Memorial Award winners for 1976 and 1978, and the novel won a National Book Award in 1979.

O'Brien's first published book was *If I Die in a Combat Zone, Box Me Up and Ship Me Home*, a book O'Brien calls a war memoir rather than a novel because while the dialogue is largely invented, the book relates his actual experiences in Vietnam. Parts of the book first appeared in *Playboy*, the *Washington Post*, the *Minneapolis Tribune*, and the *Worthington Daily Globe*. Although a revised edition, which O'Brien stripped of what he refers to as "purple prose," was published in 1979, he still calls the book "trash," a reference to what he feels was his lack of literary skill. Moreover, O'Brien now

Tim O'Brien

suspects that his perspective was limited: "Can the foot soldier teach anything important about war merely for having been there? I think not. He can tell war stories." Despite these strictures, the work stands as one of the more sensitive and literate depictions of the Vietnam War.

The beginning of *If I Die in a Combat Zone* sets the theme for the book: " 'It's incredible, it really is, isn't it? Ever think you'd be humping along some crazy-ass trail like this one, jumping up and down out of the dirt, jumping like a goddamn bullfrog, dodging bullets all day? Don't know about you, but I sure as hell never thought *I'd* ever be going all day like this. Back in Cleveland I'd still be asleep.' Barney smiled. 'Jesus, you ever see anything like this?' " These words sum up the view toward his own experiences in Vietnam that O'Brien expresses in this book. He naively assumed upon his induction, for example, that he would never be sent to fight. As he told a reporter in 1979, "I didn't know how to work a gun. I had a college education and figured they'd put me behind a typewriter. I guess I deceived myself." In many ways, therefore, the story is about the education of a somewhat bemused Midwestern boy who is suddenly thrust into the harsh world of bullets and land mines.

The book is a string of individual stories which, taken together, chronicle O'Brien's experiences just before and during the war and reflect his mental state while in Vietnam. Although some episodes are grippingly realistic, such as the story in the chapter "Mori" about the Viet Cong woman who bleeds to death from a gunshot wound, others take on an unreal, dreamlike quality.

The style of *If I Die in a Combat Zone* was described by Chris Waters as "lucid, relaxed, razor-sharp, and consiously dispassionate . . . without fuss or rhetoric." Although it includes many quotations from philosophy and literature, the work does not become didactic or shrill. As critics have pointed out, O'Brien's style seems to have been influenced by that of Ernest Hemingway. In *If I Die in a Combat Zone* O'Brien strives to craft a prose which does nothing more than tell the story simply, in clear language. When applied to strictly physical incidents, as in "Mori," O'Brien's style seems effortless. On the other hand, when applied to moral considerations, such as the nature of courage, the style sometimes becomes labored. For example, in the chapter "Courage Is a Certain Kind of Persevering," the debate between the fiery Major Callicles and O'Brien is hardly more than a thinly disguised, clumsy Socratic debate.

O'Brien's second book, *Northern Lights* (1975), is often viewed as a logical extension of *If I Die in a Combat Zone* and as an attempt by O'Brien to flush his system of the poisons of his experience in Vietnam. Instead of fighting enemy soldiers, however, the characters in this novel have to fight one another, themselves, and their paternity in a setting even bleaker than Vietnam. The book invites comparison with several of Hemingway's works, especially *The Sun Also Rises*, and critics have pointed out stylistic parallels and similar characters and incidents. Some critics, such as Roger Sale, declare that O'Brien "has read [*The Sun Also Rises*] too often, let it sink into him too deeply" while at the same time admitting that *Northern Lights* does show a certain artistic independence.

The novel's opening scene appears increasingly ironic as the book progresses. Unable to sleep the night before his brother Harvey returns from Vietnam, Perry, "sweating and anemic and flabby," gives a demonstration of civilian firepower by emptying a can of aerosol insecticide onto the mosquitoes crowding his bedroom screen. "Killed a billion of them," he states in a tone like that of a satisfied general after a battle. In this act, however, Perry summons and demonstrates nearly all the physical courage he has ever had. He has always been afraid of everything physical, including animals, deep water, and guns. When his physical courage has been tested, he has failed every time. In contrast to Perry is Harvey, nicknamed "the Bull." Harvey is apparently everything Perry is not when it comes to physical courage, and his loss of an eye in Vietnam seems merely the logical consequence of a life filled with vigor and manly derring-do. Because their father put a premium on prowess, Harvey had always been the favored son.

At the center of the work is the cross-country ski trip the two brothers take after Harvey's return. Unafraid of the wilderness, Harvey talks Perry into skiing back home after a ski race at which Harvey not only fails to place but also manages to lose his girl friend Addie. As they ski home, Perry and Harvey gradually reverse roles, and Harvey must finally be rescued by the supposedly hapless and cowardly Perry. Harvey proves to be physically inept, whereas Perry proves to be the cunning one who can survive. Harvey's bad eye takes on a moral and spiritual significance as his mind and body gradually fail him to the point where even his lungs give out, overwhelmed by asthma and infection.

The novel's tone is powerful. The description of the cross-country skiing trip is particularly vivid, with its setting in a pristine, snow-covered landscape which is pitiless and uncaring. The impossibility of actually becoming part of this world is impressed on Perry, for example, when he spots a doe in the forest: "Without thinking, he called to it as if calling a dog for petting. The doe looked at him oddly. Then she arched her back, raising her head to reach higher bark, all the while watching him. She was frail and hungry-looking. In greeting, Perry called again and raised one of his poles. He was struck by the desire to hail the beast, and he called once again and the doe continued to watch. Her eyes were cautious but not unfriendly. Then the wind changed. The doe's head jerked and held for a moment in a sharp, electric pose of perfect alertness, and then it bolted, and Perry realized they'd never met, and the doe was gone." As the novel progresses, Perry comes to realize that it is possible to live in such a world without ever really becoming part of it; but Harvey never realizes that for all his animal instincts, he is still a human being, less adept at staying alive than even a frail doe.

Despite Harvey's prominence in the novel, the book is really about Perry, the only character who changes in the course of the work. As Roger Sale remarks, "the more adventurous Harvey cannot learn as much from adventure as can the introspective and withdrawing Perry." Only Perry reconciles his inner conflicts, overcomes his fear of the wilderness by being baptized symbolically in Pliney's Pond, and sells his dead father's house despite Harvey's protests. Harvey, on the other hand, can think of nothing but escaping to some faraway adventure in Africa, Mexico, or Alaska, just as earlier he could think of nothing but the nearly disastrous adventure in the Minnesota wilderness. The novel closes with Harvey's constant comment on his plans: " 'Doesn't it sound great?' Harvey kept saying. 'Doesn't it?' " Only Perry grows enough to move on to a new and better life.

O'Brien's third work, *Going After Cacciato* (1978), was not a commercial success, selling only 12,000 copies, but the book was well received critically. Several chapters of it had previously been published as short stories in *Shenandoah, Esquire, Redbook, Ploughshares,* the *Massachusetts Review, Gallery,* and *Denver Quarterly,* and their publication had whetted critical appetites. Gene Lyons remarked,

Dust jacket

"If better realistic fiction has been written about Vietnam I have not seen it. . . . The war story that O'Brien is telling now deserves our attention." After the novel was published, John Updike stated that O'Brien was "reaching for a masterpiece."

This novel has been compared fairly frequently to works by Hemingway and to Joseph Heller's *Catch-22* (1961). It is often pointed out, for example, that *Going After Cacciato* starts precisely where Heller's World War II novel stops, with the hero's resolve to run away from the war. *Going After Cacciato,* however, is even more fantastic than *Catch-22*; while the events in Heller's novel are presented as having happened, most of O'Brien's novel reports the fantastic daydream of one of the characters. Despite certain stylistic resemblances, O'Brien's novel is much less like Hemingway's work than *Northern Lights.* Hemingway and Heller may be starting points, but neither provides the guiding principles of the novel.

Cacciato (an Italian word meaning "the pursued") decides to escape Vietnam and the army by fleeing overland to Paris, an ingenious plan which could arise only in the mind of the "awful dumb" Cacciato. The patrol sent to capture him fails, and that is the last that is seen of the AWOL soldier. Paul Berlin, however, fantasizes about what it would be like to chase Cacciato all the way to Paris, and this fantastic journey takes up the bulk of the novel, which is a combination of Berlin's memories and imaginings while he stands guard one night in a watchtower by the South China Sea.

O'Brien slides easily back and forth between time present and time past, between reality and fantasy, but the story remains clear. After the patrol has failed to capture Cacciato, Berlin asks, "What happened, and what might have happened," and it is upon Berlin's answers to these questions that the novel is built, as he reviews the deaths of Billy Boy Watkins, Frenchie Tucker, Bernie Lynn, Sidney Martin, Pederson, Rudy Chassler, Buff, and Ready Mix, and speculates about the various stops on the road to Paris—Mandalay, Delhi, Tehran, Athens. Interjected into this narrative are Berlin's thoughts as he stands guard, bringing the reader back to the present reality of Berlin's life.

Despite its realistic descriptions of war, *Going After Cacciato* is comic. Even Berlin himself thinks it at least possible to reach Paris in the manner he envisions. In his fantasy, Cacciato and the patrol are able to deal with numerous critical situations. All that is needed is to ignore a few practical improbabilities, such as the ability to walk around Tehran armed to the teeth. Moreover, Berlin's dream is the perfect stratagem for honorably getting away from the war: he escapes without deserting his post or his obligations, and in his dream he is also honorable because it is his duty to pursue Cacciato, all the way to Paris if necessary. In the end, even his fantasy comes back to the humiliation he suffered his first time in combat—one of the chief reasons for Berlin's dream of escape.

O'Brien is now writing a novel entitled "The Nuclear Age" and has given readings from sections. A recent article reports that the book is "the story of a kid growing up in the 1950s with bombshelters and fallout, and strontium 90 in the milk; in the first chapter, he converts a basement ping pong table into a fallout shelter because he's scared." The article also quotes O'Brien as saying that the novel is "sort of funny, sort of sad. I want people to laugh, . . .but I also want them to feel my uneasiness and fear about these things." The inspiration of the book, though it is set further back in time than his other books, is still much the same: war or rumor of war will figure prominently.

—*Everett C. Wilkie, Jr.*

Tillie Olsen

(14 January 1912 or 1913-)

SELECTED BOOKS: *Tell Me a Riddle* (Philadelphia: Lippincott, 1961; London: Faber, 1964);
Yonnondio: From the Thirties (New York: Delacorte, 1974; London: Faber, 1974);
Silences (New York: Delacorte, 1978; London: Faber, 1978).

Tillie Olsen recounts in her 1978 book *Silences* that she first read Rebecca Harding Davis's *Life in the Iron Mills* in a water-stained volume of the *Atlantic Monthly* (dated April 1861) which she had bought for ten cents in an Omaha junk shop when she was fifteen. She says she did not then know the name of the author of the work, published anonymously, "which meant increasingly more to me over the years, saying, with a few other books, 'Literature can be made out of the lives of despised people,' and 'You, too, must write.' "

Born Tillie Lerner in Nebraska, Olsen has lived in San Francisco most of her life laboring to make literature out of "the lives of despised people"—when she was not herself a member of the world of "everyday" jobs. Olsen's origin, identification, and life are primarily working-class. Her stories are shaped from material she has drawn from the lives of her immigrant Russian parents and other "foreigners"; housebound women and their cold, hungry children; coal miners in Wyoming; farm laborers in the Dakotas; diggers in underground sewers; packing house butchers in Omaha; merchant sailors—working people with whom she has shared much of her life.

Tillie Lerner is shown with Malcolm Cowley, Edward Dahlberg, Ford Madox Ford, John Howard Lawson, and others in a cartoon representing prominent authors attending the American Writers Congress in 1935. One of the two American women caricatured in the cartoon printed in the *New Masses* (April 1935), Lerner is drawn as a thin, sharp-featured, intense young woman. At the time, she was already recognized and respected widely for her writing. Two of her poems , a short story ("The Iron Throat," part of the first chapter of her novel in progress, *Yonnondio,* 1974), and an article ("The Strike") had appeared in various issues of the first volume of *The Partisan* (later the *Partisan Review*) between March and October 1934. The *New Republic* published her "Thousand-Dollar Vagrant," an autobiographical essay, the same year.

The next record of Olsen's published work was a short story,"Help Her to Believe," which appeared twenty-two years later in the *Pacific Spectator.* Tillie Lerner, silenced for more than two decades, endured—surviving "the unnatural thwarting of what struggles to come into being but cannot,"—to emerge as Tillie Olsen and be heard by some critics as the strongest, the purest, the most passionate poetic voice speaking in the United States today for the speechless "despised people"—workers, women, blacks.

Robert Coles observed that "Everything Tillie Olsen has written has become almost immediately a classic," while Alice Walker has written that "there are few writers who manage in their work and in the sharing of their understanding to actually help us to live, to work, to create, day by day." Margaret Atwood says in *New York Times Book Review*: "Few writers have gained such wide respect based on such a small body of published work. . . . Among women writers in the United States, 'respect' is too pale a word: 'reverence' is more like it."

The aural element in her writing, love for her

"incomparable medium, literature," and her theories about literature have made Olsen an increasingly popular reader and lecturer. She has appeared at scores of places in the United States and abroad to read her work aloud and discuss it for literary and academic groups. Annie Gottlieb wrote of *Yonnondio* in the *New York Times Book Review* that "it should be read aloud by firelight." And certainly much of Olsen's work merits the sort of praise which Joyce Carol Oates gave to the short story, "Tell Me a Riddle," saying that it deserves "repeated readings and the close attention reserved for poetry."

Olsen has recorded portions of her work for the Lamont Poetry Room Collection (Widener Library, Harvard) and for Pacifica. Sally Cunneen reports in the *Christian Century* that Olsen "often gives readings to small groups, particularly to young writers." Aside from her work, much that we know about Olsen comes from reports of her interaction with young writers at meetings where she reads and then discusses her work. Olsen said the cost of "discontinuity" imposed on her own writing by "(that pattern still urged on women by a society that prefers that they adjust, not itself) is of such a weight of things unsaid, an accumulation of material so great, that everything starts up something else in me; what should take weeks, takes me sometimes months to write; what should take months, takes years." Olsen went on to say of her writing self, "You see I am a destroyed person." A young man asked her, "Why no bitterness?" Olsen responded: "Because I have been so fortunate in my life. I have been able to do *something*—to make these few stories—when so many like me have been denied the opportunity to come to any expression of their lives. . . . How can I be bitter when I have been able to do what so few of my sex and class have had the chance to do?"

Yonnondio's beginnings, some of the circumstances that forced Olsen to lay her novel aside, the loss of the manuscript, its accidental recovery, and its reconstruction (as distinct from rewriting) are mentioned by the author in several places, particularly in "A Note About This Book" at the end of the 1974 Delacorte edition, and in *Silences*. Olsen says that she began the book when she was nineteen, in 1932, in Faribault, Minnesota, and worked on it intermittently in Omaha, Stockton, Venice (California), Los Angeles, and San Francisco.

Episodes of the book dramatize oppressive conditions which Olsen yearned to change. According to Cunneen, Olsen "was just out of high school" when she was jailed in Kansas City for trying to organize packinghouse workers. Shortly after she was released from jail, she began working on *Yonnondio*, during a severe attack of pleurisy, and continued working on it intermittently as she moved about the country. Arriving in San Francisco, she became involved again in union activities, worked at union headquarters, and began writing for left-wing journals. Soon after, perhaps early in 1937, the manuscript of *Yonnondio* was set aside.

During the twenty years that followed, she married Jack Olsen, a printer and union man, and worked at various jobs while raising their four daughters: Karla, Julie, Katherine Jo, and Laurie. She worked in industry, as a transcriber in a dairy equipment company, and, as she says, "full time on temporary jobs, a Kelly, a Western Agency girl (girl!), wandering from office to office, always hoping to manage two, three writing months ahead. Eventually there was time." But she did not return to *Yonnondio*.

The book which she "conceived primarily as a novel of the 1930s," was recovered about forty years later, "intermixed with other old papers . . . during the process of searching for another manuscript." A more thorough search, Olsen reports, turned up "odd tattered pages, lines in yellowed notebooks, scraps. Other parts, once in existence, seem irrevocably lost."

Electing to reconstruct the unfinished work which she believes "bespeaks the consciousness and roots" of the 1930s, "if not its events," Olsen describes "the choices and omissions, the combinings and reconstruction." She concludes that as a result "the book ceased to be solely the work of that long ago young writer and, in arduous partnership, became this older one's as well. But it is all the old manuscripts—no rewriting, no new writing."

Yonnondio is the story of the family of Jim Holbrook and his wife Anna, and their children. It is presented primarily through the eyes of their oldest child, Mazie, who is six-and-a-half when the story begins in a Wyoming coal-mining town. The point of view, however, shifts to the mother, Anna, and less frequently to Jim and other minor characters after the family moves to the city. And the reader's attention is drawn back and forth during the story, from interior preceptions to the external world.

In search of safer work, Jim Holbrook moves his family from the coal-mining town to try farming in South Dakota. But, as a tenant, he owes more money at the end of the year than he has made; the Holbrooks must move on. Returning to a city dominated by packinghouses, Jim finds work on a sewer-digging crew and later in a packinghouse. In these settings the family endures cold, hunger, drought, heat, illness, the daily fear of injury or death to the working father, rape within marriage for the mother, and privation in the children's lives.

Even so, the Holbrooks are not defeated by the hardships, fears, and terrors that beset them. Throughout the story, Olsen's women cope, endure, survive, and triumph in spirit. This is especially true in the case of the girl, Mazie, and her mother, Anna. From the beginning, Mazie is shown as aware of the terror of the earth, and of its beauty, and of the importance of being, of knowing: "Mazie lay under the hot Wyoming sun, between the outhouse and the garbage dump. . . . 'I am Mazie Holbrook,' she said softly. "I am a-knowen things. I can diaper a baby. I can tell ghost stories. I know words and words. Tipple. Edjication. Bug dust. Supertendent. . . . A phrase trembled into her mind, 'Bowels of earth. . . .' It means the mine. Bowels is the stummy. Earth is a stummy and mebbe she ets the men that come down."

Tillie Olsen

Mazie's imagination, her response to beauty, and her desire to know are shown in a question she asks a friendly neighbor, Elias Caldwell: " 'Stars,' she began. 'What are they now? Splinters offn the moon, I've heard it said. But more likely they're lamps in houses up there, or flowers growing in the night. I'd like to smell the smell that would be comin offn those flowers.' "

Later, when the girl comes to visit him as he is dying, Caldwell attests to the vitality of Anna, Mazie's mother: "Mazie, live, don't exist. Learn from your mother, who has had everything to grind out life and yet has kept life. Alive, felt what's real, known what's real. . . . 'Better,' your mother says, 'to be a cripple and alive than dead, not able to feel anything.' But there is more—to rebel against what will not let life be."

Caldwell's perception of Anna's strength foreshadows the struggles of the Holbrooks after they move from the farm to the city. The story includes an episode of rape within marriage that almost claims the pregnant mother's life. The husband, Jim, soaked in alcohol and clawing awkwardly for affection and sexual relief, forces himself upon Anna: "Cant screw my own wife. Expect me to go to a whore? Hold Still." Anna aborts and struggles for survival during a summer-long heat wave and drought.

In her endurance, the rich dimensions of Anna's character emerge—her determination to sustain, nurture, and educate her children. Despite the corrosive effect of the rape on conjugal love, the mother is reconciled with her husband: ". . .'Oh Jim.' Giving in, collapsing into his reaching embrace. 'The children . . . What's going to happen with them? How we going to look out for them in this damn world? . . . Seems like we cant do nothing for them.' "

Anna continues her preoccupation with ways of providing education for the children, and conveys her tenderness: "Arm and arm, they sat down under the catalpa. . . . She began stroking Mazie's hair. . . . A fragile old remembered comfort streamed from the stroking fingers into Mazie. . . . Mazie felt the strange happiness in her mother's body. . . . Soft wove the bliss around hurt and fear and want and shame—the old worn fragile bliss, a new frail selfless bliss, healing and transforming."

And still later, as her health improves, Anna again becomes a vital and affirmative force in the family. In the novel's last scene, it is night. Jim lies on a pallet outside the house "below the stoop," while the children are listening to a borrowed crystal set: "far sound, human and stellar, pulsing, pulsing. . . ." The long sweltering brings heat lightning—an illusion of relief. Anna goes to her husband, "Jim, wake up. Come in, come in. . . . Here, I'll help you. The air's changin, Jim. I see for it to end tomorrow, at least get tolerable. Come in and get freshened up." With these words the reconstructed novel stops.

In a note on the following page, beginning

"Reader," the author observes, "it was not to have ended here, but it is nearly forty years since this book had to be set aside, never to come to completion.

"These pages you have read," Olsen continues, "are all that is deemed publishable of it. Only fragments, rough drafts, outlines, scraps remain—telling what might have been." The author's note is followed by a passage from Whitman's poem on a lost Indian tribe that gives the novel its title: "Yonnondio! Yonnondio!—unlimn'd they disappear."

Several reviewers of the novel compared it with the short stories in *Tell Me a Riddle,* noting as Bell Gale Chevigny does in the *Village Voice* that the novel "lays the ground" for her later and greater story, *Tell Me a Riddle.* John Alfred Avant, to give another example, found the novel "a flawed but extraordinary early work" which foreshadows the short stories that bring Olsen's "art to completion."

Most of the reviewers also record the influence of *Life in the Iron Mills* on Olsen's work and comment upon her use of language. Jack Salzman, for instance, characterizes Olsen as "one of the greatest prose stylists now writing." In the same essay in the *Washington Post,* he describes *Yonnondio* as "the best novel" of the proletarian movement of the 1930s and insists that "Mrs. Olsen's richness of style, her depth of characterization make *Yonnondio* a work which must not—cannot—be restricted by a particular time or period . . . She is a consummate artist."

Annie Gottlieb in the *New York Times Book Review* points to Olsen's knowledge of "what a great weight poor women carry," and her "deep sympathy for the restlessness and degraded pride of the men." She says that with *Yonnondio* "(as perhaps with the poetry of Sylvia Plath) motherhood must finally be counted among the circumstances that can simultaneously hinder and nourish genius." Chevigny finds that *Yonnondio* expressed "Olsen's life project of snatching beauty from destruction. The heart of meaning in this book, the key to its rhythm, is the phoenix rebirth of spirit."

The talent that could have disappeared with the manuscript of *Yonnondio* was recovered slowly through Olsen's conviction and determination that "You, too, must write!" Her account of the period of "my own silences" is set down on less than three pages in *Silences* beginning: "In the twenty years [roughly 1936-1956] I bore and reared my children, usually had to work on a paid job as well, the simplest circumstances for creation did not exist." She observes that "It is no accident that the first work I considered publishable began: 'I stand here ironing, and what you asked me moves tormented back and forth with the iron.' "

That work, the short story "Help Her to Believe," was written between 1953 and 1954 and appeared in the *Pacific Spectator.* The opening line of the story provides a symbolic gesture of weary repetitive work to parallel the self-searching thoughts of a mother who often feels helpless. Back and forth the mother reviews the circumstances and privations that have shaped (perhaps marred) the love and understanding she shares with her nineteen-year-old daughter. The mother elects, however, not to interfere with her daughter's life—not to "come in and talk" to one of the teachers who believes the daughter is "a youngster who needs help."

"Let her be," the mother concludes. "So all that is in her will not bloom—but in how many does it? There is still enough left to live by."

Another short story, "Hey Sailor, What Ship?," written from 1953 to 1955, is about the divisive effects of circumstances and time on political and personal ties. Whitey, a lonely alcoholic merchant seaman, is cast adrift by his old political comrades and friends, Lennie and Helen, who have married and settled down. "Understand. The death of the brotherhood. Once, once an injury to one is an injury to all. Once, once they had to live for each other. Understand. Once they had been young together." But later, Whitey's "drinking and cussing had become too much and Lennie forbade the house to him unless he were 'O.K.'—because of the children." ("Hey Sailor, What Ship?" was originally published in *New Campus Writing,* number two, edited by Nolan Miller, 1957.)

The short story "Baptism" was published in *Prairie Schooner.* Like "Hey Sailor, What Ship?," it explores some circumstances and pressures that make people drift apart. In this instance, two young girls are being separated by racism, despite the efforts of both mothers to preserve their daughters' friendship. One of the girls asks "Oh why is it like it is and why do I have to care?" The girl's mother caresses and quiets her daughter and thinks—but does not speak aloud: "caring asks doing. It is a long baptism into the seas of humankind, my daughter. Better immersion than to live untouched. . . . Yet how will you sustain?"

Olsen's novella *Tell Me a Riddle,* which also delineates divisive forces that corrode and mar love, won the O. Henry Award as best American short fiction of 1961. In this work the destructive factors are in the characters' temperaments, and in the poverty that beset the early years of their marriage, and in the loss of the revolutionary idealism the

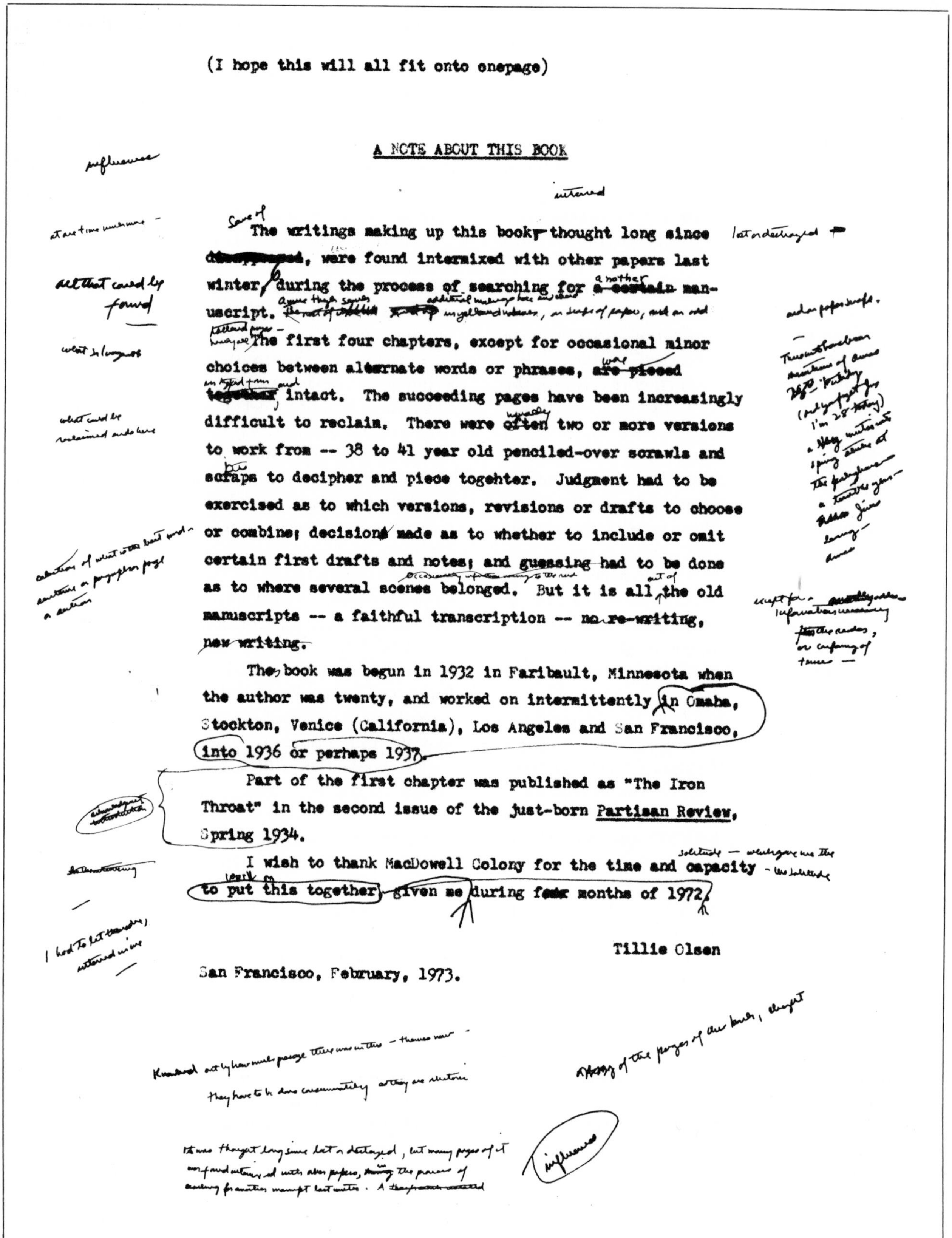

(I hope this will all fit onto onepage)

A NOTE ABOUT THIS BOOK

The writings making up this book, thought long since [redacted], were found intermixed with other papers last winter, during the process of searching for a certain manuscript. The first four chapters, except for occasional minor choices between alternate words or phrases, are pieced together intact. The succeeding pages have been increasingly difficult to reclaim. There were often two or more versions to work from -- 38 to 41 year old penciled-over scrawls and scraps to decipher and piece togehter. Judgment had to be exercised as to which versions, revisions or drafts to choose or combine; decisions made as to whether to include or omit certain first drafts and notes; and guessing had to be done as to where several scenes belonged. But it is all the old manuscripts -- a faithful transcription -- no re-writing, new writing.

The book was begun in 1932 in Faribault, Minnesota when the author was twenty, and worked on intermittently in Omaha, Stockton, Venice (California), Los Angeles and San Francisco, into 1936 or perhaps 1937.

Part of the first chapter was published as "The Iron Throat" in the second issue of the just-born Partisan Review, Spring 1934.

I wish to thank MacDowell Colony for the time and capacity to put this together given me during four months of 1972.

Tillie Olsen

San Francisco, February, 1973.

Tell Me a Riddle, *revised typescript*

aging couple had shared in "that world of their youth." Olsen depicts the caustic bitterness of the dying woman matched against her defensive husband. Only in the woman's mumbling dying words does the reader become aware of "that world of their youth," of the joy, the passion, the belief they shared—and the trust they lost. The husband hears and responds: " 'Aaah, children,' he said out loud, 'how we believed, how we belonged.' And he yearned to package for each of the children, the grandchildren, for everyone, *that joyous certainty, that sense of mattering, of moving and being moved, of being one and indivisible with the great of the past, with all that freed, ennobled man.*"

Tell Me a Riddle was collected with "I Stand Here Ironing" (originally "Help Her to Believe"), "Hey Sailor, What Ship?," and "O Yes" (originally "Baptism") and published under the title *Tell Me a Riddle* (1961).

The four short stories collected in *Tell Me a Riddle* have been anthologized fifty-three times, appearing in such books as *Fifty Years of the American Story, 1919-1970*; *Fifty Best American Short Stories, 1915-1965*; *The Norton Introduction to Literature, The Modern Tradition*; and in *Elements of Literature*. The pieces have been adapted for performance on numerous college campuses and in several stage productions. The Caravan Theatre's *Tell Me a Riddle* was cited by the Boston *Globe* as one of the ten best productions of 1978.

The publication of *Tell Me a Riddle* brought national attention to Olsen and her work. Gene Barto characterized the author as seeing and conveying sharply the "essential tragedy . . . the downward movement of life." Reviewers generally pointed to Olsen's dependence upon personal experience. Some such as the unnamed critic of the *Christian Science Monitor* found that she made only "partial transition" from experience to art. Others, Irving Howe in the *New Republic* for example, observed that she "felt very deeply and pondered and imaginatively absorbed." Several pointed to the author's age, or mentioned the fact that her career had been interrupted by raising a family, but most concluded as did the reviewer for *Time* that the four stories in the collection "were worth waiting for."

On the occasion of the collection's republication ten years later Julian Moynahan noted that *Tell Me a Riddle,* "like Faulkner's *The Bear* and Melville's *Benito Cereno* . . . carries us through despair to a renewal of hope. As a great work of literary art, it will be read as long as the American language lasts."

Olsen's third book, *Silences,* was published in 1978, four years after *Yonnondio,* and about a quarter of a century after she began "Help Her to Believe" (1953-1954). *Silences* consists of two previously published essays, revised from talks presented for academic consumption nearly a decade apart, as well as a "Biographical Interpretation" or "essay-afterword" to the Feminist Press Reprint of Rebecca Harding Davis's *Life in the Iron Mills,* and two sections of "essential deepenings and expansions" of more formal writing.

In Olsen's words, the book "is concerned with the relationship of circumstances—including class, color, sex; the times, climate into which one is born—to the creation of literature." And she insists on the organic growth of her meditations: "This book is not an orthodoxly written work of academic scholarship. Do not approach it as such. Nor did it come into being through choosing a subject, then researching for it. The substance herein was long in accumulation, garnered over fifty years, near a lifetime; the thought came slow, hard-won; the talks and essay, the book itself, elicited.

"A passion and a purpose inform its pages: love for my incomparable medium, literature; hatred for all that, societally rooted, unnecessarily lessens it; slows, impairs, silences writers.

"It is written to re-dedicate and encourage."

The first essay in *Silences* originated as a seminar presentation entitled "Death of the Creative Process," delivered at the Radcliffe Institute for Independent Study while Olsen was a Fellow there in 1962-1964. The essay was adapted from her notes and published as "Silences: When Writers Don't Write" in *Harper's.* The second essay, "One Out of Twelve: Writers Who Are Women in Our Century," demonstrates Olsen's links as an avowed feminist/humanist to the women's movement and the academic community. The essay developed from notes of a talk she presented in 1971 at the Modern Language Association Forum on Women Writers in the Twentieth Century, and it was then published in *College English.* The third essay included in *Silences* is the "Biographical Interpretation" for Davis's *Life in the Iron Mills.* Davis's career exemplifies dramatically the points made in Olsen's essay, "One Out of Twelve."

Reviews of *Silences* were in a few instances less appreciative than those of *Tell Me a Riddle* and *Yonnondio.* For example, Joyce Carol Oates begins her comments on *Silences* by praising *Tell Me a Riddle.* There is no piece of recent fiction, Oates says, that is "more powerfully moving." Yet the best she can say of *Silences* is that one can sympathize with the author's passion. Oates finds that this work "that sets itself up as a literary manifesto of the women's movement," is marred by "inconsistencies, . . . questionable statements offered as facts, . . . anger, . . . [and] failure to confront troublesome questions."

On the other hand, Margaret Atwood's evaluation in the *New York Times Book Review* begins with the observation that "Tillie Olsen's is a unique voice" and concludes that "the tone is right" in *Silences.* Atwood praises the "stylistic breathlessness—the elliptical prose" as reminiscent of a biblical messenger. And she insists that Olsen's comments on the circumstances that silence art are important to those who want to understand how it is "generated or subverted." Adrienne Rich describes *Silences* as a "prose poem of Olsen's unique connection and resonance with other writers, and with losses, the empty spaces she, above all, has been equipped to recognize."

Olsen's effectiveness in serving her feminist/humanist ideals and literary values as writer, teacher, and critic has been widely recognized. In 1979 she was awarded the honorary degree Doctor of Arts and Letters by the University of Nebraska. In 1980 the Unitarian Universalist Women's Federation conferred on her its annual Ministry to Women Award. Also in 1980, in conjunction with its issuance of stamps commemorating Emily and Charlotte Brontë, George Eliot, and Elizabeth Gaskell, the British Post Office selected Olsen for a special award as "the American woman writer best exemplifying in our time the ideals and literary excellence of the four."

Sometimes described as a Depression-era high-school dropout, Olsen is quick to insist that she received more formal education than most of her generation who never got through the eighth grade. She finished the eleventh grade, and observes that the public libraries were her college. Olsen has been identified with the academic community and its supportive organizations at least since "Help Her to Believe" appeared in 1956 in the *Pacific Spectator,* a periodical published by the Pacific Coast Committee for the Humanities of the American Council of Learned Societies.

Olsen held a Stanford University Creative Writing Center Fellowship in 1956-1957, and was awarded a Ford Foundation grant in literature for 1959. She received a fellowship for independent study from the Radcliffe Institute for 1964, and a grant in literature for 1967 from the National Endowment for the Arts. Other honors include a Literary Award in 1975 from the American Academy and Institute of Arts and Letters for "very nearly constituting a new form of fiction." A year later, in 1976, she received a Guggenheim Fellowship.

Olsen has held academic appointments at a number of outstanding colleges and universities including the following: professor and writer-in-residence at Amherst College, 1969-1970; visiting lecturer at Stanford University, 1972, for the Graduate Writing Seminar and for the first course on women and literature; writer-in-residence at Massachusetts Institute of Technology, 1973-1974; distinguished visiting professor at the University of Massachusetts, Boston, 1974; Board of Regents visiting lecturer at the University of California, San Diego, 1978; and the International Visiting Scholar to four Scandinavian universities in 1980.

She continues to be a much sought-after guest at literary events, and she continues to write, reporting that she is "still struggling with several books, including a book in a special form about aging and confronting dying—one drawing much testimony, like *Silences,* from both the obscure and the well known."

—Carolyn and Ernest Rhodes

Other:

"Hey Sailor, What Ship?," in *New Campus Writing,* no. 2, ed. Nolan Miller (New York: Putnam's, 1957), pp. 199-213;

"Tell Me a Riddle," in *New World Writing,* no. 16, ed. Stewart Richardson and Corlies M. Smith (Philadelphia: Lippincott, 1960), pp. 11-57;

"A Biographical Interpretation," in *Life in the Iron Mills,* by Rebecca Harding Davis (Old Westbury, N.Y.: Feminist Press, 1972).

Periodical Publications:

"I Want You Women Up North to Know," *Partisan,* 1 (March 1934): 4;

"There is a Lesson," *Partisan,* 1 (April 1934): 4;

"The Iron Throat," *Partisan Review,* 1 (April-May 1934): 3-9;

"Thousand-Dollar Vagrant," *New Republic,* 80 (29 August 1934): 67-69;

"The Strike," *Partisan Review,* 1 (September-October 1934): 3-9;

"Help Her to Believe," *Pacific Spectator,* 10 (Winter 1956): 55-63;

"Baptism," *Prairie Schooner,* 31 (Spring 1957): 70-80;

"Silences: When Writers Don't Write," *Harper's,* 231 (October 1965): 153-161;

"Requa," *Iowa Review,* 1 (Summer 1970): 54-74;

"Women Who Are Writers in Our Century: One Out of Twelve," *College English,* 34 (October 1972): 6-17.

References:

Sandy Boucher, "Tillie Olsen: The Weight of Things Unsaid," *Ms.* (September 1974): 26-30;

Sally Cunneen, "Tillie Olsen: Storyteller of Working America," *Christian Century*, 97 (21 May 1980): 570-574;

Florence Howe, "Literacy and Literature," *PMLA*, 89 (May 1974): 433-441;

Annette Bennington McElhiney, "Alternative Responses to Life in Tillie Olsen's Work," *Frontiers*, 2 (Spring 1977): 76-91;

Ellen Cronan Rose, "Limning: or Why Tillie Writes," *Hollins Critic*, 13 (April 1976): 1-13;

Alix Kates Shulman, "Overcoming Silences: Teaching Writing for Women," *Harvard Educational Review*, 49 (November 1979): 527-533;

Catherine R. Stimpson, "Tillie Olsen: Witness as Servant," *Polit: A Journal for Literature and Politics*, 1 (Fall 1977): 1-12;

Kenneth Turan, "Breaking Silence," *New West*, 28 (28 August 1978): 55-59.

Papers:

Portions of the manuscript version of *Yonnondio* are in the Berg Collection of English and American Literature in the New York Public Library.

Jayne Anne Phillips
(1952-)

BOOKS: *Sweethearts* (Carrboro: N.C.: Truck Press, 1976);

Counting (New York: Vehicle Editions, 1978);

Black Tickets (New York: Delacorte/Seymour Lawrence, 1979).

Jayne Anne Phillips's debut with a major publisher in 1979 won her acclaim as one of America's most promising writers. She had already won the Fels Award in Fiction from the Coordinating Council of Literary Magazines, the St. Lawrence Award for Fiction, and a National Endowment for the Arts Fellowship. The dust jacket of *Black Tickets* (1979) contained the enthusiastic praise of Rosellen Brown, Frederick Busch, Raymond Carver, Frank Conroy, Annie Dillard, Robie Macauley, Tim O'Brien, and Tillie Olsen, and reviewers were also complimentary. In 1980 Phillips became the first winner of the Sue Kaufman Prize for First Fiction presented by the American Academy and Institute of Arts and Letters.

Phillips was born and raised in Buckhannon, West Virginia, a middle-class community, and began writing poetry while in high school. She graduated from West Virginia University and received a master of fine arts degree from the University of Iowa. She has traveled throughout the country, especially in the West, and taught briefly at Humboldt State University in Arcata, California. Her poetry has appeared in magazines such as *New Letters* and *Paris Review*. Her first two books, *Sweethearts* (1976) and *Counting* (1978) were both published by small presses and consist of extremely short stories, some of them prose poems.

Soon after Phillips gave Delacorte editor Seymour Lawrence a copy of *Sweethearts* at a writer's conference in 1978, he wrote her, "You're a real writer. Bring your stories to Boston." The publication of *Black Tickets* followed. The twenty-seven stories in *Black Tickets* are of three types. Sixteen are very short stylistic exercises, usually one paragraph in length. The other eleven, of conventional length, present two contrasting views of life. One group of stories deals with grotesques—drug addicts, prostitutes, a male nurse for a rich homosexual invalid, a Son-of-Sam-like murderer—while the other group deals with the ordinariness and the tragedies of family life. Phillips explores the banality of horror and the horror of the banal through her examination of sex, violence, innocence, loneliness, illness, madness, various forms of love and lovelessness, and numerous failures at communicating and at feeling.

The briefer stories, most of which appear in *Sweethearts*, are placed between the long ones as interchapters. Compact, elliptical, and densely written, they are often obscure, but the best of them, such as "Slave," have the same sensitivity and insight as the longer stories. In "Slave" a young woman and her lover discuss her sexual needs: "she told him that although she liked men she seldom had orgasms with them but only with herself. They talked about it patiently. After that she wanted to make love with him less because her power was exposed and solidified. He wanted to make love with her more but was self-conscious because he was

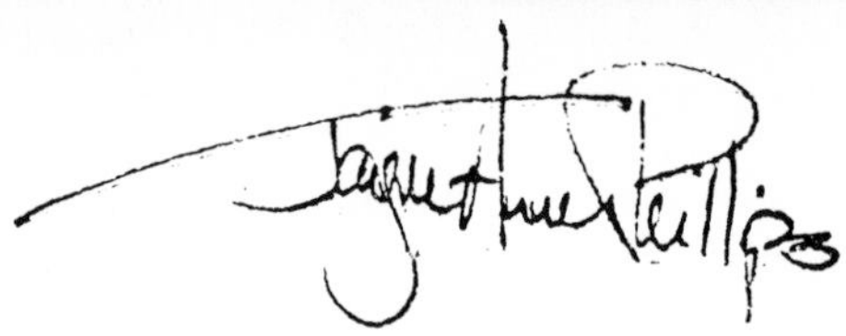

unsure of his power. She felt he was no longer like her but was less than her, and she didn't want him. The relationship cooled."

Longer stories, such as "Country," about a young man's obsession with a sixteen-year-old girl who is part Negro; "The Patron," about the male nurse; "El Paso," about a stripper and her cowboy lover; and "Black Tickets," about drug dealers, provide glimpses of sadness and depravity. Phillips is skilled at underscoring the sordidness of a place, as in "El Paso": "I remember there was always dog puke on the sidewalks in El Paso. All those strays get the sweats around noon and bring up the garbage they ate in the back alleys of beanerys at dawn." She is also good at conveying a sense of physical exertion, as when young male dancers perform in "The Patron": "Their eyes fix on the unseen; they dive and come back to it, magnetized. . . . Smooth and perfect but shaking, muscles a hidden vibrato. And when they finish they are drenched. Eyes still focused, point of light in the pupil like they are hurt with something sharp and making room."

Two more noteworthy stories about grotesques are "Gemcrack" and "Lechery." The narrator-murderer of "Gemcrack" kills when an imaginary voice he calls his "Uncle" speaks to him: "He comes at me out of everyone's mouth until I know he is the only one talking. . . . He tells me what to do in his voice that whines and excites, his old voice that talks in the eyes of the reeling prophets and clattering cans in the streets. He knows languages with no letters." His insanity has a logic of its own making and a perverse innocence that is the ultimate evasion of responsibility. The protagonist of "Lechery" is an unquestioning victim of circumstances. An orphan bought for thirty dollars when she was twelve by junkies who play sexual games with her, she is now, at fourteen, a prostitute who entices younger boys from school yards: "I do things they've never seen. I could let them touch but no. I arrange their hands and feet, keep them here forever." Once again Phillips portrays an unusual kind of innocence: the child prostitute calls herself "pure, driven snow." While Phillips's style in these stories is sometimes in pattern. She stops and counts; so many stitches across, so many down. Yes, she is on the right track. Its pattern ~~slides~~ back and ~~forth~~, intricate appears and disappears

But feeling something (spun) deeply can teach you something. Don't you want to learn anything?

I'm learning all the time, she says. (She keeps knitting. It is yarn the color of cream she winds) In her hands she folds yarn the color of cream; she works it with her long blue needles, piercing, returning, winding ~~skeins~~. Yarn cascades from her hands in long panels, luxuriant, perfect

Occasionally I try to buy her a subscription to Ms., Rolling Stone, The Daily Worker. The Smithsonian magazine Wall Bees.

I don't want to read that stuff, she says. Just save your money. Everyones going to need all they can get.

Often, I need to look at my mothers old photographs. I see her sitting in knee-high grass with a white gardenia in her hair. I see her dressed up as the groom in a mock wedding at a sorority party; her black hair pulled back and her mouth lovely in its blood red lipstick. I see her in her cadet nurse's uniform, formally posed. The photographer has painted her lashes too lushly, too long; but her scarlet mouth is correct. She didn't finish her training

The war ended too soon. She came home to nurse only her mother, and met my father at a dance. She married him in two weeks, and it took twenty-three years to divorce him. Her mother advised against marrying so quickly. "Whats your hurry" she asked from her bed.

~~The war ended too soon. She didn't finish her training; she came home to nurse only her mother.~~ My mother doesn't forget her mother.

Never one bedsore, she ~~my mother~~ says. I turned her every fifteen minutes. I kept her skin ~~so~~ soft, and kept her ~~she was~~ clean. even ~~to~~ to the end of it.

She sighs. I did all I could. And I was glad to do it. I'm glad I don't have to feel guilty.

(1)

"Home," manuscript

overly flamboyant, they move the reader through their treatment of desperation as commonplace.

A quieter desperation and a more subdued style characterize Phillips's family stories set in the rural South. In "Snow" a blind couple in South Carolina try to lead normal lives with their two children, while in "1934" a Virginia mother and her daughter cope with an increasingly insane husband and father who had once been their town's leading citizen. "The Heavenly Animal," "Souvenir," and "Home" present different treatments of a similar situation: an educated, unmarried woman in her twenties returns home to visit her divorced or widowed parent or parents. The stories examine loneliness and hopelessness, efforts to establish human contact, to feel for others as the characters know they should feel, and to love without hesitation. In "The Heavenly Animal" the divorced father who refuses to speak to his ex-wife asks their daughter to stop "All this running around you're doing. . . . You need a family. . . . No one will ever help you but your family."

The best story in *Black Tickets,* and the only one with anything remotely resembling humor, is "Home." The narrator's mother is such a consummate worrier that she even worries about celebrities: "I'm afraid Walter Cronkite has had it, says Mom. Roger Mudd always does the news now. . . . Something is going on." The mother wants her daughter to feel guilty about neglecting her, and she is disturbed by her daughter's sexuality. When an old lover of the daughter's visits, the mother hears their lovemaking and confronts her daughter: "I heard you, I heard it. . . . Here, in my own house. Please, how much do you expect me to take? I don't know what to do about anything."

These family stories suggest that awareness of individual failings is intensified when families are together and that these failings must be confronted even if no good will come of the confrontation. Phillips has said, "I'm interested in what home now consists of. Because we move around so much, families are forced to be immediate; they must stand on their relationships, rather than on stereotypes or assumptions or a common history." The strength of these stories suggests that the family may be a fruitful subject for Phillips's future work.

Black Tickets was greeted enthusiastically by the critics. In *Newsweek* Peter S. Prescott called Phillips "an authentic and original voice" and her debut "just cause for celebration." Joseph Epstein, in the *Hudson Review,* said that her "stories are firmly imagined, written in a prose style that is quite unlike any other." In the *New York Review of Books,* Thomas R. Edwards praised her "remarkably alert and resourceful writing" and her ability to find the "beauty" in the horrors she describes. Nona Balakian wrote in the *New York Times,* "Like Fellini and De Chirico, Miss Phillips hears the inner poem—and metaphors explode on every page, ambiguous, disturbing." In the *Times Literary Supplement,* Carol Rumens said Phillips's "use of language is richly sensuous. She takes street slang all the way to poetry and back, hovering on the edge of surrealism." John Irving wrote in the *New York Times Book Review,* "her strongest writing makes the grotesque tragically real and necessary, and never purely eye-catching or sensational," adding that even in her failures, Phillips "is admirably ambitious."

The reviewers also had reservations, however, mainly about the shorter stories. Rumens said they "suggest an advanced Creative Writing class doing stream-of-consciousness exercises," while in the *Village Voice,* Laurie Stone complained that "too commonly, Phillips's self-consciously poetic prose blocks drama and obscures meaning." Edwards was justifiably upset at the similar tones of the stories: "in such heavy concentration, horror begins to seem predictable, and then positively funny." Irving objected to a lack of discipline, suggesting that Phillips's stories might have been improved by judicious cutting: "this fine book is punctuated with tiny voiceprints, little oddities too precious to the author . . . to be thrown away."

Phillips has identified the influences on her stories as Flannery O'Connor, Katherine Anne Porter, Eudora Welty, William Faulkner, Sherwood Anderson, Gabriel Garcia Marquez, and William Burroughs. Because she has not yet written enough to develop a distinctively personal style, Phillips's work frequently echoes these and other writers. She seems likely to find her own voice in the future. John Irving has expressed the hope that Phillips is working on a novel, "because she seems at her deepest and broadest when she sustains a narrative, manipulates a plot, develops characters through more than one phase of their life or their behavior. I believe she would shine in a novel." Phillips's biggest problem may be learning to cope with the high expectations so many have for her.

—*Michael Adams*

Interview:

James N. Baker, " 'Being Led by a Whisper,' " *Newsweek,* 94 (22 October 1979): 116,118.

Tom Robbins
(1936-)

SELECTED BOOKS: *Another Roadside Attraction* (New York: Doubleday, 1971; London: W. H. Allen, 1973);
Even Cowgirls Get the Blues (Boston: Houghton Mifflin, 1976; London: Corgi, 1977);
Still Life with Woodpecker (New York: Bantam, 1980).

Tom Robbins has been dubbed the Prince of the Paperback Literati, a title he certainly deserves because he has managed to attract such a large reading audience among late-teen and college readers. Robbins has joined the list of popular writers of the first rank, and after the spectacular success of his first three novels critics mention him alongside Thomas Pynchon, Kurt Vonnegut, Ken Kesey, and Robert M. Pirsig. Reviewers frequently describe him as one of the foremost writers of the West Coast or Californian school, who emphasize the themes of personal freedom, the pursuit of higher states of being through Eastern mysticism, the escape from the confining life of urban California to the openness of the pastoral Pacific Northwest. Like the writings of his mentors, Robbins's own novels exhibit an elaborate style, a delight in words for their own sake, and an open, at times anarchical, attitude toward strict narrative form.

Robbins's zealous care for privacy makes biographical information about him difficult to obtain. Thomas Eugene Robbins was born in Blowing Rock, North Carolina. He was educated in rural Virginia schools, attended Washington and Lee University from 1950 to 1952, then the Richmond Professional Institute (now Virginia Commonwealth University), and finally the University of Washington, which he left in 1960. After a brief stint as a copy editor for the *Richmond Times-Dispatch*, he went West to the *Seattle Times*, where he worked as copy editor and art critic. Tom Robbins now lives alone and very privately in the small town of Burlington, Washington. He is divorced from his second wife and has one son, Fleetwood Star, by that marriage.

While in Seattle he became interested in writing a story about the body of Christ and read as many books as he could on early Christianity. By early 1970 he had invented an engaging, sacrilegious narrative about a picaro named Plucky Purcell, who steals the body of Jesus from its secret tomb in the Vatican and spirits it back to rural Washington State. *Another Roadside Attraction* (1971) is a vigorous story of Plucky and his friends John Paul Ziller, his wife Amanda, and their sidekick Mon Cul (an intractable baboon), all of whom inhabit a roadside zoo called the Capt. Kendrick Memorial Hot Dog Wildlife Preserve, formerly Mom's Little Dixie Diner. When Purcell arrives there with the mummified Jesus, he and John Paul decide to commandeer a high-altitude research balloon and take Christ's body up to heaven. Their plan to get the balloon succeeds, but Purcell is killed by security guards. John Paul ascends in the balloon accompanied by his faithful baboon, transporting the body of Christ to its eternal home. The book is full of wit and exuberant writing, and a plot that could stand a bit of discipline. Its most appealing character is properly named Amanda, the loving one. She emanates peace and a sense of dignity that give life to Robbins's preachments on human freedom. Plucky Purcell is a marvelous creature of released energy channeled into genuine fun, and his counterpart, Marx Marvelous, is an articulate narrator and spokesman for the New Physics-Eastern Mysticism philosophy that is salient in Robbins's fiction. The other characters are less fully developed, but what the novel lacks in characterization it makes up for in zaniness of plot and exuberance of language.

Another Roadside Attraction developed its audience slowly in spite of very encouraging reviews, largely because it was marketed as a hardback—to an unresponsive market. Its real market turned out to be the younger reader who could afford the cheaper paperback or borrow a tattered copy from a friend. Robbins's successes in the paperback market have continued to be substantial, and while no definitive market analyses have been conducted of his readership, reviewers and critics point to his success with the late high-school and early-college-years audience, to whom the mixture of loosely structured narrative, zany characters, and Rabelaisian style have considerable appeal.

By the time Robbins's second novel appeared he had secured a modest but growing audience, an agent, and a new publisher, Bantam Books, who leased the hardback and trade paperback rights for this new novel to Houghton Mifflin. *Even Cowgirls*

Get the Blues (1976) is a refinement in Robbins's art. It shows the same zest of his earlier book, but the plot is focused and disciplined, mostly because Robbins had learned by this time to use the structure of the journey as a major organizing principle in the narrative. The beloved Amanda is replaced by the Ultimate Hitchhiker, Sissy Hankshaw, a native Virginian who is blessed (or cursed) with extraordinarily large, active, and appealing thumbs. In her thumbing peregrinations across the United States, she has occasion to visit the Rubber Rose Ranch, a Dakota health spa devoted to shedding fat and toning the muscles of suburban housewives. It is run by Bonanza Jellybean and her cowgirls, whom Sissy joins in an attempt to find freedom from herself, as she participates in their communal search for that same freedom. They yearn for an open, sexual, unchauvinistic world, much like that of the Chink, a wizened hermit who lives near the ranch and who has absorbed his philosophy of living from the Clock people, a tribe of Indians, and from Eastern philosophy. The novel ends in semiapocalypse as federal agents destroy the Rubber Rose Ranch. After returning to the East Coast, Sissy has one of her thumbs whittled down to size surgically, and the world settles down to a tedium that one expects will span all time until the Second Coming.

Sissy Hankshaw's attempts to find freedom in her life are those of a free and whole spirit to find some space in a constantly narrowing culture. The novel's end seems to suggest that people cannot have that freedom; they have to be satisfied with a part of it, which may be worse than stultification. Sissy is left more a freak because part of her is grotesquely normal (her surgically altered thumb) and the other part freakish but genuine (her real thumb). The Ranch world has been put in its place, and the real world goes on.

Even Cowgirls Get the Blues is a tighter, better written novel than *Another Roadside Attraction*. What comes across in *Another Roadside Attraction* as pretentiousness of diction and cleverness in plotting appears as a more mature style and surer narrative skill in *Even Cowgirls Get the Blues*. In a review in *Prairie Schooner*, Raymond J. Wilson III captures pointedly the differing impact of these two books: "In *Another Roadside Attraction* Robbins is like a comedian striving for a joke on every line and getting a laugh every fourth line. In *Even Cowgirls Get the Blues* Robbins still strives for a joke on every line; but this time he hits it at least half the time."

Robbins's most recent novel pursues the themes of the earlier novels through a parody of the oriental romance. *Still Life with Woodpecker* (1980)

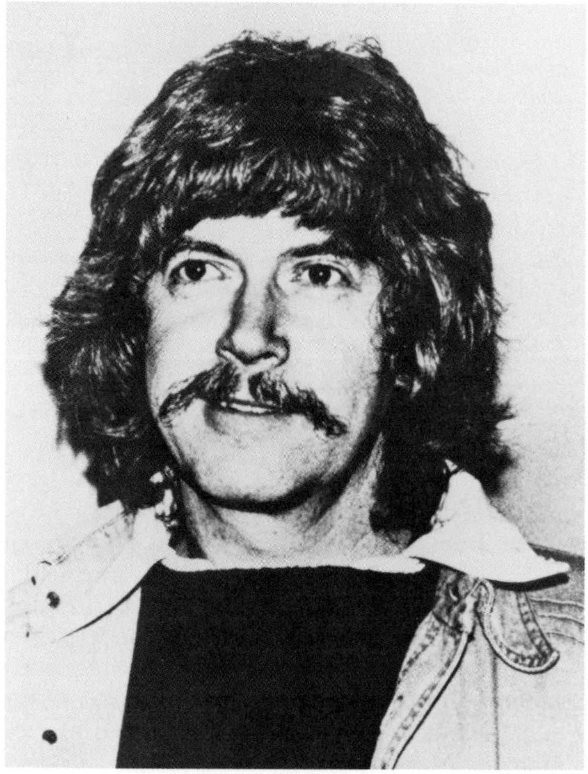

Tom Robbins

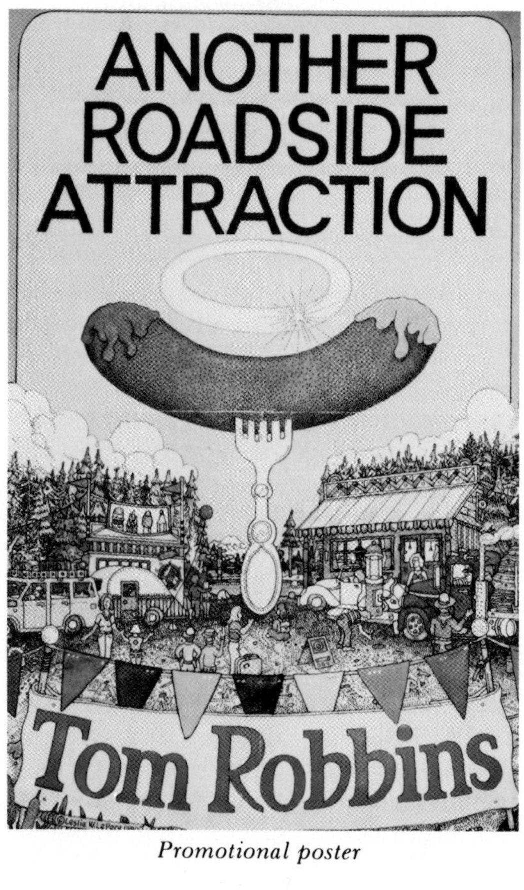

Promotional poster

chronicles the love affair of Princess Leigh-Cheri Furstenburg-Barcalona and her friendly bomber, Bernard Mickey Wrangle, alias the Woodpecker, destroyer of the chemistry building at the University of Wisconsin. Princess Leigh-Cheri is the daughter of King Max and Queen Tilli, the ousted monarchs of the Pacific island paradise of Mu; they now live with the princess in much reduced circumstances in an old house on Puget Sound. The story is framed by an author's monologue having to do with his efforts to type out his narrative on a Remington SL-3 tyepwriter, which at the end fails him, and he has to complete the novel in longhand. Princess Leigh rather predictably becomes separated from Bernard and affianced to the billionaire Arab sportsman A'ben Fizel, who promises to build her a marvelous pyramid reminiscent of the one on a pack of Camel cigarettes, since to Leigh-Cheri pyramids symbolize the inherent cosmic power of redheaded people (most notably Bernard), and the pyramid on the pack of Camels represents the immutability of all pyramids. Through Pyramid Power she hopes to be reunited with Bernard, and, ironically, she is. After Fizel's gift pyramid is completed, Bernard shows up, and the two lovers are imprisoned in its inner chamber, reminiscent of Aida and Antigone. They manage to escape live burial when the princess stealthily plants some of the Woodpecker's dynamite against the tomb's door. They survive the blast, and, both now nearly stone-deaf, live more or less happily ever after.

In the last two pages of the novel, Robbins states his theme most effectively: "When the mystery of the connection [between lovers] goes, love goes." Leigh-Cheri and the Woodpecker embody a truth as old as romance itself, that the "connection" allows lovers to weave a fabric of their own and create their own world. The message of Robbins's last novel is not as strong as that of the earlier two, and while the plot seems more intricately interlaced, it has the complexity and exoticism of grand opera but little of its brilliance. Leigh-Cheri is a pale shadow of Amanda and Sissy, and Bernard is a rather dull bomber. Leigh-Cheri's kingdom is just not a fun place to be, but anyone can enjoy the Roadside Zoo or the Rubber Rose Ranch any day of the week.

Robbins enjoys a kind of formless tale-spinning and self-conscious verbalizing; but if the reader looks closely at the master of this technique, Pynchon, he sees that casualness in form and diction are deceptive, that there is always a logic behind looseness at its best. The same can be said about Robbins's Shandyan excursions. Although they are clever, they do not do much to further the story or the art of the novel. Sissy Hankshaw was a thoroughly engaging figure caught in an oppressive world, and her plight made for good fiction. Bernard Mickey Wrangle and Princess Leigh-Cheri are drab and predictable lovers moving in a rather aimless and surprisingly predictable plot. Critical response to this novel so far bears out that judgment, finding it somewhat pretentious and dull.

Robbins's contribution to the West Coast novel lies in his athletic style and iconoclastic attitude toward form. He refuses to be disciplined by the critics. His message is like the dying call of the whooping cranes in *Even Cowgirls Get the Blues*, a plea for freedom, naturalness, and peace, but it is a rather lonely voice echoing the concerns of an earlier decade, even an earlier generation. Mitchell Ross comments in his *New York Times Magazine* profile of Robbins that he and his school fill their books "with literary fireworks; [their technique] leaves room for the suggestion of profundity; it permits the characters to spout all sorts of heavy, bogus wisdom—and it leaves the center of the book hollow." *Still Life with Woodpecker* leaves Robbins open to such criticism, but the earlier beauties of *Even Cowgirls Get the Blues* still give promise of a more earnest, more profound expression of this novelist's art at some future time.

—*R. H. Miller*

Periodical Publication:

"Why I Live Where I Live," *Esquire* (October 1980): 82-83.

References:

"Five W's for the Counterculture," *Horizon*, 19 (May 1977): 70;

Patricia E. Cleary Miller, "Reconciling Science and Mysticism: Characterization in the Novels of Tom Robbins," Ph.D. dissertation, University of Kansas, 1979;

Robert L. Nadeau, "Physics and Cosmology in the Fiction of Tom Robbins," *Critique*, 29 (1978): 63-74;

Mitchell S. Ross, "The Prince of the Paperback Literati," *New York Times Magazine*, 12 February 1978, pp. 16ff.

Anne Roiphe

(25 December 1935-)

BOOKS: *Digging Out,* as Anne Richardson (New York: McGraw-Hill, 1966);

Up the Sandbox! (New York: Simon & Schuster, 1970);

Long Division (New York: Simon & Schuster, 1972);

Torch Song (New York: Farrar, Straus & Giroux, 1977; Toronto: McGraw-Hill, 1977);

Generation Without Memory: A Jewish Journey in Christian America (New York: Linden/Simon & Schuster, 1981).

Anne Richardson Roiphe, novelist and journalist, is perhaps best known for her second novel, *Up the Sandbox!* (1970), which gained her recognition as a writer concerned with feminist issues. While Roiphe claims "There was no feminism" when she was writing *Up the Sandbox!* and that she simply explored problems emerging from her "own life experience," all four of her novels and many of her essays present the multifaceted problems of the contemporary woman who wishes to find fulfillment and a sense of identity, often in nontraditional ways. In addition to an exploration of crises peculiar to the modern woman, Roiphe examines other major conflicts prevalent in an age preoccupied with alienation and estrangement, such as divorce, hostility between parent and child, the rejection of traditional religious values, token liberalism, and the poignancy of old age. This examination is presented with a feminine vision. The ambivalence surrounding and often engulfing all areas of human relationships appears as a key theme in her works.

Born Anne Roth in New York City, Roiphe has spent most of her life there. Her affection for New York emerges in her novels, where its diversity and excitement help to shape her protagonists' personalities. After graduating from Sarah Lawrence College in 1957, Roiphe went to Europe to pursue her studies and then married Jack Richardson in 1958. Following a 1963 divorce, she married Herman Roiphe, a psychoanalyst, in 1967. Now the mother of five daughters, two of them stepdaughters, Roiphe has contributed several articles to leading magazines drawing on her experiences as a parent.

Roiphe's first novel, *Digging Out* (1966), published under the name Anne Richardson, has as its protagonist Laura Smith, daughter of a wealthy Park Avenue Jewish family. Laura is well educated, sophisticated, sensitive, and deeply unhappy. She is involved in the process of "digging out" of her past and of rejecting her heritage—a past she finds empty and sterile and a heritage she denounces as devoid of value. Laura's search for her own identity coincides with, and is made possible by, her mother's slow, painful death from cancer. The mother, Rose Tumarkin Smith, dies during the Christmas season; Christmas festivities provide an ironic backdrop to Rose's death and to Laura's rebirth in a new identity.

Roiphe tells two stories—Laura's and her family's—in alternating chapters. Laura's thoughts, reactions, and anxieties are narrated in first person. Juxtaposed to Laura's extreme subjectivity are the chapters related in third person, which provide a seemingly objective account of various relatives, all of whom appear eccentric, selfish, shallow, or inept. In addition to these "primary sources" and "secondary sources," as Roiphe labels them, there are four short chapters called Christmas stories, written by Laura as she watches her mother die. She composes them because she finds herself "thinking in terms of parables." Two of these stories have Jewish "pedlars" as central characters, poor, fearful men who lose what they love most. One story depicts a rabbi who blinds his deaf son to make him unaware of what pleasures he has lost because of his inability to hear; the rabbi, a saintly man, wants to insure that his son will love God. The third parable, like the others, is a story of love and loss; a widow adopts a foundling who gives her life meaning, but when the adopted daughter has matured, she abandons her mother by eloping and taking with her the widow's savings. The widow dies from grief. These four parables, created because "it was Christmastime," mirror the themes found in the primary and secondary sources.

While Laura and her mother have never had a close, warm relationship, both are inexorably tied together; when one dies, a part of the other dies, too. Roiphe delves into the bonds holding parent and child: the struggle for independence, the need for rebellion and rejection, and the concomitant instinct for dependency. Laura sees her mother as a vain, useless woman who has made a failure of her life in pursuit of all the wrong goals; Rose is the Jewish princess reduced by illness to a babbling infantilism. Because of her shallowness, she has lived an unhappy life, neglected by her husband and resented by her daughter. While Laura sits by her mother's bedside and observes in minute detail all of the signs of decay in Rose's body, her resentment about her loveless, yet well-ordered, childhood becomes interwoven with her pity for and likeness to her mother. Alternately repelled and attracted, she senses and fears her own bodily decay occuring simultaneously with Rose's.

"I could go alone. I could go no other way. I would become the first American in my family." In rejecting her family and her traditions, she welcomes rootlessness and assimilation. Roiphe offers only these rather ambiguous values as the replacements Laura needs. The repeated contrast between the joyless opulence of the Smiths' life-style and the relentless agony and indignity of Rose's death leaves the reader, along with Laura, drained of conventional emotions.

Anne Roiphe

Laura's response to her mother is also colored by the revelations about her relatives. Laura condemns them mentally, along with her German governess, whose parents become Nazis while she serves Jewish families, as incapable of any love other than self-love and as being motivated always by self-preservation. Larua finds the Jewish rituals empty and the traditions, clung to mindlessly by her family, reactionary and destructive. She wishes to reject everything from her past and to seek love and comfort in another, non-Jewish environment. After her mother's death, Laura plans her escape from "the tribe," refusing adamantly to continue suffering "someone else's atonement." Now that her mother is buried, she can "leave them chanting in the temple, forming businesses with each other and exchanging magic words." Laura then asserts her new identity:

Digging Out received almost unanimous praise as a first novel of interest, energy, and skill. Several critics pointed out that, like most first novels, *Digging Out* is based on a quest for identity and that it fits squarely in the genre of the American-Jewish experience novel. However, they were also quick to applaud Roiphe for her intelligent and deft handling of the narrative in the alternating chapters and for her ability to penetrate the history of an immigrant family which comes to America to pursue the American dream and succeeds. Critics also praised Roiphe's realistic treatment of slow, painful death while lamenting the large number of characters in a novel of such brevity.

With her second novel, *Up the Sandbox!*, Roiphe enjoyed both popular and critical acclaim. The central character, Margaret Reynolds, is the wife of Paul, a graduate student in social history, and the mother of two young children, Elizabeth and Peter. The novel's setting, Manhattan's Upper West Side, is, one reviewer noted, "as emblematic of New York as the lions at the Public Library." Margaret's daily routine consists of caring for her children, taking them to the park and watching them play in the sandbox, cooking meals for her family, and resolving any marital discord in the bedroom at night. The tedium of her daily life confuses Margaret; it is a life for which she was unprepared by her college education. Though she is not very skillful at keeping her apartment and her children in order, she rejects the shallow, materialistic world of her pampered mother, who spends her afternoons playing bridge and offers to send her maid to restore cleanliness to Margaret's apartment.

Like Walter Mitty, Margaret escapes the ambiguities of her existence by fantasies of glory and excitement. Though she is physically bound to the sandbox each day, her dreams provide her with feminist achievements that significantly transcend her traditional roles of wife and mother. In one daydream, Margaret is a member of a black revolutionary group, PROWL, and mistress of its leader; the group's aim is to blow up the George Washington Bridge. In other fantasies, she is a doctor at a New York hospital, an anthropologist on the Amazon, a Mother of Peace sent to Viet Nam, and a star reporter who wins an interview with Fidel Castro in Cuba. Although each of her daydreams places her in a position of power and honor, Margaret never feels fulfilled—even in her fantasy life. She discovers that the black militant leader's ambitions for his life after the revolution are as bourgeois as those of the middle class he condemns. The blowing up of the bridge is marred by the accidental presence of a derelict who becomes an innocent victim. Margaret's seduction of Castro provides another disappointment, for Castro reveals that he is a woman in disguise. When Margaret becomes dangerously ill from arrow poison during her anthropological trip on the Amazon, in her delirium she wants only to return to Paul and her children, asking their forgiveness. The novel offers no resolution to Margaret's dilemma; she is left at the end with the prospect of an unplanned third pregnancy about which she feels ambiguous.

Roiphe moves Margaret deftly between dream and reality. Chapters alternate with such headings as "In Week One," a chronicle of the frustrations and joys of real life, and "Out of Week One," the narrative of Margaret's life as an uncertain radical in PROWL. While *Digging Out* utilizes the same narrative technique of alternating chapters, Roiphe is more experimental in *Up the Sandbox!*. Instead of the more traditional flashback, she presents another level of reality—the imagination. In both novels Roiphe relies heavily on narrative and interior monologue rather than on dialogue. Margaret Reynolds is more clearly drawn than is Laura Smith, for Margaret's ambivalence toward her life, marriage, revolution, motherhood, and feminism is presented with insight and sympathy rather than hostility. Margaret frequently questions whether the need to be a separate, fulfilled self is legitimately hers or is imposed on her by society. The novel is composed of questions, not answers.

Roiphe displays a talent for satire in this novel as she cleverly pierces some of the conventional responses of feminists, militants, and liberals. Margaret sees her life as one of necessary compromises; progress and a Barnard education have done little to change its demands on her. "Despite computers and digit telephone numbers, nuclear fission," she reflects, "my life hardly differs from that of an Indian squaw settled in a teepee on the same Manhattan land centuries ago." She knows she is "no Penelope, no romantic heroine or creature of historical importance," but though she cannot "build a bridge across a jungle and plant a city," she can "make another human being." She has the "final defiance" of a "creation no authority can prevent—a birth." While this ability is not always enough to make her life satisfying, Margaret is never willing to denounce her roles of wife and mother; she will continue to compromise, dream, and nurture.

In 1972 *Up the Sandbox!* was made into a movie with a screenplay by dramatist Paul Zindel, starring Barbra Streisand as Margaret Reynolds. The movie stresses the comic overtones of the novel and moves swiftly back and forth between fantasy and reality. Though it was a commercial success, Roiphe was not pleased with the film adaptation of her novel, largely because she believed it tampered with her own creation.

Roiphe's third novel, *Long Division* (1972), is another psychological exploration of a woman, Emily Brimberg Johnson, who questions the values of marriage, motherhood, and self-fulfillment. The novel relates the story of Emily's car trip from New York to Juarez, Mexico, with her ten-year-old daughter, Sarah, in pursuit of a quick Mexican divorce. Emily has adored and served her husband, a painter, who has humiliated her, ignored her, and been unfaithful to her. Finally, he leaves her, and she is faced with a terrible freedom. Sarah is resentful and sullen, and the trip to Mexico borders on being a succession of nightmares.

Again relying more on narrative and interior monologue than on dialogue, Roiphe maintains a somewhat uncertain line between the real and the grotesque. The reader is never sure if Emily is awake or dreaming. During a tour of the Hershey chocolate factory in Pennsylvania, Sarah falls into a vat of chocolate and cannot be returned to her mother until the end of the tour. Later they pick up three hitchhikers who turn out be religious fanatics; they persuade Emily to go to a bizarre tent-revival meeting. Emily's one sexual escapade, with a dentist attending a convention at her hotel, ends in failure; he blames his impotence on her bad breath. Through all of her misadventures, Emily retains a romantic naivete that marks her as an easy victim. She buys any brown paper parcel offered to her in the expectation of finding a pornographic treasure; in every case she is duped. The grimmest nightmare occurs when she and Sarah are held captive by a group of old people in the Texas desert, people who are lonely and abandoned and determined to adopt a daughter and granddaughter. This parent-child conflict reinforces the ongoing struggle between Emily and Sarah. Their relationship is filled with hostility, attraction, and repulsion. When Sarah is kidnapped by gypsies, Emily does not at first report the incident to the police. When Sarah is recovered, however, both mother and daughter affirm their need for each other.

Emily sees herself as a wandering Jewess, a defector, a tribal renegade. She is Laura Smith at thirty-five, having renounced the religion and traditions of her family, who worship only on high holidays. By marrying her Episcopalian painter and refusing to suffer anyone's atonement, Emily believed she had found freedom and a new identity. *Long Division* catalogues in bleak, grim detail the limits and emptiness of that freedom, but Emily does not lose her faith in the romantic ideals that have failed her.

While the novel was generally well received, several critics judged it less successful than Roiphe's previous novels. They found the heroine less interesting than Laura Smith or Margaret Reynolds, and her interior monologues dull. Also lacking was the caustic humor of *Up the Sandbox!*. Most critics praised the energy of the novel and its exploration of "decent" mid-America, an area Emily finds as barren as New York and more nightmarish in its deceptive surface simplicity. Roiphe wrote a screenplay for *Long Division*, but it has not been made into a movie.

Roiphe's fourth and most recent novel, *Torch Song* (1977), has as its protagonist Marjorie Weiss Morrison, a character similar to her earlier heroines. Marjorie, like Emily in *Long Division*, is a willing victim. She is a Barnard graduate of the mid-1950s, a daughter of wealthy Jewish parents, and a member of an avant-garde, quasi-intellectual Greenwich village crowd that meets at the White Horse Tavern. Marjorie's parents, like Larua Smith's, are trapped in a marriage bound by quarrels, infidelity, and selfishness. Marjorie's asthmatic brother, Irwin, rebels by becoming an Orthodox Jew, a commitment which embarrasses his parents and his sister. Irwin's antifeminism is one of the sources of conflict between the brother and sister. Possibly as a rebellion against the materialism as well as the traditions of her family, Marjorie finds herself drawn to a blond, tall, would-be author, Jim Morrison.

First as his girlfriend and later as his wife, Marjorie allows herself to become the slave and victim of Morrison, a writer she compares to Thomas Mann. He uses and humiliates her in New York, Paris, Munich, and again in New York—mostly because she willingly allows him to do so. Marjorie lies to and steals from her family in the name of Jim's artistic need. She convinces herself that she can help him overcome his many sicknesses. Jim is a totally self-absorbed decadent, awash in a mire of alcoholism and sexual aberration. In the six years they are together, Marjorie and Jim never have a conventional sexual experience, though they manage at her insistence to produce a child. Jim has no regard for his daughter, Faith, and after his work has made him relatively famous he abandons Marjorie for another woman.

The novel ends, as it begins, with Marjorie happily married to a pediatrician who is able to provide her with the life she claims she has wanted. Roiphe uses the flashback technique to present the central narrative, the story of Marjorie's adoration and worship of Jim. The major question arising from the novel concerns Marjorie's growth and awareness. By participating in a six-year stint of grotesque humiliation and sickness which she is unable to modify, Marjorie becomes almost as abnormal as Jim and becomes guilty of his excesses by association. She is never able to cut the ties herself, and if he had not finally found her unnecessary to his well-being, her torture as well as their daughter's would have continued. Marjorie excuses herself, maintaining that she was an innocent, that "Jim distracted me from myself. He filled me with circle.

The pull towards Israel is rooted deep in the Jewish traditions

In the Seder that ends with the words next year in Jerusalem—with the ancient knowledge that God could only be worshipped in one temple in one place—and the yearning for completion. The beginning and the end of the circle—If the Diaspora . . . Zionism is also political—a response to the insanity of Anti-Semitism that promises to return and return—a response to the indigestible quality of Jewishness that has not yet been permitted to merge into the christian centuries of adoption. Zionism is a response to the Holocaust. The redemption of the holy land restores faith in the Jewish destiny and its faith spring like a phoenix from the ashes of Dachau and Auschwitz. But Zionism political or religious, is still mystical in nature. It requires a merging of self with the past and the destiny of the people, a melding of self into. It requires a passionate emotional commitment to the redemption—it is not a position for rationalists—for universalists, for the alienated and the balanced. It requires unthinking devotion. It gives mystical rewards of togetherness. It is not an easy position to adopt late in life without the necessary loyalties and bonds having run through the days of ones childhood, when ideas and ideals and feelings flowed freely mingling causes making rivers of passionate positions.

My nephew nicks his head on the side of his bed as he tumbles in for the night. Be careful says my brother. "Yes" says my nephew standing 3 ft tall in his baseball pajamas. "I remember, you told me, the head is the most important part of a little Jewish boy." Someone had asked Rabbi Kahtel about skiing and swimming and baseball. Of course Jews are free to do these things says Rabbi Kahtel, but the emphasis on the physical is Greek not Jewish—our emphasis is on the soul—our work is to bring the Messiah by perfecting our spiritual selves. 17th c. Poland swimming into the 20th century says my brother.—Those people are crazies—what do they have 10,000 rebbes? They don't believe in birth control, abortion, womens rights. They are sheep that respond to a leader like mindless robots. Mitzvah mobiles indeed—its disgusting. You don't like their singing and dancing, their chanting I ask. "Compared to Bach, to Mozart" he says—"like the Beatles compared to Beethoven." My brother is a scientist not a mystic and its for sure his head is his most important part—He was not the type to go off dancing with Baal Shem Tov—had he been there he would have laughed.

Generation Without Memory, *manuscript*

expectations of dreadful and wonderful things." If the reader is to reject Jim's sadism, however, he must also reject Marjorie's long-term masochism. Though Marjorie asserts that "nothing burns and purifies like a first love," the reader finds it all too easy to condemn such a destructive love, and his identification with Marjorie becomes very strained. Because Marjorie's willingness to be victimized is never credibly explained, the novel is seriously flawed.

As in her earlier novels, Roiphe presents here a woman concerned with finding her identity and sometimes dismayed to discover that it depends solely on a man. Marjorie punishes herself for old, instinctive, even tribal, guilts by choosing a cruel man to love and follow. She hopes to escape by having a child, but motherhood is not protection enough from the misery Jim inflicts. In her second marriage, which is very briefly related, Marjorie has somehow many years later inexplicably turned into a partner rather than a victim. Roiphe does not narrate the transformation. Because of the ambiguities surrounding Marjorie's motivations, critics did not respond as favorably to *Torch Song* as they did to Roiphe's previous novels.

In addition to her fiction Roiphe has contributed many articles on a wide range of subjects to major magazines. She is a frequent contributor to the *New York Times Magazine* and has written articles for that publication on such subjects as "The Waltons" (18 November 1974) and "The American Family" (18 February 1973), both of which are television dramas. Other articles include "The Mad Diary of a Manhattan Ecologist" (17 October 1971), "Good-by John Dewey, Hello Cotton Mather" (19 January 1975), "Confessions of a Compulsive-Impulsive Buyer" (10 March 1974), and "The Trouble at Sarah Lawrence" (20 March 1977). Roiphe's articles deal primarily with problems confronting the contemporary family and its individual members. The conflict between parents and children as the children seek to become separate selves, a frequent theme in her novels, is also a recurrent topic in her nonfiction, whether she is reviewing television's portrayal of the family, discussing religious fanaticism among teenagers, examining inconsistencies in Freud and women's liberation, or exploring teenagers' sexual mores.

The essay "Christmas Comes to a Jewish Home" (*New York Times*, 21 December 1978) sparked an immediate and continued controversy. Roiphe's attitude toward her Jewish heritage, as reflected in *Digging Out*, has been viewed by many of her readers as one of defection or betrayal. In "Christmas Comes to a Jewish Home," she opted for rationalism and skepticism and rejected Jewish antifeminism. Although her family had adopted Christmas rituals, she pointed out that they were not Christians but humanists, people much like her fictional characters.

In her most recent book, *Generation Without Memory* (1981), Roiphe cross-examines her earlier attitudes. After an unsatisfying psychoanalysis, she has undertaken a search for meaning in her Jewish heritage. *Generation Without Memory* contains a description of Roiphe's privileged, assimilated childhood; material from interviews she has conducted with rabbis, psychiatrists, and others; and a chronicle of her thoughts and feelings as her quest progresses. Describing the book as "part autobiography, part journalism and part essay" in the *New York Times Book Review*, Eli N. Evans criticized it for such flaws as shallowness and disorganization, but summed up, "as the faltering first steps of an assimilated woman back to Judaism it has a topical resonance."

Roiphe's finest novel may well be her first one, *Digging Out*. It was her initial experimentation with narrative technique, and, while *Up the Sandbox!* may exploit a more clever technique, the poignancy and credibility of *Digging Out* make this novel more memorable. Though *Up the Sandbox!* is Roiphe's most popular novel, it is also the most dated. The fantasies and humor are locked into a particular era and historical and social background. Her later novels fail primarily because of her female protagonists, who suffer too willingly and needlessly, and whose guilt ultimately must rest on their own shoulders. She does not convince the reader that society is to blame for their victimization.

Roiphe's work, both fiction and nonfiction, consistently confronts the problems of modern American life that are faced by the contemporary American woman. While her scope is limited, the seriousness of her subject is not. Her novels are all studies of an intensely personal, feminine vision. Roiphe's readers find no simple answers in her fiction; instead, she depicts life in all of its ambiguities. Her characters are skeptical about traditional values and uncertain about their ability to adopt or create new ones. Willing to experiment and take chances in her work, Roiphe continues to write.

—*Ruth L. Strickland*

References:

Walter Clemons, "Walking Nightmare," *Newsweek*, 80 (23 October 1972): 112-113;

Valentine Cunningham, "Faust things Faust," *Times Literary Supplement*, 25 March 1977, p. 334;

Elizabeth Easton, "Up the Sandbox!" *Saturday Review*, 54 (6 February 1971): 31;

Eli N. Evans, "Looking For Roots," *New York Times Book Review*, 7 June 1981, pp. 12-13;

Irma Pascal Heldman, "Love as a Bridge," *Time*, 97 (25 January 1971): 74-75;

Stanley Kauffmann, "Welcome," *New Republic*, 156 (4 March 1967): 22, 40;

Nora Sayre, "Certain Aspects of Death," *Nation*, 205 (11 September 1967): 219-220;

Sayre, "Breaking up and working loose: *Long Division*," *New York Times Book Review*, 5 November 1972, pp. 5, 22;

L. E. Sissman, "Books: Second Time Around," *New Yorker*, 47 (17 April 1971): 145-146.

Gilbert Sorrentino
(27 April 1929-)

BOOKS: *The Darkness Surrounds Us* (Highlands, N.C.: Jargon Books, 1960);

Black and White (New York: Totem Press/Corinth Books, 1964);

The Sky Changes (New York: Hill & Wang, 1966);

The Perfect Fiction (New York: Norton, 1968);

Steelwork (New York: Pantheon Books, 1970);

Imaginative Qualities of Actual Things (New York: Pantheon Books, 1971);

Corrosive Sublimate (Los Angeles: Black Sparrow Press, 1971);

Splendide-Hôtel (New York: New Directions, 1973);

Flawless Play Restored: The Masque of Fungo (Los Angeles: Black Sparrow Press, 1974);

A Dozen Oranges (Santa Barbara, Cal.: Black Sparrow Press, 1976);

Sulpiciae Elegidia/Elegiacs of Sulpicia (Mt. Horeb, Wis.: Perishable Press, 1977);

White Sail (Santa Barbara, Cal.: Black Sparrow Press, 1977);

The Orangery (Austin: University of Texas Press, 1978);

Mulligan Stew (New York: Grove, 1979);

Aberration of Starlight (New York: Random House, 1980);

Crystal Vision (Berkeley, Cal.: North Point Press, 1981);

Selected Poems: 1958-1980 (Santa Barbara, Cal.: Black Sparrow Press, 1981).

"I like to synthesize; I hate analysis. I don't like to take a subject and break it down into parts; I like to take disparate parts and put them together and see what happens," Gilbert Sorrentino told Barry Alpert in *Vort* magazine. "For me, life is right in front of you. Mysterious because it is not hidden. I'm interested in surfaces and flashes, episodes. . . . I'm an episodic and a synthetic writer." This art of synthesis, evident even in his earliest published fiction, has distinguished Gilbert Sorrentino as one of America's most important and interesting writers since 1960.

Gilbert Sorrentino was born in Brooklyn, New York, to August and Ann Sorrentino. His first serious attempt at fiction was a short story written while he was a first-year student at Brooklyn College in 1950. His story won an award in Brooklyn College's literary magazine in 1956. Sorrentino's course work was interrupted from 1951 to 1953, when he served in the U.S. Army medical corps. During that time, he wrote what he describes as an "impressionistic" sketch of the bordellos in the Mexican border towns, later sending this to William Carlos Williams and initiating a friendship that lasted until Williams's death in 1963. After leaving the army, Sorrentino began a vast novel "about my old neighborhood. But that was the true novel, you know, the narrator growing up, Studs Lonigan, that kind of stuff. Ah, sensitive plant facing life!" Though instructive for him, the novel was "hopeless" and was assigned to the drawer. He returned to Brooklyn College in 1955.

In 1956, Sorrentino and friends from Brooklyn College began *Neon*, a literary magazine he edited through six issues, with contributions from such writers as Williams, Ezra Pound, Hubert Selby, Jr., Paul Goodman, Max Finstein, Joel Oppenheimer, Charles Olson, Fielding Dawson, Joe Early, LeRoi Jones, and Ron Loewinsohn. In 1957, the year he left school, Sorrentino started a book of sketches based on the people in the Brooklyn neighborhood where he grew up, a project which became, though radically altered, the source for his second novel. In the early 1960s he wrote and served in various editorial roles for *Kulchur*, a magazine that brought together a diverse group of writers from the Black

Mountain School, the New York School, and the Beats, all loosely united in their opposition to the official academic poetry and fiction of the period.

In 1961 he began writing *The Sky Changes*, which was finished in 1964 and published in 1966. The novel records the destruction of a marriage as the husband and wife, accompanied by their two children and a nameless driver, journey across a desolate American landscape in the foolish hope that their marriage might be rescued. Written in a cold style and with an unrelenting tone of misery and numbed emotion, the novel is a carefully structured set of episodes for which place names serve as titles. In "Columbus, Ohio," for instance, we have, "Columbus. After that businessman. The usual car lots. The usual drive-ins. Nobody in the streets. The Midwest is made up of police and drive-ins. Pinched-faced car-hops. Their whole hearts full of alum, secreted into the blood. She won't get out here, she would die here, his children would be swept up by the wind, the rain would dissolve them."

Concerning the lack of narrative, Sorrentino said in an interview in *Grosseteste Review*, "The past, the present, the future are mixed together in order to show very clearly that there is really no past that is worse than the present and there is no future that will be better than the present. The mood is darkness. I wanted to create a world that was black and without hope. Therefore, the idea of a narrative line . . . was completely uninteresting to me in making this book. It is a collaboration, a synthesis, of events."

Steelwork (1970) is again a synthesis and collaboration, though here structured around time rather than space, moving even further away from the idea of the well-made story of plot and character analysis. Each section is a brief, crystalline evocation of the people, places, and attitudes of Sorrentino's Brooklyn neighborhood from 1935 to 1951. In the *Grosseteste Review* interview, Sorrentino says that the novel "works in terms of the fugue, counterpoint, complimentary irony, and sketchy narration, either backward or forward. . . . The point of all this, I suppose, to be fair and not lead you down the garden path, is that there are no characters in *Steelwork* except the neighborhood itself. I was interested in the 'character' of the neighborhood. The neighborhood is the protagonist." Amid the multilayered tones of this novel, however, is one of comedy, a tone that becomes salient in all the future work.

Imaginative Qualities of Actual Things (1971), completed while Sorrentino was still serving as an editor at Grove Press (1965-1970), uses as materials

Gilbert Sorrentino

what he had experienced in the avant-garde art community of New York during the 1960s. Both hilariously funny and bitterly satiric, the novel uncovers the pretensions and corruption of painters, writers, and hangers-on in that art world. While each chapter is largely devoted to one of eight characters, the novel proceeds by way of digression, anecdote, asides, and itemizations, all filtered through a narrator whose rage and urbane wit mix into a strangely compassionate yet unsentimental treatment of these meretricious, sometimes gifted artists. Concerning one of the characters, the narrator says, "There is a certain kind of artisan whose task it is to amuse the rich. Bart started out as a very different kind of man, and then, at a point in his life, found himself becoming interested in wanting to be the other kind of man. There is nothing tragic in this. Had he continued as he started, he would have been a mediocre painter, and a slightly better sculptor. As it turned out, he became a remarkably successful and wealthy decorator, who pleased people, gave critics something to write about, and so on. There is nothing tragic in this, it's simply another manifestation of the destruction that this book is scratching the surface of."

Imaginative Qualities of Actual Things signaled both an end and a departure for Sorrentino. The community he wrote about was already scattering, but a number of its members were not pleased with what they perceived as portraits of themselves or friends in the book. By this time

Sorrentino himself had stepped outside this community in order to have more time to write, finally quitting his job at Grove Press for the same reason. More important, the technical achievements in this novel opened up a world of possibilities for future novels, "of doing anything I damn well pleased."

This freedom led first to *Splendide-Hôtel* (1973), a short book consisting of twenty-six sections, each developed around a letter of the alphabet. These prose poems are a mixture of criticism and fiction, calling back to service some of the names used in Sorrentino's previous novels as well as inventing ones to be used in future works. Originating in his reading of Arthur Rimbaud's poem "Voyelles," the collection became exquisitely rendered exercises in style whose points of reference are the lives and work of Rimbaud and Williams. In this book Sorrentino's conception of catalogues or lists, which he had employed as early as *Steelwork*, is fully developed, so that the list becomes as important in his fiction as character and story. In its proliferation of words outside of narrative function, the list is a "kind of exhaustion of the substantive. . . . Simply taking a noun and making it do the work of many sentences. It's also a kind of insistence on the reality of words *per se*." In 1974 Black Sparrow Press published *Flawless Play Restored: The Masque of Fungo*, a Johnsonian antimasque whose conventions of private jokes, spectacle, and masquerading perfectly fit the design and themes of his next novel, wherein this antimasque serves as a centerpiece.

"Doing anything I damn well pleased" then produced *Mulligan Stew* (1979), begun in 1971 and finished in 1975. The novel was turned down by twenty-five publishers before Grove Press, just emerging from years of financial indebtedness to Random House, accepted it. An enormous undertaking that in print is nearly four hundred and fifty pages, the book is literally a synthesis of almost everything Sorrentino had read and written in the past twenty-five years. The novel established him as a major comic writer, causing reviewers to place him with Joyce, Sterne, and Rabelais. Despite its length, the novel is tightly written, each section requiring different styles and methods of construction as Sorrentino's protagonist plies himself to, among others, imitations of the detective story, the Western, the Jewish novel, pornography, scholarship, Elizabethan diction, and finally, to imitations of his imitations. In the midst of composing the novel, Sorrentino told Barry Alpert, "I've always used everything I can put my hands on. I hardly ever throw anything away." The completed novel testifies to the collector's inclusiveness.

In spite of the novel's difficulties, sections of it were published in such mainstream magazines and periodicals as *Atlantic Monthly*, *Partisan Review*, and *TriQuarterly*. Almost by way of rumor, the novel achieved a reputation before the book was ever published, an irony for a writer who fifteen years before "couldn't pay them to take anything I wrote." After publication, reviewers responded with lavish praise, for the first time taking notice of a Sorrentino novel as it was published rather than delaying reviews for months and then confining remarks to a few paragraphs.

While *Mulligan Stew* was making the rounds of publishers and being rejected by all but Grove, Sorrentino completed another ambitious novel, now entitled *Crystal Vision*, which will be published by North Point Press in 1981. It too was turned down by almost as many publishers as *Mulligan Stew*, both before and after *Mulligan Stew* had received such widespread critical fame. But while *Crystal Vision* was being rejected, Sorrentino wrote *Aberration of Starlight* (1980). Like his previous work in that it synthesizes materials from various sources, one of which is the poetry from his collection *The Orangery* (1978), the novel also has narrative development. Told from four different points of view, it relates the events in an approximately thirty-six hour period at a boardinghouse for summer vacationers in Budd Lake, New Jersey, in 1939. Neither nostalgic nor sentimental, the novel sets down the tone and temper of the times as they are reflected in and act upon the four major characters, a divorced woman, her ten-year-old son, her father, and a man whom she meets and falls in love with at the resort. Philip Roth remarked that "had James Joyce come to Budd Lake, New Jersey, for a summer vacation in 1939, he might have written a novel about the people there as lively with narrative ingenuity, and as close to the humble facts of ordinary life, as Sorrentino has in *Aberration of Starlight*." Currently, Sorrentino is working on another novel and is preparing his selected poems, which Black Sparrow Press will issue in 1981. He lives in New York City with his wife, Vicki, and son Christopher.

In his *Grosseteste* interview, Sorrentino described, in relation to a poem by Thomas Nashe, what he sees as both the motive and pleasure of the writer, an attitude that has certainly guided his own career from beginning to present. "To realize that was written so many centuries ago and that it has survived as something utterly beautiful, a construction of language that will strike anyone with a sense

86.

(all drenched in deshabille) (i.e., the professional pauper);
Georgia, ladies of the evening, the Limehouse blues, lovin' Sam the Sheik of
(am what he am); (than whom which)
Alabam', the South Sea moon, Nellie Kelly, being on the Alamo, Rose of the Rio
(who ate the moldy casserole);
Grande, stumbling, being 'way down yonder in New Orleans, Annabelle, Barney Google,
("all the news from shit to hint"); (the most-flute king);
the bugle call rag, Charleston, dizzy fingers, raggedy Ann, that old gang of his,
(cf. "Anomie in Cincinnati");
being all alone by the telephone, the day that Sally went away, the Indian love
(vide Further Adventures by Venus Furze);
call, someone who could make him feel glad just to be sad, memory lane, nobody's
(or "Framed!");
sweetheart, a prisoner's song, Rose Marie, sugar cake, a photograph to tell his . . .
and ¶ He like to fainted from ennui when entertaining thoughts of
troubles to, the Bam, Bam, Bamy shore, Cecilia, gypsy eyes blazing, Rose with the
(partial as he was to opera stockings); (read: "mountings")
turned-down hose, drinking songs, the hills of home, jalousie, a cottage small by
(where a pall of smoke did plash); (courtesy Texas-Pacific RR);
a waterfall, when lights were low, the song of the vagabonds, Sunny, that ukulele
(E.R.A.);
lady, Valencia, baby face, the birth of the blues, hard-luck stories that they
(with determined mien)
handed him, desert songs, horses, climbing the highest mountain, stars peek-a-
(vide "Honky Myths in Western Architecture")
booing down, little white houses, when nighttime came stealing, the moonlight on
(fondly floodlights flotsam fowl); (played a trick on him); (k) (k)
the Ganges, muddy water, his little nest of heavenly blue, playing and dancing,
(day left); (greetings from Lake Valentine, N.J.)
gypsies, the Riff song, when day was done, a broken heart among his souvenirs,
(and other novelty acts);
Bill, crazy words and crazy tunes, a dancing tambourine, a funny face, looking
(peep?)
over a four-leaf clover, Mississippi mud, his blue heaven, when his heart stood
(vide Farm Desertion in 1918-19); and ¶ His head was a Calabash of dreariness about
still, Paree, the rangers' song, Rio Rita, Sam, the old accordion man, going along
(known to all as the lewd lineman); (and Kasha for two);
singing a song, the varsity drag, Miss Annabelle Lee, his land and their land,
(and fog in the brain); (a windowpane)
a pain in his tum-tum, crazy rhythm, women crazy for him, rain and darkness too,
(and his pornographic prong); (the "sweetheart of Racine");
a ding-dong daddy, a red, red rose, Jeannine, the Manhattan serenade, one kiss,
(those WAC-y women)
shortnin' bread, stout-hearted men, sweethearts on parade, a rainbow round his
(and the egg in his beer);
shoulder, the sail on his dreamboat, those tears in his eyes, deep night, a talking
(cf. Venereal Vagrants);
picture of her, vagabond lovers, magic spells that were everywhere, moaning low,
(whispered in crepuscular confessional);
his sin, the one rose that was left in his heart, pagan love songs, the lonely hours,
(that go "jingle-jingle");
stardust, wedding bells, that thing called love, a man who ain't got a friend, a
plus ¶ How his rheumy eyes snapped vengefully when he heard tales of
bench in the park, Betty Co-Ed, biding his time, any Russian play, a cheerful little

Mulligan Stew, *revised typescript*

of language as thrilling as long as English survives; I don't think that there's anything more interesting for a man to do than to make language work that way, to make a perfect beauty out of all the rubbish in the world and in his own mind."

—*John O'Brien*

Periodical Publications:

FICTION:

"The Moon in Its Flight," *New American Review*, no. 13 (1971): 153-163;

"Decades," *Esquire*, 88 (August 1977): 95-96, 138-140;

"Land of Cotton," *Harper's*, 255 (November 1977): 73-76.

NONFICTION:

"*Neon, Kulchur*, Etc.," *TriQuarterly*, no. 43 (Fall 1978): 298-316.

Interviews:

David Ossman, *The Sullen Art* (New York: Corinth, 1963), pp. 46-53;

John O'Brien, "Imaginative Qualities of Gilbert Sorrentino: An Interview," *Grosseteste Review*, 6, nos. 1-4 (1973): 69-84;

Barry Alpert, "Gilbert Sorrentino: An Interview," *Vort*, no. 6 (Fall 1974): 3-30.

References:

Robert L. Caserio, "Gilbert Sorrentino's Prose Fiction," *Vort*, no. 6 (Fall 1974): 63-69;

Stephen Emerson, "Imaginative Qualities of Actual Things," *Vort*, no. 6 (Fall 1974): 85-89;

John O'Brien, "Gilbert Sorrentino: Some Various Looks," *Vort*, no. 6 (Fall 1974): 79-85;

Donald Phelps, *Covering Ground: Essays for Now* (New York: Corinth, 1969), pp. 3-6;

Review of Contemporary Fiction, special Sorrentino number (Spring 1981).

Papers:

Sorrentino's papers are being collected at the University of Delaware.

Max Steele

(30 March 1922-)

BOOKS: *Debby* (New York: Harper, 1950; London: Secker & Warburg, 1950); republished as *The Goblins Must Go Barefoot* (New York: Harper & Row, 1966);

Where She Brushed Her Hair and Other Stories (New York: Harper & Row, 1968);

The Cat and the Coffee Drinkers (New York: Harper & Row, 1969).

Although a large part of Max Steele's literary reputation rests on his skillful short stories, he made his first major impact with his novel *Debby* (1950, republished in 1966 as *The Goblins Must Go Barefoot*), written when Steele was only twenty-six years old. The novel received a great deal of attention as the Harper Prize Novel for 1950. The judges, Katherine Anne Porter, Glenway Wescott, and Joseph Henry Jackson, were unanimous in judging *Debby* a moving and accomplished novel.

Debby is not only set in the South, but it is discernibly Southern in its focus on the Merrill family and the Southern milieu. Max Steele himself has a soft Southern accent that marks him as a son of his region. Henry Maxwell Steele was born in Greenville, South Carolina, where he received his early education. He began his college work in 1939 at Furman University in Greenville, South Carolina, and left after his sophomore year for the University of North Carolina. During World War II his work at Chapel Hill was interrupted by service in the U.S. Army Air Force. His assignment as a meteorology cadet took him to Vanderbilt University during 1943-1944 and to UCLA in 1944. After the war he returned to Chapel Hill and received his B.A. in English in 1946. In 1944, Steele's career as a published short-story writer began when *Harper's Magazine* published "Grandfather and Chow Dog." His short stories have been published in major magazines ever since.

As *The Goblins Must Go Barefoot*, Steele's revised title for *Debby*, suggests, the world that the reader enters requires careful stepping. It is a world of choices and consequences. While its orientation is Southern, it mirrors the drama of the twentieth century from the Great Depression to World War II and makes that world personal through a poignant focus—that of a feebleminded woman—on a particular family. Although the point of view of *Debby* is unusual, it speaks of realities that would touch the lives of most readers.

Reality comes to Steele's readers through the perspective of Deborah Hall, a woman with a child's mind, who leaves a mental institution to work for the Merrills at the time of the birth of Mrs. Merrill's last child, a baby boy. When the novel ends, fourteen years later, Mrs. Merrill is recovering from a nearly fatal stroke, and Debby, who in those fourteen years has found her own mother role with Mrs. Merrill's children (and is, in a sense, her double), is dying. Because of the focus on Debby's perceptions, *Debby* might put readers in mind of the Benjy section of *The Sound and the Fury* (1929), though Steele was not imitating Faulkner, and he portrays more of the norm of life—its griefs, joys, its small moments. The Merrills could, as the saying goes, live next door. Unlike Benjy, Debby not only has a sense of the present, but she also comes to some resolutions about her past. And there is humor in the novel. Typical of such moments of humor is Debby's thinking when she hears Mr. Merrill say that Doctor Bronston could have "saved his breath": "All her life Deborah had puzzled about that: what you did with your breath when you saved it. Was that the breath you used when you panted after running; or did you use it in your sleep? She rather fancied that some time during the night you went sound to sleep—all over—and quit breathing for a few times and used the breath you saved during the day. That was why people died in the night. They had forgotten to save any breath during the day. Some days, she knew sometimes for weeks, she forgot to hold her breath for a little while."

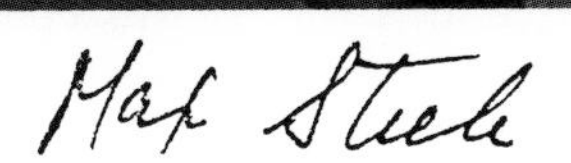

Like many American writers of the twentieth century, Steele went to Paris. In 1951-1952 he studied art at the Academie Julienne. Commenting on Steele's work, the director of the Beaux Arts wrote to the Veterans Administration: "M. Steele has a refreshing contempt for reality." The experience was probably most useful to Steele for training the writer's eye and helping him to define his views of his own culture. He studied French at the Sorbonne during 1952-1954. He was also an advisory editor for the *Paris Review*. During his five years in Paris he wrote several stories about Americans in Paris for *Harper's Magazine*.

Although Steele continued in earnest as a writer, his career began to develop in other ways once he was back in the United States. He has natural talent as a lecturer: to hear Steele talk about a story and to hear him read from it is a delightful experience, as his alma mater recognized. During 1956-1958 he was a lecturer in the department of English at the University of North Carolina at Chapel Hill; he held the same post at the University of California at San

Francisco in 1962-1964 and for several summers beginning in 1970 at the University of California at Davis. In 1967 Steele was named director of the creative writing program at Chapel Hill, a position he has held ever since. In recognition of his skill as a teacher, the university honored him with a Standard Oil Award for excellence in undergraduate teaching. In 1972 Steele was promoted to the rank of professor.

Many of Steele's stories were gathered together in *Where She Brushed Her Hair and Other Stories* (1968), which provides a good sampling of Steele's range. The most notable stories of the collection are the first, "The Cat and the Coffee Drinkers," and the last, the title piece, but others also display his gift. Originally published in the *New Yorker*, "The Cat and the Coffee Drinkers" relates the experience of a young boy who attends Miss Effie Barr's kindergarten. Although private kindergartens like the one Miss Effie runs were common in the South, Miss Effie is an exceptional teacher. She teaches her five-year-old pupils how to drink coffee—and a good deal about life and death. An astute editor recognized that Steele's story would have great appeal for children, and in 1969—with only a few changes—the story was published as a children's book. Illustrations by Erik Blegvad add to the charm of a story that appeals to adults and children. Other stories in *Where She Brushed Her Hair* emphasize Steele's ability in reflecting a young boy's experience, as in *Debby* Steele had great success in creating the Merrills' sons, Britt and Glen. "Big Goat, Little Goat" and "The Glass-Brick Apartment" recount experiences beyond the understanding of the boy who views the complexities of the adult world, especially of his family. The stories that capture the child's perspective are among the most Southern because they capture the ambience of a Southern family. Steele also seems particularly Southern in such tall tales as "Hereby Hangs a Tale," "Hear the Wind Blow," and "Promiscuous Unbound." Steele loves to gather jokes and has even taught courses in contemporary American humor and contemporary British humor.

"Where She Brushed Her Hair" was first published in the *Carolina Quarterly* (Fall 1966) under the title "Fiction, Fact and Dream." The revised title better evokes the poetry of the piece, whereas the original identified the writer's interest in dreams and in using them in his fiction. The writer/narrator of the story asks a psychiatrist friend: "But why is it that stories have value and people will pay for them and yet everyone is bored by dreams?" He proceeds then to present one of his dreams and the story that emerged from it—a story that touches deeply the mystery of life and the essence of the artist's being. The "She" of the short story is the writer's mother, who insisted that in the private time when she brushed her hair she was most herself. In that private time she was also, and in a positive sense, a Southern lady. The narrator touches on the magic of the lady's private time: "It is only when she comes here to comb and brush her hair, not a hundred strokes, but a thousand, that she persuades her soul back into her body, recoups her strength, apportions her energy to the one most in need of it at the moment, thanks her God for her magnificent body and vitality, her appetite, digestion, and health. This is the gift for which she is most thankful, and where does health show the better advantage than in a beautiful head of hair? Where, even the Bible asks, is a woman's glory?" Years later, the writer shares again, in his dream and then in his story, the glory of the magic of an annunciation.

Steele married Diana Whittinghill on 31 December 1960 in Windy Hill, South Carolina. They have two sons, Oliver Whittinghill and Kevin Russell. The Steeles were divorced in 1980. During his summers Steele often teaches in Squaw Valley, California, at the Community of Writers Workshop. He continues to write stories and is at work on a novel, "The Gorgon and the Bridegroom." He also continues to teach young writers at Chapel Hill.

There has been a modest beginning of critical commentary on Max Steele. *Debby* and *Where She Brushed Her Hair* were both widely reviewed, but critical discussion seldom attends publication of an individual short story. Nevertheless, Steele has quietly maintained his visibility with his stories, and several have made their way into anthologies. Reviews and newspaper features on Steele have been gathered in the North Carolina Collection at the University of North Carolina in Chapel Hill. We may expect new critical interest to follow publication of "The Gorgon and the Bridegroom."

—*Joseph M. Flora*

Other:

William Blackburn, ed., *Love Boy: The Letters of Mac Hyman*, introduction by Steele (Baton Rouge: Louisiana State University Press, 1969).

Periodical Publications:

"Grandfather and Chow Dog," *Harper's Magazine*, 189 (August 1944): 219-222;

"All the Wet Animals," *Harper's Magazine*, 190 (May 1945): 504-510;

THE GORGON AND THE BRIDEGROOM

The truth was he had not been in love with his wife when he married her. But now on this strange terrace which seemed to float in the fog rising from the Bay, Ross FALLON ~~Chadwick~~ was as beset by jealousy as if he never known another woman in his entire life. She was no where to be found in the enormous rooms at this party full of some of the oddest people and he had too much dignity to go prying around through the gardens though he had circled all the ~~garden~~ brick paths ~~andxat~~ on this level, the one above, and was now looking down into the only one he had not gone through. His grandmother had said: "Don't ever marry a woman till you've seen her mother" and " A woman can raise a man to her level but a man can't do the same for a woman." But then, judging from his grandmother, he would never have wanted to marry one of her daughters [redacted]. But then he could remember only a few things about his own mother, her only daughter who had died when he was three.

At the moment Ross did not know which hills these were, Berkely or Oakland, whose house, whose party, or how long he had been here on the terrace, or who the young man was hovering somewhere near him. He was not much of a drinker, but here, angry, among strangers, he had allowed a Japanese butler with a phenomenal memory to take his empty glasses and hand him full ones. The view far below of ~~Berkeleyxandx0akland~~ the east bay cities, the lights from the bridges, and the nest of lights, where a moment before San Francisco had risen ~~towered~~ brilliant as a Christmas tree, still pleased him but the drinks and the hovering presence of the young man and the disappearance of his wife were producing in him a physical sensation of near panic. He felt unsure,

"The Gorgon and the Bridegroom," corrected typescript for a work in progress

"Ah Love! Ah Me!," *Collier's*, 116 (3 November 1945): 82;

"I Became a Mohammedan," *Atlantic Monthly*, 176 (December 1945): 127, 129-130;

"Chief Rainbow and the Kids in Paris," *Harper's Magazine*, 205 (December 1952): 68-74;

"Forget the Geraniums," *Harper's Magazine*, 207 (October 1953): 69-74;

"James Thurber, The Art of Fiction," by Steele and George Plimpton, *Paris Review*, 10 (Fall 1955): 35-45; reprinted in *Thurber: A Collection of Critical Essays*, ed. Charles S. Holmes (Englewood Cliffs, N. J.: Prentice-Hall, 1974), pp. 106-116;

"The Silent Scream," *Esquire*, 54 (September 1960): 172-175;

"Rock Like a Fool," *Red Clay Reader*, 4 (1967): 25-29;

"The Most Unbelievable Character I'll Ever Forget," *Lillabulero*, 1 (Winter 1967): 31-33;

"Color the Daydream Yellow," *Quarterly Review of Literature*, 15 (Fall 1968): 443-457;

"The Ragged Halo," *South Carolina Review*, 1 (November 1968): 23-37;

"The Long Vacation," *Cosmopolitan* (November 1969): 160-168;

"My Mother's Night Out," *McCall's*, 104 (October 1976): 174-175, 216, 218, 221-223;

"The Girl from Carthage," *McCall's*, 104 (November 1976): 176-177, 233-238;

"About Love and Grasshoppers," *Redbook*, 149 (May 1977): 126-127, 206-207, 209, 211-212.

William Wharton

BOOKS: *Birdy* (New York: Knopf, 1978; London: Cape, 1979);
Dad (New York: Knopf, 1981).

Despite the major success of his first novel, *Birdy* (1978), and the publication of a second, William Wharton remains largely a mystery to the general public because he writes under the Wharton pseudonym to protect his privacy. Born in Philadelphia, Wharton is now in his mid-fifties and has for the past twenty-five years made his living as a painter. When the oldest of the Whartons' four children "got into the beginning of the television age," the family moved to Europe, living alternately in Spain, Germany, Italy, and France until they had to settle in one place for the children to go to school. For the past fifteen years they have lived almost exclusively in France, spending weekdays on a houseboat near Paris, weekends in a Paris apartment, and the summer months in an old converted water mill between Paris and Geneva.

Birdy is the story of a boy growing up in a poor neighborhood outside Philadelphia during the Depression years. Birdy is bored by school and girls. His only friend is Al, whose aggressive qualities mesh positively with Birdy's gentle, dreamy personality. Birdy's consuming interest is birds, first pigeons and then canaries, for which he builds a backyard aviary. As he becomes more deeply involved in studying and caring for his birds, his entire development comes to center on them. He makes a scientific study of flight and undertakes an exercise program to prepare himself to fly, which he eventually attempts from the top of a water tower and survives.

Birdy tries dating, but he finds girls uninteresting. In his dreams, which begin eerily to predict reality in some instances, he picks a bird mate, Perta, with whom to raise families of "wonderful children." Birdy's absorption in the bird world that he creates enables him to survive without disillusionment the grim realities of growing up in a real world that places no value on illusions. As graduation approaches, Birdy and Al drift apart, each destined to grapple with his harshest reality yet fighting in World War II. They come together again in an army hospital in Kentucky. A series of experiences in the war has left Birdy apparently deranged mentally, and Al is brought in by a psychiatrist who thinks he might be able to help penetrate Birdy's catatonic state.

Wharton begins his novel at this point and unfolds the story through a series of flashbacks from the alternate points of view of Al and Birdy. This method, which Wharton calls the "running present, first person, multiple voices," strikes some critics as difficult, but the author feels at ease with it. In an interview for *Contemporary Authors* he said, "I prefer it to the third person and find limiting my position to a single narrator too confining," describing his approach as somewhere between the novel and play form. The friendship of Al and Birdy, which Robert R. Harris called in the *New Republic* "one of the best rendered boyhood relationships in recent fiction," has more than narrative and plot significance. Wharton explains, "I consider Birdy and Al to be two aspects of a single person: on one side, the husbanding, loving, protective; on the other, the aggressive, dominant, fear ridden. There is continual interaction between the two. The question of which will be manifest in the course of a young male's growth is important."

Concluding his review, Robert Harris said, "Almost by definition, first novels contain hesitancies, an unsureness when it comes to fully engaging the imagination. *Birdy* is extraordinary because it lacks any tentativeness; it grabs and holds as its heroes grapple with life and flight." Although the reviews were generally favorable, Wharton feels that many reviewers missed what he considers the novel's main points. Misinterpreted as a crazy kid, Birdy simply had a "personal reality he tried to live with, and his illusion failed him, as most people's do sooner or later," Wharton explains. "I feel one of the book's main themes is that neither fight nor flight is adequate, that fantasy is necessary as a coping system." And the surprise ending, which has been variously praised and damned, is meant to convey the message that "there are no endings. . . . We tend to hook beginnings and endings onto things, constructing stories, something we can grab hold of."

The book's explicit detail about birds necessitated no research on Wharton's part; raising birds has been a hobby of his since childhood. Writing has been a longtime hobby as well, he says, but *Birdy* is the first book he attempted to have published. Knopf, the only publisher Wharton offered the book to, accepted it as "a literary shot in the dark," he claims, and its success surprised both publisher and author. It has been published in a paperback edition by Avon and is under option for a movie.

Birdy made Wharton a 1979 runner-up for the Pulitzer Prize for fiction, and winner of the 1980 American Book Award. In a letter to the American Book Award Committee, Wharton expressed his gratitude for the 1980 award and defended such awards: "I came from a family where there were no books, where reading was sissy, ruined the eyes and encouraged Protestant or Communist ideas. It would have helped very much to have had visible to me the kind of public presentation you've attempted. Perhaps then I wouldn't have been over 50 years old before I published my first book."

In *Dad* (1981), Wharton again draws on personal experience to tell the story of John Tremont's efforts to help his sick parents. A middle-aged painter living with his wife and children in France, John flies back to California after his mother has had a heart attack. In a reversal of the usual parent-child roles, John stays with his father while his mother is hospitalized and quickly discovers how helpless the elder Tremont has become through years of domination by his bossy, neurotic wife. John works hard at helping his father break the patterns of dependence and develop facets of his personality that have been previously suppressed. But almost as soon as Dad has achieved a more positive way of life, he learns he has cancer. For reasons that are never fully determined, he awakens from the necessary surgery a mindless, incontinent old man.

John cares for his father through the minutely detailed everyday problems engendered by his helplessness, which ends in a near-miraculous breakthrough that seems to restore Dad to his preoperative state of health. The next hurdle, which finally proves insurmountable, comes when John's mother returns home from the hospital. As he witnesses the debilitating encounters that take place between his parents and gradually comes to understand that the well-being of either threatens the health of the other, he relives the psychic maimings of his own childhood.

During John's stay in California, his nineteen-year-old son Billy arrives unexpectedly, having tired of his studies at the University of California at Santa

Dust jacket

Cruz and having decided to return to France with his father to finish writing a book he has begun. Billy's appearance in the story allows the examination of a second father-son relationship. This one suffers as much as the first from sheer age and cultural differences, but both demonstrate the ample affection that usually overcomes and survives such differences.

In *Dad,* Wharton again experiments with narrative technique. The story of the ailing elderly parents is presented through a series of flashbacks, with John as first-person narrator, while he and Billy drive to Philadelphia to catch a plane for France. Interspersed with this story are chapters in which Billy becomes the first-person narrator, mainly to describe the automobile trip, but also telling his own story and revealing his feelings about his father. A third voice enters the novel, at first occasionally and briefly, with dreamlike, lyrical reminiscences that increase in frequency and length, hinting at another life as a farmer in New Jersey. These passages turn out to be Dad's descriptions of a separate existence he has constructed in his mind; he is, says a psychiatrist, a "successful schizophrenic," using his fantasy as an "alternate coping system."

Dad is most believable when John describes the exhausting confusions of caring for his father. After a long night during which Dad has twice wandered away from his bed and into trouble before John awoke and became aware of it, John says, "I'm dead tired. It's almost six-thirty now. . . . This time I decide to do it differently. I close off the side of the bed with chairs again. Then I lie across the foot of his bed with my hand on his left foot. I don't want to tie him down. I go to sleep like that. . . ."

Dad is often flawed by self-conscious writing, awkward metaphors (as when John's plane is descending and he sees "azure and turquoise glimmers of swimming pools set in necklaces of houses"), and stereotyped secondary characters (benevolent hippies, inhumane doctors). More seriously, John often comes across as primly self-righteous in both his roles, as son and father, and the metamorphosis in Dad's real-life characters is in some aspects incredible. Even with John's encouragement, it seems unlikely that Dad would change from a lifelong conservative to a bearded motorcycle rider who frequents the Salvation Army store in search of zany costumes and cruises down to the beach to smoke pot with his new young friends. Nor do some of the idyllic passages revealing details of Dad's alternate fantasy life seem possible either in content or style from a man of such deprived background—for example, this description of a farm chore: *"Plowing for sod corn, new-cut ground turned close, one onto the other, small tufts of grass and reeds marking the depth of furrows. Jimmy pulls, slowly, easily; and I lean, just strong enough to turn over topsoil; corduroying the earth."* Nevertheless the reader may be moved by Wharton's portrayal of the intricate emotional relationships at work in the Tremont family. Reviewing *Dad* for *Newsweek,* Walter Clemons wrote, "There is a knot of emotion in this novel that the kibitzing reader may feel Wharton hasn't sufficiently mastered and clarified. The book is raw and half-written. But it scrapes the heart."

In telephone interviews with Janet Huck of *Newsweek* and Sybil S. Steinberg of *Publishers Weekly,* Wharton described his writing methods and talked about his third book, tentatively titled "A Midnight Clear" and scheduled for publication in fall 1982. In it he continues the exploration of fantasy that has figured importantly in his past writing and seems likely, from his discussion of ideas under consideration, to do so in the future.

—Jean W. Ross

References:

Walter Clemons, "Fathers and Sons," *Newsweek,* 97 (1 June 1981): 82;

Benjamin DeMott, "Fathers and Sons," *New York Times Book Review,* 24 May 1981, p. 8;

Paul Gray, "Flights of Fact and Fancy," *Time,* 113 (15 January 1979): 73-74;

Robert R. Harris, Review of *Birdy, New Republic,* 180 (February 1979): 40;

Julian Moynahan, "Crazy to Fly," *New York Times Book Review,* 21 January 1979, pp. 8, 30;

Katha Pollitt, Review of *Birdy, Saturday Review,* 6 (3 February 1979): 43-44;

Peter S. Prescott, "Birdman," *Newsweek,* 93 (8 January 1979): 62;

Sybil S. Steinberg, "PW Interviews William Wharton," *Publishers Weekly,* 219 (24 April 1981): 14-16.

Books for Further Reading: Recent Contributions to Literary History

This list is a selection of new books on various aspects and periods of literary and cultural history; biographies, memoirs, and correspondence of literary people and their associates; facsimiles of manuscripts; and primary bibliographies. Not included are volumes in general reference series, literary criticism, bibliographies of criticism and books listed elsewhere in this volume or in earlier volumes of *DLB*

Alpers, Antony. *The Life of Katherine Mansfield.* New York: Viking, 1980.

Bannister, Henry S. *Donn Byrne: A Descriptive Bibliography, 1912-1935.* New York: Garland, 1980.

Beal, Peter, comp. *Index of English Literary Manuscripts, Volume I: 1450-1625.* New York: Bowker, 1980.

Bedell, Madelon. *The Alcotts: Biography of a Family.* New York: Potter, 1980.

Bennett, Betty T., ed. *The Letters of Mary Wollstonecraft Shelley: Volume I: "A Part of the Elect."* Baltimore: Johns Hopkins University Press, 1980.

Berkson, Bill and Joseph LeSueur, eds. *Homage to Frank O'Hara.* Berkeley: Creative Arts Book Company, 1980.

Birkin, Andrew. *J.M. Barrie & the Lost Boys.* New York: Crown, 1980.

Bogan, Louise. *Journey Around My Room: The Autobiography of Louise Bogan.* Ed. Ruth Limmer. New York: Viking, 1980.

Brasch, James D. and Joseph Sigman. *Hemingway's Library: A Composite Record.* New York: Garland, 1980.

Brian, Denis. *Tallulah, Darling: A Biography of Tallulah Bankhead.* New York: Macmillan, 1980.

Cassady, Carolyn. *Heart Beat: My Life with Jack and Neal.* Berkeley: Creative Arts Book Company, 1980.

Cotton, Nancy. *Women Playwrights in England: c. 1363-1750.* Lewisburg, Pa.: Bucknell University Press, 1980.

Cowley, Malcolm. *The Dream of the Golden Mountains: Remembering the 1930's.* New York: Viking, 1980.

Cowley. *The View from 80.* New York: Viking, 1980.

Crick, Bernard. *George Orwell: A Life.* Boston: Atlantic/Little, Brown, 1981.

Davies, Hunter. *William Wordsworth: A Biography.* New York: Atheneum, 1980.

DeMott, Robert. *Steinbeck's Reading: A Catalogue of Books Owned and Borrowed.* New York: Garland, 1980.

Dorsey, John, ed. *On Mencken.* New York: Knopf, 1980.

Dunne, Philip. *Take Two: A Life in Movies and Politics.* New York & San Francisco: McGraw-Hill/San Francisco Book Company, 1980.

Edel, Leon, ed. *The Letters of Henry James, Volume 3: 1883-1895.* Cambridge: Harvard University Press, 1980.

Foley, Martha. *The Story of Story Magazine*. Ed. Jay Neugeboren. New York: Norton, 1980.

Fowler, Will. *The Second Handshake*. Secaucus, N.J.: Lyle Stuart, 1980.

Franklin, Benjamin, V, ed. *Boston Printers, Publishers and Booksellers: 1640-1800*. Boston: G. K. Hall, 1980.

Franklin, Ralph, ed. *The Manuscript Books of Emily Dickinson: A Facsimile Edition*, 2 vols. Cambridge: Harvard University Press, 1981.

Furlong, Monica. *Merton: A Biography*. New York: Harper & Row, 1980.

Fussell, Paul. *Abroad: British Literary Traveling Between the Wars*. New York & Oxford: Oxford University Press, 1980.

Garnett, David. *Great Friends: Portraits of Seventeen Writers*. New York: Atheneum, 1980.

Gayle, Addison. *Richard Wright: Ordeal of a Native Son*. Garden City: Doubleday, 1980.

Girodias, Maurice. *The Frog Prince: An Autobiography*. New York: Crown, 1980.

Goreau, Angeline. *Reconstructing Aphra: A Social Biography of Aphra Behn*. New York: Dial, 1980.

Graves, Richard Perceval. *A. E. Housman: The Scholar-Poet*. New York: Scribners, 1980.

Gribben, Alan. *Mark Twain's Library: A Reconstruction*. Boston: G. K. Hall, 1980.

Greene, Graham. *Ways of Escape*. New York: Simon & Schuster, 1981.

Hager, Philip E. and Desmond Taylor. *The Novels of World War I: An Annotated Bibliography*. New York: Garland, 1980.

Haney, Lynn. *Naked at the Feast: A Biography of Josephine Baker*. New York: Dodd, Mead, 1980.

Haver, Ronald. *David O. Selznick's Hollywood*. New York: Knopf, 1980.

Henderson, Bill, ed. *The Art of Literary Publishing: Editors on Their Craft*. Yonkers, N.Y.: Pushcart Press, 1980.

Heymann, C. David. *American Aristocracy: The Lives and Times of James Russell, Amy, and Robert Lowell*. New York: Dodd, Mead, 1980.

Honan, Park. *Matthew Arnold: A Life*. New York: McGraw-Hill, 1981.

Howell, John M. *John Gardner: A Bibliographical Profile*. Carbondale & Edwardsville: Southern Illinois University Press, 1980.

Huston, John. *John Huston: An Open Book*. New York: Knopf, 1980.

Isherwood, Christopher. *My Guru and His Disciple*. New York: Farrar, Straus & Giroux, 1980.

Kaplan, Justin. *Walt Whitman: A Life*. New York: Simon & Schuster, 1980.

Kauffmann, Stanley. *Albums of Early Life*. Boston: Ticknor & Fields, 1980.

Kennedy, Richard S. *Dreams in the Mirror: A Biography of E. E. Cummings*. New York: Liveright, 1980.

King, Richard H. *A Southern Renaissance: The Cultural Awakening of the American South, 1930-1955*. New York: Oxford University Press, 1980.

Kraus, Michelle P. *Allen Ginsberg: An Annotated Bibliography, 1969-1977*. Metuchen, N.J.: Scarecrow Press, 1980.

Laurence, Dan. H., ed. *Bernard Shaw, Early Texts: Play Manuscripts in Facsimile*. New York: Garland, 1980.

Layman, Richard. *Shadow Man: The Life of Dashiell Hammett*. New York & London: Harcourt Brace Jovanovich/Bruccoli Clark, 1981.

Lehmann, John. *The Strange Destiny of Rupert Brooke*. New York: Holt, Rinehart & Winston, 1981.

Levy, Paul. *Moore: G. E. Moore and the Cambridge Apostles*. New York: Holt, Rinehart & Winston, 1980.

Ludington, Townsend. *John Dos Passos: A Twentieth Century Odyssey*. New York: Dutton, 1980.

Lyon, James K. *Bertolt Brecht in America*. Princeton: Princeton University Press, 1980.

MacMahon, Candace W. *Elizabeth Bishop: A Bibliography, 1927-1979*. Charlottesville: University Press of Virginia, 1980.

MacNiven, Ian S. and Harry T. Moore, eds. *Literary Lifelines: the Richard Aldington—Lawrence Durrell Correspondence*. New York: Viking, 1981.

MacShane, Frank. *The Life of John O'Hara*. New York: Dutton, 1980.

Margolis, John D. *Joseph Wood Krutch: A Writer's Life*. Knoxville: University of Tennessee Press, 1980.

Martin, Robert Bernard. *Tennyson: The Unquiet Heart*. New York & Oxford: Oxford University Press, 1980.

McNally, Dennis. *Desolate Angel: Jack Kerouac, the Beat Generation, and America*. New York: McGraw-Hill, 1980.

Mellow, James R. *Nathaniel Hawthorne in His Times*. Boston: Houghton Mifflin, 1980.

Mencken, H. L. *A Choice of Days*. Ed. Edward L. Galligan. New York: Knopf, 1980.

Meyers, Jeffrey. *Katherine Mansfield: A Biography*. New York: New Directions, 1980.

Minter, David. *William Faulkner: His Life and Work*. Baltimore & London: Johns Hopkins University Press, 1980.

Monsarrat, Ann. *An Uneasy Victorian: Thackeray the Man 1811-1863. New York: Dodd, Mead, 1980.*

Moore, Harry T. and Dale S. Montague, eds. *Frieda Lawrence and Her Circle: Letters from, to and about Frieda Lawrence*. Hamden, Conn.: Archon, 1981.

Morgan, Ted. *Maugham.* New York: Simon & Schuster, 1980.

Morley, Frank. *Literary Britain: A Reader's Guide to Its Writers and Landmarks.* New York: Harper & Row, 1980.

Morley, Sheridan. *Gertrude Lawrence: A Biography.* New York: McGraw-Hill, 1981.

Mosedale, John. *The Men Who Invented Broadway: Damon Runyon, Walter Winchell & Their World.* New York: Marek, 1981.

Nelson, Randy F. *Almanac of American Letters.* Los Altos, Cal.: William Kaufman, 1980.

Nicolson, Nigel and Joanne Trautmann, eds. *The Letters of Virginia Woolf, Volume Six, 1936-1941.* New York: Harcourt Brace Jovanovich, 1980.

Pearson, John. *The Sitwells.* New York & London: Harcourt Brace Jovanovich, 1980.

Phelps, Robert, trans. *Letters from Colette.* New York: Farrar, Straus & Giroux, 1980.

Platt, Charles. *Dream Makers: The Uncommon People Who Write Science Fiction.* New York: Berkley, 1980.

Quennell, Peter. *The Wanton Chase: An Autobiography from 1939.* New York: Atheneum, 1980.

Raskin, Jonah. *My Search for B. Traven.* New York: Methuen, 1980.

Riordan, Mary Marguerite. *Lillian Hellman: A Bibliography, 1926-1978.* Metuchen, N. J.: Scarecrow Press, 1980.

Rubin, Louis D., Jr., ed. *The American South: Portrait of a Culture.* Baton Rouge: Louisiana State University Press, 1980.

Sagar, Keith. *The Life of D. H. Lawrence.* New York: Pantheon, 1980.

Scott-Kilvert, Ian, ed. *British Writers, Volume 3: Daniel Defoe to the Gothic Novel.* New York: Scribners, 1980.

Sokolov, Raymond. *Wayward Reporter: The Life of A. J. Liebling.* New York: Harper & Row, 1980.

Steegmuller, Francis, trans. *The Letters of Gustave Flaubert 1830-1857.* Cambridge: Harvard University Press, 1980.

Stempel, Tom. *Screenwriter: The Life and Times of Nunnally Johnson.* San Diego & New York: Barnes, 1980.

Stern, Madeleine B. *Publishers for Mass Entertainment in Nineteenth Century America.* Boston: G. K. Hall, 1980.

Strouse, Jean. *Alice James.* Boston: Houghton Mifflin, 1980.

Wexler, Joyce. *Laura Riding: A Bibliography.* New York: Garland, 1980.

Wilson, Edmund. *The Thirties: From Diaries and Notebooks of the Period.* New York: Farrar, Straus & Giroux, 1980.

Contributors

Michael Adams . . . . *Louisiana State University*
Max L. Autrey . . . . *Drake University*
Doris Bargen . . . . *Amherst College*
Judith S. Baughman . . . . *University of South Carolina*
Winifred Farrant Bevilacqua . . . . *University of Turin*
Joan Bischoff . . . . *Slippery Rock State College*
Joan Bobbitt . . . . *Clemson University*
Ashley Brown . . . . *University of South Carolina*
J. D. Brown . . . . *University of Oregon*
Jerry H. Bryant . . . . *California State University, Hayward*
William Burke . . . . *Northern Arizona University*
Keen Butterworth . . . . *University of South Carolina*
R. V. Cassill . . . . *Providence, Rhode Island*
Bill Crider . . . . *Howard Payne University*
Susan Currier . . . . *California Polytechnic State University*
Katherine Elias . . . . *Seattle, Washington*
Welch D. Everman . . . . *Madison, Wisconsin*
Joseph M. Flora . . . . *University of North Carolina, Chapel Hill*
Anne Hobson Freeman . . . . *Richmond, Virginia*
Louis Gallo . . . . *Columbia College*
Donald J. Greiner . . . . *University of South Carolina*
Ina Rae Hark . . . . *University of South Carolina*
Mark Harris . . . . *University of South Carolina*
Jeffrey Helterman . . . . *University of South Carolina*
Patricia Kane . . . . *Macalester College*
Brooks Landon . . . . *University of Iowa*
Norman Lavers . . . . *Arkansas State University*
Nancy Lucas . . . . *California Polytechnic State University*
Carol MacCurdy . . . . *University of Southwestern Louisiana*
John R. May . . . . *Louisiana State University*
Larry McCaffery . . . . *San Diego State University*
R. H. Miller . . . . *University of Louisville*
Gene M. Moore . . . . *Virginia Commonwealth University*
Anne Newman . . . . *University of North Carolina, Charlotte*
Elizabeth Werth Oakman . . . . *Columbia, South Carolina*
John O'Brien . . . . *Elmwood Park, Illinois*
Stephen Jan Parker . . . . *University of Kansas*
J. Douglas Perry, Jr. . . . . *Simmons College*
Peter J. Reed . . . . *University of Minnesota*
Carolyn Rhodes . . . . *Old Dominion University*
Ernest Rhodes . . . . *Old Dominion University*
Jean W. Ross . . . . *Columbia, South Carolina*
Walter W. Ross . . . . *Columbia, South Carolina*

Paula W. Shirley .... *Columbia College*
Willard Spiegelman .... *Southern Methodist University*
Ruth L. Strickland .... *University of South Carolina*
David M. Taylor .... *Livingston University*
Susan Wells .... *Wayne State University*
Alden Whitman .... *Southampton, New York*
Everett C. Wilkie, Jr. .... *John Carter Brown Library, Brown University*
Jean Wyrick .... *Colorado State University*
Richard Ziegfeld .... *University of South Carolina*

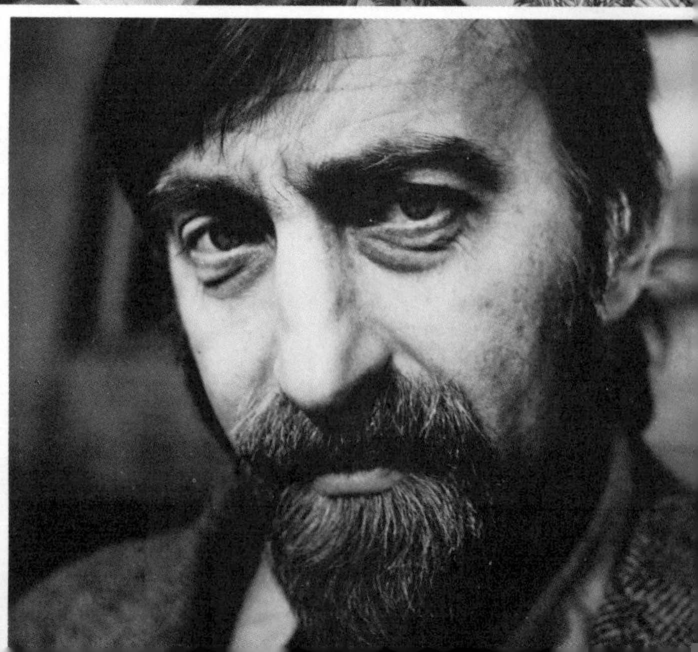